Fourth Edition

A Guide to
the SQL Standard

A user's guide to
the standard database language SQL

C. J. Date
with
Hugh Darwen

▲▲ ADDISON-WESLEY

An imprint of Addison-Wesley Longman, Inc.

Reading, Massachusetts • Harlow, England • Menlo Park, California • Berkeley, California
Don Mills, Ontario • Sydney • Bonn • Amsterdam • Tokyo • Mexico City

Library of Congress Cataloging-in-Publication Data

Date, C. J.
    A guide to the SQL standard : a user's guide to the standard database language
SQL / by C. J. Date with Hugh Darwen. —4th ed.
      p. cm.

    Includes bibliographical references and index.
    ISBN 0-201-96426-0
    1. SQL (Computer program language) 2. Query languages (computer
science) I. Darwen, Hugh. II. Date, C. J. Guide to the SQL
standard. III. Title.
QA76.73.S67D38   1997
005.75'6—dc20
                                              96-35776
                                               CIP

Many of the designations used by manufacturers and sellers to distinguish their products are claimed as trademarks. Where those designations appear in this book, and Addison-Wesley was aware of a trademark claim, the designations have been printed in initial caps or all caps.

The programs and applications presented in this book have been included for their instructional value. They have been tested with care, but are not guaranteed for any particular purpose. The publisher does not offer any warranties or representations, nor does it accept any liabilities with respect to the programs or applications.

Access the latest information about Addison-Wesley titles from our World Wide Web page:
http/www.aw.com/cseng/

Printed in the United States of America.

1 2 3 4 5 6 7 8 9 10—MA-0099989796

It is only fitting to dedicate this book to
the many people responsible, directly or indirectly,
for the rise of SQL to its present preeminent position—
the original SQL language designers at IBM,
the implementers of the IBM prototype System R
and the numerous products, IBM and nonIBM,
derived from that prototype,
and the ISO and ANSI SQL standards committees.
I hope this book
does justice to their efforts.

Preface to the Third Edition

The purpose of this book is to describe the official standard version of the database language SQL. SQL has been adopted as an international standard by the International Organization for Standardization (ISO) and as a national standard in many countries, including in particular the United States, where it is now an American National Standards Institute (ANSI) standard and a Federal Information Processing Standard (FIPS) as well. In addition, of course, numerous SQL-based products (well over 100 of them at the last count) have been available in the marketplace for several years. There can thus be no doubt that, from a commercial point of view at least, SQL represents an extremely important feature of the database world—which is of course the principal justification for this book.

Now, it is customary when producing a new edition of a book to reprint the prefaces from earlier editions. In the case of the present book, however, the third edition is to all intents and purposes a totally new book, because it deals with a totally new version of SQL—namely, the version that until now has been referred to, informally, as *SQL2*, but henceforth will probably be referred to, still informally, as "SQL/92.*" SQL/92, which ISO and various national standards bodies (ANSI in particular) have been working on for several years, represents a major set of extensions to the earlier SQL standard. (Just how major they are can be gauged from the fact that the official standard document has grown more than sixfold—from roughly 100 pages to well over 600—to accommodate them.) As a result, the third edition of this book is, as already indicated, quite different from the previous

---

*The formal name is *Database Language SQL:1992*. Formal publications also seem to use the informal abbreviation "SQL-92" (with a "-" separator instead of a "/"). We prefer "SQL/92," partly because "SQL-92" leads to ugly formations such as "SQL-92-compliant."

two; it is certainly (and regrettably) much longer than it used to be, and its structure has changed considerably. One consequence of these changes is that the previous prefaces are no longer very relevant, and I have therefore decided to drop them. Another is that there are in fact so many differences between this edition and the previous two that it is frankly not worth even trying to summarize them.

The subject of this book, then, is the new SQL standard SQL/92 (and the unqualified name "SQL" is used throughout the body of the text to refer to this new version of the language). Now, some readers will be aware that I have already discussed the SQL language at considerable length in several other books, including the following in particular:*

- *A Guide to INGRES* (Addison-Wesley, 1987)
- *A Guide to SQL/DS* (Addison-Wesley, 1988)
- *A Guide to SYBASE and SQL Server* (Addison-Wesley, 1992)
- *A Guide to DB2* (Addison-Wesley, 4th edition, 1992)

Thus, I am very conscious that I might be accused of writing the same book over and over again "until I get it right." However, the treatment of SQL in the present book differs from that in those other books in a number of significant ways:

- As already explained, the emphasis is on the official standard version of SQL instead of a product-specific dialect. The book should thus be relevant to *anyone* interested in the SQL language and SQL implementations—not just those from "the IBM world," which is where SQL originated, but also those with an interest in SQL implementations for, e.g., DEC, Unisys, ICL, ..., and other platforms.

- The emphasis in the standard on the use of SQL for programmed (as opposed to interactive) access to the database has many ramifications and repercussions on the way the book is structured and the way the material is presented. In some ways the discussions are almost the reverse of what they were in those other books; those books concentrated primarily on interactive SQL and discussed programming SQL at the end, almost as an afterthought. The present book, by contrast, necessarily deals almost exclusively with the use of SQL by application programs.

- The treatment is more thorough. All aspects of the language are discussed in detail. In the other books, by contrast, I was not aiming at any such completeness, and it was expedient to simplify and/or ignore certain aspects of the language.

---

*Colin White was coauthor on the SQL/DS and DB2 books and David McGoveran was principal author on the SYBASE book.

■ At the same time, the book is (I hope) more "user-friendly" than the official standard, in that it includes a more tutorial treatment of the material, with plenty of examples. The official standard is not very easy to read—partly because it necessarily reflects the structure of the SQL language itself, which in some ways is very ill-structured (despite the fact that the "S" in SQL originally stood for "Structured"!), and partly too because it presents the language in a most confusing mixture of bottom-up and top-down styles. In this book, by contrast, the material is organized much more along functional lines; thus, there is (e.g.) a chapter on integrity, a chapter on views, a chapter on security, and so on. For pedagogic reasons, moreover, certain more complicated topics, such as date and time support and dynamic SQL, are ignored entirely in the earlier chapters (except for a few forward pointers), thus allowing the presentation to flow in what I hope is a more natural and understandable manner.

■ It follows from the previous two paragraphs that the book is intended both as a work of reference and as a tutorial guide; it includes both formal definitions and numerous worked examples. As such, I hope it will prove useful both to SQL *users* (i.e., SQL application programmers) and to SQL *implementers* (i.e., DBMS designers and developers). *HOWEVER, I MUST MAKE IT AS CLEAR AS I CAN THAT THE BOOK IS NOT INTENDED TO REPLACE THE OFFICIAL STANDARD DOCUMENT, BUT TO COMPLEMENT IT.*

The book as a whole is divided into the following major parts:

   I. Introduction
  II. Some Preliminaries
 III. Data Definition and Manipulation
 IV. Data Control
  V. Advanced Topics

Part I sets the scene by explaining in general terms what the standard is all about and presenting an overview of the major concepts and facilities of the SQL language. The reader should study at least the overview chapter (Chapter 2) fairly carefully before moving on to later parts of the book.

Part II covers a number of fundamental issues, such as what constitutes a legal identifier and what the scope of names is. It also describes certain common underlying constructs such as schemas, sessions, and modules. Much of this material is provided primarily for reference, however; it is not necessary, and probably not even a good idea, to study these chapters exhaustively before moving on to later parts of the book.

Part III addresses what might be considered the heart of the SQL language— the basic SQL data objects and operators, the rules for defining those objects, the rules for combining those operators to form expressions, and so on. In particular, it describes the SQL data manipulation statements, i.e., the statements for retrieving and updating SQL data.

Part IV describes SQL's integrity and security support, including in particular its support for primary and foreign keys.

Finally, Part V discusses a number of more esoteric aspects of the standard, including such topics as missing information, date and time support, temporary tables, and so forth.

In addition, there are several appendixes: one giving a BNF grammar for the SQL language, another explaining the requirements for compliance with the standard, another giving an overview of some currently proposed future extensions ("SQL3"), and so on.

The book as a whole is intended to be reasonably self-contained. The only background assumed of the reader is a general interest in the SQL language; all necessary terms and concepts are defined and explained as they are introduced. *Note:* Most of the examples are based on the familiar suppliers-and-parts database (see Chapter 2). I make no apology for trotting out this old warhorse still one more time; basing the examples on such a familiar database should, I hope, make it easy for the reader to relate to those examples, and should also facilitate comparisons between the standard version of SQL and specific vendor implementations—in particular, the implementations described in the books mentioned above (*A Guide to DB2* and the rest). In some respects, in fact, this book can be seen as a complement to those other books.

A NOTE ON THE TEXT

As mentioned above, the official standard is not particularly easy to read. In places, in fact, it is well-nigh impenetrable. The following extract is perhaps worse than most but is not atypical:

> "*However, because global temporary table contents are distinct within SQL-sessions, and created local temporary tables are distinct within <module>s within SQL-sessions, the effective <schema name> of the schema in which the global temporary table or the created local temporary table is instantiated is an implementation-dependent <schema name> that may be thought of as having been effectively derived from the <schema name> of the schema in which the global temporary table or created local temporary table is defined and the implementation-dependent SQL-session identifier associated with the SQL-session.*"

This sentence is taken from a section of the standard entitled—and intended to explain the SQL concept of—"Tables."

Of course, it is precisely because the standard is so hard to understand that a book like this one can serve a useful purpose. But complexity alone is not the end of the story. The sentence quoted above is not just hard to understand, it is actually *wrong* (tables are not instantiated in schemas, table *descriptors* are). Which brings us to the next point: The standard contains all too many errors, both of omission and of commission. As a consequence, the task of reading and understanding it is made much more difficult than it might have been. So too is the task of describing and explaining it!—at least when the topic under discussion is one that is subject to the aforementioned errors. The best that can be done in such cases is to make it quite clear that the topic in question is indeed one that the standard does not deal with in a fully satisfactory manner, and of course to try to explain too what the errors seem to be. Appendix D provides a consolidated and annotated list of such topics, to serve as a basis for future discussion and investigation.

There is one more point to be made on the subject of the text, as follows: To be quite honest, I am somewhat embarrassed at the inordinate number of footnotes the book contains. I am only too well aware that too many footnotes can quickly become annoying, and can indeed seriously impede readability. But the fact is that any description of SQL is almost forced into a heavy use of footnotes if it wants to be primarily tutorial in nature and yet reasonably comprehensive at the same time. The reason is that SQL involves so many inconsistencies, exceptions, and special cases that treating everything "in line"—i.e., at the same level of description—makes it very difficult to see the forest for the trees. (Indeed, this is another reason why the standard itself is so difficult to understand.) Thus, there are numerous places in this book where the major idea is described "in line" in the main body of the text, and exceptions and the like (which must at least be mentioned, for reasons of accuracy and completeness) are relegated to a footnote. It might be best simply to ignore all footnotes on a first reading.

ACKNOWLEDGMENTS

Although I have dropped the prefaces from the first two editions, it does not seem appropriate to drop the acknowledgments to the various friends and colleagues who helped with those editions—so here goes. First, I am delighted to acknowledge my debt to the following people, who helped with numerous technical and procedural questions and reviewed various drafts of the manuscripts of those editions: Lynn Francis, Randell Flint, Carol Joyce, Geoff Sharman, and Phil Shaw. Phil in particular reviewed both editions very carefully and made numerous helpful comments and suggestions. I would also like to acknowledge the many seminar and presentation attendees, too numerous to mention individually, who offered constructive comments on those two editions.

Turning now to the third edition specifically, I would like to thank my coauthor Hugh Darwen for his invaluable contribution. Hugh is one of the UK representatives to the ISO SQL committee, and as such was able to obtain answers to the numerous technical questions that arose during my study of the official standard documents. In addition, he reviewed the entire manuscript, and indeed also wrote the first drafts of certain chapters (though I hasten to add that I am responsible for the final version of the text, and must therefore assume responsibility for any remaining errors it might contain). *Note:* The text does include a number of comments and personal opinions, generally introduced with a phrase such as "in this writer's opinion." Hugh has asked me to make it clear that he agrees with the opinions in question; in other words, "this writer" should be taken to mean both of us!

I am also indebted to the other reviewers of this edition, namely Tony Gordon, David McGoveran, Phil Shaw (again), and Mike Sykes, for their careful and constructive comments on the manuscript.

Third, I am deeply indebted to my long-suffering family, especially my wife Lindy, for her support throughout this project and so many others.

Last, I am (as always) grateful to my editor, Elydia Davis, and to the staff at Addison-Wesley for their assistance and their continually high standards of professionalism. It has been (as always) a pleasure to work with them.

Healdsburg, California   C. J. Date
1992 (revised 1996)

Hugh Darwen adds:
My role in the production of this book has been primarily that of advisor and technical reviewer, tasks made utterly nontrivial by Chris Date's meticulous questioning and his insistence on a complete understanding of everything. To answer his (hundreds of) questions, I, in turn, have leaned heavily on my fellow British members of the ISO Database Languages committee, Ed Dee, Mike Sykes, and Tony Gordon. I am especially grateful to Jim Melton, the editor of the SQL2 and SQL3 international standards, for similar assistance while he was in the throes of preparing the final SQL2 draft for publication. I am grateful to all members of this committee for an enjoyable and sometimes exhilarating collaboration under the excellent chairmanship of our *rapporteur*, Len Gallagher.

To participate in international standardization can be to distance oneself somewhat from one's employer's immediate business. My involvement was at my own initiative, and I am deeply grateful to Stuart Colvin, who was my manager in 1988, for the initial support, encouragement, and long-term vision, which have happily been continued by his several successors and superiors at the Warwick Software Development Laboratory of IBM.

Further acknowledgments added 1996: What I wrote in 1992 still stands, of course, but IBM's Warwick Software Development Laboratory, alas, does not. IBM's fortunes during the past few years are so well known as to obviate the need for explanation. That I have been able to participate in our recovery and to continue my active involvement in SQL standardization is due to the support, for which I am deeply grateful, of my manager, John Peters, and his manager (and former lab director), Tony Temple. The US National Institute for Science and Technology has also undergone cutback and redirection, a consequence of which was Len Gallagher's resignation in May, 1996, from the post of Database Languages Rapporteur which he had filled since 1986. The fine reputation he has gained from this contribution is well merited, and he will be sorely missed by me and all my fellow standardizers.

Shrewley Common, England   Hugh Darwen
1992 (revised 1996)

Preface to the Fourth Edition

Several changes have occurred in the SQL standards world since the previous edition of this book was published. First of all, a major new component, the Call-Level Interface (SQL/CLI), was added to the standard in 1995. Second, another major new component, the Persistent Stored Modules feature (SQL/PSM), is currently under development (and indeed nearing completion); SQL/PSM is not yet part of the standard but is virtually certain to become so in the near future. Third, the original standard itself has been significantly changed and corrected through the publication of two Technical Corrigenda, one in 1994 and one in 1996. Taken together, these changes are more than sufficient to justify this new (fourth) edition. At the same time, I have taken the opportunity to extend and improve the text throughout in numerous ways, and in particular to correct a few errors. It is not an exaggeration to say that scarcely a sentence survives intact from the third edition.

ACKNOWLEDGMENTS

Once again I must thank my coauthor Hugh Darwen for his invaluable contribution (especially in connection with the SQL/PSM and SQL3 appendixes). I would also like to thank Paul Cotton and Frank Pellow for their help with the material on SQL/CLI; Peter Pistor for pointing out an error in the treatment of foreign keys in the previous edition; Mike Sykes for assistance with questions regarding SQL's date and time support (especially in connection with time zones); and Mel Zimowski for assistance with questions regarding SQL's "global transaction" support. I am also indebted to Nelson Mattos, Frank Pellow, and Jeff Richey for their careful reviews of the manuscript.

Finally, I am (as always) deeply indebted to my wife, Lindy, for her support throughout this project; to my editor, Elydia Davis, for her usual sterling job; and to the staff at Addison-Wesley for their usual help and professionalism. Once again it has been a pleasure to work with them.

Healdsburg, California   C. J. Date
1996

Contents

PART IV   DATA CONTROL

_____

PART V   ADVANCED TOPICS

APPENDIXES

INTRODUCTION

This introductory part of the book consists of two chapters, one giving some pertinent background information and the other a brief overview of the SQL language. Readers are recommended to study at least the second of these two chapters fairly carefully before moving on to later portions of the book.

1

Why SQL Is Important

1.1 BACKGROUND

The name "SQL"—the official pronunciation is "ess-cue-ell," although many people pronounce it "sequel"—was originally an abbreviation for *Structured Query Language*. In its standard incarnation, however, the name is "just a name" and is not considered to be an abbreviation for anything at all. Be that as it may, the SQL language consists of a set of facilities for defining, accessing, and otherwise managing *SQL-data*.* In order to understand why and how SQL has become so widespread and so generally important, it is helpful to have an appreciation of some of the major developments in database technology over the past 25 years or so. We therefore begin by summarizing those developments.

1. In 1970, E. F. Codd, at that time a member of the IBM Research Laboratory in San Jose, California, published a now classic paper, "A Relational Model of Data for Large Shared Data Banks" (*Communications of the ACM 13,* No. 6, June 1970), in which he laid down a set of abstract principles that he proposed should serve as a foundation for database management: the so-called

---

*As subsequent paragraphs make clear, SQL was originally meant to be a language for managing *relational* data, but the standard has evolved to the point where it is now a long way from being truly relational; hence the "SQL-data" terminology.

relational model. The entire field of relational database technology has its origins in that paper.

2. Codd's ideas led directly to a great deal of experimentation and research in universities, industrial research laboratories, and similar establishments, and that activity in turn led to the numerous products now available that are based on the relational approach. The many advantages of that approach are too well known to need repeating here; see, e.g., Chapter 1 ("Why Relational?") in C. J. Date, *Relational Database Writings 1985–1989* (Addison-Wesley, 1990), for a brief summary of some of them.

3. One particular aspect of the research just referred to was the design and prototype implementation of a variety of relational languages. A relational language is a language that realizes, in some concrete syntactic form, some or all of the features of the abstract relational model. Several such languages were designed in the early and mid 1970s, but the most significant (from a commercial point of view, at any rate) was the "Structured English Query Language" SEQUEL, first defined by Donald Chamberlin and others at IBM Research in 1974, and first implemented in an IBM prototype called SEQUEL-XRM in 1974–75.

4. Partly as a result of experience with SEQUEL-XRM, a revised version of SEQUEL called SEQUEL/2 was defined in 1976–77. (The name was subsequently changed to SQL for legal reasons.) Work began on another, more ambitious, IBM prototype called System R. System R, an implementation of a large subset of the SEQUEL/2 (or SQL) language, became operational in 1977 and was subsequently installed in a number of user sites, both internal IBM sites and also (under a set of joint study agreements) selected IBM customer sites. *Note:* A number of further changes were made to the SQL language during the lifetime of the System R project, partly in response to user suggestions. For instance, an EXISTS function was added to test whether some specified data existed in the database.

5. Thanks in large part to the success and acceptance of System R at those user sites, it became generally apparent in the late 1970s that sooner or later IBM would develop commercial products based on the System R technology—specifically, products that implemented the SQL language. As a result, other vendors did not wait for IBM but began to develop their own SQL-based products. (At least one such product, ORACLE from Relational Software Inc.—subsequently renamed Oracle Corporation—actually beat IBM's own products to the market.) Then, in 1981, IBM did announce an SQL product,*

---

*Note that we are assuming the "ess-cue-ell" pronunciation here. We will favor this pronunciation in this book, even though it is not to everyone's taste, in order to be consistent with the official standard.

called SQL/DS, for the VSE environment. IBM followed that announcement with one for a VM version of SQL/DS (1982), and another for an MVS product called DB2 that was broadly compatible with SQL/DS (1983).

6. Over the next several years, numerous other vendors also announced SQL products. Those announcements included both entirely new products such as DG/SQL (Data General Corporation, 1984) and SYBASE (Sybase Inc., 1986), and SQL interfaces to established products such as INGRES (Relational Technology Inc., 1981, 1985) and the IDM (Britton-Lee Inc., 1982, 1985).* The current situation (1996) is that there are well over 100 products in the marketplace that support some dialect of SQL, running on machines that range all the way from comparatively small personal computers to the largest mainframes. *SQL has become the* de facto *standard in the database world.*

7. Furthermore, of course, SQL is now an *official* standard also. In 1982, the American National Standards Institute (ANSI) chartered its Database Committee X3H2 to develop a proposal for a standard relational language. The X3H2 proposal, which was finally ratified by ANSI in 1986, consisted essentially of the IBM dialect of SQL, "warts and all" (except that a few—in this writer's opinion, far too few—minor IBM idiosyncrasies were removed). And in 1987, the ANSI standard was also accepted as an international standard by the International Organization for Standardization (ISO). *Note:* That original standard version of SQL is often referred to, informally, as "SQL/86."

The foregoing is not the end of the story, of course. In 1989, the original SQL standard was extended to include an (optional) *Integrity Enhancement Feature,* IEF; by analogy with "SQL/86," that extended version is often referred to, again informally, as "SQL/89." Also in 1989, a related standard called *Database Language Embedded SQL* was adopted, at least in the United States. And various versions of SQL have been adopted at various subsequent times as

- an X/Open standard (for open systems)
- an SAA standard (for IBM systems)
- a Federal Information Processing Standard or FIPS (for US Federal Government systems)

In addition, a consortium of vendors known as the SQL Access Group has been working for several years to define a set of facilities to support interoperability

---

*To keep the record straight, we note that (a) Relational Technology Inc. later changed its name to Ingres Corporation and was subsequently acquired, first by ASK Computer Systems Inc., later by Computer Associates International Inc., and (b) Britton-Lee Inc. changed its name to ShareBase Corporation (and changed the name of its product to ShareBase also), and was subsequently acquired by Teradata Corporation, which later merged with NCR Corporation.

among disparate SQL implementations. The first results of that effort saw the light of day in July 1991, when a prototype implementation of such interoperability involving ten different application systems and nine different database management systems was demonstrated. *Note:* The SQL Access Group became part of X/Open in December 1994 and is now officially known as the X/Open SQL Access Group.

Last, the ISO and ANSI committees have been working for many years on the definition of a greatly expanded version of the original standard, referred to informally as "SQL2" (more recently "SQL/92"). That expanded version became a ratified standard—"International Standard ISO/IEC 9075:1992, *Database Language SQL*"—in late 1992. That standard was then further extended in 1995 by the addition of an important new feature, the *Call-Level Interface* feature (SQL/CLI); it was also significantly changed and corrected through the publication of two *Technical Corrigenda*, one in 1994 and one in 1996.* The principal purpose of this book is to describe the version of the SQL/92 standard that is current at the time of writing, including in particular the important extensions and corrections just mentioned.

Note: To repeat, we are primarily concerned in this book with the SQL/92 version of SQL, which is the version normally meant when people refer to "the SQL standard." In this book, therefore, we will take the unqualified name "SQL" (also terms such as "standard SQL," "the standard," "the official standard," etc.) to refer to this version. When we need to refer to some specific dialect other than the current standard version, we will always use an appropriately qualified name, such as "SQL/86" or "SQL/89" or "X/Open SQL" (etc.).

One final point of a historical nature: The original version of SQL was intended for standalone, interactive, "direct" use. However, facilities were added later to allow the invocation of SQL operations from an application program written in a language such as C or Pascal or PL/I. By contrast, the standard concentrates almost exclusively on these latter facilities (i.e., for application programming), presumably on the grounds that standardization is much more significant for portability of programs than it is for interactive interfaces. This emphasis is reflected in the structure of this book, as will be seen.

1.2 IS A STANDARD DESIRABLE?

Before going any further, we should perhaps briefly consider the question of whether an SQL standard is a good thing. On the one hand, the advantages are fairly obvious:

---

*Another major new extension, the *Persistent Stored Modules* feature (SQL/PSM), is under development at the time of writing. SQL/PSM is not yet part of the standard, but it is likely to become so in the near future; we therefore examine it—or, at least, the current version of it—in detail in Appendix E.

- *Reduced training costs:* Application developers can move from one environment to another without the need for expensive retraining.

- *Application portability:* Applications—in particular, applications developed by third-party software vendors—can run unchanged in a variety of different hardware and software environments. Applications can be developed on one platform (e.g., a workstation) and then run on another (e.g., a mainframe).

- *Application longevity:* Standard languages are assured of a reasonably long lifetime. Applications developed using such languages can therefore be assured of a reasonably long lifetime also (other things being equal).

- *Intersystem communication:* Different systems can more easily communicate with one another (in this regard, note the work of the X/Open SQL Access Group, mentioned briefly in the previous section).

- *Customer choice:* If all products support the same interface, customers can concentrate on the problem of choosing the implementation that best meets their own particular needs, without having to get involved in the additional complexity of choosing among different interfaces (possibly widely different interfaces).

We should perhaps stress the point that many of the foregoing advantages apply in principle but *not* necessarily in practice (this word of caution is particularly relevant in the case of the "application portability" advantage!). And, of course, there are some significant disadvantages too:

- *A standard can stifle creativity:* Implementers might effectively be prevented from providing "the best" solution (or even just a good one) to some problem because the standard already prescribes some alternative, less satisfactory, solution to that same problem.

- *SQL in particular is very far from ideal as a relational language:* This criticism has been elaborated by the present writers in many places; see, e.g., the books *Relational Database: Selected Writings, Relational Database Writings 1985–1989, Relational Database Writings 1989–1991,* and *Relational Database Writings 1991–1994,* published by Addison-Wesley in 1986, 1990, 1992, and 1995, respectively. To quote from the first of these books:

  "[It] cannot be denied that SQL in its present form leaves rather a lot to be desired—even that, in some important respects, it fails to realize the full potential of the relational model."

  The basic problem (in this writer's opinion) is that, although there are well-established principles for the design of formal languages, there is little evidence that SQL was ever designed in accordance with any such principles. As a result, the language is filled with numerous restrictions, *ad hoc* constructs, and annoying special rules. These factors in turn make the language difficult to define, describe, teach, learn, remember, apply, and implement.

- *Standard SQL especially is additionally deficient in a number of respects:* Over and above the deficiencies mentioned under the previous point (i.e., deficiencies that are intrinsic to the original SQL language *per se*), standard SQL in particular suffers from certain additional deficiencies. Specifically, it fails to include any support at all for several features that are clearly needed in practice (e.g., a truth-valued or Boolean data type), and it leaves as "implementation-defined" or "implementation-dependent" (see below) many aspects that would much better be spelled out as part of the standard (e.g., the column names of the tables that result from evaluating certain table expressions—see Chapter 11). As a result, it seems likely that every realistic implementation of the standard will necessarily include many implementation-specific extensions and variations, and hence that no two "standard" SQL implementations will ever be truly identical.

Note: The (important) difference between the concepts "implementation-defined" and "implementation-dependent" is as follows:

- *Implementation-defined* means that an implementation is free to decide how it will implement the SQL feature in question, but the result of that decision must be documented.

- *Implementation-dependent* effectively means "undefined." Again, the implementation is free to decide how it will implement the feature in question, but the result of that decision need not be documented (it might even vary from release to release).

Examples of the two cases are the maximum length of a character string (implementation-defined) and the physical representation of data in storage (implementation-dependent).

Anyway, to return to our main discussion: Regardless of the potential drawbacks identified above, the situation is that the standard exists, vendors are scrambling to support it, and customers are demanding such support. Hence this book.

2

An Overview of SQL

2.1 INTRODUCTION

The aim of this chapter is to present a brief and very informal overview of some of the major facilities of standard SQL, and thereby to pave the way for an understanding of the more formal and thorough treatment of the material in subsequent chapters. The chapter is very loosely based on Chapter 1 ("Relational Database: An Overview") from C. J. Date, *Relational Database: Selected Writings* (Addison-Wesley, 1986). *Note:* One point that is worth making right at the outset is the following: Space obviously does not permit us to make any detailed comparisons between the facilities of the standard and those of existing SQL products; however, readers who happen to be familiar with commercial SQL implementations might be in for a few surprises.

    The primary function of the SQL language is to support the definition, manipulation, and control of data in SQL databases.* An *SQL database* is a database that is perceived by the user as a collection of *tables*; a *table* in turn consists of one or

---

*As explained in Chapter 1, SQL was originally meant for use with *relational* databases. However, the standard never uses the term *relation* at all (it uses *table* instead, SQL tables being a rough approximation to the mathematical concept of a relation). What is more, it does not use the term *database* either!—at least, not in any formal sense. Instead, it talks about *SQL-data*, which is "any data described by schemas [i.e., SQL-schemas—see Section 2.8] that is under the control of an SQL-implementation in an SQL-environment."

S

SNO	SNAME	STATUS	CITY
S1	Smith	20	London
S2	Jones	10	Paris
S3	Blake	30	Paris
S4	Clark	20	London
S5	Adams	30	Athens

P

PNO	PNAME	COLOR	WEIGHT	CITY
P1	Nut	Red	12	London
P2	Bolt	Green	17	Paris
P3	Screw	Blue	17	Rome
P4	Screw	Red	14	London
P5	Cam	Blue	12	Paris
P6	Cog	Red	19	London

SP

SNO	PNO	QTY
S1	P1	300
S1	P2	200
S1	P3	400
S1	P4	200
S1	P5	100
S1	P6	100
S2	P1	300
S2	P2	400
S3	P2	200
S4	P2	200
S4	P4	300
S4	P5	400

Fig. 2.1 The suppliers-and-parts database (sample values)

more *columns* and zero or more *rows*, each row containing one *scalar value* for each column ("scalar" here meaning simply "elementary"). An example, the suppliers-and-parts database, is shown in Fig. 2.1. We will be using this database throughout this book as the basis for examples, so it is worth taking a little time to familiarize yourself with it now.

We explain the figure as follows. First of all, the three tables S, P, and SP represent, respectively, suppliers, parts, and shipments of parts by suppliers. Note that each table can be thought of, loosely, as a *file*, with the rows representing records and the columns fields. Unlike the records of a typical file, however, the rows in such a table are *unordered* (the *representation* of a table—on paper, for example—necessarily shows the rows in some order, of course, but that ordering is an artefact of the representation; it is, to repeat, not part of the concept of a table *per se*, as that concept is understood in SQL).

Now, SQL statements in general, and SQL "data manipulation" statements in particular (i.e., SQL statements that perform data retrieval or updating operations), can be invoked either interactively or from within an application program. Fig. 2.2 illustrates both cases; it shows a data retrieval operation—actually a SELECT statement*—being invoked both (a) interactively and (b) from within a PL/I program. In general:

- *Interactive invocation* (also called *direct* invocation) means the statement in question is invoked from some terminal. If the statement causes data to be retrieved, that data is displayed at that terminal.

---

*Not all retrieval operations are SELECT statements.

(a) *Interactive (direct) invocation:*

```
        SELECT  S.CITY                Result:    CITY
        FROM    S
        WHERE   S.SNO = 'S4' ;                   London
```

(b) *Invocation from a PL/I program:*

```
    EXEC SQL SELECT  S.CITY INTO :SC    Result:   SC
             FROM    S
             WHERE   S.SNO = 'S4' ;               London
```

Fig. 2.2 SQL retrieval example

■ *Invocation from within an application program* means the statement is invoked as part of the process of executing that program. If the statement causes data to be retrieved, that data is fetched into an input area within that program—"SC" in Fig. 2.2(b).* *A note on terminology:* The application program is said to be a *host* program, and the language in which it is written—PL/I in Fig. 2.2(b)—a *host language.*

One further introductory remark: The reader will have noticed that we used *qualified column names* (S.CITY, S.SNO) in the SELECT statements in Fig. 2.2. Actually SQL allows the qualifiers to be omitted in many contexts (including, in particular, the SELECT and WHERE clauses of a SELECT statement), provided no ambiguity results from such omission. Thus, for example, the two SELECT clauses of Fig. 2.2 could both have been abbreviated to just "SELECT CITY." However, it is not wrong to include the qualifiers as we have done, and it is often good practice to do so. In this book, therefore, we will usually show the qualifiers explicitly, even when they are not strictly necessary—except, of course, in contexts where they are expressly prohibited (an example of such a context is the left hand side of a SET clause assignment in an UPDATE statement; see Section 2.3).

2.2   DATA DEFINITION

Fig. 2.1, the suppliers-and-parts database, of course represents that database as it appears at some specific time. Fig. 2.3, by contrast, shows (in outline) how the database would be *defined.* We explain that definition as follows:

---

*There are several distinct ways of invoking SQL from an application program, as we will see in Chapter 6. Fig. 2.2(b) illustrates one of the most important, namely "embedded SQL."

```
CREATE TABLE S   ( SNO      CHAR(5),
                   SNAME    CHAR(20),
                   STATUS   DECIMAL(3),
                   CITY     CHAR(15),
                   PRIMARY KEY ( SNO ) )

CREATE TABLE P   ( PNO      CHAR(6),
                   PNAME    CHAR(20),
                   COLOR    CHAR(6),
                   WEIGHT   DECIMAL(3),
                   CITY     CHAR(15),
                   PRIMARY KEY ( PNO ) )

CREATE TABLE SP  ( SNO      CHAR(5),
                   PNO      CHAR(6),
                   QTY      DECIMAL(5),
                   PRIMARY KEY ( SNO, PNO ),
                   FOREIGN KEY ( SNO ) REFERENCES S,
                   FOREIGN KEY ( PNO ) REFERENCES P )
```

Fig. 2.3 Data definition example

- The three CREATE TABLE statements define three tables with the specified names and specified named columns (with specified data types). All three tables will initially be empty (i.e., contain no rows). Note that column names must be unique within their containing table.

- Within table S, column SNO is defined as the *primary key*—meaning that, at any given time, no two distinct rows of the table will ever have the same SNO value. Similarly for column PNO in table P and the combination of columns (SNO,PNO) in table SP. *Note:* Primary key columns are indicated by double underlining in Fig. 2.1. We will make use of this convention in figures throughout this book.*

- Within table SP, columns SNO and PNO are defined as *foreign* keys, referencing tables S and P respectively. What this means, loosely speaking, is that every value appearing in column SP.SNO must also appear in column S.SNO (the primary key) of table S, and likewise every value appearing in column SP.PNO must also appear in column P.PNO (the primary key) of table P. The intuitive (and correct) interpretation of these constraints is that a shipment cannot exist unless the corresponding supplier and part exist also.

Data can subsequently be entered into the tables via the SQL INSERT statement, discussed in the next section.

---

*The reader should not infer from our convention that the primary key of any given table is always known to SQL. On the contrary, it is known if and only if the table is a "base" table (see later in this section) *and* the user has explicitly chosen to provide a PRIMARY KEY specification for that table.

Actually there are two kinds of tables that can be defined in SQL, *base tables* and *viewed tables* (more usually referred to simply as *views*). The tables of Fig. 2.3 are all base tables. Note, therefore, that CREATE TABLE creates a base table specifically. There is a separate CREATE VIEW statement for creating views (see Section 2.5).

■ A base table is a "real" table—i.e., a table that "really exists" (or, at least, can be thought of as "really existing"). There might even be physical stored records, and possibly physical access paths such as indexes, in one or more stored files, that directly support that table in physical storage.

■ By contrast, a view is a "virtual" table—i.e., a table that does not "really exist" in the foregoing sense, but looks to the user as if it did. Views are defined, in a manner to be explained in Section 2.5, in terms of one or more underlying base tables (and/or other views).

Note: The foregoing explanations should not be construed as meaning that a base table is a *physically stored* table—i.e., a collection of physically adjacent, physically stored records, each one consisting of a direct copy of a row of the base table. In principle, in fact, a base table need have no direct stored counterpart at all! Base tables are best thought of as an *abstraction* of some collection of stored data—an abstraction in which numerous storage-level details (such as physical data location, physical ordering, physical data encodings, physical access paths, etc.) are concealed from the user. Thus, there can be any number of differences between a base table and its stored representation. The point is, however, that users can always *think* of base tables as "really existing," while not having to concern themselves with how the data is physically represented in storage. Views on the other hand do not "really exist" in this sense; views are merely a different way of looking at the data in the base tables.

2.3   DATA MANIPULATION

There are four basic SQL data manipulation operations—SELECT, INSERT, UPDATE, and DELETE. We have already given an example of SELECT (two versions) in Fig. 2.2. Fig. 2.4 gives examples of the other three operations, the so-called update operations. *Note:* The term "update" unfortunately has two meanings in SQL: It is used generically to refer to the three operations INSERT, UPDATE, and DELETE as a class, and also specifically to refer to the UPDATE operation *per se*. We will distinguish between the two meanings in this book by always using lower case when the generic meaning is intended and upper case when the specific meaning is intended.

Note that the UPDATE and DELETE operations of Fig. 2.4 are each "multi-row"—that is, each of them operates on several rows at once, conceptually speak-

```
INSERT                              Result:   Specified row
INTO SP ( SNO, PNO, QTY )                     inserted into
VALUES  ('S5','P1',1000 )                     table SP

UPDATE S                            Result:   STATUS doubled
SET    STATUS = 2 * S.STATUS                  for suppliers in
WHERE  S.CITY = 'London'                      London (i.e., S1
                                              and S4)

DELETE                              Result:   Rows deleted from
FROM   P                                      table P for parts
WHERE  P.WEIGHT > 15                          P2, P3, and P6
```

Fig. 2.4 Update examples

ing, not just on one row at a time. The same is true in general for INSERT operations (although the INSERT of Fig. 2.4 is actually single-row), and also for retrieval operations. In the case of retrieval, however, standard SQL does not permit a multi-row retrieval operation (e.g., a multi-row SELECT) to be executed as a separate statement in its own right;* instead, it is necessary to define a *cursor* having the desired multi-row collection as its "scope," and then to access the rows in that scope one at a time by means of that cursor. For tutorial reasons, however, we defer discussion of cursors to Section 2.4, and pretend for the time being that a multi-row retrieval operation can indeed be executed as a statement in its own right. Note that single-row SELECTs *can* be executed in this way, as illustrated in Fig. 2.2.

The SELECT operation has the general form "SELECT–FROM–WHERE," as illustrated in Fig. 2.5. (*Note:* The symbol "<>" in that figure stands for "not equals.") Observe that the result of the SELECT is another table (one that is

```
SELECT DISTINCT P.COLOR, P.CITY   Result:   ┌─────────┬───────────┐
FROM   P                                    │ COLOR   │ CITY      │
WHERE  P.WEIGHT > 10                        ├─────────┼───────────┤
AND    P.CITY <> 'Paris'                    │ Red     │ London    │
                                            │ Blue    │ Rome      │
                                            │ --Red-----London--- │
                                            │ --Red-----London--- │
                                            └─────────┴───────────┘
                                            (two rows eliminated
                                            because of DISTINCT)
```

Fig. 2.5 The basic "SELECT–FROM–WHERE" (example)

---

*At least, not from an application program. Multi-row retrieval operations can be executed in their own right in "direct SQL" (i.e., interactively).

derived from an existing table, not one that already exists in the database). Note too that:

- If the WHERE clause is omitted, the result table contains all of the rows of the FROM table.
- If the DISTINCT option is omitted, the result table might contain duplicate rows (in the example, four rows will be returned if DISTINCT is omitted, two if it is included).

Join

One of the most crucially important features of SQL systems is their support for the relational *join* operator. It is this operator that makes it possible to retrieve data from two, three, four, . . . or any number of tables, all in a single statement. An example is given in Fig. 2.6; the query is "For each part supplied, retrieve part number and names of all cities in which there is located a supplier who supplies the part." The term "join" arises from the fact that (in the example) tables SP and S are conceptually being *joined* on their common SNO column before the PNO and CITY values are extracted. Note that the references to columns S.SNO and SP.SNO in the WHERE clause *must* be qualified in this example, to avoid ambiguity.

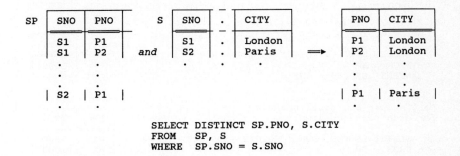

```
SELECT DISTINCT SP.PNO, S.CITY
FROM     SP, S
WHERE    SP.SNO = S.SNO
```

Fig. 2.6 Example involving a join

It should be mentioned that (unlike SQL/86 and SQL/89) SQL/92 also includes an *explicit* join feature. Using this feature, the query of Fig. 2.6 could alternatively have been written as follows:

```
SELECT DISTINCT SP.PNO, S.CITY
FROM     SP NATURAL JOIN S
```

The key word NATURAL indicates the type of join required. Refer to Chapter 11 for further explanation.

Aggregate Functions

SQL provides a set of builtin *aggregate functions:* COUNT, SUM, AVG, MAX, MIN, and COUNT(*) (the asterisk "*" denotes an entire row of the table concerned). Examples are given in Fig. 2.7. The final example in that figure also illustrates the GROUP BY clause, which is used to divide a table (conceptually) into groups so that an aggregate function such as SUM can be applied to each individual group. Note, incidentally, that the first three examples are all single-row SELECTs. Note too the use of the AS clause (in all four examples) to specify a name for the column resulting from the use of the aggregate function, which otherwise would be given an implementation-dependent name (refer back to Chapter 1 if you need to refresh your memory regarding the meaning of the term "implementation-dependent").

Number of suppliers:

```
    SELECT  COUNT(*) AS N1
    FROM    S
```

Result:

N1
5

Number of suppliers supplying parts:

```
    SELECT  COUNT ( DISTINCT SP.SNO ) AS N2
    FROM    SP
```

Result:

N2
4

Total quantity of part P2:

```
    SELECT  SUM ( SP.QTY ) AS TOT1
    FROM    SP
    WHERE   SP.PNO = 'P2'
```

Result:

TOT1
1000

Part number and total quantity for each part supplied:

```
    SELECT  SP.PNO, SUM ( SP.QTY ) AS TOT2
    FROM    SP
    GROUP   BY SP.PNO
```

Result:

PNO	TOT2
P1	600
P2	1000
P3	400
P4	500
P5	500
P6	100

Fig. 2.7 SQL aggregate function examples

2.4   CURSOR OPERATIONS

As mentioned in Section 2.3, the standard does not permit a multi-row retrieval operation to be executed as a statement in its own right (except in "direct SQL").

The reason for this state of affairs is that the standard is primarily concerned with the use of SQL in conjunction with programming languages such as PL/I and COBOL, and such languages are generally not well equipped to deal with collections of many rows as single operands. What is needed, therefore, is a mechanism for stepping through such a collection and picking off the rows one by one; and *cursors* provide such a mechanism. A cursor is an SQL object that is associated (via an appropriate declaration) with a specific retrieval operation.* To access the desired rows, the user must:

1. OPEN the cursor, which (conceptually) makes the desired collection of rows available for subsequent retrieval;

2. Use FETCH repeatedly on the opened cursor, which (on each execution) steps that cursor to the next row in the collection and retrieves that row; and finally

3. CLOSE the cursor when all desired rows have been retrieved.

Special forms of UPDATE and DELETE are provided for updating or deleting the row on which the cursor is currently positioned. An example is given (in outline—many important details are omitted) in Fig. 2.8. *Note:* The example is written in PL/I. The standard does support other languages as well, of course, but the rules for using SQL with those other languages are essentially the same as those for PL/I (see Chapter 6 for further discussion). For definiteness, therefore, we adopt PL/I as the basis for our programming examples, here and throughout most of the book.

```
EXEC SQL DECLARE C1 CURSOR FOR
          SELECT SP.SNO, SP.QTY
          FROM    SP
          WHERE   SP.PNO = 'P2' ;

DECLARE X CHAR(5) ;
DECLARE Y FIXED DECIMAL(5) ;
DECLARE Z FIXED DECIMAL(3) ;

EXEC SQL OPEN C1 ;
DO for all rows accessible via cursor C1 ;
   EXEC SQL FETCH C1 INTO :X, :Y ;
   process X and Y ;
   EXEC SQL UPDATE SP
            SET    QTY = QTY + :Z
            WHERE  CURRENT OF C1 ;
END ;
EXEC SQL CLOSE C1 ;
```

Fig. 2.8 Example of the use of a cursor

---

*More accurately, a specific *table expression*. See Chapters 10 and 11.

Note: As mentioned in Section 2.1 (in a footnote), the SQL standard provides several different ways of invoking SQL operations from an application program. Fig. 2.8 illustrates the method most commonly used, which involves explicitly interleaving SQL statements and host language statements in the program source text ("embedded SQL"). Embedded SQL statements must be prefixed with EXEC SQL, for purposes of recognition. They can include references to host language variables; such references must be prefixed with a colon (":"), again for purposes of recognition. For more details, see Chapter 6.

2.5   VIEWS

Recall from Section 2.2 that a view, or "viewed table," is a (named) *virtual* table—i.e., a named table that (unlike a base table) does not "really exist" but looks to the user as if it did. Views are not directly supported by their own data, separate from the data in the base tables; instead, they simply serve as different ways of looking at the data in those base tables. Thus, they are defined in terms of other tables (base tables and/or views). Fig. 2.9 shows the definition of a view called LS ("London suppliers").

```
CREATE VIEW LS
    AS SELECT  S.SNO, S.SNAME, S.STATUS
        FROM   S
        WHERE  S.CITY = 'London'
```

Fig. 2.9 CREATE VIEW (example)

View LS acts as a kind of *window*, through which the user can see the SNO, SNAME, and STATUS values (only) of rows in base table S for which the CITY value is London (only). The SELECT defining the view is *not* executed when the view is created but is merely remembered by the system in some way (actually by saving it in the appropriate *schema*—see Section 2.8). But to the user it now appears as if a table called LS really does exist in the database. Fig. 2.10 shows an example of a retrieval against that table.

```
SELECT  LS.SNO
FROM    LS
WHERE   LS.STATUS < 50
```

Result:

SNO
S1
S4

Fig. 2.10 Retrieval against a view (example)

Operations against a view are effectively handled by replacing *references* to the view by the expression that *defines* the view. In the example, the system logically merges the remembered SELECT of Fig. 2.9 with the SELECT of Fig. 2.10 to give the modified SELECT shown in Fig. 2.11 (note the clause "AS LS"). And that modified SELECT in turn is readily seen to be equivalent to the simplified version shown in Fig. 2.12. Thus, the original SELECT on the view is effectively converted into an equivalent SELECT on the underlying base table, and that equivalent SELECT is then executed in the normal way.

```
SELECT  LS.SNO
FROM    ( SELECT  S.SNO, S.SNAME, S.STATUS
          FROM    S
          WHERE   S.CITY = 'London' ) AS LS
WHERE   LS.STATUS < 50
```

Fig. 2.11 Modified SELECT

```
SELECT  S.SNO                          Result:    SNO
FROM    S                                         ────
WHERE   S.CITY = 'London'                         S1
AND     S.STATUS < 50                             S4
```

Fig. 2.12 Equivalent SELECT against the base table

Update operations are handled in a similar fashion; however, update operations on views are subject to a number of restrictions in SQL, details of which are beyond the scope of this chapter. Simplifying matters somewhat, standard SQL allows update operations on a view only if that view consists of a simple row-and-column subset of a single underlying base table (for example, it cannot involve a join). See Chapter 13 for further discussion.

Two more examples of views (both nonupdatable in SQL) are shown in Fig. 2.13.

```
CREATE VIEW PQ
    AS SELECT SP.PNO, SUM ( SP.QTY ) AS TOTQ
       FROM    SP
       GROUP   BY SP.PNO

CREATE VIEW CITY_PAIRS
    AS SELECT DISTINCT S.CITY AS SCITY, P.CITY AS PCITY
       FROM    S, SP, P
       WHERE   S.SNO = SP.SNO
       AND     SP.PNO = P.PNO
```

Fig. 2.13 Additional view examples

2.6   SECURITY AND INTEGRITY

As mentioned in Section 2.1, SQL provides facilities for data control as well as for data definition and manipulation. Those control facilities include (among other things) certain *security* and *integrity* features, which we now briefly discuss.

Security

There are two principal aspects to security in SQL, the view mechanism and the GRANT operation. First, views. Views can be used to *hide* sensitive data from unauthorized users. Some examples of views that might be used in this way are shown in Fig. 2.14; the first shows information only for red parts, the second shows information only for parts that are supplied by the current user of the view, the third shows information for suppliers but hides the status values, and the fourth shows average shipment quantity per part but hides the individual quantities. *Note:* "SELECT *" is shorthand for a SELECT clause that lists all columns of the table; for example, "SELECT * FROM P" is shorthand for "SELECT P.PNO, P.PNAME, P.COLOR, P.WEIGHT, P.CITY FROM P."

```
CREATE VIEW RED_PARTS
     AS SELECT *
        FROM   P
        WHERE  P.COLOR = 'Red'

CREATE VIEW MY_PARTS
     AS SELECT *
        FROM   P
        WHERE  P.PNO IN
             ( SELECT SP.PNO
               FROM   SP
               WHERE  SP.SNO = CURRENT_USER )

CREATE VIEW STATUS_HIDDEN
     AS SELECT S.SNO, S.SNAME, S.CITY
        FROM   S

CREATE VIEW AVG_QTYS
     AS SELECT SP.PNO, AVG ( SP.QTY ) AS AVGQ
        FROM   SP
        GROUP  BY SP.PNO
```

Fig. 2.14 Using views to hide data (examples)

Second, the GRANT operation. To execute any SQL statement at all, the user must hold the appropriate *privilege* for the combination of operation and operand(s) concerned (otherwise the statement will be rejected). The possible privileges include SELECT, INSERT, UPDATE, and DELETE (representing in each case the privilege to perform the indicated operation on the table in question), plus certain others that are beyond the scope of this introductory chapter. INSERT and UPDATE privileges can be further restricted to just specific columns. Privileges are granted as follows:

- A user who creates a table (base table or view) is automatically granted all applicable privileges on that table, "with the grant option."

- Any user holding a privilege "with the grant option" can in turn grant that privilege to another user, and moreover can optionally pass the grant option on to that other user also (in which case that user in turn can go on to grant the privilege to a third party, and so on).

- Granting privileges is performed by means of the GRANT operation, some examples of which are shown in Fig. 2.15. Note that the last example refers to a view (table LS), not a base table; the user receiving the privilege in that example is allowed to perform SELECT operations on view LS, but *not* necessarily on the underlying base table S.

```
GRANT INSERT, UPDATE, DELETE ON SP TO JOE

GRANT SELECT ON SP TO ALICE WITH GRANT OPTION

GRANT UPDATE ( STATUS ) ON S TO JUDY

GRANT DELETE ON SP TO BONNIE, CLYDE

GRANT SELECT ON LS TO FRED
```

Fig. 2.15: GRANT examples

Note: In the interest of accuracy, we should mention that the standard does not in fact talk in terms of "users" at all, but rather in terms of what it calls *authorization identifiers*. In Fig. 2.15, for example, JOE, ALICE, JUDY, BONNIE, CLYDE, and FRED are really all authorization identifiers. See Chapters 4 and 15 for further discussion.

Integrity

The term "integrity" refers to the correctness of the data in the database. Standard SQL allows certain *integrity constraints* to be defined by a variety of means—e.g., via appropriate options on CREATE TABLE. Any attempt to perform an update that would violate any defined constraint is rejected, and the database remains unchanged. Here are some of the ways in which constraints can be defined:

- *UNIQUE:* Can be specified for any column or combination of columns within a specified base table. Any attempt to introduce a row having the same value in the specified column or column combination as some existing row will be rejected.

- *PRIMARY KEY:* A special case of UNIQUE, already discussed briefly in Section 2.2.

- *FOREIGN KEY:* Also discussed briefly in Section 2.2.

- *CHECK:* Can be specified for any column or combination of columns in any base table or combination of base tables. Any attempt to update the database in a way that would cause the specified CHECK constraint to fail will be rejected.

The foregoing list is not intended to be exhaustive; see Chapter 14 for a comprehensive discussion.

Two further integrity features should also be mentioned, data type checking and "the check option." First, SQL will reject any attempt to violate data type specifications—e.g., an attempt to insert a character string value into a column defined as DECIMAL. Second, SQL also supports the clause WITH CHECK OPTION on CREATE VIEW. For details of WITH CHECK OPTION, the reader is referred to Chapter 13.

2.7   RECOVERY AND CONCURRENCY

Standard SQL includes support for the conventional transaction concept. A tutorial on transaction management and the associated notions of recovery and concurrency would be out of place here; such tutorials can be found in many places—see, e.g., C. J. Date, *An Introduction to Database Systems* (6th edition, Addison-Wesley, 1995). We defer detailed discussion of the relevant SQL features to Chapter 5; what follows is only the briefest of sketches.

- A transaction (more precisely, an *SQL-transaction*) is a sequence of operations that is guaranteed to be atomic for recovery purposes. Every transaction terminates by executing either a COMMIT operation (normal termination) or a ROLLBACK operation (abnormal termination).*

- Database updates made by a given transaction *T1* are not made visible to any distinct transaction *T2* until and unless *T1* successfully executes a COMMIT.† Successful execution of COMMIT causes all updates made by the

---

*Or some equivalent to COMMIT or ROLLBACK. Exactly how a given transaction terminates depends on the environment in which the transaction executes (see Chapter 5).

†Here we are describing the way conventional transaction management is supposed to work. It is not clear that standard SQL actually does work this way—and in fact it definitely does not, if transaction *T2* executes at isolation level READ UNCOMMITTED. See Chapter 5 for further discussion.

transaction to be made visible to other transactions; such updates are said to be *committed*, and are guaranteed never to be canceled. If the transaction executes a ROLLBACK instead, all updates made by the transaction are canceled (*rolled back*).

■ By default, the interleaved execution of a set of concurrent transactions is required to be *serializable*, in the sense that it must produce the same result as executing those same transactions one at a time in some (unspecified) serial order. However, the standard explicitly provides options that permit certain violations of serializability. See the discussion of *isolation level* in Chapter 5, Section 5.4.

2.8   SCHEMAS AND CATALOGS

Note: The standard uses both "schemata" and "schemas" as the plural of "schema." We prefer the latter form.

Standard SQL operations are always performed within the context of an *SQL-environment* ("environment" for short), which includes among other things an arbitrary number of *catalogs*, grouped into clusters. Each catalog in turn contains an arbitrary number of *SQL-schemas*. None of these concepts is explained very well in the standard, but the intent seems to be somewhat as follows:

■ An *SQL-environment* represents the combination of

   a. a particular instance of a particular SQL database management system (DBMS) that is

   b. executing at a particular computer site, together with

   c. the collection of all databases accessible to that DBMS instance at that site, together with

   d. the collection of all users and programs at that site that are able to use that DBMS instance to access those databases.

For example, a single copy of IBM's DB2 DBMS (MVS version), executing on a single MVS system, together with the set of all DB2 databases under the control of that copy of DB2 and the set of all users and programs on that MVS system that can use that copy of DB2 to access those DB2 databases, might together constitute such an "environment." *Note:* Since the term "database" is not formally defined within the standard, we are within our rights in assuming that a single environment might contain any number of databases, not necessarily just one.

Actually, the standard does *not* say that an SQL-environment is limited to a single site; in fact, it strongly suggests the opposite, because it explicitly requires an "SQL-connection" to be established between the "SQL-client" and an "SQL-server" before any database processing can be done, with the implication that the SQL-client and SQL-server might be at different sites (and the further implication that the database will actually reside at the server site, not the client site). However, it certainly does not preclude the single-site case either, and we will stay with the single-site interpretation for now. See Section 2.9 and Appendix D for further discussion.

SQL operations are not allowed to span environments.

■ Each *catalog* within a given environment consists of a set of *schemas* (more correctly, *SQL-schemas*), the entries in which, taken together, describe what might reasonably (but not officially!) be regarded as a *database*. That is, each catalog effectively describes a certain set of base tables, views, and so on, that somehow—in some implementation-defined way—constitute a logically related collection of data within the given environment.

■ Catalogs are grouped in an implementation-defined way into *clusters*. The intent seems to be that a given cluster should consist of the set of all catalogs that describe any objects that are accessible to a given user. Each SQL-session (see Section 2.9) has exactly one associated cluster, which defines the totality of SQL-data available to that SQL-session. *Note:* It is implementation-defined whether the same catalog can appear in distinct clusters.

We stated above that SQL operations are not allowed to span environments. More specifically, they are not allowed to span clusters *within* an environment.

■ Each *schema* within a given catalog contains entries that describe some individual user's portion of the complete "database" as described by the overall catalog; or, to put it another way, each catalog is effectively partitioned into schemas, one for each user who has created objects that are described by that catalog. (This explanation is slightly oversimplified: A given user can be responsible for any number of schemas, not necessarily just one, within a given catalog.)

Exactly what schemas in general look like is not defined, but every catalog is required to contain one particular schema called the *Information Schema*, whose contents *are* precisely defined. More specifically, the Information Schema (within a given catalog) consists of a set of SQL tables whose contents effectively echo, in a precisely defined way, all of the definitions from all of the other schemas in the catalog in question. See Chapter 21.

SQL objects such as base tables, views, integrity constraints, etc., always exist within the context of some particular schema (within some catalog within some environment), and are thereby considered to "belong to" or "be owned by" the schema in question.* Creating a new object—e.g., a base table—causes an

---

*More precisely, they are considered to belong to the unique authorization identifier—i.e., user, loosely speaking—that is associated with that schema. See Chapter 4.

entry (a *descriptor*) describing that object to be placed in the relevant schema. Note, however, that SQL operations are explicitly allowed to span schemas, and even catalogs (and hence, perhaps, "databases"); for example, it is possible to join tables that are described by distinct schemas or distinct catalogs. The only requirement is that all of those schemas and catalogs be part of the same cluster.

The schema name is used as the high-level qualifier for names of objects that belong to the schema (schema names must be unique within their containing catalog). Likewise, schemas always belong to some catalog, and the catalog name is used as the high-level qualifier for names of schemas in the catalog in question (catalog names must be unique within the environment). Note, however, that in practice these high-level qualifiers will frequently be omitted; the standard includes an elaborate system of *defaults*, by which appropriate catalog and schema names are assumed if nothing is specified explicitly (see Chapters 3–6 for details).

2.9 SESSIONS AND CONNECTIONS

SQL operations are invoked by *SQL-agents*. An SQL-agent can be thought of as the execution of an application program; it starts execution under the control of an SQL-environment component called the *SQL-client*, and remains "bound" to that SQL-client throughout its execution. In order to carry out any database operations, the SQL-agent must first ask the SQL-client to establish an *SQL-connection* to some *SQL-server* (another component of the overall SQL-environment). The SQL-server, in turn, is the component that will actually perform the database operations requested by the SQL-agent. (As mentioned in the previous section, the database can be thought of as residing at the server site.) *Note:* In practice the SQL-client and SQL-server might, and frequently will, be at one and the same site, but they need not be; the intent is to provide a basis for true remote data access, in which an SQL-agent at one site is able to execute SQL operations on data at some distinct site, possibly a site that is geographically remote.

Establishing the necessary SQL-connection between client and server is performed by means of the CONNECT statement, which also has the effect of initiating an *SQL-session* over the SQL-connection. Once the SQL-connection has been established and the SQL-session initiated, the SQL-agent can carry out any number of *SQL-transactions* over that SQL-connection (see Section 2.7), until such time as it executes a DISCONNECT statement, which breaks the SQL-connection and terminates the SQL-session.

Note: Actually matters are rather more complex than the foregoing paragraph suggests. In fact, a given SQL-agent can establish *any number* of SQL-connections and SQL-sessions, one after another; each time such a connection and session are established, the immediately preceding connection and session are put into a *dormant* state. Further, it is always possible to switch back to (i.e., reawaken) a dormant connection and session by means of another statement, SET

CONNECTION. Switching from one connection (and session) to another can even be done while a transaction is running, implying that a single transaction can span several connections (and sessions). See Chapter 5 and Appendix D for further discussion.

We should mention that (as with the business of using catalog and schema names as high-level qualifiers) explicit CONNECT and DISCONNECT operations can frequently be omitted in practice; again the standard includes an elaborate system of defaults, by which default connections and sessions are established and terminated at appropriate times if nothing is specified explicitly. See Chapter 5 for further discussion.

PART **II**

SOME PRELIMINARIES

This part of the book might be thought of as the "necessary evils" part. Its purpose is (a) to spell out the rules for a number of fundamental aspects of the SQL language, such as what it is that constitutes a legal SQL identifier and what the scope of SQL names is, and (b) to define and explain certain common underlying concepts and constructs, such as schemas, sessions, and modules. *CAVEAT:* Much of this material is provided primarily for reference; it is NOT necessary to read these chapters exhaustively before moving on to later parts of the book—*in fact, it is probably better not even to try, owing to the excessive complexity of much of the subject matter.* However, later parts of the book will necessarily refer back to these chapters from time to time (especially Chapter 6).

3

Basic Language Elements

3.1   SQL LANGUAGE CHARACTERS

The most primitive language elements of all are the individual characters of the
SQL language character set. The characters of that character set—the *SQL language characters*—are used to construct higher-level (nonprimitive) elements of
the language. The SQL language characters are the upper case letters A–Z, the
lower case letters a–z, the digits 0–9, and a set of *SQL special characters*, consisting of a *space* character and the following additional characters:*

> " % & ' ( ) * + , - . / : ; < = > ? _ |

For the remainder of this chapter, the term "character" will be taken to mean an
SQL language character specifically, barring explicit statements to the contrary.

Note: A given SQL-implementation (see Chapter 4 for an explanation of this
term) can support any number of distinct character sets; however, it *must* support
a character set called SQL_TEXT that includes all of the SQL language characters,
and possibly other characters as well. The whole subject of character sets is quite
complex, and for this reason we defer detailed discussion to Chapter 19. The

---

*For the reader's information, the only use of the ampersand ("&") is in SQL embedded in MUMPS.

reader is warned, however, that our discussion of identifiers in Section 3.4 below is therefore not quite complete (it will be completed in Chapter 19, Section 19.8).

3.2   TOKENS AND SEPARATORS

Tokens and separators represent lexical units in the language. We discuss *tokens* first. A token is either a *delimiter* or a *nondelimiter*; the difference is that a delimiter *might* (but need not) be followed by a separator, whereas a nondelimiter *must* be followed by either a separator or a delimiter.

- A *delimiter* is any of the following:

    a. a character string literal (see Chapter 7 for a discussion of literals);

    b. a date, time, timestamp, or interval string (see Chapter 17);

    c. a "delimited identifier" (see Section 3.4 below);

    d. an SQL special character; or

    e. one of the following symbols*—

    > <>   >=   <= || ..   [   ]

- A *nondelimiter* is any of the following:

    a. a literal of type unsigned numeric, national character string, or bit string (including hexadecimal string);

    b. a "regular identifier" (see Section 3.4 below); or

    c. a key word (see Section 3.3 below).

Turning now to separators: A *separator* is any combination of spaces and/or newline markers and/or comments. (As already explained, delimiter tokens can optionally be followed by a separator, and nondelimiter tokens must be followed by either a separator or a delimiter.) *Spaces* are self-explanatory. A *newline marker* is an implementation-defined end-of-line indicator. A *comment* consists of two immediately adjacent hyphens ("- -"), followed by any sequence of zero or more characters (not necessarily SQL language characters), terminating with a newline marker. *Note:* The syntax notation introduced later in this chapter (in Section 3.6) simply ignores separators, for the most part.

No token is allowed to include any separators, except possibly for:

- Character string literals (including national character string literals)—see Chapters 7 and 19;

---

*For the reader's information, the only use of the double period ("..") is in SQL embedded in Ada or Pascal, and the only use of brackets ("[" and "]") is in SQL embedded in Pascal or C.

- Bit string literals (including hexadecimal string literals)—see Chapter 7;
- Timestamp strings and "day-time intervals" (a special case of interval strings)—see Chapter 17;
- Delimited identifiers—see Section 3.4 below.

In the foregoing cases certain embedded separators are both allowed and significant, as will be seen.

3.3   KEY WORDS

A *key word* is a word that has one or more prescribed meanings in the SQL language itself. Some key words are reserved (i.e., cannot be used as a regular identifier), others are not. Here first is a list of those that are reserved:

```
ABSOLUTE  ACTION  ADD  ALL  ALLOCATE  ALTER  AND  ANY  ARE
AS  ASC  ASSERTION  AT  AUTHORIZATION  AVG

BEGIN  BETWEEN  BIT  BIT_LENGTH  BOTH  BY

CASCADE  CASCADED  CASE  CAST  CATALOG  CHAR  CHARACTER
CHAR_LENGTH  CHARACTER_LENGTH  CHECK  CLOSE  COALESCE
COLLATE  COLLATION  COLUMN  COMMIT  CONNECT  CONNECTION
CONSTRAINT  CONSTRAINTS  CONTINUE  CONVERT  CORRESPONDING
COUNT  CREATE  CROSS  CURRENT  CURRENT_DATE  CURRENT_TIME
CURRENT_TIMESTAMP  CURRENT_USER  CURSOR

DATE  DAY  DEALLOCATE  DEC  DECIMAL  DECLARE  DEFAULT
DEFERRABLE  DEFERRED  DELETE  DESC  DESCRIBE  DESCRIPTOR
DIAGNOSTICS  DISCONNECT  DISTINCT  DOMAIN  DOUBLE  DROP

ELSE  END  END-EXEC  ESCAPE  EXCEPT  EXCEPTION  EXEC  EXECUTE
EXISTS  EXTERNAL  EXTRACT

FALSE  FETCH  FIRST  FLOAT  FOR  FOREIGN  FOUND  FROM  FULL

GET  GLOBAL  GO  GOTO  GRANT  GROUP

HAVING  HOUR

IDENTITY  IMMEDIATE  IN  INDICATOR  INITIALLY  INNER  INPUT
INSENSITIVE  INSERT  INT  INTEGER  INTERSECT  INTERVAL  INTO
IS  ISOLATION

JOIN

KEY

LANGUAGE  LAST  LEADING  LEFT  LEVEL  LIKE  LOCAL  LOWER

MATCH  MAX  MIN  MINUTE  MODULE  MONTH

NAMES  NATIONAL  NATURAL  NCHAR  NEXT  NO  NOT  NULL  NULLIF
NUMERIC

OCTET_LENGTH  OF  ON  ONLY  OPEN  OPTION  OR  ORDER  OUTER
OUTPUT  OVERLAPS
```

```
PARTIAL   POSITION   PRECISION   PREPARE   PRESERVE   PRIMARY
PRIOR   PRIVILEGES   PROCEDURE   PUBLIC

READ   REAL   REFERENCES   RELATIVE   RESTRICT   REVOKE   RIGHT
ROLLBACK   ROWS

SCHEMA   SCROLL   SECOND   SECTION   SELECT   SESSION
SESSION_USER   SET   SIZE   SMALLINT   SOME   SQL   SQLCODE
SQLERROR   SQLSTATE   SUBSTRING   SUM   SYSTEM_USER

TABLE   TEMPORARY   THEN   TIME   TIMESTAMP   TIMEZONE_HOUR
TIMEZONE_MINUTE   TO   TRAILING   TRANSACTION   TRANSLATE
TRANSLATION   TRIM   TRUE

UNION   UNIQUE   UNKNOWN   UPDATE   UPPER   USAGE   USER   USING

VALUE   VALUES   VARCHAR   VARYING   VIEW

WHEN   WHENEVER   WHERE   WITH   WORK   WRITE

YEAR

ZONE
```

And here is a list of those that are not reserved:

```
ADA
C   CATALOG_NAME   CHARACTER_SET_CATALOG   CHARACTER_SET_NAME
CHARACTER_SET_SCHEMA   CLASS_ORIGIN   COBOL   COLLATION_CATALOG
COLLATION_NAME   COLLATION_SCHEMA   COLUMN_NAME
COMMAND_FUNCTION   COMMITTED   CONDITION_NUMBER
CONNECTION_NAME   CONSTRAINT_CATALOG   CONSTRAINT_NAME
CONSTRAINT_SCHEMA   CURSOR_NAME

DATA   DATETIME_INTERVAL_CODE   DATETIME_INTERVAL_PRECISION
DYNAMIC_FUNCTION

FORTRAN

LENGTH

MESSAGE_LENGTH   MESSAGE_OCTET_LENGTH   MORE   MUMPS

NAME   NULLABLE   NUMBER

PAD   PASCAL   PLI

REPEATABLE   RETURNED_LENGTH   RETURNED_OCTET_LENGTH
RETURNED_SQLSTATE   ROW_COUNT

SCALE   SCHEMA_NAME   SERIALIZABLE   SERVER_NAME   SPACE
SUBCLASS_ORIGIN

TABLE_NAME   TYPE

UNCOMMITTED   UNNAMED
```

Points to note:

1. The rule by which it is determined within the standard that one key word needs to be reserved while another need not is not clear to this writer. In practice, it is probably wise to treat all key words as reserved.

2. Within key words, upper case and lower case letters are treated as inter-changeable; thus, e.g., "WHERE" and "where" represent the same key word. In this book we will adhere to the convention (as the standard itself does) that key words are always shown in all upper case.

3. The standard document also includes a list of some 60 or so *potential* reserved words, i.e., additional words that are likely to become reserved words in some future version of the standard. We do not give that list here, but simply note the following (a direct extract from the standard): "Readers must understand that there is no guarantee that all of [the words in this list] will, in fact, become reserved words in any future revision; furthermore, it is almost certain that additional words will be added to [the list] as any possible future revision emerges." *Caveat lector.*

3.4   IDENTIFIERS AND NAMES

An *identifier* is either a regular identifier or a delimited identifier.

- A *regular* identifier is a string of not more than 128 characters, of which the first must be a letter (upper or lower case), while the rest can be any combi-nation of upper or lower case letters, digits, and the underscore character ("_"). No reserved key word can be used as a regular identifier.* *Note:* Like key words, regular identifiers are case-insensitive; thus, e.g., ABC, abc, and aBc are all the same identifier, and they can be used interchangeably.

- A *delimited* identifier is any string of not more than 128 characters (not nec-essarily SQL language characters) enclosed in double quotes;† for example, SELECT is not a valid regular identifier, because it is identical to a reserved key word, but "SELECT" is a valid delimited identifier. Within such a string, the double quote character itself is represented by a pair of immediately adja-cent double quotes (such a pair of double quotes counting, of course, as a sin-gle character with respect to the 128-character limit).

For the sake of simplicity, all identifiers used in examples in this book will be regular identifiers, and the unqualified term *identifier* will be taken to mean a reg-

---

*The standard provides options by which the letters and digits in a regular identifier can be different from the letters and digits (A–Z, a–z, 0–9) of the SQL language character set. We ignore this possibil-ity throughout this book, except in Chapter 19. Refer to Chapter 19, Section 19.8, for further discus-sion.

†We follow the standard here in using *double quote* to mean what is more conventionally called a quo-tation mark ("). We use *single quote* to refer to the apostrophe (').

ular identifier specifically, barring any explicit statement to the contrary. Furthermore, we will never include any lower case letters in any of our identifiers.

The following are all identifiers in the foregoing sense:

- authorization identifiers
- catalog names
- range variable names
  (i.e., "correlation names"—see Chapter 11)
- module names
- procedure names
- parameter names
  (except that a colon prefix is required—see Chapter 6)
- cursor names
- statement names

The following have names that consist of an identifier in the foregoing sense, preceded by a qualifier that is a catalog name (separated from the identifier by a period):

- schemas

The following have names that consist of an identifier in the foregoing sense, preceded by a qualifier that is a schema name (separated from the identifier by a period):

- domains
- base tables
- views
- constraints
- character sets
- collations
- translations
- conversions

Note: Collations, translations, and *conversions* all have to do with the general topic of character sets and are discussed, along with character sets *per se,* in Chapter 19. However, we remark here that in the case of conversions the (implicit or explicit, unqualified) schema name *must* be INFORMATION_SCHEMA; i.e., conversions are always considered to belong to an Information Schema. Note further that the standard also talks about *character repertoire* names and *form-of-use* names (again, see Chapter 19 for more information). However, both of these are ultimately defined to be character set names; we therefore exclude them from the foregoing list.

The following have names that consist of an identifier in the foregoing sense, preceded by the key word MODULE (separated from the identifier by a period):

- declared local temporary tables
  (referred to as "Type 1" temporary tables in Chapter 18)

The following have names that consist of an identifier in the foregoing sense, preceded by a qualifier that is a base table name or view name (separated from the identifier by a period):

- columns within base tables and views

Note: All columns within named tables (i.e., base tables and views) are required by the standard to be named; those names are specified—possibly implicitly, in the case of views—as part of the base table or view definition. The standard also includes a set of rules defining names of columns within *un*named tables (i.e., tables that result from evaluating some table expression), but those column names are sometimes system-generated (and implementation-dependent) and concealed from the user. Refer to Chapter 11, Section 11.7, for further explanation.

We close this section by reminding the reader that, as mentioned in Chapter 2, the standard provides a set of default rules by which high-level components can often be omitted from what would otherwise be qualified names. Thus, e.g., the catalog name component might be omitted from a schema name, in which case an appropriate catalog name will be assumed by default. If a high-level qualifier is omitted from a given name, the period that would have separated that qualifier from the rest of the name is omitted too. The default rules are spelled out in detail at appropriate points in the chapters that follow—primarily Chapters 4, 6, and 11.

3.5 SCOPE OF NAMES

In this section we summarize SQL's name scoping rules. First, the following must be unique within the SQL-environment:

- authorization identifiers
  (note that the identifier PUBLIC is not allowed as an authorization identifier)
- catalog names*
- module names

---

*Actually the standard says only that catalog names have to be unique within their containing *cluster* (see Chapter 2). But clusters themselves seem to be unnamed!—or, at best, to have names that are implementation-defined. It looks to this writer as if the cluster notion was grafted on to the standard at a late stage in its development and never properly integrated with other features.

The following must be unique within their containing catalog:

- schema names
  (note that no schema can have an unqualified name of DEFINITION_
  SCHEMA, and every catalog must include exactly one schema with the
  unqualified name INFORMATION_SCHEMA)

The following must be unique within the applicable schema:

- domain names
- table names
  ("table" here includes both base tables and views, i.e., a base table and a view
  cannot have the same unqualified name)
- constraint names
- character set names
- collation names
- translation names
- conversion names
  (as explained in the previous section, the schema in this case is always the
  applicable Information Schema)

The following must be unique within their containing module:

- procedure names
- cursor names
- statement names
- declared local temporary table names

The following must be unique within their containing procedure:

- parameter names

The following must be unique within their containing table:

- base table column names
- view column names

Finally, range variable names are unique within a certain scope as defined in
Chapter 11, Section 11.3. Points to note:

1. When we say that names of a certain type must be unique within a certain
   scope, we mean they must be unique with respect to all names *of that type*
   within that scope. Thus, when we say, for example, that domain names and
   constraint names must be unique within their containing schema, we mean that
   no two domains within a given schema can have the same name, and likewise

for constraints. However, a domain and a constraint within a given schema can have the same name if desired (the practice is not recommended).

2. All columns within named tables (i.e., base tables and views) are required by the standard to have names that are unique within their containing table. In certain circumstances, however, columns within *un*named tables—i.e., tables that result from evaluating some table expression—are (very unfortunately, in this writer's opinion) allowed to have nonunique names. In this book we will generally assume that *all* columns have names that are unique within their containing table, barring some explicit statement to the contrary. Refer to Chapter 11, Section 11.7, for further explanation.

3. Certain objects, namely *SQL-servers, SQL-sessions, SQL-connections, SQL-transactions,* and *SQL-agents* (see Chapters 4 and 5), are omitted from the lists given in this section because, although those objects most certainly do have names, those names are not necessarily identifiers (qualified or unqualified) as defined above.

4. Finally, certain objects that are used in connection with the *dynamic SQL* feature (see Chapter 20) are also omitted from the lists given above because, although those objects do have names that are indeed identifiers as defined above, those identifiers are *generated* by the user at run time. The objects in question are *SQL descriptor areas*, certain *cursors*, and certain *statements*. Furthermore, those user-generated names* can be defined to have either LOCAL or GLOBAL scope; LOCAL means the scope is the containing *module*, GLOBAL means it is the current *SQL-session*.† See Chapter 20 for further details.

3.6   NOTATION

The syntax of SQL language elements is specified in this book by means of a variant of the well known BNF notation. The variant in question is defined as follows:

- Special characters and material in upper case must be written exactly as shown. Material in lower case represents a syntactic category that appears on the left hand side of another production rule, and hence must eventually be replaced by specific values chosen by the user. *Note:* In this book, however, some of the production rules at the lowest level of detail, such as the rules that

---

*Which are represented in an implementation-defined character set, incidentally (see Chapter 19).

†The key words are not well chosen, because (as we will see in Chapters 5 and 6) sessions and modules do not have a global-to-local kind of relationship: One session can be associated with many modules and one module can be associated with many sessions.

define the construction of an identifier, are not shown in explicit BNF style but are instead explained in ordinary prose.

- Vertical bars "|" are used to separate alternatives.

- Square brackets "[" and "]" are used to indicate that the material enclosed in those brackets is optional; i.e., it consists of a set of one or more items (separated by vertical bars if there are more than one) from which at most one is to be chosen.

- Braces "{" and "}" are used to indicate that the material enclosed in those braces consists of a set of two or more items (separated by vertical bars) from which exactly one is to be chosen.

By way of example, we show a possible set of production rules for the syntactic category "unsigned numeric literal" (see Chapter 7 for a full description of literals):

```
unsigned-numeric-literal
    ::=    unsigned-exact-numeric-literal
         | unsigned-approximate-numeric-literal

unsigned-exact-numeric-literal
    ::=    unsigned-integer [ . [ unsigned-integer ] ]
         | . unsigned-integer

unsigned-approximate-numeric-literal
    ::=    unsigned-exact-numeric-literal  E  signed-integer

signed-integer
    ::=  [ + | - ] unsigned-integer
```

The category "unsigned integer" is not further defined here; i.e., it is a *terminal category* with respect to this simple example. (Note, incidentally, that although the production rules shown in this example include numerous embedded spaces for readability reasons, "unsigned numeric literals" are tokens—see Section 3.2— and in fact must *not* include any such spaces.)

Here is another example to illustrate the use of braces (this rule shows the syntax of the *fold* function, which is used to replace upper case letters by their lower case equivalents or *vice versa*):

```
fold-function-reference
    ::=  { LOWER | UPPER } ( character-string-expression )
```

---

*Except that the standard distinguishes syntactic categories by enclosing them in angle brackets, whereas we use hyphenated word strings. For example, we use *unsigned-integer* where the standard uses *<unsigned integer>*. In less formal contexts, we drop the hyphens and enclose the term in double quotes—for example, "unsigned integer" (see the discussion above). If there is no risk of confusion we might even drop the double quotes as well.

So far our BNF notation is essentially the same as that used in the SQL standard itself.* However, we introduce two further simplifying conventions of our own, as follows. First, we define a *syntactic unit* to be either (a) a syntactic category (i.e., something that appears on the left hand side of some BNF production rule), or (b) whatever is contained between a pair of matching square brackets or matching braces. Then:

- If *xyz* is a syntactic unit, then *xyz-list* is a syntactic unit consisting of a sequence of one or more *xyz*'s in which each pair of adjacent *xyz*'s is separated by at least one separator (i.e., a space, comment, or newline marker).

- If *xyz* is a syntactic unit, then *xyz-commalist* is a syntactic unit consisting of a sequence of one or more *xyz*'s in which each pair of adjacent *xyz*'s is separated by a comma (as well as zero or more spaces and/or comments and/or newline markers).

These two conventions have the net effect of reducing the overall length and number of production rules required. Here is an example to illustrate their use (a simplified variant of the first few production rules for the CREATE SCHEMA statement, which is discussed in detail in Chapter 4 and later chapters):

```
schema-definition
    ::=    CREATE SCHEMA [ schema ] [ AUTHORIZATION user ]
                [ schema-element-list ]

schema-element
    ::=    base-table-definition
         | view-definition

base-table-definition
    ::=    CREATE TABLE base-table
                ( base-table-element-commalist )

base-table-element
    ::=    column-definition
         | base-table-constraint-definition
```

And so on.

One further point regarding notation: In our BNF we follow the convention that if *xyz* is an SQL object type (e.g., "schema"), then in syntax rules the syntactic category *xyz* stands for the *name* of an object of that type. For example, in the syntax rule already discussed—

```
schema-definition
    ::=    CREATE SCHEMA [ schema ] [ AUTHORIZATION user ]
                [ schema-element-list ]
```

—the syntactic category "schema" stands for a schema name.

Note: We often deliberately use names for syntactic categories that are different from those in the SQL standard. Our primary reason for doing this is that the SQL standard nomenclature is often not very apt (in some cases, in fact, it is positively misleading). As one example, the standard actually uses "qualified identifier" to mean, quite specifically, an identifier that is *not* qualified . . . As a second example, it uses "table definition" to refer to what we called a "base table definition" above. The standard's usage here obscures the important fact that a *view* is also a defined table, and hence that "table definition" ought to include "view definition" as a special case.

To pursue this latter point a moment longer: In fact, SQL is generally ambivalent as to the meaning of the term "table"—sometimes it uses it to mean either a base table or a view, sometimes it uses it to mean a base table explicitly. In this book we will use "table" to mean *any* kind of table (base table, view, or more generally the result of evaluating any arbitrary table expression); we will use "base table" explicitly when a base table is what we mean.

4

Catalogs and Schemas

4.1   THE SQL-ENVIRONMENT

As explained in Chapter 2, the SQL standard starts with the concept of an *SQL-environment*, which is effectively an abstraction of the notion of an operational DBMS installation (including client and server components). More precisely, an SQL-environment is defined to consist of the following components:

- an *SQL-implementation*;
- any number of *authorization identifiers* ("authIDs");
- any number of *modules*;
- any number of *catalogs*;
- "SQL-data" as described by the *SQL-schemas* in those catalogs;
- optionally, other implementation-defined components.

We elaborate on these concepts briefly, as follows.

- First, the *SQL-implementation* can be thought of, informally, as just the DBMS itself (i.e., the DBMS *instance*)—or possibly the combination of several such instances, since it can involve any number of *SQL-server* components (see Chapter 5). It must support standard SQL operations to at least Entry level (see Appendix B), together with at least one *binding style* (direct

SQL, embedded SQL, "module," or the SQL Call-Level Interface—see Chapter 6).

- Second, an *authorization identifier* ("authID" for short) can be thought of, also informally, as the name by which some user is known to the system; indeed, we will often use the term *user* in this book instead of "authorization identifier" or "authID." Please note, however, that the standard does not really know anything about users as such, it knows only about authIDs.

- Third, a *module* consists essentially of a set of SQL statements that can be executed by a given "compilation unit" (i.e., application program, loosely speaking). Note that, regardless of binding style, SQL statements are *always* considered to be contained within some module, at least conceptually.*

- Finally, *catalogs* and *SQL-schemas* ("schemas" for short) are discussed in more detail in Sections 4.2 and 4.3 below.

We remind the reader that SQL operations are not allowed to span SQL-environments, although they *are* allowed to span schemas, and even catalogs (but not clusters of catalogs), within the same SQL-environment. And we will see in Chapter 5 that SQL operations also cannot span *SQL-servers*,† even within the same SQL-environment, because within a given transaction only one connection, and hence only one server, can be current at any one time.

4.2   CATALOGS

A catalog is a named collection of SQL-schemas within an SQL-environment. For example, a given SQL-environment might include two catalogs called TEST_CAT and PRODUCTION_CAT, describing test and production versions of "the same" database; moving an application over from test to production might then be essentially just a matter of recompilation (provided the application in question did not explicitly mention either catalog by name, of course—see the remarks on default catalog names below). Or different catalogs might correspond to databases at different sites, if the SQL-environment supported some kind of distributed processing.

---

*Except for (a) the nonexecutable statements WHENEVER and BEGIN and END DECLARE SECTION, which appear in embedded SQL only, and (b) certain "standalone" CREATE SCHEMA statements. For a discussion of the second of these two possibilities—it is not clear that it actually *is* a possibility, but if it is it is much the more important of the two—see the subsection "Standalone CREATE SCHEMA Statements" at the end of this chapter.

†There are a few somewhat trivial exceptions to this statement, namely CONNECT, DISCONNECT, SET CONNECTION, COMMIT, ROLLBACK, and SET TRANSACTION. See Chapter 5.

The standard does not provide any explicit mechanism for creating and dropping (i.e., destroying) catalogs; instead, catalogs are created and dropped in some implementation-defined manner.

As explained in Chapter 3, the catalog name serves as the high-level qualifier for the names of schemas that are contained within the catalog in question. If some schema reference omits the catalog name, a *default* catalog name is assumed, as follows:*

- If the schema reference appears within the SCHEMA clause (or is implied by the AUTHORIZATION clause) of a module definition—see the subsection "Module Definition" in Chapter 6, Section 6.2—then an implementation-defined catalog name is assumed.

- If the schema reference appears as the schema name (or is implied by the AUTHORIZATION clause) of a CREATE SCHEMA statement, then the catalog name associated with the containing module is assumed.†

- If the schema reference appears in a CREATE SCHEMA statement (other than as described in the previous paragraph), then the catalog name for the schema currently being defined is assumed.

- Otherwise, the catalog name associated with the module that contains the schema reference is assumed (again, see the subsection "Module Definition" in Chapter 6, Section 6.2).

Note: When we talk about a "schema reference," the reader should understand that the most frequent occurrence of such a construct is likely to be as a qualifier—implicit or explicit—in a reference to some other object, such as a base table.

4.3   SCHEMAS

A schema (more correctly, an *SQL-schema*) is a named collection of *descriptors* within a catalog. A descriptor in turn (to quote the standard) is "a coded description of an SQL object [that includes] all of the information about the object that a conforming SQL-implementation requires." Each schema contains descriptors for the following types of objects (in general):

- domains
- base tables

---

*Unless the reference appears in direct SQL, dynamic SQL, or an SQL statement invoked via the Call-Level Interface, in which case the SQL-session default catalog name is taken as the default.

†Note that there always is such a containing module, unless the CREATE SCHEMA is "standalone," in which case an implementation-defined catalog name is assumed. See the subsection "Standalone CREATE SCHEMA Statements" at the end of this chapter.

- views
- constraints
- privileges
- character sets
- collations
- translations

Note: The astute reader might observe a couple of discrepancies between the foregoing list and the list of objects that were stated in Chapter 3 to have names that were "unique within schema." First, *privileges* (see Chapter 15) are described in schemas but do not have names. Second, *conversions* (see Chapter 19) have names but are not described in schemas.*

Schemas are created and dropped (i.e., destroyed) by means of the CREATE and DROP SCHEMA statements, which we now discuss. First, CREATE SCHEMA. The syntax is:

```
CREATE SCHEMA [ schema ] [ AUTHORIZATION user ]
              [ DEFAULT CHARACTER SET character-set ]
              [ schema-element-list ]
```

At least one of "schema" and "AUTHORIZATION user" must appear (see below). We defer explanation of the optional DEFAULT CHARACTER SET clause to Chapter 19. The possible "schema elements" are as follows:

- domain definitions
- base table definitions
- view definitions
- grant statements
- constraint definitions
- character set definitions
- collation definitions
- translation definitions

Each of the above is explained in detail later in this book. However, there is one point that needs to be made now: Each of the foregoing can appear *either* as a "schema element" within a CREATE SCHEMA statement as indicated above *or* as an independent operation in its own right. The difference between the two cases is that an independent operation is not allowed to include any references to objects

---

*More precisely, all conversion descriptors are considered to be part of the applicable Information Schema specifically. See Chapter 21.

that have not yet been defined, whereas a schema element *can* include references to other schema elements that appear later within the same CREATE SCHEMA statement. Suppose, for example, that base tables S and P (suppliers and parts) have not yet been defined. Then the following base table definition for base table SP (shipments)—

```
CREATE TABLE SP ( ... ,
                  FOREIGN KEY ( SNO ) REFERENCES S,
                  FOREIGN KEY ( PNO ) REFERENCES P )
```

—would not be permitted as an independent operation at all, since it references both S and P, but *would* be permitted within a CREATE SCHEMA statement if the base table definitions for S and P appeared subsequently within that same CREATE SCHEMA statement.

To return to the "schema" and "AUTHORIZATION user" specifications: As already mentioned, at least one and possibly both of these specifications will appear; their purpose is to provide a name for the new schema and to identify the schema's owner, respectively. The effect of omitting one or other of these specifications is as follows:

- If the "schema" specification is omitted, then the "user" value from "AUTHORIZATION user" is taken as the schema name.*

- If "AUTHORIZATION user" is omitted, then the authID of the containing module is taken as the schema owner†—or, if that module does not have an explicit authID, then the SQL-session authID is taken instead. Once again, see the subsection "Module Definition" in Chapter 6, Section 6.2.

We turn now to DROP SCHEMA. The syntax is:

```
DROP SCHEMA schema { RESTRICT | CASCADE }
```

If RESTRICT is specified, the operation will fail if the specified schema is nonempty; otherwise it will succeed, and the specified schema will be destroyed (i.e., it will be deleted from the relevant catalog).

If CASCADE is specified, the operation will always succeed, and will cascade to drop not only the specified schema *per se*, but also all objects contained in that schema, all objects described by that schema, and all objects anywhere that reference objects within that schema. Furthermore, the implied DROP that is executed for all those other objects also includes the CASCADE option (wherever

---

*I.e., as the *unqualified* schema name. The corresponding catalog name is decided as explained in Section 4.2 above.

†We are assuming here that the CREATE SCHEMA is not "standalone." See the subsection "Standalone CREATE SCHEMA Statements" at the end of this section.

such an option is legal), and so objects that reference *those* objects will be dropped too, etc., etc.* Indeed, the overall effect appears so drastic that we respectfully suggest that CASCADE be reserved for very special occasions indeed.

As explained in Chapter 3, schema names (including the implicit or explicit catalog-name component) serve as the high-level qualifier for the names of objects that are described by the schema in question. If a reference to such an object omits the schema name, a *default* schema name is assumed, as follows:†

■   If the reference appears within a CREATE SCHEMA statement, then the schema name for the schema currently being defined is assumed.

■   Otherwise, the schema name associated with the module that contains the reference is assumed (note that such a module does always exist—see the subsection "Module Definition" in Chapter 6, Section 6.2).

Standalone CREATE SCHEMA Statements

The standard refers repeatedly to the idea that, regardless of binding style, all SQL statements—at least, all executable SQL statements—are always contained within some module, with the sole possible exception of CREATE SCHEMA statements, which might be "standalone." The reason for the exception is compatibility with SQL/86 and SQL/89, where CREATE SCHEMA statements *had* to be standalone; in fact, the only "official" way of performing data definition operations of any kind in SQL/86 and SQL/89 was in the context of such a standalone CREATE SCHEMA statement (although most vendors went beyond the standard in this respect and allowed data definition operations to be performed from within application programs).

It is now generally agreed that forcing CREATE SCHEMA statements to be standalone was a mistake in SQL/86 and SQL/89. For reasons of compatibility, however (and also because some vendors did in fact implement some kind of standalone schema processor), the standard does still permit CREATE SCHEMA statements to stand alone.‡ But it is not intended that such should be the normal

---

*These remarks are slightly overstated (but only slightly!): Dropping certain objects—e.g., domains—with the CASCADE option merely *alters* referencing objects in certain ways instead of dropping them entirely.

†Unless the reference appears in direct SQL, dynamic SQL, or an SQL statement invoked via the Call-Level Interface, in which case the SQL-session default schema name is taken as the default.

‡It would be more accurate to say that it does not explicitly prohibit such a possibility. Certainly it is not clear from the standard how CREATE SCHEMA (or any other statement, come to that) can possibly *not* be contained within a module.

method of operation. In subsequent chapters, therefore, we will generally assume that, indeed, there always is a containing module; here we simply summarize those features of the standard that seem to rely on the possibility that CREATE SCHEMA statements might somehow be "standalone."

■   If the standalone CREATE SCHEMA does not include an AUTHORIZATION clause, then the owner of the new schema is taken to be the SQL-session authID instead of the module authID (see Chapter 5, Section 5.3).

■   Identifiers and character string literals appearing within a standalone CREATE SCHEMA are assumed by default to be using *either* the SQL language character set (see Chapter 3) *or* the default character set of the schema (see Chapter 19).

5

Connections, Sessions, and Transactions

CAVEAT: It is probably best not to worry too much about the material of this chapter (except perhaps for those portions having to do with transactions). Most of the concepts discussed were not originally part of SQL at all but were added at a later stage; they have little to do with database management as such, and subsequent chapters do not depend on them very much. What is more, they show clear signs of not having been properly thought through (see Appendix D for further discussion). The reader is warned.

5.1 SQL-AGENTS

As explained in Chapter 2, an *SQL-agent* can be thought of as the execution of an application program (the standard defines it as "an implementation-dependent entity that causes the execution of SQL-statements"). A given SQL-agent operates under the control of an *SQL-client*, and remains "bound" to that SQL-client (in an implementation-defined way) throughout its execution. Of course, different SQL-agents can operate under different SQL-clients, but from the point of view of any given SQL-agent there is always just one corresponding SQL-client.

Before it can issue any database requests, the SQL-agent must first establish an *SQL-connection* between the SQL-client and an *SQL-server*. The SQL-server can be thought of as the place where the database actually resides. The SQL-agent establishes the SQL-connection to the SQL-server by executing a CONNECT statement (possibly implicitly). Then, so long as the SQL-agent has at least one such SQL-connection available to it, it can issue SQL requests over those connections; all such SQL requests are executed by the corresponding SQL-server (except for CONNECT, DISCONNECT, SET CONNECTION, and GET DIAGNOSTICS requests, which are executed by the SQL-client instead). Further, the SQL-agent can execute *SQL-transactions* over those connections (indeed, most SQL requests *must* be contained within some SQL-transaction). Note, however, that each SQL-transaction initiated by a given SQL-agent must be executed in its entirety before the next can begin; in other words, SQL-transactions cannot be nested.

Establishing an SQL-connection also initiates an *SQL-session* over that SQL-connection. The SQL-session acts as a holder for certain pieces of "global" context information—for example, certain *session default values* (see Section 5.3).

As was also mentioned in Chapter 2, an SQL-agent can establish any number of SQL-connections, and thus initiate any number of SQL-sessions; it is not necessary to terminate the current SQL-connection before starting up a new one. However, starting up a new connection makes the previous one *dormant*—only one connection can actually be *current* at any given time. Likewise, only one SQL-session can be current at any time, namely the SQL-session that is associated with the current SQL-connection; SQL-sessions that are associated with dormant SQL-connections are themselves considered to be dormant also. The SET CONNECTION statement allows the SQL-agent to make a dormant SQL-connection (and SQL-session) current again—thereby, of course, making the previously current SQL-connection (and SQL-session) dormant.

Note that switching between connections can be done even while a transaction is running, implying that a single transaction can span several connections, and therefore several servers* (though implementations are explicitly permitted not to support this capability). All connections over which a given transaction has performed some database operation are said to be *active* with respect to that transaction.†

Note: As we have just seen, SQL-transactions can span servers; however, indi-

---

*And therefore several *SQL-sessions* also. Such a state of affairs does not accord well with the usual intuitive interpretation of the terms "transaction" and "session," but it is what the standard allows. Note, therefore, that the relationship between transactions and sessions is many-to-many; a given transaction can have any number of corresponding sessions (though only one "active" session at a time), and a given session can have any number of corresponding transactions (though only one transaction at a time).

†The terminology is not very good! If a given transaction has $n + 1$ active connections at some given time, then n of those connections will be dormant at that time—so "dormant" does not imply "inactive" (and "inactive" does not imply "dormant" either). Further, the current connection is not necessarily active, so "current" does not imply "active" either (and "active" certainly does not imply "current").

vidual SQL operations cannot,* because they cannot span connections (they are always performed over the *current* connection). It follows that SQL's multi-server support does not amount to full distributed database support, because it does not provide *location independence* (defined as the ability for users to behave, at least from a logical standpoint, as if the data were all stored at a single "location" or server).

Finally, when the SQL-agent has finished with a given SQL-connection and SQL-session, it must execute a DISCONNECT statement (again possibly implicitly), which has the effect of breaking the specified SQL-connection and terminating the corresponding SQL-session. The connection to be terminated should not be "active" (if it were, it would not make sense to say that the SQL-agent had finished with it).

We now proceed to elaborate on the concepts *SQL-connection, SQL-session,* and *SQL-transaction.*

5.2   SQL-CONNECTIONS

CONNECT

SQL-connections can be established either explicitly or implicitly. The explicit case is handled by means of an explicit CONNECT statement; the implicit case occurs if an SQL-agent invokes a procedure (see Chapter 6) when there is no current SQL-connection, in which case the system automatically issues an implicit CONNECT TO DEFAULT on the SQL-agent's behalf (except as noted at the end of this subsection). Here is the syntax of CONNECT:

```
CONNECT TO { DEFAULT
           | string1 [ AS string2 ] [ USER string3 ] }
```

Each of *string1, string2,* and *string3* is a literal, parameter, or host variable, of type character string in each case. *Note:* The phrase "parameter or host variable" appears many times in the standard, and many times in the present book. In all cases, the significance is as follows: If the context is the module language (see Chapter 6, Section 6.2), then a parameter is required; if the context is embedded SQL (see Chapter 6, Section 6.3), then a host variable is required.

- *Case 1* (DEFAULT): An SQL-connection is established to a *default SQL-server.* A *default SQL-connection* is established and a *default SQL-session* is initiated. None of these "default" concepts is further defined in the standard.

---

*As we pointed out in Chapter 4, there are a few somewhat trivial exceptions to this statement, namely CONNECT, DISCONNECT, SET CONNECTION, COMMIT, ROLLBACK, and SET TRANSACTION.

- *Case 2* (otherwise): An SQL-connection is established to the SQL-server identified (in an implementation-defined way) by the value of *string1*. The value of *string2*, if specified, becomes the name of the new SQL-connection; if *string2* is omitted, it defaults to the value of *string1*. The value of *string3*, if specified, defines an authorization identifier for the new SQL-session; if *string3* is omitted, it defaults to an implementation-defined value.

In both cases:

1. The new SQL-connection and SQL-session become current and the previously current connection and session (if any) become dormant.

2. It is an error if the SQL-agent already has an SQL-connection with the same name, or if DEFAULT is specified and the SQL-agent already has a default SQL-connection.

3. It is an error if the SQL-agent has an SQL-transaction in progress and the SQL-implementation does not support multi-server transactions (in other words, CONNECT can be issued from within a transaction only if the implementation does support multi-server transactions).

As mentioned above, if an SQL-agent invokes a procedure and there is no current SQL-connection, the system will automatically issue an implicit CONNECT TO DEFAULT on the SQL-agent's behalf*—*unless* the SQL-agent has previously executed any explicit CONNECT, SET CONNECTION, or DISCONNECT statements. If the latter is the case, an attempt to invoke a procedure when there is no current SQL-connection is treated as an error. In other words, the general intent is that a given SQL-agent should *either* use explicit CONNECTs, DISCONNECTs, etc., *or* perform all such operations implicitly; mixing the two approaches is not allowed, with the minor exception that any number of implicit CONNECTs etc. can be performed before the first explicit one.

SET CONNECTION

SET CONNECTION is used to switch to a dormant SQL-connection and SQL-session (making them current and the previously current ones dormant). The syntax is:

```
SET CONNECTION { DEFAULT | string }
```

---

*Or an implicit SET CONNECTION DEFAULT, if the SQL-agent has an associated default SQL-connection. This possibility is intended to cater for the situation in which a communication failure occurs and the current connection is the implicit default connection; to recover from such a failure, the system will try an implicit SET CONNECTION DEFAULT.

String here is a literal, parameter, or host variable, of type character string, whose value is an SQL-connection name.

- *Case 1* (DEFAULT): The default SQL-connection and default SQL-session are made current.

- *Case 2* (otherwise): The SQL-connection whose name is given by the value of *string* and the corresponding SQL-session are made current.

In both cases:

1. The *context information* for the revived SQL-connection and SQL-session is restored to the state it was in when that SQL-connection and SQL-session became dormant. *Note:* "Context information" includes such things as the SQL-session name (see Section 5.3), the name of the associated SQL-session module (again, see Section 5.3), the current position for all open cursors (see Chapter 10), various session default values (once again, see Section 5.3), and so forth. (For a complete list, the reader is referred to the official standard document.) See Appendix D for further discussion.

2. It is an error if the SQL-agent has an SQL-transaction in progress and the SQL-implementation does not support multi-server transactions (in other words, SET CONNECTION can be issued from within a transaction only if the implementation does support multi-server transactions).

It is not an error if the specified SQL-connection is in fact the current SQL-connection, i.e., is in fact not dormant.

DISCONNECT

SQL-connections (and the corresponding SQL-sessions) are terminated either explicitly, by means of an explicit DISCONNECT statement, or implicitly. We consider the explicit case first. Here is the syntax of DISCONNECT:

```
DISCONNECT { DEFAULT | CURRENT | ALL | string }
```

Once again, *string* is a literal, parameter, or host variable, of type character string, whose value is an SQL-connection name.

- *Case 1* (DEFAULT): The default SQL-connection is terminated. It is an error if that SQL-connection is neither current nor dormant.

- *Case 2* (CURRENT): The current SQL-connection is terminated. It is an error if there is no current SQL-connection.

- *Case 3* (ALL): The current SQL-connection (if any) and all dormant SQL-connections (if any) are terminated.

- *Case 4* (otherwise): The SQL-connection whose name is given by the value of *string* is terminated. It is an error if the specified SQL-connection is neither current nor dormant.

In all cases, it is an error if any of the SQL-connections to be terminated is active (refer back to Section 5.1 for an explanation of this term).

To turn now to the implicit case: According to the standard, an SQL-connection is terminated implicitly "following the last call to a procedure within the last active module, or . . . the last execution of a direct SQL statement through the direct invocation of SQL." It goes on to say that "the mechanism and rules by which an SQL-implementation determines whether [a given procedure call] is the last call within the last active module or [a given direct SQL statement execution is] the last execution of a direct SQL statement through the direct invocation of SQL are implementation-defined." Be that as it may, let us assume that the implementation is indeed able to determine, somehow, that implicit disconnection is required. Then, if the SQL-connection in question is still active (meaning an SQL-transaction is still running, i.e., has not issued either a COMMIT or a ROLLBACK):

- If an unrecoverable error has occurred in the SQL-transaction, the system automatically executes a ROLLBACK; otherwise, it automatically executes either a ROLLBACK or a COMMIT (it is implementation-dependent which).

- It then automatically executes the required DISCONNECT.

5.3   SQL-SESSIONS

Each SQL-session has an implementation-dependent name that is unique with respect to all SQL-sessions currently existing in the SQL-environment; this name is used (conceptually) in the definition of certain "temporary schemas" that are used to hold descriptors for certain "temporary tables" (see Chapter 18). Each SQL-session also has a number of associated *session default values* for use in certain contexts (the contexts in question are explained elsewhere in this book). Those default values are as follows:

- a default authorization identifier
- a default catalog name
- a default schema name
- a default time zone
- a default character set name

Each of these items is set to an implementation-defined "default default" when the SQL-session is initiated,* but can subsequently be changed by means of a SET SESSION AUTHORIZATION statement, SET CATALOG statement, SET SCHEMA statement, SET TIME ZONE statement, or SET NAMES statement, as appropriate. SET CATALOG, SET SCHEMA, and SET NAMES have to do with the dynamic SQL feature (also with direct SQL and the Call-Level Interface) and are discussed in Chapter 20; SET TIME ZONE has to do with SQL's date and time support and is discussed in Chapter 17; SET SESSION AUTHORIZATION is discussed immediately following. The syntax is:

```
SET SESSION AUTHORIZATION { string | authID-function }
```

Here *string* is, once again, a literal, parameter, or host variable (of type character string in each case), whose value is an authorization identifier, and "authID function" is any of the following:

```
USER
CURRENT_USER
SESSION_USER
SYSTEM_USER
```

The default authorization identifier for the current SQL-session is set to the indicated value. *Note:* USER, CURRENT_USER, SESSION_USER, and SYSTEM_USER are all niladic builtin functions† that return an authorization identifier.‡ For further explanation, see Chapters 7 and 15.

It is an error to attempt to SET SESSION AUTHORIZATION if the SQL-agent has an SQL-transaction in progress.

Each SQL-session also has an associated implementation-defined "SQL-session module" that is distinct from all other modules currently existing in the same SQL-environment. The purpose of the SQL-session module is to act as a container for "global prepared statements" (see Chapter 20).§ The standard states that the definition of the SQL-session module must include the specification "SCHEMA schema" (see Chapter 6 for an explanation of this specification), where the value of "schema" is implementation-dependent. *Note:* Actually, these remarks concerning the SQL-session module seem to have little operational significance.

---

*The default authorization identifier can also be set explicitly by means of the USER option on the CONNECT statement. See Section 5.2.

†The term "niladic builtin function," meaning a builtin function that takes no arguments, is not used in the standard, but there does not seem to be any term that *is* used for the concept either, at least not consistently (the phrase "time-varying system variable" is used at one point). In this book we will stay with our term.

‡Actually, the value returned by SYSTEM_USER might be an *operating system* identifier rather than an authorization identifier as such. See Chapters 7 and 15.

§We speculate that statements of "direct SQL" (see Chapter 6) and SQL statements invoked through the Call-Level Interface (see Chapter 23) are also supposed to belong to the SQL-session module.

Probably they were included in the standard purely so that there should be no exception to the general rule that SQL statements are *always*, at least conceptually, contained within some module (except possibly for certain CREATE SCHEMA statements, as explained in Chapter 4). Again, refer to Chapter 6 for further discussion.

5.4   SQL-TRANSACTIONS

An *SQL-transaction* is a *logical unit of work*; i.e., it is a sequence of SQL operations—both data manipulation and data definition operations, in general*—that is guaranteed to be atomic for the purposes of recovery. *Note:* Individual SQL statements are *always* atomic, in the sense that they either execute in their entirety or leave the database unchanged—they cannot fail in the middle and leave the database in an inconsistent state.

An SQL-transaction is initiated when the relevant SQL-agent executes a "transaction-initiating" SQL statement (see below) and the SQL-agent does not already have an SQL-transaction in progress. Note, therefore, that (as mentioned in Section 5.1) SQL-transactions cannot be nested. Note too that transaction initiation is always implicit—there is no explicit "BEGIN TRANSACTION" statement.

An SQL-transaction terminates either with a COMMIT statement ("termination with commit") or with a ROLLBACK statement ("termination with rollback"). Changes made to SQL-data by a given SQL-transaction *T1* do not become visible to any distinct transaction *T2* until and unless transaction *T1* terminates with commit.† Termination with commit causes all changes made by the transaction to become visible to other transactions; such changes are said to be committed, and are guaranteed never to be canceled. Termination with rollback causes all changes made by the transaction to be canceled; such changes will never become visible to other transactions at all.

Transaction-Initiating Statements

The following SQL statements are *not* transaction-initiating:

---

*Whether data manipulation and data definition operations can in fact be mixed together in the same SQL-transaction is implementation-defined.

†Actually the standard never quite seems to say this, though it probably meant to (see the remarks on the subject of "dirty write" at the end of this section). Note too that this entire paragraph assumes that all transactions execute at isolation level READ COMMITTED, REPEATABLE READ, or SERIALIZABLE; special considerations apply to transactions executing at READ UNCOMMITTED isolation level (see the subsection "Concurrency" at the end of this section).

```
CONNECT
SET CONNECTION
DISCONNECT
SET SESSION AUTHORIZATION
SET CATALOG
SET SCHEMA
SET NAMES
SET TIME ZONE
SET TRANSACTION
SET CONSTRAINTS
COMMIT
ROLLBACK
GET DIAGNOSTICS
```

Nor, of course, are the nonexecutable statements DECLARE CURSOR, DECLARE LOCAL TEMPORARY TABLE, BEGIN DECLARE SECTION, END DECLARE SECTION, and WHENEVER. All other SQL statements are transaction-initiating, except possibly for the EXECUTE and EXECUTE IMMEDIATE statements (see Chapter 20), which are transaction-initiating if and only if their target—i.e., the SQL statement to be executed by the EXECUTE or EXECUTE IMMEDIATE in question—is transaction-initiating in turn. Refer to Chapter 6 for a complete list of SQL statements.

Note: SET SESSION AUTHORIZATION and SET TRANSACTION can be executed only if no transaction is in progress. As already explained in Section 5.2, it is implementation-defined as to whether the same is true of CONNECT and SET CONNECTION. All other (executable) SQL statements can be executed only in the context of a transaction.

COMMIT AND ROLLBACK

As indicated above, an SQL-transaction terminates by executing either a COMMIT operation (successful termination) or a ROLLBACK operation (unsuccessful termination). Here first are the specifics of COMMIT. The syntax is:

```
COMMIT [ WORK ]
```

An implicit CLOSE is executed for every open cursor (see Chapter 10). An implicit SET CONSTRAINTS ALL IMMEDIATE is executed for each active SQL-connection (see Chapter 14). An implicit DELETE FROM *T* is executed for every temporary table *T* for which ON COMMIT DELETE was specified (see Chapter 18). All changes made to SQL-data by this SQL-transaction since its initiation are committed (i.e., made permanent). The SQL-transaction is terminated successfully* ("termination with commit"). *Note:* Presumably all active

---

*Assuming the COMMIT itself succeeds. If instead it fails—which it might do if, e.g., the implicit SET CONSTRAINTS ALL IMMEDIATE fails—then the SQL-transaction fails also and is terminated with rollback.

SQL-connections are made inactive, though the standard does not say as much.

The optional specification WORK is a pure noiseword and can be omitted without affecting the semantics of the operation.

And here are the specifics of ROLLBACK. The syntax is:

```
ROLLBACK [ WORK ]
```

An implicit CLOSE is executed for every open cursor (see Chapter 10). All changes made to SQL-data by this SQL-transaction since its initiation are canceled (i.e., undone). The SQL-transaction is terminated unsuccessfully ("termination with rollback"). Again, the optional specification WORK is a pure noiseword and can be omitted without affecting the semantics of the operation. *Note:* Presumably all active SQL-connections are made inactive, though the standard does not say as much.

One last point regarding transaction termination: The standard explicitly permits an SQL-implementation to use nonSQL statements (i.e., statements other than COMMIT and ROLLBACK) to terminate transactions, in order to allow that implementation to act as just one "resource manager" within some larger context— e.g., to allow an SQL-transaction to access some nonSQL database. (Such a transaction is sometimes referred to as a "global" transaction.) No matter what statements are used to terminate a transaction, however, successful termination must cause the actions defined for COMMIT to be performed, and unsuccessful termination must cause the actions defined for ROLLBACK to be performed.

SET TRANSACTION

The SET TRANSACTION statement is used to define certain characteristics of the next SQL-transaction to be initiated (note that SET TRANSACTION can be executed only when no SQL-transaction is in progress, and is not itself transaction-initiating). The characteristics in question are the *access mode*, the *diagnostics area size*, and the *isolation level*. The syntax is:

```
SET TRANSACTION option-commalist
```

where "option commalist" contains at most one *access mode* option, at most one *diagnostics area size* option, and at most one *isolation level* option (at least one option in total, of course).

- The *access mode* option is either READ ONLY or READ WRITE. If neither is specified, READ WRITE is assumed, unless READ UNCOMMITTED isolation level is specified, in which case READ ONLY is assumed. If READ WRITE is specified, the isolation level must not be READ UNCOMMITTED.

READ ONLY prohibits updates, of course, except to temporary tables (see Chapter 18); the standard does not say whether it also prohibits "SQL schema statements," which imply updates to *schemas*.*

- The *diagnostics area size* option takes the form DIAGNOSTICS SIZE *n*, where *n* is a literal, parameter, or host variable of type exact numeric with a scale of zero. The value of *n* (which must be greater than zero) specifies the number of "conditions" that can be held at any given time in the "diagnostics area" for this transaction (see Chapter 22 for further discussion). If the diagnostics area size option is omitted, an implementation-defined value (at least 1) is assumed for *n*.

- The *isolation level* option takes the form ISOLATION LEVEL *isolation*, where *isolation* is READ UNCOMMITTED, READ COMMITTED, REPEATABLE READ, or SERIALIZABLE.† The default is SERIALIZABLE; if any of the other three is specified, the implementation is free to assign some greater level, where "greater" is defined in terms of the ordering SERIALIZABLE > REPEATABLE READ > READ COMMITTED > READ UNCOMMITTED. For further explanation, see the subsection "Concurrency" below.

SET TRANSACTION has no effect on transactions subsequent to the next one. If a transaction is initiated for which no corresponding SET TRANSACTION has been performed, the effect is as if such a SET TRANSACTION *had* been performed with all options set to their default value (presumably, though the standard does not actually say as much).

SET CONSTRAINTS

The SET CONSTRAINTS statement is used to define the *constraint mode* (IMMEDIATE or DEFERRED) for certain integrity constraints with respect to either the next SQL-transaction to be initiated (if there is no SQL-transaction currently in progress) or the current SQL-transaction (otherwise). We defer detailed discussion of this statement to Chapter 14, except to note that:

---

*What it does say is that READ ONLY "applies only to viewed tables and persistent base tables." It is relevant to point out that Information Schemas are defined to consist of a collection of "viewed tables" (see Chapter 21).

†SERIALIZABLE is *not* an appropriate key word here. Serializability is a property of the interleaved execution of a set of concurrent transactions, not a property of any individual transaction considered independently. A better key word might have been just ISOLATED (perhaps FULLY ISOLATED).

- As we have already seen, transactions can span sessions; however, the effects of SET CONSTRAINTS are specifically defined by the standard to apply to the current session only. Note the contrast with SET TRANSACTION, whose effects are specifically defined to be "transaction-wide."

- SET CONSTRAINTS has no effect on transactions subsequent to either the current one (if a transaction is currently in progress) or the next one (otherwise). If a transaction starts execution within a session for which no corresponding SET CONSTRAINTS has been performed, the constraint mode for any given constraint depends on whether that constraint was defined to be INITIALLY IMMEDIATE or INITIALLY DEFERRED. Refer to Chapter 14 for further discussion.

Concurrency

If all transactions execute at isolation level SERIALIZABLE (the default), then the interleaved execution of any set of concurrent transactions is guaranteed to be *serializable*, in the sense that it will produce the same effect as some (unspecified) serial execution of those same transactions one at a time. However, if any transaction executes at a lower isolation level, then serializability can be violated in a number of different ways. The standard defines three such ways: "dirty read," "nonrepeatable read," and "phantoms" (with the implication that these are the *only* permitted serializability violations). Here are informal explanations of each of the three:

- *Dirty read:* Suppose transaction *T1* performs an update on some row, transaction *T2* then retrieves that row, and transaction *T1* then terminates with rollback. Transaction *T2* has then seen a row that no longer exists, and in a sense never did exist (because transaction *T1* effectively never ran).

- *Nonrepeatable read:* Suppose transaction *T1* retrieves some row, transaction *T2* then updates that row, and transaction *T1* then retrieves the "same" row again. Transaction *T1* has now retrieved the "same" row twice but seen two different values for it.

- *Phantoms:* Suppose transaction *T1* retrieves the collection of all rows that satisfy some condition (e.g., all supplier rows satisfying the condition that the supplier city is Paris). Suppose that transaction *T2* then inserts a new row satisfying that same condition. If transaction *T1* now repeats its retrieval request, it will see a row that it did not previously see—a "phantom."

More discussion of the foregoing possibilities can be found in C. J. Date, *An Introduction to Database Systems* (6th edition, Addison-Wesley, 1995). None of them could occur in a serial execution, of course (and, to repeat, none of them can occur if all transactions execute at isolation level SERIALIZABLE).

The various isolation levels are defined in terms of which of the foregoing violations of serializability they permit. They are summarized in the following table ("Y" means the indicated violation can occur, "N" means it cannot).

isolation level	dirty read	nonrepeatable read	phantom
READ UNCOMMITTED	Y	Y	Y
READ COMMITTED	N	Y	Y
REPEATABLE READ	N	N	Y
SERIALIZABLE	N	N	N

The standard's attempt to characterize isolation levels in terms of serializability violations has been the subject of some criticism. To quote from Hal Berenson *et al.*, "A Critique of ANSI SQL Isolation Levels," published in the Proceedings of the 1995 ACM SIGMOD International Conference on Management of Data, San Jose, Calif. (May 23rd-25th, 1995): "[The SQL/92] definitions fail to properly characterize several popular isolation levels, including the standard locking implementations of the levels covered." The paper goes on to point out in particular that the standard fails to prohibit *dirty write* (defined as the possibility that two transactions *T1* and *T2* might both perform an update on the same row before either transaction terminates).

It does seem to be true that the standard does not prohibit dirty writes explicitly. What it does say is this:

- "The execution of concurrent SQL-transactions at isolation level SERIALIZABLE is guaranteed to be serializable." In other words, if all SQL-transactions operate at isolation level SERIALIZABLE, the implementation is *required* to prohibit dirty writes, since dirty writes would certainly violate serializability.

- "The four isolation levels guarantee that . . . no updates will be lost." This claim is just wishful thinking; the definitions of the four isolation levels by themselves do *not* provide any such guarantee. However, it does indicate that the standard definers *intended* to prohibit dirty writes.

- "Changes made [by one SQL-transaction] cannot be perceived by other SQL-transactions [except those with isolation level READ UNCOMMITTED] until the former SQL-transaction terminates with a <commit statement>." The question here is, what exactly does *perceived* mean? Would it be possible for a transaction to update a piece of "dirty data" without "perceiving" it?

A couple of final points in connection with this overall topic:

- The standard states that "regardless of . . . isolation level, [the various serializability violations] shall not occur during the implied reading of schema definitions performed on behalf of executing [a given SQL statement], the

checking of integrity constraints, and the execution of referential actions . . . ."
The implications of this requirement are left as a subject for the reader to meditate on.

■   An implementation that supports any isolation level other than
SERIALIZABLE (which is, of course, the only totally *safe* level) would normally provide some explicit concurrency control facilities—typically explicit
LOCK statements—in order to allow users to write their applications in such
a way as to guarantee safety in the absence of such a guarantee from the system itself. For example, IBM's DB2 product (MVS version) supports isolation
levels corresponding to the standard levels READ UNCOMMITTED, READ
COMMITTED, and SERIALIZABLE. But it also provides an explicit
LOCK TABLE statement, which allows users operating at a level other
than SERIALIZABLE to acquire explicit locks, over and above the ones that
DB2 will acquire automatically to enforce that level. The standard, however,
includes no such explicit concurrency control mechanisms.

6

Binding Styles

6.1 INTRODUCTION

As mentioned in Chapter 4, any given SQL-implementation is required to support at least one *binding style*. This concept is not very precisely defined in the standard, but basically it refers to the possible methods by which SQL operations can be invoked, or in other words to the various possible SQL interfaces that an implementation might be expected to support. Currently, the standard specifies four such interfaces: *module, embedded SQL,* the *Call-Level Interface*, and *direct SQL*. We defer detailed consideration of the Call-Level Interface (CLI) to Chapter 23; the other three cases are explained in the present chapter.

6.2 THE MODULE LANGUAGE

We start with modules, since the module binding style is in a sense the most fundamental of all.* The module concept originated with the ANSI committee—i.e., ANSI/X3H2—that defined the very first of the various SQL standards, *viz.* the one that subsequently became known as "SQL/86." Recall that the prime emphasis in

---

*This is true so far as the standard is concerned. In practice, however, embedded SQL is usually much more important (and CLI is likely to become so), both from the user's perspective and from the implementer's.

every one of the SQL standards is on the *application programming* aspects of the SQL language. In attempting to define SQL/86, therefore, the ANSI/X3H2 committee was faced with a significant (though nontechnical) problem, namely as follows: ANSI-standard versions of languages such as COBOL and PL/I were already defined, and ANSI committees (e.g., ANSI/X3J4, in the case of COBOL) already existed to maintain and protect those standard definitions. Extending each of those standard languages separately to include the required SQL functionality would have involved a considerable amount of work—work, moreover, that generally would have had little to do with database management *per se*—and would have delayed the appearance of an SQL standard by many years. Consequently, the committee adopted the so-called *module* approach.

The *module language* is basically just a small language for expressing SQL operations in pure SQL syntactic form. The general idea is that any *compilation unit* (e.g., a PL/I "external procedure") that wants to interact with an SQL database has one or more associated *modules*, each consisting essentially of a set of *procedures*; and each procedure in turn consists essentially of a set of *parameter definitions* and a single *SQL statement* formulated in terms of those parameters. For example:

```
PROCEDURE DELETE_PART
             ( SQLSTATE,
               :PNO_PARAM CHAR(6) ) ;
          DELETE FROM P WHERE P.PNO = :PNO_PARAM ;
```

Note the SQLSTATE parameter, which is used to pass a status code back to the program that invokes the procedure. A SQLSTATE value of 00000 means that the SQL statement executed to completion and no errors occurred; a value of 02000 means that no rows were found to satisfy the request; other values are discussed in Chapter 22. *Note:* SQLSTATE and SQLCODE—see later in this section—are the only exceptions to the general rule that parameter names must have a colon prefix (as illustrated by the case of the parameter :PNO_PARAM in the example above).

The procedure shown above might be invoked from a PL/I program as follows:

```
DCL RETCODE CHAR(5) ;
DCL PNO_ARG CHAR(6) ;
DCL DELETE_PART ENTRY ( CHAR(5), CHAR(6) ) ;
   .......
PNO_ARG = 'P2' ;                /* for example                */
CALL DELETE_PART ( RETCODE, PNO_ARG ) ;
IF RETCODE = '00000'
THEN ... ;                      /* delete operation succeeded */
ELSE ... ;                      /* some exception occurred    */
```

Note (for readers who might be unfamiliar with PL/I): DCL is just a permitted PL/I abbreviation for DECLARE; an ENTRY declaration is just a definition of an external "entry point" (i.e., a name by which some piece of external code can be invoked).

The module language thus provides the ability for programs written in host languages such as PL/I, COBOL, etc., to execute SQL operations without requiring any change to the syntax or semantics of those languages. All that is required is:

1. The ability on the part of the host language to invoke procedures that are written in a different language and are separately compiled, together with

2. A defined correspondence between host and module language data types (for the purposes of passing arguments to those procedures and results back to the host).

In other words, the relationship between the host language and standard SQL is analogous to—actually identical to—that between two host languages: The host language program calls a separately compiled program (i.e., external procedure) that happens to be written in SQL, instead of in the host language under consideration or in some other host language.

As indicated above, each compilation unit can be associated with any number of modules during its execution. (One module per compilation unit is probably the normal case, however, and we will generally assume this case in our discussions.) How the association between compilation units and modules is established is implementation-defined; so too are the mechanisms by which modules are created and dropped. It is also implementation-defined as to whether one compilation unit can pass control to another at execution time.

Note carefully that, at least from a conceptual point of view, there is *always* a module at execution time, even if the binding style is "embedded SQL" or "direct" (see Sections 6.3 and 6.4) or the Call-Level Interface (see Chapter 23). To repeat from Chapter 4, therefore, a module can be thought of essentially as a set of SQL statements available for execution by a given compilation unit, and SQL statements are *always*—conceptually, at least—executed in the context of some module;* even statements that are "prepared and executed dynamically," or invoked via the Call-Level Interface, are considered to belong to a module, as we will see in Chapters 20 and 23.

Here then is a definition of the module language.

Module Definition

```
module-definition
    ::=    MODULE [ module ] [ NAMES ARE character-set ]
           LANGUAGE language
         [ SCHEMA schema ] [ AUTHORIZATION user ]
         [ temporary-table-definition-list ]
           module-element-list
```

---

*Except possibly for certain "standalone" CREATE SCHEMA statements, as explained in Chapter 4.

Points to note:

1. If "module" is omitted, the module is unnamed. No two modules within the same SQL-environment can have the same name, but any number can be unnamed. *Note:* The module must be named if the LANGUAGE clause specifies ADA (see paragraph 3 below).

2. We defer explanation of the optional NAMES clause to Chapter 19.

3. The LANGUAGE clause specifies the host language from which procedures within the module will be invoked. The "language" specification can be any one of the following: ADA, C, COBOL, FORTRAN, MUMPS, PASCAL, and PLI (*not* "PL/I", notice).

4. At least one of "SCHEMA schema" and "AUTHORIZATION user" must appear (see below).

5. We defer explanation of the optional list of temporary table definitions to Chapter 18.

6. The possible "module elements" are as follows:

   - cursor definitions

   - dynamic cursor definitions

   - procedures

   Cursor definitions are explained in detail in Chapters 20 (dynamic cursors) and 10 (others); procedures are discussed in the next subsection below.

The purpose of the "SCHEMA schema" and "AUTHORIZATION user" specifications is as follows:

- First, the SCHEMA specification provides a default schema name for use in object references within the module that do not include any schema name explicitly.* If the SCHEMA specification is omitted, then the "user" value from "AUTHORIZATION user" is used as the schema name (note that "AUTHORIZATION user" must be specified if "SCHEMA schema" is omitted). Observe, therefore, that every module *always* has an associated schema. *Note:* If "SCHEMA schema" is specified but defines only an unqualified schema name, an implementation-defined catalog name is assumed by default. The same is true if "SCHEMA schema" is omitted, which—as we have just seen—is equivalent to specifying "SCHEMA user" ("user" here being taken as an *un*qualified schema name).

---

*Apart from object references within a CREATE SCHEMA statement, for which the schema name for the schema currently being defined is taken as the default. Also, we are ignoring object references within direct SQL, dynamic SQL, and SQL statements invoked via CLI, for all of which the SQL-session default schema name is taken as the default.

■ Second, the AUTHORIZATION specification can be thought of as identifying the module's *owner* (though the standard does not actually talk in terms of modules being "owned" as such). The specified user, or rather the specified *authorization identifier*, must hold all necessary privileges for all SQL operations to be executed from within the module. If the AUTHORIZATION specification is omitted, then the module does not have an explicit owner; instead, a "user" value is assumed *at run time* that is identical to the authID for the SQL-session. In other words, it is the SQL-session authID that has to hold all the necessary privileges in this case. See Chapter 5, Section 5.3, for a discussion of SQL-sessions.

Procedure Definition

```
procedure-definition
    ::=    PROCEDURE procedure
           ( parameter-definition-commalist ) ;
             SQL-statement ;

parameter-definition
    ::=    parameter data-type
         | SQLCODE
         | SQLSTATE
```

Points to note:

1. The procedure name must be unique within its containing module.

2. The parentheses surrounding the commalist of parameter definitions can be omitted. However, if they are, then the commas must be omitted too, thereby transforming the "commalist" into a "list." *Note:* This alternative "list" format is supported only for compatibility with SQL/89, and constitutes a "deprecated feature" in SQL/92—meaning that it is a feature that is retained only for compatibility reasons and is likely to be dropped in some future version of the standard. See Appendix C.

3. The list or commalist of parameter definitions must include SQLCODE, SQLSTATE, or both. Both of these are used to return status information; the difference between them is that most SQLCODE values are implementation-defined, whereas many SQLSTATE values are defined within the standard.* In fact, the *only* SQLCODE values that are defined within the standard are as follows:

   ■ A value of 0 means the SQL statement completed execution satisfactorily and *either* no errors occurred *or* a warning condition exists. (A *warning* is

---

*In fact, SQLCODE too is now a "deprecated feature" and is likely to be dropped at some future time.

a noncatastrophic error; for example, a warning is raised on retrieval of a character string value into a target—see the next subsection below—that is too small to hold that string. See Chapter 7, Section 7.6.)

- A value of +100 means no rows were found to satisfy the request.

- A positive value other than +100 means the SQL statement completed execution satisfactorily but a warning condition exists.

- A negative value means some catastrophic error occurred (the SQL statement did not complete execution satisfactorily; in particular, it had no effect on the data values in the database).

Parameters and Arguments

Every parameter definition (other than the definitions of the SQLCODE and SQLSTATE parameters) consists of a parameter name—including a colon prefix—and a data type specification (see Chapter 7). Note that the data type here is an *SQL* data type, not a host language data type; note too that the syntax does specifically require a data type here, not a domain (see Chapters 7 and 8). Parameters are used to represent:

1. *Targets* (i.e., host program variables into which data values are to be retrieved). In this capacity, a parameter can be used, e.g., as the operand of an INTO clause on a FETCH or single-row SELECT statement.

2. *Data values* that are to be passed from the host program (e.g., a value that is to be used within a WHERE clause to control a database search).

Let p be a parameter (other than SQLCODE or SQLSTATE) to procedure P. Then (a) if the single SQL statement contained in P assigns a value to p, then p is an *output parameter*; (b) otherwise, p is an *input parameter*.* Arguments corresponding to output parameters must be specified as simple host variables; arguments corresponding to input parameters, by contrast, can be specified as arbitrary scalar expressions. In other words, arguments corresponding to output parameters must be "passed by reference," and assignment to such a parameter really means assignment to the corresponding argument; arguments corresponding to input parameters, by contrast, can be "passed by value," and assignment to such a parameter is not allowed. *Note:* SQLSTATE and SQLCODE can be thought of as output parameters more or less by definition, but they cannot be the target of any operation that explicitly assigns a value to them.

Now we turn to the "data type" portion of a parameter definition. That data type is, as already mentioned, an SQL type, not a host language type. When the

---

*A slight oversimplification. See Appendix D.

procedure is invoked, however, the corresponding argument will be of some host language type. The range of SQL types that can be specified therefore depends on the range of types supported by the host language in question; not all SQL types can be specified for all host languages. By way of example, the following table shows the legal parameter types—i.e., SQL types—and the corresponding host language argument types in the particular case of PL/I. For further information, the reader is referred to the official standard document.

SQL parameter	PL/I argument
CHARACTER (sn)	CHARACTER (pn)
CHARACTER VARYING (sn)	CHARACTER VARYING (pn)
BIT (n)	BIT (n)
BIT VARYING (n)	BIT VARYING (n)
DECIMAL (p,q)	FIXED DECIMAL (p,q)
INTEGER	FIXED BINARY (p1)
SMALLINT	FIXED BINARY (p2)
FLOAT (p)	FLOAT BINARY (p)

Points to note:

1. Arguments corresponding to SQLCODE and SQLSTATE must have PL/I data types FIXED BINARY (n) and CHARACTER (5), respectively (where n is implementation-defined but must be at least 15).

2. The character length *pn* must be the maximum possible octet length equivalent to *sn* (see Chapter 7 for an explanation of character lengths and octet lengths).

3. The binary precisions *p1* and *p2* are implementation-defined (though *p2* must presumably not be greater than *p1*).

SQL Statements

SQL statements fall into a number of different categories, as follows:

- SQL schema statements
- SQL data statements
- SQL transaction statements
- SQL connection statements
- SQL session statements
- SQL diagnostics statements
- SQL exception declaration
- SQL dynamic statements

Note: For the purposes of this classification, BEGIN and END DECLARE SECTION are not regarded as SQL statements at all, and they cannot appear within procedures. DECLARE CURSOR, DECLARE LOCAL TEMPORARY TABLE, and WHENEVER are regarded as SQL statements, but they still cannot appear within procedures. In fact, BEGIN and END DECLARE SECTION and WHENEVER can appear only in embedded SQL (see Section 6.3).

The following are *SQL schema statements*, also referred to in this book (except for CREATE and DROP ASSERTION and GRANT and REVOKE) as *data definition* statements:

```
CREATE SCHEMA, DROP SCHEMA
CREATE DOMAIN, ALTER DOMAIN, DROP DOMAIN
CREATE TABLE, ALTER TABLE, DROP TABLE
CREATE VIEW, DROP VIEW
CREATE CHARACTER SET, DROP CHARACTER SET
CREATE COLLATION, DROP COLLATION
CREATE TRANSLATION, DROP TRANSLATION
CREATE ASSERTION, DROP ASSERTION
GRANT, REVOKE
```

The following are *SQL data statements*, also referred to in this book as *data manipulation* statements:*

```
DECLARE CURSOR
DECLARE LOCAL TEMPORARY TABLE
OPEN, CLOSE
FETCH, "positioned" UPDATE, "positioned" DELETE
SELECT, INSERT, "searched" UPDATE, "searched" DELETE
```

Note: Actually the standard contradicts itself on the question of whether or not DECLARE CURSOR and DECLARE TEMPORARY TABLE are SQL data statements. Anyway, whether they are or not, it is certainly true that they cannot appear within procedures.

The following are *SQL transaction statements:*

```
SET TRANSACTION
SET CONSTRAINTS
COMMIT, ROLLBACK
```

The following are *SQL connection statements:*

```
CONNECT, DISCONNECT
SET CONNECTION
```

The following are *SQL session statements:*

```
SET SESSION AUTHORIZATION
SET CATALOG
SET SCHEMA
SET TIME ZONE
SET NAMES
```

---

*Most of the SQL dynamic statements (see Chapter 20) are also regarded as SQL data statements; so too is the multi-row retrieval statement of direct SQL (see Section 6.4).

The following is the only *SQL diagnostics statement:*

GET DIAGNOSTICS

The following is the only *SQL exception declaration:*

WHENEVER

We defer discussion of the *SQL dynamic statements* to Chapter 20.

Another Example

We close this section with another example of the use of the module language. The purpose of the example is to illustrate the point that, as mentioned above, parameters—more specifically, *output* parameters—also serve as the mechanism by which values can be returned to the invoking program (more correctly, to the invoking *SQL-agent*). Of course, this point has already been illustrated for the special case of the SQLSTATE parameter by the DELETE example discussed near the beginning of this section.

Procedure:

```
PROCEDURE GET_WEIGHT
            ( SQLSTATE,
              :PNO_PARAM    CHAR(6),
              :WEIGHT_PARAM DECIMAL(3)
    SELECT P.WEIGHT
    INTO   :WEIGHT_PARAM
    FROM   P
    WHERE  P.PNO = :PNO_PARAM ;
```

Possible invocation from PL/I:

```
DCL RETCODE     CHAR(5) ;
DCL PNO_ARG     CHAR(6) ;
DCL WEIGHT_ARG DECIMAL(3) ;
DCL GET_WEIGHT ENTRY ( CHAR(5), CHAR(6), DECIMAL(3) ) ;
  .......
PNO_ARG = 'P2' ;              /* for example               */
CALL GET_WEIGHT ( RETCODE, PNO_ARG, WEIGHT_ARG ) ;
IF RETCODE = '00000'
THEN ... ;                    /* WEIGHT_ARG = retrieved value */
ELSE ... ;                    /* some exception occurred   */
```

6.3   EMBEDDED SQL

The ANSI/X3H2 committee did not necessarily intend (or even primarily intend) that users actually code direct calls to the module language as discussed in Section 6.2 above. Instead, the more usual method of operation is to embed SQL statements directly into the text of the host language program, as illustrated by Figs. 2.2(b) and 2.8 in Chapter 2. An embedded SQL example corresponding to the module language example near the beginning of the previous section might appear as shown below. *Note:* The example is incomplete; the SQLSTATE and PNO declarations need to be nested within an "embedded SQL declare section," delimited by BEGIN and END DECLARE SECTION statements (see later). We remind the reader that, like parameters in the module language, host language variable names in embedded SQL statements must have a colon prefix (as we saw in Chapter 2).

```
DCL SQLSTATE CHAR(5) ;
DCL PNO CHAR(6) ;
    ........
PNO = 'P2' ;                       /* for example            */
EXEC SQL DELETE FROM P WHERE P.PNO = :PNO ;
IF SQLSTATE = '00000'
THEN ... ;                         /* delete operation succeeded */
ELSE ... ;                         /* some exception occurred */
```

Note that no explicit definition of procedure DELETE_PART is now needed.

However, embedded SQL is not a *fundamental* part of the SQL standard as such. Instead, the embedded SQL code shown above is defined to be a mere syntactic shorthand for the module language version (including the explicit procedure definition and the explicit call) shown in the previous section. The standard defines a set of rules by which a conceptual module is derived from a given program that contains embedded SQL statements. We omit the details here, since they are essentially straightforward (though tedious), except to remark that (a) that derived module is either unnamed or has a name that is implementation-dependent; (b) the "SCHEMA schema" specification in that derived module is implementation-dependent; (c) there is no "AUTHORIZATION user" specification.

Here is another example—an embedded SQL version of the SELECT example from the end of the previous section. This time we do show the necessary BEGIN and END DECLARE SECTION statements.

```
EXEC SQL BEGIN DECLARE SECTION ;

    DCL SQLSTATE CHAR(5) ;
    DCL PNO      CHAR(6) ;
    DCL WEIGHT   FIXED DECIMAL(3) ;

EXEC SQL END DECLARE SECTION ;

PNO = 'P2' ;                       /* for example            */
EXEC SQL SELECT P.WEIGHT
         INTO   :WEIGHT
         FROM   P
         WHERE  P.PNO = :PNO ;
IF SQLSTATE = '00000'
THEN ... ;                         /* WEIGHT = retrieved value */
ELSE ... ;                         /* some exception occurred */
```

Points to note:

1. Embedded SQL statements are prefixed by EXEC SQL* (so that they can easily be distinguished from statements of the host language), and are terminated as follows:

---

*Except in MUMPS, which uses the prefix "&SQL(" (ampersand–SQL–left parenthesis) instead.

```
Ada       --   semicolon
C         --   semicolon
COBOL     --   END-EXEC
FORTRAN   --   absence of continuation character
               (i.e., no explicit terminator exists)
MUMPS     --   right parenthesis
Pascal    --   semicolon
PL/I      --   semicolon
```

2. An executable SQL statement can appear wherever an executable host statement can appear. Note that we say "executable" SQL statement here; the reason is that certain SQL statements are *not* executable—for example,
   DECLARE CURSOR is not, nor is WHENEVER (see paragraph 8 below),
   and nor are BEGIN and END DECLARE SECTION.

3. SQL statements (from now on we will usually drop the qualifier "embedded")
   can include references to host variables. As already mentioned, such references must be prefixed with a colon to distinguish them from names of SQL
   objects (in particular, from SQL column names). They must not identify
   arrays or structures, nor can they be qualified or subscripted. They can appear
   in SQL statements in the same positions that parameter references can appear
   in the module language (see Section 6.2).

4. All host variables that will be referenced in SQL statements must be defined
   within an *embedded SQL declare section*, bracketed by the statements BEGIN
   and END DECLARE SECTION. Such host variable definitions are deliberately limited to certain simple forms (e.g., arrays and structures are not permitted); the reader is referred to the standard document for details. A given
   program can include any number of embedded SQL declare sections. A given
   host variable definition must physically appear in the host program source text
   before any reference to that host variable in an embedded SQL statement.

5. Every embedded SQL program should include either a host variable called
   SQLCODE (SQLCOD in FORTRAN), or a host variable called SQLSTATE
   (SQLSTA in FORTRAN), or both.* After any SQL statement has been executed, a status value is returned to the program in SQLCODE or SQLSTATE
   or both. See Chapter 22 for further discussion of SQLCODE and SQLSTATE.

6. Host variables must have a data type appropriate to the purposes for which
   they are used. In particular, a host variable that is to be used as a target must
   have a data type that is compatible with that of the SQL value to be assigned
   to that target; likewise, a host variable that is to be used as a source must have
   a data type that is compatible with that of the SQL column to which values of
   that source are to be assigned. Similar remarks apply to a host variable that is
   to be used in an SQL comparison, or indeed in any kind of SQL expression.

---

*This statement is surely true in practice. Actually the standard does allow an embedded SQL program
to include neither SQLSTATE nor SQLCODE, but such a program would then seem not to be able to
obtain the status information it needs.

For details of what it means for host and SQL data types to be compatible in the foregoing sense, refer to the subsection "Parameters and Arguments" in the previous section.

7. Host variables and SQL columns can have the same name.

8. Every executable SQL statement (except for GET DIAGNOSTICS—see Chapter 22) should in principle be followed by a test of the returned SQLCODE or SQLSTATE value. The WHENEVER statement is provided to simplify this process. The WHENEVER statement has the syntax:

```
EXEC SQL WHENEVER condition action terminator
```

where "terminator" is as explained in paragraph 1 above, "condition" is either SQLERROR or NOT FOUND, and "action" is either CONTINUE or a GO TO statement.* WHENEVER is not an executable statement; rather, it is a directive to the SQL language processor. "WHENEVER condition GO TO label" causes that processor to insert an "IF condition GO TO label" statement after each executable SQL statement it encounters; "WHENEVER condition CONTINUE" causes it not to insert any such statements, the implication being that the programmer will insert such statements by hand. The two "conditions" are defined as follows:

```
NOT FOUND    means    no data was found
                      (SQLCODE = +100; SQLSTATE = 02xxx)
SQLERROR     means    an error occurred
                      (SQLCODE < 0; see Chapter 22 for SQLSTATE)
```

Note that there is no "SQLWARNING" condition; that is, the WHENEVER statement provides no assistance with dealing with SQL warnings (SQLCODE = a nonnegative value, possibly 0, other than +100; see Chapter 22 for the corresponding SQLSTATE values).

Each WHENEVER statement the SQL processor encounters on its sequential scan through the program text for a particular condition overrides the previous one for that condition.

6.4   DIRECT SQL

The term "direct SQL" refers to that part of the standard that permits execution of SQL statements from an interactive terminal, with results being returned to that terminal. The following SQL statements (only) can be executed interactively:

---

*"GO TO" can be spelled as shown here, as two words, or as one word without the space ("GOTO").

- SQL schema statements
- SQL transaction statements
- SQL connection statements
- SQL session statements
- direct SQL data statements

All of these categories were explained in Section 6.2, except for the last one. A *direct SQL data statement* is a DECLARE LOCAL TEMPORARY TABLE statement, an INSERT statement, a searched UPDATE statement, a searched DELETE statement, or a multi-row retrieval statement. Temporary tables are discussed in Chapter 18, and INSERT, searched UPDATE, and searched DELETE are discussed in Chapter 9; multi-row retrievals are discussed immediately following.

Briefly, a *multi-row retrieval** is a statement that retrieves an entire collection of zero, one, two, . . ., or any number of rows. It takes the form:

```
table-expression
[ ORDER BY order-item-commalist ]
```

(much as in a cursor definition—see Chapter 10 for further discussion). Here are some examples:

```
SELECT  S.SNO, S.CITY
FROM    S
ORDER   BY SNO ;

S NATURAL JOIN SP
ORDER BY SNO, PNO ;

SELECT DISTINCT SP.PNO, S.CITY
FROM    SP NATURAL JOIN S
ORDER   BY PNO, CITY ;
```

The direct SQL feature also supports the interactive execution of *implementation-defined* statements. All statements entered interactively, implementation-defined or otherwise, must terminate in a semicolon, as shown in the examples above.

The implementation-defined statements just mentioned are not the only aspect of the direct SQL feature to be implementation-defined. To quote the standard: "The method of invoking direct SQL statements, the method of raising conditions that result from the execution of direct SQL statements, the method of accessing the diagnostics information that results from the execution of direct SQL statements, and the method of returning results . . . are all implementation-defined"

---

*The standard term is "direct select statement: multiple rows," but this terminology is misleading, because the operation is not necessarily a SELECT at all.

(slightly paraphrased). Moreover, there is supposed to be an implicit implementation-defined module* to which the direct SQL statements are considered to belong (though in fact the standard never seems to come out and say as much explicitly— see Appendix D). Numerous additional aspects of direct SQL are also implementation-defined. In view of all of this lack of specificity, it seems best in this book just to ignore direct SQL (for the most part) from this point forward.

---

*We suspect that the SQL-session module might be intended here. See Chapter 5, Section 5.3.

PART III

DATA DEFINITION AND MANIPULATION

This part of the book addresses what might be considered the core of the SQL language—the basic SQL data objects and operators, the rules for defining or creating those objects, the rules for combining those operators to form expressions, and so on. In particular, it describes the SQL statements for retrieving data from, and updating data in, SQL databases. (It is convenient to continue in the harmless pretense that there is such a thing as "an SQL database.")

7

Scalar Objects, Operators, and Expressions

7.1 INTRODUCTION

In this chapter we describe the scalar (i.e., elementary) objects and operators supported by SQL. The basic data object is the *individual scalar value*; for example, the object appearing at the intersection of a given row and a given column of a given table is a scalar value. Each such value is of some particular *scalar data type*. For each such data type, there is an associated format for writing *scalar literals* of that type. Scalar data types and literals are discussed in Sections 7.2 and 7.3, respectively.

Scalar objects can be operated upon by means of certain *scalar operators*. For example, two numeric values can be added together by means of the scalar arithmetic operator "+", and can be tested for equality by means of the scalar comparison operator "=". In addition, SQL provides:

- Certain *scalar functions* (e.g., the POSITION and SUBSTRING functions), which can also be regarded as scalar operators; and

■   Certain *aggregate functions* (e.g., the SUM and AVG functions), which have the effect of reducing some *aggregate*, or collection of scalar values, to a single scalar value. *Note:* Although they take aggregate arguments, they return scalar values, and so aggregate function references can appear in some contexts (but not all!—see Section 7.5) in which scalar values are allowed.

Scalar objects, operators, and functions can be combined in various ways to form *scalar expressions*. The scalar operators and functions available for each data type, and the corresponding scalar expressions, are discussed in Section 7.4. Section 7.5 then discusses the aggregate functions. Finally, Section 7.6 considers the generic operations of *scalar assignment* and *scalar comparison*.

A couple of notes on terminology:

1. The standard does not make much use of the qualifier "scalar," referring instead simply to *values, data types, operators,* and so on. We prefer to use the qualifier, except occasionally where the context makes it unnecessary. The problem with the unqualified usage is that it usurps very general terms such as "value" and gives them very specific meanings, thereby making it difficult to talk about other specific cases or the more general case—for example, to talk about the value of a table expression (see Chapter 11) as opposed to that of a scalar one.

2. The standard uses the term *set functions* to refer to aggregate functions (despite the fact that the aggregate argument is not necessarily a set, since it can include duplicates, which sets by definition do not). It has no term for an aggregate *per se*.

Finally, a few more preliminary remarks:

1. In addition to the data types discussed in Section 7.2 immediately following, SQL also supports a variety of *date and time* data types. We defer all discussion of those data types to Chapter 17.

2. The SQL support for *character strings* includes a large number of options and complications that we prefer not to get into at this comparatively early point in the book. We therefore defer detailed discussion of this topic also, to Chapter 19.

3. No description of scalar data in SQL would be complete without a detailed explanation of *nulls*, which are SQL's way of representing the fact that some scalar value is missing for some reason. The fact is, however, that nulls give rise to an inordinate amount of undesirable and unnecessary complexity. *WE THEREFORE CHOOSE TO DEFER ALL DISCUSSION OF NULLS AND RELATED MATTERS TO CHAPTER 16* (except for the occasional unavoidable brief mention or forward pointer). The reader is warned, therefore, that many of our discussions prior to that point will need to be revisited and extended when that chapter is reached.

7.2   DATA TYPES

SQL supports the following scalar data types.

CHARACTER(n)	Fixed length string of exactly n characters ($n > 0$)
CHARACTER VARYING(n)	Varying length string of up to n characters ($n > 0$)
BIT(n)	Fixed length string of exactly n bits ($n > 0$)
BIT VARYING(n)	Varying length string of up to n bits ($n > 0$)
NUMERIC(p,q)	Decimal number, p digits and sign, with assumed decimal point q digits from the right ($0 \le q \le p, p > 0$)
DECIMAL(p,q)	Decimal number, m digits and sign, with assumed decimal point q digits from the right ($0 \le q \le p \le m, p > 0$—see below for an explanation of m)
INTEGER	Signed integer, decimal or binary (see below)
SMALLINT	Signed integer, decimal or binary (see below)
FLOAT(p)	Floating point number N, say, represented by a signed binary fraction f of m binary digits ($-1 < f < +1, 0 < p \le m$—see below for an explanation of m) and a signed binary integer exponent e, such that $N = f * (10 ** e)$
	Note: The symbol "**" here stands for exponentiation. Note, however, that SQL does not in fact support any such operator (see Section 7.4).

Points to note:

1. The string length specifications (n), the precision specifications (p and m), and the scale specifications (q) must all be unsigned decimal integers.

2. The following abbreviations and alternative spellings are permitted:

   - CHARACTER is an abbreviation for CHARACTER(1).
   - CHAR is an abbreviation for CHARACTER.
   - VARCHAR is an abbreviation for CHARACTER VARYING (or CHAR VARYING).
   - INT is an abbreviation for INTEGER.
   - NUMERIC(p) is an abbreviation for NUMERIC(p,0).
   - NUMERIC is an abbreviation for NUMERIC(p), where p is implementation-defined.
   - DEC is an abbreviation for DECIMAL.
   - DECIMAL(p) is an abbreviation for DECIMAL(p,0).

- DECIMAL is an abbreviation for DECIMAL(p), where p is implementation-defined.

- FLOAT is an abbreviation for FLOAT(p), where p is implementation-defined.

- REAL is an alternative spelling for FLOAT(s), where s is implementation-defined.

- DOUBLE PRECISION is an alternative spelling for FLOAT(d), where d is implementation-defined.

3. The following items are all implementation-defined:

   - The maximum value of n, the declared length of a character string (fixed or varying length);

   - The maximum value of n, the declared length of a bit string (fixed or varying length);

   - Whether INTEGER and SMALLINT are decimal or binary (though they must be the same);

   - The actual precision for INTEGER and SMALLINT (though the latter must not exceed the former);

   - The maximum value of p, the declared precision for NUMERIC and DECIMAL;

   - The default precision for NUMERIC and DECIMAL if there is no declared precision;

   - The actual precision m for DECIMAL (though the actual precision m must not be less than the declared or implied precision p);

   - The maximum value of p, the declared precision for FLOAT;

   - The default precision for FLOAT if there is no declared precision;

   - The actual precision m for FLOAT (though the actual precision m must be greater than or equal to the declared or implied precision p);

   - The actual precisions s and d for REAL and DOUBLE PRECISION (though d must be greater than s).

4. Data types CHARACTER and CHARACTER VARYING are known collectively as character string data types. Data types BIT and BIT VARYING are known collectively as bit string data types. Character and bit string data types are known collectively as string data types.

5. Data types NUMERIC, DECIMAL, INTEGER, and SMALLINT are known collectively as exact numeric data types. Data type FLOAT and the "alternative spelling" data types REAL and DOUBLE PRECISION are known col-

lectively as approximate numeric data types. Exact and approximate numeric data types are known collectively as numeric data types.

6. *(With acknowledgments to Phil Shaw:)* It is worth pointing out explicitly the distinction between NUMERIC and DECIMAL. NUMERIC(p,q) means that the precision must be *exactly p* digits; DECIMAL(p,q) means that it must be *at least p* digits, with the actual precision being implementation-defined. Thus, e.g., the implementation might store both NUMERIC and DECIMAL values as packed decimal. NUMERIC(2,1) and DECIMAL(2,1) items could then both be stored as two-byte packed decimal values. Since two-byte packed decimal fields can actually hold three digits plus a sign, the DECIMAL items would be allowed to have values in the range –99.9 to +99.9; the NUMERIC items, by contrast, would be constrained to values in the range –9.9 to +9.9. In other words, the range of NUMERIC values is strictly defined, for maximum portability, whereas the range of DECIMAL values adjusts to the implementation, for maximum exploitation of the capabilities of that implementation.

Domains

Domains represent an absolutely fundamental component of the theoretical relational model (see Chapter 1, Section 1.1). This is not the place to go into details; suffice it to say that the SQL standard unfortunately includes only an *extremely weak* form of support for the domain concept. Within the standard, in fact, almost the only purpose of domains is to serve as a means of factoring out column data type specifications. In the case of suppliers and parts, for example, we might define a domain called CITIES, as follows:

```
CREATE DOMAIN CITIES CHAR(15)
```

Now, instead of defining columns S.CITY and P.CITY explicitly as CHAR(15), we could define each to be "based on" the CITIES domain:

```
CREATE TABLE S ( ... , CITY CITIES, ... )

CREATE TABLE P ( ... , CITY CITIES, ... )
```

The CITIES definition thus effectively serves as a shorthand.

Note: Domains in SQL do provide slightly more functionality than the foregoing rather trivial example might suggest (see Chapter 8). However, one thing they most definitely do not do is *constrain comparisons.* In the relational model, the comparison (e.g.) S.CITY = P.CITY is valid only if the two CITY columns are defined on the same domain. In SQL, by contrast, it is valid only if they are of *compatible data types* (see Section 7.6), regardless of what the domains are or even whether any (SQL-style) domains are involved at all.

7.3   LITERALS

The various kinds of scalar literal values supported in SQL are as follows.

character string	Written as a sequence of characters enclosed in single quotes (the single quote character itself being represented as usual within a character string literal by two immediately adjacent single quotes)

Examples: `'123 Main St.'`   `'Pig'`   `'honey don''t'`

bit string	Written *either* as a sequence of zeros and ones enclosed in single quotes and preceded by the letter B *or* as a sequence of hexadecimal digits enclosed in single quotes and preceded by the letter X

Examples: `B'11000001'`   `B'0101'`   `B'0'`
`X'C1'`   `X'5'`   `X'beef'`

Note: The hexadecimal digits are 0–9 and A–F (and the latter can be either upper or lower case). They represent the bit strings 0000 through 1111 in the usual way. Thus, the 1st and 4th of the examples above represent the same value, as do the 2nd and 5th.

exact numeric	Written as a signed or unsigned decimal number, possibly with a decimal point

Examples: `4`   `7.`   `-95.7`   `+364.05`   `0.007`   `.6333`

approximate numeric	Written as an exact numeric literal, followed by the letter E, followed by a signed or unsigned decimal integer

Examples: `4E3`   `-95.7E46`   `+364E-5`   `0.7E1`   `-.15E-15`

Note: The expression *x*E*y* represents the value $x * (10 ** y)$. Internally, approximate numeric values are "normalized" in such a way that the x portion lies in the range $-1 < x < +1$; e.g., the literal 4E6 will be treated as if it had been written as 0.4E7 instead.

Points to note:

1. The terms "signed numeric literal," "unsigned numeric literal," and "hexadecimal literal" are also sometimes used, each with the obvious meaning.

2. The standard also includes an extended format for writing string literals when the literal in question spans several text lines. In this extended format, the literal value is divided up into segments, each with its own opening and closing single quote, and adjacent segments are separated by any separator that includes a newline marker. (Recall from Chapter 3 that, in general, a separa-

tor in SQL is any combination of spaces and/or newline markers and/or comments.) Here is an example of such a literal (of type character string):

```
'The White House■'                          -- Segment 1
'1600 Pennsylvania Avenue■'                  -- Segment 2
'Washington DC 20500'                        -- Segment 3
```

This example is logically equivalent to the following:

```
'The White House■1600 Pennsylvania Avenue■Washington DC 20500'
```

Data Types of Literals

The data type of a given literal is derived as indicated below from the form in which the literal is written.

character string	CHARACTER(n), where n is the number of characters in the literal as written
bit string	BIT(n), where n is the number of bits (specified or implied) in the literal as written
exact numeric	NUMERIC(p,q), where p is the number of digits in the literal as written and q is the number of digits in the fractional part of the literal as written
approximate numeric	FLOAT(p), where p is the number of digits preceding the E in the literal as written

7.4   SCALAR OPERATORS AND FUNCTIONS

SQL provides a number of builtin scalar operators and functions that can be used in the construction of scalar expressions. We summarize those operators and functions below (in alphabetic order), for purposes of reference; note, however, that discussion of all functions having to do with dates and times is deferred to Chapter 17, and discussion of certain functions having to do with character strings is deferred to Chapter 19. For a discussion of *aggregate* functions, see Section 7.5.

■ Arithmetic operators

The usual arithmetic operators "+", "-", "*", and "/" are supported, all with the usual meanings.

■ BIT_LENGTH

Returns the length of a given character string or bit string in bits. The string in question is specified by means of an arbitrary string expression.

- CASE

  See the subsection "CASE Operations" below.

- CAST

  Converts a given scalar value to a given scalar data type. The syntax is:

  ```
  CAST ( scalar-expression AS { data-type | domain } )
  ```

  The value of the scalar expression is converted either to "data type" (if "data type" is specified explicitly), or to the data type underlying "domain" (otherwise).* *Note:* Not all pairs of data types are mutually convertible; for example, conversions between numbers and bit strings are not supported. The reader is referred to the official standard document for details of precisely which data types can be converted to which. Further, certain conversions can lead to overflow exceptions in fairly obvious ways. We omit the details here.

- CHARACTER_LENGTH or CHAR_LENGTH

  Returns the length of a given string either in characters or in "octets." The string in question is specified by means of an arbitrary string expression; the result is the length in characters if the string is of type character, the length in octets otherwise. See OCTET_LENGTH below for an explanation of octets.

- Concatenation

  The concatenation operator "||" can be used to concatenate two character strings or two bit strings. It is written as an infix operation; e.g., the expression INITIALS || LASTNAME can be used to concatenate the values of INITIALS and LASTNAME (in that order). The arguments can be specified as any character string or bit string expressions, so long as they are both character strings or both bit strings (and, in the case of character strings, they both have the same character set—see Chapter 19).

- COLLATE

  See Chapter 19.

- CONVERT

  See Chapter 19.

- CURRENT_DATE

  See Chapter 17.

- CURRENT_TIME

  See Chapter 17.

---

*It is an error if "domain" is specified and the converted value fails to satisfy some integrity constraint associated with "domain" (see Chapters 8 and 14). Apart from this consideration, however, "domain" here serves (as usual in SQL) merely as shorthand for the underlying data type.

- CURRENT_TIMESTAMP

  See Chapter 17.

- CURRENT_USER

  Returns a character string representing the current authorization ID. See Chapter 15 for further explanation.

- EXTRACT

  See Chapter 17.

- LOWER and UPPER

  Return a character string that is identical to a given character string, except that all upper case letters are replaced by their lower case equivalents (for LOWER), or *vice versa* (for UPPER). The string argument can be specified as any character string expression. *Note:* LOWER and UPPER are referred to generically as *fold* functions.

- OCTET_LENGTH

  Returns the length of a given string in "octets." The string in question is specified by means of an arbitrary string expression; the result is the bit length of the string—see BIT_LENGTH above—divided by 8 (ignoring any remainder from the division).

- POSITION

  Returns the position within a given string (*string1*) of another given string (*string2*). Here *string1* and *string2* are specified as arbitrary string expressions, except that they must both be character strings or both bit strings (and, in the case of character strings, they must both have the same character set—see Chapter 19). More precisely, the expression POSITION (*string2* IN *string1*) is defined to return a value as follows:

  1. If *string2* is of length zero,* the result is one;

  2. Otherwise, if *string2* occurs as a substring within *string1*, the result is one greater than the number of characters or bits (as applicable) in *string1* that precede the first such occurrence;

  3. Otherwise, the result is zero.

- SESSION_USER

  Returns a character string representing the SQL-session authorization ID. See Chapter 15 for further explanation.

---

*Note that a character string can have a length of zero even though zero is not valid as a value for *n* in the data type declaration CHARACTER(*n*), and similarly for bit strings.

- SUBSTRING

  Extracts a substring from a given string. For example, the expression SUBSTRING (S.SNAME FROM 1 FOR 3) extracts the first three characters of the specified supplier name. In general, the string argument can be specified as any character or bit string expression, and the FROM and FOR arguments can be specified as any numeric expressions (of type exact numeric with a scale of zero). If the key word FOR and its associated argument expression are omitted, the effect is to extract the entire right hand portion of the given string, starting at the specified FROM position.

- SYSTEM_USER

  Returns a character string representing the ID of the operating system user who invoked the module containing the SYSTEM_USER reference.

- TRANSLATE

  See Chapter 19.

- TRIM

  Returns a character string that is identical to a given character string, except that leading and/or trailing pad characters are removed. More precisely, the expression TRIM (*ltb pad* FROM *string*), where *string* is an arbitrary character string expression, *ltb* is LEADING, TRAILING, or BOTH, and *pad* is a character string expression that evaluates to a single character (from the same character set as *string*—see Chapter 19), removes leading and/or trailing (as specified) *pad* characters from *string*. If *ltb* is omitted, BOTH is assumed. If *pad* is omitted, the pad character is assumed to be a space. If *ltb* and *pad* are both omitted, the key word FROM must be omitted too.

  Note: One of the principal uses of TRIM is in connection with varying length character strings. Suppose column C of base table T is of data type CHARACTER VARYING(100), say. In a host language such as COBOL that does not support such a data type, any host variable, H say, corresponding to column C will have to be defined to be of type character string with *fixed* length 100. Now suppose that H has the value "Smith" followed by 95 spaces. Then the statement

  ```
  INSERT
  INTO T ( ..., C, ... )
  VALUES ( ..., :H, ... )
  ```

  will set C to the value "Smith" followed by 95 spaces. By contrast, the statement

  ```
  INSERT
  INTO T ( ..., C, ... )
  VALUES ( ..., TRIM (:H), ... )
  ```

  will set C to just "Smith" (with no trailing spaces).

- USER

    Same as CURRENT_USER.

CASE operations

A CASE operation returns one of a specified set of scalar values, depending on some condition. The general format is

```
CASE
    when-clause-list
    ELSE scalar-expression
END
```

where a "when clause" takes the form

```
WHEN conditional-expression THEN scalar-expression
```

The when-clauses are processed in sequence as written. As soon as one is found for which the conditional expression evaluates to *true*, the value of the corresponding scalar expression is taken as the overall result, and the evaluation process stops. If none of the conditional expressions evaluates to *true*, the value of the scalar expression in the ELSE clause is taken as the overall result. Here is an example:

```
CASE
    WHEN S.STATUS > 25 THEN 'Fine'
    WHEN S.STATUS > 20 THEN 'Acceptable'
    WHEN S.STATUS > 15 THEN 'Mediocre'
    WHEN S.STATUS > 10 THEN 'Not too good'
    WHEN S.STATUS >  5 THEN 'Dubious'
    ELSE                  'Last resort'
END
```

A second CASE format also exists. It effectively serves as shorthand for a special case of the first format. The syntax is

```
CASE scalar-expression-1
    type-2-when-clause-list
    ELSE scalar-expression-4
END
```

where a "type 2 when clause" takes the form

```
WHEN scalar-expression-2 THEN scalar-expression-3
```

This CASE expression is defined to be equivalent to a CASE operation of the first format in which each when-clause includes a conditional expression of the form "scalar-expression-1 = scalar-expression-2." For example, the CASE expression

```
CASE P.COLOR
   WHEN 'Red'     THEN 4
   WHEN 'Yellow'  THEN 3
   WHEN 'Blue'    THEN 2
   WHEN 'Green'   THEN 1
   ELSE           0
END
```

is equivalent to the CASE operation

```
CASE
   WHEN P.COLOR = 'Red'     THEN 4
   WHEN P.COLOR = 'Yellow'  THEN 3
   WHEN P.COLOR = 'Blue'    THEN 2
   WHEN P.COLOR = 'Green'   THEN 1
   ELSE                     0
END
```

Note: There are a couple of other variants of the basic CASE operation, NULLIF and COALESCE, both having to do with nulls. As already indicated, we defer detailed discussion of everything to do with nulls to Chapter 16.

Scalar Expressions

A scalar expression is an expression that evaluates to a scalar value. Generally speaking, such expressions can appear wherever a *literal* of the appropriate type is permitted (e.g., as operands in SELECT and WHERE clauses). Unfortunately, however, there are numerous exceptions to this general rule. Such exceptions are noted at appropriate points in the text. *Note:* For details regarding the data type, precision, etc., of the result of a scalar expression, the reader is referred to the official standard document. Note, however, that CAST can be used (up to a point) to *force* the result to be of a prescribed data type, precision, etc.

There are basically five kinds of scalar expressions, characterized according to the data type of the value they represent: numeric, character string, bit string, "datetime," and interval expressions. Here we consider the first three kinds only; as already explained, detailed discussion of dates and times (including intervals) is deferred to Chapter 17.

First, *numeric* expressions:

```
numeric-expression
    ::=    numeric-term
         | numeric-expression { + | - } numeric-term

numeric-term
    ::=    numeric-factor
         | numeric-term { * | / } numeric-factor

numeric-factor
    ::=    [ + | - ] numeric-primary
```

A "numeric primary" is any of the following:

- a column name, possibly qualified;
- a parameter, host variable, or unsigned numeric literal;
- a reference to a scalar function (possibly CASE or CAST) or aggregate function;
- a scalar expression in parentheses;
- a table expression in parentheses (see Chapter 11).

In each case, of course, the "numeric primary" must yield a value of data type numeric. In the last case, moreover, the table expression must evaluate to a table containing exactly one column and exactly one row; the value of the expression is then taken to be, precisely, the single scalar value contained within that table. *Note:* The standard refers to such an expression as a *scalar subquery*. It is an error if a scalar subquery yields a table of more than one row. If instead it yields a table of no rows at all, then the expression is interpreted as null (see Chapter 16).

Incidentally, the syntax rules imply that (e.g.) "X−−3" is a valid numeric expression, containing two immediately adjacent minus signs. However, that "−−3" will not be interpreted (as the user might expect) as "+3"; instead, the "−−" will be taken as marking the beginning of a *comment*.

Here are some examples of numeric expressions.

```
S.STATUS

P.WEIGHT * 454

SALARY + COMMISSION + BONUS

( QTY + 1500 ) / 75.2

( CHAR_LENGTH ( S.SNAME ) - 1 ) * 2

50 - ( AVG ( SP.QTY ) / 100 )

( SELECT S.STATUS FROM S WHERE S.SNO = 'S3' )
```

We turn now to *character string* expressions:

```
character-string-expression
    ::=    character-string-concatenation
         | character-string-primary

character-string-concatenation
    ::=    character-string-expression
                    || character-string-primary
```

Note: The symbol "‖" here represents the concatenation operator—it should not be confused with the vertical bar "|" that is used to separate alternatives in the grammar.

A "character string primary" is syntactically identical to a "numeric primary"—but, of course, it must yield a value of data type character string instead of numeric. Here are some examples of character string expressions.

```
P.PNAME

INITIALS || LASTNAME

MIN ( P.COLOR )

USER

SUBSTRING ( S.SNAME FROM 1 FOR 3 )

( CASE WHEN P.WEIGHT < 50
  THEN 'Light' ELSE 'Heavy' END ) || ' ' || 'part'
```

Finally, a *bit string* expression is syntactically similar to a character string expression, but of course the "bit string primary" operands must yield values of type bit string, not character string.

7.5   AGGREGATE FUNCTIONS

SQL provides a set of five builtin aggregate functions: COUNT, SUM, AVG, MAX, and MIN.* Apart from the special case of COUNT(*)—see below—each of these functions operates on a certain *aggregate*, namely the collection of scalar values in some column of some table (often a *derived* table, i.e., a table derived in some way from the given base tables), and produces a single scalar result value, defined as follows:

```
COUNT    number of scalar values in the column

SUM      sum of the scalar values in the column

AVG      average of the scalar values in the column

MAX      largest scalar value in the column

MIN      smallest scalar value in the column
```

As indicated in Section 7.4, an aggregate function reference is a special case of a scalar "primary," and so can be used within scalar expressions. The syntax is:

```
aggregate-function-reference
    ::=    COUNT(*)
       | { AVG | MAX | MIN | SUM | COUNT }
              ( [ ALL | DISTINCT ] scalar-expression )
```

Points to note:

1. For details regarding the data type (etc.) of the result of an aggregate function invocation, the reader is referred to the official standard document.

---

*EXISTS and UNIQUE (see Chapter 12) can also be considered as aggregate functions of a kind; however, they differ from the functions discussed in the present section in that (a) their argument is specified in a different syntactic style (actually a more logical style), and (b) they return a truth value instead of (e.g.) a number or a character string, and "truth value" is not an SQL data type.

2. For SUM and AVG the argument must be of type numeric.

3. Except for the special case of COUNT(*), the argument expression can option-ally be preceded by the key word DISTINCT, to indicate that redundant dupli-cate values are to be eliminated from the argument before the function is applied. The alternative to DISTINCT is ALL; ALL is assumed if nothing is specified. We remark that DISTINCT is legal but unavailing in the case of MAX and MIN.

4. The special function COUNT(*)—DISTINCT not allowed—is provided to count all rows in a table without any duplicate elimination.

5. (We mention this point for completeness.) Any nulls in the argument are always eliminated before the aggregate function is applied, regardless of whether DISTINCT is specified, except for the case of COUNT(*), where nulls are handled just like nonnull values.

6. (Again we mention this point for completeness.) If the argument happens to be empty, COUNT returns a result of zero; the others all return null.

7. The argument expression cannot include any aggregate function references or table expressions. Thus, for example, an expression such as

```
SELECT AVG ( SUM ( QTY ) ) AS AQ        -- *** ILLEGAL *** !!!
FROM    ...
```

is *** *ILLEGAL* ***. By contrast, the more complex expression

```
SELECT AVG ( X ) AS AQ
FROM    ( SELECT SUM ( QTY ) AS X ... )
   ...
```

is legal! Refer to Chapter 11 for a full discussion of such matters.

8. If an aggregate function reference appears within a table expression that is in turn nested within another table expression, and its argument expression includes a column reference whose implicit or explicit range variable quali-fier has that "outer" table expression as its scope, then that column reference must be the only column reference within that argument expression. Furthermore, the aggregate function reference in question must appear either within a SELECT clause or within a table expression within a HAVING clause, and in the HAVING case the table expression nesting must be "direct"—i.e., no other table expression can intervene between the two table expressions in question. (Again we mention this rule only for completeness. It is very difficult to explain it in intuitive terms, in part because it seems to be logically unnecessary; at the very least, it is more restrictive than it needs to be.)

Note: In addition to the foregoing eight points, there are a number of further restrictions on the use of aggregate functions; they are documented in Chapter 11, Section 11.6, subsections "The SELECT Clause" and "The WHERE Clause," and Chapter 14, Section 14.1.

Here then are some examples. Each of the expressions shown below could serve as the basis for a single-row SELECT statement (see Chapter 9) or could be nested within some more complex expression such as a table expression (see Chapter 11).

Example 1: Get the total number of suppliers.

```
SELECT  COUNT(*) AS N1
FROM    S
```

Result: A table consisting of a single column, called N1, and a single row, containing the scalar value 5 (given our usual sample data values).

Example 2: Get the total number of suppliers currently supplying parts.

```
SELECT  COUNT ( DISTINCT SP.SNO ) AS N2
FROM    SP
```

Result: A table consisting of a single column N2 and a single row, containing the scalar value 4.

Example 3: Get the number of shipments for part P2.

```
SELECT  COUNT(*) AS N3
FROM    SP
WHERE   SP.PNO = 'P2'
```

Result: A table consisting of a single column N3 and a single row, containing the scalar value 4.

Example 4: Get the total quantity of part P2 supplied.

```
SELECT  SUM ( SP.QTY ) AS TOT1
FROM    SP
WHERE   SP.PNO = 'P2'
```

Result: A table consisting of a single column TOT1 and a single row, containing the scalar value 1000.

Example 5: Get supplier numbers for suppliers with status less than the current maximum status in the S table.

```
SELECT  S.SNO
FROM    S
WHERE   S.STATUS <
        ( SELECT MAX ( S.STATUS )
          FROM   S )
```

Result: A table consisting of a single column, called SNO, containing the scalar values S1, S2, and S4. Note that we have not bothered to introduce a column name for the single column of the (single-row!) intermediate result table produced by the scalar subquery on the right hand side of the comparison in the WHERE clause. The reason is that we do not need to refer to that column by name anywhere. By contrast, we always make sure in our examples that the *final* result table does have a proper name for every column.

Example 6: Get supplier numbers for suppliers whose status is greater than or equal to the average for their particular city.

```
SELECT  SX.SNO
FROM    S SX
WHERE   SX.STATUS >=
      ( SELECT AVG ( SY.STATUS )
        FROM    S SY
        WHERE   SY.CITY = SX.CITY )
```

Result: A table consisting of a single column, SNO, containing the scalar values S1, S3, S4, and S5. *Note:* The scalar subquery in this example involves an *outer reference*—namely, SX.CITY. See Chapter 12 for further discussion of outer references.

7.6   ASSIGNMENTS AND COMPARISONS

Assignments

Scalar assignment operations are performed when scalar values are retrieved from the database (e.g., via SELECT) or entered into the database (e.g., via UPDATE). In general, such an assignment involves assigning the value of some scalar expression (the *source*) to some scalar object (the *target*), where the source and target must be of compatible SQL data types. Type compatibility is defined in SQL as follows:

1. All numeric types are compatible with one another.
2. All character string types are compatible with one another.*
3. All bit string types are compatible with one another.
4. There are no other instances of compatibility (other than those having to do with dates and times—see Chapter 17).

Assignments are performed as follows:

1. For a numeric assignment, the source is converted if necessary to the data type of the target (including precision, and scale if applicable) before the assignment is performed. It is an error if the conversion causes significant digits to be lost.
2. For a character string assignment:

---

*A slight oversimplification. See Chapter 19 for further discussion.

- If the target is fixed length, then for retrieval operations the source string is conceptually truncated on the right or padded on the right with space characters (as necessary) to make it the same length as the target before the assignment is performed. For update operations the same rules apply, except that it is an error if truncation is required and it would cause any nonspace characters to be lost.

- If the target is varying length, its current actual length is set to the lesser of its declared maximum length and the length of the source, and the assignment is then performed as in the fixed length case.

3. Bit string assignments are performed in a like manner, except that:

- Any necessary padding is with 0-bits instead of space characters.

- For update operations truncation is not allowed.

Note that assignment targets in INSERT and UPDATE operations—i.e., target *columns*—must be specified by means of *unqualified* column names. See Chapter 3 for a discussion of qualified and unqualified names.

Comparisons

Comparisons are performed under many circumstances—for example, when duplicate values are eliminated (see, e.g., the discussion of DISTINCT in Section 7.5 above and elsewhere). A comparison is also one kind of *conditional expression* (though not the only kind); conditional expressions are used in, e.g., CASE operations (see Section 7.4 above), in WHERE clauses (see Chapter 11), and elsewhere. *Note:* In principle, conditional expressions could be regarded as a special kind of scalar expression, except that they evaluate to a truth value instead of to one of the SQL-supported data types.

The *basic* form of a comparison (but we stress the point that there are many other forms, over and above this "basic" form) looks like this:

```
scalar-expression comparison-operator scalar-expression
```

Points to note:

1. The two "scalar expression" comparands must be *compatible* (as that term is defined under "Assignments" above). In other words, they must be scalar expressions of the same kind—i.e., both numeric or both character string or . . . (etc.). The data types are *not* required to be absolutely identical.

2. The comparison operator must be one of the following: =, <, <=, >, >=, or <> ("not equals").*

---

*We remark that, for character strings at least, the behavior of these comparison operators—including in particular the most fundamental one of all, the "equals" operator!—is not always as straightforward as might be expected. Refer to Chapter 19, Section 19.7, especially the subsection "Indeterminate Table Expressions," for further discussion.

Comparisons are evaluated as follows:

1. Numbers compare algebraically (negative values are considered to be smaller than positive values, regardless of their absolute magnitude). Note that it might be necessary to convert either or both of the comparands to some other (numeric) type before the comparison can be performed.

2. Character strings are compared character by character from left to right. The individual pairwise comparisons are performed in accordance with the appropriate *collating sequence* (see Chapter 19). If every pairwise comparison yields "equal," the character strings are equal; otherwise, the first pairwise comparison that does not yield "equal" determines the overall result. *Note:* If two character strings of different lengths are to be compared, then:

   ▪ If PAD SPACE applies to the collating sequence in question (arguably "the normal case"), then the shorter string is conceptually padded at the right with spaces to make it the same length as the longer before the comparison is done.

   ▪ If instead NO PAD applies, a character string *c1* that is shorter than some other character string *c2*, but "compares equal" to that leading substring of *c2* that is the same length as *c1*, is considered to be less than *c2* even if all remaining characters of *c2* are spaces. For example, if *c1* and *c2* have the values "xyz" (length 3) and "xyz*" (length 4, with the "*" representing a space), respectively, then *c1* < *c2* under NO PAD.

   See Chapter 19 for further discussion of PAD SPACE *vs.* NO PAD and other matters having to do with character string comparisons.

3. Bit strings are compared bit by bit from left to right. The individual pairwise comparisons are performed in accordance with the convention that a 0-bit is less than a 1-bit. If every pairwise comparison yields "equal," the bit strings are equal; otherwise, the first pairwise comparison that does not yield "equal" determines the overall result. *Note:* A bit string *b1* that is shorter than some other bit string *b2*, but "compares equal" to that leading substring of *b2* that is the same length as *b1*, is always considered to be less than *b2* even if all remaining bits of *b2* are 0-bits. For example, if *b1* and *b2* have the values "101" (length 3) and "1010" (length 4), then *b1* < *b2*.

Here are some examples of comparisons.

```
SP.SNO = 'S1'

P.WEIGHT * 454 > 1000

SUBSTRING ( P.CITY FROM 1 FOR 1 ) = 'L'

SUM ( SP.QTY ) > 500
```

8

Data Definition:
Domains and Base Tables

8.1   INTRODUCTION

Domains and base tables are initially defined by means of the statements CREATE
DOMAIN and CREATE TABLE, respectively. These statements can be executed
as independent operations in their own right, or they can be executed as "schema
elements" within a CREATE SCHEMA operation, as explained in Chapter 4.
Once created, domain and base table definitions can subsequently be:

- Changed in various ways by means of the statements ALTER DOMAIN and
  ALTER TABLE;

- Deleted entirely by means of the statements DROP DOMAIN and DROP
  TABLE.

Unlike their CREATE counterparts, however, these ALTER and DROP statements must be executed as independent operations—they cannot appear as schema
elements within a CREATE SCHEMA statement.

Note carefully that (as explained in Chapter 4) every domain and every base
table always belongs to some schema, even if the corresponding CREATE statement is executed "independently." It follows that creating a new domain or base
table ("independently" or otherwise), or altering or dropping an existing domain

or base table (necessarily "independently"), thus has the effect—among other things—of updating the relevant schema in the appropriate manner.

Note: The reader will observe from the foregoing paragraphs that the term "TABLE" in CREATE, ALTER, and DROP TABLE refers to a base table specifically.* This fact is a trifle unfortunate, since base tables are only one special case—albeit an important one—of tables in general. Now, we cannot change the syntax of SQL, but (as mentioned at the end of Chapter 3) we will be careful in this book, in our prose explanations, always to say "base table" when we mean a base table specifically, and to reserve the term "table," unqualified, to mean any kind of table (base table or view or intermediate result or final result or . . .).

We now proceed to discuss the foregoing ideas in detail. *Note:* In what follows, we choose to discuss domains before base tables, because domains are actually much more fundamental in a theoretical sense—even though, as mentioned in the previous chapter, SQL's support for the domain concept is very weak, and indeed does not even have to be used.

8.2   DOMAINS

CREATE DOMAIN

As suggested in Chapter 7, a domain definition in SQL is essentially nothing more than a kind of factored-out column data type specification that can be shared by any number of actual columns in any number of actual base tables. Domains are defined using CREATE DOMAIN:†

```
domain-definition
    ::=   CREATE DOMAIN domain [ AS ] data-type
                      [ default-definition ]
                      [ domain-constraint-definition-list ]
```

---

*We have argued elsewhere (see, e.g., C. J. Date, *An Introduction to Database Systems*, 6th edition, Addison-Wesley, 1995) that in addition it really refers to a table *variable* rather than to a table *per se*. A table variable is a variable in the conventional programming language sense, but one that happens to take tables as its values (different tables at different times). For example, Fig. 2.1 in Chapter 2 shows the current table values of three table variables called S, P, and SP. If we perform an update on (say) table variable S, the effect, conceptually speaking, is to replace the current table value *en bloc* by another such value (probably not very different from the previous one). Unfortunately SQL does not explicitly make the logical distinction between table values and table variables (though it would be better if it did); since this is a book about SQL, we will downplay that distinction also.

†We say that CREATE DOMAIN "defines" or "creates" a domain, but (as indicated in Section 8.1) what is really happening is that a domain definition or *descriptor* is being created and entered into the relevant schema. An analogous remark applies to all forms of CREATE, of course. By the same token, ALTER operations *change* descriptors in schemas, and DROP operations *delete* descriptors from schemas. It is usual (and convenient) not to be this precise, however, but to speak of creating or altering or dropping domains (and so forth) *per se*, and we will usually follow this latter practice ourselves in this book.

Here "domain" is the name for the new domain,* "data type" is the underlying data type for that domain, and the optional "default definition" and "domain constraint definition list" specify a default value and a set of integrity constraints that will apply to every column† defined on the domain. Default values are discussed in more detail below; constraints (of all kinds) are discussed in Chapter 14. *Note:* The optional "AS" is a pure noiseword and can be omitted without affecting the semantics of the operation.

The optional "default definition" takes the form

```
DEFAULT { literal | niladic-function | NULL }
```

where "niladic function" is any of the following:

```
USER
CURRENT_USER
SESSION_USER
SYSTEM_USER
CURRENT_DATE
CURRENT_TIME
CURRENT_TIMESTAMP
```

(see Chapter 15 for an explanation of the first four of these and Chapter 17 for the rest). Here is an example:

```
CREATE DOMAIN CITIES CHAR(15) DEFAULT '???'

CREATE TABLE S ( ... , CITY CITIES, ... )
```

If the user now inserts a row into table S and does not provide a value for the CITY column within that row, then the value "???" will be placed in that position by default. Thus, the general purpose of a default definition is to specify a value to be placed in some column—a *default value*, or simply a *default*—if the user does not provide a value on INSERT. "DEFAULT literal" means that the default is the specified literal; "DEFAULT niladic-function" means that the default is the value of the specified function at the time of the INSERT; and "DEFAULT NULL" means that the default is null (see Chapter 16).

If CREATE DOMAIN does not specify an explicit default, the domain in question initially has no default value. However, one can be added later by means of ALTER DOMAIN (see below). ALTER DOMAIN can also be used to remove the default value from a domain that does have one (again, see below).

For further discussion of defaults, see Section 8.3.

---

*If the name is qualified by a schema name and the CREATE DOMAIN appears within the context of a CREATE SCHEMA statement, then that schema name must identify the schema that would have been assumed by default anyway, *viz.* the schema being created (see Chapter 4, Section 4.3).

†Well, not quite *every* column; if a column has its own explicit default definition, then that definition takes precedence over one specified at the domain level. By contrast, the integrity constraints do indeed apply to every column defined on the domain (they are logically ANDed with any other constraints that might apply to the column in question).

ALTER DOMAIN

Just as a new domain can be created at any time via CREATE DOMAIN, so an existing domain can be *altered* at any time (in a variety of ways) via ALTER DOMAIN:

```
domain-alteration
    ::=   ALTER DOMAIN domain domain-alteration-action

domain-alteration-action
    ::=   domain-default-alteration-action
        | domain-constraint-alteration-action

domain-default-alteration-action
    ::=   SET default-definition
        | DROP DEFAULT

domain-constraint-alteration-action
    ::=   ADD domain-constraint-definition
        | DROP CONSTRAINT constraint
```

As the syntax suggests, ALTER DOMAIN allows (a) a new default definition to be attached ("SET") to an existing domain (replacing the previous one, if any) or an existing default definition to be removed ("DROP DEFAULT"); it also allows (b) a new constraint to be attached ("ADD") to an existing domain (being ANDed to existing constraints, if any) or an existing constraint to be removed ("DROP CONSTRAINT"). Here we discuss possibility (a) only; refer to Chapter 14 for a discussion of possibility (b).

■   *SET:* The new default automatically applies to all columns defined on the domain, except for columns that have their own explicit default (see Section 8.3 below).

■   *DROP:* The existing default definition is copied down to all columns defined on the domain (except for columns that have their own explicit default) before it is removed from the domain.

DROP DOMAIN

Finally, an existing domain can be dropped by means of DROP DOMAIN:

```
DROP DOMAIN domain { RESTRICT | CASCADE }
```

If RESTRICT is specified, then (a) if "domain" is referenced in any column definition or (within a CAST operation) in any view definition (see Chapter 13) or integrity constraint (see Chapter 14), the DROP DOMAIN will fail; (b) otherwise it will succeed, and the specified domain will be dropped. If CASCADE is specified, the DROP DOMAIN will always succeed; any referencing views and integrity constraints will implicitly be dropped also (in the case of referencing views, that implied DROP will also include the CASCADE option). Referencing columns will not be dropped, but will effectively be "altered" as follows:

- Instead of being defined on the now dropped domain, they will now be considered to be defined directly on the underlying data type of that domain instead.

- If they previously had no explicit default, they will now be considered to have the explicit default (if any) defined for the now dropped domain.*

- They will also effectively inherit any integrity constraints that were previously associated with the now dropped domain.

8.3   BASE TABLES

As indicated in Section 8.1, a base table is an important special case of the more general concept "table." Let us therefore begin by making that general concept more precise. A *table* in an SQL system consists of a row of *column headings*, together with zero or more *data rows* (different numbers of data rows at different times, in general). For a given table:

- The column heading row specifies one or more columns (giving, among other things, a data type for each).

- Each data row contains exactly one scalar value† for each of the columns specified in the column heading row. Further, all values in a given column are of the same data type, namely the data type specified for that column in the column heading row.

The number of data rows in a given table is called the *cardinality* of that table and the number of columns is called the *degree* (though in fact neither of these terms is much used in SQL contexts). *Note:* The unqualified term "row" invariably refers to a *data* row, not to the column heading row, and we will follow this convention in the present book from this point forward.

Several points arise in connection with the foregoing definition.

1. First, note that in the relational model no table is ever permitted to contain any duplicate rows. That is, every true relational table is guaranteed to contain a genuine mathematical *set* of rows (sets in mathematics do not have duplicate members). In SQL, however, this discipline is—very unfortunately, in this

---

*Likewise, if they previously had no explicit collation, they will now be considered to have the collation (if any) defined for the now dropped domain. See Chapter 19 for a discussion of collations.
†That "exactly one" will become "at most one" when we take nulls into account. See Chapter 16.

writer's opinion—not enforced,* and SQL tables are indeed permitted to contain duplicate rows. In this book, however, we will never permit duplicate rows in any of our tables, and we recommend strongly that users follow this same discipline in practice.

Note: Because of the foregoing, SQL tables are sometimes said to contain *bags* of rows (a *bag*, also known as a *multiset*, is a collection that does permit duplicate members).

2. Observe that the definition makes no mention of *row ordering*. As explained in Chapter 2, the rows of an SQL table have no ordering (and the same is true of true relational tables). It is possible, as we will see in Chapter 10, to *impose* an ordering on the rows when they are accessed through a cursor; however, imposing such an ordering should not be thought of as "ordering the table," but rather as converting the table into something that is not a table, but instead a *sequence* or *ordered list* of rows.

3. In contrast to the previous point, the columns of a table are considered to be ordered, left to right (at least, *SQL* tables possess such an ordering, though true relational tables do not). For example, in the suppliers table S (see Fig. 2.1 in Chapter 2), column SNO is the first column, column SNAME is the second column, and so on. In practice, however, there are very few situations in which such ordering is important; in the interests of simplicity, therefore, we will ignore it in this book wherever possible.

To turn now to base tables specifically: A base table is an *autonomous, named* table. By "autonomous," we mean that the table exists in its own right—unlike (e.g.) a view, which does not exist in its own right but is derived from one or more base tables (it is merely an alternative way of looking at the data in those base tables). By "named," we mean that the table is explicitly given a name via an appropriate CREATE statement—unlike (e.g.) a table that is merely the result of executing some query against the database, which does not have any explicit name of its own and has only ephemeral existence.

CREATE TABLE

Base tables are defined by means of the CREATE TABLE statement. The syntax is as follows:†

---

*Actually the situation is worse than this sentence suggests; it is not merely that the discipline is not enforced, but rather that SQL actually includes certain options, such as the ALL option on UNION, that are specifically designed to *generate* tables with duplicate rows (in general).

†Ignoring temporary tables. We remind the reader that (as mentioned in Chapter 3 and elsewhere) we are deferring everything to do with temporary tables to Chapter 18.

```
base-table-definition
   ::=    CREATE TABLE base-table
              ( base-table-element-commalist )
```

Here "base table" is the name for the new (and initially empty) base table,* and each "base table element" is either a column definition or a base table constraint definition. Column definitions are discussed below; constraints (of all kinds) are discussed in Chapter 14. Refer to Fig. 2.3 in Chapter 2 for some examples of CREATE TABLE. *Note:* The syntax permits column definitions and base table constraint definitions to be arbitrarily interspersed. In this book we adopt the convention that the column definitions always come first.

The syntax of "column definition" is:

```
column-definition
   ::=    column { data-type | domain }
              [ default-definition ]
              [ column-constraint-definition-list ]
```

Here "column" is the unqualified name for the column in question, "data type" or "domain" specifies the corresponding data type (see Section 8.2 above), and the optional "default definition" is discussed immediately below. (Once again, all discussion of constraints is deferred to Chapter 14.)

The optional "default definition" takes the form

```
DEFAULT { literal | niladic-function | NULL }
```

(exactly like a default definition in CREATE or ALTER DOMAIN). The effect is to specify an explicit default for the column in question. In general, therefore, the default value for a given column is determined as follows:

- If the column has an explicit DEFAULT clause, then the value specified in that clause is the default.

- Otherwise, if the column is defined on a domain and that domain has an explicit DEFAULT clause, then the value specified in that clause is the default.

- Otherwise, the default is null.

Note that if the default for a given column is explicitly or implicitly defined to be null, but that column is also defined to be NOT NULL (see Chapter 16), then that column effectively has no default at all—implying that a value *must* be provided for the column on INSERT. Informally, we will refer to such a column as one that "has no default." *Note:* In SQL/89 (but not in SQL/92), explicitly specifying both DEFAULT NULL and NOT NULL for the same column was illegal.

---

*If the name is qualified by a schema name and the CREATE TABLE appears within the context of a CREATE SCHEMA statement, then that schema name must identify the schema that would have been assumed by default anyway, *viz.* the schema being created (see Chapter 4, Section 4.3).

Observe, incidentally, that omitting the default definition for a given column and specifying DEFAULT NULL explicitly for that column are *not* equivalent (because the former permits the column to inherit a domain-level default, while the latter does not).

ALTER TABLE

Just as an existing domain can be altered via ALTER DOMAIN, so an existing base table can be altered (in a variety of ways) via ALTER TABLE:

```
base-table-alteration
    ::=    ALTER TABLE base-table base-table-alteration-action

base-table-alteration-action
    ::=    column-alteration-action
         | base-table-constraint-alteration-action

column-alteration-action
    ::=    ADD [ COLUMN ] column-definition
         | ALTER [ COLUMN ] column
                { SET default-definition | DROP DEFAULT }
         | DROP [ COLUMN ] column { RESTRICT | CASCADE }

base-table-constraint-alteration-action
    ::=    ADD base-table-constraint-definition
         | DROP CONSTRAINT constraint { RESTRICT | CASCADE }
```

As the syntax suggests, ALTER TABLE allows (a) a new column to be added to, or an existing column to be altered in, or an existing column to be removed from, an existing base table; it also allows (b) a new integrity constraint to be attached to, or an existing integrity constraint to be removed from, an existing base table. Here we discuss possibility (a) only; refer to Chapter 14 for a discussion of possibility (b).

Here is an example of ADD COLUMN:*

```
ALTER TABLE S ADD COLUMN DISCOUNT SMALLINT DEFAULT -1
```

This statement adds a new fifth column called DISCOUNT to base table S. All existing S rows are extended to include a value for the new column; that value is −1 in every such row. *Note:* If (a) the new column had been defined on a domain instead of having its own data type specification, and (b) that domain had a default definition, and (c) the new column did *not* have its own default definition, then (d) the value of the new column in existing rows would have been set to the default defined for the domain.

---

*The optional key word COLUMN in ADD COLUMN is a pure noiseword and can be omitted without affecting the semantics of the operation. The same is true for ALTER COLUMN and DROP COLUMN.

The foregoing example is sufficient to explain ADD COLUMN. ALTER COLUMN allows a new default definition to be attached ("SET") to an existing base table column (replacing the previous default definition, if any) or an existing default definition to be removed. DROP COLUMN allows an existing base table column to be removed; note, however, that the operation will fail (a) if it attempts to remove the only column from a single-column base table, or (b) if RESTRICT is specified and the column in question is referenced in any view definition (see Chapter 13) or any integrity constraint* (see Chapter 14). If CASCADE is specified instead of RESTRICT, the DROP COLUMN will always succeed (unless it attempts to remove the only column from a single-column base table), and furthermore will cascade to drop all such referencing views and integrity constraints (in the case of referencing views, that implied DROP will also include the CASCADE option).

DROP TABLE

Finally, an existing base table can be dropped by means of DROP TABLE:

```
DROP TABLE base-table { RESTRICT | CASCADE }
```

If RESTRICT is specified, then (a) if "base table" is referenced in any view definition (see Chapter 13) or integrity constraint† (see Chapter 14), the DROP TABLE will fail; (b) otherwise it will succeed, and the specified base table will be dropped. If CASCADE is specified, the DROP TABLE will always succeed; any referencing views and integrity constraints will implicitly be dropped also (in the case of referencing views, that implied DROP will also include the CASCADE option).

---

*Excluding base table integrity constraints that both (a) are specified as part of the definition of the base table containing the column to be dropped and (b) do not reference any column other than the one to be dropped.

†Excluding base table integrity constraints that both (a) are specified as part of the definition of the base table to be dropped and (b) do not reference any base table other than the one to be dropped.

9

Data Manipulation: Noncursor Operations

9.1 INTRODUCTION

As explained briefly in Chapter 2, the SQL data manipulation operations can be divided into two broad classes, those that involve cursors and those that do not. In this chapter we restrict our attention to those that do not; cursor operations will be discussed in Chapter 10. Thus, the operations we will be discussing in the present chapter are the following:

```
SELECT (single-row)
INSERT
UPDATE (searched)
DELETE (searched)
```

Note: For tutorial reasons, we assume throughout this chapter that all named tables—at least, all those that are to be updated, i.e., those that are the target of an INSERT, UPDATE, or DELETE operation—are base tables. The special considerations that apply to views are deferred to Chapter 13. We also ignore the possibility of errors (for the most part); in particular, we ignore the possibility that any integrity violations might occur (e.g., we assume that no attempt is made to introduce a row that violates a primary or foreign key constraint, or to enter a value into a column that is of the wrong data type, etc., etc.).

9.2   SINGLE-ROW SELECT

As explained in Chapter 2, the noncursor SELECT operation in standard SQL is *not* the fully general (multi-row) SELECT operation that readers might already be familiar with; instead, it is what is usually called a *single-row SELECT*, i.e., a SELECT that retrieves *at most one* row. For example:

```
SELECT P.WEIGHT, P.COLOR
INTO   :WEIGHT_PARAM, :COLOR_PARAM
FROM   P
WHERE  P.PNO = 'P4'
```

It is an error if the result table, i.e., the table to be retrieved, contains more than one row (not possible in the example, because PNO is the primary key for table P).

Here are some more examples. The reader should confirm that they are all valid, in the sense that at most one row will indeed be retrieved in each case.

```
SELECT S.SNO, S.SNAME, S.STATUS, S.CITY
INTO   :SNO_PARAM, :SNAME_PARAM, :STATUS_PARAM, :CITY_PARAM
FROM   S
WHERE  S.SNO = 'S7'

SELECT AVG ( SP.QTY )
INTO   :AVG_QTY_PARAM
FROM   SP

SELECT MAX ( SP.QTY ) - MIN ( SP.QTY )
INTO   :ARITH_PARAM
FROM   SP
WHERE  SP.PNO = 'P4'
```

The general syntax is:*

```
  SELECT [ ALL | DISTINCT ] select-item-commalist
  INTO   target-commalist
  FROM   table-reference-commalist
[ WHERE  conditional-expression ]
[ GROUP  BY column-commalist ]
[ HAVING conditional-expression ]
```

Explanation:

1. If neither ALL nor DISTINCT is specified, ALL is assumed.

2. Each "select item" is a scalar expression, typically but not necessarily involving one or more columns of table *T1* (see paragraph 4 below for an explanation of "table *T1*"). *Note:* It is possible to assign names to the columns that result from evaluating the select-items. It is also possible to use certain shorthands (involving the use of asterisks) for specifying certain commalists of

---

*Observe that a single-row SELECT is limited to being what in Chapter 11 we will call a "select expression," instead of the more general "table expression." The reason for this slight lack of orthogonality is probably just historical accident. (The concept of *orthogonality* is explained in Appendix C.)

select-items. We omit the details here; see Chapter 11, Section 11.6, for further discussion.

3. Each "target" is a parameter or host variable (refer to Chapter 5, Section 5.2, if you need to refresh your memory regarding the meaning of this phrase). There must be exactly one target for each select-item; the target identified by the *i*th entry in the target-commalist corresponds to the *i*th select-item.

4. We make no attempt at this juncture to explain the FROM, WHERE, GROUP BY, and HAVING clauses in any detail (those explanations are deferred to Chapter 11). However, note that, no matter which of those clauses are specified and which omitted, the conceptual result of evaluating them is always a table, which for the purposes of this explanation we refer to as table *T1* (even though it is in fact unnamed). *Note:* Table *T1* might be a "grouped" table (see Chapter 11), but if it is it must contain at most one group (it is an error otherwise). We can then reinterpret the name *T1* as referring to the table that is exactly that single group if indeed there is such a group, or to an empty table otherwise.

5. Let *T2* be the table that is obtained by evaluating the specified select-items against table *T1*.

6. Let *T3* be the table that is obtained by eliminating redundant duplicate rows from table *T2* if DISTINCT is specified, or a table that is identical to table *T2* otherwise.

7. If table *T3* contains exactly one row, that row is retrieved; if it contains no rows, a "not found" condition occurs; if it contains more than one row, an error occurs.

9.3 INSERT

The INSERT statement is used to insert new rows into a named table. Two examples are given below; the first inserts a single row, the second inserts several rows (at least potentially). *Note:* In that second example we assume we have another named table, TEMP, with columns SNO and CITY, such that the data types of columns TEMP.SNO and TEMP.CITY are compatible with those of columns S.SNO and S.CITY, respectively.

```
INSERT
INTO    S ( SNO, CITY, SNAME )
VALUES ( :SNO_PARAM, DEFAULT, :SNAME_PARAM )

INSERT
INTO    TEMP ( SNO, CITY )
        SELECT  S.SNO, S.CITY
        FROM    S
        WHERE   S.STATUS > :STATUS_PARAM
```

The general syntax is:

```
INSERT INTO table [ ( column-commalist ) ] source
```

where "table" identifies the target table, the optional "column commalist" identifies some or all of the columns of that table (by their *un*qualified column names), and "source" is explained below. Omitting the parenthesized commalist of column names—the practice is not recommended—is equivalent to specifying all of the columns of the target table, in their left-to-right order within that table.

The "source" in an INSERT statement is either a *table expression* (i.e., an expression that evaluates to a table of zero or more rows—see Chapter 11), or an expression of the form

```
DEFAULT VALUES
```

The parenthesized commalist of column names must be omitted if DEFAULT VALUES is specified.
Explanation:

1. If an INSERT statement contains an explicit commalist of column names that omits one or more columns of the target table *T*, then every row inserted into *T* by that statement will contain the appropriate default (possibly null) in each column so omitted. It is an error if a column is omitted and that column has no default.

2. If a source of DEFAULT VALUES is specified, a single row is inserted into the target table *T* that contains the appropriate default (possibly null) in every column. It is an error if any column has no default.

3. The full syntax of table expressions is quite complex, and for that reason we defer the details to Chapter 11. However, we give an outline explanation of two special cases here—basically (though not quite!) the only two that were supported in SQL/89.

   - *Case 1:* The table expression takes the form

     ```
     VALUES ( insert-item-commalist )
     ```

     where each "insert item" is either a scalar expression or one of the self-explanatory key words DEFAULT or NULL. The effect is to insert a single row into the target table. The value specified by the *i*th insert-item is inserted into the column identified by the *i*th entry in the (explicit or implicit) commalist of column names in the INTO clause.

   - *Case 2:* The table expression takes the form

```
    SELECT ...
    FROM   ...
[ WHERE   ... ]
[ GROUP  BY ... ]
[ HAVING ... ]
```

The effect is to insert a collection of (potentially) any number of rows into the target table. The table expression is evaluated to yield an intermediate result table R. Each row of R in turn is then treated as if the scalar values in that row were specified as the insert-items in the single-row version of INSERT as discussed under Case 1.

9.4   SEARCHED UPDATE

The searched UPDATE statement is used to update rows in a named table without using a cursor. The operation is multi-row, in general; i.e., the statement updates zero, one, two, . . ., or any number of rows in a single operation. Here is an example (a variation on an example from Chapter 2):

```
UPDATE S
SET    STATUS = 2 * S.STATUS
WHERE  S.CITY = :CITY_PARAM
```

The general syntax is:

```
UPDATE table
  SET    assignment-commalist
[ WHERE  conditional-expression ]
```

where "table" identifies the target table (T, say), "assignment-commalist" is discussed below, and "conditional expression" identifies the rows of T that are to be updated. (Conditional expressions are discussed in detail in Chapter 12.) Omitting the WHERE clause means that the UPDATE is to be applied to all rows of T.

Each assignment in the assignment-commalist takes the form

```
column = update-item
```

where "column" is the *un*qualified name of a column of table T, and "update item" (like "insert item"—see Section 9.3) is either a scalar expression or one of the self-explanatory key words DEFAULT or NULL. The rows of T that satisfy the conditional expression in the WHERE clause (or all rows of T, if the WHERE clause is omitted) are updated in accordance with the assignments in the SET clause. *Note:* For each row to be updated, any reference within an update-item to a column of table T denotes the value of that column in that row before any of the assignments have been performed. The example at the beginning of this section provides an illustration of this point.

We close this section with another, more complex, example. The example is somewhat contrived, but is intended to illustrate the point that one possible form of scalar expression is a *scalar subquery* that extracts a data value from somewhere else in the database:

```
UPDATE P
SET    CITY = ( SELECT S.CITY
                FROM    S
                WHERE   S.SNO = 'S5' )
WHERE  P.COLOR = 'Red'
```

The effect of this UPDATE is to set the city for each red part to be the same as the city for supplier S5.

9.5   SEARCHED DELETE

The searched DELETE statement is used to delete rows in a named table without using a cursor. The operation is multi-row, in general; i.e., the statement deletes zero, one, two, . . ., or any number of rows in a single operation. Here is an example (again a variation on an example from Chapter 2):

```
DELETE
FROM    P
WHERE   P.WEIGHT > :WEIGHT_PARAM
```

The general syntax is:

```
  DELETE
  FROM    table
[ WHERE   conditional-expression ]
```

where "table" identifies the target table (*T*, say) and "conditional expression" identifies the rows of *T* that are to be deleted. (Once again, conditional expressions are discussed in detail in Chapter 12.) Omitting the WHERE clause means that the DELETE is to be applied to all rows of *T*.

10

Data Manipulation:
Cursor Operations

10.1 INTRODUCTION

The basic concept of cursor-based access was explained in Chapter 2 (Section 2.4); refer back to that section if you need to refresh your memory regarding the general idea. In this chapter we consider cursor operations in detail. The operations in question are:

```
OPEN
FETCH
UPDATE (positioned) -- i.e., UPDATE ... CURRENT ...
DELETE (positioned) -- i.e., DELETE ... CURRENT ...
CLOSE
```

The plan of the chapter is as follows. Following this introductory section, Section 10.2 explains exactly what a cursor is and what is involved in defining a cursor. Section 10.3 then discusses the five cursor operations listed above. Finally, Sections 10.4 and 10.5 present a comprehensive example that ties together many of the ideas introduced in the prior sections; Section 10.4 gives a module language version of the example, Section 10.5 gives an embedded SQL equivalent. *Note:* As in the previous chapter, we assume for simplicity that all named tables—at least all those to be updated, i.e., those that are the target of an UPDATE or DELETE

CURRENT operation—are base tables; the special considerations that apply to views are deferred to Chapter 13. We also (for the most part) ignore the possibility of run-time errors.

10.2   CURSORS

A cursor consists essentially of a kind of *pointer* that can be used to run through an ordered collection of rows, pointing to each of the rows in that collection in turn and thus providing addressability to those rows one at a time. If cursor *C* is pointing to row *R*, it is said to be *positioned on* (or just "on") that row *R*. Further, if "cursor *C* is updatable" (see the subsection "Cursor Definition" below), then that row *R* can then be updated via the "positioned," or CURRENT, form of the UPDATE and DELETE operations (UPDATE ... WHERE CURRENT OF *C*, DELETE ... WHERE CURRENT OF *C*). In other words, for a positioned UPDATE or DELETE, the cursor must be in the "on state"—i.e., it must be positioned on some row.

Each cursor has an associated *table expression*,* specified as part of the statement that defines the cursor. The expression can be *parameterized* by means of parameters (in the module language) or host variables (in embedded SQL). For example:

```
DECLARE X CURSOR
     FOR SELECT SP.SNO, SP.QTY
         FROM    SP
         WHERE   SP.PNO = :PNO_PARAM
         ORDER   BY SNO
```

This statement defines a cursor called X, with associated table expression "SELECT ... WHERE SP.PNO = :PNO_PARAM" (:PNO_PARAM is a parameter). That table expression is not evaluated at this time; DECLARE CURSOR is a purely declarative operation. The expression *is* (conceptually) evaluated when cursor X is opened (see Section 10.3). The collection of rows resulting from that evaluation then becomes associated with cursor X, and remains so until cursor X is closed (again, see Section 10.3). Furthermore, that collection of rows is *ordered* in accordance with the ORDER BY clause ("ORDER BY SNO") in the cursor definition for cursor X.

Note: If the expression is parameterized, as it is in the example, the values of the corresponding arguments are conceptually fixed at OPEN time; in other words, changing the values of those arguments after the cursor has been opened has no effect on the collection of rows accessible via that opening of that cursor.

---

*The standard calls it a *query* expression, and ascribes a different (more restrictive) meaning to the term "table expression." Our use of the term is explained in Chapter 11.

Analogous remarks apply to the use of the niladic builtin functions CURRENT_USER, CURRENT_TIME, etc., within a cursor definition.

While it is open, therefore, a cursor designates a certain collection of rows and a certain ordering for that collection. It also designates a certain *position* with respect to that ordering. The possible positions are as follows:

- *on* some specific row ("on" state)
- *before* some specific row ("before" state)
- *after* the last row ("after last" state)

Cursor state is affected by a variety of operations, as follows:

- OPEN positions the cursor before the first row.
- FETCH NEXT positions the cursor on the next row or (if there is no next row) after the last row. FETCH PRIOR positions the cursor on the prior row or (if there is no prior row) before the first row. See Section 10.3 for the effects of other FETCH formats (FIRST, LAST, ABSOLUTE *n*, RELATIVE *n*).
- If the cursor is on some row and that row is deleted via that cursor (by means of an appropriate DELETE CURRENT operation), the cursor is positioned before the next row or (if there is no next row) after the last row.*

Note that a cursor can be "before the first row" or "after the last row" even in the special case where the collection of rows is empty.

All cursors are in the closed state at transaction initiation and are forced (if open) into the closed state at transaction termination. While the transaction is executing, however, the same cursor can be opened and closed any number of times. And if the cursor definition is parameterized, then the arguments corresponding to those parameters can have different values on different openings, implying that the same cursor can be associated with different collections of rows on different openings (within a single transaction or otherwise).

Cursor Definition

For definiteness, we assume until further notice that we are working with the module language rather than embedded SQL. Recall from Chapter 6 that cursor definitions are one type of "module element" (*procedures* being the other; cursor

---

*Update operations that either use some distinct cursor or do not use a cursor at all would seem to have similar potential for changing cursor state and positioning (in a "side effect" kind of way, moreover). However, all the standard has to say on such matters is that if a row is to be updated or deleted via a given cursor, and that row has been subjected to such an update (presumably while the given cursor was positioned on it, though the standard does not say as much), then a warning is raised, but the UPDATE or DELETE CURRENT completes execution in the usual way. See Appendix D for further discussion.

definitions and procedures can be arbitrarily interspersed within the module, except that any given cursor definition must physically precede all procedures that reference that cursor). The syntax for a cursor definition is:

```
DECLARE cursor [ INSENSITIVE ] [ SCROLL ] CURSOR
        FOR cursor-specification
```

And a "cursor specification" looks like this:

```
  table-expression
[ ORDER BY order-item-commalist ]
[ FOR { READ ONLY | UPDATE [ OF column-commalist ] } ]
```

Explanation:

1. Let *T* be the table identified by the table expression at OPEN time. So far as this cursor opening is concerned, the rows of *T* are effectively ordered in accordance with the specifications of the explicit or implicit ORDER BY clause (see the next subsection below). *Note:* We follow the standard here in referring to that ordered collection of rows as a "table," despite the fact that the rows of a table are unordered by definition. In the next section we will use the more descriptive (but still rather sloppy) term *ordered table*.

2. If INSENSITIVE is specified, OPEN effectively causes a *separate copy of T* to be created, and the cursor accesses that copy; thus, updates that affect *T* while this cursor is open, either made via other cursors or made without cursors at all, will not be visible through this opening of this cursor. (In other words, INSENSITIVE means the user definitely wants not to "sense" such updates through this cursor.) UPDATE and DELETE CURRENT operations are not allowed via an INSENSITIVE cursor.

   If INSENSITIVE is not specified,* no separate copy of *T* is created; thus, the cursor accesses *T* directly (see the note at the end of the present subsection for further discussion of what it means for the cursor to "access *T* directly"). Whether updates that affect *T* made via other cursors, or made without cursors at all, will be visible through this cursor is implementation-dependent.

3. If SCROLL is specified, all forms of FETCH (see the next section) are legal against this cursor. If SCROLL is not specified, only FETCH NEXT is legal.

4. We defer a detailed explanation of table expressions to Chapter 11. However, the general purpose of the table expression in the context under discussion is to define the table *T* that will be accessible via the cursor when the cursor is opened. That table *T* will be updatable via the cursor (i.e., UPDATE and

---

*There is no explicit SENSITIVE option in SQL/92. One is planned for SQL3, but specifying SENSITIVE is not quite the same as not specifying INSENSITIVE! See Appendix F.

DELETE CURRENT operations will be allowed, or "the cursor will be updatable," to use a sloppy but common expression) if and only if both of the following are true:

- *T* itself is *SQL-updatable*—i.e., the table expression defining *T* would define an SQL-updatable view if it appeared in the context of a view definition (see Chapter 13).
- The cursor definition does not specify either INSENSITIVE or FOR READ ONLY.

5. If FOR READ ONLY is specified, UPDATE and DELETE CURRENT operations via this cursor will not be allowed. If FOR UPDATE is specified:

- *T* must be SQL-updatable (it is an error otherwise).
- If "OF column-commalist" is specified, every column name in the commalist must be the *un*qualified name of a column of *T*. Omitting "OF column-commalist" is equivalent to specifying all columns of *T*.
- UPDATE CURRENT operations via this cursor on columns *not* identified in the explicit or implicit "OF column-commalist" will not be allowed.
- UPDATE CURRENT operations via this cursor on columns that are mentioned in the ORDER BY clause will not be allowed, even if they *are* mentioned (explicitly or implicitly) in the FOR UPDATE clause.
- UPDATE CURRENT operations via this cursor on columns that are mentioned (explicitly or implicitly) in the FOR UPDATE clause and not mentioned in the ORDER BY clause will be allowed.
- DELETE CURRENT operations via this cursor will be allowed.

If neither FOR READ ONLY nor FOR UPDATE is specified, then:

- If *T* is not SQL-updatable or if INSENSITIVE, SCROLL, or ORDER BY is specified, FOR READ ONLY is assumed. (Note that the combination of specifications INSENSITIVE and FOR UPDATE is definitely illegal, but the combinations (a) SCROLL and FOR UPDATE and (b) ORDER BY and FOR UPDATE are both legal—assuming in both cases, of course, that *T* is SQL-updatable.)
- Otherwise FOR UPDATE is assumed (without "OF column-commalist").

Note: If cursor *C* is updatable, then the table expression in the definition of *C* must be regarded not (as it normally would be) as conceptually evaluating to a *brand new* table that is somehow derived from the tables in the database, but rather as actually *designating* a table in the database that will be subject to update. Consider, for example, the table expression "SELECT S.SNO, S.CITY FROM S." Ordinarily, that expression would be regarded as evaluating to a "brand new" table that is derived in the obvious way from base table S. But in the cursor definition

```
DECLARE X CURSOR
    FOR SELECT S.SNO, S.CITY
        FROM    S
```

that very same table expression must now be regarding as "designating" base table S itself, and UPDATE ... CURRENT and DELETE ... CURRENT operations via cursor X will indeed update that base table.*

The ORDER BY Clause

As indicated in the subsection "Cursor Definition" above, the ORDER BY clause specifies a commalist of order-items. Each order-item takes the form:

```
{ column | unsigned-integer } [ ASC | DESC ]
```

The left-to-right sequence of order-items in the ORDER BY clause corresponds to major-to-minor ordering in accordance with familiar convention. Again, let *T* be the table associated with (this opening of) the cursor in question. Usually each order-item consists of a simple column name (*un*qualified, observe), identifying a column of table *T*, with an optional specification of ASC or DESC; ASC (the default) means ascending order and DESC means descending order. Alternatively, an order-item can consist of an unsigned decimal integer, as in the following example:

```
DECLARE Y CURSOR
    FOR SELECT SP.PNO, AVG ( SP.QTY )
        FROM    SP
        GROUP   BY SP.PNO
        ORDER   BY 2
```

The integer refers to the ordinal (left-to-right) position of the column within *T*. This feature makes it possible to define an ordering on the basis of a column that does not have a proper, user-known name (in the example, the "2" refers to the column of averages).

Note, however, that it is never necessary to use the foregoing trick, because it is always possible to introduce a proper, user-known name for a column that would not otherwise have one. For example:

```
DECLARE Y CURSOR
    FOR SELECT SP.PNO, AVG ( SP.QTY ) AS AQ
        FROM    SP
        GROUP   BY SP.PNO
        ORDER   BY AQ
```

---

*The situation is analogous to that which arises in programming languages in connection with arguments and parameters: Arguments corresponding to output parameters must be passed by reference, while arguments corresponding to input parameters can be passed by value. Indeed, the same situation arises in SQL itself in connection with the module language, as we saw in Chapter 6 (Section 6.2).

For this reason, integer order-items are regarded as a "deprecated feature" of the standard, and are likely to be dropped at some future time.

Note that each order-item must identify a column of T itself, not just a column of some table from which T is derived. Thus, for example, the following is *** *ILLEGAL* *** :

```
DECLARE Z CURSOR
    FOR SELECT S.SNO
        FROM   S
        ORDER  BY CITY                  -- *** ILLEGAL *** !!!
```

Finally, if no ORDER BY clause is specified, the rows of T will have an implementation-dependent ordering. Likewise, if an ORDER BY clause is specified but does not define a *total* ordering, then the relative order of rows within T that have the same value for the order-item(s) will again be implementation-dependent. For example:

```
DECLARE W CURSOR
    FOR SELECT SP.SNO, SP.PNO, SP.QTY
        FROM   SP
        ORDER  BY SNO
```

Here the relative order of SP rows with the same PNO value will be implementation-dependent.

10.3   CURSOR-BASED MANIPULATION STATEMENTS

OPEN

For each cursor definition in a given module, there must be exactly one procedure (not "at least one," and not "at most one" either!) in that module whose purpose is to open the cursor in question. The OPEN statement takes the form

```
OPEN cursor
```

where "cursor" identifies a cursor (C, say). Cursor C must currently be in the closed state. The table expression in the definition of C is evaluated, using the argument values specified in the OPEN procedure invocation for any parameters referenced in that table expression, to yield a certain collection of rows as explained in Section 10.2. An ordering for that collection is defined, also as explained in Section 10.2, and cursor C is placed in the open state and positioned before the row that is first according to that ordering within that collection. As mentioned in the previous section, we will henceforth refer to that collection of rows together with the associated ordering as the *ordered table* for this particular opening of cursor C.

Here is an example of a procedure that opens the cursor X defined near the beginning of Section 10.2:

```
PROCEDURE OPENX
   ( SQLSTATE,
     :PNO_PARAM CHAR(6) ) ;
     OPEN X ;
```

Note that any parameter mentioned in the definition of a given cursor *must* be defined in the procedure that opens that cursor.

FETCH

The FETCH statement takes the form

```
FETCH [ [ row-selector ] FROM ] cursor INTO target-commalist
```

where "cursor" identifies a cursor (C, say), "target-commalist" is a commalist of parameters (in the module language) or host variables (in embedded SQL), and "row selector" is any of the following:

```
NEXT
PRIOR
FIRST
LAST
ABSOLUTE n
RELATIVE n
```

Points to note:

1. NEXT is the only legal "row selector" unless "cursor" is defined with the SCROLL option.
2. FROM is basically just a noiseword* (though it is required if "row selector" is specified explicitly).
3. NEXT is assumed if "row selector" is omitted.
4. The specification n in the ABSOLUTE and RELATIVE cases must be a literal, parameter, or host variable of data type exact numeric with a scale of zero.
5. The meanings of NEXT, PRIOR, FIRST, and LAST are self-explanatory.
6. "ABSOLUTE n" refers to the nth row in the ordered table T currently associated with cursor C (a negative value of n means counting backward from the end of T).
7. "RELATIVE n" refers to the nth row in the ordered table T, counting relative to the row on which cursor C is currently positioned (again, a negative value of n means counting backward).

---

*Not a very *good* noiseword at that, since the retrieval is not "from the cursor," it is from the row the cursor is positioned on.

8. The target commalist must contain exactly one target for each column of *T*;
the *i*th target in that commalist corresponds to the *i*th column of *T* (remember
that tables have a left-to-right column ordering in SQL).

Cursor *C* must currently be open. Assuming that "row selector" does identify
a row of *T*—i.e., there is a NEXT row or PRIOR row or FIRST row or LAST row,
as applicable, in the case of NEXT/PRIOR/FIRST/LAST, or the value of *n* identifies a row between the first and last row (inclusive), in the case of ABSOLUTE
n or RELATIVE *n**—then cursor *C* is positioned on that row, values are retrieved
from that row, and assignments are made to targets in accordance with the specifications in the INTO clause.† If "row selector" does not identify a row of *T*—i.e.,
there is no NEXT row or PRIOR row or FIRST row or LAST row, as applicable,
in the case of NEXT/PRIOR/FIRST/LAST, or the value of *n* is out of range, in the
case of ABSOLUTE *n* or RELATIVE *n*—then no data is retrieved, and cursor *C*
is positioned "after the last row" or "before the first row," depending on whether
"row selector" was attempting to move forward or backward from cursor *C*'s previous position. Note that (to repeat from Section 10.2) cursor *C* can be "after the
last row" or "before the first row" even if *T* is empty.

Here is an example of FETCH, again using the cursor X defined near the
beginning of Section 10.2:

```
FETCH NEXT FROM X INTO :SNO_PARAM, :QTY_PARAM
```

Positioned UPDATE

The positioned UPDATE statement takes the form

```
UPDATE table
SET    assignment-commalist
WHERE  CURRENT OF cursor
```

where "cursor" identifies a cursor (*C*, say), "table" identifies the ordered table (*T*,
say) currently associated with *C*, and the SET clause is exactly as for searched
UPDATE (see Chapter 9, Section 9.4). Cursor *C* must currently be open, must be
"updatable," and must be positioned on a row of *T*. That row is updated in accordance with the assignments in the SET clause. Each column to be updated must

---

*A value of zero for *n* means the current row for RELATIVE but is out of range for ABSOLUTE.

†Assume for definiteness that (as stated in Section 10.2) we are working with the module language, not
embedded SQL. In this context, it is usual to talk in terms of the *i*th value retrieved being assigned to
the *i*th parameter in the target commalist. More correctly, of course, that *i*th value is assigned to the
argument (i.e., the host language variable) *corresponding* to that *i*th parameter—i.e., it is not target
parameters *per se*, but rather the arguments corresponding to those parameters, to which values are
assigned on retrieval.

have been mentioned in an (explicit or implicit) FOR UPDATE clause in the definition of cursor *C* and must *not* have been mentioned in the associated ORDER BY clause (if any).

Example:

```
UPDATE SP
SET    QTY = SP.QTY + :INCR_PARAM
WHERE  CURRENT OF X
```

Positioned DELETE

The positioned DELETE statement takes the form

```
DELETE
FROM   table
WHERE  CURRENT OF cursor
```

where "cursor" identifies a cursor (*C*, say) and "table" identifies the ordered table (*T*, say) currently associated with *C*. Cursor *C* must currently be open, must be "updatable," and must be positioned on a row of *T*. That row is deleted.

Example:

```
DELETE
FROM   SP
WHERE  CURRENT OF X
```

Cursor X will now be positioned before the row immediately following the row just deleted, or after the last row if no such immediately following row exists.

CLOSE

The CLOSE statement takes the form

```
CLOSE cursor
```

where "cursor" identifies a cursor (*C*, say). Cursor *C* (which must currently be open) is placed in the closed state.

Example:

```
CLOSE X
```

10.4   A COMPREHENSIVE EXAMPLE (MODULE VERSION)

We conclude with a somewhat contrived, but accurate, example that shows how many of the ideas introduced in this chapter and earlier chapters fit together. The host program is written in PL/I. It accepts four input values: a part number (GIVENPNO), a city name (GIVENCIT), a status increment (GIVENINC), and a status level (GIVENLVL). It then scans all suppliers of the part identified by GIVENPNO. For each such supplier, if the supplier city is GIVENCIT, the status is increased by GIVENINC; otherwise, if the status is less than GIVENLVL, the supplier is deleted, together with all shipments for that supplier. In all cases supplier information is displayed to the user ("PUT SKIP LIST"), with an indication of how that particular supplier was handled by the program.

Note: Observe that the code deletes shipment rows *before* deleting the corresponding supplier row. The reason is, of course, that if we attempted to delete the supplier first, and the supplier in question did in fact have some corresponding shipments, the DELETE might fail, because of the foreign key constraint from shipments to suppliers (see Chapter 14). We remark that careful concurrency control needs to be applied here in order to prevent some concurrent transaction from (e.g.) inserting another shipment for the current supplier between our two DELETEs. Unfortunately, the standard does not include any explicit concurrency control facilities (explicit locking, etc.) that would permit us to apply such controls. For that reason, we choose to set the transaction isolation level to SERIALIZABLE (see Chapter 5, Section 5.4), in order to ensure that violations of serializability such as the one just mentioned cannot occur.

Here then is the host program:

```
PLIEX: PROC OPTIONS (MAIN) ;

        /* program input */

        DCL GIVENPNO        CHAR(6) ;
        DCL GIVENCIT        CHAR(15) ;
        DCL GIVENINC        FIXED DECIMAL(3) ;
        DCL GIVENLVL        FIXED DECIMAL(3) ;

        /* targets for "FETCH SUPPLIER" */

        DCL SNO             CHAR(5) ;
        DCL SNAME           CHAR(20) ;
        DCL STATUS          FIXED DECIMAL(3) ;
        DCL CITY            CHAR(15) ;

        /* housekeeping variables */

        DCL DISP            CHAR(7) ;
        DCL MORE_SUPPLIERS BIT(1) ;

        /* SQL return code variable */

        DCL RETCODE         CHAR(5) ;

        /* SQL entry point declarations, in alphabetical order */

        DCL CLOSE_PROC      ENTRY ( CHAR(5) ) ;
        DCL COMMIT_PROC     ENTRY ( CHAR(5) ) ;
        DCL CONNECT_PROC    ENTRY ( CHAR(5), CHAR(8) ) ;
        DCL DELETE_S_PROC   ENTRY ( CHAR(5) ) ;
        DCL DELETE_SP_PROC  ENTRY ( CHAR(5), CHAR(5) ) ;
        DCL DISCONNECT_PROC ENTRY ( CHAR(5), CHAR(8) ) ;
```

```
DCL FETCH_PROC         ENTRY ( CHAR(5), CHAR(5),
                                       CHAR(20),
                                       FIXED DECIMAL(3),
                                       CHAR(15) ) ;
DCL OPEN_PROC          ENTRY ( CHAR(5), CHAR(6) ) ;
DCL ROLLBACK_PROC      ENTRY ( CHAR(5) ) ;
DCL SET_TRAN_PROC      ENTRY ( CHAR(5) ) ;
DCL UPDATE_PROC        ENTRY ( CHAR(5), FIXED DECIMAL(3) ) ;

/* database exception handler */

ON CONDITION ( DBEXCEPTION )
BEGIN ;
   PUT SKIP LIST ( RETCODE ) ;
   CALL ROLLBACK_PROC ( RETCODE ) ;
   PUT SKIP LIST ( RETCODE ) ;
   GO TO QUIT ;
END ;

/* connect to server */

CALL CONNECT_PROC ( RETCODE, 'SERVER42' ) ;
IF ¬ ( RETCODE = '00000' )
THEN SIGNAL CONDITION ( DBEXCEPTION ) ;

/* set isolation level SERIALIZABLE */

CALL SET_TRAN_PROC ( RETCODE ) ;
IF ¬ ( RETCODE = '00000' )
THEN SIGNAL CONDITION ( DBEXCEPTION ) ;

/* main program logic */

GET LIST ( GIVENPNO, GIVENCIT, GIVENINC, GIVENLVL ) ;
CALL OPEN_PROC ( RETCODE, GIVENPNO ) ;
IF ¬ ( RETCODE = '00000' )
THEN SIGNAL CONDITION ( DBEXCEPTION ) ;
MORE_SUPPLIERS = '1'B ;
DO WHILE ( MORE_SUPPLIERS ) ;
   CALL FETCH_PROC ( RETCODE, SNO, SNAME, STATUS, CITY ) ;
   SELECT ;           /* a PL/I SELECT, not a SQL SELECT */
      WHEN ( RETCODE = '02000' )
         MORE_SUPPLIERS = '0'B ;
      WHEN ¬ ( RETCODE = '02000' | RETCODE = '00000' )
         SIGNAL CONDITION ( DBEXCEPTION ) ;
      WHEN ( RETCODE = '00000' )
         DO ;
            DISP = '        ' ;
            IF CITY = CIVENCIT
            THEN
               DO ;
                  CALL UPDATE_PROC
                     ( RETCODE, SNO, GIVENINC ) ;
                  IF ¬ ( RETCODE = '00000' )
                  THEN SIGNAL CONDITION ( DBEXCEPTION )
                  DISP = 'UPDATED' ;
               END ;
            ELSE
            IF STATUS < GIVENLVL
            THEN
               DO ;
                  CALL DELETE_SP_PROC ( RETCODE, SNO ) ;
```

```
                        IF ¬ ( RETCODE = '00000'
                             | RETCODE = '02000' )
                        THEN SIGNAL CONDITION ( DBEXCEPTION )
                        CALL DELETE_S_PROC ( RETCODE, SNO ) ;
                        IF ¬ ( RETCODE = '00000' )
                        THEN SIGNAL CONDITION ( DBEXCEPTION )
                        DISP = 'DELETED' ;
                   END ;
                PUT SKIP LIST
                        ( SNO, SNAME, STATUS, CITY, DISP ) ;
             END ;    /* WHEN ( RETCODE = '00000' ) ... */
     END ;    /* PL/I SELECT */
   END ;    /* DO WHILE */
   CALL CLOSE_PROC ( RETCODE ) ;
   IF ¬ ( RETCODE = '00000' )
   THEN SIGNAL CONDITION ( DBEXCEPTION ) ;
   CALL COMMIT_PROC ( RETCODE ) ;
   IF ¬ ( RETCODE = '00000' )
   THEN SIGNAL CONDITION ( DBEXCEPTION ) ;
   CALL DISCONNECT_PROC ( RETCODE, 'SERVER42' ) ;
   IF ¬ ( RETCODE = '00000' )
   THEN SIGNAL CONDITION ( DBEXCEPTION ) ;
QUIT: RETURN ;
   END ;    /* PLIEX */
```

And here is the corresponding module:

```
MODULE SQLEXMOD
        LANGUAGE PLI
        SCHEMA CJD_CATALOG.CJD_SCHEMA
        AUTHORIZATION CJD
        DECLARE Z CURSOR FOR
            SELECT S.SNO, S.SNAME, S.STATUS, S.CITY
            FROM   S
            WHERE  S.SNO IN
                 ( SELECT SP.SNO
                   FROM   SP
                   WHERE  SP.PNO = :PNO )
            FOR UPDATE OF STATUS

PROCEDURE CLOSE_PROC
        ( SQLSTATE ) ;
        CLOSE Z ;

PROCEDURE COMMIT_PROC
        ( SQLSTATE ) ;
        COMMIT ;

PROCEDURE CONNECT_PROC
        ( SQLSTATE,
         :SERVERID CHAR(8) ) ;
         CONNECT TO :SERVERID ;

PROCEDURE DELETE_S_PROC
        ( SQLSTATE ) ;
        DELETE FROM S WHERE CURRENT OF Z ;

PROCEDURE DELETE_SP_PROC
        ( SQLSTATE,
         :SNO CHAR(5) ) ;
         DELETE FROM SP WHERE SP.SNO = :SNO ;
```

```
PROCEDURE DISCONNECT_PROC
    ( SQLSTATE,
     :SERVERID CHAR(8) ) ;
      DISCONNECT :SERVERID ;

PROCEDURE FETCH_PROC
    ( SQLSTATE,
     :SNO    CHAR(5),
     :SNAME   CHAR(20),
     :STATUS DECIMAL(3),
     :CITY    CHAR(20) ) ;
      FETCH NEXT FROM Z INTO :SNO, :SNAME, :STATUS, :CITY ;

PROCEDURE OPEN_PROC
    ( SQLSTATE,
     :PNO CHAR(6) ) ;
      OPEN Z ;

PROCEDURE ROLLBACK_PROC
    ( SQLSTATE ) ;
      ROLLBACK ;

PROCEDURE SET_TRAN_PROC
    ( SQLSTATE ) ;
      SET TRANSACTION ISOLATION LEVEL SERIALIZABLE ;

PROCEDURE UPDATE_PROC
    ( SQLSTATE,
     :GIVENINC DECIMAL(3) ) ;
      UPDATE S
      SET     STATUS = S.STATUS + :GIVENINC
      WHERE   CURRENT OF Z ;
```

10.5   A COMPREHENSIVE EXAMPLE (EMBEDDED SQL VERSION)

A host language program with embedded SQL statements—an "embedded SQL host program"—consists of an otherwise standard host program plus a set of embedded SQL declare sections, a set of embedded cursor definitions, a set of embedded exception declarations, and a set of embedded SQL statements. These various components can be arbitrarily interspersed in the source text, except that, first, a given host variable definition must physically precede any reference to that variable (as mentioned in Chapter 6); second, a given embedded cursor definition must physically precede any reference to that cursor. We show below an embedded SQL version of the example from the previous section.

```
SQLEX: PROC OPTIONS (MAIN) ;

        EXEC SQL BEGIN DECLARE SECTION ;

            /* program input */

            DCL GIVENPNO        CHAR(6) ;
            DCL GIVENCIT        CHAR(15) ;
            DCL GIVENINC        FIXED DECIMAL(3) ;
            DCL GIVENLVL        FIXED DECIMAL(3) ;

            /* targets for "FETCH SUPPLIER" */

            DCL SNO             CHAR(5) ;
            DCL SNAME           CHAR(20) ;
            DCL STATUS          FIXED DECIMAL(3) ;
            DCL CITY            CHAR(15) ;

            /* SQL return code variable */

            DCL SQLSTATE        CHAR(5) ;

        EXEC SQL END DECLARE SECTION ;

        /* housekeeping variables */

        DCL DISP            CHAR(7) ;
        DCL MORE_SUPPLIERS BIT(1) ;

        /* exception declarations */

        EXEC SQL WHENEVER NOT FOUND CONTINUE ;
        EXEC SQL WHENEVER SQLERROR  CONTINUE ;

        /* database exception handler */

        ON CONDITION ( DBEXCEPTION )
        BEGIN ;
           PUT SKIP LIST ( SQLSTATE ) ;
           EXEC SQL ROLLBACK ;
           PUT SKIP LIST ( SQLSTATE ) ;
           GO TO QUIT ;
        END ;

        /* cursor definition */

        EXEC SQL DECLARE Z CURSOR FOR
            SELECT S.SNO, S.SNAME, S.STATUS, S.CITY
            FROM    S
            WHERE   S.SNO IN
                  ( SELECT SP.SNO
                    FROM    SP
                    WHERE   SP.PNO = :GIVENPNO ) ;

        EXEC SQL CONNECT TO 'SERVER42' ;
        IF ¬ ( SQLSTATE = '00000' )
        THEN SIGNAL CONDITION ( DBEXCEPTION ) ;

        EXEC SQL SET TRANSACTION ISOLATION LEVEL SERIALIZABLE ;
        IF ¬ ( SQLSTATE = '00000' )
        THEN SIGNAL CONDITION ( DBEXCEPTION ) ;
```

```
GET LIST ( GIVENPNO, GIVENCIT, GIVENINC, GIVENLVL ) ;

EXEC SQL OPEN Z ;
IF ¬ ( SQLSTATE = '00000' )
THEN SIGNAL CONDITION ( DBEXCEPTION ) ;

MORE_SUPPLIERS = '1'B ;

DO WHILE ( MORE_SUPPLIERS ) ;

   EXEC SQL FETCH Z INTO :SNO, :SNAME, :STATUS, :CITY ;

   SELECT ;            /* a PL/I SELECT, not a SQL SELECT */

      WHEN ( SQLSTATE  = '02000' )
         MORE_SUPPLIERS = '0'B ;

      WHEN ¬ ( SQLSTATE = '02000' | SQLSTATE = '00000' )
         SIGNAL CONDITION ( DBEXCEPTION ) ;

      WHEN ( SQLSTATE = '00000' )
         DO ;
            DISP = '          ' ;
            IF CITY = GIVENCIT
            THEN
               DO ;
                  EXEC SQL UPDATE S
                           SET     STATUS =
                                   S.STATUS + :GIVENINC
                           WHERE   CURRENT OF Z ;
                  IF ¬ ( SQLSTATE = '00000' )
                  THEN SIGNAL CONDITION ( DBEXCEPTION ) ;
                  DISP = 'UPDATED' ;
               END ;
            ELSE
            IF STATUS < GIVENLVL
            THEN
               DO ;
                  EXEC SQL DELETE
                           FROM    SP
                           WHERE   SP.SNO = :SNO ;
                  IF ¬ ( SQLSTATE = '00000'
                       | SQLSTATE = '02000' )
                  THEN SIGNAL CONDITION ( DBEXCEPTION ) ;
                  EXEC SQL DELETE
                           FROM    S
                           WHERE   CURRENT OF Z ;
                  IF ¬ ( SQLSTATE = '00000' )
                  THEN SIGNAL CONDITION ( DBEXCEPTION ) ;
                  DISP = 'DELETED' ;
               END ;
            PUT SKIP LIST
                  ( SNO, SNAME, STATUS, CITY, DISP ) ;
         END ;   /* WHEN ( SQLSTATE = '00000' ) ... */
   END ;   /* PL/I SELECT */
END ;   /* DO WHILE */

EXEC SQL CLOSE Z ;
IF ¬ ( SQLSTATE = '00000' )
THEN SIGNAL CONDITION ( DBEXCEPTION ) ;
```

```
       EXEC SQL COMMIT ;
       IF ¬ ( SQLSTATE = '00000' )
       THEN SIGNAL CONDITION ( DBEXCEPTION ) ;

       EXEC SQL DISCONNECT 'SERVER42' ;
       IF ¬ ( SQLSTATE = '00000' )
       THEN SIGNAL CONDITION ( DBEXCEPTION ) ;

QUIT: RETURN ;
       END ;   /* SQLEX */
```

11

Table Expressions

11.1 INTRODUCTION

In this chapter we explain the crucially important construct "table expression," which appears in numerous contexts throughout the SQL language; in many ways, in fact, it can be regarded as being at the top of the syntax tree. *Note:* As mentioned in Chapter 10, the standard refers to this construct as a *query* expression, and ascribes a different (more restrictive) meaning to the term "table expression." We prefer our term, because the whole point is, precisely, that the expression does evaluate to a table (actually an *unnamed* table). By contrast, what the standard calls a "table expression" is merely a special case (it corresponds to what we refer to as a "select expression" below, minus the SELECT clause itself).

We begin by giving the full BNF definition of "table expression," for purposes of subsequent reference. We then go on to explain that definition piecemeal in the sections that follow.

```
table-expression
    ::=   join-table-expression
        | nonjoin-table-expression

join-table-expression
    ::=   table-reference CROSS JOIN table-reference
        | table-reference [ NATURAL ] [ join-type ] JOIN
              table-reference [ ON conditional-expression
                              | USING ( column-commalist ) ]
        | ( join-table-expression )
```

```
table-reference
    ::=    join-table-expression
        |  table [ [ AS ] range-variable
                       [ ( column-commalist ) ] ]
        |  ( table-expression ) [ AS ] range-variable
                                   [ ( column-commalist ) ]

join-type
    ::=    INNER
        |  LEFT [ OUTER ]
        |  RIGHT [ OUTER ]
        |  FULL [ OUTER ]
        |  UNION

nonjoin-table-expression
    ::=    nonjoin-table-term
        |  table-expression { UNION | EXCEPT } [ ALL ]
               [ CORRESPONDING [ BY ( column-commalist ) ] ]
                    table-term

nonjoin-table-term
    ::=    nonjoin-table-primary
        |  table-term INTERSECT [ ALL ]
               [ CORRESPONDING [ BY ( column-commalist ) ] ]
                    table-primary

table-term
    ::=    join-table-expression
        |  nonjoin-table-term

table-primary
    ::=    join-table-expression
        |  nonjoin-table-primary

nonjoin-table-primary
    ::=    ( nonjoin-table-expression )
        |  select-expression
        |  TABLE table
        |  table-constructor

table-constructor
    ::=    VALUES row-constructor-commalist

row-constructor
    ::=    ( row-component-commalist ) | ( table-expression )

select-expression
    ::=    SELECT [ ALL | DISTINCT ] select-item-commalist
             FROM table-reference-commalist
               [ WHERE conditional-expression ]
                 [ GROUP BY column-commalist ]
                   [ HAVING conditional-expression ]

select-item
    ::=    scalar-expression [ [ AS ] column ]
        |  [ range-variable . ] *
```

11.2   JOIN EXPRESSIONS

First of all, table expressions in general are divided into join and nonjoin table expressions:*

```
table-expression
    ::=   join-table-expression
        | nonjoin-table-expression
```

In this section we consider the first of these two cases only. Broadly speaking, a join table expression (*join expression* for short) represents an explicit join of some kind between two tables, each of which is represented by a "table reference" (see Section 11.3, later). More precisely, a join expression is either (a) a "cross join" or (b) a join involving an explicit or implicit "join type" (or it might consist of a join expression in parentheses; however, the parentheses are included purely for syntactic reasons and have no effect on the semantics of the expression):

```
join-table-expression
    ::=   table-reference CROSS JOIN table-reference
        | table-reference [ NATURAL ] [ join-type ] JOIN
              table-reference [ ON conditional-expression
                             | USING ( column-commalist ) ]
        | ( join-table-expression )
```

Cross Join

"Cross join" is just another term for what is more accurately called the *extended Cartesian product* (usually abbreviated to just *Cartesian product* in SQL contexts). Let A and B be the tables resulting from evaluation of the two table references. Then the expression "A CROSS JOIN B" evaluates to a table consisting of all possible rows R such that R is the concatenation of a row from A and a row from B.†
It follows that the join expression A CROSS JOIN B is semantically identical to the following parenthesized select-expression:

```
( SELECT A.*, B.*
  FROM   A, B )
```

See Section 11.6 for an explanation of select-expressions.

---

*Do not be misled by the terminology: A nonjoin table expression might still represent a join, as we saw in Chapter 2. The point is merely that join table expressions directly involve the explicit key word JOIN and nonjoin table expressions do not.

†This definition requires a certain amount of care and refinement if either A or B includes any duplicate rows. See Appendix D.

Other Joins

The syntax for other join expressions (to repeat) is:

```
table-reference [ NATURAL ] [ join-type ]
      JOIN table-reference
            [ ON conditional-expression
            | USING ( column-commalist ) ]
```

"Join type" in turn is any of the following:

```
INNER
LEFT [ OUTER ]
RIGHT [ OUTER ]
FULL [ OUTER ]
UNION
```

Points to note:

1. NATURAL and UNION cannot both be specified.

2. If either NATURAL or UNION is specified, neither an ON clause nor a USING clause can be specified.

3. If neither NATURAL nor UNION is specified, then either an ON clause or a USING clause must be specified.

4. If "join type" is omitted, INNER is assumed by default.

Note: The optional OUTER on LEFT, RIGHT, and FULL is a mere noiseword and has no effect on the overall meaning of the expression.

LEFT, RIGHT, FULL (with or without the noiseword OUTER in each case), and UNION all have to do with nulls; we therefore defer discussion of them to Chapter 16. So we are left with the following cases to consider:

```
1. table-reference JOIN table-reference ON conditional-expression
```

```
2. table-reference JOIN table-reference USING ( column-commalist )
```

```
3. table-reference NATURAL JOIN table-reference
```

In each case, let *A* and *B* be the tables resulting from evaluation of the two table references. Then *Case 1* ("*A* JOIN *B* ON *cond*," where *cond* is a conditional expression) is defined to be semantically identical to the following parenthesized select-expression:

```
( SELECT A.*, B.*
  FROM   A, B
  WHERE  cond )
```

(again, see Section 11.6 for an explanation of select-expressions; conditional expressions are discussed in Chapter 12).

In *Case 2*, let the commalist of columns in the USING clause be *C1, C2, ..., Cn*. Each of *C1, C2, ..., Cn* must be *un*qualified and must identify both a column of *A* and a column of *B*. Then the join expression is defined to be semantically identical to a Case 1 expression in which the ON clause is of the form—

```
ON A.C1 = B.C1 AND A.C2 = B.C2 AND ... AND A.Cn = B.Cn
```

—except that (a) each of the common columns *C1, C2, ..., Cn* appears only once, not twice, in the final result, and (b) the result column ordering is different—the common columns appear first (i.e., at the left, in the order specified in the USING clause), then the other columns of *A* (in the order in which they appear in *A*), then the other columns of *B* (in the order in which they appear in *B*).

Finally, a *Case 3* expression is defined to be semantically identical to a Case 2 expression in which the commalist of columns specifies *all* of the columns that are common to *A* and *B* (in the order in which they appear in *A*). *Note:* It is possible that there are no common columns at all, in which case *A* NATURAL JOIN *B* degenerates to *A* CROSS JOIN *B*. It is also possible that either *A* or *B* has no columns at all other than common ones; for example, *A* might be the shipments table SP and *B* the table resulting from evaluation of the expression SELECT SNO FROM S. *Exercise for the reader:* What happens if neither *A* nor *B* has any columns at all other than common ones?

Here are some examples (all based as usual on the suppliers-and-parts database):

```
S JOIN SP ON S.SNO = SP.SNO

S JOIN SP USING ( SNO )

S NATURAL JOIN SP
```

These three expressions are all equivalent, except that the first produces a table with two identical SNO columns and the second and third produce a table with just one such column (the SNO column that appears between the CITY and PNO columns in the first case being eliminated in the second and third cases).

Note: Since these expressions all produce a result table that is multi-row (in general), they cannot be executed as separate statements in their own right (other than in "direct" SQL). Instead, it is necessary to define a *cursor* having the expression in question as its scope (as explained in Chapter 10), and then to retrieve the rows in that scope one by one by means of that cursor. For simplicity, however, it is convenient to assume that multi-row expressions *can* be executed in their own right, and for tutorial reasons we will make that assumption throughout the remainder of this chapter, and indeed throughout many of the chapters that follow also.

11.3   TABLE REFERENCES

A table reference is a reference to some table, either named (i.e., a base table or a view) or unnamed. Table references in SQL serve two general purposes: They specify the operands in FROM clauses in select-expressions (see Section 11.6), and they specify the operands in explicit joins (i.e., join expressions—see Section 11.2). Syntactically, a table reference consists of *either* a join expression (already discussed in Section 11.2) *or* one of the following: (a) a table name, or (b) a table expression in parentheses. In Case (a), the table reference can optionally also include an AS clause, whose purpose is to introduce a *range variable* that ranges over the table in question, and optionally to introduce a set of column names for the columns of that table as well; in Case (b), it *must* include such an AS clause. Thus, the overall syntax is:

```
table-reference
   ::=   join-table-expression
      | table [ [ AS ] range-variable
                 [ ( column-commalist ) ] ]
      | ( table-expression ) [ AS ] range-variable
                               [ ( column-commalist ) ]
```

Here is a simple "Case (a)" example:

```
S AS SX
```

Here SX denotes a range variable that ranges over the suppliers table S. *Note:* The key word AS is a mere noiseword and can be omitted without changing the meaning, thus:

```
S SX
```

In order to explain the range variable concept, we consider the following example: "Get all pairs of supplier numbers such that the two suppliers concerned are located in the same city." One possible SQL formulation for this query is as follows:*

```
SELECT FIRST.SNO AS XX, SECOND.SNO AS YY
FROM   S AS FIRST, S AS SECOND
WHERE  FIRST.CITY = SECOND.CITY
```

This expression involves a join of table S with itself over matching cities, as we now explain. Suppose for a moment that we had two separate copies of table S, the "first" copy and the "second" copy. Then the logic of the query is as follows: We need to examine all possible pairs of supplier rows, one from the first copy of S and one from the second, and to retrieve the two supplier numbers from such a pair of rows if and only if the two CITY values are equal. We thus need to be able to reference two supplier rows at the same time. In order to distinguish between the two references, therefore, we introduce the two *range variables* FIRST and SECOND, each of which "ranges over" table S (for the duration of the evaluation of

---

*This formulation uses AS clauses in the SELECT clause as well as in the FROM clause. See Section 11.6 for a discussion of the use of AS clauses in the SELECT clause.

the containing table expression). At any particular time during that evaluation, FIRST represents some row from the "first" copy of table S and SECOND represents some row from the "second" copy. Thus, the overall result is found by examining all possible pairs of FIRST and SECOND rows and checking the WHERE condition in every case:

XX	YY
S1	S1
S1	S4
S2	S2
S2	S3
S3	S2
S3	S3
S4	S1
S4	S4
S5	S5

Note: We can tidy up this result by extending the WHERE clause as follows:

```
SELECT  FIRST.SNO AS XX, SECOND.SNO AS YY
FROM    S AS FIRST, S AS SECOND
WHERE   FIRST.CITY = SECOND.CITY
AND     FIRST.SNO < SECOND.SNO
```

The effect of the additional condition FIRST.SNO < SECOND.SNO is twofold:

- It eliminates pairs of supplier numbers of the form (x,x);
- It guarantees that the pairs (x,y) and (y,x) will not both appear.

Result:

XX	YY
S1	S4
S2	S3

This example is the first in this chapter involving a table expression in which the explicit use of range variables is necessary. However, it is never wrong to introduce such variables, even when they are not explicitly required, and sometimes they can help to make the expression clearer. They can also save writing, if table names are on the lengthy side.

In general, then, a range variable is a variable that ranges over some specified table—i.e., a variable whose permitted values are rows of that table. In other words, if range variable R ranges over table T, then, at any given time, the expression "R" represents some row of T. For example, consider the query "Get supplier numbers for suppliers in Paris with status > 20." A "natural" formulation of this query in SQL would be:

```
SELECT  S.SNO
FROM    S
WHERE   S.CITY = 'Paris'
AND     S.STATUS > 20
```

However, it could equally well be expressed as follows:

```
SELECT  SX.SNO
FROM    S AS SX
WHERE   SX.CITY = 'Paris'
AND     SX.STATUS > 20
```

The range variable here is SX, and it ranges over table S.

As a matter of fact, SQL *always* requires select-expressions (and join expressions also) to be formulated in terms of range variables. If no such variables are specified explicitly, then SQL assumes the existence of *implicit* range variables with the same name(s) as the corresponding table(s). For example, the expression

```
SELECT  T.C
FROM    T
    .....
```

(where *T* is a table name) is treated by SQL as if it had been written as follows:

```
SELECT  T.C
FROM    T AS T
    .....
```

—in other words, "*T*" itself is an implicit range variable name, representing a range variable called *T* that ranges over the table called *T*.*

Note: The standard does not use the term "range variable." Instead, it refers to names such as SX in the example above as "correlation names," and does not say what kind of object is denoted by such names. "Range variable" is the orthodox term, however, and in this book we will stick with it.

The table corresponding to a given range variable is not necessarily a named table (i.e., base table or view). For example, consider the following expression (which involves a "Case (b)" table reference):

```
SELECT  JX.SNO, JX.CITY, JX.PNO
FROM    ( S NATURAL JOIN SP ) AS JX
```

In this example, the range variable JX ranges over an unnamed table—to be specific, the table that is the natural join of tables S and SP over supplier numbers.

---

*There is actually a tiny difference between "SELECT *T.C* FROM *T*" and "SELECT *T.C* FROM *T* AS *T*," as follows. In the first case, references elsewhere in the overall table expression—e.g., in a WHERE clause—to column *T.C* can optionally be qualified by a schema name (why?). In the second case, such references *must* be of the form "*T.C*" only. See the paragraph later in this section beginning "Note finally" (immediately preceding the subsection "Range Variables and Join Expressions").

Here is another example of a table reference involving an AS clause, to illustrate the introduction of column names for the result (the result, that is, of evaluating the table expression nested within the table reference):

```
SELECT JSNO, JCITY, JPNO
FROM   ( S NATURAL JOIN SP )
          AS JX ( JSNO, JSNAME, JSTATUS, JCITY, JPNO, JQTY )
```

Again the expression S NATURAL JOIN SP evaluates to the table that is the natural join of tables S and SP over supplier numbers (and JX is a range variable that ranges over that table). The columns of that table are then given names (in left-to-right order) JSNO, JSNAME, JSTATUS, JCITY, JPNO, and JQTY. Note that the column-commalist, if specified, must include a name (*un*qualified) for every column in the relevant table, and must not specify any name more than once.

To repeat a remark from the beginning of this section, table references serve two distinct purposes: They specify the operands in FROM clauses (within select-expressions), and they specify the operands in explicit joins (i.e., join expressions). We have now seen too that every table reference serves to introduce a range variable, at least implicitly. The *scope* of that range variable—i.e., the context within which it can be referenced and within which its name must be unique—is defined as follows. It might help to observe that the rules are somewhat (but only somewhat!) analogous to the rules regarding the scope of names in a block-structured language such as Algol 60 or Pascal.

- If the table reference represents a FROM-clause operand, then the scope is the select-expression that immediately contains that FROM clause (i.e., the SELECT clause, the FROM clause itself, the WHERE clause if any, the GROUP BY clause if any, and the HAVING clause if any, that go to make up that select-expression)—*excluding* any select-expression or join expression that is nested anywhere within the original select-expression in which another range variable is introduced with the same name.

- If the table reference represents a JOIN operand, then the scope is the join expression that immediately contains that JOIN—*excluding* any select-expression or join expression that is nested anywhere within the original join expression in which another range variable is introduced with the same name.

  Note: The foregoing paragraph does not quite tell the whole story. If the join expression containing the table reference represents an operand within a FROM clause, then the scope extends out to include the select-expression that immediately contains that FROM clause as well. Thus, e.g., the following is legal:

```
SELECT DISTINCT SP.PNO, S.CITY
FROM   SP NATURAL JOIN S
```

The intent seems to be that the scope in such a case should be just as if the join expression were replaced by the two join operands separated by a comma. In the example, therefore, the scope of the range variables S and SP is exactly as it would be in the expression

```
SELECT ...
FROM   SP, S
```

One very counterintuitive consequence of this unorthodox scoping rule is illustrated by the following example: The result of the expression

```
SELECT DISTINCT SP.*
FROM   SP NATURAL JOIN S
```

will include columns PNO and QTY but *not* column SNO, because—believe it or not—there is no column "SP.SNO" in the result of the join expression* (indeed, specifying SP.SNO in the SELECT clause would be a syntax error). Instead, there is a column called simply SNO, without any qualifier, that is the result of a kind of "merging" of columns S.SNO and SP.SNO.

The whole question of the scope of range variable names in the context of a join expression is quite complex. We therefore offer an extended discussion of the question in the next subsection below ("Range Variables and Join Expressions").

If a reference appears in (e.g.) a WHERE or GROUP BY clause to an unqualified column name, that reference must be within the scope of a range variable whose associated table includes a column with the specified name, and that range variable is then taken as the implicit qualifier. (If there is more than one such range variable, then the "nearest"—i.e., the one with the most local scope—is taken as the qualifier. If the "nearest" is not uniquely determined it is an error, except for the case where (a) there are exactly two such "nearest," (b) they represent the two operands of a NATURAL JOIN or JOIN ... USING expression, and (c) the column reference is a reference to a common column of those operands. Note in this latter case that no possible explicit qualifier exists—i.e., the column reference *must* be unqualified in this situation.)

Note finally that if an explicit range variable is introduced for a given table, then for naming purposes it effectively replaces that table throughout its scope. Thus, for example, the following is *** *ILLEGAL* ***:

```
SELECT  S.SNO                          -- *** ILLEGAL *** !!!
FROM    S AS SX
WHERE   S.CITY = 'Paris'               -- *** ILLEGAL *** !!!
AND     S.STATUS > 20                  -- *** ILLEGAL *** !!!
```

(all of the "S." qualifiers should be replaced by "SX.").

---

*Note, therefore, that omitting the key word DISTINCT in the example could cause the result to include duplicate rows.

Range Variables and Join Expressions

Note: The discussions of this section are based (with acknowledgments) on a private communication from Phil Shaw.

Consider this example:

```
( ( T1 JOIN T2 ON cond-1 )
    JOIN
  ( T3 JOIN T4 ON cond-2 )
    ON cond-3 )
```

Here *cond-1* is the join condition for the join of *T1* and *T2*, *cond-2* is the join condition for the join of *T3* and *T4*, and *cond-3* is the join condition for the join of the results of the other two joins. Then:

- *cond-1* can reference *T1* and *T2* but not *T3* or *T4*;
- *cond-2* can reference *T3* and *T4* but not *T1* or *T2*;
- *cond-3* can reference all four of *T1*, *T2*, *T3*, and *T4*.

And if the overall expression appears as the operand of a FROM clause, then the associated SELECT clause, WHERE clause, etc., can also reference all four of *T1*, *T2*, *T3*, and *T4*.

Now let us modify the example slightly to introduce explicit range variables *TA* and *TB* for the two intermediate joins:

```
( ( T1 JOIN T2 ON cond-1 ) AS TA
    JOIN
  ( T3 JOIN T4 ON cond-2 ) AS TB
    ON cond-3 )
```

The rules are now as follows:

- *cond-1* can reference *T1* and *T2* but not *T3*, *T4*, *TA*, or *TB*;
- *cond-2* can reference *T3* and *T4* but not *T1*, *T2*, *TA*, or *TB*;
- *cond-3* can reference *TA* and *TB* but not *T1*, *T2*, *T3*, or *T4*.

And (again) if the overall expression appears as the operand of a FROM clause, then the associated SELECT clause, WHERE clause, etc., can also reference *TA* and *TB* but not *T1*, *T2*, *T3*, or *T4*.

Now let us modify the example once again to introduce an explicit range variable *TC* for the overall result:

```
( ( T1 JOIN T2 ON cond-1 ) AS TA
    JOIN
  ( T3 JOIN T4 ON cond-2 ) AS TB
    ON cond-3 ) AS TC
```

The rules are now as follows:

- *cond-1* can reference *T1* and *T2* but not *T3*, *T4*, *TA*, *TB*, or *TC*;
- *cond-2* can reference *T3* and *T4* but not *T1*, *T2*, *TA*, *TB*, or *TC*;
- *cond-3* can reference *TA* and *TB* but not *T1*, *T2*, *T3*, *T4*, or *TC*.

And (once again) if the overall expression appears as the operand of a FROM clause, then the associated SELECT clause, WHERE clause, etc., can reference *TC* but not *T1*, *T2*, *T3*, *T4*, *TA*, or *TB*.

11.4   UNIONS, DIFFERENCES, AND INTERSECTIONS

The SQL UNION, EXCEPT, and INTERSECT operations are based on the well-known union, difference, and intersection operations of set theory. The two tables that represent the direct operands of the union, difference, or intersection must be of the same degree (i.e., they must have the same number of columns), and corresponding columns must be of compatible data types (refer to Chapter 7, Section 7.6, for an explanation of data type compatibility). For details regarding the data types (precision, scale, etc.) of columns of the result, the reader is referred to the official standard document.

UNION and EXCEPT appear in "nonjoin table expressions" and INTERSECT appears in "nonjoin table terms." Here is a summary of the syntax:

```
nonjoin-table-expression
    ::=    nonjoin-table-term
        |  table-expression { UNION | EXCEPT } [ ALL ]
                   [ CORRESPONDING [ BY ( column-commalist ) ] ]
                         table-term

nonjoin-table-term
    ::=    nonjoin-table-primary
        |  table-term INTERSECT [ ALL ]
                   [ CORRESPONDING [ BY ( column-commalist ) ] ]
                         table-primary
```

A "table term" is either a join expression (explained in Section 11.2 above) or a "nonjoin table term" (explained in the present section); a "table primary" is either a join expression (again, see Section 11.2 above) or a "nonjoin table primary." This last construct ("nonjoin table primary") is explained in Section 11.5; for the purposes of the present section, however, we simply assume that the construct is understood (it might, for example, be a select-expression, of the form SELECT–FROM–WHERE), and concentrate instead on "nonjoin table expressions" and "nonjoin table terms."

INTERSECT

To fix our ideas, let us focus first on the "nonjoin table term"

```
table-term INTERSECT [ ALL ]
    [ CORRESPONDING [ BY ( column-commalist ) ] ] table-primary
```

Let us agree to refer to such an expression (for the moment) as an *intersection*. Let *A* and *B* be the tables resulting from evaluation of the table-term and table-primary, respectively. Then the various possible intersections we have to consider are as follows*—

```
1. A INTERSECT CORRESPONDING BY ( column-commalist ) B

2. A INTERSECT CORRESPONDING B

3. A INTERSECT B
```

—plus three further cases that are identical to the ones above except that they additionally include the option ALL.

In *Case 1*, let the commalist of columns in the BY clause be *C1, C2, ..., Cn*. Each of *C1, C2, ..., Cn* must be *un*qualified and must identify both a column of *A* and a column of *B*. This case is defined to be semantically identical to an expression of the form

```
( ( SELECT C1, C2, ..., Cn FROM A )
    INTERSECT
  ( SELECT C1, C2, ..., Cn FROM B ) )
```

In other words: Let *AC* be a table that is derived from *A* by dropping all columns not mentioned in the BY clause, and let *BC* be a table that is derived from *B* analogously. Then the result of the intersection is a table of *n* columns; a given row *R* appears in that result if and only if *R* appears in *AC and* in *BC*.† The result does not contain any duplicate rows.

Here is an example of Case 1:

```
( SELECT * FROM P )
    INTERSECT CORRESPONDING BY ( PNO )
        ( S NATURAL JOIN SP )
```

---

*Conceptually, that is. The three cases shown are not intended to reflect valid SQL syntax. Specifically, the operands to INTERSECT *cannot* be specified as simple table names, contrary to what the "intersections" shown suggest. A similar remark applies to UNION and EXCEPT (see later).

†This definition is slightly oversimplified. To be more precise: Let *R* be a row that is a duplicate of some row in *AC and* a duplicate of some row in *BC*. Then the result contains (a) exactly one duplicate of every such row *R*, (b) no row that is not a duplicate of some such row *R*. (The point is that two rows can be duplicates without actually being identical, owing to the fact that two scalar values in turn can "compare equal" without being identical; e.g., the INTEGER value 3 and the NUMERIC(2,1) value 3.0 "compare equal." See also Chapter 19, Section 19.7, subsection "Indeterminate Table Expressions.")

The standard does specify the data types of the columns of the result of the INTERSECT and thereby does effectively specify, out of potentially many distinct duplicates of *R*, which particular one is to appear in that result. We omit the details here, but note one bizarre consequence of them—namely, that the result might quite legitimately include a row that does not appear in either operand!

Remarks analogous to the foregoing apply to all forms of INTERSECT (also to all forms of UNION and EXCEPT, of course). For brevity, we will let this footnote serve as our only explicit coverage of all such cases.

The result is a table of part numbers, containing just those part numbers that are common to (a) the parts table P and (b) the natural join of the suppliers and shipments tables (S and SP) over supplier numbers.

A *Case 2* intersection is defined to be semantically identical to a Case 1 intersection in which the commalist of columns specifies *all* of the columns that are common to *A* and *B*.* Here is an example:

```
( SELECT * FROM P )
    INTERSECT CORRESPONDING
        ( S NATURAL JOIN SP )
```

The columns that are common to the two operands here are PNO and CITY. Thus, the result is a table of part-number/city-name pairs, containing just those pairs that appear in both (a) the parts table P and (b) the natural join of the suppliers and shipments tables over supplier numbers.

Finally, a *Case 3* intersection is performed, not by matching columns with the same name as in Cases 1 and 2, but by matching columns with the same *ordinal position*. That is, the ith column of *A* is matched with the ith column of *B* (for all i in the range 1 to n, where n is the degree—recall that *A* and *B* must have the same degree). The result will also have degree n; a given row will appear in that result if and only if it appears in both *A* and *B*. Once again, the result will not contain any duplicate rows.

The ALL versions of the three cases are analogous, except that the result can include duplicate rows. More precisely, suppose a given row *R* appears exactly m times in the first operand and exactly n times in the second ($m \geq 0$, $n \geq 0$). Then row *R* will appear exactly p times in the result, where p is the lesser of m and n.†

UNION

Now we turn our attention to "nonjoin table expressions" of the form

```
table-expression UNION [ ALL ]
    [ CORRESPONDING [ BY ( column-commalist ) ] ] table-term
```

Let us agree to refer to such an expression (for the moment) as a *union*. Let *A* and *B* be the tables resulting from evaluation of the table-expression and table-term, respectively. Then the various possible cases to consider are exactly analogous to

---

*It is an error if the set of common column names is empty (contrast the state of affairs with NATURAL JOIN).

†Note the difference between INTERSECT and SELECT with regard to duplicate elimination. With SELECT, the user can specify ALL or DISTINCT, and ALL is the default; with INTERSECT, the user can specify only ALL explicitly (omitting the specification is like specifying "DISTINCT"), and "DISTINCT" (by omission) is the default. A similar remark applies to UNION and EXCEPT (see later). We remind the reader that, in our opinion, duplicate rows are *always* ill-advised.

the intersection cases discussed above; in other words, the cases are conceptually as follows—

1. `A UNION CORRESPONDING BY ( column-commalist ) B`

2. `A UNION CORRESPONDING B`

3. `A UNION B`

—plus three further cases that are identical to the ones above except that they additionally include the option ALL.* They are (of course) defined analogously to the intersection cases, except that, for UNION, a given row appears in the result if and only if it appears in *at least one* of the two operands. By default, the result does not contain any duplicate rows. If ALL is specified, however, then suppose again that a given row R appears exactly m times in the first operand and exactly n times in the second ($m \geq 0$, $n \geq 0$). Then row R will appear exactly p times in the result, where $p - m + n$.

EXCEPT

Finally, EXCEPT. The various possible cases (which we will refer to as *differences*) are again analogous to the intersection cases—

1. `A EXCEPT CORRESPONDING BY ( column-commalist ) B`

2. `A EXCEPT CORRESPONDING B`

3. `A EXCEPT B`

—plus three further cases that are identical to the ones above except that they additionally include the option ALL.† Again the three cases are defined analogously to the intersection cases, except that, for EXCEPT, a given row appears in the result if and only if it appears in the first operand and not in the second. By default, again, the result does not contain any duplicate rows. If ALL is specified, however, then suppose once again that a given row R appears exactly m times in the first operand and exactly n times in the second ($m \geq 0$, $n \geq 0$). Then row R will appear exactly p times in the result, where p is the greater of $m - n$ and zero.

A Note on Syntax

It is worth explicitly pointing out some inconsistencies between the syntax rules for NATURAL JOIN and those for UNION (and INTERSECT and EXCEPT; we focus on UNION here for simplicity). Assume that A and B are named tables.

---

*The three unions shown are not intended to reflect valid SQL syntax.

†Once again the syntax is not meant to be accurate.

Assume too that tables *A* and *B* are such that the data type compatibility (etc.) requirements for UNION are satisfied. Then the following expressions are syntactically legal or syntactically illegal as indicated:

```
A NATURAL JOIN B                                          -- legal

A UNION B                                                 -- illegal

TABLE A UNION TABLE B                                     -- legal

TABLE A NATURAL JOIN TABLE B                              -- illegal

SELECT * FROM A UNION SELECT * FROM B                     -- legal

SELECT * FROM A NATURAL JOIN SELECT * FROM B              -- illegal

(TABLE A) UNION (TABLE B)                                 -- legal

(TABLE A) NATURAL JOIN (TABLE B)                          -- illegal

(TABLE A) AS AA NATURAL JOIN (TABLE B) AS BB             -- legal
```

Note: The construct "TABLE *T*" (where *T* is a table name) is explained in the next section.

11.5   TABLE PRIMARIES

As indicated in the previous section, a "table primary" is used to specify the second operand of an intersection. To repeat from that section, a "table primary" is either a join expression (see Section 11.2) or a "nonjoin table primary." A "nonjoin table primary," in turn, is one of the following:

- A nonjoin table expression enclosed in parentheses, in which case the value is just the value of that enclosed expression (see Section 11.4; the parentheses are included purely for syntactic reasons and have no effect on the semantics);

- A select-expression (explained in Section 11.6, later);

- An expression of the form "TABLE table";

- A "table constructor."

The last two cases are discussed in the present section.

First, the expression "TABLE table" (where "table" is some named table—i.e., it is, specifically, a base table or a view) is defined to be semantically identical to the parenthesized select-expression

```
( SELECT * FROM table )
```

(see Section 11.6). Here is an example:

```
TABLE SP
```

(Incidentally, contrast the use of the key word TABLE here to refer to *any* named table—views as well as base tables—with the use of the same key word in, e.g., CREATE TABLE, where it refers to base tables specifically.)

Second, a "table constructor" takes the form

```
VALUES row-constructor-commalist
```

In other words, a table constructor consists of the key word VALUES followed by a commalist of row constructors. Each such row constructor specifies one row, and the table constructor then evaluates to a table that is the "UNION ALL" of those rows (loosely speaking). For example, the table constructor

```
VALUES ( 'S1', 'Smith', 20, 'London' ),
       ( 'S2', 'Jones', 10, 'Paris'  ),
       ( 'S3', 'Blake', 30, 'Paris'  ),
       ( 'S4', 'Clark', 20, 'London' ),
       ( 'S5', 'Adams', 30, 'Athens' )
```

evaluates to a table that is identical to the suppliers table S shown in Fig. 2.1 (except for column names—see Section 11.7).

A row constructor in turn takes one of the following two general forms:

```
( row-component-commalist ) | ( table-expression )
```

In other words, a row constructor consists of either (a) a parenthesized commalist of "row components" or (b) a parenthesized table expression, where:

1. A "row component" is identical to an "insert item" or "update item" as defined in Chapter 9; i.e., it is a scalar expression or one of the key words DEFAULT or NULL. (DEFAULT and NULL are permitted only if the row constructor is being used to specify the source, or part of the source, for an INSERT operation.) The value of the row constructor is the row formed by the specified row component values. *Note:* If the commalist contains just one row component, the surrounding parentheses can optionally be omitted.

2. The parenthesized table expression must evaluate to a table containing exactly one row, in which case the value of the row constructor is taken to be, precisely, that single row. *Note:* The standard refers to such an expression as a *row subquery*. It is an error if a row subquery yields a table of more than one row; if instead it yields a table of no rows at all, the value of the row constructor is taken to be a row of all nulls.*

Here are some examples of row constructors. Note that the second of these examples would be valid only in the context of an INSERT statement.

---

*Here is as good a place as any to mention that a table expression in parentheses that is *not* limited to producing at most one row (as row and scalar subqueries are) is known as a *table* subquery. Observe that table, row, and scalar subqueries are syntactically identical, except that scalar subqueries are required to be of degree one.

```
( 'S1', 'Smith', 20, 'London' )

( 'S1', 'Smith', DEFAULT, 'London' )

( 'S1' )

'S1'

( SELECT S.STATUS, S.CITY FROM S WHERE S.SNO = 'S4' )
```

Note: Let T be a named table with the same column names and corresponding data types as the suppliers base table S. Then it is worth pointing out that the following two INSERTs are semantically distinct:

```
1. INSERT INTO T VALUES ( SELECT * FROM S WHERE SNO = 'S6' )

2. INSERT INTO T        ( SELECT * FROM S WHERE SNO = 'S6' )
```

Assuming in both cases that there is no row for supplier S6 in base table S, the first inserts an all-null row into table T, while the second inserts no rows at all. The reason is as follows:

1. In the first case, the table expression representing the rows to be inserted is in fact a table constructor that involves exactly one row constructor. That row constructor in turn is a row subquery that produces a table of no rows at all, and so is taken (as explained above) to be a row of all nulls.

2. In the second case, the table expression is basically just a regular SELECT–FROM–WHERE expression that produces a table of no rows.

Of course, we assume for the sake of the example that every column of table T does permit nulls.

11.6   SELECT EXPRESSIONS

A select-expression can be thought of, loosely, as a table expression that does not involve any JOINs, UNIONs, EXCEPTs, or INTERSECTs ("loosely," because, of course, such operators might be involved in expressions that are *nested inside* the select-expression). The syntax is:

```
SELECT [ ALL | DISTINCT ] select-item-commalist
   FROM table-reference-commalist
      [ WHERE conditional-expression ]
         [ GROUP BY column-commalist ]
            [ HAVING conditional-expression ]
```

We explain the various clauses of a select-expression one by one in the subsections that follow.

The SELECT Clause

The SELECT clause takes the form

```
SELECT [ ALL | DISTINCT ] select-item-commalist
```

(see below for a detailed discussion of select-items). *Note:* The following explanation is partly a repeat of material already presented in Chapter 9, Section 9.2.

1. If neither ALL nor DISTINCT is specified, ALL is assumed.

2. We assume for the sake of this explanation that the FROM, WHERE, GROUP BY, and HAVING clauses have already been evaluated. No matter which of those clauses are specified and which omitted, the conceptual result of evaluating them is always a table,* which we will refer to as table *T1* (even though that conceptual result is in fact unnamed).

3. Let *T2* be the table that is obtained by evaluating the specified select-items against table *T1*.

4. Let *T3* be the table that is obtained by eliminating redundant duplicate rows from table *T2* if DISTINCT is specified, or a table that is identical to table *T2* otherwise.

5. Table *T3* is the final result.

We turn now to an explanation of select-items. There are two cases to consider, of which the second is really just shorthand for a commalist of select-items of the first form; thus, the first case is really more fundamental.

Case 1: The select-item takes the form

```
scalar-expression [ [ AS ] column ]
```

- The scalar expression will typically but not necessarily involve one or more columns of table *T1* (see paragraph 2 above for an explanation of "table *T1*"). For each row of table *T1*, the scalar expression is evaluated, to yield a scalar result. The commalist of such scalar results corresponding to evaluation of all select-items in the SELECT clause against a single row of table *T1* constitutes a single row of table *T2* (see paragraph 3 above for an explanation of "table *T2*"). If the select-item includes an AS clause, the *un*qualified column name "column" from that clause is assigned as the name of the corresponding column of table *T2*.† *Note:* Once again, the optional key word AS is just noise and can be omitted without affecting the meaning.

---

*Possibly a "grouped" table (see the subsections on GROUP BY and HAVING later in this section).

†Because it is, specifically, the name of a column of table *T2*, not table *T1*, any name introduced by such an AS clause cannot be used in the WHERE, GROUP BY, and HAVING clauses (if any) directly involved in the construction of that table *T1*. It can, however, be referenced in an associated ORDER BY clause in a cursor definition or (in direct SQL) a multi-row retrieval, and also in an "outer" table expression that contains the select-expression under discussion nested within it.

- If a select-item includes an aggregate function reference *and* the select-expression does not include a GROUP BY clause (see below), then no select-item in the SELECT clause can include any reference to a column of table *T1* unless that column reference represents the argument, or part of the argument, to such an aggregate function reference. Thus, for example, the following is *** *ILLEGAL* ***—

```
SELECT SP.PNO, AVG ( SP.QTY ) AS AQ    -- *** ILLEGAL *** !!!
FROM   SP
```

—because (a) there is no GROUP BY clause *and* (b) the SELECT clause includes an aggregate function reference *and* (c) the SELECT clause also includes a reference to a column of "table *T1*" (i.e., base table SP, in the example) that is not contained within such an aggregate function reference. By contrast, the following is legal:

```
SELECT AVG ( SP.QTY ) AS AQ, SUM ( SP.QTY ) AS SQ
FROM   SP
```

Case 2: The select-item takes the form

```
[ range-variable . ] *
```

- If the qualifier is omitted (i.e., the select-item is just an unqualified asterisk), then this select-item must be the *only* select-item in the SELECT clause. This form is shorthand for a commalist of all of the columns of table *T1*, in left-to-right order.*

- If the qualifier is included (i.e., the select-item consists of an asterisk qualified by a range variable name *R*, thus: "*R.**"), then the select-item represents a commalist of all of the columns of the table associated with range variable *R*, in left-to-right order.† (Recall that a table name can and often will be used as an implicit range variable. Thus, the select-item will frequently be of the form "*T.**" rather than "*R.**".)

- If an "asterisk-style" select-item, qualified or unqualified, appears within a view definition or integrity constraint (see Chapters 13 and 14, respectively), it will be expanded out at the time that view or constraint is created. Thus (e.g.) adding a new column to the corresponding table at some later time will not affect that view or constraint.

---

*Except in the context of an EXISTS condition (see Chapter 12, Section 12.7).

†As we saw in Section 11.3, a weird exception to this rule occurs if *T1* is the result of evaluating a join expression. To repeat the example from that section, the select-item "SP.*" in the select-expression "SELECT SP.* FROM SP NATURAL JOIN S" stands for "SP.PNO, SP.QTY"—*not* for "SP.SNO, SP.PNO, SP.QTY"!

The FROM Clause

The FROM clause takes the form

```
FROM table-reference-commalist
```

Let the table references in the commalist evaluate to tables *A, B, ..., C,* respectively. Then the result of evaluating the FROM clause is a table that is equal to the Cartesian product of *A, B, ..., C.** *Note:* The Cartesian product of a single table *T* is defined to be equal to *T.* In other words, it is (of course) legal for the FROM clause to contain just a single table reference.

The WHERE Clause

The WHERE clause takes the form

```
WHERE conditional-expression
```

Let *T* be the result of evaluating the immediately preceding FROM clause. Then the result of the WHERE clause is a table that is derived from *T* by eliminating all rows for which the conditional expression does not evaluate to *true.* If the WHERE clause is omitted, the result is simply *T.*

Note: WHERE clauses are subject to a couple of rather complex syntactic restrictions which we simply state here without further elaboration:

1. If the conditional expression contains a table expression that in turn contains an aggregate function reference, then the expression representing the aggregate function argument must not reference any column of *T.*

2. If the conditional expression "directly" contains an aggregate function reference—i.e., the aggregate function reference appears directly within the conditional expression *per se,* not within another expression nested within that conditional expression (where that other expression is either a table expression or another aggregate function reference)—then:

    - The WHERE clause must be nested within either a SELECT clause or a HAVING clause.

    - The expression representing the aggregate function argument must be, not an arbitrary scalar expression, but very specifically an "outer reference" (see Chapter 12, Section 12.5, for an explanation of this term).

---

*Again we remark that the definition of Cartesian product requires a certain amount of care and refinement if any duplicate rows are involved. See Appendix D.

The GROUP BY Clause

The GROUP BY clause takes the form

```
GROUP BY column-commalist
```

We introduce this clause by means of an example. Consider the following query: "For each part supplied, get the part number and the total shipment quantity for that part." A possible SQL formulation is as follows:

```
SELECT  PNO, SUM ( SP.QTY ) AS PQTY
FROM    SP
GROUP   BY SP.PNO
```

Given our usual sample data (Fig. 2.1), the result is:

PNO	PQTY
P1	600
P2	1000
P3	400
P4	500
P5	500
P6	100

This result is obtained by (conceptually) rearranging base table SP into *groups of rows*, one group for each distinct part number, and then extracting the corresponding part number and average part quantity from each such group.

More generally, let T be the result of evaluating the immediately preceding FROM clause and WHERE clause (if any). Each "column" in the column-commalist in the GROUP BY clause must be the (optionally qualified) name of a column of T. The result of the GROUP BY clause is a *grouped table*—i.e., a set of groups of rows, derived from T by conceptually rearranging it into the minimum number of groups such that within any one group all rows have the same value for the combination of columns identified by the GROUP BY clause. Note carefully, therefore, that this result is thus *not* a proper table. However, a GROUP BY clause never appears without a corresponding SELECT clause whose effect is to derive a proper table from that improper intermediate result, so not much harm is done by this temporary deviation from the pure tabular framework. *Note:* Columns mentioned in the GROUP BY clause are known as *grouping columns*.

If a select-expression includes a GROUP BY clause, then there are restrictions on the form that the SELECT clause can take. To be specific, each select-item in the SELECT clause (including any that are implied by an asterisk shorthand) must be *single-valued per group*. Thus, such select-items must not include any reference to any column of table T that is not one of the grouping columns—*unless* that reference represents the argument, or part of the argument, to one of the aggregate functions, whose effect is to reduce some collection of scalar values from a group to a single such value.

The HAVING Clause

The HAVING clause takes the form

```
HAVING conditional-expression
```

Let *G* be the grouped table resulting from the evaluation of the immediately preceding FROM clause, WHERE clause (if any), and GROUP BY clause (if any). If there is no GROUP BY clause, then *G* is taken to be the result of evaluating the FROM and WHERE clauses, considered as a grouped table that contains a single group;* in other words, there is effectively an implicit GROUP BY clause that specifies *no grouping columns at all.*† The result of the HAVING clause is a grouped table that is derived from *G* by eliminating all groups for which the conditional expression does not evaluate to *true. Note:* Scalar expressions in a HAVING clause must be single-valued per group (like scalar expressions in the SELECT clause if there is a GROUP BY clause, as discussed in the previous subsection).

If the HAVING clause is omitted but the GROUP BY clause is included, the result is simply *G*. If the HAVING and GROUP BY clauses are both omitted, the result is simply the "proper"—i.e., nongrouped—table *T* resulting from the FROM and WHERE clauses.

Examples

Here are some examples of select-expressions, most of them presented without additional discussion.

Example 1: Get part numbers for all parts supplied.

```
SELECT DISTINCT SP.PNO
FROM    SP
```

Example 2: Get supplier numbers for suppliers in Paris with status > 20.

```
SELECT S.SNO
FROM    S
WHERE   S.CITY = 'Paris'
AND     S.STATUS > 20
```

Example 3: Get all supplier-number/part-number combinations such that the supplier and part in question are located in the same city.

```
SELECT S.SNO, P.PNO
FROM    S, P
WHERE   S.CITY = P.CITY
```

---

*This is what the standard says, though logically it should say *at most one* group (there should be no group at all if the FROM and WHERE clauses yield an empty table).

†Note, however, that such a GROUP BY clause cannot be stated explicitly. More important, note the implication that if a select-expression includes a HAVING clause and no GROUP BY clause, the SELECT and HAVING clauses cannot include any references to columns of *T* (where *T* is the result of evaluating the FROM and WHERE clauses) except within aggregate function references.

Example 4: Get all supplier-number/part-number combinations such that the supplier city follows the part city in alphabetical order. (We are assuming a "sensible" collating sequence here! See Chapter 19.)

```
SELECT  S.SNO, P.PNO
FROM    S, P
WHERE   S.CITY > P.CITY
```

Example 5: Get all supplier-number/part-number combinations such that the supplier and part in question are located in the same city, but omitting suppliers with status 20.

```
SELECT  S.SNO, P.PNO
FROM    S, P
WHERE   S.CITY = P.CITY
AND     S.STATUS <> 20
```

Example 6: Get all pairs of city names such that a supplier located in the first city supplies a part stored in the second city.

```
SELECT  DISTINCT S.CITY AS SCITY, P.CITY AS PCITY
FROM    S, SP, P
WHERE   S.SNO = SP.SNO
AND     SP.PNO = P.PNO
```

Example 7: Get all pairs of supplier numbers such that the two suppliers concerned are located in the same city.

```
SELECT  FIRST.SNO AS XX, SECOND.SNO AS YY
FROM    S AS FIRST, S AS SECOND
WHERE   FIRST.CITY = SECOND.CITY
```

This example was discussed in detail in Section 11.3 above.

Example 8: For each part supplied, get the part number, maximum quantity, and minimum quantity supplied of that part, excluding shipments by supplier S1.

```
SELECT  SP.PNO, MAX ( SP.QTY ) AS XXX, MIN ( SP.QTY ) AS YYY
FROM    SP
WHERE   SP.SNO <> 'S1'
GROUP   BY SP.PNO
```

Result:

PNO	XXX	YYY
P1	300	300
P2	400	200
P4	300	300
P5	400	400

Example 9: Get part numbers for all parts supplied by more than one supplier.

```
SELECT  SP.PNO
FROM    SP
GROUP   BY SP.PNO
HAVING  COUNT(*) > 1
```

Example 10: For all red and blue parts such that the total quantity supplied is greater than 350 (excluding from the total all shipments for which the quantity is less than or equal to 200), get the part number, the weight in grams, the color, and the maximum quantity supplied of that part. We assume for the sake of the example that weights are given in table P in pounds.

```
SELECT  P.PNO,
        'Weight in grams =' AS TEXT1,
        P.WEIGHT * 454 AS GMWT,
        P.COLOR,
        'Max quantity =' AS TEXT2,
        MAX ( SP.QTY ) AS MQY
FROM    P, SP
WHERE   P.PNO = SP.PNO
AND     ( P.COLOR = 'Red' OR P.COLOR = 'Blue')
AND     SP.QTY > 200
GROUP   BY P.PNO, P.WEIGHT, P.COLOR
HAVING  SUM ( SP.QTY ) > 350
```

Explanation: We explain this example in some detail in order to provide a kind of summary of some of the material discussed earlier in this section. First note that, as explained in the foregoing subsections, the clauses of a select-expression are conceptually executed in the order suggested by that in which they are written—with the sole exception of the SELECT clause itself, which is executed last. In the example, therefore, we can imagine the result being constructed as follows:

1. *FROM:* The FROM clause is evaluated to yield a new table that is the Cartesian product of tables P and SP.

2. *WHERE:* The result of Step 1 is reduced by the elimination of all rows that do not satisfy the WHERE clause. In the example, rows not satisfying the conditional expression

```
    P.PNO = SP.PNO AND
( P.COLOR = 'Red' OR P.COLOR = 'Blue') AND
    SP.QTY > 200
```

are eliminated.

3. *GROUP BY:* The result of Step 2 is grouped by values of the columns named in the GROUP BY clause. In the example, those columns are P.PNO, P.WEIGHT, and P.COLOR.

4. *HAVING:* Groups not satisfying the condition

```
    SUM ( SP.QTY ) > 350
```

are eliminated from the result of Step 3.

5. *SELECT:* Each group in the result of Step 4 generates a single result row, as follows. First, the part number, weight, color, and maximum quantity are extracted from the group. Second, the weight is converted to grams. Third, the two literal strings "Weight in grams =" and "Max quantity =" are inserted at the

appropriate points in the row. Note, incidentally, that—as the phrase "appropriate points in the row" suggests—we are relying here on the fact that columns of tables have a left-to-right ordering in SQL. The literal strings would not make much sense if they did not appear at those "appropriate points."

The final result looks like this:

PNO	TEXT1	GMWT	COLOR	TEXT2	MQY
P1	Weight in grams =	5448	Red	Max quantity =	300
P5	Weight in grams =	5448	Blue	Max quantity =	400
P3	Weight in grams =	7718	Blue	Max quantity =	400

Note: To return to the GROUP BY clause for a moment: In theory P.PNO alone would be sufficient as the grouping column in this example, since P.WEIGHT and P.COLOR are themselves single-valued per part number. What is more, SQL is aware of this latter fact, since PNO was defined to be the primary key for table P! Nevertheless, an error condition will still be raised if P.WEIGHT and P.COLOR are omitted from the GROUP BY clause, because they are mentioned in the SELECT clause.

Example 11: For each shipment, define a *revised shipment quantity* thus: (a) if the specified quantity SP.QTY is greater than 250, then an incremented quantity equal to that specified quantity plus 50; (b) otherwise, a decremented quantity equal to that specified quantity minus 50. Then, for each shipment such that the revised quantity is greater than 100, get the supplier number, part number, and revised quantity.

First attempt:.

```
SELECT  SP.SNO, SP.PNO,
        ( CASE
              WHEN SP.QTY > 250 THEN SP.QTY + 50
              ELSE                   SP.QTY - 50
          END ) AS REVQTY
FROM    SP
WHERE   ( CASE
              WHEN SP.QTY > 250 THEN SP.QTY + 50
              ELSE                   SP.QTY - 50
          END ) > 100
```

Here is a better formulation, using a select-expression in the FROM clause:

```
SELECT SNO, PNO, REVQTY
FROM ( SELECT SP.SNO, SP.PNO,
                ( CASE
                      WHEN SP.QTY > 250 THEN SP.QTY + 50
                      ELSE                   SP.QTY - 50
                  END ) AS REVQTY
        FROM    SP ) AS POINTLESS
WHERE  REVQTY > 100
```

This second formulation is preferable to the first because:

- It involves less writing—the CASE expression is written out once, not twice.
- It is likely to perform better too—the CASE expression can be evaluated once per shipment row instead of twice. (Such would be the case with the first formulation only if the implementation is able to recognize and factor out common subexpressions.)

Note: The clause AS POINTLESS is required in the second formulation because of SQL's syntax rules (see Section 11.3), even though the range variable introduced by that clause, POINTLESS, is never explicitly referenced.

Example 12: Define a *versatile supplier*, VS, to be a supplier who (a) supplies at least one part and (b) supplies at least as many different parts as the average for suppliers in the same city as VS. For each versatile supplier, get the supplier number, name, status, and city, together with the number of different parts supplied and the average number of different parts supplied by suppliers in the same city.

```
SELECT  SNO, SNAME, STATUS, CITY, PCT, APCT
FROM    S
        NATURAL JOIN
      ( SELECT SNO, COUNT(*) AS PCT
        FROM    SP
        GROUP   BY SP.SNO ) AS POINTLESS1
        NATURAL JOIN
      ( SELECT CITY, AVG ( PCT ) AS APCT
        FROM    S
                NATURAL JOIN
              ( SELECT SNO, COUNT(*) AS PCT
                FROM    SP
                GROUP   BY SNO ) AS POINTLESS2
        GROUP   BY CITY ) AS POINTLESS3
WHERE   PCT > APCT
```

The meaning of this expression is not immediately apparent! The purpose of the example is to show a select-expression involving a reasonably complex degree of nesting; in practice, however, such complex expressions are probably best built up a step at a time from smaller subexpressions. We leave it as an exercise for the reader to determine how the single-expression formulation shown above might have been arrived at. *Note:* As in the previous example, the clauses AS POINTLESS1, AS POINTLESS2, and AS POINTLESS3 are required by SQL's syntax rules, even though the range variables introduced by those clauses are never explicitly referenced.

A Note on Redundancy

It is worth mentioning that the GROUP BY and HAVING clauses are actually redundant—i.e., for every select-expression that involves such a clause, there is a semantically equivalent one that does not.* We illustrate the point by giving alternative solutions to two of the examples from the previous subsection.

---

*This observation is valid in SQL/92 but was not so in SQL/89.

Example 8 (solution avoiding GROUP BY): For each part supplied, get the part number, maximum quantity, and minimum quantity supplied of that part, excluding shipments by supplier S1.

```
SELECT DISTINCT SP.PNO, ( SELECT MAX ( SPX.QTY )
                          FROM   SP AS SPX
                          WHERE  SPX.PNO = SP.PNO ) AS XXX,
                        ( SELECT MIN ( SPX.QTY )
                          FROM   SP AS SPX
                          WHERE  SPX.PNO = SP.PNO ) AS YYY
       FROM    SP
       WHERE   SP.SNO <> 'S1'
```

Example 9 (solution avoiding HAVING): Get part numbers for all parts supplied by more than one supplier.

```
SELECT DISTINCT SP.PNO
FROM    SP
WHERE   (SELECT COUNT(*)
         FROM    SP AS SPX
         WHERE   SPX.PNO = SP.PNO) > 1
```

While on the subject of redundancy, we should point out that explicit range variables too are logically redundant—meaning again that for every select-expression that involves such a construct, there is a semantically equivalent one that does not (or, rather, *should* not).* We illustrate the point by giving (a) an alternative solution to Example 7 from the previous subsection, and (b) another alternative solution to Example 8.

Example 7 (solution avoiding range variables FIRST and SECOND): Get all pairs of supplier numbers such that the two suppliers concerned are located in the same city.

```
SELECT XX, YY
FROM ( SELECT SNO AS XX, CITY FROM S ) AS POINTLESS1
       NATURAL JOIN
     ( SELECT SNO AS YY, CITY FROM S ) AS POINTLESS2
```

Note: It is true that this formulation does include two explicit range variables, POINTLESS1 and POINTLESS2, but logically it ought not to; certainly those range variables are never explicitly referenced. They are there only because SQL has a syntax rule to the effect that a table reference specified as a table expression in parentheses *must* have an associated AS clause that explicitly introduces such a range variable. See Section 11.3 once again.

Example 8 (solution avoiding range variables: For each part supplied, get the part number, maximum quantity, and minimum quantity supplied of that part, excluding shipments by supplier S1.

---

*Again this observation is valid in SQL/92 but was not so in SQL/89.

```
SELECT ZZZ AS PNO, ( SELECT MAX ( QTY )
                     FROM    SP
                     WHERE   PNO = ZZZ ) AS XXX,
                   ( SELECT MIN ( QTY )
                     FROM    SP
                     WHERE   PNO = ZZZ ) AS YYY
FROM ( SELECT DISTINCT PNO AS ZZZ
       FROM    SP
       WHERE   SNO <> 'S1' ) AS POINTLESS
```

11.7   DERIVED TABLE COLUMN NAMES

A *derived table* is the table that results from the evaluation of a table expression. In Sections 11.1-11.6 above, we have explained how such tables are conceptually constructed. One question we have not addressed, however (at least, not properly), is that of how the columns of such tables are *named*. In this section we consider this question in detail.

1. First of all, of course, every column of a base table has an *explicitly defined* name. (The same is effectively true for views too—see Chapter 13.) All such column names are unique within their containing table.

2. Second, if "*xyz*" is a table expression of any kind, then "(*xyz*)" is a table expression with identical semantics. In particular, therefore, the column names of the result of evaluating the table expression "(*xyz*)" are identical to those of the result of evaluating the table expression "*xyz*".

3. *Join expressions:* CROSS JOIN and "JOIN ... ON" are both defined in terms of select-expressions. "JOIN ... USING" is defined in terms of "JOIN ... ON." NATURAL JOIN is defined in terms of "JOIN ... USING." Thus, all of these cases ultimately reduce to the select-expression case (see paragraph 9 below).

4. *Table references:* We ignore the "join expression" case, since it has already been covered in the previous paragraph. A table reference that includes an AS clause with a commalist of column names evaluates to a table with column names as specified in that AS clause. A table reference that either includes an AS clause without a commalist of column names, or does not include an AS clause at all, evaluates to a table that inherits column names in the obvious way from the "table" or "table expression" component of that table reference.

5. *INTERSECT:* An intersection that specifies a BY clause with a commalist of column names evaluates to a table with column names as specified in that BY clause. An intersection that specifies a CORRESPONDING clause without a BY clause is defined to be shorthand for a special case of an intersection that does have a BY clause. And an intersection that matches columns on their ordinal position evaluates to a table in which column names are determined as follows:

- If the *i*th column of both operand tables is called *C*, then the *i*th column of the result is also called *C*.

- Otherwise, the *i*th column of the result has a name that is unique within its containing table but is otherwise implementation-dependent.

6. *UNION and EXCEPT:* The INTERSECT rules apply to UNION and EXCEPT also, *mutatis mutandis*.

7. *TABLE:* A table expression of the form "TABLE table" evaluates to a table that inherits column names in the obvious way from its "table" argument.

8. *Table constructors:* The result of evaluating a "table constructor" is a table in which each column has a name that is unique within its containing table but is otherwise implementation-dependent.

9. *Select-expressions:* As explained in Section 11.6, the value of a select-expression is determined by evaluating the FROM, WHERE, GROUP BY, HAVING, and SELECT clauses, in that order.

   - *FROM:* The result of evaluating the FROM clause is a table, *T1* say, that is equal to the Cartesian product of the tables identified by the table references in that FROM clause. Each column of *T1* inherits its name from the corresponding column of the applicable operand table. Note that the column names of *T1* are thus not necessarily unique within *T1*.*

   - *WHERE:* The result of evaluating the WHERE clause, table *T2* say, inherits its column names from table *T1*.

   - *GROUP BY:* As explained in Section 11.6, evaluating the GROUP BY clause yields an "improper" (i.e., grouped) table, G1 say, so it is a little difficult to say precisely what the column names of that table are. Perhaps the best way to think of the situation is to regard *each group* as having the same column names as table *T2*. Furthermore, those column names can be partitioned into two disjoint subsets, namely those that refer to grouping columns (i.e., columns mentioned in the GROUP BY clause) and those that do not. Names from the first subset can appear in the corresponding SELECT clause (and HAVING clause, if any) directly; names from the second subset can appear in those clauses only in the context of an aggregate function reference.

   - *HAVING:* The result of evaluating the HAVING clause, table G2 say, inherits its column names from table *G1*.

---

*There are fundamentally only two ways in which a table can be produced that does have nonunique column names, and this is the more important of the two (the other is illustrated by the example "SELECT *C*, *C* FROM *T*"). Nonunique column names are best avoided; indeed, certain SQL operations—NATURAL JOIN is a case in point—*require* column names to be unique, and raise an error if this requirement is violated. See the official standard document for further details.

- *SELECT:* After any necessary expansion of "asterisk-style" select-items, the SELECT clause effectively specifies a commalist of scalar expressions, each optionally accompanied by an AS clause. The result of evaluating that clause is a table, *T* say, that is derived from table *G2* by evaluating those scalar expressions as explained in Section 11.6. Table *T* contains one column for each such scalar expression, with a column name defined as follows:

  - If the scalar expression has an accompanying AS clause, then the column name is the name specified in that clause.

  - Otherwise, if the scalar expression consists simply of a possibly qualified column name, then the column name is the unqualified version of that name.

  - Otherwise, the column has a name that is unique within its containing table but is otherwise implementation-dependent.

Note that, as a consequence of the foregoing rules, every table in SQL/92 does have a name for every column (an improvement over SQL/89, incidentally). It is, however, unfortunately still the case (as it was in SQL/89) that column names are not necessarily unique within their containing table (though they are so in the case of *named* tables, i.e., base tables and views). It is also unfortunately the case that some column names in derived tables are implementation-dependent (i.e, not specified in the standard). Finally, it is also the case that those implementation-dependent column names are not made visible to the user;* that is, they cannot be referenced in, e.g., a SELECT or WHERE clause.

---

*Except via DESCRIBE OUTPUT (see Chapter 20).

12

Conditional Expressions

12.1 INTRODUCTION

In this chapter we explain another vitally important SQL concept, *viz.* conditional expressions, which (like table expressions, the subject of the previous chapter) appear in numerous contexts throughout the SQL language. In particular, of course, conditional expressions are used in WHERE, ON, and HAVING clauses to qualify or disqualify rows or groups during evaluation of table expressions. *Note:* Once again, we are departing here from official standard terminology; the standard refers to conditional expressions as "search conditions," and does not use the term "conditional expression" at all.

As in the previous chapter, we begin by giving the full BNF definition for the construct under consideration, for purposes of subsequent reference. We then go on to explain that definition piecemeal in the sections that follow. We remind the reader, however, that we are still ignoring everything (or almost everything) to do with nulls; conditional expressions, perhaps more than most other parts of the language, require significantly extended treatment when the implications (and complications) of nulls are taken into account, and certain conditional expression formats, not shown below, are provided purely to deal with certain aspects of "the nulls question."

```
conditional-expression
    ::=   conditional-term
        | conditional-expression OR conditional-term
```

```
conditional-term
    ::=    conditional-factor
         | conditional-term AND conditional-factor

conditional-factor
    ::=    [ NOT ] conditional-test

conditional-test
    ::=    conditional-primary [ IS [ NOT ] { TRUE | FALSE } ]

conditional-primary
    ::=    simple-condition | ( conditional-expression )

simple-condition
    ::=    comparison-condition
         | between-condition
         | like-condition
         | in-condition
         | match-condition
         | all-or-any-condition
         | exists-condition
         | unique-condition

comparison-condition
    ::=    row-constructor comparison-operator row-constructor

comparison-operator
    ::=    = | < | <= | > | >= | <>

between-condition
    ::=    row-constructor [ NOT ] BETWEEN row-constructor
                                         AND row-constructor

like-condition
    ::=    character-string-expression [ NOT ] LIKE pattern
                                        [ ESCAPE escape ]

in-condition
    ::=    row-constructor [ NOT ] IN ( table-expression )
         | scalar-expression [ NOT ] IN
                            ( scalar-expression-commalist )

match-condition
    ::=    row-constructor MATCH [ UNIQUE ] ( table-expression )

all-or-any-condition
    ::=    row-constructor
              comparison-operator { ALL | ANY | SOME }
                                       ( table-expression )

exists-condition
    ::=    EXISTS ( table-expression )

unique-condition
    ::=    UNIQUE ( table-expression )
```

Note: The parenthesized table expression in "match condition," "all-or-any condition," "exists condition," "unique condition," and the first form of "in condition" is in fact a *table subquery* (see Chapter 11).

For completeness, we should mention that there are two further "simple conditions," one, IS [NOT] NULL, having to do with nulls and the other, OVERLAPS, with dates and times. These two conditions are described in Chapters 16 and 17, respectively. In addition, "match conditions" have certain options, not shown above, that once again have to do with nulls; those options are also described in Chapter 16.

12.2 GENERAL REMARKS

In general, a conditional expression is an expression that evaluates to a truth value (*true* or *false*). As the syntax shows, such an expression is basically a collection of "conditional primaries," combined together using the logical operators AND, OR, and NOT, and parentheses to enforce a desired order of evaluation. Each such "conditional primary" in turn (a) is either a "simple condition" or a conditional expression enclosed in parentheses, and (b) is optionally followed by one of the following:

```
IS TRUE
IS NOT TRUE
IS FALSE
IS NOT FALSE
```

We explain these latter four expressions by means of the following truth table. Let *p* be a conditional primary. Then the meanings of the four expressions are as indicated:*

p	true	false
p IS TRUE	true	false
p IS NOT TRUE	false	true
p IS FALSE	false	true
p IS NOT FALSE	true	false

A "simple condition" is any of the following:

- a comparison-condition
- a between-condition
- a like-condition
- an in-condition
- a match-condition
- an all-or-any-condition
- an exists-condition
- a unique-condition

---

*The expressions were introduced primarily in an attempt to overcome certain problems that arise over nulls. They are, rather obviously, of limited usefulness in the context of the present chapter. See Chapter 16 for further discussion.

One further general remark: As will be seen, many of the foregoing "simple conditions" involve one or more *row constructors* (see, e.g., the discussion of comparison conditions in Section 12.3 immediately following). It is worth pointing out that, in practice, such a row constructor will more often than not consist of the special case that is simply a scalar expression, without surrounding parentheses. Many of our examples will illustrate this special case.

12.3 COMPARISON CONDITIONS

The syntax of a comparison condition (*comparison* for short) is as follows:

```
row-constructor comparison-operator row-constructor
```

Here:

- The comparison operator must be one of the following: =, <, <=, >, >=, or <> ("not equals").

- A "row constructor" is exactly as defined in Chapter 11. In other words, it is either a commalist of "row components" or a table expression, enclosed in parentheses in each case—except that (as always for row constructors):

  a. In the first case, the parentheses can be omitted if the commalist contains just one component.

  b. In the second case (where the row constructor is in fact a row subquery), the table expression must evaluate to a table containing at most one row.*

  See Chapter 11, Section 11.5, for further discussion.

Let the two row constructors evaluate to rows *Left* and *Right*, respectively. *Left* and *Right* must be of the same degree (i.e., they must contain the same number, n say, of scalar values each). Let i range from 1 to n, and let the ith components of *Left* and *Right* be Li and Ri, respectively. The data type of Li must be compatible with that of Ri (see Chapter 7, Section 7.6, for an explanation of data type compatibility). Then the result of the comparison condition is defined as follows:

- "*Left = Right*" is *true* if and only if for all i, "$Li = Ri$" is *true*

- "*Left <> Right*" is *true* if and only if there exists some j such that "$Lj <> Rj$" is *true*

- "*Left < Right*" is *true* if and only if there exists some j such that "$Lj < Rj$" is *true* and for all $i < j$, "$Li = Ri$" is *true*

- "*Left > Right*" is *true* if and only if there exists some j such that "$Lj > Rj$" is *true* and for all $i < j$, "$Li = Ri$" is *true*

---

*We remind the reader that if it evaluates to a table of no rows at all, it is effectively converted to a table of exactly one row, every component of which is null.

■ "*Left <= Right*" is *true* if and only if "*Left < Right*" is *true* or "*Left = Right*" is *true*

■ "*Left >= Right*" is *true* if and only if "*Left > Right*" is *true* or "*Left = Right*" is *true*

Finally, of course, "*Left op Right*" (where *op* stands for any of =, <>, <, <=, >, >=) is *false* if and only if it is not *true*.*

Here is a fairly nontrivial example of the use of a comparison. The query is "Get supplier numbers for suppliers who are located in the same city as supplier S1":

```
SELECT  S.SNO
FROM    S
WHERE   S.CITY = ( SELECT  S.CITY
                   FROM    S
                   WHERE   S.SNO = 'S1' )
```

And here is an example of a comparison involving rows of degree greater than one:

```
( SELECT  S.STATUS, S.CITY
  FROM    S
  WHERE   S.SNO = 'S1' )   =   ( 20, 'London' )
```

Given the sample data of Fig. 2.1, this expression evaluates to *true*.

12.4   BETWEEN AND LIKE CONDITIONS

BETWEEN Conditions

Between-conditions are really nothing more than shorthands. The syntax is

```
row-constructor [ NOT ] BETWEEN
                        row-constructor AND row-constructor
```

The semantics are as follows. First, the between-condition

```
y BETWEEN x AND z
```

is defined to be semantically equivalent to

```
x <= y AND y <= z
```

(note that the range includes the two extreme values). Second, the between-condition

```
y NOT BETWEEN x AND z
```

---

*Perhaps we should point out that this apparently trite observation ceases to be valid when nulls are taken into account. See Chapter 16.

is defined to be semantically equivalent to

```
NOT ( y BETWEEN x AND z )
```

Here is an example of the use of a between-condition:

```
SELECT  P.PNO
FROM    P
WHERE   P.WEIGHT BETWEEN 16 AND 19
```

LIKE Conditions

Like-conditions are intended for simple pattern matching on character strings—i.e., for testing a given character string to see whether it conforms to some prescribed pattern. The syntax is:

```
character-string-expression [ NOT ] LIKE pattern
                                   [ ESCAPE escape ]
```

Here "pattern" is represented by an arbitrary character string expression, and "escape" (if specified) is represented by a character string expression that evaluates to a character string of length one (in other words, to a single character). Here is an example:

```
SELECT  P.PNO, P.PNAME
FROM    P
WHERE   P.PNAME LIKE 'C%'
```

("Get part numbers and names for parts whose names begin with the letter C"). *Result:*

PNO	PNAME
P5	Cam
P6	Cog

In general, provided no ESCAPE clause is specified, characters within "pattern" are interpreted as follows:

- The underscore character (_) stands for *any single character.*

- The percent character (%) stands for *any sequence of n characters* (where *n* can be zero).

- All other characters stand for themselves.*

---

*Note that it is possible that $c1 = c2$ is *true* and yet $c1$ LIKE $c2$ is *false*! E.g., suppose $c1$ and $c2$ are "xyz" (length 3) and "xyz*" (length 4, with the "*" representing a space), respectively, and suppose PAD SPACE applies.

In the example, therefore, the query returns rows from table P for which the PNAME value begins with an upper case C and has any sequence of zero or more characters following that C.

Here are some more examples:

```
ADDRESS LIKE '%Berkeley%'   --   will evaluate to true if
                                 ADDRESS contains the string
                                 "Berkeley" anywhere inside it

SNO LIKE 'S__'              --   will evaluate to true if SNO
                                 is exactly 3 characters long
                                 and the first is "S"

PNAME LIKE '%c___'          --   will evaluate to true if PNAME
                                 is 4 characters long or more
                                 and the last but three is "c"

MYTEXT LIKE '=_%'           --   will evaluate to true if
         ESCAPE '='              MYTEXT begins with an
                                 underscore character (see
                                 below)
```

In this last example, the character "=" has been specified as the escape character, which means that the special interpretation given to the characters "_" and "%" can be disabled, if desired, by preceding such characters with an "=" character.

Finally, the like-condition

```
x NOT LIKE y [ ESCAPE z ]
```

is defined to be semantically equivalent to

```
NOT ( x LIKE y [ ESCAPE z ] )
```

12.5   IN AND MATCH CONDITIONS

IN Conditions

In-conditions come in two different formats, of which the second is effectively just shorthand for a special case of the first (it is provided principally for compatibility with SQL/89), and the first is just a different spelling for an all-or-any-condition (see Section 12.6). From a logical standpoint, therefore, in-conditions are wholly redundant. However, they do display a certain degree of intuitive attractiveness, so in this section we discuss them in a little more detail than they might otherwise be felt to deserve.

Format 1: The first, more general, format of an in-condition is as follows:

```
row-constructor [ NOT ] IN ( table-expression )
```

This expression is defined to be semantically identical to

```
row-constructor =ANY  ( table-expression )
```

if NOT is not specified, and to

```
row-constructor <>ALL ( table-expression )
```

otherwise (see Section 12.6). However, IN and NOT IN are perhaps easier to understand intuitively than =ANY and <>ALL. Here is an example of IN:

```
SELECT DISTINCT S.SNAME
FROM    S
WHERE   S.SNO IN
      ( SELECT SP.SNO
        FROM    SP
        WHERE   SP.PNO = 'P2' )
```

("Get names of suppliers who supply part P2"). *Explanation:* The system evaluates the inner select-expression first (conceptually, at any rate), to yield the set of supplier numbers S1, S2, S3, S4. It then evaluates the outer select-expression to obtain the names of suppliers whose supplier numbers are included in that set.

Here is a more complex example, involving several levels of nesting:

```
SELECT DISTINCT S.SNAME
FROM    S
WHERE   S.SNO IN
      ( SELECT SP.SNO
        FROM    SP
        WHERE   SP.PNO IN
              ( SELECT P.PNO
                FROM    P
                WHERE   P.COLOR = 'Red' ) )
```

("Get supplier names for suppliers who supply at least one red part").

We repeat this latter example with all explicit name qualifiers omitted, in order to make another point:

```
SELECT DISTINCT SNAME
FROM    S
WHERE   SNO IN
      ( SELECT SNO
        FROM    SP
        WHERE   PNO IN
              ( SELECT PNO
                FROM    P
                WHERE   COLOR = 'Red' ) )
```

In this formulation, each unqualified column name is *implicitly* qualified by a range variable name defined (explicitly or implicitly) in the nearest applicable FROM clause. (For full details of how implicit qualifiers are determined, see Chapter 11 or refer to the official standard document. Explicit qualification is to be recommended in practice if there is any possible doubt.)

We show another example of IN in order to introduce yet another concept, namely "outer reference." The query is "Get names of suppliers who supply part

P2" (the same as the first example in this section; the following is another possible formulation of that query).

```
SELECT DISTINCT S.SNAME
FROM    S
WHERE   'P2' IN
        ( SELECT SP.PNO
          FROM    SP
          WHERE   SP.SNO = S.SNO )
```

This example differs from the previous ones in that the inner table expression cannot be evaluated once and for all before the outer one is evaluated, because that inner expression depends on a *variable*, namely S.SNO, whose value changes as the system examines different rows of table S. Conceptually, therefore, evaluation proceeds as follows:

1. The system examines some row of table S, say the row for S1. The variable S.SNO thus currently has the value S1, so the system evaluates the inner table expression

    ```
    ( SELECT SP.PNO
      FROM    SP
      WHERE   SP.SNO = 'S1' )
    ```

    to obtain the set P1, P2, P3, P4, P5, P6. Now it can complete its processing for S1; it will select the SNAME value for S1, namely Smith, if and only if P2 is in this set (which of course it is).

2. Next the system moves on to repeat this kind of processing for another supplier row, and so on, until all rows of table S have been dealt with.

In this example, the reference to "S.SNO" in the inner table expression is an *outer reference*—that is, it is a reference to an (explicit or implicit) range variable that is not defined within the table expression in question, but rather in some "outer" table expression.* *Note:* We have introduced this concept in the context of in-conditions, but of course outer references can appear in other contexts also. Examples of such other contexts are given in Sections 12.7 and 12.8 later.

Here is another example involving an outer reference, this time with explicit range variables. The query is "Get supplier numbers for suppliers who supply at least one part supplied by supplier S2."

```
SELECT DISTINCT SPX.SNO
FROM    SP AS SPX
WHERE   SPX.PNO IN
        ( SELECT SPY.PNO
          FROM    SP AS SPY
          WHERE   SPY.SNO = 'S2' )
```

---

*A parenthesized table expression that includes an outer reference (like the one appearing on the right hand side of the IN condition in the example) is sometimes referred to as a *correlated subquery*.

Result:

SNO
S1
S2
S3
S4

Note: Explicit range variables are not *required* in this example. Here is a formulation of the query without them:

```
SELECT  DISTINCT SP.SNO
FROM    SP
WHERE   SP.PNO IN
      ( SELECT  SP.PNO
        FROM    SP
        WHERE   SP.SNO = 'S2' )
```

Here, however, references to SP in the inner expression do not mean the same thing as references to SP in the outer expression. The two "SP"s are really *two different variables.* Introducing explicit range variables SPX and SPY, as in the previous formulation, makes this fact clearer.

We turn now to the second (and simpler) form of the in-condition. Here is the syntax.

Format 2: The second in-condition format is:

```
scalar-expression [ NOT ] IN ( scalar-expression-commalist )
```

Note that the scalar expression on the left hand side can be regarded as a special case of a row constructor. And, if *rhs* is the commalist of scalar expressions enclosed in parentheses on the right hand side, that entire right hand side is defined to be semantically identical to a parenthesized table expression of the form

```
( VALUES rhs )
```

(observe that this table expression must necessarily evaluate to a table containing a single column). Thus "Format 2" is indeed equivalent to a special case of "Format 1," as stated previously. Here is an example of the use of "Format 2":

```
SELECT P.PNO
FROM   P
WHERE  P.WEIGHT IN ( 12, 16, 17 )
```

Of course, a "Format 2" in-condition can be defined in a more intuitive fashion, as follows: The in-condition

```
x IN ( x1, x2, ..., xn )
```

is defined to be semantically equivalent to

```
x = x1 OR x = x2 OR ... OR x = xn
```

The negated form can also be defined more intuitively, thus: The in-condition

```
x NOT IN ( rhs )
```

is defined to be semantically equivalent to

```
NOT ( x IN ( rhs ) )
```

MATCH Conditions

A match-condition takes the form

```
row-constructor MATCH [ UNIQUE ] ( table-expression )
```

Let *R1* be the row that results from evaluating "row constructor" and let *T* be the table that results from evaluating "table expression." Then, if UNIQUE is specified, the match-condition evaluates to *true* if and only if *T* contains *exactly* one row, *R2* say, such that the comparison condition

```
R1 = R2
```

evaluates to *true*. If UNIQUE is not specified, the match-condition evaluates to *true* if and only if *T* contains *at least* one row, *R2* say, such that the comparison condition

```
R1 = R2
```

evaluates to *true*. Note, therefore, that if UNIQUE is not specified, the match-condition is equivalent to the following in-condition:*

```
row-constructor IN ( table-expression )
```

Here is an example of the use of MATCH:

```
SELECT SP.*
FROM   SP
WHERE  NOT ( SP.SNO MATCH UNIQUE ( SELECT S.SNO FROM S ) )
```

("Get shipments that do not have exactly one matching supplier in the suppliers table"). Such a query might be useful in checking the integrity of the database, because, of course, there should not *be* any such shipments if the database is correct. See Chapter 14 for a detailed discussion of integrity. *Note:* In the example, the UNIQUE is actually redundant (why?).

---

*This equivalence is valid only in the absence of nulls.

12.6 ALL-OR-ANY CONDITIONS

An all-or-any condition has the general form

```
row-constructor
    comparison-operator { ALL | ANY | SOME }
                              ( table-expression )
```

where the comparison operator is any of the usual set (=, <, <=, >, >=, or <>), and SOME is just a different spelling for ANY. In general, an all-or-any condition evaluates to *true* if and only if the corresponding comparison condition without the ALL (respectively ANY) evaluates to *true* for all (respectively any) of the rows in the table represented by the table expression. (*Note:* If that table is empty, the ALL conditions return *true*, the ANY conditions return *false*.) Here is an example ("Get part names for parts whose weight is greater than that of every blue part"):

```
SELECT DISTINCT PX.PNAME
FROM    P AS PX
WHERE   PX.WEIGHT >ALL ( SELECT DISTINCT PY.WEIGHT
                         FROM    P AS PY
                         WHERE   PY.COLOR = 'Blue' )
```

Result:

PNAME
Cog

Explanation: The nested table expression returns the set of weights for blue parts, namely the set 17, 12. The outer SELECT then returns the name of the only part whose weight is greater than every value in this set, namely part P6. In general, of course, the final result might contain any number of part names (including zero).

Note: A word of caution is appropriate here, at least for native English speakers. The fact is, all-or-any conditions are seriously error-prone. A very natural English formulation of the foregoing query would use the word "any" in place of "every," which could easily lead to the (incorrect) use of >ANY instead of >ALL. Analogous criticisms apply to every one of the ANY and ALL operators.

12.7 EXISTS CONDITIONS

Exists-conditions are used to test whether a specified table—usually a derived table—contains at least one row (i.e., to test whether the table in question is nonempty). The syntax is:

```
EXISTS ( table-expression )
```

The condition evaluates to *false* if the table expression evaluates to an empty table, the value *true* otherwise. Here are some examples.

Example 1: Get supplier names for suppliers who supply at least one part.

```
SELECT DISTINCT S.SNAME
FROM    S
WHERE   EXISTS
      ( SELECT *
        FROM    SP
        WHERE   SP.SNO = S.SNO )
```

The exists-condition here is testing for the existence of a row in table SP that satisfies the condition that its SNO component has a value that is equal to the value
represented by the outer reference S.SNO. Points to note:

1. Observe first that the EXISTS argument is a select-expression in which the
   SELECT clause is of the form "SELECT *"; in practice, EXISTS arguments
   are almost always of this form. However, that "*" is almost meaningless—it
   could be replaced by almost anything without affecting the result of evaluating the exists-condition. Partly for this reason, the standard says that in this
   context the "*" does not stand for "all of the columns of the table" but is effectively replaced by an arbitrary literal (e.g., 42).

2. Observe too that the EXISTS argument includes an outer reference
   ("S.SNO"). In practice, EXISTS arguments will almost always include at
   least one such reference.

Example 2: Get supplier names for suppliers who do not supply at least one part.

```
SELECT DISTINCT S.SNAME
FROM    S
WHERE   NOT EXISTS
      ( SELECT *
        FROM    SP
        WHERE   SP.SNO = S.SNO )
```

Example 3: Get supplier names for suppliers who supply all parts.

```
SELECT DISTINCT S.SNAME
FROM    S
WHERE   NOT EXISTS
      ( SELECT *
        FROM    P
        WHERE   NOT EXISTS
            ( SELECT *
              FROM    SP
              WHERE   S.SNO = SP.SNO
              AND     SP.PNO = P.PNO ) )
```

This SQL formulation corresponds to the following informal English statement of
the query: "Get supplier names for suppliers such that there does not exist a part
that they do not supply."

12.8 UNIQUE CONDITIONS

Unique-conditions are used to test that every row within some table is unique (i.e.,
there are no duplicates). The syntax is:

```
UNIQUE ( table-expression )
```

The condition evaluates to *true* if the table expression evaluates to a table in which the rows are all distinct, the value *false* otherwise. Note in particular, therefore, that the condition will always evaluate to *true* if the argument table contains just one row or is empty (i.e., contains no rows at all). It will also necessarily evaluate to *true* if the argument is of the form "SELECT DISTINCT ..." (or any of several other table expression formats that guarantee that there will be no duplicates in the result—for instance, a union without the ALL option).

Here is an example ("Get names of suppliers who supply at least two distinct parts in the same quantity"):

```
SELECT DISTINCT S.SNAME
FROM    S
WHERE   NOT UNIQUE ( SELECT SP.QTY
                     FROM    SP
                     WHERE   SP.SNO = S.SNO )
```

Note: The reader might realize that we are making a virtue of necessity here. We have mentioned the point several times in this book that it is our opinion that tables should *never* be allowed to contain duplicate rows. If that discipline were followed, of course, then UNIQUE would be useless (because it would always evaluate to *true*). We contrived the "realistic" example above in order to illustrate a "realistic" application of a unique-condition, but the reader should not infer from that example that the system *must* permit duplicate rows in order to support queries such as the one discussed. Here, for example, is a formulation of that query that does not involve UNIQUE:

```
SELECT DISTINCT S.SNAME
FROM    S
WHERE   EXISTS ( SELECT * FROM SP SPX WHERE
        EXISTS ( SELECT * FROM SP SPY WHERE
                 SPX.SNO = S.SNO AND
                 SPY.SNO = S.SNO AND
                 SPX.QTY = SPY.QTY AND
                 SPX.PNO <> SPY.PNO ) )
```

("get names of suppliers such that there exist at least two shipments for the supplier in question with the same quantity but different part numbers").

12.9   A FINAL REMARK

We close this chapter by reminding the reader yet again that throughout this chapter we have ignored almost everything to do with nulls. *Every one* of the conditional expression formats we have discussed in the foregoing sections will need to be revisited when we reach Chapter 16.

13

Views

13.1 INTRODUCTION

Throughout our discussion of data manipulation operations in Chapters 9 and 10, we deliberately assumed for simplicity that all named tables were base tables. Now we turn our attention to the special considerations that apply to views (or *viewed tables*, to use the official term).

Recall from Chapter 2 that a view is a named, virtual table; i.e., it is a named table that does not exist in its own right, but looks to the user as if it did. In other words, the data that is visible through a given view "really belongs" to—or, at least, is *derived from*—some underlying base table (or base tables, plural) rather than to the view *per se*. Thus, views are not supported by any separately distinguishable underlying data of their own. Instead, all that happens when a view is created is that the *definition* of that view in terms of other named tables (base tables and/or other views) is remembered by the system in some way (actually by keeping it in the appropriate *schema*—see Chapter 21). Here is an example:

```
CREATE VIEW GOODSUPPS
    AS SELECT S.SNO, S.STATUS, S.CITY
       FROM    S
       WHERE   S.STATUS > 15
```

Note the similarities to the definition of a cursor: As with a cursor definition, a view definition includes a table expression whose purpose is to define a certain "scope" (as we called it in Chapter 2); and, again as with a cursor definition, that table expression is not evaluated at the time of definition, but is instead merely remembered by the system, under the specified name. (Unlike a cursor definition, however, a view definition cannot include any references to parameters or host variables. One reason for this difference is that a view, once created, persists until it is dropped, while a cursor persists only so long as the program that is using it is executing. Another difference is that a view definition cannot include an ORDER BY clause, since views are *tables* and tables, by definition, are unordered.)

Once a view has been created, to the user it is as if there really were a table in the database with the specified name. In the example, it is as if there really were a table called GOODSUPPS, with rows and columns as shown in the unshaded portions (only) of Fig. 13.1.

GOODSUPPS	SNO	SNAME	STATUS	CITY
	S1	Smith	20	London
	S2	Jones	10	Paris
	S3	Blake	30	Paris
	S4	Clark	20	London
	S5	Adams	30	Athens

Fig. 13.1   GOODSUPPS as a view of base table S
(unshaded portions only)

Here is an example of a table expression involving GOODSUPPS:

```
SELECT GOODSUPPS.*
FROM    GOODSUPPS
WHERE   GOODSUPPS.CITY <> 'London'
```

The system will translate this expression, involving the view GOODSUPPS, into an equivalent expression involving the underlying base table S instead. The translation is done by "merging" the specified expression with the view-defining expression that was saved in the schema—which means, loosely, replacing references to the view *name* by the corresponding view *definition*. More precisely, the process involves replacing the clause "FROM GOODSUPPS" by a clause of the form "FROM (exp) AS GOODSUPPS," where *exp* is the defining expression for the view. In the example, therefore, the result of the translation process is an expression that looks something like this:

```
SELECT GOODSUPPS.*
FROM    ( SELECT  S.SNO, S.STATUS, S.CITY
          FROM    S
          WHERE   S.STATUS > 15 ) AS GOODSUPPS
WHERE   GOODSUPPS.CITY <> 'London'
```

And this expression can now be evaluated in the usual way, since it references only "real" (base) tables, not virtual ones.

The translation process just illustrated—or something very like it, at any rate—applies to update operations also. For example, the UPDATE operation

```
UPDATE GOODSUPPS
SET    CITY = 'New York'
WHERE  GOODSUPPS.CITY = 'Paris'
```

effectively translates to:

```
UPDATE S
SET    CITY = 'New York'
WHERE  S.STATUS > 15
AND    S.CITY = 'Paris'
```

And, of course, INSERT and DELETE operations are handled in the same general way. For example, the INSERT operation

```
INSERT
INTO   GOODSUPPS ( SNO, STATUS, CITY )
VALUES ( 'S6', 25, 'Madrid' )
```

effectively translates to:

```
INSERT
INTO   S ( SNO, SNAME, STATUS, CITY )
VALUES ( 'S6', DEFAULT, 25, 'Madrid' )
```

Note that SNAME, which is excluded from the GOODSUPPS view, will necessarily be set to the applicable default value in any rows inserted via that view (of course, it is an error if that column has no default). Likewise, the DELETE operation

```
DELETE
FROM   GOODSUPPS
WHERE  GOODSUPPS.CITY = 'New York'
```

effectively translates to:

```
DELETE
FROM   S
WHERE  S.STATUS > 15
AND    S.CITY = 'New York'
```

As we have seen, views are defined by means of the statement CREATE VIEW. There is also a DROP VIEW statement, for dropping an existing view (note, however, that there is no ALTER VIEW statement). Like CREATE DOMAIN and CREATE TABLE, CREATE VIEW can be executed as an independent operation in its own right, or it can be executed as a "schema element" within a CREATE SCHEMA statement; DROP VIEW, however, like DROP DOMAIN and DROP TABLE, must be executed as an independent operation— it cannot appear within a CREATE SCHEMA statement. Note, however, that every view does belong to some schema, even if the corresponding CREATE statement is executed "independently," and creating a new view ("independently" or otherwise), or dropping an existing view (necessarily "independently"), thus has the effect—among other things—of updating the relevant schema in the appropriate manner.

13.2   DATA DEFINITION OPERATIONS

CREATE VIEW

The general syntax of CREATE VIEW is:

```
view-definition
    ::=    CREATE VIEW view [ ( column-commalist ) ]
                AS table-expression
                    [ WITH [ CASCADED | LOCAL ] CHECK OPTION ]
```

Here "view" is the name of the new view,* the "column commalist" (if specified) lists the unqualified names of the columns of the view, the table expression defines the scope of the view, and the optional WITH ... CHECK OPTION clause is explained in Section 13.4, later. See Examples 1–4 below for a discussion of what it means for the commalist of column names to be omitted. *Note:* The AS in CREATE VIEW is (for a change) *not* a mere noiseword and must not be omitted.

As noted in Section 13.1, the table expression in CREATE VIEW cannot include any parameter or host variable references. It also cannot include any references, either direct or indirect, to the name of the view currently being defined; in other words, no recursion is permitted, either direct or indirect, among view definitions. Further, no column in the result of evaluating the table expression is allowed to have a "coercibility" property of **no collating sequence** (see Chapter 19 for an explanation of this point).

Here then are some examples of CREATE VIEW:

```
1. CREATE VIEW REDPARTS ( PNO, PNAME, WEIGHT, CITY )
        AS SELECT P.PNO, P.PNAME, P.WEIGHT, P.CITY
           FROM    P
           WHERE   P.COLOR = 'Red'
```

The effect of this statement is to create a new view called REDPARTS, with four columns called PNO, PNAME, WEIGHT, and CITY, corresponding respectively to the four columns PNO, PNAME, WEIGHT, and CITY of the underlying table P. *Note:* For the sake of the example, we have specified column names for the newly created view explicitly, even though those exact same names would otherwise have been inherited from the underlying table anyway. The general rules are as follows:

---

*If the name is qualified by a schema name and the CREATE VIEW appears within the context of a CREATE SCHEMA statement, then that schema name must identify the schema that would have been assumed by default anyway, *viz.* the schema being created (see Chapter 4, Section 4.3).

■ First, every column of the view must indeed have a proper, user-known column name that is unique within the view.

■ Second, the view will inherit its column names from the underlying table (where by "underlying table" we mean the table that results from the evaluation of the table expression) *unless* new column names are specified explicitly.

Thus, explicit specification of column names is *required* only if some column of the underlying table has a name that is implementation-dependent (see Chapter 11, Section 11.7), and/or two columns of that underlying table have the same name. (Of course, such explicit specification is never wrong, even when it is not actually required.) Note, however, that if explicit specification is used, explicit names must be specified for *all* columns of the view, even if some of those columns would otherwise have had an obvious inherited name.

```
2. CREATE VIEW LREDPARTS
        AS SELECT REDPARTS.PNO, REDPARTS.WEIGHT
           FROM    REDPARTS
           WHERE   REDPARTS.CITY = 'London'
```

It is perfectly possible to define a view in terms of other views, as this example illustrates. The column names for LREDPARTS (inherited from REDPARTS) are PNO and WEIGHT.

```
3. CREATE VIEW CITYPAIRS ( SCITY, PCITY )
        AS SELECT DISTINCT S.CITY, P.CITY
           FROM    S, SP, P
           WHERE   S.SNO = SP.SNO
           AND     SP.PNO = P.PNO
```

The meaning of this view is as follows: A pair of city names (x,y) will appear in the view if and only if a supplier located in city x supplies a part stored in city y. For example, supplier S1 supplies part P1; supplier S1 is located in London and part P1 is stored in London; and so the pair (London,London) appears in the view. Notice that the definition of this view involves a join (actually a "3-way join"), so that this is an example of a view that is derived from several underlying base tables. Note also that the names of the two columns of the result of evaluating the table expression are both CITY, and hence that new column names *must* be specified explicitly in this example.

Note: The following definition would have produced the same effect:

```
CREATE VIEW CITYPAIRS
        AS SELECT DISTINCT S.CITY AS SCITY, P.CITY AS PCITY
           FROM    S, SP, P
           WHERE   S.SNO = SP.SNO
           AND     SP.PNO = P.PNO
```

(compare Example 6 in Chapter 11, Section 11.6, subsection "Examples"). In fact, the ability to specify new column names in the CREATE VIEW clause is logically unnecessary (another redundant feature, in fact); it is provided primarily for compatibility with SQL/89, which did not support the AS clause on select-items.

```
4. CREATE VIEW PQ
       AS SELECT SP.PNO, SUM ( SP.QTY ) AS TOTQTY
          FROM    SP
          GROUP   BY SP.PNO
```

The column names for this view are PNO and TOTQTY. Notice that, although this view is derived from a single underlying base table, it is not just a simple row-and-column subset of that base table—unlike the views REDPARTS and GOODSUPPS shown earlier.* Rather, it is a kind of *statistical summary* of that underlying table.

DROP VIEW

An existing view can be dropped by means of DROP VIEW—syntax:

```
DROP VIEW view { RESTRICT | CASCADE }
```

If RESTRICT is specified, then (a) if "view" is referenced in any other view definition or in an integrity constraint (see Chapter 14), the DROP VIEW will fail; (b) otherwise it will succeed, and the specified view will be dropped. If CASCADE is specified, the DROP VIEW will always succeed, and any referencing views and integrity constraints will automatically be dropped too (in the case of referencing views, that implied DROP will also include the CASCADE option).

13.3   DATA MANIPULATION OPERATIONS

We have already explained in outline (in Section 13.1) how retrieval operations on a view are translated into equivalent operations on the underlying base table(s). In the case of retrieval operations, that translation process is reasonably straightforward and works perfectly well.† In the case of update operations, however, the situation is more complex, as we will see.

The basic point is that *not all views are updatable.* We demonstrate this point by means of the two views GOODSUPPS and CITYPAIRS from Sections 13.1 and 13.2 respectively. For convenience we repeat their definitions below:

---

*Note that we explicitly do not say here that view LREDPARTS is a row-and-column subset of its underlying base table. Actually LREDPARTS *is* a row-and-column subset of its underlying base table (namely, base table P), but only because (a) it is a row-and-column subset of its underlying table REDPARTS, and (b) that underlying table in turn is a row-and-column subset of *its* underlying table P.

†It is worth mentioning that this statement was not true for SQL/89. Furthermore, it is still not true for certain commercial SQL products at the time of writing; i.e., certain retrievals on certain views using certain products will still be found to fail in surprising ways.

```
CREATE VIEW GOODSUPPS
     AS SELECT S.SNO, S.STATUS, S.CITY
        FROM   S
        WHERE  S.STATUS > 15

CREATE VIEW CITYPAIRS
     AS SELECT DISTINCT S.CITY AS SCITY, P.CITY AS PCITY
        FROM   S, SP, P
        WHERE  S.SNO = SP.SNO
        AND    SP.PNO = P.PNO
```

Of these two views, GOODSUPPS is logically updatable, while CITYPAIRS is logically not. It is instructive to examine why this is so.* In the case of GOODSUPPS:

- We can INSERT a new row into the view—say the row (S6,40,Rome)—by actually inserting the corresponding row (S6,DEFAULT,40,Rome) into the underlying base table.

- We can DELETE an existing row from the view—say the row (S1,20,London)— by actually deleting the corresponding row (S1,Smith,20,London) from the underlying base table.

- We can UPDATE an existing value in the view—say the CITY value for supplier S1 (namely London), to change it to Rome—by actually making that change in the corresponding row in the underlying base table.

Now consider the view CITYPAIRS. Suppose we tried to insert the row (Paris,Oslo) into that view. What could such an INSERT possibly signify?—i.e., what updates (INSERTs or otherwise) on the underlying data could such an INSERT possibly correspond to? We might try saying that "Paris" means the supplier is either S2 or S3, so that we need to insert a row into base table SP for either S2 or S3—but which one? And what about that "Oslo"? There are currently *no* parts in Oslo, so we would have to insert a row into base table P as well—but we have no part number for that row. Thus we see that:

- First, the original INSERT probably cannot be supported at all, because column P.PNO almost certainly does not have a default.

- Second, even if column P.PNO does have a default, there is still no *unique* set of updates on the underlying tables that has precisely the desired effect on view CITYPAIRS.

In other words, the original INSERT is an intrinsically unsupportable operation.

---

*The reader is warned that the analysis that follows is not particularly rigorous or deep (though it is correct as far as it goes). Recent investigations have shown that many more views are logically updatable than was previously thought. For further discussion, see "Updating Union, Intersection, and Difference Views" and "Updating Joins and Other Views," both by C. J. Date and David McGoveran, in *Database Programming & Design 7,* No. 6 (June 1994) and No. 8 (August 1994), republished in C. J. Date, *Relational Database Writings 1991–1994* (Addison-Wesley, 1995).

Similar arguments can be made to show that UPDATE and DELETE operations are also intrinsically not supportable on this view (in general). Thus we see that some views are inherently updatable, whereas others are inherently not. *Note the word "inherently" here.* It is not just a question of some systems being able to support certain updates while others cannot. *No* system can consistently support updates such as the foregoing INSERT on a view such as CITYPAIRS unaided (by "unaided" here, we mean "without help from some human user").

Turning now to SQL specifically: In this book, of course, we are concerned not so much with what is theoretically possible, but rather with what SQL will allow (which is a very different thing!). We therefore introduce the term *SQL-updatable* (not a standard term): We say that a view is SQL-updatable—meaning that it is updatable so far as SQL is concerned—if and only if all of the following conditions 1-8 below hold:*

1. The table expression that defines the scope of the view is either a select-expression or an expression of the form "TABLE table." As explained in Chapter 11, however, an expression of this latter form is effectively equivalent to a certain select-expression anyway; thus, we can consider the table expression that defines the scope of the view just to *be* a select-expression without loss of generality.

2. The SELECT clause of that select-expression does not include the key word DISTINCT.

3. Every select-item in that SELECT clause (after any necessary expansion of "asterisk-style" select-items) consists of a possibly qualified column name (optionally accompanied by an AS clause), representing a simple direct reference to a column of the underlying table (see paragraph 5 below).

4. The FROM clause of that select-expression contains exactly one table reference.

5. That table reference identifies either a base table or an SQL-updatable view. *Note:* From this point forward, we will refer to the table identified by that table reference as *the* (single) underlying table on which the SQL-updatable view in question is immediately defined.

6. That select-expression does not include a WHERE clause that includes a nested table expression that includes a FROM clause that includes a reference to the same table as is referenced in the FROM clause mentioned in paragraph 4 above.

---

*It might help to point out that conditions 1–8 effectively mean that a view is SQL-updatable if and only if it boils down to being a row-and-column subset of a single underlying base table—like views GOODSUPPS, REDPARTS, and LREDPARTS from Sections 13.1 and 13.2. In other words, a view is SQL-updatable (loosely speaking) if it is defined to be a direct row-and-column subset of some base table or a direct row-and-column subset of some other SQL-updatable view.

7. That select-expression does not include a GROUP BY clause.

8. That select-expression does not include a HAVING clause.

Finally, to state the obvious (well, maybe it is not so obvious): The operations INSERT, UPDATE, and DELETE can be applied to a given view if and only if that view is SQL-updatable as defined above. Observe in particular that UPDATE either *can* or *cannot* be applied to a given view; it is not possible to have some columns updatable and others not within the same view (although some commercial products do support such a capability). Observe too that updatability is "all or nothing," in the sense that *either* all three of INSERT, UPDATE, or DELETE can be applied to a given view *or* none of them can; it is not possible for (e.g.) DELETE to be applicable but INSERT not (although, again, some commercial products do go beyond the standard in this regard).

Note: It has to be said that the list of conditions stated above is excessively stringent. In fact, *every single one* of them is actually stronger than is logically necessary. However, this is not the place to go into details; as already mentioned, we are concerned in this book not so much with what is logically possible, but rather with what SQL allows.

One final point: Note that the fact that a given view is SQL-updatable does *not* mean that all updates against that view will necessarily succeed. For one thing, there is always the question of integrity constraints to be taken into account (see Chapter 14). For another, a view that omits a column of the underlying base table that has no default will certainly not be able to support INSERT operations (as we have already seen).

13.4 THE CHECK OPTION

The topic of this section, the check option, also has to do with view updating; however, the topic is sufficiently complex that it seems advisable to devote a separate section to it.* *Note:* We are thus concerned in this section with SQL-updatable views only. Throughout what follows, therefore, we will just assume for simplicity that all views mentioned are SQL-updatable. Indeed, the check option can be specified for a given view only if the view in question is SQL-updatable.

First we consider the case of a view that is defined directly in terms of a base table. Consider view GOODSUPPS once again (which is defined directly in terms of base table S). As explained in Section 13.3, this view certainly is SQL-updatable. But consider the following UPDATE:

---

*For further elaboration of the ideas underlying the discussion that follows, the reader is referred to the chapter "Without Check Option" in C. J. Date and Hugh Darwen, *Relational Database Writings 1989–1991* (Addison-Wesley, 1992), also the two articles on view updating mentioned in an earlier footnote.

```
UPDATE GOODSUPPS
SET    STATUS = 10
WHERE  GOODSUPPS.SNO = 'S1'
```

Should this UPDATE be accepted? If it is, it will have the effect of removing the row for supplier S1 from the view, since that row will no longer satisfy the view-defining condition ("STATUS > 15"). Likewise, the INSERT operation

```
INSERT
INTO    GOODSUPPS ( SNO, STATUS, CITY )
VALUES ( 'S8', 7, 'Stockholm' )
```

(if accepted) will create a new supplier row, but that row will instantly vanish from the view.

The check option is designed to avoid such counterintuitive behavior. If the clause

```
WITH CHECK OPTION
```

is included in the definition of a view, then all INSERTs and UPDATEs on that view will be checked to ensure that the newly INSERTed or UPDATEd rows do indeed satisfy the view-defining condition. If they do not, the update will be rejected. Thus, if the definition of view GOODSUPPS had included the check option, the two update operations shown above would both have been rejected.

Note: As we will see in the next subsection, the clause WITH CHECK OPTION can optionally include either a CASCADED or a LOCAL specification (CASCADED is assumed if neither is specified). For the case under discussion however—namely, the case of a view defined directly in terms of a base table— the CASCADED *vs.* LOCAL distinction is irrelevant.

We remark that, logically speaking, the view-defining condition for a given view is actually an *integrity constraint* on that view (though SQL does not refer to it as such). It follows that, again logically speaking, the check option should *always* be specified for an SQL-updatable view. Unfortunately, however, SQL does not enforce this rule.

Views on Views

To summarize the situation so far:

- Updates on a base table are of course checked against the integrity constraints that apply to that base table (see Chapter 14).

- Updates on a view derived directly from a base table will *a fortiori* be checked against the integrity constraints that apply to that base table. If the check option is specified for the view in question, updates on that view will additionally be checked against the integrity constraint that is the defining condition for the view, as we have just seen.

But what about a view that is derived directly, not from a base table, but from another view? (Note that such a view must be derived from *just one* directly underlying view, since by definition we are concerned with SQL-updatable views only.) In other words, if view *V2* is defined in terms of view *V1*, thus—

```
CREATE VIEW V2
     AS SELECT ...
        FROM   V1
        WHERE  ...
      [ WITH [ CASCADED | LOCAL ] CHECK OPTION ]
```

—what integrity constraints will be checked when updates are attempted on view *V2*? The answer to this question depends on what is specified for view *V2*:

1. If *V2* has no check option, then updates on *V2* are checked against all of the integrity constraints that are checked for updates on *V1*, but *not* against the defining condition for *V2*.

2. If *V2* has a LOCAL check option, then again updates on *V2* are checked against all of the integrity constraints that are checked for updates on *V1, and* against the integrity constraint that is the defining condition for *V2*.

3. If *V2* has a CASCADED check option, then updates on *V2* are checked against all of the integrity constraints that would be checked for updates on *V1* if *V1* also had a CASCADED check option (regardless of whether it actually does) *and* against the integrity constraint that is the defining condition for *V2*. In other words, updates on *V2* are checked against the integrity constraints for the underlying base table *and* against the defining condition for every view between that base table and *V2* itself *and* against the defining condition for *V2* itself.

In what follows, we will refer to these three possibilities as *Check Option Rules 1, 2, and 3*. In order to illustrate the effects of these rules, we modify our GOODSUPPS example, as follows. First, we define another view over base table S:

```
CREATE VIEW MEDSUPPS
     AS SELECT S.SNO, S.STATUS, S.CITY
        FROM   S
        WHERE  S.STATUS < 25
      [ WITH [ CASCADED | LOCAL ] CHECK OPTION ]
```

With our usual sample data, view MEDSUPPS ("medium suppliers") will include rows for suppliers S1, S2, and S4 (with status 20, 10, and 20, respectively), and no others. *Note:* We show the check option in square brackets, and the CASCADED *vs.* LOCAL option likewise, simply to remind readers of the degree of optionality involved (and similarly for the redefined version of view GOODSUPPS— see below).

Now we redefine view GOODSUPPS in terms of MEDSUPPS instead of directly in terms of base table S:

```
CREATE VIEW GOODSUPPS
    AS SELECT MEDSUPPS.SNO, MEDSUPPS.STATUS, MEDSUPPS.CITY
       FROM    MEDSUPPS
       WHERE   MEDSUPPS.STATUS > 15
     [ WITH [ CASCADED | LOCAL ] CHECK OPTION ]
```

This view will include rows for suppliers S1 and S4 only (both with status 20). Fig. 13.2 illustrates the situation at this point.

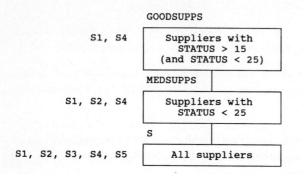

Fig. 13.2 Views GOODSUPPS and MEDSUPPS and base table S

Now the question is: What happens if either or both of these views has some form of check option specified? There are obviously nine possible cases to consider, as indicated by the following table:

	none	LOCAL	CASCADED	◄— MEDSUPPS
none	Case 1	Case 2	Case 3	
LOCAL	Case 4	Case 5	Case 6	
CASCADED	Case 7	Case 8	Case 9	

▲
|
GOODSUPPS

We now proceed to consider these nine cases in detail. To fix our ideas, we consider specifically what happens with respect to the following two UPDATE operations ("Update 1" and "Update 2") in each case:

```
UPDATE GOODSUPPS                              -- Update 1
SET    STATUS = GOODSUPPS.STATUS + 20

UPDATE GOODSUPPS                              -- Update 2
SET    STATUS = GOODSUPPS.STATUS - 20
```

Note: For the sake of the discussion that follows we assume, perhaps a little unrealistically, that the user does not know that all suppliers visible in GOODSUPPS also have STATUS < 25. Certainly this latter fact is not explicit in the GOODSUPPS definition.

Case 1: Neither view has the check option.

In this case, Update 1 has the astonishing effect that *table GOODSUPPS becomes empty!*—suppliers S1 and S4 will each now have status 40, and thus will no longer appear in view MEDSUPPS, and hence *a fortiori* will no longer appear in view GOODSUPPS either. Note very carefully the counterintuitive nature of this result. The user of view GOODSUPPS believes, correctly, that all suppliers visible in that view have STATUS > 15, and surely has a right to expect that *increasing* those STATUS values cannot possibly violate that condition, and so cannot possibly have any strange side effects.

Update 2 also has the effect that table GOODSUPPS becomes empty (though the result is arguably a little less surprising in this case)—suppliers S1 and S4 will each now have status 0, and thus will no longer satisfy the defining condition for view GOODSUPPS (though they will still appear in MEDSUPPS).

Case 2: MEDSUPPS has a LOCAL check option, GOODSUPPS has no check option.

Clearly, the way to avoid the anomalous behavior described under Case 1 for Update 1 is to have the system check updates on GOODSUPPS against the defining condition for MEDSUPPS. Suppose, therefore, that we specify a LOCAL check option for MEDSUPPS (but not for GOODSUPPS, since the defining condition for GOODSUPPS is not an issue, for the moment). The question now is: Will that MEDSUPPS check option be inherited by GOODSUPPS?—i.e., will it apply to updates on GOODSUPPS, as well as to updates on MEDSUPPS directly? By virtue of Check Option Rules 1 and 2 taken together, we see that the answer to this question is *yes* (and so Update 1 is rejected, as desired).

Note, however, that from the perspective of the GOODSUPPS user, Update 1 certainly *looks* reasonable; there is no way it can violate the GOODSUPPS defining condition (STATUS > 15). Yet it fails! Moreover, the user will receive diagnostic information from the system to the effect that there has been a check option violation—even though, so far as the user is concerned, there *is* no check option. Thus, it could be argued that "encapsulation" (of a kind) has been violated: The user cannot think in terms of view GOODSUPPS in isolation, but has to have some awareness of the definition of that view in terms of its underlying table (and similarly for that table in turn, if that table in turn is another view, and so on, recursively—assuming, of course, that all of those views also have a check option).

Anyway, to repeat: Specifying a LOCAL check option for MEDSUPPS does seem to solve the Update 1 problem. But does it really? Suppose MEDSUPPS were defined in terms of another view, *V* say (instead of directly in terms of base table S); suppose further that view *V* had no check option. Then updates on GOODSUPPS would *not* be checked against the defining condition for view *V*. For example, if MEDSUPPS were defined simply as SELECT * FROM *V* and *V* were defined as

```
SELECT  S.SNO, S.STATUS, S.CITY
FROM    S
WHERE   S.STATUS < 25
```

(without a check option, but otherwise just like our original MEDSUPPS), then the LOCAL check option on MEDSUPPS would be useless; Update 1 on GOODSUPPS would not be checked against the condition STATUS < 25, and the surprising result would still occur.

Note finally that Update 2 is certainly *not* rejected under Case 2. So Case 2 is far from being a perfect solution to our overall problem (namely, the problem of ensuring that all updates are treated correctly in all circumstances).

Case 3: MEDSUPPS has a CASCADED check option, GOODSUPPS has no check option.

Here again updates on GOODSUPPS will be checked against the defining condition for MEDSUPPS. They will *also* be checked against the defining condition for the table underlying MEDSUPPS, if that table in turn is another view (and so on, recursively, regardless of whether those views have a check option in turn), by virtue of Check Option Rules 1 and 3 taken together. *Net effect:* Update 1 is treated correctly. However, Update 2 is not.

Case 4: MEDSUPPS has no check option, GOODSUPPS has a LOCAL check option.

This case deals correctly with Update 2 but not Update 1. Further, if MEDSUPPS were defined on top of another view *V* (instead of base table S), we would be in a Case 1, 2, or 3 situation (*q.v.*), with *V* playing the role of MEDSUPPS and MEDSUPPS playing the role of GOODSUPPS.

The remaining five cases do all deal correctly with both Update 1 and Update 2. However, they are not all equally acceptable solutions to the overall problem— which is, to repeat, the problem of ensuring that all updates are treated correctly in all circumstances.

Case 5: MEDSUPPS and GOODSUPPS both have a LOCAL check option.

Here, if another view *V* were to be defined on top of GOODSUPPS, we could be in a Case 2 or 8 situation (*q.v.*), with *V* playing the role of GOODSUPPS and GOODSUPPS playing the role of MEDSUPPS.

Case 6: MEDSUPPS has a CASCADED check option, GOODSUPPS has a LOCAL check option.

Here, if another view *V* were to be defined on top of GOODSUPPS, we would be in a Case 2, 5, or 8 situation (*q.v.*), with *V* playing the role of GOODSUPPS and GOODSUPPS playing the role of MEDSUPPS.

Case 7: MEDSUPPS has no check option, GOODSUPPS has a CASCADED check option.

Here, if MEDSUPPS were defined on top of another view *V*, we could be in a Case 1 or 4 situation (*q.v.*), with *V* playing the role of MEDSUPPS and MEDSUPPS playing the role of GOODSUPPS.

Case 8: MEDSUPPS has a LOCAL check option, GOODSUPPS has a CASCADED check option.

Here, if MEDSUPPS were defined on top of another view *V*, we would be back in a Case 4, 5, or 6 situation (*q.v.*), with *V* playing the role of MEDSUPPS and MEDSUPPS playing the role of GOODSUPPS.

Case 9: MEDSUPPS and GOODSUPPS both have a CASCADED check option.

This case deals correctly with all updates, and continues to do so if additional views are introduced (e.g.) on top of GOODSUPPS or between GOODSUPPS and MEDSUPPS, provided those additional views also have the CASCADED check option.

We can summarize the foregoing analysis as follows. First, if all views do have a check option, then all updates will be handled correctly, and it makes no difference whether those check options are specified as LOCAL or CASCADED or any mixture. But if any view is permitted to have no check option at all, then (in general) certain updates will be treated incorrectly; further, more updates will be treated incorrectly if some views have only a LOCAL check option instead of a CASCADED one (again in general). Thus, we recommend that all views—all SQL-updatable views, that is—be defined with the CASCADED check option.

PART **IV**

DATA CONTROL

This part of the book consists of two chapters, one on integrity and one on security. The integrity chapter discusses the various kinds of *integrity constraints* supported by SQL, with special attention to foreign key ("referential") constraints. The security chapter discusses the various *privileges* that users (more precisely, "authorization IDs") must possess in order to perform SQL operations.

14

Integrity

14.1 INTRODUCTION

SQL provides a variety of methods for defining *integrity constraints* that are to be enforced by the SQL-implementation. An integrity constraint (*constraint* for short) is basically just a conditional expression—see Chapter 12—that is required not to evaluate to *false*. Indeed, some constraints are actually specified in terms of the conditional expression syntax of Chapter 12, as we will see; others, by contrast, are not, but instead use a special syntax of their own (though that special syntax is defined to be just shorthand for an equivalent formulation in terms of conditional expressions). Here is a simple example ("total shipment quantity must be less than 500,000"):

```
CREATE ASSERTION IC35
      CHECK ( ( SELECT SUM ( SP.QTY ) FROM SP ) < 500000 )
```

Note: As this example suggests, certain constraints—specifically, those that we will be referring to in this chapter as *general* constraints (see below, also Section 14.3)—are referred to in the standard not as constraints *per se* but rather as *assertions*. We prefer our own term.

When a user attempts to create a new constraint, the system checks that the constraint is satisfied by all existing data in the database. If it is not, the new constraint cannot be accepted; otherwise, the constraint *is* accepted, and is enforced from that point forward (meaning that any attempt to perform an update that would violate the constraint will henceforth be rejected), until such time as the constraint is dropped.

All constraints have a *constraint name*; if the user does not specify such a name explicitly, the system will implicitly provide an implementation-dependent one anyway. In the example above, "IC35" ("integrity constraint number 35") is the constraint name. (In fact, explicit constraint names *must* be specified in the case of general constraints, which is what constraint IC35 is.) If an update is attempted that would violate some constraint if it were actually executed, the name of that constraint will be made available to the user as part of the relevant diagnostic information (see Chapter 22).

For the purposes of this chapter, we divide integrity constraints into the following broad categories:

1. domain constraints
2. general constraints
3. base table constraints (including "column constraints")

We explain these categories very briefly as follows:

1. *Domain constraints* are constraints that are associated with a specific domain, and apply to every column (in every base table) that is defined on that domain.*
2. *General constraints* are constraints that apply to arbitrary combinations of columns in arbitrary combinations of base tables.
3. *Base table constraints* are constraints that are associated with some specific base table (the precise meaning of "associated with" here will be explained in Section 14.4). "Column constraints" are syntactic shorthands for certain common base table constraints.

The plan of the chapter is as follows. Following this introductory section, Section 14.2 discusses domain constraints, Section 14.3 general constraints, and Section 14.4 base table constraints (including column constraints). Section 14.5 then deals with a very important special case of base table constraints, namely *foreign key* constraints. Finally, Section 14.6 addresses the question of when integrity checking is actually performed; prior to that point, we will simply assume where necessary that such checking is performed whenever any update operation is attempted.

---

*They also apply to attempts to CAST a specified scalar value to the data type underlying a specified domain. We do not discuss this case further in this chapter. See Chapter 7, Section 7.4.

Note: Integrity constraints are subject to certain syntactic restrictions which we might as well get out of the way here. Let the conditional expression contained within (or effectively implied by) some given constraint be *C*. Then:

1. If *C* includes an aggregate function reference, that reference must be contained within a subquery (except perhaps in the context of a general constraint—see Appendix D).

2. *C* cannot include any references to parameters or host variables (because, of course, constraints are independent of specific applications).

3. *C* cannot include any references to any of the niladic functions USER, CURRENT_USER, SESSION_USER, SYSTEM_USER, CURRENT_DATE, CURRENT_TIME, or CURRENT_TIMESTAMP (refer to Chapters 15 and 17 for detailed discussion of these functions). The rationale for this restriction is that such references will return different values on different invocations, in general.

4. *C* must not be "possibly nondeterministic." See Chapter 19, Section 19.7, subsection "Indeterminate Table Expressions," for an explanation of this term.

5. There are also some restrictions having to do with *temporary tables*. See Chapter 18 for details.

A couple of final introductory remarks:

1. It is sometimes conceptually useful to regard the entire database as being subject to just one giant integrity constraint, which is the conjunction ("logical AND") of all of the individually specified constraints. In particular, note that every base table is required to satisfy, not only all of the general and base table constraints that apply to that table directly, but also all of the domain constraints that apply to columns within that table.

2. For completeness, we remind the reader that there are two additional features of the standard that can be regarded as integrity features of a kind, namely *data type checking* and *the check option:*

   - First, SQL will reject any attempt to violate data type specifications on INSERT or UPDATE—e.g., an attempt to insert a string value into a column defined as numeric.

   - Second, SQL will reject any attempt to perform an INSERT or UPDATE on a view that violates the defining condition for that view (and possibly for views on which that view is defined), so long as an appropriate check option is in effect. Refer to Chapter 13 for a detailed discussion of the check option.

14.2   DOMAIN CONSTRAINTS

Domain constraints can be initially specified by means of CREATE DOMAIN, and can be added to or dropped from an existing domain by means of ALTER DOMAIN. However, it is perhaps surprising to find that domain constraints are *not* dropped—at least, not exactly—by DROP DOMAIN, as we will see.

CREATE DOMAIN

To repeat from Chapter 8, the syntax of a domain definition is as follows:

```
domain-definition
    ::=    CREATE DOMAIN domain [ AS ] data-type
                        [ default-definition ]
                        [ domain-constraint-definition-list ]
```

A "domain constraint definition" in turn looks like this:

```
[ CONSTRAINT constraint ] CHECK ( conditional-expression )
```

Here the optional specification "CONSTRAINT constraint" defines a name for the new constraint,* and "conditional expression" defines the constraint *per se*. If the specification "CONSTRAINT constraint" is omitted, the constraint is given an implementation-dependent name. (Note that the syntax is indeed "CONSTRAINT constraint," whereas in a general constraint—see Section 14.3 or the example in Section 14.1—it is "ASSERTION constraint.") *Note:* Circular references are not allowed; that is, domain constraints must not be defined, either directly or indirectly, in terms of the domain to which they apply. Thus, for example, a given domain constraint must not refer to a base table that includes a column that is defined on the domain to which the constraint in question applies. See Appendix D for further discussion.

Here is an example of a domain definition that includes a domain constraint:

```
CREATE DOMAIN CITIES CHAR(15)
        DEFAULT '???'
        CONSTRAINT ICCITIES
           CHECK ( VALUE IN ( 'Athens', 'Dublin', 'London',
                              'Madrid', 'New York', 'Oslo',
                              'Paris', 'Rome', 'Stockholm',
                              '???' ) )
```

---

*If the name is qualified by a schema name and the constraint definition appears within the context of a CREATE SCHEMA statement, then that schema name must identify the schema that would have been assumed by default anyway, *viz.* the schema being created (see Chapter 4, Section 4.3).

Suppose some user attempts (via an INSERT or UPDATE operation) to place a scalar value *v* into some column defined on domain *D*. Then:

- Let *DC* be a domain constraint for *D*, and let *CE* be the conditional expression specified in *DC*.

- Let *ce* be the conditional expression obtained by replacing every occurrence of the special symbol VALUE in *CE* by the value *v*.

- If *ce* evaluates to *false*, then the attempted INSERT or UPDATE is considered to violate the constraint *DC*, and so is rejected.

Note: The special symbol VALUE can be used in a domain constraint *and nowhere else.** It stands for the scalar value in question, i.e., the value for which the constraint is to be checked (*v* in the foregoing discussion). VALUE inherits its data type—CHAR(15) in the example—from the applicable domain.

It is perhaps worth pointing out that, somewhat surprisingly, NOT NULL is *not* a valid domain constraint (though it is a valid column constraint, as we will see in Section 14.4). Thus, for example, the following is *** *ILLEGAL* ***:

```
CREATE DOMAIN CITIES CHAR(15) NOT NULL -- *** ILLEGAL *** !!!
```

The correct way to specify that nulls are not allowed for a given domain is as illustrated by the following example:

```
CREATE DOMAIN CITIES CHAR(15)
            CHECK ( VALUE IS NOT NULL )
```

Note, incidentally, that the constraint in this example has no user-specified name.

ALTER DOMAIN

Recall from Chapter 8 that ALTER DOMAIN supports "domain constraint alteration actions" of two possible forms:

```
domain-constraint-alteration-action
    ::=    ADD domain-constraint-definition
         | DROP CONSTRAINT constraint
```

ADD permits a new constraint to be specified for an existing domain (the new constraint does not replace any existing constraints for the domain in question but is logically ANDed on to them). DROP permits an existing domain constraint to be removed.

---

*The same key word VALUE is also used in dynamic SQL, but with a completely different meaning. See Chapter 20.

DROP DOMAIN

As mentioned in Chapter 8 (at the end of Section 8.2), dropping a domain that has any domain constraints does *not* drop those constraints, but instead effectively converts them into base table constraints and attaches them to every base table that includes a column defined on the domain in question.* Note the contrast with ALTER DOMAIN ... DROP CONSTRAINT; this latter operation really does drop the constraint (effectively for all columns defined on the domain in question).

14.3   GENERAL CONSTRAINTS

CREATE ASSERTION

As mentioned in the introduction to this chapter, we use the term "general constraint" to mean a constraint of arbitrary complexity, involving an arbitrary collection of columns from an arbitrary collection of base tables. Such constraints are created by CREATE ASSERTION—syntax:

```
CREATE ASSERTION constraint CHECK ( conditional-expression )
```

Here "constraint" is the name of the new constraint† (as mentioned in Section 14.1, a general constraint must indeed have a user-specified name). Here are some examples:

1. Every supplier has status greater than four:

```
CREATE ASSERTION IC13 CHECK
      ( ( SELECT MIN ( S.STATUS ) FROM S ) > 4 )
```

2. Every part has a positive weight:

```
CREATE ASSERTION IC18 CHECK
      ( NOT EXISTS ( SELECT * FROM P
                            WHERE  NOT ( P.WEIGHT > 0 ) ) )
```

---

*It would be conceptually clearer to regard this operation as a two-step process: First, convert each such domain constraint into a *column* constraint (by replacing each occurrence of VALUE by the relevant column name) for every column defined on the domain; second, convert each such column constraint into the equivalent base table constraint and attach it to the relevant base table. Such an explanation would make it clear that if base table *T* includes two or more columns defined on domain *D*, and *D* is dropped, then *T* will acquire two or more base table constraints accordingly. The problem with this explanation is that the first step might fail, in that it might generate syntactically invalid column constraints! See Appendix D.

†If the name is qualified by a schema name and the CREATE ASSERTION appears within the context of a CREATE SCHEMA statement, then that schema name must identify the schema that would have been assumed by default anyway, *viz.* the schema being created (see Chapter 4, Section 4.3).

Note: Examples 1 and 2 are conceptually very similar ("weight positive" means "weight greater than zero," which is of the same logical form as "status greater than four"), so either could alternatively be expressed in the syntactic style of the other.*

3. All red parts must be stored in London:

```
CREATE ASSERTION IC99 CHECK
       ( NOT EXISTS ( SELECT * FROM P
                      WHERE  P.COLOR = 'Red'
                      AND    P.CITY <> 'London' ) )
```

"There does not exist a part where the color is red and the city is not London."

4. No shipment has a total weight (part weight times shipment quantity) greater than 20,000:

```
CREATE ASSERTION IC46 CHECK
       ( NOT EXISTS ( SELECT * FROM P, SP
                      WHERE  P.PNO = SP.PNO
                      AND  ( P.WEIGHT * SP.QTY ) > 20000 ) )
```

5. No supplier with status less than 20 can supply any part in a quantity greater than 500:

```
CREATE ASSERTION IC95 CHECK
       ( NOT EXISTS ( SELECT * FROM S
                      WHERE  S.STATUS < 20
                      AND    EXISTS
                           ( SELECT * FROM SP
                             WHERE  SP.SNO = S.SNO
                             AND    SP.QTY > 500 ) ) )
```

Observe that most of the foregoing examples—effectively all of them, in fact—involve a conditional expression that begins with "NOT EXISTS." This state of affairs is perhaps to be expected, because integrity constraints are usually of the form "Every *x* satisfies *y*," which in turn usually has to be expressed in SQL as "No *x* does not satisfy *y*"; however, it does serve to stress the fundamental importance of the EXISTS operator. (It is only fair to point out, however, that EXISTS in general, and NOT EXISTS in particular, hold traps for the unwary in SQL, as will be explained in Chapter 16.) We will return to this question of the form of the conditional expression in Section 14.4 below.

Incidentally, it is probably worth mentioning that expressing constraints as base table constraints instead of as general constraints—which can *always* be

---

*There is a subtle point here. The constraint in Example 2 will evaluate to *true* if table P is empty; by contrast, the constraint in Example 1 will evaluate to *unknown* if table S is empty (see Chapter 16 for further discussion). For this reason the formulation of Example 2 is perhaps to be preferred.

done—will often have the effect of eliminating the need for that preliminary "NOT EXISTS." In Section 14.4 below, we will show "base table constraint" counterparts of the five examples given above. We should perhaps point out the converse too—namely, that base table constraints (including "column constraints") can *always* be reformulated as general constraints.* Domain constraints, by contrast, cannot be expressed as general constraints (why not?).

DROP ASSERTION

General constraints—that is, constraints created by means of CREATE ASSERTION—can be dropped by means of DROP ASSERTION. Syntax:

```
DROP ASSERTION constraint
```

The specified constraint is dropped. Note that, unlike all forms of DROP discussed earlier in this book, DROP ASSERTION does not offer a RESTRICT *vs.* CASCADE option.

14.4 BASE TABLE AND COLUMN CONSTRAINTS

To repeat from Section 14.1, base table constraints are constraints that are associated with a specific base table. Note carefully, however, that *associated with a specific base table* does not mean that such a constraint cannot refer to other base tables; on the contrary, in fact, some such constraints (foreign key constraints in particular) almost certainly *will* refer to other base tables. Rather, it means simply that the constraint cannot exist if the associated base table does not exist, and in particular that dropping the base table will drop the constraint too. In fact, as suggested in the previous section, base table constraints are essentially just shorthand; there is nothing that can be expressed by means of a base table constraint that cannot alternatively be expressed as a general constraint—*except* for the "referential action" portion of a foreign key constraint (see Section 14.5).

Base table constraints can be initially specified by means of CREATE TABLE, and can be added to or dropped from an existing base table by means of ALTER TABLE. Also, as just mentioned, DROP TABLE automatically drops any base table constraints that were previously associated with the base table in question.

CREATE TABLE

As we saw in Chapter 8, a base table definition takes the form "CREATE TABLE base-table" followed by a parenthesized commalist of "base table elements," where

---

*Except for the "referential action" portion of foreign key constraints. See Section 14.6.

each "base table element" is either a column definition or a base table constraint definition.* A base table constraint definition in turn is any of the following:

1. a candidate key definition
2. a foreign key definition
3. a "check constraint" definition

Each of these can optionally be preceded by "CONSTRAINT constraint" (exactly as for domain constraints), in order to provide a name for the new constraint. For brevity, we will omit this option from our further discussions of the syntax below.

Candidate key definitions: In the relational model, a *candidate key* is basically just a unique identifier—that is, a column or combination of columns with the properties that:

1. At any given time, no two rows of the table have the same value for that column or column combination.
2. No proper subset of the columns within that column combination has the uniqueness property (i.e., none of the columns mentioned is irrelevant for unique identification purposes).

A given table in the relational model can have any number of candidate keys;† however, it is customary (at least in the case of base tables specifically) to designate just one of those candidate keys as the *primary* key. If one candidate key is designated as primary, then the remaining candidate keys, if any, are said to be *alternate* keys (again, so far as the relational model is concerned).

In SQL, a candidate key definition (supported for base tables only, please note) takes the form

```
{ PRIMARY KEY | UNIQUE } ( column-commalist )
```

where each "column" is the *un*qualified name of a column of the base table in question. The identified column or combination of columns constitutes a candidate key for that table. For a given base table, at most one candidate key definition can specify PRIMARY KEY.

We can define the semantics of a candidate key definition (a trifle loosely) in terms of a "check constraint," as follows: The database will satisfy the candidate key constraint shown above if and only if it satisfies the check constraint (*q.v.*)

---

*We remind the reader that the syntax permits column definitions and base table constraint definitions to be arbitrarily interspersed. In this book, however, we adopt the convention that the column definitions always come first.

†At least one, because tables in the relational model never contain duplicate rows. SQL, however, unfortunately permits tables that have no candidate keys at all (i.e., tables that contain duplicate rows).

```
CHECK ( UNIQUE ( SELECT column-commalist FROM T ) )
```

where *T* is the base table whose definition contains the candidate key definition in question (refer back to Chapter 12 if you need to refresh your memory regarding unique-conditions). Also, if the candidate key definition specifies PRIMARY KEY rather than UNIQUE, each component column is additionally assumed to be NOT NULL, even if NOT NULL is not specified explicitly (see Chapter 16). *Note:* Henceforth, we will refer to a candidate key definition that specifies PRIMARY KEY as a *primary* key definition specifically.

Foreign key definitions: In the relational model, a *foreign key* is a column or combination of columns in one base table *T2* whose values are required to match values of some candidate key—usually the primary key—in some base table *T1* (again, speaking a little loosely). For example, in the suppliers-and-parts database, column SP.SNO of table SP is a foreign key matching the primary key S.SNO of table S; every supplier number value appearing in column SP.SNO must also appear in column S.SNO (for otherwise the database would not be consistent). Likewise, column SP.PNO of table SP is a foreign key matching the primary key P.PNO of table P; every part number value appearing in column SP.PNO must also appear in column P.PNO.

In SQL, a foreign key definition takes the form

```
FOREIGN KEY ( column-commalist ) references-definition
```

where each "column" is the *un*qualified name of a column of the base table in question (the identified column or combination of columns constituting a foreign key within that table), and "references definition" is explained in Section 14.5. *Note:* The full details of foreign key definitions are quite complex; we therefore defer discussion of those details to Section 14.5. However, we give a couple of examples here—namely, definitions for the two foreign keys in the suppliers table SP:

```
FOREIGN KEY ( SNO ) REFERENCES S

FOREIGN KEY ( PNO ) REFERENCES P
```

We can define the semantics of a foreign key definition (a trifle loosely once again) in terms of a "check constraint," as follows: The database will satisfy the foreign key constraint

```
FOREIGN KEY fk REFERENCES T ( ck )
```

if and only if it satisfies the check constraint (*q.v.*)

```
CHECK ( fk MATCH ( SELECT ck FROM T ) )
```

Refer back to Chapter 12 if you need to refresh your memory regarding match-conditions.

Check constraint definitions: A "check constraint definition" takes the form

```
CHECK ( conditional-expression )
```

Suppose some user attempts a certain update on base table *T*. That attempt is considered to violate a check constraint for *T* if the conditional expression specified within that constraint would evaluate to *false* if the update were in fact performed—or, to state matters a little less precisely, if the specified conditional expression evaluates to *false* for any row of *T*.

Note: It is that phrase—"for any row"—that makes the preliminary NOT EXISTS found in the typical general constraint unnecessary in the equivalent base table constraint. In other words, where the typical general constraint says something like "NOT EXISTS *x* WHERE NOT *y*," the equivalent base table constraint says simply "*y*".* Here, for instance, are "base table constraint" analogs of the "general constraint" examples from Section 14.3. Each is intended to be part of the CREATE TABLE for the relevant base table (which implies, incidentally, that the table-name qualifiers could optionally be dropped from many of the qualified column names; e.g., "S.STATUS" in Example 1 could be abbreviated to just "STATUS," if desired).

1. Every supplier has status greater than four:

```
CONSTRAINT IC13 CHECK ( S.STATUS > 4 )
```

2. Every part has a positive weight:

```
CONSTRAINT IC18 CHECK ( P.WEIGHT > 0 )
```

3. All red parts must be stored in London:

```
CONSTRAINT IC99 CHECK ( P.COLOR <> 'Red' OR
                        P.CITY <> 'London' )
```

"For any given part, either the color is not red or the city is not London."

4. No shipment has a total weight (part weight times shipment quantity) greater than 20,000:

```
CONSTRAINT IC46 CHECK
        ( SP.QTY * ( SELECT P.WEIGHT FROM P
                     WHERE  P.PNO = SP.PNO ) <= 20000 )
```

---

*The explicit or implicit conditional expression in *any* constraint is required to conform to certain rules of "well-formedness." Specifically, all range variables (explicit or otherwise) must be *quantified.* In general constraints, the quantifiers are explicit; in base table and domain constraints, certain quantifiers are implicit (this is why these latter constraints tend to be more succinct and—arguably—easier to understand). Note that in this context, the aggregate functions SUM, etc., can be regarded as quantifiers of a kind; so too can the UNIQUE operator in a unique-condition.

This constraint must be specified as part of the CREATE TABLE for base table SP. Here, by contrast, is a logically analogous constraint that would have to be specified as part of the CREATE TABLE for base table P instead:

```
CONSTRAINT IC46 CHECK
        ( NOT EXISTS ( SELECT * FROM SP
                       WHERE  SP.PNO = P.PNO
                       AND  ( SP.QTY * P.WEIGHT ) > 20000 ) )
```

5. No supplier with status less than 20 can supply any part in a quantity greater than 500:

```
CONSTRAINT IC95 CHECK
        ( SP.QTY <= 500 OR ( SELECT S.STATUS FROM S
                             WHERE  S.SNO = SP.SNO ) >= 20 )
```

Again this constraint must be specified as part of the CREATE TABLE for base table SP.

One slightly counterintuitive consequence of the foregoing is worth pointing out explicitly. The base table check constraint CHECK(y) is defined to be equivalent to the general constraint

```
NOT EXISTS ( SELECT * FROM T WHERE NOT ( y ) )
```

where T is the base table to which y is attached. It follows that the original constraint y will *always* be satisfied if T is empty, no matter what form y might take (even if, e.g., y is of the form "T must contain at least one row"!—or even the form "T must contain –5 rows," or the form "1 = 0," come to that).

ALTER TABLE

Recall from Chapter 8 that ALTER TABLE supports "base table constraint alteration actions" of two possible forms:

```
base-table-constraint-alteration-action
    ::=    ADD base-table-constraint-definition
         | DROP CONSTRAINT constraint { RESTRICT | CASCADE }
```

ADD permits a new constraint to be defined for an existing base table (the new constraint does not replace any existing constraints for the base table in question but is logically ANDed on to them). DROP permits an existing base table constraint to be removed. RESTRICT and CASCADE have meaning only if the constraint is a candidate key definition:* An attempt to drop a candidate key definition will fail if any foreign key references that candidate key, unless CASCADE is specified, in which case all such foreign key definitions will be dropped too.

---

*Though strangely enough one or the other must apparently always be specified, even if the constraint is not a candidate key definition.

Column Constraints

If a base table constraint applies to a single column within a single base table, it can optionally be specified (in abbreviated syntactic form, in most cases) as part of the definition of the column in question, instead of as a distinct "base table element." That is, a column definition can optionally include any number of "column constraint definitions." A column constraint definition in turn can be any of the following:

1. NOT NULL
2. PRIMARY KEY or UNIQUE
3. a "references definition"
4. a "check constraint" definition

Each of these can optionally be preceded by "CONSTRAINT constraint," exactly as for domain and base table constraints. For brevity, we will omit this option from our discussions below; note, however, that if the option *is* specified, it is inherited by the base table constraint that the column constraint is defined to be shorthand for.

NOT NULL: Specifying NOT NULL for a column *C* is defined to be shorthand for specifying the base table constraint

```
CHECK ( C IS NOT NULL )
```

for the base table that contains *C*. See Chapter 16.

PRIMARY KEY and UNIQUE: Specifying PRIMARY KEY or UNIQUE for a column *C* is defined to be shorthand for specifying the base table constraint

```
PRIMARY KEY ( C )
```

or

```
UNIQUE ( C )
```

(as appropriate) for the base table that contains *C*.

References definition: Specifying a references-definition, *ref-def* say, for a column *C* is defined to be shorthand for specifying the base table constraint

```
FOREIGN KEY ( C ) ref-def
```

for the base table that contains *C*. Refer to Section 14.5 below for further discussion.

Check constraint: Specifying a check constraint for a column *C* is defined to be shorthand for specifying that very same check constraint as a base table constraint for the base table that contains *C*. Note, however, that *C* must be the only column referenced within that check constraint.*

---

*Given that this is so, it might have been nice to allow the special symbol VALUE to be used in a column constraint (analogous to the use of VALUE in a domain constraint), and then to prohibit *all* explicit column references within the check constraint.

Column constraints can be specified only within a column definition. Thus, they must be defined when the column *per se* is defined, either by means of CREATE TABLE or by means of ALTER TABLE. Once defined, however, they logically become *base table* constraints; thus, they can be dropped from an existing base table by means of ALTER TABLE ... DROP CONSTRAINT (or by DROP TABLE, of course), but there is no way to add a new column constraint to an existing column or to remove an existing column constraint from an existing column.

14.5   FOREIGN KEYS

We begin this section with a quick overview of the relevant ideas from the relational model. We then go on to examine the details of SQL's support for those ideas.

1. First, as explained in the previous section, a foreign key in the relational model is basically a column or combination of columns in one base table *T2* whose values are required to match values of some candidate key (usually the primary key) in some base table *T1*. For example, columns SNO and PNO in the shipments table SP are foreign keys that match the primary keys SNO and PNO of the suppliers table and parts table, respectively—meaning that every value appearing in column SP.SNO must also appear in column S.SNO, and every value appearing in column SP.PNO must also appear in column P.PNO. Of course, the converse is *not* a requirement—i.e., a primary key value can exist without a matching foreign key value. For example, given the suppliers-and-parts sample data of Fig. 2.1, supplier S5 currently does not supply any parts, and hence the value S5 occurs in column S.SNO but not in column SP.SNO.

2. *Terminology:* A given foreign key value represents a *reference* from the rows containing it to the row containing the matching candidate key value. For that reason, the problem of ensuring that every foreign key value does in fact match a value of the corresponding candidate key is known as the *referential integrity* problem. The base table containing the foreign key is called the *referencing table*; the base table containing the matching candidate key is called the *referenced table*. The integrity constraint is called a *referential constraint* or *foreign key constraint*.

3. The referenced table *T1* and the referencing table *T2* in our (loose) definition of "foreign key" in paragraph 1 above do not have to be distinct. That is, a base table might include a foreign key whose values are required to match values of some candidate key within that very same base table. An example might be a base table CHILDOF with columns CHILD and MOTHER, where each MOTHER is in turn a CHILD of some other MOTHER (etc.). Here CHILD is a candidate key and MOTHER is a foreign key matching CHILD (i.e., the MOTHER value in a given row must be equal to the CHILD value in some other row).

4. The foregoing example is actually just a special case of the more general situation in which there is a *referential cycle*—i.e., a cycle of base tables *T1, T2, T3, ..., Tn*, such that *T1* includes a foreign key matching some candidate key in *T2*, *T2* includes a foreign key matching some candidate key in *T3*, and so on, ..., and *Tn* includes a foreign key matching some candidate key in *T1*. We remark that, in order to specify such a cycle, it will be necessary to specify at least one of the foreign keys by means of ALTER TABLE ... ADD instead of by means of CREATE TABLE, because a foreign key definition cannot refer to a base table that does not yet exist.*

5. The CHILDOF example also serves to illustrate another point—namely, that foreign key values might sometimes be missing, and foreign keys might therefore sometimes have to have "nulls allowed." In the case at hand, there will presumably be at least one CHILD whose mother in turn is not represented as a CHILD in any CHILDOF row. Thus, we will be forced in the present section to discuss nulls, albeit briefly! As always, we defer as much of the detail as possible to Chapter 16; the basic point, however, is that we must now modify our earlier definition of *foreign key* slightly, as follows: A foreign key is a column or combination of columns in the referencing table *T2* such that, for each row of *T2*, that column or column combination *either* is null *or* contains a value that matches the value of the relevant candidate key in some row of the referenced table *T1*.†

Let us now turn to SQL specifically. Remember that a foreign key constraint is a special case of a base table constraint, and so foreign key definitions appear within CREATE (or ALTER) TABLE statements. The syntax is as follows:

```
FOREIGN KEY ( column-commalist ) references-definition
```

(optionally preceded, like all base table constraint definitions, by "CONSTRAINT constraint"; we omit this option for brevity). The "references definition" in turn takes the form:

```
REFERENCES base-table [ ( column-commalist ) ]
[ MATCH { FULL | PARTIAL } ]
[ ON DELETE { NO ACTION | CASCADE | SET DEFAULT | SET NULL } ]
[ ON UPDATE { NO ACTION | CASCADE | SET DEFAULT | SET NULL } ]
```

---

*Unless all of the CREATE TABLEs involved appear as elements within the same CREATE SCHEMA operation. Since individual SQL statements are supposed to be "atomic," the elements within a single CREATE SCHEMA must be thought of as effectively all being executed simultaneously, as discussed in Chapters 4 and 5.

†This is the definition usually given in discussions of the relational model, and it is the definition adopted in SQL. We remark, however, that considerable controversy exists regarding nulls in general, and nulls in foreign keys in particular. See the chapter entitled "Notes Toward a Reconstituted Definition of the Relational Model," in C. J. Date and Hugh Darwen, *Relational Database Writings 1989–1991* (Addison-Wesley, 1992), for further discussion.

Explanation:

1. The "column commalist" in the FOREIGN KEY clause per se (i.e., not the one in the references-definition) identifies the column or combination of columns that constitutes the foreign key. Each column must be identified by its *unqual-ified* name.

2. The "base table" in the references-definition identifies the referenced table.

3. The optional "column commalist" in the references-definition must be the same (except possibly for the sequence in which the columns are listed) as the "column commalist" in some candidate key definition for the referenced table (again, each column must be identified by its *unqualified* name). Omitting that second column commalist is equivalent to specifying a column commalist that is identical to that in the *primary* key definition for the referenced table (the referenced table must possess a defined primary key in this case).

4. The optional MATCH specification has to do with nulls. We defer further dis-cussion to Chapter 16.

5. The optional ON DELETE and ON UPDATE clauses (which can appear in either order) are explained in the subsection "Referential Actions" below. Here we simply note that omitting either clause is equivalent to specifying that clause with the NO ACTION option.

Here is an example:

```
CREATE TABLE SP
     ( SNO ... , PNO ... , QTY ... ,
       PRIMARY KEY ( SNO, PNO ),
       FOREIGN KEY ( SNO ) REFERENCES S,
       FOREIGN KEY ( PNO ) REFERENCES P )
```

The first of the two FOREIGN KEY clauses here states that column SP.SNO is a foreign key matching the primary key of base table S (note that base table S must have a defined primary key for this references-definition to be legal). The second FOREIGN KEY clause is analogous.

Points to note:

1. It so happens in the example that each of the two foreign keys is a component of the primary key of the containing base table. However, it is certainly *not* a requirement that such be the case. In fact, *any column* (or column combina-tion) within a given base table can be a foreign key. For example, column CITY of base table S might be a foreign key, if the database included another base table representing cities.

2. As mentioned in Section 14.4, if a foreign key is single-column (as in both of the examples above), the references-definition can be included directly in the column definition instead of being made part of a separate FOREIGN KEY clause. For example:

```
CREATE TABLE SP
    ( SNO ... REFERENCES S,
      PNO ... REFERENCES P,
      QTY ... ,
      PRIMARY KEY ( SNO, PNO ) )
```

As explained earlier, however, references-definitions that are part of an individual column definition are defined to be merely a shorthand for corresponding base table foreign key definitions.

3. As was also explained earlier, a given foreign key is allowed to match *any candidate key* in the referenced table. In our examples, however, we will adopt the convention that foreign keys always reference primary keys, never alternate keys.

4. A given foreign key and its matching candidate key must contain the same number of columns, n say; the ith column of the foreign key corresponds to the ith column of the matching candidate key ($i = 1$ to n), and corresponding columns must have the same data type (not just compatible data types, observe, but *exactly the same* data type; see Appendix D for further discussion of this point).

5. Let $T2$ and $T1$ be a referencing table and the corresponding referenced table, respectively, and let $T2.FK$ and $T1.CK$ be the foreign key and matching candidate key in those two tables. Assume for the moment that the foreign key definition includes neither an ON DELETE clause nor an ON UPDATE clause. Then, in order to maintain the referential constraint between $T2.FK$ and $T1.CK$, the system will simply reject any operation that would violate it.* The operations that will be rejected are:

   ▪ *Case 1:* An INSERT on $T2$ or an UPDATE on $T2.FK$ that would introduce a value for $T2.FK$ that does not exist as a value of $T1.CK$.

   ▪ *Case 2:* A DELETE on $T1$ or an UPDATE on $T1.CK$ that would leave "dangling references" in $T2$ (i.e., rows in $T2$ that have no corresponding row in $T1$).

   If on the other hand the foreign key definition does include either an ON DELETE clause or an ON UPDATE clause, then Case 2 updates will not necessarily be rejected after all. (Case 1 updates will always be rejected out of hand, however, regardless of whether there is an ON DELETE clause or an ON UPDATE clause.) See the subsection "Referential Actions" immediately following.

---

*"Simply reject" is not quite accurate for Case 2 updates (*q.v.*). Instead, what happens—at least conceptually—for Case 2 is that the system actually does the update, and then undoes it again if the referential constraint is now violated. But the net effect is indeed as if the update had simply been rejected in the first place.

Referential Actions

The general idea behind "referential actions" is that it might sometimes be possible to maintain referential integrity, not by simply rejecting an update that would violate it, but rather by performing another, compensating update in addition to the one originally requested. For example, instead of simply rejecting an attempt to delete the row for supplier S1 from the suppliers table (on the grounds that there are rows for supplier S1 in the shipments table), it might be better to go ahead and delete that supplier row *and* delete the matching shipment rows as well. Certainly referential integrity will be maintained that way.

Suppose once again, therefore, that *T2* and *T1* are a referencing table and the corresponding referenced table, respectively, and *T2.FK* and *T1.CK* are the relevant foreign key and matching candidate key. Suppose, moreover, that *T2.FK* has an associated ON DELETE clause and an associated ON UPDATE clause.

- The ON DELETE clause defines the *delete rule* for the referenced table *T1* with respect to this foreign key—that is, it defines what happens if an attempt is made to delete some "target" row from *T1* and there exist rows in *T2* that match that target row. The possible specifications ("referential actions") are NO ACTION, CASCADE, SET DEFAULT, and SET NULL, with meanings as follows:

  a. *NO ACTION:* Specifying NO ACTION is equivalent to omitting the ON DELETE clause entirely, the effect of which has already been explained.

  b. *CASCADE:* The DELETE "cascades" to delete all matching rows in *T2* also.*

    Note that *T2* might in turn be referenced by some foreign key in some base table *T3*. If it is, then if any DELETE on *T1* cascades to some row *R2* in *T2*, then the effect is exactly as if an attempt had been made to DELETE that row *R2* directly; i.e., it depends on the delete rule specified for the foreign key from *T3* to *T2*. And so on, recursively, to any number of levels.

  c. *SET DEFAULT:* In this case, every component of the foreign key must have a defined default value. The target row is deleted, and each component of the foreign key is set to the applicable default value in all matching rows in *T2*. Note that in this case a row must already exist in *T1* in which each component of the candidate key *T1.CK* has the appropriate default value (unless the default for some foreign key component is in fact null—see Chapter 16).

---

*It might be helpful to point out that the CASCADE option on the ON DELETE clause is somewhat analogous to the CASCADE option on various DROP statements. Likewise, the NO ACTION option on ON DELETE is analogous—though somewhat less so—to the RESTRICT option on DROP. The important difference is that the options are specified *dynamically* (at run time) in the case of DROP, but *statically* (as part of the data definition) in the case of DELETE.

d. *SET NULL:* In this case, every component of the foreign key must have "nulls allowed." The target row is deleted and each component of the foreign key is set to null in all matching rows in *T2*.

■ The ON UPDATE clause defines the *update rule* for the referenced candidate key *T1.CK* with respect to this foreign key—that is, it defines what happens if an attempt is made to UPDATE the candidate key *CK* within some "target" row of *T1* and there exist rows in *T2* that match that target row. The possible specifications ("referential actions") are the same as for the ON DELETE clause—i.e., NO ACTION, CASCADE, SET DEFAULT, and SET NULL— with meanings as follows:

a. *NO ACTION:* Specifying NO ACTION is equivalent to omitting the ON UPDATE clause entirely, the effect of which has already been explained.

b. *CASCADE:* The UPDATE "cascades" to update the foreign key (in the same way) in all matching rows of *T2* also.

c. *SET DEFAULT:* The target row is updated, and components of the foreign key that correspond to updated components of the candidate key are set to the applicable default value in all matching rows in *T2*. (Those foreign key components must have a defined default value.) Note that in this case, a row must already exist in *T1* in which each component of the candidate key *T1.CK* has the appropriate value (unless the default for some foreign key component is in fact null—see Chapter 16).

d. *SET NULL:* The target row is updated, and components of the foreign key that correspond to updated components of the candidate key are set to null in all matching rows in *T2*. (Those foreign key components must have "nulls allowed.")

Note that *T2.FK* might be a candidate key, or part of a candidate key, for *T2* that is referenced in turn by some foreign key in some base table *T3*. If it is, then if any UPDATE on *T1.CK* cascades to some row *R2* in *T2*, or if any UPDATE on *T1.CK* or DELETE on *T1* sets *T2.FK* to a default value or null in some row *R2* in *T2*, then the effect is exactly as if an attempt had been made to UPDATE that row *R2* directly; i.e., it depends on the update rule specified for the foreign key from *T3* to *T2*. And so on, recursively, to any number of levels.

Here is an example:

```
CREATE TABLE SP
      ( SNO ... , PNO ... , QTY ... ,
        PRIMARY KEY ( SNO, PNO ),
        FOREIGN KEY ( SNO ) REFERENCES S
                            ON DELETE CASCADE
                            ON UPDATE CASCADE,
        FOREIGN KEY ( PNO ) REFERENCES P
                            ON DELETE CASCADE
                            ON UPDATE CASCADE )
```

With this definition for base table SP, an attempt to delete a specific supplier row or part row will cascade to delete all shipment rows for that supplier or part as well; likewise, an attempt to update the primary key value in a specific supplier row or part row will cascade to update the foreign key value in the same way in all shipment rows for that supplier or part as well.

Guaranteeing Predictable Behavior

It is well known that certain combinations of

1. referential structures (i.e., sets of base tables that are interrelated via referential constraints), along with

2. referential action specifications, and

3. actual data values in the database

can lead to conflict situations and can potentially cause unpredictable behavior on the part of the implementation; see, e.g., Chapters 5 and 6 ("Referential Integrity and Foreign Keys, Parts I and II") in C. J. Date, *Relational Database Writings 1985–1989* (Addison-Wesley, 1990). The details are beyond the scope of this book; suffice it to say that the SQL standard identifies cases involving such potential unpredictability and requires the implementation to treat them as run-time errors—i.e., the attempted update must be rejected at run time and an exception condition raised. Such exceptions can occur on DELETEs and candidate key UPDATEs against certain referenced tables.*

14.6   DEFERRED CONSTRAINT CHECKING

Up to this point we have been assuming that all integrity constraints are checked "immediately," i.e., as the final step in executing any SQL statement—and, if any constraint is found to be violated, the offending SQL statement is simply rejected, so that its overall effect on the database is nil. Sometimes, however, it is necessary that certain constraints not be checked until some later time, on the grounds that if they were to be checked "immediately" they would always fail. Here is an example (involving a referential cycle):

■ Suppose we have two base tables, *T1* and *T2*, each of which includes a foreign key that references some candidate key of the other, and suppose we start with both tables empty. Then, if all foreign key checking is done immediately, there

---

*A helpful analysis and explanation of this aspect of the standard can be found in Bruce M. Horowitz, "A Run-Time Execution Model for Referential Integrity Maintenance," published in the Proceedings of the 8th International Data Engineering Conference (February 1992).

is no way to get started: Any attempt to insert a row into either table will fail, because there is no target row in the other table that it can possibly reference.

The facilities described immediately following are intended to address such situations.

1. At any given time, with respect to any given transaction, any given constraint must be in one of two "modes," *immediate* or *deferred*.* *Immediate* means the constraint is checked "immediately" (as explained above); *deferred* means it is not.†

2. Any given constraint definition can optionally include either or both of the following:

```
INITIALLY { DEFERRED | IMMEDIATE }

[ NOT ] DEFERRABLE
```

These specifications appear as the final syntactic component of the constraint definition. They can appear in either order.

- INITIALLY DEFERRED and NOT DEFERRABLE are mutually exclusive. If neither INITIALLY DEFERRED nor INITIALLY IMMEDIATE is specified, INITIALLY IMMEDIATE is implied. If INITIALLY IMMEDIATE is specified or implied, then if neither DEFERRABLE nor NOT DEFERRABLE is specified, NOT DEFERRABLE is implied. If INITIALLY DEFERRED is specified, then (as already explained) NOT DEFERRABLE must not be specified; DEFERRABLE can be specified, but is implied anyway.

- INITIALLY DEFERRED and INITIALLY IMMEDIATE specify the "initial" mode of the constraint—i.e., its mode immediately after it is defined and at the start of every transaction‡—as *deferred* or *immediate*, respectively.

- DEFERRABLE and NOT DEFERRABLE specify whether or not this constraint can ever be in *deferred* mode. DEFERRABLE means it can; NOT DEFERRABLE means it cannot.

---

*The standard *says* the mode is "with respect to any given transaction," but it ought probably to say "with respect to *any given session within* any given transaction" (see Chapter 5).

†This paragraph is true in general terms, but there are some constraints where deferred checking seems to make no sense. Domain constraints are a case in point, and a strong argument could be made that the same is true for NOT NULL and candidate key constraints. Indeed, if candidate key *CK* is referenced by some foreign key, then the standard *requires* the candidate key constraint for *CK* to be NOT DEFERRABLE.

‡The standard *says* the initial mode applies "at the start of every transaction," but it ought probably to say it applies "at the start of *every session within* every transaction" (see Chapter 5).

3. The SET CONSTRAINTS statement is used to set the mode for specified constraints with respect to the current transaction and current session (or the next transaction to be initiated in the current session, if the SQL-agent has no transaction currently executing). The syntax is:

```
SET CONSTRAINTS { constraint-commalist | ALL }
                { DEFERRED | IMMEDIATE }
```

Each "constraint" mentioned by name must be DEFERRABLE; ALL is shorthand for "all DEFERRABLE constraints." If DEFERRED is specified, the mode of all indicated constraints is set to *deferred*. If IMMEDIATE is specified, the mode of all indicated constraints is set to *immediate*, and those constraints are then checked; if any check fails, the SET CONSTRAINTS fails, and the mode of all indicated constraints remains unchanged. Note that because of paragraph 4 below, the checks should not fail if the SET CONSTRAINTS statement is executed while the SQL-agent has no current transaction.

4. COMMIT implies SET CONSTRAINTS ALL IMMEDIATE (for every active SQL-session for the applicable SQL-transaction). If some implied integrity check then fails, the COMMIT fails, and the transaction fails also (i.e., is rolled back).

To revert to the example mentioned at the beginning of this section (the referential cycle involving two tables): We could deal with the problem using the foregoing facilities as indicated by the following pseudocode.
Data definitions:

```
CREATE TABLE T1 ...
        CONSTRAINT T1FK FOREIGN KEY ... REFERENCES T2
                INITIALLY DEFERRED

CREATE TABLE T2 ...
        CONSTRAINT T2FK FOREIGN KEY ... REFERENCES T1
                INITIALLY DEFERRED
```

SQL-transaction:

```
INSERT INTO T1 ( ... ) VALUES ( ... )

INSERT INTO T2 ( ... ) VALUES ( ... )

SET CONSTRAINTS T1FK, T2FK IMMEDIATE

IF SQLSTATE = code meaning "SET CONSTRAINTS failed"
THEN ROLLBACK                           -- cancel the INSERTs
```

15

Security

15.1 INTRODUCTION

As explained in Chapter 4, every domain, every base table, every view, and every integrity constraint—also every character set, every collation, and every translation (see Chapter 19)—is described by some *schema*. As also explained in that chapter, every schema in turn has an associated user, the schema *owner*, who can be regarded as the owner not only of the schema *per se*, but of everything described by that schema also.

Now, users can certainly operate on data they do not themselves own. If their operation is to succeed, however, the user that does own the data must first have granted them the appropriate *access privilege* for that operation and that data.* Access privileges ("privileges" for short) are thus SQL's mechanism for providing *data security*. Accordingly, the SQL standard specifies a set of *Access Rules*, which define the privileges needed for various combinations of data objects and operations. It also defines two statements, GRANT and REVOKE, that allow users to grant privileges to one another and subsequently to revoke such privileges. In this chapter, we examine these ideas in some detail.

We remind the reader that, despite our use of the term "user" above (and elsewhere in this book), the standard does not in fact talk in such terms at all, but rather

---

*The granting might have been indirect. See the discussion of the grant option in Section 15.5.

in terms of what it calls "authorization identifiers" (*authIDs* for short). In this chapter, we will still use the term *user* from time to time for intuitive reasons, but the reader should understand that our use of that term is only informal. Thus, the mapping between authIDs and real users as understood by the external operating system is completely implementation-defined;* in particular, there is no reason why a single authID should not map to an entire *group* of real users, and indeed there are reasons why this might be a good idea in practice.

The plan of the chapter is as follows. Following this brief introduction, Section 15.2 discusses certain special authIDs that need to be understood in order to appreciate the overall SQL security mechanism in general. Section 15.3 then summarizes the various privileges that are defined within the standard, indicating which privileges are needed for which operations on which objects. Section 15.4 describes the GRANT and REVOKE statements. Finally, Section 15.5 discusses "the grant option" and the associated notion of *grant authority*, and Section 15.6 discusses the RESTRICT *vs.* CASCADE option on REVOKE.

15.2   AUTHORIZATION IDENTIFIERS

There are a number of special authIDs that need to be understood and clearly distinguished in any discussion of SQL security: the *current* authID, the *module* authID, the *SQL-session* authID, and the *schema* authID. (Any or all of these various authIDs might have the same *value*, of course, but conceptually speaking they are all distinct.)

1. The *current* authID identifies what might be thought of as "the current user." It is the authID against which authorization checking is actually done. For example, an attempt to perform a DELETE operation against some base table causes the system to check that the current authID holds the privilege to perform DELETE operations on that base table. As another example, an attempt to ALTER some base table causes the system to check that the current authID is the owner of the schema to which that base table belongs (see below).

    The current authID is taken to be the module authID for the module containing the SQL statement in question (if that module has an authID—see below), or the SQL-session authID for the current SQL-session otherwise. As mentioned in Chapter 7, the niladic builtin function CURRENT_USER (which can be abbreviated to just USER) returns the current authID.

2. The *module* authID for a given module identifies the owner of that module (if such an owner exists—see Chapter 6, Section 6.2). It is established by means

---

*The standard says it is implementation-*dependent*, but this is surely an error in the standard.

of the AUTHORIZATION clause on the MODULE statement that defines that module (again, see Chapter 6); if that clause is omitted, the module has no owner, and hence no authID.

The standard does not say what privileges (if any) are needed to create a module, because the whole mechanism for creating modules is implementation-defined anyway. Presumably the intent is that some external agency will control that mechanism in an appropriate manner.

3. The *SQL-session* authID serves as a default authID for use in contexts where no other authID is provided to override it. It is initially established by means of the USER clause on the CONNECT statement that initiates the SQL-session (if that clause is omitted, the initial SQL-session authID is implementation-defined), but can subsequently be changed by means of the statement SET SESSION AUTHORIZATION. See Chapter 5, Section 5.3, for a discussion of CONNECT and SET SESSION AUTHORIZATION. *Note:* No particular privileges are required in order to execute these two statements; however, the implementation is explicitly permitted to impose implementation-defined restrictions on them, so that, for example, CONNECT might be prohibited from setting the SQL-session authID to anything other than the applicable module authID.

As mentioned in Chapter 7, the niladic builtin function SESSION_USER returns the SQL-session authID.

4. The *schema* authID for a given schema identifies the owner of that schema (and hence the owner of everything described by that schema also). It is established by means of the AUTHORIZATION clause on the CREATE SCHEMA statement that creates that schema (see Chapter 4, Section 4.3); if that clause is omitted, the owner of the schema is taken to be the owner, if any, of the module that contains the CREATE SCHEMA statement, or the SQL-session authID if that module has no owner. (It is also taken to be the SQL-session authID if the CREATE SCHEMA is "standalone" and does not include an AUTHORIZATION clause.)

The privileges needed to execute a CREATE SCHEMA operation are implementation-defined. Presumably the intent is that some external agency will decide who is allowed to create new schemas.

Note that, as a consequence of all of the foregoing, if, for example, an application uses several modules, say one with owner *A*, one with owner *B*, and one with no owner, and if the session authID is *C*, then authorization checking will be done variously against *A*, *B*, or *C*, depending on which module contains the SQL statement that is currently executing. Thus, e.g., *A* might be able to update some base table that *B* and *C* cannot.

15.3   PRIVILEGES AND ACCESS RULES

The following list summarizes all of the privileges that are defined in the standard. *Note:* The privileges listed, excluding USAGE, are sometimes referred to collectively as *table privileges*, where "table"—somewhat unusually for the standard—means any named table, not just a base table specifically (i.e., table privileges apply to views as well as base tables).

■   *USAGE:* Privilege to use a specific domain (or character set, collation, or translation—see Chapter 19).

■   *SELECT:* Privilege to access all of the columns of a specific named table, including any columns added to that table later.

■   *INSERT(x):* Privilege to INSERT into a specific named column x of a specific named table.

■   *INSERT:* Privilege to INSERT into all columns of a specific named table; implies INSERT(x) privilege for all columns x of that table, including any columns added to that table later.

■   *UPDATE(x):* Privilege to UPDATE a specific named column x of a specific named table.

■   *UPDATE:* Privilege to UPDATE all columns of a specific named table; implies UPDATE(x) for all columns x of that table, including any columns added to that table later.

■   *DELETE:* Privilege to DELETE rows from a specific named table.

■   *REFERENCES(x):* Privilege to reference a specific named column x of a specific named table in integrity constraints. Note that despite the name, this privilege is required for *all* integrity constraints, not just referential constraints.

■   *REFERENCES:* Privilege to reference all columns of a specific named table in integrity constraints; implies REFERENCES(x) for all columns x of that table, including any columns added to that table later.

We now present a summary of the SQL Access Rules for each SQL statement (more accurately, each pertinent SQL construct) previously discussed in this book.* SQL constructs previously discussed but not mentioned in the following summary are defined in the standard as having "Access Rules: None."

■   *CREATE SCHEMA:* Requires implementation-defined privileges.

■   *DROP SCHEMA, CREATE/ALTER/DROP DOMAIN, CREATE/ALTER/DROP TABLE, CREATE/DROP VIEW, CREATE/DROP ASSERTION* (excluding

---

*The only pertinent constructs not previously discussed are character sets, collations, and translations. To CREATE or DROP such an object, the current authID must be the same as the authID of the affected schema. Any use of such an object requires the USAGE privilege on the object in question.

CREATEs executed as "schema elements" within CREATE SCHEMA): The current authID must be the same as the authID of the affected schema.

■ *CAST:* The operation CAST (... AS domain) requires USAGE on "domain."

■ *Column definition:* Defining a column on "domain" requires USAGE on "domain."

■ *Table reference:* Requires SELECT on the referenced table (except for table references within integrity constraints, *q.v.*).

■ *Column reference:* Requires SELECT on the base table or view containing the referenced column (except for column references within integrity constraints, *q.v.*). *Note:* A *column reference* is just an implicitly or explicitly qualified column name.

■ *Integrity constraint:* Requires REFERENCES(x) on every column x referenced, or REFERENCES(x) for at least one column x of table T if T is referenced but no particular column of T is.

■ *INSERT:* Requires INSERT(x) for every column x explicitly mentioned, or INSERT on the target table if no columns are explicitly mentioned.

■ *UPDATE:* Requires UPDATE(x) for every target column x.

■ *DELETE:* Requires DELETE on the target table.

■ *GRANT and REVOKE:* See Section 15.4, later.

Certain implications and ramifications of the foregoing are worth spelling out explicitly.

1. First, we should explain that the owner of any object—i.e., the user who creates the object in question—is automatically granted all privileges that make sense for that object. For example, in the case of a base table, the owner is automatically granted the SELECT, INSERT, UPDATE, DELETE, and REFERENCES privileges on that base table, with "grant authority" in each case (see Section 15.5). The "user" granting all of these privileges is considered to be a hypothetical user with the special—syntactically invalid!—authID _SYSTEM.

2. Likewise, in the case of a view, the owner is automatically granted the SELECT and REFERENCES privileges on that view. If the view is SQL-updatable (see Chapter 13) *and* the owner holds the INSERT privilege and/or the UPDATE privilege and/or the DELETE privilege on the (single) underlying table of the view (again, see Chapter 13), then the owner is automatically granted the INSERT and/or UPDATE and/or DELETE privileges (as applicable) on that view also. Each of these privileges will include "grant authority" if and only if the user already holds the corresponding privilege on the underlying table with grant authority. Again, the authID granting all of these privileges is considered to be _SYSTEM.

3. Note that CREATE VIEW involves a table expression, which in turn involves one or more table references, and so requires the SELECT privilege on every named table (base table or view) identified by those table references, at any level of nesting.

4. In order to define a foreign key, the user needs the REFERENCES privilege on every column of the referenced candidate key. More generally, in order to define *any* integrity constraint, the user needs the REFERENCES privilege on every referenced column of every referenced named table—except in the special case of a constraint that references some named table but does not mention any specific column of that table (an example might be a constraint to the effect that the count of suppliers must be less than 100). In this special case, the user needs only the REFERENCES privilege on *at least one* column of the referenced named table.

5. INSERT by definition always inserts whole rows into the target table. If the user does not have the INSERT privilege for some column of that table, then the user cannot explicitly mention that column in the INSERT; that column will thus be set to the applicable default value in the new row.

6. Note that the UPDATE statement (e.g.)

```
UPDATE T SET C = 1 ...
```

requires the UPDATE privilege on column *C* of table *T*, whereas the UPDATE statement (e.g.)

```
UPDATE T SET C = T.C + 1 ...
```

requires the SELECT privilege on *T* as well, because of the column reference *T.C*.

15.4   GRANT AND REVOKE

As indicated in the previous section, the owner of an object is automatically granted all privileges that make sense for that object. Furthermore, those privileges are granted "with the grant option." In general, if a privilege is granted "with the grant option," we say that the recipient of the privilege has *grant authority* (not a standard term) for that privilege, which means that the recipient can in turn grant that same privilege—with or without the grant option—to some further user, and so on.

Granting privileges is done by means of the GRANT statement, which is discussed in detail below. Thus, the owner of an object can use the GRANT statement to grant privileges on that object to other users; furthermore, such a GRANT statement can optionally include the specification WITH GRANT OPTION, and if it does, then the recipient can grant the same privilege to a third party, etc., etc. However, we defer detailed discussion of the grant option to Section 15.5, and concentrate in the present section on the use of GRANT (and REVOKE) without that option.

Note: GRANT (like CREATE DOMAIN, CREATE TABLE, etc.) can be executed as an independent operation in its own right, or it can be executed as a "schema element" within a CREATE SCHEMA statement (see Chapter 4). REVOKE must be executed as an independent operation.

We remark that GRANT and REVOKE might logically be thought of as "CREATE AUTHORIZATION" and "DROP AUTHORIZATION," respectively— except that (a) there is no such thing as an "authorization" in the standard (there are "privilege descriptors" instead), and (b) unlike objects that truly are created and dropped by means of explicit CREATE and DROP statements, those "authorizations" (or privilege descriptors, rather) have no names.

GRANT

The general format of GRANT is

```
GRANT privileges ON object TO users [ WITH GRANT OPTION ]
```

where:

- "Privileges" is a commalist of privileges or the phrase ALL PRIVILEGES. *Note:* ALL PRIVILEGES does not literally mean all privileges—it means all privileges on "object" for which the current authID (i.e., the user issuing the GRANT) has grant authority. Also, the privilege "INSERT(x,y)" (where x and y are commalists of column names) is defined to be shorthand for the commalist of privileges "INSERT(x), INSERT(y)" (and similarly for UPDATE and REFERENCES).

- "Object" is one of the following:

```
  DOMAIN domain
[ TABLE ] table
  CHARACTER SET character-set
  COLLATION collation
  TRANSLATION translation
```

Note that the key word "TABLE" is optional in the TABLE case, and furthermore that in this context (unlike some others in SQL), "table" means *any* named table—i.e., it includes views as well as base tables. If "object" specifies anything other than a table, "privileges" must specify USAGE (only). If "object" specifies a table, "privileges" can specify any collection of table privileges; any columns mentioned explicitly (e.g., column x in "INSERT(x)") must belong to the specified table.

- "Users" is either a commalist of authIDs or the special key word PUBLIC. PUBLIC means, loosely, all authIDs known to the system (including authIDs defined at any time subsequent to execution of the GRANT operation). More precisely, "granting to PUBLIC" means that, at any given time, every authID known to the system at that time is considered to hold all privileges that have been granted to PUBLIC and not (yet) revoked from PUBLIC.

- WITH GRANT OPTION is discussed in Section 15.5.

The specified privileges on the specified object are granted to each of the specified authIDs. The user issuing the GRANT—i.e., the current authID—must hold all of the specified privileges and must have grant authority for each of them; no user can grant a privilege not held by that user with the grant option.*

Note: More precisely, we should say, not that privileges are granted, but rather that privilege *descriptors* are *created*. Each such descriptor indicates that a certain *grantor* authID has granted a certain *grantee* authID the authority to perform a certain *operation* on a certain *object*. It is particularly important to be clear on the distinction between a privilege and a privilege descriptor when considering what happens if, e.g., users *U1* and *U2* both grant the same privilege *P* on the same object *O* to another user *U3*, and *U1* then revokes *P* on *O* from *U3* (the two GRANTs create two descriptors, and the REVOKE drops one of them; thus *U3* still holds *P* on *O*). Most of the time, however, it is not necessary to be quite so precise.

Here are some examples of GRANT, mostly repeated from Chapter 2 (Section 2.6):

```
GRANT INSERT, UPDATE, DELETE ON SP TO JOE

GRANT SELECT ON SP TO ALICE WITH GRANT OPTION

GRANT UPDATE ( STATUS ) ON S TO JUDY

GRANT DELETE ON SP TO BONNIE, CLYDE

GRANT SELECT ON GOODSUPPS TO FRED
```

(GOODSUPPS here is the view that served as the basis for most of our examples in Chapter 13.)

We conclude this discussion of GRANT by repeating the point from Section 15.3 that if user *U* holds the SELECT, INSERT, UPDATE, or REFERENCES privilege (in the last three cases non-column-specific) on base table *T*, and a new column *C* is added to *T*, user *U*'s privileges are automatically extended to include the relevant privilege on the new column *C*.

---

*This statement is undeniably true. According to the standard, however, it is not actually an error if some of the privileges a user tries to grant are not held by that user with the grant option (or indeed not held by that user at all); all that happens is that the privileges in question are not granted, and a "completion condition" (see Chapter 22) is raised. An analogous remark applies to REVOKE also.

REVOKE

The general format of REVOKE is

```
REVOKE [ GRANT OPTION FOR ] privileges ON object FROM users
                              { RESTRICT | CASCADE }
```

where "privileges," "object," and "users" are as for GRANT, and the GRANT OPTION FOR and RESTRICT *vs.* CASCADE specifications are discussed in Section 15.5 and Section 15.6, respectively. The specified privileges on the specified object are revoked from each of the specified authIDs (more precisely, the corresponding privilege descriptors are dropped—refer back to the discussion of GRANT above for an explanation of privilege descriptors). *Note:* The user issuing the REVOKE—i.e., the current authID—must have been the user who granted the privileges in the first place.

Dropping a domain, base table, column, or view* causes an automatic REVOKE ... CASCADE for all privileges on the dropped object for all users.

15.5   THE GRANT OPTION

If user *U1* has the authority to grant a privilege *P* to another user *U2*, then user *U1* also has the authority to grant that privilege *P* to user *U2* "with the grant option" (by specifying WITH GRANT OPTION on the GRANT statement). Passing the grant option along from *U1* to *U2* in this manner means that *U2* in turn now has grant authority on *P*, and so can grant *P* to some third user *U3*. And therefore, of course, *U2* also has the authority to pass the grant option for *P* along to *U3* as well, etc., etc. For example:

```
U1: GRANT SELECT ON TABLE S TO U2 WITH GRANT OPTION

U2: GRANT SELECT ON TABLE S TO U3 WITH GRANT OPTION

U3: GRANT SELECT ON TABLE S TO U4 WITH GRANT OPTION
```

And so on.

The analogous optional specification GRANT OPTION FOR on the REVOKE statement means that the issuing user is not trying to revoke the specified privileges *per se*, but only to revoke grant authority for those privileges. In this case, of course, the user issuing the REVOKE—i.e., the current authID—must have executed the original GRANT with the grant option in the first place. For example:

```
U3: REVOKE GRANT OPTION FOR SELECT ON TABLE S FROM U4 RESTRICT
```

---

*Or character set, collation, or translation.

The RESTRICT *vs.* CASCADE option on REVOKE is discussed in Section 15.6 immediately following.

15.6   RESTRICT vs. CASCADE

Consider again the sequence of GRANTs shown in the previous section:

```
U1: GRANT SELECT ON TABLE S TO U2 WITH GRANT OPTION

U2: GRANT SELECT ON TABLE S TO U3 WITH GRANT OPTION

U3: GRANT SELECT ON TABLE S TO U4 WITH GRANT OPTION
```

What happens if user *U1* now tries to revoke "SELECT ON TABLE S" from user *U2*?—

```
U1: REVOKE SELECT ON TABLE S FROM U2 ...
```

If this REVOKE were to do *precisely* (and *only*) what it says, then *U2* would no longer hold the specified privilege, but *U3* and *U4* still would. However, those privileges held by *U3* and *U4* would now be *abandoned*—meaning that they were originally derived from the privilege held by *U2*, and that privilege no longer exists.

The possibility of abandoned privileges is the justification (or, at least, part of that justification) for the RESTRICT *vs.* CASCADE option on REVOKE. The basic idea is that abandoned privileges are prohibited. Thus, if CASCADE is specified, the REVOKE succeeds, and cascades down to revoke any privileges that would otherwise be abandoned. If RESTRICT is specified, the REVOKE succeeds only if revoking the privileges identified explicitly in the REVOKE operation *and no others* would not leave any abandoned privileges. In the example, therefore, the REVOKE will fail if RESTRICT is specified, but will succeed (and will revoke *U3*'s and *U4*'s privileges as well) if CASCADE is specified. By contrast, user *U3* could successfully revoke "SELECT ON S" from user *U4* with a mere RESTRICT specification (assuming, of course, that *U4* has not gone on to grant the privilege to some further user *U5*, etc.).

Now, it is not only privileges to which the notion of abandonment applies. For example, a view would become abandoned if its owner were to lose the SELECT privilege on some table that is used in the definition of that view. Analogous remarks apply to constraints also. Again, REVOKE ... RESTRICT will fail if it would lead to any abandoned objects; REVOKE ... CASCADE will succeed, and will cause those abandoned objects to be *dropped* (a rather more severe side effect, it seems to this writer, than merely revoking some privilege would be).

In a like manner, certain objects (domains, columns, modules, schemas) would become "lost" if USAGE of some relevant character set were to be revoked, and certain objects (domains, columns, collations, character sets) would be "impacted" if USAGE of some relevant collation were to be revoked (refer to Chapter 19 for a discussion of character sets and collations). Like abandoned objects, lost and impacted objects are prohibited, and the meaning of the REVOKE *vs.* CASCADE option on REVOKE is extended accordingly: REVOKE ... RESTRICT will fail if it would lead to any lost or impacted objects; REVOKE ... CASCADE will succeed, and will cause those lost or impacted objects to be dropped.

What all this means is that the effects of REVOKE ... CASCADE could be quite drastic!—especially since (a) those implied DROPs are defined to include the CASCADE option (where applicable), and (b) all such implied DROPs are performed "without further Access Rule checking" (to quote the standard), meaning that the user issuing the REVOKE might be destroying objects not owned by that user. It follows that, in practice, the REVOKE ... CASCADE operation probably needs to be used with a considerable degree of circumspection.

PART **V**

ADVANCED TOPICS

This, the final part of the book, discusses a number of more esoteric aspects of SQL. By and large, it is not necessary to understand all of this material in detail in order to get a broad appreciation of what SQL is all about (with the possible exception of the topic of Chapter 16, "Missing Information and Nulls"). Needless to say, however, a proper understanding of these topics *is* essential to a full appreciation of the scope of the SQL standard.

16

Missing Information and Nulls

CAVEAT: It is only fair to the reader to explain at the outset that the topic of this chapter CANNOT be described in a manner that is simultaneously both comprehensive and comprehensible. The reason is that the theoretical ideas on which the relevant SQL features are based and—even more so—those SQL features per se are themselves not fully consistent; indeed, in some ways they are fundamentally at odds with the way the world behaves. This is not the place to go into details; the interested reader can find extensive discussion of the problem in four books:

- *Relational Database: Selected Writings (1986)*
- *Relational Database Writings 1985–1989 (1990)*
- *Relational Database Writings 1989–1991 (1992)*
- *Relational Database Writings 1991–1994 (1995)*

(all by the present author(s) and published by Addison-Wesley).

16.1   INTRODUCTION

With the foregoing caveat out of the way, let us get down to some specifics. First of all, SQL represents the fact that some piece of information is missing by means of a special marker called a *null*. For example, we might say, loosely, that the weight of some part, say part P7, is null. What we mean by such a remark is, more precisely, that:

- We know that part P7 exists;
- Also, of course, it does have a weight, because all parts have a weight;
- However, we do not know what that weight is.

In other words, we do not know a genuine weight value that can sensibly be put in the WEIGHT position in the row in table P for that part. Instead, therefore, we *mark* that position as "null," and we interpret that mark to mean, precisely, that we do not know what the real value is.

Now, informally we often think of such a position as "containing a null," or of the corresponding value as "being null," and such terms are certainly the ones most often heard in SQL contexts. But the previous paragraph should serve to show that such a manner of speaking *is* only informal, and indeed not very accurate. That is why the expression *null value*, which is heard very frequently (and indeed is used throughout the standard), is to be deprecated: The whole point about nulls is precisely that they are not values. *Note:* How nulls are actually represented in the system is implementation-dependent; however, that representation must be such that the system can distinguish nulls from all possible nonnull values. As the standard puts it: "A null value is an implementation-dependent special value that is distinct from all nonnull values . . . There is effectively only one null value."

The reader will recall from Chapter 8 that columns in base tables usually have an associated default value, and that default value is often defined, explicitly or implicitly, to be null. Furthermore, columns in base tables always *permit* nulls, unless there is an integrity constraint—probably just a NOT NULL column constraint—that explicitly bans them from the column in question (see Chapter 14). But even though nulls can thus appear as "values" in certain columns in certain tables, they do not have a data type (precisely because they are *not* truly values). And partly for this reason, they cannot be assigned as "values" of parameters or host variables (at least, not directly; see the subsection "Indicator Parameters and Variables" in Section 16.2).

We now proceed to explore the detailed effects of the foregoing ideas on the SQL language. Section 16.2 discusses scalar values and scalar expressions; Section 16.3 describes *three-valued logic* and its implications for conditional expressions; Section 16.4 considers table expressions, and in particular introduces some new table operators called "outer joins"; and Section 16.5 examines the implications for integrity constraints. Finally, Section 16.6 offers a specific recommendation.

16.2   EFFECT OF NULLS ON SCALAR EXPRESSIONS

"Literals"

SQL provides a special construct, represented by the key word NULL, that might be thought of in some respects as a kind of literal representation of null. However, this construct certainly cannot appear in all contexts in which literals can appear; as the standard puts it, "there is no <literal> for a null value, although the key word NULL is used in some places to indicate that a null value is desired." To be specific, the "literal" NULL can appear in the following contexts *only.**

1. As a default specification within a column or domain definition—i.e., DEFAULT NULL

2. As an insert-item specifying a "value" to be placed in a column position on INSERT

3. As an update-item specifying a "value" to be placed in a column position on UPDATE

4. As a CAST source operand—i.e., CAST (NULL AS ...)

5. As a CASE result—i.e., CASE ... THEN NULL ... END, or CASE ... ELSE NULL END

6. As part of a referential specification—i.e., SET NULL

Number 1 in this list was discussed in Chapter 8, Numbers 2 and 3 were discussed in Chapter 9, and Number 6 is discussed in Section 16.5 later. The other two are discussed in the subsection "Scalar Operators and Functions" below. First, however, there are a few specific consequences of the foregoing that are worth pointing out explicitly:

- It is not possible to specify NULL explicitly as a select-item—e.g., "SELECT NULL" is illegal.

- It is not possible to specify NULL explicitly as an operand of a scalar expression—e.g., "X + NULL" is illegal.

- It is not possible to specify NULL explicitly as an operand of a conditional expression—e.g., "WHERE X = NULL" is illegal.

---

*SQL also provides two constructs, "IS NULL" and its converse "IS NOT NULL," for use in conditional expressions (see Sections 14.4 and 16.3). However, these constructs should *not* be regarded as containing the "literal" NULL; instead, they should be seen as distinct constructs in their own right, representing certain truth-valued functions. Indeed, the expressions "*x* IS NULL" and "*x* IS NOT NULL" might better have been written IS_NULL(x) and NOT (IS_NULL(x)), respectively.

Scalar Operators and Functions

Let x and y each be of some numeric data type. Then if x is null, each of the expressions $+x$ and $-x$ is defined to evaluate to null. And if x is null or y is null or both, then each of the expressions

```
x + y      x - y      x * y      x / y
```

is also defined to evaluate to null. These definitions are all justified by the intended interpretation of null as "value unknown"; after all, if x is unknown, then obviously (e.g.) x + 1 is unknown too.*

Analogous considerations apply to all other data types and all other scalar operations (including scalar functions); that is, if any operand evaluates to null, then the result of the operation or function is defined to evaluate to null also. In particular, the operation CAST (x AS ...) evaluates to null if x evaluates to null.† The only operation that needs any further attention is the CASE operation, which we now discuss.

1. First, as indicated above, any THEN clause and/or the ELSE clause within a CASE operation can specify explicitly that the result of that CASE operation (if that clause in fact provides the result) is NULL. In fact, if the ELSE clause is omitted, an ELSE clause of "ELSE NULL" is assumed by default.

2. Second, two shorthand forms of CASE are provided specifically to deal with certain nulls-related issues, as follows:

   - The expression NULLIF(x,y) is defined to be equivalent to the expression

     ```
     CASE WHEN x = y THEN NULL ELSE x END
     ```

     In other words, NULLIF(x,y) returns null if its operands are equal (see Section 16.3), and returns its first operand otherwise.

   - The expression COALESCE(x,y) is defined to be equivalent to the expression

     ```
     CASE WHEN x IS NOT NULL THEN x ELSE y END
     ```

     More generally, COALESCE($x,y,...,z$) returns null if and only if its operands all evaluate to null; otherwise it returns the value of its first nonnull operand. See Section 16.3 for a discussion of "IS NOT NULL."

Aggregate Functions

To repeat a couple of points already made in Chapter 7: First, the aggregate functions (SUM, AVG, etc.) do *not* behave in accordance with the rules for scalar oper-

---

*"Justified" is perhaps a little strong here. Observe, for example, that according to that "justification" the expression $x - x$, which logically should always yield zero, actually yields null if x is null.

†We remark that the expression CAST (NULL AS ...) provides a way of producing a kind of "null literal" of a specific data type. For example, the expression "X + NULL" is illegal, as already explained, but the more complex expression "X + CAST (NULL AS INTEGER)" is legal (and its value is null).

ators ("+" etc.) explained above, but instead simply ignore any nulls in their argument (except for COUNT(*)). Note, therefore, that (for example) the SUM function cannot be explained as simply an iterated addition. Second, if the argument to such a function happens to evaluate to an empty set, the functions all—quite incorrectly, in this writer's opinion—return null (except for COUNT, which does return the correct result, *viz.* zero).

Scalar Expressions

In general, the result of evaluating a scalar expression in which any of the operands evaluates to null can be deduced from the rules described above (in most cases, of course, the result is null in turn). However, there is one aberrant case: If the scalar expression is in fact a scalar subquery—see Chapter 7, Section 7.4—then normally that table expression is required to evaluate to a table containing exactly one column and exactly one row; the value of the scalar expression is then taken to be, precisely, the single scalar value contained within that table. But if the table expression evaluates to a table that contains no rows at all, the value of the scalar expression is—again, quite incorrectly!—taken to be null.

Indicator Parameters and Variables

Consider the following example of a procedure in the module language:

```
PROCEDURE GET_WEIGHT
            ( ̄SQLSTATE,
             :PNO_PARAM    CHAR(6),
             :WEIGHT_PARAM DECIMAL(3) ) ;
   SELECT P.WEIGHT
   INTO   :WEIGHT_PARAM
   FROM   P
   WHERE  P.PNO = :PNO_PARAM ;
```

Suppose there is a possibility that WEIGHT might be null for some part. The SELECT statement as shown will fail for such a part: SQLSTATE will be set to 22002, and the target ("output") parameter :WEIGHT_PARAM will be left in an undefined state. In general, if it is possible that a value to be retrieved might "be null," the user should specify an *indicator parameter* in addition to the regular target or output parameter for that value, as we now illustrate:

```
PROCEDURE GET_WEIGHT
            ( ̄SQLSTATE,
             :PNO_PARAM    CHAR(6),
             :WEIGHT_PARAM DECIMAL(3),
             :WEIGHT_INDIC DECIMAL(5) ) ;
   SELECT P.WEIGHT
   INTO   :WEIGHT_PARAM INDICATOR :WEIGHT_INDIC
   FROM   P
   WHERE  P.PNO = :PNO_PARAM ;
```

If the value to be retrieved "is null" and an indicator parameter has been specified, then that indicator parameter is set to –1 (minus one); the value of the corresponding regular parameter is undefined. If the value to be retrieved is nonnull, the indicator parameter is set to zero.* Indicator parameters are specified as shown— i.e., following the corresponding regular parameter, and optionally separated from that regular parameter by the key word INDICATOR. They must be of data type exact numeric with a scale of zero (the precise data type is implementation-defined).

The foregoing example shows the use of an indicator parameter in conjunction with an output parameter in a single-row SELECT. FETCH is treated analogously, of course. Indicator parameters can also be used with input parameters (i.e., parameters that are used merely to supply values, instead of acting as targets). For example, the UPDATE statement

```
UPDATE P
SET     WEIGHT = :WEIGHT_PARAM INDICATOR :WEIGHT_INDIC
WHERE   P.CITY = 'London'
```

will set the weight for all London parts to null if the value of WEIGHT_INDIC is negative (*any* negative value, not necessarily just –1). So also of course will the statement

```
UPDATE P
SET     WEIGHT = NULL
WHERE   P.CITY = 'London'
```

Note: Indicator parameters can also be used in conditional expressions—in particular, in WHERE clauses—but probably should not be. For example, even if the value of :WEIGHT_INDIC is negative, the following statement will *not* retrieve part numbers for parts where the weight is null. *Exercise for the reader:* What will it do? You will need at least a basic understanding of the ideas of Section 16.3 in order to answer this question.

```
SELECT  P.PNO
INTO    :PNO_PARAM
FROM    P
WHERE   P.WEIGHT = :WEIGHT_PARAM INDICATOR :WEIGHT_INDIC
```

The correct way to retrieve part numbers where the weight is null is:

```
SELECT  P.PNO
INTO    :PNO_PARAM
FROM    P
WHERE   P.WEIGHT IS NULL
```

Again, see Section 16.3.

---

*A slight oversimplification. If the value to be retrieved is nonnull and is a character or bit string of length $n1$ (characters or bits, respectively), and if the data type of the target parameter is respectively CHARACTER [VARYING] ($n2$) or BIT [VARYING] ($n2$), and if $n1 > n2$, then the result is truncated by dropping the rightmost $n1 - n2$ characters or bits, and the indicator parameter is set to $n1$ (also, a warning condition is raised).

We conclude this subsection (and section) by observing that in embedded SQL, indicator *variables* can and must be used in a manner analogous to the way indicator *parameters* are used in the module language. For example (PL/I):

```
EXEC SQL SELECT P.WEIGHT
         INTO   :WEIGHT INDICATOR :WEIGHT_INDIC
         FROM   P
         WHERE  P.PNO = :PNO ;
IF WEIGHT_INDIC < 0 THEN ... /* no WEIGHT retrieved */ ;
```

16.3   EFFECT OF NULLS ON CONDITIONAL EXPRESSIONS

Conditional expressions are also affected—dramatically so—by nulls. First let us consider the basic comparison operations introduced in Chapter 7, Section 7.5. Let x and y be compatible for comparison purposes. Then, if x is null or y is null or both, then each of the comparisons

```
x = y      x <> y
x < y      x <= y
x > y      x >= y
```

evaluates, not to *true*, nor to *false*, but rather to the *unknown* truth value. The justification for this rule (again) is the intended interpretation of null as "value unknown": If the value of x is unknown, then clearly it is *unknown* whether, e.g., "$x = 3$" is *true* (despite the fact that, as mentioned in Section 16.1, the standard explicitly states that null is "distinct from all nonnull values"!—a statement that might reasonably be taken to imply that "$x = 3$" should yield *false* if x is null).

Note very carefully that, as a particular case of the foregoing, two nulls are not considered to be equal to one another—that is, the comparison "null = null" (not intended to be valid SQL syntax) evaluates to *unknown*, not *true* (and not *false*). Thus, "$x = x$" evaluates to *unknown*, not *true*, if x is null. Likewise, "$x > x$" and "$x < x$" also both evaluate to *unknown*, not *false*, if x is null.

The concept of nulls thus leads us into a *three-valued logic* (so called because there are three truth values, namely *true*, *false*, and *unknown*). The three-valued logic truth tables for AND, OR, and NOT are shown below (t = *true*, f = *false*, u = *unknown*):

AND	t u f		OR	t u f		NOT	
t	t u f		t	t t t		t	f
u	u u f		u	t u u		u	u
f	f f f		f	t u f		f	t

Suppose, for example, that $A = 3$, $B = 4$, and C is null. Then the following logical (i.e., conditional) expressions have the indicated truth values:

```
A > B AND B > C  :   false
A > B OR  B > C  :   unknown
A < B OR  B < C  :   true
NOT ( A = C )    :   unknown
```

In Chapter 11, we stated that when SQL applies a WHERE clause to some table *T*, it eliminates all rows of *T* for which the conditional expression in that WHERE clause does not evaluate to *true*. Now, this remark is still correct as a statement of fact under three-valued logic, but it needs to be clearly understood that "not evaluating to *true*" means "evaluating either to *false* or to *unknown*." (Analogous remarks apply to the ON and HAVING clauses, of course.) We will elaborate on this point and related matters in Section 16.4.

We now proceed to investigate the implications of the foregoing ideas for conditional expressions in general.

Comparison Conditions

To repeat from Chapter 12, the syntax of a comparison condition (*comparison* for short) is:

```
row-constructor comparison-operator row-constructor
```

In Chapter 12, Section 12.3, we defined what it meant for this expression to evaluate to *true*, and we assumed, tacitly, that the expression evaluated to *false* if and only if it did not evaluate to *true*. Now, however, we have to consider what happens if any component of either of the two row constructors happens to be (or to evaluate to) null.

First we repeat the definition of the *true* cases (refer back to Chapter 12, Section 12.3, for an explanation of the notation):

- "*Left = Right*" is *true* if and only if for all *i*, "*Li = Ri*" is *true*
- "*Left <> Right*" is *true* if and only if there exists some *j* such that "*Lj <> Rj*" is *true*
- "*Left < Right*" is *true* if and only if there exists some *j* such that "*Lj < Rj*" is *true* and for all *i < j*, "*Li = Ri*" is *true*
- "*Left > Right*" is *true* if and only if there exists some *j* such that "*Lj > Rj*" is *true* and for all *i < j*, "*Li = Ri*" is *true*
- "*Left <= Right*" is *true* if and only if "*Left < Right*" is *true* or "*Left = Right*" is *true*
- "*Left >= Right*" is *true* if and only if "*Left > Right*" is *true* or "*Left = Right*" is *true*

Now we have to add the following:

- "*Left = Right*" is *false* if and only if "*Left <> Right*" is *true*
- "*Left <> Right*" is *false* if and only if "*Left = Right*" is *true*
- "*Left < Right*" is *false* if and only if "*Left >= Right*" is *true*

- "*Left > Right*" is *false* if and only if "*Left <= Right*" is *true*

- "*Left <= Right*" is *false* if and only if "*Left > Right*" is *true*

- "*Left >= Right*" is *false* if and only if "*Left < Right*" is *true*

Finally, let *op* stand for any of =, <>, <, <=, >, >=. Then:

- "*Left op Right*" is *unknown* if and only if it is not *true* and not *false*

  Here are some examples:

  ```
  ( 1, 2, NULL ) = ( 3, NULL, 4 )  :  false
  ( 1, 2, NULL ) < ( 3, NULL, 4 )  :  true
  ( 1, 2, NULL ) = ( 1, NULL, 4 )  :  unknown
  ( 1, 2, NULL ) > ( NULL, 2, 4 )  :  unknown
  ```

Of course, either *Left* or *Right* might in fact be a *row subquery*—that is, a table expression enclosed in parentheses that is normally supposed to evaluate to a table containing exactly one row. If instead it evaluates to a table that contains no rows at all, the value of the row constructor is taken—quite incorrectly!—to be a row of all nulls. This fact can lead to surprises. For example, consider the following query ("Get supplier numbers for suppliers in a different city from supplier S6"):

```
SELECT  S.SNO
FROM    S
WHERE   S.CITY <> ( SELECT  S.CITY
                    FROM    S
                    WHERE   S.SNO = 'S6' )
```

Given our usual sample data, this query will return an empty result—a result that might reasonably, but incorrectly, be interpreted to mean that every supplier is in the same city as supplier S6. Similar surprises can occur with most conditional expression formats.

Tests for Null

As mentioned in Section 16.2 above, SQL provides two special operators, IS NULL and IS NOT NULL, to test for the presence or absence of nulls. The syntax is:

```
row-constructor IS [ NOT ] NULL
```

(an additional case of "simple condition"—see Chapter 12). First we consider the case where the row constructor is a simple scalar, *x* say:

- The conditional expression "*x* IS NULL" evaluates to *true* if *x* evaluates to null and to *false* otherwise.

- The conditional expression "*x* IS NOT NULL" is defined to be equivalent to the conditional expression "NOT (*x* IS NULL)."

For example, suppose again that $A = 3$, $B = 4$, and C is null. Then the following conditional expressions have the indicated truth values:

```
C IS NULL       :   true
A IS NULL       :   false
B IS NOT NULL   :   true
```

Note that IS NULL and IS NOT NULL never return *unknown*.

The more general case, in which x is not a scalar expression but a general row constructor, with scalar components $x1, x2, ..., xn$ say, is defined as follows:

- The expression

  ```
  ( x1, x2, ..., xn ) IS NULL
  ```

  is defined to be equivalent to the expression

  ```
  ( x1 IS NULL ) AND
  ( x2 IS NULL ) AND
      .....       AND
  ( xn IS NULL )
  ```

- The expression

  ```
  ( x1, x2, ..., xn ) IS NOT NULL
  ```

  is defined to be equivalent to the expression

  ```
  ( x1 IS NOT NULL ) AND
  ( x2 IS NOT NULL ) AND
      ........        AND
  ( xn IS NOT NULL )
  ```

- The expression

  ```
  NOT ( x1, x2, ..., xn ) IS NULL
  ```

  is defined to be equivalent to the expression

  ```
  NOT ( ( x1, x2, ..., xn ) IS NULL )
  ```

- The expression

  ```
  NOT ( x1, x2, ..., xn ) IS NOT NULL
  ```

  is defined to be equivalent to the expression

  ```
  NOT ( ( x1, x2, ..., xn ) IS NOT NULL )
  ```

Observe, therefore, that the expressions

```
x IS NOT NULL
```

and

```
NOT x IS NULL
```

are no longer equivalent, in general! For example, if *x* has two components, *x1* and *x2*, then the first is equivalent to

```
x1 IS NOT NULL AND x2 IS NOT NULL
```

The second is equivalent to

```
x1 IS NOT NULL OR x2 IS NOT NULL
```

Tests for True, False, Unknown

As we saw in Chapter 12, any "conditional primary" *p* (*p* is either a "simple condition," *q.v.*, or a conditional expression enclosed in parentheses) can optionally be followed by one of the following:

```
IS TRUE
IS NOT TRUE
IS FALSE
IS NOT FALSE
```

Now we have two more tests to add to this list:

```
IS UNKNOWN
IS NOT UNKNOWN
```

We explain the various possibilities by extending the truth table from Chapter 12, Section 12.2. Note that like IS NULL and IS NOT NULL, these tests never return *unknown*.

p	true	false	unknown
p IS TRUE	true	false	false
p IS NOT TRUE	false	true	true
p IS FALSE	false	true	false
p IS NOT FALSE	true	false	true
p IS UNKNOWN	false	false	true
p IS NOT UNKNOWN	true	true	false

Observe, therefore, that the expressions

```
p IS NOT TRUE
```

and

```
NOT p
```

are no longer equivalent, in general! For example, if *p* is *unknown*, the first expression evaluates to *true*, but the second evaluates to *unknown*.*

---

*In other words, the NOT in NOT TRUE is not the "NOT" of three-valued logic. Then again, the NOT of three-valued logic is not the "not" of ordinary English . . .

BETWEEN Conditions

The between-condition

```
y BETWEEN x AND z
```

is still defined (as in Chapter 12) to be semantically equivalent to

```
x <= y AND y <= z
```

but, of course, either of the two component expressions can now evaluate to *unknown*, giving an overall result of *unknown* (if the other component expression evaluates to *true* or *unknown*) or *false* (otherwise). NOT BETWEEN is revised accordingly.

LIKE Conditions

The like-condition

```
character-string-expression [ NOT ] LIKE pattern
                                    [ ESCAPE escape ]
```

evaluates to *unknown* if any of its operands "character string expression," "pattern," or "escape" evaluates to null (otherwise it evaluates to *true* or *false* as explained in Chapter 12). NOT LIKE is revised accordingly.

IN Conditions

A "Format 1" in-condition is equivalent to an all-or-any condition involving the comparison operator =ANY (or <>ALL, in the negated case); see the subsection on all-or-any conditions immediately following. The "Format 2" in-condition

```
x IN ( x1, x2, ..., xn )
```

is still defined (as in Chapter 12) to be semantically equivalent to

```
x = x1 OR x = x2 OR ... OR x = xn
```

but, of course, any of the component expressions can now evaluate to *unknown*, thus possibly giving an overall result of *unknown*. NOT IN is revised accordingly.

All-or-Any Conditions

Let *op* stand for any of =, <>, <, <=, >, >=. Then the all-or-any condition

```
x op ALL ( table-expression )
```

evaluates to *true* if the expression

```
x op y
```

evaluates to *true* for every *y* in the result of evaluating the table expression (or if that result is empty); it evaluates to *false* if the expression

```
x  op  y
```

evaluates to *false* for at least one *y* in the result of evaluating that table expression; and it evaluates to *unknown* otherwise. Likewise, the all-or-any condition

```
x  op ANY  ( table-expression )
```

evaluates to *true* if the expression

```
x  op  y
```

evaluates to *true* for at least one *y* in the result of evaluating the table expression; it evaluates to *false* if the expression

```
x  op  y
```

evaluates to *false* for every *y* in the result of evaluating that table expression (or if that result is empty); and it evaluates to *unknown* otherwise.

MATCH Conditions

The syntax of match-conditions includes a "PARTIAL or FULL" option, not shown and not discussed in Chapter 12, that can affect the result if nulls are present:

```
row-constructor MATCH [ UNIQUE ]
                [ PARTIAL | FULL ] ( table-expression )
```

There are six cases to consider, depending on (a) whether the UNIQUE option is missing or specified and (b) whether the "PARTIAL or FULL" option is missing or specified (and if specified, which it is). We refer to the six cases as indicated by the following table:*

	missing	PARTIAL	FULL
missing	Case 1	Case 2	Case 3
UNIQUE	Case 4	Case 5	Case 6

In all cases, let *R1* be the row that results from evaluating the row constructor and let *T* be the table that results from evaluating the table expression. It is worth pointing out immediately that PARTIAL and FULL have no effect, and thus can safely be ignored, if either (a) *R1* and *T* are both of degree one (i.e., contain

---

*We cannot resist the temptation to point out that this table includes certain row-and-column positions for which information is missing for some reason, and yet those positions do *not* "contain a null." There is probably a moral here.

just one scalar value and one column, respectively), or (b) every component of *R1* has "nulls not allowed." However, the general rules are as follows.

■   *Case 1* (no UNIQUE, no PARTIAL or FULL):

The result is *true* if either (a) any component of *R1* is null, or (b) *T* contains at least one row, *R2* say, such that the comparison condition "*R1 = R2*" evaluates to *true*; otherwise the result is *false*.

■   *Case 2* (no UNIQUE, PARTIAL specified):

The result is *true* if either (a) every component of *R1* is null, or (b) *T* contains at least one row, *R2* say, such that each nonnull component within *R1* is equal to its counterpart in *R2*; otherwise the result is *false*.

■   *Case 3* (no UNIQUE, FULL specified):

The result is *true* if either (a) every component of *R1* is null, or (b) every component of *R1* is nonnull and *T* contains at least one row, *R2* say, such that the comparison condition "*R1 = R2*" evaluates to *true*; otherwise the result is *false*.

■   *Case 4* (UNIQUE, no PARTIAL or FULL):

The result is *true* if either (a) any component of *R1* is null, or (b) *T* contains exactly one row, *R2* say, such that the comparison condition "*R1 = R2*" evaluates to *true*; otherwise the result is *false*.

■   *Case 5* (UNIQUE, PARTIAL specified):

The result is *true* if either (a) every component of *R1* is null, or (b) *T* contains exactly one row, *R2* say, such that each nonnull component within *R1* is equal to its counterpart in *R2*; otherwise the result is *false*.

■   *Case 6* (UNIQUE, FULL specified):

The result is *true* if either (a) every component of *R1* is null, or (b) every component of *R1* is nonnull and *T* contains exactly one row, *R2* say, such that the comparison condition "*R1 = R2*" evaluates to *true*; otherwise the result is *false*.

The standard makes use of the MATCH condition in its definition of foreign key constraints and referential actions. See Section 16.5.

EXISTS Conditions

The definition of EXISTS is not affected by nulls; to repeat from Chapter 12, the expression "EXISTS (table-expression)" is defined to return the value *false* if the table expression evaluates to an empty table, the value *true* otherwise. However, as mentioned in Chapter 14, there are certainly some traps for the unwary in this area. Consider the query (repeated from Chapter 12, Section 12.6) "Get part names for parts whose weight is greater than that of every blue part." Here is a superfi-

cially plausible—but actually *** *INCORRECT* ***—formulation of this query
using EXISTS (or rather NOT EXISTS):

```
SELECT DISTINCT PX.PNAME              -- *** INCORRECT *** !!!
FROM    P AS PX
WHERE   NOT EXISTS
      ( SELECT *
        FROM    P AS PY
        WHERE   PY.COLOR = 'Blue'
        AND     PY.WEIGHT >= PX.WEIGHT )
```

To paraphrase: "Get part names for parts, PX say, such that there does not exist a
blue part, PY say, with the same or a greater weight."

On the face of it, this SQL expression certainly *looks* as if it ought to be logically correct. Yet there are at least two situations in which it gives the wrong
answer! Before we can examine those situations in detail, however, we first have
to agree on exactly what the original query is intended to mean (always a challenge
if nulls are involved). Here is a more precise statement: "Get part names for parts
known to have a weight greater than that of every part that (a) *is known to be* blue
and (b) *has a known weight*." Let us assume that this restatement does indeed cap-
ture the intended meaning of the query. Now consider the following possibilities:

1. Suppose every blue part has a null weight. Then the SQL expression shown
   incorrectly yields a result consisting of all part names, because:

   - The EXISTS argument evaluates to an empty set for every row in table P.

   - The EXISTS condition therefore evaluates to *false* for every part.

   - The negation of that condition therefore evaluates to *true* for every part.

   - Thus, the final result includes all part names, instead of none of them (the
     correct solution in this case).

2. Suppose there exists at least one part (not necessarily a blue part) with a null
   weight. Then the SQL expression shown yields a result incorrectly including
   the names of all such parts, because:

   - The EXISTS argument evaluates to an empty set for each such part.

   - The EXISTS condition therefore evaluates to *false* for each such part.

   - The negation of that condition therefore evaluates to *true* for each such part.

   - Thus, the final result includes the names of all such parts, yet the parts in
     question are certainly not "known to have a weight greater than that of
     every blue part."

The real problem, of course, is that the user intuitively, and quite justifiably,
expects EXISTS in SQL to behave like the "existential quantifier" EXISTS of
(three-valued) logic, but it does not. In the case at hand, we would like the EXISTS

to return *unknown* (the logically correct response) if PX.WEIGHT or PY.WEIGHT is null—but, as we have seen, it returns *false* instead.

Perhaps we should point out that the given SQL expression *is* a correct formulation of the query in the absence of nulls.*

UNIQUE Conditions

The expression "UNIQUE (table-expression)" is defined to return *true* if the result of evaluating the table expression contains no two distinct rows, *R1* and *R2* say, such that the comparison condition "*R1* = *R2*" evaluates to *true*; otherwise it returns *false*. Recall, however, that "*R1* = *R2*" will not evaluate to *true* if either *R1* or *R2* includes any null components; hence, e.g., if column *C* of the 5-row table *T* contains the values 1, 2, 3, NULL, and NULL, then the expression UNIQUE (SELECT *C* FROM *T*) will return *true*. Thus we see that, just as EXISTS sometimes returns *false* when *unknown* would be more logically correct, so UNIQUE sometimes returns *true* when *unknown* would be more logically correct.

The standard makes use of the UNIQUE condition in its definition of candidate key constraints. See Section 16.5.

16.4   EFFECT OF NULLS ON TABLE EXPRESSIONS

Conditional Expressions Within Table Expressions

We have already mentioned that when SQL applies a WHERE clause to some table *T*, it eliminates all rows of *T* for which the conditional expression in that WHERE clause evaluates to *false* or *unknown*. (Analogous remarks apply to ON clauses within join expressions, of course, since ON clauses are defined in terms of WHERE clauses.) Likewise, when SQL applies a HAVING clause to some grouped table *G*, it eliminates all groups of *G* for which the conditional expression in that HAVING clause evaluates to *false* or *unknown*.

The foregoing remarks apply equally to WHERE and HAVING clauses within "searched UPDATE" and "searched DELETE" statements, of course; in fact, the "table ... WHERE conditional expression" component of such statements is effectively just a slight variation on the normal SQL syntax for a certain special case of a table expression.

---

*It is worth mentioning that the discussion of this example in the previous edition of this book contained several errors (thanks to Ed Dee of Edinburgh University, Scotland, for pointing those errors out)—further evidence of the fact that it is easy to make mistakes in this area.

Duplicates

Duplicates are relevant to the DISTINCT, GROUP BY, UNION, INTERSECT, and EXCEPT operations: DISTINCT, UNION, EXCEPT, and INTERSECT (without the ALL option, in the last three cases) are all defined to eliminate redundant duplicate rows, and GROUP BY groups rows together on the basis of duplicate values in the set of grouping columns (and those sets of grouping column values can be regarded as "rows" for present purposes). The point is, however, the definition of duplicate rows requires some refinement in the presence of nulls. Let *Left* and *Right* be as defined for the subsection "Comparison Conditions" in Section 16.3 above. Then *Left* and *Right* are defined to be *duplicates* of one another if and only if, for all *i* in the range 1 to *n*, either "$Li = Ri$" is *true*, or *Li* and *Ri* are both null.

Note, therefore, that if *Left* and *Right* are duplicates of one another, it does not follow that the comparison "*Left* = *Right*" evaluates to *true!* Note too that if "UNIQUE (SELECT * FROM *T*)" evaluates to *true*, it does not imply that "SELECT * FROM *T*" and "SELECT DISTINCT * FROM *T*" have the same cardinality.

Ordering

Although not technically part of a table expression *per se*, the ORDER BY clause is used in a cursor definition* to impose an ordering on the result of such an expression. The question that arises is: What is the relative ordering for *x* and *y* if *x* is null or *y* is null or both? The answer given by the SQL standard is as follows:

■   For ordering purposes, all nulls are considered to be equal to one another.

Furthermore:

■   For ordering purposes, all nulls are considered *either* to be greater than all nonnull values *or* less than all nonnull values; however, which of the two possibilities applies is implementation-defined.

Outer Join

We discussed join expressions in some detail in Chapter 11. However, we deferred discussion of the various "outer" joins to the present chapter, on the grounds that they all had to do with nulls. We now explain these operations.

---

*Or in a multi-row retrieval operation in direct SQL.

The basic idea behind outer join is as follows. Suppose we are trying to construct the ordinary ("inner") join of two tables *T1* and *T2*. Then any row in either *T1* or *T2* that matches no row in the other table (under the relevant join condition) simply does not participate in the result. In an outer join, by contrast, such a row does participate in the result—to be more precise, it appears exactly once in the result—and the column positions that would have been filled with values from some matching row in the other table, if such a matching row had in fact existed, are filled with nulls instead. Thus, the outer join "preserves" nonmatching rows in the result, where the inner join "loses" them. *Note:* A left outer join of *T1* and *T2* (in that order) preserves rows from *T1* with no matching row in *T2*; a corresponding right outer join preserves rows from *T2* with no matching row in *T1*; and a full outer join does both.

The syntax for an outer join expression is:

```
table-reference [ NATURAL ] outer-join-type
                            JOIN table-reference
                            [ ON conditional-expression
                            | USING ( column-commalist ) ]
```

"Outer join type" here is one of the following:

```
LEFT [ OUTER ]
RIGHT [ OUTER ]
FULL [ OUTER ]
```

If NATURAL is specified, neither an ON clause nor a USING clause can be specified; otherwise, exactly one of the two *must* be specified. *Note:* The optional OUTER is a mere noiseword and has no effect on the overall meaning of the expression.

To fix our ideas, let us concentrate on *left* outer joins. Then there are three cases to consider:

```
1. table-reference LEFT JOIN table-reference
                   ON conditional-expression

2. table-reference LEFT JOIN table-reference
                   USING ( column-commalist )

3. table-reference NATURAL LEFT JOIN table-reference
```

In each case, let *A* and *B* be the tables resulting from evaluation of the two table references. Then *Case 1* ("*A* LEFT JOIN *B* ON *cond*," where *cond* is a conditional expression) can perhaps most easily be explained by defining it to be equivalent to the following pseudoSQL expression:*

It is only "pseudoSQL" for at least two reasons: (a) "NULL" is not a valid select-item; (b) "A." is not a valid row constructor and thus cannot be used as a comparand.

```
SELECT  A.*,  B.*
FROM    A, B
WHERE   cond

UNION   ALL

SELECT  A.*, NULL, NULL, ..., NULL
FROM    A
WHERE   A.* NOT IN  ( SELECT  A.*
                      FROM    A, B
                      WHERE   cond )
```

In other words, the result consists of the "UNION ALL" of (a) the corresponding *inner* join and (b) the collection of all rows of *A* that do not participate in that inner join, each one concatenated with a row of all nulls (one null for each column of *B*; the pseudoSQL expression "NULL, NULL, ..., NULL" shown above is to be understood as containing one NULL for each column of *B*). The column names of the result are identical to those of the corresponding inner join.

We remark that, in general, the result will include some rows that do not satisfy the conditional expression *cond*.

In *Case 2*, let the commalist of columns in the USING clause be *C1, C2, ..., Cn*. Each of *C1, C2, ..., Cn* must be *un*qualified and must identify both a column of *A* and a column of *B*. Then the left outer join expression is defined to be semantically identical to a Case 1 left outer join expression in which the ON clause is of the form—

```
ON A.C1 = B.C1 AND A.C2 = B.C2 AND ... AND A.Cn = B.Cn
```

—except that (a) each of the common columns *C1, C2, ..., Cn* appears only once, not twice, in the final result; (b) for each such result column, *Ci* say, the value contained in any given row is defined to be COALESCE(*A.Ci,B.Ci*) (see Section 16.2 for an explanation of COALESCE); and (c) the result column ordering is different—the common columns appear first (i.e., at the left, in the order specified in the USING clause), then the other columns of *A* (in the order in which they appear in *A*), then the other columns of *B* (in the order in which they appear in *B*).

Finally, a *Case 3* left outer join expression is defined to be semantically identical to a Case 2 left outer join expression in which the commalist of columns specifies *all* of the columns that are common to *A* and *B* (in the order in which they appear in *A*). *Note:* It is possible that there are no common columns at all, in which case *A* NATURAL LEFT JOIN *B* degenerates to *A* CROSS JOIN *B*.

Here are some examples (all based as usual on the suppliers-and-parts database):

```
S LEFT JOIN SP ON S.SNO = SP.SNO
```

```
S LEFT JOIN SP USING ( SNO )
```

```
S LEFT NATURAL JOIN SP
```

These three expressions are all equivalent, except that the first produces a table with two SNO columns and the second and third produce a table with just one such column (the SNO column that appears between the CITY and PNO columns in the first case being eliminated in the second and third cases). For example, the result from the first expression looks like this (assuming, as always, data values as given in Fig. 2.1, and using lines of dashes "---" to represent nulls):

SNO	SNAME	STATUS	CITY	SNO	PNO	QTY
S1	Smith	20	London	S1	P1	300
S1	Smith	20	London	S1	P2	200
S1	Smith	20	London	S1	P3	400
S1	Smith	20	London	S1	P4	200
S1	Smith	20	London	S1	P5	100
S1	Smith	20	London	S1	P6	100
S2	Jones	10	Paris	S2	P1	300
S2	Jones	10	Paris	S2	P2	400
S3	Blake	30	Paris	S3	P2	200
S4	Clark	20	London	S4	P2	200
S4	Clark	20	London	S4	P4	300
S4	Clark	20	London	S4	P5	400
S5	Adams	30	Athens	---	---	---

Here by contrast is the result from the second (or third) expression:

SNO	SNAME	STATUS	CITY	PNO	QTY
S1	Smith	20	London	P1	300
S1	Smith	20	London	P2	200
S1	Smith	20	London	P3	400
S1	Smith	20	London	P4	200
S1	Smith	20	London	P5	100
S1	Smith	20	London	P6	100
S2	Jones	10	Paris	P1	300
S2	Jones	10	Paris	P2	400
S3	Blake	30	Paris	P2	200
S4	Clark	20	London	P2	200
S4	Clark	20	London	P4	300
S4	Clark	20	London	P5	400
S5	Adams	30	Athens	---	---

Definitions of the RIGHT and FULL outer joins are left as an exercise for the reader.

Union Join

"Union join," like outer join, is represented by an additional version of the explicit join expressions introduced in Chapter 11.* The syntax is:

```
table-reference UNION JOIN table-reference
```

---

*We deliberately make no attempt here to explain the operation in intuitive terms. It seems to be an attempt (but an inaccurate attempt) to define what is more usually known as *outer union*. Even if it were defined correctly, however, it is this writer's opinion that it would still not be worth trying to explain it intuitively, for reasons beyond the scope of this text. The interested reader is referred to Warden's paper "Into the Unknown" (included in C. J. Date, *Relational Database Writings 1985–1989*, Addison-Wesley, 1990) for a detailed—and critical—discussion of outer union.

Let *A* and *B* be the tables resulting from evaluation of the two table references. Then the union join expression can most easily be explained by defining it to be equivalent to the following pseudoSQL expression:

```
SELECT A.*, NULL, NULL, ..., NULL
FROM    A

UNION   ALL

SELECT NULL, NULL, ..., NULL, B.*
FROM    B
```

In other words, the result is constructed by (a) extending each operand table with all of the columns of the other operand; (b) filling those added columns with nulls; and finally (c) taking the "UNION ALL" (*not* the UNION, observe, despite the fact that the syntax specifies just "UNION") of those two extended tables. The column names of the result are identical to those of the Cartesian product of *A* and *B* (and are thus not necessarily unique within that result).

16.5 EFFECT OF NULLS ON INTEGRITY CONSTRAINTS

As explained in Chapter 14, an integrity constraint is basically a conditional expression that must not evaluate to *false*. Note, therefore, that the constraint is not considered to be violated if it evaluates to *unknown*. Technically, of course, we should say in such a case that it is *not known* whether the constraint is violated, but, just as SQL regards *unknown* as *false* for the purposes of a WHERE clause, so it regards *unknown* as *true* for the purposes of an integrity constraint (speaking a trifle loosely).

The foregoing remarks are directly applicable to domain constraints, general constraints ("assertions"), and check constraints, and effectively dispose of the issue for those three cases.* Candidate key and foreign key definitions require additional consideration, however.

---

*Perhaps we should point out, however, that since (a) as explained in Chapter 14, constraints typically begin (explicitly or implicitly) with "NOT EXISTS," and (b) as explained in Section 16.3, NOT EXISTS sometimes returns *true* when *unknown* would be more logically correct, therefore (c) updates will sometimes succeed when they really ought not to. For example, consider what the system will do, given the constraint "All red parts must be stored in London," with an attempt to INSERT a part row in which the COLOR is "Red" but the CITY is null. This row surely does violate the real-world constraint that the SQL constraint is attempting to enforce, but the INSERT will succeed. Note too that this criticism would still be valid, at least in the case of general constraints though possibly not for base table ones, even if SQL were changed—as it probably should be—to reject updates that cause some constraint to evaluate to *unknown*.

Candidate Keys

Ignoring the optional constraint name specification, a candidate key definition takes the form

```
{ PRIMARY KEY | UNIQUE } ( column-commalist )
```

As explained in Chapter 14, the database will satisfy this candidate key constraint if and only if it satisfies the "check constraint"

```
CHECK ( UNIQUE ( SELECT column-commalist FROM T )
        [ AND column-commalist IS NOT NULL ] )
```

where T is the base table that contains the candidate key in question (and where the "AND column-commalist IS NOT NULL" portion of the constraint applies only for PRIMARY KEY, not for UNIQUE). In other words, SQL's definition of "uniqueness" for candidate keys is identical to its definition of "uniqueness" in the context of the UNIQUE condition.

Note in particular, therefore, that if the candidate key consists of a single column—and is not in fact the *primary* key—then that column can contain *any number* of nulls (together with any number of nonnull values, all of which must be distinct). More generally, let *CK* be some candidate key, possibly involving several columns, for some base table *T*, and let *ck2* be a new value for *CK* that some user is attempting to introduce (via an INSERT or UPDATE operation) into table *T*. That INSERT or UPDATE will be rejected if *ck2* is the same as some value for *CK, ck1* say, that already exists in some distinct row within table *T*. What then does it mean for the two values *ck1* and *ck2* to be "the same"? It turns out that *no two* of the following three statements are equivalent:

1. *ck1* and *ck2* are the same for the purposes of a comparison condition
2. *ck1* and *ck2* are the same for the purposes of candidate key uniqueness
3. *ck1* and *ck2* are the same for the purposes of duplicate elimination

Number 1 is defined in accordance with the rules of three-valued logic; Number 2 is defined in accordance with the rules for the UNIQUE condition; and Number 3 is defined in accordance with the definition of duplicates in Section 16.4 above. Suppose, for example, that *CK* involves just one column. Then if *ck1* and *ck2* are both null, Number 1 gives *unknown*, Number 2 gives *false*, and Number 3 gives *true*. However, it is at least true that if Number 1 gives *true*, Number 2 must necessarily give *true*, and if Number 2 gives *true*, then Number 3 must necessarily give *true*.

Note: While all of the foregoing is true (in SQL) for candidate keys in general, matters are considerably simpler for *primary* keys, because no component of a primary key value is allowed (in SQL) to be null. The three statements 1., 2., and 3. above are all equivalent (in SQL) for primary keys.

Foreign Keys

Ignoring the optional constraint name specification, a foreign key definition takes the form

```
FOREIGN KEY ( column-commalist )
REFERENCES base-table [ ( column-commalist ) ]
[ MATCH { FULL | PARTIAL } ]
[ ON DELETE { NO ACTION | CASCADE | SET DEFAULT | SET NULL } ]
[ ON UPDATE { NO ACTION | CASCADE | SET DEFAULT | SET NULL } ]
```

We did not discuss the MATCH option in Chapter 14 because (once again) it had significance only in the presence of nulls; we now explain it, as follows. First we note that the option has no effect, and can thus safely be ignored, if either (a) the foreign key consists of a single column, or (b) every component column of the foreign key has "nulls not allowed" (refer back to the explanation of the MATCH condition in Section 16.3). However, the general rules are as follows. Let us agree for the moment to ignore the ON DELETE and ON UPDATE clauses. Then the database will satisfy the foreign key constraint shown above if and only if it satisfies the "check constraint"

```
CHECK ( fk MATCH [ PARTIAL | FULL ] ( SELECT ck FROM T ) )
```

where (a) *fk* is a row constructor corresponding to the column-commalist that represents the foreign key, (b) *ck* is a select-item-commalist identical to the column-commalist that represents the referenced candidate key, (c) *T* is the base table that contains that candidate key, and (d) PARTIAL is specified if and only if PARTIAL appears in the foreign key definition (and similarly for FULL). In other words, SQL's definition of "matching" for a foreign-key/candidate-key pair is identical to its definition of "matching" in the context of the MATCH condition.* Specifically:

- If neither PARTIAL nor FULL is specified:

  The referential constraint is satisfied if and only if, for each row *R2* of the referencing table, either (a) at least one component of *R2.fk* is null, or (b) *T* contains exactly one row, *R1* say, such that the comparison condition "*R2.fk = R1.ck*" evaluates to *true*.

- If PARTIAL is specified:

  The referential constraint is satisfied if and only if, for each row *R2* of the referencing table, either (a) every component of *R2.fk* is null, or (b) *T* contains at least one row, *R1* say, such that each nonnull component within *R2.fk* is equal to its counterpart in *R1.ck*.

---

*Note that there is no need to state UNIQUE in the "equivalent" MATCH condition, because *ck* represents a candidate key and so is necessarily "unique."

- If FULL is specified:

  The referential constraint is satisfied if and only if, for each row $R2$ of the referencing table, either (a) every component of $R2.fk$ is null, or (b) every component of $R2.fk$ is nonnull and T contains exactly one row, $R1$ say, such that the comparison condition "$R2.fk = R1.ck$" evaluates to *true*.

In all three cases, an INSERT on the referencing table, or an UPDATE on the foreign key in the referencing table, that would violate the referential constraint will fail.

Nulls also have implications for the "referential actions" specified in the ON DELETE and ON UPDATE clauses. In order to explain those implications, we must first define the concept of *referencing rows*.* Let $T2$ and $T1$ be a referencing table and the corresponding referenced table, and let $T2.FK$ and $T1.CK$ be the foreign key and corresponding candidate key, respectively. Then:

- For a given row $R1$ of $T1$, the rows $R2$ of $T2$ for which "$R2.fk = R1.ck$" evaluates to *true*—or, if PARTIAL is specified, the rows $R2$ of $T2$ for which the nonnull components of $R2.fk$ are equal to their counterparts in $R1.ck$—are said to be the *referencing rows* for $R1$.

- Furthermore, in the PARTIAL case, a referencing row for $R1$ is said to reference $R1$ *exclusively* if it is not a referencing row for any row of $T1$ other than $R1$. (The point here is that $T1.CK$ might involve several columns, at least one of which might permit nulls. Thus we might have, e.g., two distinct rows of $T1$, both including a CK value of (x,null), say. Any referencing row for either of these two distinct rows will necessarily be a referencing row for the other as well, and so will not reference either row *exclusively*.)†

Now we can explain the effect of the ON DELETE clause. Recall that the possible specifications are NO ACTION, CASCADE, SET DEFAULT, and SET NULL. We assume that the user has attempted to delete row $R1$ from table $T1$.

1. *NO ACTION:* The DELETE fails if it would cause the referential constraint to be no longer satisfied. See above for an explanation of what it means for the constraint to be satisfied in the various possible cases (FULL, PARTIAL, neither FULL nor PARTIAL).

---

*The standard calls them *matching* rows, but this term is misleading because "matching" here does *not* mean "matching in accordance with the rules of the MATCH condition (as previously discussed)."

†The standard term for referencing rows that reference some row exclusively is "unique matching rows," but this term is misleading because it is the *referenced row* that is supposed to be unique, not the *referencing* rows.

2. *CASCADE:* Row *R1* is deleted and the DELETE cascades to delete all referencing rows for *R1* also—or, for PARTIAL, all rows that reference *R1* exclusively.

3. *SET DEFAULT:* Row *R1* is deleted and each component of the foreign key is set to the applicable default value in all referencing rows for *R1*—or, for PARTIAL, in all rows that reference *R1* exclusively.

4. *SET NULL:* Row *R1* is deleted and each component of the foreign key is set to null in all referencing rows for *R1*—or, for PARTIAL, in all rows that reference *R1* exclusively.

And here are the specifics of the ON UPDATE clause. Again, the possible specifications are NO ACTION, CASCADE, SET DEFAULT, and SET NULL. We assume that the user has attempted to update the relevant candidate key within row *R1* of table *T1*.

1. *NO ACTION:* The UPDATE fails if it would cause the referential constraint to be no longer satisfied. See above for an explanation of what it means for the constraint to be satisfied in the various possible cases (FULL, PARTIAL, neither FULL nor PARTIAL).

2. *CASCADE:* Row *R1* is updated and the UPDATE "cascades" to update the foreign key (in the same way) in all referencing rows for *R1* also—or, for PARTIAL, in all rows that reference *R1* exclusively, in which case only those "corresponding" components of the foreign key that were previously nonnull are updated.

3. *SET DEFAULT:* Row *R1* is updated and each component of the foreign key that corresponds to a component that has been changed in row *R1* is set to the applicable default value in all referencing rows for *R1*—or, for PARTIAL, in all rows that reference *R1* exclusively, in which case only those "corresponding" components of the foreign key that were previously nonnull are set to their default.

4. *SET NULL:* Row *R1* is updated and each component of the foreign key that corresponds to a component that has been changed in row *R1* is set to null in all referencing rows for *R1*—or, for PARTIAL, in all rows that reference *R1* exclusively, in which case only those "corresponding" components of the foreign key that were previously nonnull are set to null.

16.6   A RECOMMENDATION

Avoid nulls.

17

Dates and Times

17.1 INTRODUCTION

SQL includes an extensive set of features for support of dates and times. Unfortunately, however, that support is quite complex (this remark is not intended as a criticism—the fact is, many aspects of dates and times are *inherently* complex, as is well known). Therefore, rather than discussing the features in question in detail in Chapter 7 ("Scalar Objects, Operators, and Expressions")—even though such a discussion would most logically have belonged in that chapter—it seemed better to relegate it to this later part of the book.

A note on terminology: Following the standard, we use the term "datetime" to mean "date or time or timestamp"; for example, we use the term "datetime data types" to mean the data types DATE and TIME and TIMESTAMP collectively (with or without the WITH TIME ZONE option, in the last two cases). Note, however, that there is also an INTERVAL data type, which, though certainly part of the overall date and time support, is not classified as a "datetime" data type *per se*.

17.2 DATA TYPES

As just mentioned, SQL supports an INTERVAL data type and several "datetime" data types. Intervals and datetimes each involve one or more of the following components:

```
YEAR
MONTH
DAY
HOUR
MINUTE
SECOND
```

These components are known collectively as *datetime fields* (note that intervals involve datetime fields even though intervals are not considered as datetimes).

The intuitive interpretation of the various fields is obvious. The significance of their ordering is also obvious: YEAR is the most significant, then MONTH, and so on, down to SECOND (least significant). A given interval or datetime need not include a value for every datetime field, but there must not be any gaps—i.e., the values it does include must correspond to a contiguous nonempty subsequence of the full sequence as shown above (the specific rules vary with the specific data type—see below). Each field value is always a decimal integer, except possibly for SECOND values, which can optionally include a fractional portion (again, the specific rules vary with the specific data type).

Intervals

An interval is a period of time, such as "3 years" or "90 days" or "5 minutes 30 seconds." For example, subtracting the time "9:00 AM" from the time "10:15 AM" yields the interval "1 hour 15 minutes." (*Note:* The expressions "3 years," "10:15 AM," etc., are not meant to be valid SQL literals.) There are two kinds of intervals, *year-month* intervals and *day-time* intervals. A year-month interval consists of a YEAR component or a MONTH component or both, in that order; a day-time interval consists of any contiguous nonempty subsequence of a DAY component, an HOUR component, a MINUTE component, and a SECOND component, in that order.* Hence the syntax of an INTERVAL data type definition is

```
INTERVAL start [ TO end ]
```

where "start" and "end" are each one of YEAR, MONTH, DAY, HOUR, MINUTE, and SECOND, optionally followed—in the case of "start" only—by an unsigned integer in parentheses giving a *precision* for the corresponding item. *Note:* Since datetime field values are always integers, the corresponding *scale* is always zero (except possibly for SECOND; these remarks on precision and scale will be refined slightly for SECOND in a moment).

---

*The reason for drawing a sharp distinction between year-month and day-time intervals—and hence, in particular, for not permitting MONTH and DAY components to appear within the same interval— is basically that (of course) different months have different numbers of days. As a result, an interval such as "2 months 10 days," if permitted, would be ambiguous. (Would it or would it not be the same interval as "70 days"? Or "71 days"? Or "72 days"? What about February?) Consider the effect of such complications on assignments, comparisons, date arithmetic, etc.

Here are some examples of interval data type definitions:

```
INTERVAL YEAR
INTERVAL YEAR TO MONTH
INTERVAL MONTH
INTERVAL DAY (3)
INTERVAL HOUR (3) TO MINUTE
INTERVAL SECOND (5,3)
INTERVAL DAY (3) TO SECOND (3)
```

Each of these could be the data type specification within a base table column definition or domain definition. Points to note:

1. If "TO end" is omitted, the interval type involves just the datetime field specified as "start." If "TO end" is stated explicitly, the interval type involves all datetime fields from "start" to "end" inclusive ("start" must be more significant than "end").

2. If "start" specifies YEAR, "end" (if stated) must specify MONTH. If "start" specifies MONTH or SECOND, "TO end" must be omitted.

3. A precision p ($p > 0$) can always be specified for "start." The maximum value is implementation-defined, but must be at least 2 (which is the default).

4. If "start" is SECOND and if a "start" precision p is specified explicitly, then:

   - That value p specifies the number of digits in the *integer* portion (only) of the SECOND field.

   - The number of significant digits q ($q \geq 0$) in the fractional portion can optionally be specified too. The syntax is SECOND(p,q).* The maximum value of q is implementation-defined, but must be at least 6 (which is the default).

5. If and only if "end" is SECOND, the number of significant digits in the *fractional* portion of the "end" field can optionally be specified too. The syntax is SECOND(q), where q is as defined above (note that the syntax is just (q), not (p,q)—p is always 2 in this context).

6. The value of the leading (most significant) field within an interval is unconstrained; thus, e.g., an interval might specify "45 hours," "90 minutes," "18 months," etc. The value of a field that is not in the leading position is constrained as indicated below:

---

*Note the difference between these rules and the rules for NUMERIC and DECIMAL data. Consider NUMERIC, for example. The specification NUMERIC(p,q) means p digits in total, with an assumed decimal point q digits from the right (i.e., the integer portion is $p - q$ digits and the fraction is q digits). By contrast, the specification SECOND(p,q) means $p + q$ digits in total, with p digits in the integer portion and q digits in the fraction. In other words, the value p in the specification SECOND(p,q) does *not* represent a "precision" as that term is usually understood (i.e., total number of significant digits).

```
MONTH   : 0 to 11
HOUR    : 0 to 23
MINUTE  : 0 to 59
SECOND  : 0.000... to 59.999...
```

7. Values of type INTERVAL can be either positive or negative; e.g., "–5 years" is a legal interval. In other words, intervals are always considered to be signed.

Datetimes

A datetime represents an absolute position on the timeline (for DATE and TIMESTAMP)* or an absolute time of day (for TIME). For example, a date or a timestamp might both represent "January 18th, 1941"; the date, however, would be accurate only to the day, while the timestamp might be accurate to the microsecond, or even further. A time might represent "7:30 AM." *Note:* The expressions "January 18th, 1941" and "7:30 AM" are not meant to be valid SQL literals.

The datetime data types are DATE, TIME (optionally WITH TIME ZONE), and TIMESTAMP (again, optionally WITH TIME ZONE). We defer discussion of the optional WITH TIME ZONE specification to Section 17.4. Ignoring that specification for now, then, we can say that DATEs consist of a YEAR component, a MONTH component, and a DAY component, in that order; TIMEs consist of an HOUR component, a MINUTE component, and a SECOND component, in that order; and TIMESTAMPs value consist of a YEAR component, a MONTH component, a DAY component, an HOUR component, a MINUTE component, and a SECOND component, in that order. Thus, the syntax of a datetime data type definition is one of the following—

```
DATE
TIME
TIMESTAMP
```

—optionally followed, in the case of TIME and TIMESTAMP, by an unsigned integer value q in parentheses giving the number of significant digits in the fractional portion of the SECOND field of the specified data type. The maximum value of q is implementation-defined (but must be at least 6); the default is 0 for TIME and 6 for TIMESTAMP. Here are some examples of datetime data type definitions:

```
DATE
TIME
TIME (6)
TIMESTAMP
TIMESTAMP (10)
```

---

*Note that "absolute position on the timeline" really means a *relative* position with respect to a specific origin, namely midnight on the day preceding January 1st, 1 AD. Note too that dates and timestamps are always positive (no BC values), and times and timestamps are always expressed in terms of a 24-hour clock (no AM or PM qualifiers—our informal examples to the contrary notwithstanding).

Each of these could be the data type specification within a base table column definition or domain definition. Points to note:

1. Field values within a datetime are constrained as indicated below:

```
YEAR   : 0001 to 9999
MONTH  : 01 to 12
DAY    : 01 to 31
HOUR   : 00 to 23
MINUTE : 00 to 59
SECOND : 00.000... to 61.999...
```

2. Observe that MONTH values range from 1 to 12 in a datetime but from 0 to 11 in an interval (assuming in the interval case that the YEAR field is present, for otherwise the MONTH field would be unconstrained and could possibly have a value greater than 11).

3. The curious upper limit on SECOND values in a datetime is explained by the following excerpt from the standard: "On occasion, UTC [see Section 17.4 for an explanation of UTC] is adjusted by the omission . . . or insertion of a *leap second* in order to maintain synchronization with sidereal time. [This possibility] implies that sometimes, but very rarely, a particular minute will contain 59, 61, or 62 seconds." *Note:* Datetime arithmetic (see Section 17.6) that involves leap seconds produces an implementation-defined result; in fact, datetime arithmetic that involves *any* irregularity in the calendar always produces an implementation-defined result.

4. All other fields have the same range for both datetimes and intervals, except that, as already mentioned, the leading field of an interval, whatever it happens to be, is unconstrained. If it is a YEAR field, it can even have a value greater than 9999 (although, to repeat, the YEAR component of a datetime cannot).

5. Permitted datetime values are thus as follows:

   - *DATE:* Legal dates in the range 0001-01-01 (January 1st, 1 AD) to 9999-12-31 (December 31st, 9999 AD) inclusive
   - *TIME:* Legal times in the range 00:00:00... to 23:59:61.999... inclusive
   - *TIMESTAMP:* Legal timestamps in the range 0001-01-01 00:00:00... to 9999-12-31 23:59:61.999... inclusive

   DATE and TIMESTAMP values are further constrained by the rules of the Gregorian calendar; thus, e.g., invalid dates such as 1999-04-31 ("April 31st, 1999") or 1900-02-29 ("February 29th, 1900") are not permitted.

17.3 LITERALS

Note: We continue to ignore the question of time zones. See Section 17.4 for a discussion of the effect of time zone support on literals.

Datetime literals are of three kinds—date literals, time literals, and timestamp literals. The syntax is shown below.

date   Written as the key word DATE followed by a *date string* of the form '*yyyy-mm-dd*'

   Examples: `DATE '1941-01-18'`
         `DATE '1999-12-25'`

time   Written as the key word TIME followed by a *time string* of the form '*hh:mm:ss[.[nnnnnn]]*'

   Examples: `TIME '09:30:00'`
         `TIME '17:45:45.75'`

timestamp   Written as the key word TIMESTAMP followed by a *timestamp string* of the form '*yyyy-mm-dd hh:mm:ss[.[nnnnnn]]*'

   Examples: `TIMESTAMP '1998-04-28 12:00:00.000000'`
         `TIMESTAMP '1944-10-17 18:30:45'`

Points to note:

1. As indicated, the enclosing single quotes are considered to be part of the date, time, or timestamp string (as applicable).

2. The YEAR, MONTH, DAY (etc., etc.) components are all unsigned decimal integers of exactly four digits (for the YEAR component) and exactly two digits (for everything else except the *nnnnnn*—i.e., fractional—portion of the SECOND component, which can include as many digits as necessary).

3. As indicated, the *nnnnnn* portion of the SECOND component can optionally be omitted, in which case that component has no fractional portion; and if the *nnnnnn* portion is omitted, the preceding decimal point can optionally be omitted also.

4. A timestamp literal must include exactly one space between the date and time portions.

5. The data type of a datetime literal is derived in an obvious manner from the way in which the literal is written.

Turning now to interval literals: Interval literals are of two kinds, namely year-month literals and day-time literals. The syntax is shown below.

year-month   Written as the key word INTERVAL, followed by a (year-month) *interval string* consisting of an opening single quote, an optinal sign, either or both of *yyyy* and *mm* (with a hyphen separator if both are specified), and a closing single quote, followed by YEAR, MONTH, or YEAR TO MONTH (as applicable)

   Examples: `INTERVAL '-1' YEAR`
         `INTERVAL '2-6' YEAR TO MONTH`

day-time   Written as the key word INTERVAL, followed by a (day-time) *interval string* consisting of an opening single quote, an optional sign, a contiguous nonempty subsequence of *dd*, *hh*, *mm*, and *ss*[.[*nnnnnn*]] (with a space separator between *dd* and the rest, if *dd* is specified, and colon separators elsewhere), and a closing single quote, followed by the appropriate "*start* [TO *end*]" specification

Examples:
```
INTERVAL '1' MINUTE
INTERVAL '2 12' DAY TO HOUR
INTERVAL '2:12:35' HOUR TO SECOND
INTERVAL '-4.50' SECOND
```

Points to note:

1. As indicated, the enclosing single quotes and the optional sign are considered to be part of the interval string.

2. The YEAR, MONTH, DAY (etc., etc.) components are all unsigned decimal integers of not more than four digits (for the YEAR component) and not more than two digits (for everything else except the *nnnnnn*—i.e., fractional—portion of the SECOND component, which can include as many digits as necessary).

3. As indicated, the *nnnnnn* portion of a SECOND value can optionally be omitted, in which case that value has no fractional portion; and if the *nnnnnn* portion is omitted, the preceding decimal point can optionally be omitted also.

4. The data type of an interval literal is derived in an obvious manner from the way in which the literal is written.

17.4   TIME ZONES

CAVEAT: It is in this area that much of the complexity referred to in Section 17.1 lies. What is more, SQL's time zone support is not only complicated, it is also somewhat confused—even incorrect or self-contradictory in some places. For this reason, the descriptions that follow are not always consistent with the standard as currently specified, but instead reflect informed guesses on the part of the writer as to how the standard might be revised and corrected in the near future. The reader should thus understand that the material is liable to subsequent revision, at least at the detail level. Refer to Appendix D for further discussion.

The foregoing caveat notwithstanding, the basic point is quite simple: Natural language expressions such as "10:00 AM" are inherently ambiguous—their interpretation can depend on the time zone in which they are used. For example, the very same point in time might be referred to as "10:00 AM" by someone in San Francisco, California, as "6:00 PM" by someone in London, England, and as "8:00 PM" by someone in Helsinki, Finland. In other words, these three expressions, even though their *external representations* are all different, might all have the same *denotation*—i.e., they might all denote the same absolute point in time. The data types TIME WITH TIME ZONE and TIMESTAMP WITH TIME ZONE are intended to serve as a basis for dealing with such issues.

Note: For simplicity, let us agree to concentrate on times specifically (everything having to do with times and time zones is equally applicable to *timestamps* and time zones also, *mutatis mutandis;* we can therefore ignore timestamps, for the most part, except when there is some specific point to be made regarding them).

First of all, we must make it clear that TIME WITH TIME ZONE really is a new data type; i.e., it is not just a variation on the data type TIME as already discussed (although of course there are many points of similarity). So how do the data types differ? The intended distinction seems to be as follows:

- A "without time zone" value is really a *local* time—that is, it is the time given by a (correct!) local clock. Thus, for example, the values 10:00 AM in San Francisco and 10:00 AM in London will "compare equal" if they represent "without time zone" times, even though they denote different absolute times.

- By contrast, "with time zone" values can be thought if as being *corrected for time zone differences;* thus, for example, the values 10:00 AM in San Francisco, 6:00 PM in London, and 8:00 PM in Helsinki will all "compare equal" if they represent "with time zone" values, because they all denote the same absolute time.

"With time zone" times are represented internally in terms of *Coordinated Universal Time*, UTC.* The UTC value corresponding to the three "with time zone" values above is 6:00 PM (more precisely, it is 18:00:00, since UTC is based on a 24-hour clock). Thus, each of those values will be represented internally as "6:00 PM" (and will thus indeed "compare equal" to the other two, as just mentioned).

In order to convert a given local time value to UTC, it is necessary to subtract an appropriate *time zone displacement value* from that local time value;† that is,

```
UTC time  =  local time - time zone displacement
```

For example, the normal time zone displacement value for San Francisco would be "–8 hours"; for Helsinki, it would be "+2 hours"; and for London, it would be zero. (We say the *normal* time zone displacement value, because we wish to ignore the complications caused by Daylight Savings Time and related matters.) In other words, San Francisco is eight hours behind GMT, Helsinki is two hours ahead.

---

*The abbreviation *is* UTC, not CUT. UTC corresponds to what used to be (and often still is) referred to as Greenwich Mean Time, GMT.

†The standard contradicts itself on this issue, stating at some points that the arithmetic should go the other way—that is, the equation should be UTC time = local time + time zone displacement. However, there are good reasons to believe our equation is the correct one, and we assume throughout what follows that it is.

We now proceed to examine SQL's support for the foregoing ideas in some detail.

Time Zone Displacement Values

As already indicated, the value that must be subtracted from a given local time value in order to obtain the corresponding UTC value is called a *time zone displacement value*. Time zone displacement values are of the form INTERVAL HOUR TO MINUTE; possible values range from −12:59 to +13:00 inclusive.* The HOUR and MINUTE components of a time zone displacement value are referred to as TIMEZONE_HOUR and TIMEZONE_MINUTE, respectively.

Let t be a local time value, and let tz be the corresponding (possibly negative) time zone displacement value; i.e., t is to be understood as a local time within the time zone identified by tz. Let the absolute (unsigned) values of the TIMEZONE_HOUR and TIMEZONE_MINUTE components of tz be tzh and tzm, respectively. Then we can be more specific regarding the local-to-UTC time conversion process, as follows:

- If tz is negative, the UTC time corresponding to t is t + tzh hours + tzm minutes.

- If tz is positive, the UTC time corresponding to t is t − tzh hours − tzm minutes.

The slightly counterintuitive nature of the foregoing is worth pointing out explicitly. For instance, the normal time zone displacement value for San Francisco is "−08:00," as we have seen. In order to specify the local time "10:00 AM" as a "with time zone" literal, therefore, a user in San Francisco has to write an expression of the form "10 − 8" (simplifing the syntax somewhat); however, that expression "evaluates" to 18, not 2!—that is, it denotes UTC time 18:00:00, with an associated time zone displacement value of −08:00.

Now (as mentioned in Chapter 5), each SQL-session has an associated *default time zone displacement value,* to be used when such a value is required and none is explicitly provided by the user. This value is initialized to an implementation-defined default (a "default default") when the SQL-session is initiated, but can subsequently be changed at any time by means of the SET TIME ZONE operation—syntax:

```
SET TIME ZONE { displacement | LOCAL }
```

The default time zone displacement value for the current SQL-session is set to the specified value ("displacement" is an interval expression—see Section 17.6—of type INTERVAL HOUR TO MINUTE; LOCAL refers to the initial implementation-defined SQL-session "default default").

---

*The range *is* −12:59 to +13:00, not (as might have been expected) −11:59 to +12:00, because (as the standard puts it) it is "governed by political decisions . . . rather than by any natural law."

Data Types

The specification WITH TIME ZONE can optionally be included in a TIME or TIMEZONE data type definition—i.e., in a base table column definition or domain definition (following the parenthesized SECOND fraction precision specification "(q)", if included). To fix our ideas, we consider one specific case:

- Let C be a base table column of type TIME WITH TIME ZONE.
- Let t be a value in column C.

Then t will consist of the combination of (a) a UTC time value, together with (b) TIMEZONE_HOUR and TIMEZONE_MINUTE components,[*] representing the time zone displacement value specified when t was originally entered into C (via an INSERT or UPDATE operation). That time zone displacement value—tz, say—can be specified explicitly as part of the scalar expression (within that INSERT or UPDATE) from which t is derived; if no such value tz is specified explicitly, the current SQL-session default time zone displacement value is considered to be specified implicitly.

Literals

Time and timestamp literals can include an optional time zone displacement value specification (immediately preceding the closing single quote). Here are a couple of examples:

```
TIME '10:00:00-08:00'

TIMESTAMP '1944-10-17 18:30:45+02:00'
```

The specified time zone displacement value is subtracted from the specified local time (or timestamp) value to obtain the corresponding UTC value. Thus, for example, the "with time zone" TIME literal shown above will be represented internally as UTC value 18:00:00, displacement value –08:00.

Examples

It is time to consider some examples. Suppose table FLIGHTS is defined as follows:

```
CREATE TABLE FLIGHTS
    ( FNO CHAR(6) PRIMARY KEY,          -- flight number
      DEP TIME WITH TIME ZONE,          -- departure time
      ARR TIME WITH TIME ZONE,          -- arrival time
      ... )
```

---

[*]Actually, the standard is not clear on whether values such as t really do include those components; at some points it seems to say they do, at others it seems to regard values such as t as consisting of just the time portion alone. The first possibility seems more reasonable, which is why we adopt it here.

Suppose table FLIGHTS is currently empty, and a user in San Francisco executes the following INSERT statement:

```
INSERT INTO FLIGHTS ( FNO, DEP, ... )
        VALUES ( 'AA682', TIME '10:00:00-08:00', ... )
```

(for simplicity we ignore arrival time). The FLIGHTS table now looks something like this (only relevant portions shown):

FNO	DEP UTC time	SFO time zone displacement
AA682	18:00:00	-08:00

SFO = San Francisco

Observe that the local time value (10:00 AM) has been converted to UTC; we have annotated the column heading for column DEP to make this point explicit (we do not mean to suggest that the standard prescribes any such annotation, of course.) Observe too that the time zone displacement value –08:00 has been preserved along with that UTC value in the database (again we do not mean to suggest that the standard prescribes any annotation such as that shown). *Note:* The effect would be the same if the time zone displacement value specification "–08:00" had been omitted from the original INSERT (provided the San Francisco default time zone displacement value had been set appropriately, of course).

Now suppose some user executes the following SELECT statement:

```
SELECT  FLIGHTS.FNO, FLIGHTS.DEP
FROM    FLIGHTS
WHERE   FLIGHTS.FNO = 'AA682'
```

The result looks like this:

FNO	DEP UTC time	SFO time zone displacement
AA682	18:00:00	-08:00

Suppose, by contrast, that the SELECT statement looked like this:

```
SELECT  FLIGHTS.FNO, FLIGHTS.DEP AT LOCAL
FROM    FLIGHTS
WHERE   FLIGHTS.FNO = 'AA682'
```

(note the AT LOCAL specification on FLIGHTS.DEP in the SELECT clause). Then the time zone displacement value in the result will be the applicable SQL-session default value. For example, if the SELECT were executed in Helsinki (default time zone displacement value "+02:00"), the result would be:

FNO	DEP UTC time	HEL time zone displacement
AA682	18:00:00	+02:00

HEL = Helsinki

If it were executed in London (default time zone displacement value "+00.00"), the result would be:

FNO	DEP UTC time	*LHR time zone displacement*	LHR = London
AA682	18:00:00	+00:00	

And if it were executed in San Francisco (default time zone displacement value "–08:00"), the result would be the same as if AT LOCAL had not been specified at all.

Finally, suppose the user (no matter where he or she happens to be located) actually wants to be able to determine the flight departure time in terms of *Helsinki* time. Then the following SELECT will suffice:

```
SELECT FLIGHTS.FNO,
       FLIGHTS.DEP AT TIME ZONE INTERVAL '+02:00' HOUR TO MINUTE
FROM   FLIGHTS
WHERE  FLIGHTS.FNO = 'AA682'
```

The user has asked for the value of FLIGHTS.DEP to be displayed with a "+02:00" time displacement value. *Result:*

FNO	DEP UTC time	*HEL time zone displacement*
AA682	18:00:00	+02:00

Refer to Section 17.6 for further explanation of the AT TIME ZONE option.

17.5 DATA CONVERSION

As we saw in Chapter 7, the CAST operator is used to perform explicit data type conversions of all kinds. Simplifying matters slightly (by ignoring nulls!), the general syntax is as follows:

```
CAST ( scalar-expression AS { data-type | domain } )
```

In particular, CAST provides a basis for dealing with datetimes and intervals in a host language that has no directly equivalent data types, because it can be used to convert other scalar values (e.g., character strings and numbers) to the various datetime and interval data types and *vice versa.*

CAST also allows datetime values to be converted from one datetime data type to another. Specifically, a date or a time can be converted to a timestamp, and a timestamp can be converted to a date or a time (for the details of these conversions, especially with respect to the manner in which time zones are handled, we refer the reader to the official standard). Note in particular, however, that no conversions are supported between dates and times, nor between datetimes and intervals, nor between year-month intervals and day-time intervals.

In the remainder of this section, we concentrate on (a) conversions between non-datetime values and datetimes and (b) conversions between non-interval values and intervals.

Conversions Involving Datetimes

- A character string can be converted to a date, time, or timestamp so long as the value of that character string represents either a literal of the appropriate type or a string of the appropriate type (without the enclosing single quotes in the latter case). The character string can also include leading or trailing spaces, which will be ignored. The result of the conversion is a date, time, or timestamp with the obvious value.

- A date, time, or timestamp can be converted to a fixed or varying length character string. The result of the conversion is a character string representing the value of the date, time, or timestamp as a literal of the appropriate type (padded at the right with spaces if necessary in the fixed length case).

Conversions Involving Intervals

- A character string can be converted to an interval so long as the value of that character string represents either a literal of the appropriate type or a string of the appropriate type (without the enclosing single quotes in the latter case). The character string can also include leading or trailing spaces, which will be ignored. The result of the conversion is an interval with the obvious value.

- An interval can be converted to a fixed or varying length character string. The result of the conversion is a character string representing the value of the interval as a literal of the appropriate type (padded at the right with spaces if necessary in the fixed length case).

- An exact numeric value can be converted to an interval involving just one datetime field. The result of the conversion is an interval with the obvious value.

- An interval can be converted to an exact numeric value, so long as the interval involves just one datetime field. The result of the conversion is a number with the obvious value.

Certain of the foregoing conversions can lead to overflow exceptions in fairly obvious ways. We omit the details here.

17.6   SCALAR OPERATORS AND FUNCTIONS

The usual arithmetic operators "+", "–", "*", and "/" can be used to perform certain calculations involving datetimes and intervals; for example, a date and an interval can be added to yield another date. The details are somewhat complicated, however; we therefore choose to discuss the other operators (actually functions) first.

- CURRENT_DATE

  Returns the current date, i.e., the date "today." *Note:* When any given SQL statement is executed, all references within that statement to CURRENT_DATE are (to paraphrase the standard) "effectively evaluated simultaneously"; i.e., they are all based on a single reading of the local clock. Thus, e.g., the conditional expression "CURRENT_DATE = CURRENT_DATE" is guaranteed always to evaluate to true. Analogous remarks apply to CURRENT_TIME and CURRENT_TIMESTAMP (see below); furthermore, all references to any of these three functions within a given SQL statement are always "in synch," in the sense that CURRENT_DATE and CURRENT_TIMESTAMP always designate the same date and CURRENT_TIME and CURRENT_TIMESTAMP always designate the same time.

- CURRENT_TIME

  Returns the current time in UTC, i.e., the UTC time "now," with time zone displacement value "+00:00" (e.g., invoking CURRENT_TIME at 10:00 AM local time in San Francisco will return the value TIME '18:00:00 + 00:00'). The function name can optionally be followed by an unsigned integer value q in parentheses specifying the number of significant digits in the fractional portion of the SECOND component of the value returned (see the discussion of the TIME data type in Section 17.2).

- CURRENT_TIMESTAMP

  Returns the current timestamp, i.e., the date "today" concatenated with the UTC time "now," with time zone displacement value "+00:00". The function name can optionally be followed by an unsigned integer value q in parentheses specifying the number of significant digits in the fractional portion of the SECOND component of the value returned (see the discussion of the TIMESTAMP data type in Section 17.2).

- EXTRACT

  EXTRACT is used to extract an individual datetime field value from a specified datetime or interval. More precisely, the expression EXTRACT (*field* FROM *scalar-expression*), where *field* is YEAR, MONTH, DAY, HOUR, MINUTE, SECOND, TIMEZONE_HOUR, or TIMEZONE_MINUTE, and *scalar-expression* is either a datetime expression or an interval expression, is defined to return the specified *field* value as a value with data type exact numeric, with implementation-defined precision and scale 0 (or, if SECOND is specified, implementation-defined precision and implementation-defined scale—though the scale must not be such as to lose digits).

Note that EXTRACT returns a *numeric* value (it is an additional form of "numeric primary"—see Chapter 7, Section 7.4). Note too that EXTRACT applied to a negative interval returns a negative value.

- Aggregate functions

All five of the usual aggregate functions (COUNT, MAX, MIN, SUM, AVG) can be used with intervals; only the first three (COUNT, MAX, MIN) can be used with datetimes. Each returns the obvious result.

We turn now to the arithmetic operators. First, we should warn the reader that not all operations that might appear to make sense are in fact permitted; for example, it is not permitted to divide one interval by another (e.g., "10 days" divided by "2 days") to obtain a number. The table below summarizes those operations that *are* permitted.

1st operand	operator	2nd operand	result
datetime	−	datetime	interval
datetime	+	interval	datetime
datetime	−	interval	datetime
interval	+	datetime	datetime
interval	+	interval	interval
interval	−	interval	interval
interval	*	number	interval
interval	/	number	interval
number	*	interval	interval

Points to note:

1. If two datetimes appear in the same datetime expression (basically possible only if one is being subtracted from the other), they must be both dates or both times or both timestamps.

2. If two intervals appear in the same interval expression (basically possible only if one is being added to or subtracted from the other), they must be both year-month intervals or both day-time intervals.

3. If a datetime and an interval appear in the same datetime expression (basically possible only if the interval is being added to or subtracted from the datetime), the interval must contain only datetime fields that are also contained within the datetime.

Here then is the syntax:

```
datetime-expression
    ::=    datetime-term
         | interval-expression + datetime-term
         | datetime-expression { + | - } interval-term
datetime-term
    ::=    datetime-primary
                    [ AT { LOCAL | TIME ZONE displacement } ]
interval-expression
    ::=    interval-term
         | interval-expression { + | - } interval-term
         | ( datetime expression - datetime-term ) start [ TO end ]
interval-term
    ::=    interval-factor
         | interval-term { * | / } numeric-factor
         | numeric-term * interval-factor
interval-factor
    ::=    [ + | - ] interval-primary
```

Points to note:

1 A datetime expression evaluates to a datetime; an interval expression evaluates to an interval. More precisely, a datetime expression involving dates evaluates to a date, one involving times evaluates to a time, and one involving timestamps evaluates to a timestamp. Likewise, an interval expression involving year-month intervals evaluates to a year-month interval, and one involving day-time intervals evaluates to a day-time interval.

2. For an explanation of "numeric term" and "numeric factor," see Chapter 7, Section 7.4.

3. A "datetime primary" is any of the following:

   - a possibly qualified column name;
   - a datetime literal;
   - a reference to a scalar function—possibly CASE or CAST—or aggregate function;
   - a table expression enclosed in parentheses (i.e., a scalar subquery);
   - a datetime expression enclosed in parentheses.

   In each case, of course, the datetime-primary must yield a value of one of the datetime data types.

4. An "interval primary" is analogous, except of course that it involves interval literals or expressions instead of datetime literals or expressions, and it must yield a value of type INTERVAL.*

---

*If and only if the interval primary is represented by a question mark (i.e., it constitutes a "placeholder" in a dynamically prepared SQL statement—see Chapters 20 and 23), it must include a "start [TO end]" specification.

5. A datetime term can include "AT LOCAL" or "AT TIME ZONE displacement" only if the datetime term evaluates to a time or a timestamp ("displacement" is an interval primary of type INTERVAL HOUR TO MINUTE). The effect in both cases is to cause the value of the datetime term to be adjusted in accordance with the specified time zone displacement value. For example, the value TIME '18:00:00+00:00' will be converted to the value TIME '10:00:00 – 08:00' if AT TIME ZONE INTERVAL '–08:00' HOUR TO MINUTE is specified. AT LOCAL means the current default time zone displacement value for the SQL-session.*

6. If an interval is added to or subtracted from a time or timestamp, the time zone displacement value associated with the result is the same as that associated with the time or timestamp. For example, the expression TIME '10:00:00 – 08:00' + INTERVAL '1' HOUR yields the value TIME '11:00:00 – 08:00'.

Here are some examples of datetime and interval expressions:

```
DATE '1972-08-17' - DATE '1969-10-28'
DATE '1972-08-17' - CAST ( ' DATE''1969-10-28'' ' AS DATE )

START_TIME + INTERVAL '5' MINUTE
INTERVAL '5' MINUTE + START_TIME
START_TIME - INTERVAL '4:30' MINUTE TO SECOND
START_TIME + ( 3 * INTERVAL '1:4:30' HOUR TO MINUTE )

CURRENT_TIMESTAMP + INTERVAL '1.500000' SECOND
```

Interval expressions are effectively evaluated by converting the operands to integers (e.g., the operand INTERVAL '2–6' YEAR TO MONTH might be converted to the integer 30, meaning 30 months), evaluating the resulting numeric expression, and then converting the result back to the required interval format (*start* TO *end*). We omit the details, since they are essentially straightforward.

Datetime expressions are evaluated in accordance with the Gregorian calendar and permissible datetime values. Thus, for example, the expression

```
DATE '1998-07-31' + INTERVAL '1' MONTH
```

("July 31st, 1998 plus one month") correctly evaluates to

```
DATE '1998-08-31'
```

("August 31st, 1998"). Likewise, the expression

```
DATE '1998-12-31' + INTERVAL '1' MONTH
```

("December 31st, 1998 plus one month") correctly evaluates to

```
DATE '1999-01-31'
```

---

*We remark that the meaning of LOCAL is context-dependent. In SET TIME ZONE, it means the *initial* SQL-session default time zone displacement value; in a datetime term, it means the *current* SQL-session default time zone displacement value.

("January 31st, 1999"), and the expression

```
DATE '1999-01-31' + INTERVAL '30' DAY
```

("January 31st, 1999 plus 30 days") correctly evaluates to

```
DATE '1999-03-02'
```

("March 2nd, 1999"). In general, adding an interval to a datetime is performed by adding the least significant field values, then the next least, and so on; and, as the second and third examples above illustrate, any of these individual additions has the potential of causing a carry to the next more significant datetime field. Note, however, that the next *less* significant field will *not* be adjusted; thus, for example, the expression

```
DATE '1998-08-31' + INTERVAL '1' MONTH
```

("August 31st, 1998 plus one month") apparently evaluates to

```
DATE '1998-09-31'
```

("September 31st, 1998"), and thus fails (an "invalid date" exception is raised). It does *not* evaluate (as might perhaps have been expected) to

```
DATE '1998-10-01'
```

("October 1st, 1998"), because such a result would require an adjustment to the DAY field after the MONTH addition had been performed. In other words, if interval *i* is added to date *d*, and *i* is of type year-month, then the DAY value in the result is the same as the DAY value in *d* (i.e., the DAY value does not change).

Subtraction is performed analogously, except that carries, if any, are *from*, not to, the next more significant field.

Note: If the datetime expression involves TIMEs, arithmetic on the HOUR field is performed *modulo* 24 (e.g., "10 PM" plus 4 hours gives "2 AM"). The same is not true for TIMESTAMPs, of course, where HOURs carry to or from DAYs in the normal way.

17.7   ASSIGNMENTS AND COMPARISONS

Assignments

As always in an assignment, the source and target must be of compatible data types. For datetimes and intervals, type compatibility is defined as follows:*

---

*Certain complications, beyond the scope of this text, arise from the fact that "with and without time zone" times and timestamps are really different data types (this remark applies to both assignments and comparisons, also to datetime arithmetic).

1. All dates are compatible with one another.
2. All times are compatible with one another.
3. All timestamps are compatible with one another.
4. All year-month intervals are compatible with one another.
5. All day-time intervals are compatible with one another.
6. There are no other instances of compatibility.

Cases 4 and 5 require some slight elaboration. We concentrate first on Case 4. Let the source y be a year-month interval, and let the target x be defined to be of year-month interval type. Consider what is involved in assigning y to x.

- If y and x are both of type INTERVAL YEAR TO MONTH, or both of type INTERVAL YEAR, or both of type INTERVAL MONTH, the assignment is straightforward.

- If y is of type INTERVAL YEAR but x is of type INTERVAL YEAR TO MONTH, y is effectively extended at the least significant end by attaching a MONTH field with a value of 0. The assignment is then straightforward.

- If y is of type INTERVAL MONTH but x is of type INTERVAL YEAR TO MONTH, y is effectively extended at the most significant end by attaching a YEAR field with a value of 0, and then adjusted if necessary so that it conforms to the rules for valid intervals (e.g., the value "0 years 15 months" would be adjusted to "1 year 3 months"). The assignment is then straightforward.

- If y is of type INTERVAL YEAR or INTERVAL YEAR TO MONTH but x is of type INTERVAL MONTH, y is effectively converted to type INTERVAL MONTH before the assignment is performed (e.g., "2 years" would be converted to "24 months").

- If y is of type INTERVAL MONTH or INTERVAL YEAR TO MONTH but x is of type INTERVAL YEAR, y is effectively converted to type INTERVAL YEAR before the assignment is performed (e.g., "24 months" would be converted to "2 years"). If the conversion causes a loss of information, an exception is raised.

Analogous (but somewhat tedious) considerations apply to Case 5.

Note: Certain assignments can lead to overflow exceptions in fairly obvious ways. We omit the details here.

Comparisons

The basic form of a comparison is (as always)

```
scalar-expression comparison-operator scalar-expression
```

where:

- The two comparands must be compatible (as for assignment).
- The comparison operator is one of the usual set (=, <>, <, <=, >, >=).
- Datetime comparisons are performed in accordance with chronologic ordering. Interval comparisons are performed in accordance with their sign and magnitude.
- When two intervals are to be compared, a process analogous to that described under "Assignments" might have to be carried out—i.e., either comparand (or both) might have to be extended, at either or both ends, by attaching new datetime fields with an initial value of zero, and either or both might then have to be adjusted to conform to the rules for valid intervals. The comparison is then performed in the normal manner. (The net effect is that, e.g., the intervals "1 hour" and "60 minutes" are considered to be equal.)

OVERLAPS Condition

SQL also provides a special comparison operator, OVERLAPS, to test whether two time periods overlap. The time periods in question are represented in each case either by their start and end points or by a start point and an interval (they do not both have to be represented in the same way). Thus, the syntax is

```
row-constructor OVERLAPS row-constructor
```

(an additional case of "simple condition"—see Chapter 12), where:

- The two row constructors, *Left* and *Right* say, must each consist of exactly two components.
- The first component of *Left* and *Right* must be of the same data type—DATE in both cases, TIME in both cases, or TIMESTAMP in both cases.
- The second component in each case must *either* be of the same datetime data type as the corresponding first component *or* be of an INTERVAL data type that involves only datetime fields that are also involved in the corresponding first component.

Let the two components of *Left* (in order) be *L1* and *L2* and the two components of *Right* (in order) be *R1* and *R2*, respectively. *L1* and *L2* determine a certain time period in an obvious way—either from *L1* to *L2*, if *L1* and *L2* are both datetimes, or from *L1* to *L1* + *L2*, if *L2* is an interval. (If the end point is earlier in time than the start point, or if the start point is null, then the two are conceptually interchanged before the time period is determined.*) Let *Ls* and *Le* be that start

---

*The purpose of the interchange in the case where the start point is null is simply to avoid dealing with time periods in which the end point is known but the start point is not (i.e., the start point can be unknown after the interchange only if the end point is too).

point and end point, respectively (after any necessary interchanging). Define *Rs* and *Re* analogously. Then the original OVERLAPS condition is defined to be semantically equivalent to the conditional expression

```
( Ls > Rs AND ( Ls < Re OR Le < Re ) ) OR
( Rs > Ls AND ( Rs < Le OR Re < Le ) ) OR
( Ls = Rs AND Le IS NOT NULL AND Re IS NOT NULL )
```

For example, the OVERLAPS condition

```
( TIME '08:00:00', TIME '09:00:00' )
  OVERLAPS
( TIME '08:30:00', TIME '09:30:00' )
```

evaluates to *true*. (So too does the condition that is obtained from the one just shown by replacing the end point of the second time period by null.) By contrast, the OVERLAPS condition

```
( TIME '08:00:00', TIME '09:00:00' )
  OVERLAPS
( TIME '09:00:00', TIME '09:30:00' )
```

evaluates to *false*. Note the asymmetry, incidentally; e.g., consider what happens if *Rs* = *Re*—i.e., *Right* is a time *point* rather than a time period—and it happens to coincide with (a) the start point of *Left*, (b) the end point of *Left*.

18

Temporary Tables

18.1   INTRODUCTION

So far in this book we have concerned ourselves solely with what might be called *permanent* (or *persistent*) base tables—where by "permanent" we mean that the tables in question, once created, persist in the database until such time as they are explicitly destroyed by means of an explicit DROP operation. Sometimes, however, applications have a need for tables that will be used only to pass intermediate results from one portion of the application to another, and hence will persist only for a comparatively short time (certainly not beyond the lifetime of the application in question). Furthermore, such tables are typically "private" to the application that uses them—there is no question of having to share the data they contain with other applications, concurrent or otherwise.

Now, it would of course be possible to use "permanent" tables for such purposes. However, the standard explicitly supports the concept of "temporary" tables (specifically, temporary *base* tables) that can be used to simplify the process slightly. In a nutshell, a temporary table is a base table that:

- Is explicitly stated to be TEMPORARY when it is defined;
- Is always empty at the time of first access from within the applicable module or SQL-session (see Sections 18.2 and 18.3 for an explanation of the difference between the two cases);
- Can optionally be returned to an empty state (automatically) at each COMMIT; and

- Will be dropped automatically (if it has not already been dropped explicitly) at the end of the SQL-session.

Also, transactions are allowed to update temporary tables even if those transactions have been specified to be READ ONLY.

Temporary tables in the standard fall into three types, which we might as well refer to simply as Type 1, Type 2, and Type 3. (The standard uses the terms *declared local* temporary tables, *created local* temporary tables, and *global* temporary tables, respectively; however, these terms are cumbersome, and in this writer's opinion do not serve to characterize the real differences among the three cases any better than the simple labels "Type 1," "Type 2," and "Type 3" do.) We discuss Type 1 in Section 18.2 immediately following and Types 2 and 3 in Section 18.3, later.

18.2   TYPE 1: "DECLARED" TEMPORARY TABLES

A Type 1 temporary table is *declared* (not "created," please note) by means of an appropriate DECLARE statement. Such a table can be accessed only by procedures in the module that contains the corresponding DECLARE; observe that such DECLAREs must physically precede all cursor and procedure definitions within the module in question.* *Note:* We referred to such DECLAREs as "temporary table definitions" in Chapter 6, Section 6.2.

Here then is the syntax for a "temporary table definition":

```
DECLARE LOCAL TEMPORARY TABLE MODULE . base-table
    ( base-table-element-commalist )
    [ ON COMMIT { PRESERVE | DELETE } ROWS ]
```

Here "base table" is an *un*qualified table name; note that all references to the table must be of the special form "MODULE.*table*," where *table* is the name specified as "base table" in the DECLARE. The "base table elements" are as for CREATE TABLE—in other words, each is either a column definition or a base table constraint definition (see below). The ON COMMIT clause specifies whether the table is to be automatically emptied (DELETE) or left unchanged (PRESERVE) at each COMMIT; the default is DELETE.

The current authID (i.e., the authID of the owner of the containing module, if such an owner exists, or the SQL-session authID otherwise) is automatically granted all privileges—but not "grant authority"—on the new Type 1 table. The user granting these privileges is considered to be the special authID _SYSTEM.

As indicated above, a Type 1 table is effectively private to the module in which it is declared; it cannot be accessed from any other module. If any base table

---

*Likewise, if a Type 1 temporary table is declared in a host program with embedded SQL statements, then that declaration must physically precede all references from within that program to the Type 1 table in question.

integrity constraints are specified (within the DECLARE) for such a table, those constraints are not allowed to refer to any named tables that are not themselves temporary tables in turn (of any of the three types). Furthermore, *general* constraints (specified by CREATE ASSERTION) are not allowed to reference temporary tables at all; neither are domain constraints, nor base table constraints that are attached to permanent base tables.

View definitions are allowed to reference temporary tables of Types 2 and 3, but not Type 1. Note that such a view definition might be regarded as defining a kind of "temporary view" (though this term is not used in the standard).

All Type 1 tables are automatically dropped at the end of the SQL-session; in fact, explicit DROP TABLE operations are not even permitted, and nor are ALTER TABLE operations, though such operations *are* permitted for Types 2 and 3. Indeed, Type 1 tables are not even mentioned in any Information Schema (see Chapter 21), again unlike Types 2 and 3. Overall, it seems better to think of Type 1 tables as not belonging to the database at all, and hence not being described by any schema; instead, they should be regarded as purely private objects, kept in the application's private address space along with other local variables.*

18.3   TYPES 2 AND 3: "CREATED" TEMPORARY TABLES

Type 2 and 3 temporary tables are defined by means of a CREATE TABLE statement (not a DECLARE statement) that specifies TEMPORARY. However, such a statement is really quite different in kind from a regular CREATE TABLE. It should certainly not be thought of as actually creating a new base table then and there, as a regular CREATE TABLE does (and so the syntax "CREATE TABLE" is really quite inappropriate). Instead, the table is actually created—the standard uses the term "materialized" or "instantiated"—*when it is first accessed*, either within a module (for Type 2) or within an SQL-session (for Type 3). In other words, each module activation effectively has its own private version of each Type 2 table, and each SQL-session effectively has its own private version of each Type 3 table; thus, Type 2 tables cannot be used to pass information from one module activation to another, and Type 3 tables cannot be used to pass information from one SQL-session to another.

Note: In practice there will often be a one-to-one correspondence between module activations and SQL-sessions anyway, in which case the real distinction between Type 2 and Type 3 becomes very minor indeed. And the real distinction between Type 1 and Type 2 is also fairly minor, in this writer's opinion—after all, both are "module-local"; the principal difference is merely that *any* module can

---

*Actually, the standard does regard a Type 1 table as belonging to a kind of secret schema, whose "effective <schema name> ... may be thought of as [a combination of] the implementation-dependent SQL-session identifier associated with the SQL-session and a unique implementation-dependent name associated with the <module> that contains the <temporary table declaration>."

access a Type 2 table without bothering to declare it (assuming, of course, that appropriate privileges have been granted), whereas only the module that declares it can access a Type 1 table.

Here then is the syntax for creating Type 2 and 3 tables:

```
CREATE { LOCAL | GLOBAL } TEMPORARY TABLE base-table
       ( base-table-element-commalist )
       [ ON COMMIT { PRESERVE | DELETE } ROWS ]
```

LOCAL corresponds to our "Type 2" and GLOBAL to our "Type 3." "Base table" is as for the regular CREATE TABLE,* and "base table elements" and the ON COMMIT clause are as for Type 1 tables (see Section 18.2)—*except* that any named tables referenced within any integrity constraints within the CREATE TABLE must themselves be Type 2 or Type 3 tables (for LOCAL), or just Type 3 tables (for GLOBAL).

The current authID (i.e., the authID of the owner of the containing module, if there is such a containing module and it does have an owner, or the SQL-session authID otherwise, is automatically granted all privileges, with "grant authority",† on the new Type 2 or Type 3 table. The user granting these privileges is considered to be the special authID _SYSTEM.

We remind the reader that, as stated in Section 18.2, general constraints and "permanent" base table constraints are not allowed to reference temporary tables at all, and nor are domain constraints. By contrast, view definitions are allowed to reference temporary tables of Types 2 and 3, but not Type 1. As with Type 1, all Type 2 and Type 3 tables are automatically dropped at the end of the SQL-session, unless they have already been explicitly dropped (explicit DROP and ALTER TABLE operations are allowed for Type 2 and Type 3 tables). Finally, Type 2 and Type 3 tables, unlike Type 1 tables, are described in the applicable Information Schema (again, see Chapter 21).

---

*Except that it must definitely be an *un*qualified name (furthermore, all references to the table must also be via that *un*qualified name). Type 2 and Type 3 tables are considered to belong to a schema, but that schema is *not* the one normally assumed by default. To quote the standard again: "... because global temporary table contents are distinct within SQL-sessions, and created local temporary tables are distinct within <module>s [meaning module *activations*] within SQL-sessions, the *effective* <schema name> of the schema in which [the description of] the global temporary table or the created local temporary table is instantiated is an implementation-dependent <schema name> that may be thought of as having been effectively derived from the <schema name> of the schema in which the global temporary table or created local temporary table is defined and the implementation-dependent SQL-session identifier associated with the SQL-session. In addition, the *effective* <schema name> of the schema in which [the description of] the created local temporary table is instantiated may be thought of as being further qualified by a unique implementation-dependent name associated with the <module> [meaning module *activation*] in which the created local temporary table is referenced." Well, that certainly seems clear enough.

†Any GRANT or subsequent REVOKE against the Type 2 or Type 3 table *must* specify ALL PRIVILEGES.

19

Character Data

19.1 INTRODUCTION

Traditional programming languages have tended to treat as a "character" any value that can be stored in a single addressable location in computer memory. Commonly there are 256 such values, as a direct consequence of the 8-bit byte being the typical unit of addressability. The fact that many of these values map to typical "atoms" of written language, such as letters, numerals, punctuation marks, and so on, has been the concern not of programming languages *per se*, but rather of I/O devices such as keyboards and printers. Well known coding schemes such as ASCII and EBCDIC have been used to map 8-bit values to named symbols such as "upper-case A," "lower-case q," "space," "zero," "comma," and so on. Such named symbols are often referred to as *graphemes* (though this term is not used in the SQL standard).

Traditional programming languages have also provided special operators and notation for the treatment of *character strings* (often abbreviated in this chapter to just *strings*), and the reader will no doubt be very familiar with notations for:

- Representing a character string literal by enclosing a sequence of individual characters (graphemes) in single quotes.

- Comparing two strings character by character, from the first character to the last ("left to right"), to determine whether the first is less than, equal to, or greater than the second according to some *collating sequence. Note:* Historically the collating sequence has typically been just the numerical order of the values of the 8-bit codes, treated as numbers in base 2. However, there is no intrinsic reason why the collating sequence need depend on the internal coding scheme, and the two concepts are distinguished in SQL (under the names *collation* and *form-of-use*, respectively), as we will see in Section 19.2.

- Joining two strings together to make a new string (*concatenation*).

- Extracting some contiguous portion of a given string (*substring*).

- Searching a given string from left to right to see at what *position*, if any, a given substring first occurs.

In databases, character strings have many typical uses. They are the obvious choice for representing written text and names of people, places, and things. They are a common, if less obvious, choice for codes such as part numbers, supplier numbers, and personnel numbers (even when such things really are just numbers). They have also been used, where the database language offers nothing more suitable, for highly specialized and often quite complex data that requires special software, external to the DBMS, to encode, decode, and interpret it.

SQL's support for character data embraces all of the foregoing and more besides. Additional complications arise from the increasingly compelling need to support databases with an international community of users, which in turn implies a need to cope with the ways in which computerized treatment of written text varies from one national language to another. For example:

- Different languages use different sets of graphemes.

- There is sometimes little or no correspondence between the graphemes of one language and those of another.

- Indeed, the number of distinct graphemes varies from a few dozen (in most European languages) to many thousands (notably in Chinese). In some languages there are far too many distinct symbols to be mappable to the 256 possible values of an 8-bit byte, so 16-bit coding schemes are used instead. At the same time, there is understandable reluctance to use 16-bit coding schemes for languages where 8 bits are sufficient.

- Two languages that use approximately the same alphabet can vary in their use of diacritical marks such as accents; further, accented letters are typically required to appear close to their unaccented counterparts in the collating sequence.

- Even internationally accepted coding schemes for languages based on the "Latin alphabet"* reserve some codes for national variations.

---

*So called even though it includes letters such as W and Y that were not originally part of Latin at all.

The reader will probably begin to appreciate the point that SQL's support for character data is quite complex, owing in part to difficulties such as those outlined above. However, the standard does provide an elaborate system of *defaults* to keep matters relatively simple in the majority of cases, as we will see.

19.2   PROPERTIES OF CHARACTER STRINGS

A character string is a sequence of zero or more characters, all of which are drawn from the same *character set*, which must always be specified, even for an empty string (though such specifications will often be implicit). A character set in turn is a named combination of a *character repertoire* and a *form-of-use*:

- A *character repertoire* ("repertoire" for short) is a named collection of characters.*
- A *form-of-use* is a named one-to-one mapping between the characters of some repertoire and a set of internal codes (e.g., 8-bit values).†

A character set also has one or more associated *collations*, of which exactly one is the *default* collation for that character set (see below). *Note:* It is probably worth mentioning that character repertoires and forms-of-use are provided in SQL primarily as building blocks for the construction of character sets. Character sets play a major role in the language, of course (as do collations also); character repertoires and forms-of-use *per se*, by contrast, do not.

Now, when we say that a character string is a "sequence" of (say) L characters, we mean that it consists of an ordered collection of L characters ($L \geq 0$), not necessarily all distinct. Within that ordered collection, there is exactly one, uniquely determined character at each ordinal position p ($1 \leq p \leq L$). The value L (the total number of ordinal positions within the collection) is the *character length* (or just *length*) of the string. Observe that the character length is not necessarily the same as the *octet length*, which is (informally) the amount of computer memory, in 8-bit bytes, minimally needed to accommodate the string.‡

A character string also has a pair of separate but interconnected properties that determine whether and how that string can be compared with others: a *coercibil-*

---

*It is difficult to resist pointing out that (despite the name) a character set is thus *not* a set of characters.

†Here is the standard definition of *form-of-use*: "[a] convention (or encoding) for representing characters (in character strings) ... [Something] that specifies the convention for arranging [the characters of a character set] into character strings."

‡Indeed, two strings might have the same character length but different octet lengths. More precisely, "same character length" implies "same octet length" only in the special (though common) case in which the form-of-use is a *fixed-length coding*—i.e., a form-of-use in which the same number of bits is used for every character.

ity property (the "whether"), and—unless the coercibility property specifies otherwise—a collation property (the "how").

- A *collation* (also, and more familiarly, known as a *collating sequence*) is a rule associated with a specified character set that governs the comparison of strings drawn from that set. Let *C* be a collation for character set *S*, and let *a* and *b* be any two characters (not necessarily distinct) of *S*. Then collation *C* is required to be such that exactly one of the comparisons

  ```
  a < b      a = b      a > b
  ```

  evaluates to *true* and the other two to *false* (under *C*).

  Note that the comparison $a = b$ might evaluate to *true* under *C* even if *a* and *b* are distinct characters. For example, we might define a collation called CASE_INSENSITIVITY (for the character set in question) under which each lower-case letter is considered to "compare equal" to its upper-case counterpart.

- The *coercibility* property of a given string determines which if any of possibly several collations applies to that string (speaking somewhat loosely). Coercibility is discussed in detail in Section 19.7.

To sum up, every character string has:

- A character set, being the combination of some character repertoire *R* and some form-of-use *F*;

- A length *L*;

- For every ordinal position *p* ($1 \leq p \leq L$), a *p*th character drawn from *R* and represented by an internal code determined by *F*;

- A coercibility property and (usually) an associated collation, being any of possibly several collations that apply to the string's character set.

19.3   CHARACTER SETS AND COLLATIONS

As we have just seen, every character string has an associated character set and (usually) an associated collation also. In this section we explain how character sets and collations are defined and destroyed in SQL. As the reader might expect, the relevant statements are CREATE and DROP CHARACTER SET and CREATE and DROP COLLATION, respectively. However, there is one point we should probably make clear right away, and that is that, ultimately,

1. the specific characters contained within a given character set (i.e., the character repertoire),

2. the associated character coding scheme (i.e., the form-of-use), and

3. the specific character ordering represented by a given collation,

are all defined outside the framework of SQL *per se*. In other words, all character sets and all collations are, ultimately, defined in terms of some "external" specification, as we will see.*

Note: As mentioned in Chapter 4, character set definitions and collation definitions are both "schema elements"; in other words, CREATE CHARACTER SET and CREATE COLLATION (like CREATE TABLE and various other CREATE statements) can be executed as independent operations in their own right,† or they can be included as components within a CREATE SCHEMA statement. DROP CHARACTER SET and DROP SCHEMA must be independent operations (like all other forms of DROP).

Character Sets

Here first is the syntax for a character set definition:

```
character-set-definition
    ::=  CREATE CHARACTER SET character-set [ AS ]
            GET existing-character-set
         [ COLLATE collation |
           COLLATION FROM collation-source ]
```

Here "character set" is the name of the new character set,‡ and "existing character set" is the name of some previously defined character set (as so often, the optional key word AS is just noise and can be omitted without affecting the meaning). This latter character set might have been defined by means of a CREATE CHARACTER SET operation in turn, or it might have been defined "externally," i.e., outside the scope of SQL *per se* (it might, for example, be defined in some national or international standard). *Note:* The SQL-implementation *must* support at least one "existing character set," called SQL_TEXT, whose character repertoire (also called SQL_TEXT) is required to contain:

- Every character that is used in the SQL language itself (see Chapter 3, Section 3.1), together with
- Every character that is included in any other character set supported by the SQL-implementation.

Authorization identifiers, SQL-server names, and SQL-connection names are all SQL_TEXT character strings; in particular, the niladic builtin functions USER,

---

*Note, however, that those "external" objects are considered to belong to the applicable Information Schema.

†But see Appendix D.

‡If the name is qualified by a schema name and the CREATE CHARACTER SET appears within the context of a CREATE SCHEMA statement, then that schema name must identify the schema that would have been assumed by default anyway, *viz.* the schema being created (see Chapter 4, Section 4.3).

CURRENT_USER, SESSION_USER, and SYSTEM_USER (see Chapter 15) all return character strings whose associated character set is SQL_TEXT.

"COLLATE ..." and "COLLATION FROM ..." are alternative ways of defining the *default collation* for the new character set. (See below for the syntax of the "collation source" operand of COLLATION FROM.) If neither COLLATE nor COLLATION FROM is specified, COLLATION FROM DEFAULT is assumed (see below); thus, every character set *always* has a default collation.*

A "collation source" is any of the following:

```
EXTERNAL ( 'external-collation' )
collation
DESC ( collation )
DEFAULT
translation-collation
```

We explain these possibilities as follows.

- *EXTERNAL:* "External collation" identifies some collation that is defined externally (e.g., in some national or international standard).

- *Collation:* "Collation" is the name of some existing collation (previously defined by some CREATE COLLATION operation).

- *DESC:* "Collation" is as in the previous case, and the character set being defined has a default collation that is the reverse of the one so identified.

- *DEFAULT:* The default collation is "the order of characters as they appear in the character repertoire." This latter concept is not further defined or clarified in the standard.

- *Translation collation:* The syntax for this case is

```
TRANSLATION translation [ THEN COLLATION collation ]
```

Here "collation" (once again) is the name of some existing collation. However, that existing collation does not necessarily have to be for the character set being defined, because "translation" identifies an existing *translation* (see Section 19.6) that maps strings of the character set being defined to strings of the character set to which "collation" *does* apply. If "THEN COLLATION collation" is omitted, the default collation for the target character set of "translation" is taken as the specified collation source.

Finally, we turn to DROP CHARACTER SET. The syntax is:

```
DROP CHARACTER SET character-set
```

---

*It is worth pointing out too that every collation always has a corresponding character set; that is, given some specific collation, there always exists exactly one corresponding character set to which that collation applies (see the definition of CREATE COLLATION, later).

Note that (in contrast to most other DROP statements) there is no RESTRICT *vs.* CASCADE option. However, RESTRICT is effectively implied—that is, there must be no existing references (e.g., in a column or domain definition or in an integrity constraint) to the specified character set, or the DROP will fail.

Collations

The syntax for "collation definition" is:

```
collation-definition
    ::=  CREATE COLLATION collation
           FOR  character-set
           FROM collation-source
         [ PAD SPACE | NO PAD ]
```

Here "collation" is the name of the new collation,* "character set" identifies the character set whose elements are ordered by this collation, and "collation source" defines that ordering. (We defer discussion of the optional PAD SPACE *vs.* NO PAD specification to Section 19.7, except to note that the default is PAD SPACE or NO PAD according to whether PAD SPACE or NO PAD applies to the collation specified by "collation source.") The collation source can be any of the following:

```
EXTERNAL ( 'external-collation' )
collation
DESC ( collation )
DEFAULT
translation-collation
```

(just as in the COLLATION FROM clause in CREATE CHARACTER SET). The meanings of these various possibilities are analogous to those already explained under the discussion of CREATE CHARACTER SET above.

And here is the syntax for DROP COLLATION:

```
DROP COLLATION collation
```

As with DROP CHARACTER SET, there is no RESTRICT *vs.* CASCADE option; however, the implications of this fact are not quite the same as they are for DROP CHARACTER SET. To be more specific:

- If there are any references to the specified collation in a view definition or an integrity constraint, the DROP will fail.

- Otherwise, the DROP will succeed—and, if there are any references to the now dropped collation in some other collation definition or in a character set, column, or domain definition, those references will simply be deleted without

---

*If the name is qualified by a schema name and the CREATE COLLATION appears within the context of a CREATE SCHEMA statement, then that schema name must identify the schema that would have been assumed by default anyway, *viz.* the schema being created (see Chapter 4, Section 4.3).

warning! For example, if the example collation we mentioned earlier (in Section 19.2), CASE_INSENSITIVITY, is dropped, and there exists a character set CASE_INSENSITIVE for which COLLATE CASE_INSEN-SITIVITY was specified, CASE_INSENSITIVE will be internally rede-fined as if COLLATION FROM DEFAULT had been specified instead (and so the name originally chosen for this character set could become quite inappropriate).

19.4   DATA TYPES

In Chapter 7, we said that SQL supported the following character string data types:

CHARACTER(n)   Fixed length string of exactly n characters ($n > 0$)

CHARACTER
VARYING(n)   Varying length string of up to n characters ($n > 0$)

Now, of course, we can see that a certain amount of refinement is needed. In fact, since every character string has an associated character set and (usually) an associated collation also, we must extend the basic syntax for "character string data type" (within a column or domain definition) to include optional CHARACTER SET and COLLATE specifications, thus:*

```
CHARACTER [ VARYING ] [ ( length ) ]
          [ CHARACTER SET character-set ]
          [ COLLATE collation ]
```

If the CHARACTER SET clause is omitted, the default character set for the relevant schema is assumed by default† (see later in this section for an explanation of the schema default character set). If the COLLATE clause is omitted, then:

- In the context of a column definition, for column C (say), where column C is defined on domain D (say), the collation that applies to domain D is assumed by default.

- In the context of a domain definition, or the column definition for a column that is not defined on a domain, the default collation for the (explicit or implicit) CHARACTER SET character set is assumed by default.

---

*In the interest of accuracy we should make it clear that the COLLATE clause is not technically part of the data type specification *per se*.

†Assuming that the "character string data type" specification is indeed (as stated) part of a column or domain definition. "Character string data type" specifications can also appear within CAST expressions and parameter and host variable definitions, in which case the default character set is implementation-defined. The COLLATE clause is not allowed within CAST expressions and parameter and host vari-able definitions.

In addition to the basic syntax explained above, SQL provides certain short-hands, some of which have already been described in Chapter 7 but are repeated here for completeness. *Note:* Of these shorthands, one seems to be truly useful, the others seem to be merely time-honored abbreviations.

- CHARACTER without a length specification means the same as CHARAC-TER(1).

- CHAR means the same as CHARACTER.

- VARCHAR means the same as CHARACTER VARYING (or CHAR VARYING).

- NATIONAL CHARACTER (the useful one) means the same as CHARACTER ... CHARACTER SET *ncs*, where *ncs* is the name of a particular character set that the implementation has designated as the "national" one.

- NCHAR means the same as NATIONAL CHARACTER.

The Schema Default Character Set

To repeat a remark made earlier in this section, if the CHARACTER SET speci-fication is omitted from a character string data type specification, the default char-acter set for the relevant schema is assumed by default. The default character set for a given schema is specified as part of the CREATE SCHEMA statement. The syntax of that statement, to repeat from Chapter 4, is as follows:

```
CREATE SCHEMA [ schema ] [ AUTHORIZATION user ]
              [ DEFAULT CHARACTER SET character-set ]
              [ schema-element-list ]
```

The default character set for the schema is specified by the DEFAULT CHAR-ACTER SET clause. If that clause is omitted, an implementation-defined charac-ter set is assumed by default (the "default default").

19.5   LITERALS

As explained in Chapter 7, SQL supports the familiar notation for a character string literal, *viz.* a sequence of symbols enclosed in single quotes, where each character is represented by one symbol (except for the single quote itself, which is repre-sented by two immediately adjacent single quotes). Examples are:

```
'This is a string!'
'Here''s another one.'
'SQL'
'p23'
```

and, often sadly overlooked,

```
''
```

(the empty string). *Note:* We remind the reader that SQL also supports an extended format for string literals that span several text lines. Refer to Chapter 7 for the details.

The foregoing notation is clearly sufficient to represent both the actual sequence of characters constituting the value of a literal string* and, by implication, the length of such a string. However, it is not sufficient to represent the string's character set and collation properties. Thus, certain extensions to the basic syntax are necessary.

First, to specify the *character set* for a given character string literal, the name of the character set, prefixed with an underscore, is written in front of the literal itself. For example:

```
_FRANCAIS 'Comment ça va?'
```

The characters that appear between the delimiting single quotes must all, of course, belong to the repertoire of the named character set, in this case FRANCAIS. Note, incidentally, that in the example the character set name is intended to be the same as the name of the language it is supporting, but it has an ordinary C instead of Ç ("C-cedilla"). We will return to this point in Section 19.8.

At this point SQL introduces another useful shorthand, as follows: The expression

```
N'string'
```

—where "string" is a sequence of characters (exactly as in a regular character string literal)—is defined to be shorthand for the expression

```
_national-character-set 'string'
```

where "national-character-set" is the name of the character set that the implementation has designated as the national one. *Note:* National (type N) character string literals can span several lines, just like other string literals; again, see Chapter 7 for the details.

If a character string literal is presented without an explicit accompanying character set specification, then *either* the characters of that literal must all be SQL language characters (see Chapter 3) *or* the character set of the literal defaults to:

- The relevant module's default character set, if the literal appears within a module (see Section 19.8);
- The relevant schema's default character set, if the literal appears within a standalone CREATE SCHEMA (see Section 19.4);

---

*Well, perhaps we should point out one tiny possible problem. The term "character" is presumably intended to include what used to be called "nonprintable" characters (such as carriage return, backspace, etc.) as well as graphemes such as "A", "a", etc. However, the standard makes no special provisions for writing literal strings that include such characters.

■   The default character set of the SQL-session, if the literal appears within a dynamically prepared SQL statement (see Chapters 20 and 23).

Second, to specify the *collation* for a given character string literal, the expression "COLLATE collation" (where "collation" identifies the collation required) is written immediately following the literal itself. For example:

```
'How''s it going?' COLLATE CASE_INSENSITIVITY
```

If "COLLATE collation" is not explicitly specified, the literal inherits the default collation of its explicitly or implicitly specified character set.

Note: COLLATE is really a scalar builtin function (just like, e.g., SUBSTRING); the expression "literal COLLATE collation" is really just unorthodox syntax for a certain function reference. Since the COLLATE function is available for character string expressions in general, it is discussed further in Section 19.6 ("Scalar Operators and Functions"), which follows immediately.

19.6   SCALAR OPERATORS AND FUNCTIONS

Most of the scalar operators and functions (SUBSTRING, POSITION, etc.) that either operate on or yield character strings have already been discussed in Chapter 7, Section 7.4, and the reader is referred to that chapter for further details. Three rather specialized functions, TRANSLATE, CONVERT, and COLLATE (the last of which is very important), remain to be described.

TRANSLATE

TRANSLATE translates a specified character string, character by character, into another string of the same length, using a predefined *translation* that maps a *source* character set to a *target* character set. The source and target character sets can be the same, and the mapping can be many-to-one or one-to-one.

More precisely, the expression TRANSLATE (*string* USING *translation*), where *string* is any arbitrary character string expression, returns a string whose characters are determined from those of *string* according to *translation* and whose "coercibility" (see Section 19.7) is defined to be **implicit**, with collation *C*, where *C* is the default collation for the target character set. For example, the expression

```
TRANSLATE ( 'A,B,C,D' USING PUNCTUATION_TO_SPACES )
```

will return the string

```
'A B C D'
```

(assuming that PUNCTUATION_TO_SPACES is a translation that translates commas and other punctuation marks into spaces and leaves other characters unchanged). The result string will have **implicit** coercibility, with collation the default collation for the target character set of the translation called PUNCTUATION_TO_SPACES. *Note:* The two character sets (source and target) are obviously the same, or at least very similar, in this particular example, but in general there is no reason why this need be so. Note too that the "fold" functions UPPER and LOWER discussed in Chapter 7, Section 7.4, might well be regarded as special cases of TRANSLATE.

Translations are defined using CREATE TRANSLATION, which can be performed (like all other CREATE operations, except for CREATE SCHEMA itself) either standalone or as part of a CREATE SCHEMA operation. The syntax is:

```
translation-definition
    ::=  CREATE TRANSLATION translation
              FOR   source-character-set
              TO    target-character-set
              FROM translation-source
```

Here "translation" is the name of the new translation,* "source character set" and "target character set" are the names of existing character sets, and "translation source" specifies a many-to-one or one-to-one mapping of the source character set to the target character set. The "translation source" can be any of the following:

```
EXTERNAL ( 'external-translation' )
IDENTITY
translation
```

- *EXTERNAL:* "External translation" identifies some translation that is defined externally (e.g., in some national or international standard).

- *IDENTITY:* Every character in the repertoire of the source character set must occur in the repertoire of the target character set (i.e., the source repertoire must be a subset of the target repertoire). The translation maps each character in the source to its counterpart in the target.

- *Translation:* "Translation" is the name of some existing translation (previously defined by some CREATE TRANSLATION operation).

Observe, therefore, that all translations (like all character sets and all collations) are, ultimately, defined in terms of some external specification.

Translations are destroyed via DROP TRANSLATION. The syntax is:

```
DROP TRANSLATION translation
```

Once again there is no RESTRICT *vs.* CASCADE option. Instead:

- If there are any references to the specified translation in a collation definition, view definition, or integrity constraint, the DROP will fail.

---

*If the name is qualified by a schema name and the CREATE TRANSLATION appears within the context of a CREATE SCHEMA statement, then that schema name must identify the schema that would have been assumed by default anyway, *viz.* the schema being created (see Chapter 4, Section 4.3).

■ Otherwise, the DROP will succeed; if there are any references to the now dropped translation in some character set definition, those references will simply be deleted without warning.

CONVERT

CONVERT converts a specified character string, character by character, into another string of the same length, using a predefined *form-of-use conversion* that maps a *source* character set to a *target* character set. The source and target character sets must have the same character repertoire.

More precisely, the expression CONVERT (*string* USING *conversion*), where *string* is any arbitrary character string expression, returns a string whose characters are determined from those of *string* according to *conversion* and whose "coercibility" (see Section 19.7) is defined to be **implicit**, with collation *C*, where *C* is the default collation for the target character set. For example, let EBCDIC_TO_ASCII be a conversion that converts from EBCDIC to ASCII. Then the expression

```
CONVERT ( S.CITY USING EBCDIC_TO_ASCII )
```

could be used to convert an S.CITY value (assumed to be an EBCDIC string) to its ASCII equivalent.

Note: Actually this example is slightly fraudulent (despite the fact that essentially the same example is given in the standard itself!), because EBCDIC and ASCII do not have quite the same character repertoires and thus do not satisfy the prerequisites for CONVERT. Indeed, it seems to be quite difficult to find two genuinely distinct character sets that do have exactly the same character repertoire. Furthermore, it is very unclear to this writer as to why CONVERT is provided at all, since its functionality appears to be totally subsumed by that of TRANSLATE; i.e., there is nothing that can be done with CONVERT that cannot equally well be done with TRANSLATE.

Although a conversion name can include a schema name qualifier, the schema specified *must* be the applicable Information Schema (see Chapter 21). The standard does not provide any "CREATE CONVERSION" or "DROP CONVERSION" operations, nor does it specify any privileges that might be needed to use conversions. Rather, all such matters are apparently implementation-defined.

COLLATE

The expression "*string* COLLATE *collation*" (where string is any arbitrary character string expression) returns a string that has the same value and character set as *string*, but with **explicit** coercibility (see Section 19.7) and with the specified collation. Here is an example (repeated from the end of the previous section):

```
'How''s it going?' COLLATE CASE_INSENSITIVITY
```

Note in particular that the COLLATE function can be used in a GROUP BY clause—provided the relevant grouping column is of type character string, of course—to specify a collation to be used for grouping purposes. It can also be used in an analogous manner in an ORDER BY clause to specify a collation to be used for ordering purposes.

19.7 ASSIGNMENTS AND COMPARISONS

In Chapter 7, we stated that assigning some *source* to some *target* was allowed if and only if *source* and *target* were "compatible" (i.e., had compatible data types). We further stated that "all character strings are compatible with one another." This latter statement now clearly requires some refinement. To be more specific, the definition of "compatibility" must be extended, for the purposes of assignment, to include the requirement that the source and target have *the same character set*. (Note, however, that the TRANSLATE function is available for translating strings from one character set to another. See Section 19.6 above.)

What about comparisons? In Chapter 7, we stated that any two character strings could be compared with one another; again, however, this statement now clearly requires some refinement. The general rule is as follows: Two character strings can be compared if and only if they have the same *collation* (or at least can be "coerced" to have the same collation)—which certainly implies that they must have the same character set, since (as mentioned in Section 19.3) every collation is associated with precisely one character set, but has further implications besides.

The reason for the foregoing general rule is, of course, that character string comparisons must always be performed according to some specific collating sequence. Therefore, given a comparison of the form

```
scalar-expression comparison-operator scalar-expression
```

(where for the moment we assume the comparison operator to be any one of the usual set, and the two comparands are both character string expressions), we need a set of rules to determine the specific collation that will govern the comparison. In what follows, we explain the rules adopted in SQL for this purpose.

First we consider what it means to compare two strings under some given collation. Basically, such comparisons are performed character by character, pairwise, from left to right. If the strings are of equal length, then (a) if every pairwise comparison yields "equal" under the specified collation, the character strings are equal; otherwise (b) the first pairwise comparison that does not yield "equal" determines the overall result. If the strings are of different lengths, then the rules depend on whether the collation was defined with PAD SPACE or NO PAD (refer back to Section 19.3 if you need to refresh your memory regarding these options):

- Under a PAD SPACE collation, the shorter is conceptually padded at the right with spaces to make it the same length as the longer; the rules for comparing equal-length strings are then applied.

- Under a NO PAD collation, a string *s1* that is shorter than some other string *s2*, but "compares equal" to that leading substring of *s2* that is the same length as *s1*, is considered to be less than *s2* even if all remaining characters of *s2* are spaces.

Examples: Let X, Y, Z be strings (all having the same collation *C*, and therefore necessarily all drawn from the same character set) with values as indicated:

```
X : 'ijk'        (length 3)
Y : 'ijk '       (length 5)
Z : 'ij'         (length 2)
```

Furthermore, let collation *C* be such that the familiar "Latin" alphabetic ordering is preserved. Then the following table shows the results of the indicated comparisons under collation *C* (a) if PAD SPACE applies, (b) if NO PAD applies:

Comparison	PAD SPACE	NO PAD
X = Y	true	false
X < Y	false	true
X > Z	true	true

In the last example ("X > Z") we have made the additional assumption that "space" precedes "k" under collation *C*.

Now we turn to the question of deciding what collation to use for a given comparison. That question, not surprisingly, turns on the question of what collations (if any) are associated with the two comparand strings; and *that* question leads us to the question of determining what collation (if any) is associated with the result of evaluating an arbitrary character string expression.

To this end, the standard introduces the notion of "coercibility." Every string has a *coercibility* property, the possible values of which are **explicit, implicit, coercible,** and **no collating sequence.** *Note:* It must be said immediately that the name "coercibility" does not help the cause of intuitive understanding very much— especially since three of the four possible values of the "coercibility" property apparently mean that the string in question is *not* "coercible"! Moreover, the connection between (a) the intuitive interpretation of the terms **explicit, implicit,** and so forth, on the one hand, and (b) their actual significance in the present context on the other, is tenuous at best. Accordingly, we will simply set the terms in **boldface** throughout this chapter in order to stress the fact that they are to be interpreted in a specialized and formal manner, and give only a *very* informal characterization of their intuitive meaning here. We will then follow that informal characterization with a more formal set of definitions.

First, then, the informal characterization. We remind the reader that for the comparison to be even feasible, the two comparands must at least have the same character set, and so we assume throughout the following discussion that such is indeed the case. We also assume for simplicity that all columns, values, etc., mentioned are indeed of type character string.

1. A string with **no collating sequence** can be a comparand only if the other comparand has an **explicit** collation (in which case the **explicit** collation governs the comparison). An example of a string with **no collating sequence** is the result produced by concatenating two strings, *s1* and *s2* say, where *s1* and *s2* are values from columns with different collating sequences. (Note, however, that a **no collating sequence** string can easily be given an **explicit** collation by means of the COLLATE function.) We ignore **no collating sequence** strings in paragraphs 2, 3, and 4 below.

2. A **coercible** string is always a legal comparand; its collation will be "coerced" to that of the other comparand, if necessary. (We will see later that if *both* comparands are **coercible,** they will necessarily have the same collation, so no "coercing" will be necessary.) An example of a **coercible** string would be a character string literal. We ignore **coercible** strings in paragraphs 3 and 4 below.

3. A string with an **implicit** collation can always be compared with one with an **explicit** collation (the **explicit** collation taking precedence); it can be compared with one with an **implicit** collation only if the two **implicit** collations are the same. Values from columns of base tables always have **implicit** collations. We ignore **implicit** strings in paragraph 4 below.

4. Finally, two strings both having an **explicit** collation can be compared only if the **explicit** collations are the same. The result of an invocation of the COLLATE function always has an **explicit** collation.

In all except the **no collating sequence** case, of course, we also need to specify what the associated collation *is*. Here then are the formal rules, specifying the character set, coercibility, and associated collation for the result of evaluating an arbitrary character string expression.

- The character set for a character string literal is determined as explained in Section 19.5 above. Such a string is **coercible,** with collation the default collation for its character set. (In fact, **coercible** *always* means that the corresponding collation is the default collation for the applicable character set.)

- The character set for a character string parameter or host variable can be specified by means of an explicit CHARACTER SET specification on the parameter or host variable declaration (as in a column or domain definition). If that specification is omitted, then the default is implementation-defined.

Such a string is **coercible,** with collation the default collation for its character set.

- The character set for a character string "placeholder" in dynamic SQL (denoted by a question mark) is the default character set for the SQL-session (see Chapters 20 and 23).* Such a string is **coercible,** with collation the default collation for its character set.

- Strings produced by CAST are **coercible,** with collation the default collation for their character set.

- Strings in the same column of the same base table all have the same character set and collation, as explained in Section 19.4 above. The coercibility of such strings is **implicit,** with collation C, where C is the collation defined for the column in question.

- Strings derived from a single string (other than those returned by TRANS-LATE, CONVERT, and COLLATE)—in particular, those returned by TRIM and SUBSTRING—inherit their character set, coercibility, and collation from that single string.

- Strings returned by TRANSLATE and CONVERT have the specified target character set, with **implicit** coercibility and with collation C, where C is the default collation for that character set.

- The coercibility of strings returned by COLLATE is **explicit,** with collation C, where C is the specified collation. The character set of such strings is inherited from the single string operand.

- The character set, coercibility, and collation of strings derived from two strings—which is to say, strings returned by *concatenation*—are determined as follows. Let $s1$ and $s2$ be the two operands, and let sr be the returned string. The operands must be drawn from the same character set, and sr inherits that character set. Furthermore:

  a. If $s1$ and $s2$ have the same coercibility and collation, sr inherits that coercibility and that collation.

  b. If one of $s1$ and $s2$ has an **implicit** collation C and the other is **coercible,** then sr has **implicit** collation C.

  c. If one of $s1$ and $s2$ has an **explicit** collation C and the other has an **implicit** collation, is **coercible,** or has **no collating sequence,** then sr has **explicit** collation C.

  d. If $s1$ and $s2$ have different **explicit** collations, the expression is illegal.

  e. In all other cases, the coercibility of sr is **no collating sequence.**

---

*The reader is warned that this statement is merely an educated guess on the part of the writer. The "placeholder" case is apparently overlooked in the standard.

Note: It follows from the foregoing rules that the only way in which a string that has **no collating sequence** can be generated from string(s) that do all have some collating sequence is by means of an expression of the form *s1||s2*, where *s1* and *s2* have the same character set (necessarily) but different collations, both of which are **implicit.** In all other cases, the result can have **no collating sequence** only if at least one of the operands has **no collating sequence.**

Now we can present the formal rules for character string comparisons. Let *s1* and *s2* be the two comparands (we remind the reader yet again that *s1* and *s2* must be drawn from the same character set).

- If either *s1* or *s2* has **no collating sequence,** the comparison is illegal unless the other has an **explicit** collation.

- Otherwise, if *s1* has an **explicit** collation and *s2* does not, or if *s1* and *s2* both have the same **explicit** collation, then the comparison is performed in accordance with that **explicit** collation. If *s1* and *s2* have different **explicit** collations, the comparison is illegal.

- Otherwise, if *s1* and *s2* both have the same **implicit** collation, then the comparison is performed in accordance with that **implicit** collation. If *s1* and *s2* have different **implicit** collations, the comparison is illegal.

- Otherwise, if *s1* has an **implicit** collation and *s2* is **coercible,** the comparison is performed in accordance with that **implicit** collation.

- Otherwise, *s1* and *s2* must both be **coercible,** and the comparison is performed in accordance with the default collation for the character set of *s1* and *s2*.

Finally, conditional expressions that are not just simple comparisons—expressions involving operators such as LIKE, MATCH, etc.—are defined in accordance with these same general principles. We omit the details here; they are tedious but straightforward, for the most part (but see the subsection "Indeterminate Table Expressions" at the end of this section).

Some examples are in order. Let columns C1 and C2 contain strings from the same character set, and let CASE_INSENSITIVITY be the name of a collation that, among other things, equates lower-case letters from that character set and their upper-case counterparts. Then the expression

```
C1 < C2 COLLATE CASE_INSENSITIVITY
```

is interpreted to mean some "less than" comparison of the string returned by the (trivial) expression "C1" with that returned by the (less trivial) expression "C2 COLLATE CASE_INSENSITIVITY." This latter expression returns a string with **explicit** collation CASE_INSENSITIVITY; the other expression returns a string with some **implicit** collation. The comparison is therefore performed according to the **explicit** collation (which takes precedence).

Note, incidentally, that the comparisons

```
C1 COLLATE CASE_INSENSITIVITY < C2
```

and

```
C1 COLLATE CASE_INSENSITIVITY < C2 COLLATE CASE_INSENSITIVITY
```

are both equivalent to the first one above. By contrast, the comparison

```
C1 COLLATE CASE_INSENSITIVITY < C2 COLLATE CASE_SENSITIVITY
                            -- This is *** ILLEGAL *** !!!
```

is *** *ILLEGAL* ***, since the comparands have two different **explicit** collations. Similarly, the comparison

```
C1 < C2                     -- This is *** ILLEGAL *** !!!
```

is also *** *ILLEGAL* ***, unless the two **implicit** collations for C1 and C2 happen to be the same.

Another example:

```
SP.PNO < 'P23'
```

Here the left hand side is a column name, and has some **implicit** collation; the right hand side is a literal, and so is **coercible.** The comparison is performed in accordance with the **implicit** collation (we are assuming that the character set for column SP.PNO is the same as the default character set that applies to the literal—see Section 19.5 above).

Finally, here is an example of the case in which both operands are **coercible:**

```
:THIS_VAR < 'P23'
```

Here the left hand side is a host variable and the right hand side is a literal (as in the previous example). The comparison is performed in accordance with the default collation for the character set of the comparands (we are assuming that the explicit or implicit character set for the host variable is the same as the default character set that applies to the literal—again, see Section 19.5 above).

In conclusion, we remark that the rules summarized above for determining coercibility, collation, how to evaluate comparisons, etc., are certainly quite complex, but most of the time they do lead to what one would intuitively expect.

Indeterminate Table Expressions

We have seen that two characters from a given character set might be distinct and yet be treated as equal according to some collation. We have also seen that two strings might be distinct, inasmuch as they are of different lengths, and yet be treated as equal when they are compared (at least under PAD SPACE), because the shorter of the two is conceptually padded with spaces for the purposes of the comparison. Both of these facts imply that there exist pairs of character strings *s1* and *s2* such that *s1* is distinguishable from *s2* in some way, and yet the comparison "*s1* = *s2*" evaluates to *true*. We will use the term "equal but distinguishable" to refer to such pairs of strings.*

Now, equality comparisons between character strings are performed—often implicitly—in many, many contexts; examples include MATCH, LIKE, UNIQUE, and NATURAL JOIN (assuming in all cases that the relevant operands are of type character string, of course). The kind of equality involved in all such comparisons is indeed "equal even if distinguishable." For example, suppose once again that CASE_INSENSITIVITY is a collation under which lower-case letters of the so-called Latin alphabet are treated as equal to their upper-case counterparts. Suppose also that PAD SPACE applies to this collation. Then, if the PNO columns of tables P and SP both use this collation, and if

    'P23 '

and

    'p23'

are PNO values in, respectively, some row of P and some row of SP, those two rows will be regarded as satisfying a referential constraint between the PNO columns of the two tables, despite the lower-case "p" and the missing trailing spaces in the foreign key value.

Moreover, when operators such as UNION, INTERSECT, NATURAL JOIN, GROUP BY, and DISTINCT are used in table expressions, the system might have to decide which of two or more equal but distinguishable character string values is chosen for some column in some particular result row. The standard does not lay down any rules to govern such arbitrary choices; rather, all such matters are stated to be implementation-dependent.

It follows from the foregoing that certain table expressions are *indeterminate* (the standard term is "possibly nondeterministic"), in the sense that the standard does not fully specify how they should be evaluated, and indeed they might quite legitimately give different results on different evaluations, even under the very same SQL-implementation against the very same SQL-data. For example, if table *T* has a character string column *C* with collation CASE_INSENSITIVITY, then the expression

```
SELECT MAX (C) AS MAXC
FROM    T
```

---

*Of course, it is not just strings to which this concept applies; for example, the INTEGER value 3 and the NUMERIC(2,1) value 3.0 are equal but distinguishable. However, it is strings specifically that are relevant to the present discussion.

might return "ZZZ" on one evaluation and "zzz" on another, even if no change has occurred to table *T* in the interim.

Here then are the rules.* Table expression *T* is considered by the standard to be *indeterminate* ("possibly nondeterministic") if and only if any of the following is true:

■ *T* is a *union* (without ALL), *intersection*, or *difference* (see Chapter 11, Section 11.4, for definitions of these terms), and the operand tables include a column of type character string.

■ *T* is a *select-expression* (see Chapter 11, Section 11.6), the commalist of select-items in that select-expression includes a select-item *C* of type character string, and:

   a. the commalist of select-items is preceded by the key word DISTINCT, or

   b. *C* involves a MAX or MIN reference, or

   c. *T* directly includes a GROUP BY clause and *C* is one of the grouping columns.

■ *T* is a *select-expression* that directly includes a HAVING clause and the conditional expression in that HAVING clause includes *either* a reference to a grouping column of type character string *or* a MAX or MIN reference in which the argument is of type character string.

As mentioned in Chapter 14, the standard prohibits the appearance of such indeterminate expressions within integrity constraints, on the grounds that to permit them could cause certain updates to succeed or fail unpredictably.

19.8 CHARACTER SETS FOR IDENTIFIERS

We close this chapter with a brief discussion of the character sets used to construct identifiers. *Note:* This discussion does not really belong in a chapter concerned with character *data*, but it does rely on some of the ideas introduced earlier in this chapter and would not have made much sense prior to this point.

First, we remind the reader that to specify the character set of a character string *literal*, we write the name of the character set, prefixed with an underscore, in front of the literal *per se*. For example:

```
_FRANCAIS 'Comment ça va?'
```

The same technique is used for identifiers—for example:

```
_FRANCAIS LIBERTÉ
```

---

*These rules are essentially the ones given in the standard, but they seem to be neither accurate nor complete. See Appendix D.

or even

```
_FRANCAIS LIBERTÉ . _FRANCAIS ÉGALITÉ . _FRANCAIS FRATERNITÉ
```

(this latter might be the name of a base table, qualified by the name of the containing schema, qualified by the name of the containing catalog).

Now, we pointed out previously (in Section 19.5) that the name of the character set in our examples is FRANCAIS, not FRANÇAIS—i.e., it has a Latin C instead of Ç ("C-cedilla"). The reason is that, although (as we have just seen) identifiers in general can be constructed using any character set we please, an exception is made in the case of identifiers that represent character set names themselves; such identifiers are limited to the letters A–Z (or a–z), the digits 0–9, and underscores (see Chapter 3, Section 3.4, for further discussion). And the reason for this limitation is the obvious problem of recursion that would otherwise arise. For example, if we wanted to name the character set in our example FRANÇAIS instead of FRANCAIS, then the "introducer" _FRANÇAIS would in principle have to be specified an infinite number of times.*

Note: On the other hand, a character set name (and therefore an introducer) can be qualified by a schema name that can in turn be qualified by a catalog name, and schema names and catalog names are identifiers for which character sets *can* be specified. As a consequence, the standard, although it does avoid the need for an infinite *sequence* of "introducers," does not avoid the need for an infinite *nest* of them!

If an identifier appears without an explicit character set name prefix (the normal case, of course), then *either* the characters in that identifier must all be SQL language characters (see Chapter 3) *or* the default character set for the relevant module will be assumed by default.† The default character set for a given module is specified as part of the module definition. The syntax for a module definition, to repeat from Chapter 6, is:

```
module-definition
   ::=   MODULE [ module ] [ NAMES ARE character-set ]
         LANGUAGE language
         [ SCHEMA schema ] [ AUTHORIZATION user ]
         [ temporary-table-definition-list ]
         module-element-list
```

The default character set for the module is specified by the NAMES ARE clause. If that clause is omitted, an implementation-defined character set that includes at least all characters used in the SQL language itself (see Chapter 3,

---

*In the interest of accuracy we should mention that the standard uses the term "introducer" to mean just the leading underscore. It does not seem to have a term for what we are calling an introducer, *viz.* the whole construct (underscore plus character set name).

†Unless the identifier appears within a standalone CREATE SCHEMA statement, in which case the default character set for the schema is assumed instead.

Section 3.1) is assumed by default. *Note:* An embedded SQL program can optionally include the analogous specification:

```
SQL NAMES ARE character-set
```

If this specification is omitted, an implementation-defined character set is
assumed that (again) must include at least all characters used in the SQL language
itself. *Note:* If an "SQL NAMES ARE ..." specification is stated explicitly, then
that specification must appear *within* an embedded SQL declare section, *before* any
host variable declarations within that declare section, *without* an EXEC SQL prefix, and *without* a statement terminator.

20

Dynamic SQL

Note: It is worth mentioning that the SQL Call-Level Interface feature—see Chapter 23—provides an arguably better solution to the problem that dynamic SQL is intended to address than dynamic SQL itself does (in fact, dynamic SQL would probably never have been included in the standard if the Call-Level Interface had been defined first). Readers who are interested in that problem should probably still study the present chapter, however, since it can be seen in part as a useful generic introduction to the basic concepts underlying both approaches.

20.1 INTRODUCTION

It is customary when discussing the implementation of programming languages to distinguish between *compilers* and *interpreters*. A compiler requires each source program to be subjected to some kind of preparatory processing before it can be executed; the purpose of that preliminary compilation step is to produce an executable version of the program that can subsequently be run many times, thereby amortizing the cost of actually doing the compilation over many executions. An interpreter, on the other hand, requires no such preparatory step, but just executes the source program directly—in effect, by compiling each statement "on the fly" as it encounters it at run time.

Now, it is well known that, for performance reasons, compilation "ahead of time"—i.e., prior to run time—is the preferred approach in many situations (though by no means all). Certainly many current SQL products do use such an approach. Furthermore, the SQL standard does seem to assume that the implementation will indeed use such an approach, although to be fair it never states as much explicitly.*

The trouble is, however, there are some applications—typically "general-purpose" applications, such as *ad hoc* query utilities or database design tools—for which it is simply not possible to provide all of the information needed to do the compilation prior to run time. For example, consider a natural language query application that allows end users to enter queries expressed in (say) English and responds to those queries by retrieving data from an SQL database. It is obviously not feasible to "hard-code" every possible SQL statement that might ever be needed as part of the original application source code. Instead, therefore, the application must:

1. *Generate* the necessary SQL statements dynamically (i.e., at run time) on an "as needed" basis; then

2. *Compile* such statements dynamically, by invoking the SQL compiler at run time, again on an "as needed" basis; and finally

3. *Execute* the newly compiled statements as and when necessary.

We give a small PL/I code fragment (accurate but unrealistically simple) to illustrate the foregoing process.

```
DCL SQLSOURCE CHAR VARYING (65000) ;

SQLSOURCE = 'DELETE FROM SP WHERE SP.QTY < 300' ;
EXEC SQL PREPARE SQLPREPPED FROM :SQLSOURCE ;
EXEC SQL EXECUTE SQLPREPPED ;
```

Explanation:

1. The name SQLSOURCE identifies a PL/I varying length character string variable in which the program will somehow construct the source form—i.e., character string representation—of some SQL statement (a DELETE statement, in our particular example).

2. The name SQLPREPPED, by contrast, identifies an *SQL* variable, not a PL/I variable, that will be used (conceptually) to hold the compiled form of the SQL statement whose source form is given in SQLSOURCE. *Note:* The names SQLSOURCE and SQLPREPPED are arbitrary, of course. Also, "SQL variable" is not an official standard term (see later).

---

*In fact it is at least arguable that the opposite is true, inasmuch as the standard does effectively provide for interpretive implementation through its "direct SQL" feature. However, direct SQL is very far from being computationally complete (i.e., it is quite inadequate for most applications), because it does not include anything in the way of traditional flow control constructs such as IF - THEN - ELSE or loops.

3. The assignment statement "SQLSOURCE = ... ;" assigns to SQLSOURCE the source form of an SQL DELETE statement. In practice, of course, the process of constructing such a source statement is likely to be much more complex—perhaps involving the analysis of some end user request expressed in natural language or some other form more "user-friendly" than plain SQL.

4. The PREPARE statement then takes that source statement and "prepares"—i.e., compiles—it to produce an executable version, which it stores in SQLPREPPED.

5. Finally, the EXECUTE statement executes that SQLPREPPED version and thus causes the actual DELETE to occur. Feedback information from the DELETE (SQLSTATE value, etc.) is returned exactly as if the DELETE had been directly executed in the normal way.

Note, incidentally, that since it denotes an SQL variable, not a PL/I variable, the name SQLPREPPED does *not* have a colon prefix when it is referenced in the PREPARE and EXECUTE statements. Note too that such SQL variables are not explicitly declared.

Thus we see that the standard does provide a set of features—PREPARE, EXECUTE, etc.—to permit the writing of general-purpose applications. The features in question are referred to collectively as *dynamic SQL*, and are the subject of the present chapter. By contrast, other aspects of the language are referred to collectively as *static* SQL. *Note:* Actually, the term "static SQL" is neither defined nor used in the standard; nor need it be, though it is common parlance in SQL circles. It is sufficient just to say that there is SQL, and some part of SQL is a discrete "detachable" piece called dynamic SQL.*

There are a couple of further points that we might as well get out of the way before we start getting into too much detail:

- First, the privileges needed to execute some "prepared" statement *S* are (reasonably enough) exactly the same as they would be if *S* were executed directly as part of static SQL.

- Second, as we will see in Section 20.3, "prepared" statements come in two varieties, local and global. *Local* prepared statements are considered to belong to the module containing the relevant PREPARE statement. *Global* prepared statements, by contrast, are considered to belong to the "SQL-session

---

*As we saw in Chapter 6, the standard includes a classification scheme for SQL statements, one category of which is *SQL dynamic statements*. The reader is warned, however, that this category does not include all of the statements that go to make up what most people would call dynamic SQL. Specifically, it does not include any cursor statements, not even those cursor statements that make use of the special facilities described in the present chapter. Instead, all cursor statements, static or dynamic, are classified simply as *SQL data statements*.

module," which, as the reader might recall from Chapter 5 (Section 5.3), is an implementation-defined module that is distinct from all other modules currently existing in the same SQL-environment.

20.2   WHAT IS THE PROBLEM?

Dynamic SQL is remarkably complex, even by SQL standards. Before studying it in detail, therefore, it is as well to familiarize oneself with the special problems that are faced by general-purpose application developers, for otherwise the rationale for many of the facilities provided will not be at all obvious. In this section, therefore, we describe some of those problems briefly, and sketch the relevant facilities of dynamic SQL in each case.

1. As we have already seen, a general-purpose application might need to generate SQL statements at run time. An example might be an interactive database creation utility that allows the end user to enter SQL data definition statements (e.g., CREATE TABLE, CREATE VIEW) from a workstation or terminal. This utility cannot be written in static SQL, because the SQL statements to be executed are not known until run time.

    Dynamic SQL's EXECUTE IMMEDIATE statement addresses this problem (see Section 20.3). *Note:* EXECUTE IMMEDIATE effectively combines the functions of PREPARE and EXECUTE into a single operation, loosely speaking.

2. Consider an *ad hoc* query utility that allows end users to develop and submit queries (not necessarily SQL queries *per se*) and to display the results of those queries as reports or graphs. In order to display the result of a given query, the utility needs to find out at run time how many columns there are in that result; for each such column, it also needs to find out the name, the data type, and many other things.

    Dynamic SQL includes an elaborate *descriptor* mechanism to address this problem (see Section 20.4). *Note:* Please observe that the descriptors referred to here are nothing to do with the descriptors found in schemas, whose purpose is to describe objects such as base tables, views, domains, constraints, etc., as explained in Chapter 4. Please observe too that we will use the term "descriptor" throughout this chapter to mean the dynamic SQL construct, not the schema construct.

3. Suppose the *ad hoc* query utility mentioned above also allows the user to save queries for subsequent reuse. Suppose further that the user is allowed to save a *generic form* of such queries, implying that certain *arguments* will have to be provided every time such queries are executed. For example, suppose we frequently need to find out about the suppliers in some given city. When that city is Paris, the SQL statement that must be executed—i.e., the *internal form* of the query, as executed from within the query utility—is:

```
SELECT  S.SNO, S.SNAME, S.STATUS
FROM    S
WHERE   S.CITY = 'Paris'
```

In static SQL, a generic form of this SQL statement might look something like this:

```
SELECT  S.SNO, S.SNAME, S.STATUS
FROM    S
WHERE   S.CITY = :CITY_PARAM
```

Note: CITY_PARAM here is either a parameter or a host variable, depending on whether we are using the module language or embedded SQL. To fix our ideas, we assume the latter case.

Remember, however, that we are talking about *dynamic* SQL. A moment's thought will reveal why host variables cannot be used in the same way in dynamic SQL. For one thing, it is not known at compilation time how many such variables will be needed, nor what data type they should be; for another, host variables are declared in the application program itself, and their names are not known to the end user (which would thus make it difficult for the application to prompt for arguments at run time). We therefore need some other way in dynamic SQL to mark places to be filled at run time and to supply such run-time arguments.

We have already seen that dynamic SQL provides the PREPARE statement for compiling SQL statements at run time. Furthermore, those SQL statements can include *placeholders*—i.e., they can represent *generic* statements. When such generic statements are subsequently executed, there are facilities for providing arguments to be substituted for the placeholders. The same descriptor interface as that mentioned above (for describing the columns of a query result to the application) is used to describe such placeholders, or *parameters*, to the system. Again, see Section 20.4 for detailed discussion. *Note:* "Parameters" is the standard term. However, such parameters are nothing to do with the parameters of the module language, discussed in Chapter 6. In the hope of avoiding confusion, therefore, we will (throughout the remainder of this chapter) always use "placeholders" for the dynamic SQL construct, reserving "parameters" for the module language construct.

4. In dynamic SQL, as in static SQL, multi-row retrieval is done by means of a cursor, using OPEN, FETCH, and CLOSE operations (rows retrieved via the cursor can be the target of UPDATE and DELETE CURRENT operations too). In static SQL, the DECLARE CURSOR statement includes a *cursor specification* that, among other things, defines the table to be accessed via that cursor. As a reminder, here is the syntax of "cursor specification," repeated from Chapter 10:

```
    table-expression
[ ORDER BY order-item-commalist ]
[ FOR { READ ONLY | UPDATE [ OF column-commalist ] } ]
```

There is a counterpart to DECLARE CURSOR in dynamic SQL; however, it involves a *level of indirection* between the cursor declaration *per se* and the cursor specification portion, so that this latter portion can be the subject of a separate PREPARE and can vary from one opening of the cursor to the next. See Section 20.5.

5. But even a dynamic variant of DECLARE CURSOR is inadequate if the application does not know *how many* cursors it will be required to have open concurrently during any particular invocation. For example, the *ad hoc* query utility referred to above might want to support the concurrent display of an arbitrary number of query results, each in its own window on the screen.

   Dynamic SQL therefore provides an ALLOCATE CURSOR statement, which effectively supports the generation of new cursors "on the fly." Again, see Section 20.5.

6. In static SQL, there are rules for determining the missing high-level qualifiers (catalog name and schema name) for object references when no such qualifiers are specified explicitly. Similarly, there is a rule for determining the relevant character set for identifiers and character string literals when no such character set is specified explicitly. All of these rules take effect at compilation time. Partly for that reason, however, the rules are, typically, inappropriate for applications that use dynamic SQL, because such applications are, typically, meant for use with a variety of different databases in a variety of different environments. Therefore, dynamic SQL includes special statements to specify the default catalog name, schema name, and character set name for an SQL-session, and it is these *session* defaults that are used in the dynamic SQL context. The statements in question are SET CATALOG, SET SCHEMA, and SET NAMES. See Section 20.6.

This concludes our brief survey of dynamic SQL and the kinds of problems it is intended to solve. Without further ado, let us now begin our detailed examination of the various features and facilities that dynamic SQL provides.

20.3 STATEMENT PREPARATION AND EXECUTION

In this section we discuss the basic PREPARE and EXECUTE operations and various associated facilities. We begin with the shorthand form EXECUTE IMMEDIATE.

EXECUTE IMMEDIATE

A given SQL statement can be "executed immediately"—i.e., it can be the subject of an EXECUTE IMMEDIATE statement—provided that:

- It does not contain any placeholders.

- It is *preparable* (we will define this latter term precisely in a moment; here we merely note that certain statements—e.g., EXECUTE IMMEDIATE itself— are *not* preparable).

- It does not retrieve any data; specifically, it is not a single-row SELECT statement, nor more generally a table expression of any kind (refer to Chapter 11 if you need to refresh your memory regarding table expressions). *Note:* Although table expressions in general are not normally regarded as statements *per se*,* they are nevertheless preparable, as we will see. But they cannot be the subject of an EXECUTE IMMEDIATE, for essentially the same reason that a multi-row retrieval operation cannot be executed directly in embedded SQL or the module language.

Here then is the syntax of EXECUTE IMMEDIATE:

```
EXECUTE IMMEDIATE source-statement-container
```

"Source statement container" here is a parameter or host variable, of type character string, that contains the source form of the SQL statement to be executed. Note that the source statement in question must not include an EXEC SQL prefix or a statement terminator. However, the parameter or host variable does require a colon prefix, as always.

Here is an example. Suppose again that, as in the first of the examples in Section 20.2, we have an interactive database creation utility that allows its end user to enter SQL data definition statements (CREATE TABLE, etc.) from the terminal. If that utility is written in embedded SQL, it might look something like this:

```
EXEC SQL BEGIN DECLARE SECTION ;

    /* variable to contain SQL statement (source form) */

    DCL SQLSOURCE CHAR VARYING (65000) ;

    /* SQL return code variable */

    DCL SQLSTATE CHAR (5) ;

EXEC SQL END DECLARE SECTION ;

/* code to execute SQL statements entered by end user */

GET LIST ( SQLSOURCE ) ;
DO WHILE ( SQLSOURCE ¬= '' ) ;
    EXEC SQL EXECUTE IMMEDIATE :SQLSOURCE ;
    PUT SKIP LIST ( 'Return code:', SQLSTATE ) ;
    GET LIST ( SQLSOURCE ) ;
END ;
```

---

*Except in direct SQL.

This code executes SQL statements submitted from the terminal until the end user enters an empty line.

Note: For definiteness, all examples in this chapter will be shown in embedded SQL rather than the module language. Also, for brevity we will henceforth omit the BEGIN and END DECLARE SECTION statements. We will, however, *not* omit the EXEC SQL prefixes, because it is desirable to distinguish clearly between statements of dynamic SQL *per se* and statements of the host language (PL/I in our examples).

PREPARE

As explained in Section 20.1, the basic purpose of PREPARE is to "prepare" some specified SQL statement for execution—i.e., to produce a "prepared" (or *object* or *compiled* or *executable* or, very informally, "prepped") form of that specified SQL statement. As indicated by the example in that section, there must be a *name* (i.e., an identifier) by which the prepared form of the statement can be referenced—indirectly, please note—in subsequent EXECUTE statements and elsewhere. This name, which must be supplied by the user, can be specified either directly or indirectly. Accordingly, there are two distinct PREPARE formats. The first is:

```
PREPARE prepped-statement-container
        FROM source-statement-container
```

Here "source statement container" is as for EXECUTE IMMEDIATE, and "prepped statement container" is the name of an SQL variable.* The statement in "source statement container" is compiled and the compiled form is placed in the SQL variable denoted by "prepped statement container." Here is an example (repeated from Section 20.1):

```
EXEC SQL PREPARE SQLPREPPED FROM :SQLSOURCE ;
```

Note that there is no explicit declaration of the SQL variable SQLPREPPED. Note too that if that same SQL variable has already been specified in some previous PREPARE, then the new PREPARE effectively overwrites the previous value of that variable (i.e., the result of the previous PREPARE is lost).

Now, in the foregoing example, the name SQLPREPPED is clearly "hard-coded" into the PREPARE statement. However, requiring such names always to

---

*As indicated earlier, "SQL variable" is not an official standard term. Moreover, what we are here (accurately) referring to as the name of that variable is referred to in the standard as the (user-supplied) name of the *prepared statement* instead. But it seems to this writer that this latter nomenclature is unnecessarily confusing, because it skips a significant level of indirection. It is desperately important to preserve conceptual clarity wherever possible, above all in a context that is as inherently complex as dynamic SQL is. In this chapter, therefore, we will briefly mention the standard nomenclature in passing, but we will use our own.

be hard-coded in this way would lead to an undesirable loss of flexibility and would make certain applications very awkward to write. This is the justification for the second format of PREPARE:

```
PREPARE prepped-statement-name-container
        FROM source-statement-container
```

Here "source statement container" is as before, and "prepped statement name container" is a parameter or host variable (with a colon prefix) of type character string, with octet length not greater than 128, whose *value* is an identifier. In other words, before executing the PREPARE, the user must have placed in "prepped statement name container" the (user-generated) *name* of an "SQL variable".* The PREPARE then causes the statement in "source statement container" to be compiled and the compiled form placed in that SQL variable. Again, if that SQL variable already contains the compiled form of some SQL statement, then the new PREPARE effectively overwrites the previous value of that variable (i.e., the previously compiled statement is lost).

Here is an example that makes use of the second PREPARE format:

```
SQLPREPPEDNAME = 'SQL_STMT' || N ;

EXEC SQL PREPARE :SQLPREPPEDNAME FROM :SQLSOURCE ;
```

Note: The "prepped statement name container" in the second format of PREPARE can optionally include a LOCAL or GLOBAL prefix—for example:

```
EXEC SQL PREPARE LOCAL :SQLPREPPEDNAME FROM :SQLSOURCE ;
```

LOCAL (the default) means the scope of the SQL variable name given in "prepped statement name container" is the containing module; GLOBAL means it is the current SQL-session. Every reference to "prepped statement name container" in subsequent EXECUTE statements and elsewhere must also specify LOCAL or GLOBAL, as appropriate. For simplicity, we ignore the GLOBAL possibility throughout the remainder of this chapter, thus effectively treating all SQL variable names (implicitly) as LOCAL.

Preparable Statements

We turn now to the definition of what it means for a statement to be preparable. First, such a statement cannot include any comments, host variables, or parameters. Second, it must be one of the following:

---

*The standard nomenclature is again very bad in this area—it actually refers to the "prepped statement name container" parameter or host variable as a *statement* as such! That is, it actually uses the term "statement name" (more precisely, "*extended* statement name," which seems even less appropriate) to mean the name of the specified parameter or host variable, instead of the value of that parameter or host variable. In our opinion, this is not just confusing, it is *confused*. We will stay with our own terminology.

- *SQL data statements* (also referred to in this book as *data manipulation* statements):

```
single-row SELECT (without an INTO clause)
INSERT, searched UPDATE, searched DELETE
DECLARE CURSOR (cursor specification portion only)
positioned UPDATE, positioned DELETE
```

Note: The preparable forms of the positioned UPDATE and DELETE statements differ slightly from their static SQL counterparts. See Section 20.5, later.

- *SQL schema statements* (also referred to in this book as *data definition* statements, except for CREATE and DROP ASSERTION and GRANT and REVOKE):

```
CREATE SCHEMA, DROP SCHEMA
CREATE DOMAIN, ALTER DOMAIN, DROP DOMAIN
CREATE TABLE, ALTER TABLE, DROP TABLE
CREATE VIEW, DROP VIEW
CREATE CHARACTER SET, DROP CHARACTER SET
CREATE COLLATION, DROP COLLATION
CREATE TRANSLATION, DROP TRANSLATION
CREATE ASSERTION, DROP ASSERTION
GRANT, REVOKE
```

- *SQL transaction statements:*

```
SET TRANSACTION
SET CONSTRAINTS
COMMIT, ROLLBACK
```

- *SQL session statements:*

```
SET SESSION AUTHORIZATION
SET CATALOG
SET SCHEMA
SET TIME ZONE
SET NAMES
```

- *Other statements* (as defined by the implementation)

Placeholders

A preparable statement is permitted (in general) to include any number of *placeholders*, each denoted in the source form of the statement by a question mark ("?"). The placeholders will be replaced by actual argument values when the prepared version is later executed. Here is an example:

```
SQLSOURCE = 'DELETE FROM SP WHERE SP.QTY > ? AND SP.QTY < ?' ;

EXEC SQL PREPARE SQLPREPPED FROM :SQLSOURCE ;

LOW = 100 ;
HIGH = 300 ;

EXEC SQL EXECUTE SQLPREPPED USING :LOW, :HIGH ;
```

The effect of this example is to delete all shipments with a quantity in the indicated range. *Note:* We will have a lot more to say about the EXECUTE ... USING statement later in this section—also in Section 20.4, later.

Placeholders (i.e., question marks) are permitted only where *literals* are permitted. Note in particular, therefore, that they cannot be used to represent *names* (of tables, columns, etc.). Furthermore, they are subject to the following dazzling array of additional prohibitions:*

- They cannot appear as the operand of a monadic operator. Thus, e.g., the scalar expression "+?" is illegal. (The expression "0+?", by contrast, is legal.)

- They cannot appear as both operands of a dyadic operator. Thus, e.g., the scalar expressions "?+?" and "?||?" are illegal.

- They cannot be select-items. Thus, e.g., the following is illegal:

```
SELECT ? AS X                          -- This is *** ILLEGAL *** !!!
FROM   ...
```

The following, by contrast, is legal:

```
SELECT 0 + ? AS X
FROM   ...
```

The reason is, of course, that the "+" ensures that the placeholder (question mark) must be of type numeric. Concatenation with an empty bit or character string could be used in a like manner to ensure that a given placeholder is of type BIT or CHARACTER.

- They cannot appear as both operands of a comparison operator. Thus, e.g., the following is illegal:

```
SELECT *
FROM   ...
WHERE  ? = ?                           -- This is *** ILLEGAL *** !!!
```

(but if we replaced either question mark by, say, "0+?" the comparison would then be legal).

This rule extends to corresponding components of rows, so that a comparison such as "(X,?) > (?,Y)" is legal, but "(X,?) > (Y,?)" is not. Furthermore, "((1,?),(2,?))" is not a valid table constructor,† because it has placeholders in the second column position in both rows.

---

*The general intent of these prohibitions is to ensure that placeholders can appear only in positions where the data type of the corresponding argument can be determined at PREPARE time. Note, however, that "CAST (? AS data-type)" is *always* legal, and can effectively be used to specify a placeholder of any desired data type. For example, "SELECT ? AS X FROM ..." is not legal, but "SELECT CAST (? AS REAL) AS X FROM ..." is legal.

†Except in the special case where it represents the source table expression in an INSERT statement.

- They cannot appear as both the sole scalar comparand on the left hand side and the first component of the commalist of scalar comparands on the right hand side of an IN condition. Thus, e.g., the following is illegal:

```
SELECT *
FROM   ...
WHERE  ? = ( ?, ... )             -- This is *** ILLEGAL *** !!!
```

- They cannot appear as both operands in POSITION.
- They cannot appear as the sole operand in UPPER or LOWER.
- They cannot appear as the first operand in SUBSTRING.
- They cannot appear as either the second or the third operand in TRIM.
- They cannot appear as the FROM operand in EXTRACT.
- They cannot appear as the first operand in TRANSLATE, CONVERT, or COLLATE.
- They cannot appear as the argument to an aggregate function such as MAX.
- They cannot appear as the left hand operand (or any component of the left hand operand) of IS [NOT] NULL.
- They cannot appear as the second component of either operand of OVERLAPS.
- The "result" of a THEN or ELSE clause within a CASE expression can be a placeholder only if at least one other "result" in that CASE expression is neither a placeholder nor the specification NULL.

DEALLOCATE PREPARE

The purpose of DEALLOCATE PREPARE is to "DROP" a previously prepared statement. There are two formats, corresponding to the two formats of PREPARE:

```
DEALLOCATE PREPARE { prepped-statement-container |
                     prepped-statement-name-container }
```

"Prepped statement container" and "prepped statement name container" are as for PREPARE. Note that, as already suggested under the discussion of PREPARE above, an appropriate DEALLOCATE PREPARE is executed automatically if PREPARE specifies an SQL variable (either directly or indirectly) that already contains a prepared statement.

It is worth mentioning that the standard explicitly permits—but does not require—the SQL-implementation to "DROP" existing prepared statements automatically at COMMIT (and ROLLBACK). As the standard puts it, not very elegantly: "The validity of [a prepared statement] in an SQL-transaction different from the one in which the statement was prepared is implementation-dependent."

EXECUTE

The general form of the EXECUTE statement is:

```
EXECUTE { prepped-statement-container |
          prepped-statement-name-container }
                   [ INTO places ] [ USING arguments ]
```

As the syntax suggests, the first operand is either an SQL variable that contains a prepared statement, or a parameter or host variable that contains the name of an SQL variable that in turn contains such a prepared statement. The prepared statement thus specified, either directly or indirectly, is executed. Furthermore:

- If the statement to be executed is a single-row SELECT statement, an INTO clause must be specified; "places" (see below) indicates where the retrieved data is to be placed.

- If the statement to be executed includes any placeholders, a USING clause must be specified; "arguments" (see below) provides the necessary argument values to fill the gaps corresponding to those placeholders.

Note: As already mentioned, cursor specifications are preparable; nevertheless, they cannot be the object of an EXECUTE statement. Instead, FETCH and other cursor operations have to be used, more or less as in static SQL, in order to access the data corresponding to a prepared cursor specification. See Section 20.5, later.

The "places" operand takes one of the following two forms:

```
target-commalist | SQL DESCRIPTOR descriptor
```

In the first format, each "target" is a parameter or host variable, optionally accompanied by an indicator parameter or host variable (exactly as described in Chapter 16); there must be exactly one target for each select-item in the single-row SELECT, and the target identified by the ith entry in the target commalist corresponds to the ith select-item. The second format is intended for use when (e.g.) the number of select-items is not known at compilation time. We defer further discussion of this latter case to Section 20.4 below.

The "arguments" operand also has two possible formats:

```
argument-commalist | SQL DESCRIPTOR descriptor
```

In the first format, each "argument" is a parameter or host variable, optionally accompanied by an indicator parameter or host variable (again as described in Chapter 16); there must be exactly one argument for each placeholder in the source form of the prepared statement, and the argument identified by the ith entry in the argument commalist corresponds to the ith placeholder in that statement as written. The second format is intended for use when (e.g.) the number of arguments is not known at compilation time; again, we defer further discussion of this case to Section 20.4 below.

Let us revise our example from the subsection "Placeholders" above. First, we repeat from that subsection the source form of the statement to be prepared and the corresponding PREPARE:

```
SQLSOURCE = 'DELETE FROM SP WHERE SP.QTY > ? AND SP.QTY < ?' ;
EXEC SQL PREPARE SQLPREPPED FROM :SQLSOURCE ;
```

Here now is a possible execution sequence, a little more complete and realistic than that shown previously:

```
DCL LOW  FIXED DECIMAL (5) ;
DCL HIGH FIXED DECIMAL (5) ;

/* obtain values for the arguments */

GET LIST ( LOW, HIGH ) ;

/* now perform the DELETE */

EXEC SQL EXECUTE SQLPREPPED USING :LOW, :HIGH ;
```

As already indicated, the commalist form, whether it be for "places" or for "arguments," is inappropriate in cases where the number of result columns or placeholders, or their corresponding data types, cannot be determined at compilation time. It is for this reason that the alternative "SQL DESCRIPTOR" formats are provided. The "descriptor" operand of those formats identifies something called an *SQL descriptor area*, and that brings us to a complex subject, which we discuss in the next section.

20.4   SQL DESCRIPTOR AREAS

We begin by considering a simple example. Suppose we have an application that needs to prepare and execute a single-row SELECT statement, the details of which will not be known until run time. The dynamic facilities discussed so far are inadequate to handle this case; the reason is, of course, that SELECT is different from most other SQL statements, in that it returns data to the application (others return feedback information only).

Clearly, the application needs to know something about the data values to be retrieved in order to be able to process those values properly. To be more specific, it at least needs to know how many scalar values there will be in the result row, and also what the data types, lengths, precisions, etc. (as applicable) of those values will be. If the SELECT is generated dynamically, it will usually not be possible for the application to know this information in advance; therefore, it must obtain the information dynamically. SQL descriptor areas are provided to address such requirements. In outline, the process the application must go through is as follows.

1. First, it creates an SQL descriptor area, *sda* say, using ALLOCATE DESCRIPTOR. This area can be thought of as consisting of a list or one-dimensional array of individual item descriptors—one for each of the values

in the result row that will be produced when the single-row SELECT is actually executed—together with a count of the number of entries (i.e., individual item descriptors) in that array. *Note:* ALLOCATE DESCRIPTOR does not *populate* the descriptor area, it merely allocates storage for it. However, it is necessary to assume that the application does at least know an upper bound for the number of values to be expected in the result row, in order to be able to allocate a descriptor area of adequate capacity.

2. Next, it builds and prepares the single-row SELECT. Recall from Section 20.3 that this SELECT will *not* include an INTO clause.

3. It then executes a DESCRIBE OUTPUT ... USING SQL DESCRIPTOR *sda* against the prepared single-row SELECT. The effect of this statement is to populate the descriptor area *sda*; i.e., it places a count of the number of values in the result row into *sda*, and a description (data type, etc.) of the *i*th value in the result row into the *i*th item descriptor within *sda*.

4. It then executes the prepared single-row SELECT by means of an EXECUTE statement of the form EXECUTE ... INTO SQL DESCRIPTOR *sda*. The *i*th value in the SELECTed row is retrieved into the *i*th item descriptor within *sda*.

5. It uses GET DESCRIPTOR operations repeatedly against *sda* to discover the data type, length, etc., of the retrieved values and to transfer such values, one at a time, from *sda* to other variables as desired.

So much for our introductory example. To complete this brief overview, here is a summary list of the SQL statements having to do with SQL descriptor areas:

```
ALLOCATE DESCRIPTOR, DEALLOCATE DESCRIPTOR
GET DESCRIPTOR, SET DESCRIPTOR
DESCRIBE
```

In addition, the EXECUTE, dynamic OPEN, and dynamic FETCH statements can all include clauses of the form "INTO (or USING) SQL DESCRIPTOR ..." (see Section 20.5 for a description of the dynamic OPEN and FETCH statements). We remark that the apparently redundant qualifier "SQL" in "SQL DESCRIPTOR" is *required* in the context of an INTO or USING clause and *prohibited* in all other contexts (such as, e.g., ALLOCATE DESCRIPTOR). We remark also that the key word DESCRIPTOR refers to the entire SQL descriptor area in some contexts (e.g., ALLOCATE DESCRIPTOR) but to an individual item descriptor in others (e.g., GET DESCRIPTOR).

SQLDAs

As already indicated, an SQL descriptor area—"SQLDA" for short—can be thought of as consisting of a *count*, together with a list or one-dimensional *array* of individual item descriptors that all have the same (composite) structure. Each individual item descriptor describes either

- A column of the table that results from executing some prepared statement (in the case of "places"), or
- An argument to replace some placeholder in some prepared statement (in the case of "arguments").

Note: "SQLDA" is a useful abbreviation, but it is not an official standard term. Note clearly, moreover, that several SQL products do already support some kind of SQLDA, and even refer to it by that name, but those SQLDAs are typically not the same as the "SQLDA" defined in the standard. In particular, the standard SQLDA is *encapsulated* (meaning that its internal structure is not specified in the standard and is thus *a fortiori* hidden from the user), whereas the same is typically not true of the SQLDAs in current products. The fact that the standard SQLDA is encapsulated in this way means that it should be possible to conceal the differences among different products with respect to SQLDA implementation. In order to help achieve this goal:

- The standard provides facilities for allocating and deallocating SQLDA storage that do not rely on details of how SQLDAs are actually implemented.
- It also provides facilities for moving data values into and out of SQLDAs that (again) do not rely on details of how SQLDAs are actually implemented.

These two points taken together imply (among other things) that the facilities of dynamic SQL can be used even with host languages such as COBOL and FORTRAN that do not support dynamic storage allocation or pointers.

Now, although (as just explained) users are not concerned with the actual structure of an SQLDA, it is nevertheless helpful to think of them as consisting of the aforementioned array of item descriptors (plus the count). Each such item descriptor in turn consists of a number of named components, each representing some particular aspect of the "place" or "argument" described by the item descriptor in question. We list below some of the more important of these components (together with their data type in each case); for a complete list, the reader is referred to the official standard. Note that not all components have meaning in all contexts.

```
NAME                     character string
UNNAMED                  exact numeric with scale 0
TYPE                     exact numeric with scale 0
LENGTH                   exact numeric with scale 0
RETURNED_LENGTH          exact numeric with scale 0
RETURNED_OCTET_LENGTH    exact numeric with scale 0
PRECISION                exact numeric with scale 0
SCALE                    exact numeric with scale 0
DATA                     (depends on TYPE, LENGTH, etc.)
INDICATOR                exact numeric with scale 0
```

Note the DATA component, which is used to contain an actual scalar value (e.g., a retrieved value, if the item descriptor is part of a "places" SQLDA). If the INDICATOR value is negative, the DATA value is undefined ("null"). Note also the

UNNAMED component, which is set to 1 if the NAME value is implementation-dependent (loosely, if the corresponding column is unnamed).

ALLOCATE DESCRIPTOR

The syntax of ALLOCATE DESCRIPTOR is:

```
ALLOCATE DESCRIPTOR descriptor [ WITH MAX occurrences ]
```

Here (a) "descriptor" is a literal, parameter, or host variable—*not* an identifier, please note!*—of type character string, with octet length not greater than 128, whose *value* is an identifier, and (b) "occurrences" is a literal, parameter, or host variable of type exact numeric with scale 0, whose value is a positive integer. An SQLDA is created with the value of "descriptor" as its name, of sufficient size to accommodate at least M item descriptors, where M is the value of "occurrences." If "WITH MAX occurrences" is omitted, an implementation-defined value (at least 1) is assumed for M.

Here is an example:

```
EXEC SQL ALLOCATE DESCRIPTOR 'SPIDA' WITH MAX 1000
```

If an SQLDA with the name SPIDA ("suppliers-and-parts information descriptor area") already exists, an exception is raised. Contrast the situation with PREPARE: If an SQL variable is reused (either directly or indirectly) in PREPARE, a DEALLOCATE PREPARE is performed implicitly to destroy the prepared statement previously contained in that variable.

Note: Like the "prepped statement name container" specification in the second format of PREPARE, the "descriptor" specification in ALLOCATE DESCRIPTOR can optionally include a LOCAL or GLOBAL prefix—for example:

```
EXEC SQL ALLOCATE DESCRIPTOR LOCAL 'SPIDA' WITH MAX 1000
```

The significance is analogous: LOCAL (the default) means the scope of the SQLDA name is the containing module, GLOBAL means it is the current SQL-session, and all subsequent references to "descriptor" in (e.g.) DESCRIBE statements must also specify LOCAL or GLOBAL, whichever is appropriate. For simplicity, we ignore the GLOBAL possibility throughout the remainder of this chapter.

---

*The reason it is not an identifier is, of course, the added flexibility that accrues from the possibility of using a parameter or host variable. Note, however, that the fact that it is not an identifier means that we are flouting our own syntax conventions here. In Chapter 3 we said that if *xyz* is an SQL object type, then in syntax rules the syntactic category *xyz* would stand for the *name* of an object of that type, thus writing, e.g., "CREATE SCHEMA *schema*," where *schema* stands for the name of some schema. But "descriptor" above does not stand for the name of a descriptor, it stands for a literal or the name of a parameter or the name of a host variable, whose *value* is that descriptor name.

Of course, ALLOCATE DESCRIPTOR does not *populate* the newly created SQLDA; on the contrary, every component of every individual item descriptor is initially undefined. There are several different ways of populating a given SQLDA such as the one called SPIDA in our example:

1. We can specify

```
INTO SQL DESCRIPTOR 'SPIDA'
```

   in an EXECUTE statement (in which case the prepared statement that is being executed must be a single-row SELECT). This case has already been discussed briefly in the "Overview" subsection above.

2. We can specify

```
INTO SQL DESCRIPTOR 'SPIDA'
```

   in a dynamic FETCH statement. See Section 20.5 for further discussion of this case.

3. We can specify

```
USING SQL DESCRIPTOR 'SPIDA'
```

   in a DESCRIBE INPUT or DESCRIBE OUTPUT statement. This is the recommended method for the most highly generalized type of application. We describe DESCRIBE in the subsection "DESCRIBE" below.

4. We can execute one or more statements of the form

```
SET DESCRIPTOR 'SPIDA' ...
```

   Each such statement will assign values to components within *a single item descriptor* within the SQLDA. Note, therefore, that one difference between SET DESCRIPTOR and DESCRIBE is that DESCRIBE populates the entire SQLDA *en bloc*, whereas SET DESCRIPTOR populates only a single item descriptor (and very likely only portions of that descriptor, at that). We describe SET DESCRIPTOR in the subsection "SET DESCRIPTOR" at the end of the present section.

Before we go on to explain any of these methods in detail, however, let us first dispose of DEALLOCATE DESCRIPTOR.

DEALLOCATE DESCRIPTOR

If ALLOCATE DESCRIPTOR is thought of as "CREATE SQLDA"—which is effectively what it is—then DEALLOCATE DESCRIPTOR is the corresponding DROP. The syntax is:

```
DEALLOCATE DESCRIPTOR descriptor
```

"Descriptor" here is exactly as for ALLOCATE DESCRIPTOR.

DESCRIBE

DESCRIBE causes the system to "describe" some specified prepared statement—i.e., to place descriptor information for that prepared statement into some specified SQL descriptor area. There are two formats, DESCRIBE INPUT and DESCRIBE OUTPUT; DESCRIBE INPUT is for an "arguments" area, DESCRIBE OUTPUT is for a "places" area (and thus the terms INPUT and OUTPUT are to be interpreted from the system's point of view—"arguments" are input *to* the system, and "places" are where output *from* the system is to go).

Here first is the syntax of DESCRIBE INPUT:

```
DESCRIBE INPUT { prepped-statement-container |
                 prepped-statement-name-container }
                    USING SQL DESCRIPTOR descriptor
```

"Prepped statement container" and "prepped statement name container" are as for PREPARE (as usual); whichever is specified, it must identify a prepared statement, either directly or indirectly, that involves N placeholders ($N \geq 0$). The value N is placed within the SQLDA identified by "descriptor" (where "descriptor" is as for ALLOCATE DESCRIPTOR), and a description of the ith placeholder—and hence of the ith argument to be supplied at execution time—is placed in the ith item descriptor within that SQLDA. *Note:* If N is greater than the maximum number of item descriptors that the SQLDA can accommodate, then a warning condition is raised, and no item descriptors are set (though the count is set to N).

And here is the syntax of DESCRIBE OUTPUT:

```
DESCRIBE [ OUTPUT ] { prepped-statement-container |
                      prepped-statement-name-container }
                         USING SQL DESCRIPTOR descriptor
```

Note that the key word OUTPUT is optional. Again, "prepped statement container" and "prepped statement name container" are as for PREPARE; whichever is specified, it must identify (directly or indirectly) either a prepared single-row SELECT statement or a prepared cursor specification, both of which will produce a result table of N columns ($N > 0$) at execution time (in the case of a single-row SELECT, of course, that table should have at most one row). The value N is placed within the SQLDA identified by "descriptor" (which is again as for ALLOCATE DESCRIPTOR), and a description of the ith column is placed in the ith item descriptor within that SQLDA. Again, if N is greater than the maximum number of item descriptors that the SQLDA can accommodate, then a warning condition is raised, and no item descriptors are set (though the count is set to N).

GET DESCRIPTOR

GET DESCRIPTOR is for retrieving specified information from a specified SQLDA (usually from a specified *item descriptor* within a specified SQLDA). There are two formats. The first simply retrieves a count of the number of populated item descriptors in the specified SQLDA:

```
GET DESCRIPTOR descriptor target = COUNT
```

"Descriptor" specifies an SQLDA in the usual way; "target" is a parameter or host variable of type exact numeric with scale 0. The count of the number of populated item descriptors in the specified SQLDA is placed in the specified target.

The second GET DESCRIPTOR format is:

```
GET DESCRIPTOR descriptor
               VALUE subscript assignment-commalist
```

Once again "descriptor" specifies an SQLDA in the usual way; "subscript" is a literal, parameter, or host variable of type exact numeric with scale 0, whose value i identifies the ith item descriptor in that SQLDA. The assignments in the "assignment commalist" retrieve values from that ith item descriptor. Each such assignment is of the form

```
target = source
```

where "target" is a parameter or host variable, and "source" is the name of one of the components (TYPE, LENGTH, DATA, etc.) within the item descriptor. Of course, each target must have a data type compatible with that of its source; in the special case where the source is DATA, the target must be of a data type that is consistent with the values for TYPE, LENGTH, PRECISION, SCALE, etc., in that same item descriptor.

An Example

The following somewhat lengthy example shows how the ideas discussed so far might fit together in practice. The assumption is that we need to prepare and execute a single-row SELECT statement, and we do not know at the time of writing the program how many values (or columns) are involved in the result row, nor how many placeholders are involved in the request. For simplicity, we give the text of the SELECT as an explicit character string literal below (and hence the number of columns and number of placeholders clearly *are* known), but the reader should understand that in practice the exact format of the SELECT will normally not be known so readily.

```
/* variable to hold source form of SELECT statement */
DCL SQLSOURCE CHAR VARYING (65000) ;
```

```
/* construct source form of SELECT statement; we do this */
/* via an assignment here, but in practice it might be,  */
/* e.g., built from input from the terminal              */

SQLSOURCE = 'SELECT P.CITY, P.WEIGHT, P.COLOR
            FROM    P
            WHERE   P.PNO = ?' ;

/* construct prepped form of SELECT statement */

EXEC SQL PREPARE SQLPREPPED FROM :SQLSOURCE ;

/* create SQLDAs for SELECT columns and arguments */

EXEC SQL ALLOCATE DESCRIPTOR 'SELCOLS' WITH MAX 256 ;
EXEC SQL ALLOCATE DESCRIPTOR 'SELARGS' WITH MAX 40 ;

/* populate the SQLDAs */

EXEC SQL DESCRIBE INPUT SQLPREPPED
                   USING SQL DESCRIPTOR 'SELARGS' ;
EXEC SQL DESCRIBE OUTPUT SQLPREPPED
                   USING SQL DESCRIPTOR 'SELCOLS' ;

/* code is needed here to place SELECT arguments into the */
/* SELARGS SQLDA (because for the sake of the example we  */
/* will say EXECUTE ... USING SQLDA, though EXECUTE ...   */
/* USING argument-commalist would be simpler); we omit    */
/* this code from the example, for brevity, but it would  */
/* bear some similarity to the code shown below for       */
/* retrieving results from the SELCOLS SQLDA              */

/* perform the SELECT */

EXEC SQL EXECUTE SQLPREPPED INTO SQL DESCRIPTOR 'SELCOLS'
                            USING SQL DESCRIPTOR 'SELARGS' ;

/* variable to hold column count */

DCL DEGREE FIXED BINARY (15) ;

/* how many columns are there in the result? */

EXEC SQL GET DESCRIPTOR 'SELCOLS'
                   :DEGREE = COUNT ;

/* variables to receive column information from SELCOLS */

DCL DATA_TYPE FIXED BINARY (15) ;
DCL DATA_LEN  FIXED BINARY (15) ;

/* loop control variable */

DCL I FIXED BINARY (15) ;

DO I = 1 TO DEGREE ;

   /* get data type and length of Ith result column */

   EXEC SQL GET DESCRIPTOR 'SELCOLS' VALUE :I
             :DATA_TYPE = TYPE,
             :DATA_LEN = LENGTH ;
```

```
/* can now allocate a suitable variable, say DATA_VAR, */
/* into which Ith column data value can be retrieved    */

/* get data value from Ith result column */

EXEC SQL GET DESCRIPTOR 'SELCOLS' VALUE :I
          :DATA_VAR = DATA ;

END ;

/* and so on, and so on, and so on */
```

SET DESCRIPTOR

As already indicated, SET DESCRIPTOR is for populating or updating the contents of an SQLDA, or more precisely of an individual item descriptor within an SQLDA, in piecemeal fashion. Now, it is very unlikely that anyone would want to populate an entire SQLDA using SET DESCRIPTOR; a more likely thing to do would be to populate the whole SQLDA using DESCRIBE, and then to change certain parts of it using SET DESCRIPTOR.

Why might it be desirable to overwrite the descriptor information produced by DESCRIBE? One important reason is as follows. Suppose that DESCRIBE OUTPUT reports a certain result column to be of some data type, say DECIMAL, that is not supported by the host language. In such a case, SET DESCRIPTOR could be used to change the data type specification in the corresponding item descriptor to REAL, say. The system will then know that we want to see values of that result column as REAL, even though it knows those values are actually DECIMAL (it knows this from its own "private" descriptor, which is of course not accessible to—and certainly not changeable by—the user). The system will therefore perform an appropriate data type conversion on the decimal values when they are retrieved.*

Like GET DESCRIPTOR, SET DESCRIPTOR comes in two formats. The first is used to establish the count of the number of item descriptors in the specified SQLDA that are to be populated:

```
SET DESCRIPTOR descriptor COUNT = source
```

"Descriptor" specifies an SQLDA in the usual way; "source" is a literal, parameter, or host variable of type exact numeric with scale 0. The count of the number of item descriptors to be populated in the specified SQLDA is set to the specified value. *Note:* One possible use for this first SET DESCRIPTOR format might be to initialize the COUNT to zero immediately after ALLOCATE DESCRIPTOR,

---

*The legal conversions are not necessarily identical to (nor are they limited to) those supported by CAST. Rather, the rules are all implementation-defined.

in order to reduce the risk of a program "running wild" if it inadvertently accesses an SQLDA that has not yet been the target of a DESCRIBE.

The second SET DESCRIPTOR format is:

```
SET DESCRIPTOR descriptor
            VALUE subscript assignment-commalist
```

Once again "descriptor" specifies an SQLDA in the usual way; "subscript" is a literal, parameter, or host variable of type exact numeric with scale 0, whose value *i* identifies the ith item descriptor in that SQLDA. The assignments in the "assignment commalist" update values in that *i*th item descriptor. Each such assignment is of the form

```
target = source
```

where "source" is a literal, parameter, or host variable, and "target" is the name of one of the components (TYPE, LENGTH, DATA, etc.) within the item descriptor. Of course, each source must have a data type compatible with that of its target. Here is an example of the second format:

```
EXEC SQL SET DESCRIPTOR 'SELARGS' VALUE :I
                    TYPE = 12,
                    LENGTH = 100 ;
```

Let the current value of the variable I be *i*. Then the effect of this SET DESCRIPTOR is to update the *i*th item descriptor in the SQLDA called SELARGS. The assignments to TYPE and LENGTH indicate that the data type CHARACTER VARYING (100) will be used for values of the *i*th argument (we assume that SELARGS is an "arguments" SQLDA; 12 is the standard TYPE code for CHARACTER VARYING). Once again, the reader is referred to the official standard document for details of the components included within item descriptors, for details of the values those components are permitted to have, and for an explanation of the meanings of those permitted values.

20.5   CURSOR OPERATIONS

We begin by repeating a few points previously made in Section 20.2:

- First, multi-row retrieval in dynamic SQL, like multi-row retrieval in static SQL, is done by means of a cursor, using OPEN, FETCH, and CLOSE operations (rows retrieved via the cursor can be the target of UPDATE and DELETE CURRENT operations too).

- Second, the dynamic version of DECLARE CURSOR is more flexible than the static version, in that it introduces a level of indirection between the cursor declaration *per se* and the cursor specification portion, so that this latter portion can be the subject of a separate PREPARE and can vary from cursor opening to cursor opening.

- Third, there is one additional cursor operation available in dynamic SQL, *viz.* ALLOCATE CURSOR, which effectively supports the generation of new cursors "on the fly." Note, however, that there is no corresponding DEALLOCATE CURSOR, at least not explicitly.

We now proceed to examine these ideas in detail.

DECLARE CURSOR

Cursors defined by the dynamic version of DECLARE CURSOR (or generated by ALLOCATE CURSOR) are said to be *dynamic cursors*. If the application can manage with a "hard-coded" dynamic cursor name, the dynamic version of DECLARE CURSOR will suffice. The syntax is:*

```
DECLARE cursor [ INSENSITIVE ] [ SCROLL ] CURSOR
        FOR prepped-statement-container
```

"Cursor" here is the name of the dynamic cursor; "prepped statement container" is the name of an SQL variable that—by the time the cursor is opened—will contain the prepared form of a cursor specification. Note that the operand *is* "prepped statement container," not "prepped statement *name* container" ("prepped statement name container" is the operand for ALLOCATE CURSOR, *q.v.*). Here is an example:

```
EXEC SQL DECLARE X CURSOR FOR SQLPREPPED ;
```

Before cursor X can be opened, a PREPARE must have been done to place the prepared form of a cursor specification into SQLPREPPED. Our "cursor X" example might thus continue as follows:

```
DCL SQLSOURCE CHAR VARYING (65000) ;

SQLSOURCE = 'SELECT SP.PNO, SP.QTY
             FROM    SP
             WHERE   SP.SNO = ''S2''
             ORDER   BY PNO' ;

EXEC SQL PREPARE SQLPREPPED FROM :SQLSOURCE ;
```

Now the cursor can be opened:

```
EXEC SQL OPEN X ;
```

See the subsection "OPEN and CLOSE" below for further discussion of OPEN.

---

*The only difference *vis-à-vis* the static variety is that "prepped statement container" appears in place of a cursor specification. Refer to Chapter 10 if you need to refresh your memory regarding SCROLL and INSENSITIVE.

ALLOCATE CURSOR

When DECLARE CURSOR is not appropriate (because of its insistence on a hard-coded cursor name), ALLOCATE CURSOR must be used instead. The syntax is:

```
ALLOCATE cursor-name-container [ INSENSITIVE ] [ SCROLL ]
         CURSOR FOR prepped-statement-name-container
```

Here "cursor name container" and "prepped statement name container" are both parameters or both host variables (of type character string with octet length not greater than 128 in each case). "Cursor name container" must contain a user-generated identifier that will be used to refer to the cursor that is dynamically created by the ALLOCATE CURSOR operation.* "Prepped statement name container" must contain the user-generated identifier of an SQL variable that *already contains* the prepared form of a cursor specification.

Note: "Cursor name containers," like "prepped statement name containers" and "descriptors," can optionally include a LOCAL or GLOBAL prefix. Once again, we ignore the GLOBAL possibility for simplicity, treating all cursor names as LOCAL by default.

Here is an ALLOCATE CURSOR version of our DECLARE CURSOR example above:

```
DCL SQLSOURCE       CHAR VARYING (65000) ;
DCL SQLPREPPEDNAME  CHAR VARYING (128) ;
DCL XNAME           CHAR VARYING (128) ;

SQLSOURCE = 'SELECT  SP.PNO, SP.QTY
            FROM    SP
            WHERE   SP.SNO = ''S2''
            ORDER   BY PNO' ;

SQLPREPPEDNAME = 'SELECT_STMT_1' ;

EXEC SQL PREPARE :SQLPREPPEDNAME FROM :SQLSOURCE ;

XNAME = 'CURSOR_1' ;

EXEC SQL ALLOCATE :XNAME CURSOR FOR :SQLPREPPEDNAME ;

EXEC SQL OPEN :XNAME ;
```

As mentioned at the beginning of this section, there is no "DEALLOCATE CURSOR." However, if a prepared cursor specification *C* is dropped via DEALLOCATE PREPARE, and *D* is an "allocated" dynamic cursor that is currently associated with *C* (i.e., an ALLOCATE CURSOR has been executed associating *C* with *D*), then *D* is dropped automatically.

---

*The standard uses the term "cursor name" (more precisely, "*extended* cursor name," which seems even less appropriate) to refer, very confusingly, to the name of the specified parameter or host variable, instead of to the value of that parameter or host variable. Once again it has to be said that the official terminology is not very good, and we will avoid it.

OPEN and CLOSE

The dynamic version of OPEN looks like this:

```
OPEN { cursor | cursor-name-container } [ USING arguments ]
```

"Cursor" and "cursor name container" are as for DECLARE CURSOR and ALLOCATE CURSOR, respectively. The "arguments" option has the same two possible formats as it does in EXECUTE:

```
argument-commalist | SQL DESCRIPTOR descriptor
```

The USING clause must be provided if the cursor specification associated with the cursor to be opened contains any placeholders. Here is a modified version of our ALLOCATE CURSOR example to illustrate the point:

```
DCL SQLSOURCE      CHAR VARYING (65000) ;
DCL SQLPREPPEDNAME CHAR VARYING (128) ;
DCL XNAME          CHAR VARYING (128) ;
DCL SNO            CHAR (5) ;

SQLSOURCE = 'SELECT SP.PNO, SP.QTY
             FROM    SP
             WHERE   SP.SNO = ?
             ORDER   BY PNO' ;

SQLPREPPEDNAME = 'SELECT_STMT_1' ;

EXEC SQL PREPARE :SQLPREPPEDNAME FROM :SQLSOURCE ;

XNAME = 'CURSOR_1' ;

EXEC SQL ALLOCATE :XNAME CURSOR FOR :SQLPREPPEDNAME ;

GET LIST ( SNO ) ;

EXEC SQL OPEN :XNAME USING :SNO ;
```

And, of course, the dynamic version of CLOSE looks like this:

```
CLOSE { cursor | cursor-name-container }
```

For example:

```
EXEC SQL CLOSE :XNAME ;
```

FETCH

The dynamic version of FETCH takes the form:

```
FETCH [ [ row-selector ] FROM ]
        { cursor | cursor-name-container } INTO places
```

"Cursor" and "cursor name container" are as for OPEN, "row selector" is as explained in Chapter 10, and "places" is as for EXECUTE—i.e., it takes one of the following forms:

```
target-commalist | SQL DESCRIPTOR descriptor
```

To continue with our running example:

```
EXEC SQL OPEN :XNAME USING :SNO ;

EXEC SQL ALLOCATE DESCRIPTOR 'SELCOLS' WITH MAX 256 ;

EXEC SQL DESCRIBE OUTPUT :SQLPREPPEDNAME
                USING SQL DESCRIPTOR 'SELCOLS' ;

EXEC SQL FETCH ABSOLUTE :I FROM :XNAME
                INTO SQL DESCRIPTOR 'SELCOLS' ;
```

If the host variable I has the value 42, say, this FETCH will retrieve values from the 42nd row of the ordered collection of rows associated with the current opening of the dynamic cursor whose name is given in the host variable XNAME.* Those values will be retrieved into the SQLDA called SELCOLS. The application will then have to use GET DESCRIPTOR statements to copy those values into variables of its own. Assuming for the sake of simplicity that all columns are of type SMALLINT, and nulls are not permitted for any of them, the following code could be used to display the row just fetched:

```
DCL DEGREE         FIXED BINARY (15) ;
DCL COLUMN_NAME    CHAR VARYING (128) ;
DCL COLUMN_VALUE   FIXED BINARY (15) ;
DCL COLUMN_NUMBER  FIXED BINARY (15) ;

EXEC SQL GET DESCRIPTOR 'SELCOLS' :DEGREE = COUNT ;

DO COLUMN_NUMBER = 1 TO DEGREE ;

    EXEC SQL GET DESCRIPTOR 'SELCOLS' VALUE :COLUMN_NUMBER
                              :COLUMN_NAME = NAME,
                              :COLUMN_VALUE = DATA ;

    PUT SKIP LIST ( COLUMN_NAME || ':', COLUMN_VALUE ) ;

END ;
```

Positioned UPDATE and DELETE

The dynamic SQL versions of UPDATE CURRENT and DELETE CURRENT differ from their static counterparts in certain important respects. In particular, each comes in two varieties, a preparable form and a nonpreparable form, as we will see.

---

*The "ALLOCATE :XNAME CURSOR ..." statement would have had to have specified SCROLL for this FETCH ABSOLUTE to succeed.

1. The nonpreparable form is identical to the static SQL counterpart except that the "WHERE CURRENT OF" clause can specify *either* a cursor in the usual way, as in static SQL, or a cursor name container (as is only to be expected).

2. By contrast, the preparable form:

   ▪ *Cannot* be executed except via PREPARE and EXECUTE (or EXECUTE IMMEDIATE);

   ▪ *Must* specify a cursor in the usual way, not a cursor name container; and

   ▪ *Need not* name the table in which a row is to be updated or from which a row is to be deleted, because that table is implied by the cursor specification anyway.* (Since the cursor specification is constructed at run time, the table name would typically not be known at compilation time. In order to include that table name in a positioned UPDATE or DELETE, therefore, the application would have to parse the cursor specification at run time—an undesirable and unnecessary state of affairs.)

   DELETE is simpler, and we therefore treat it first. The syntax is:

   ```
   DELETE [ FROM table ]
   WHERE  CURRENT OF { cursor | cursor-name-container }
   ```

Here is an example:

```
DELETE WHERE CURRENT OF X
```

(a preparable positioned DELETE).

   And here is the syntax for UPDATE:

   ```
   UPDATE [ table ]
   SET    assignment-commalist
   WHERE  CURRENT OF { cursor | cursor-name-container }
   ```

Since the column names of "table" (which are needed for the assignments) are almost certainly not known at compilation time, in practice the UPDATE statement is likely to be built at run time and then explicitly prepared. Let us imagine a simple application that displays the row most recently fetched in a window where the user can, if desired, update the row by overtyping the displayed values (all of which we assume to be of type SMALLINT, remember). Then a suitable UPDATE statement might be built and prepared as follows:

```
DCL DEGREE        FIXED BINARY (15) ;
DCL COLUMN_NAME   CHAR VARYING (128) ;
DCL COLUMN_VALUE  FIXED BINARY (15) ;
DCL COLUMN_NUMBER FIXED BINARY (15) ;
```

---

*Note that the same is true in static SQL! In this writer's strong opinion, it should not be necessary to name the table in the static versions of the statements either.

```
DCL SQLUPD          CHAR VARYING (65000) ;

DCL COMMA           CHAR (1) ;

EXEC SQL GET DESCRIPTOR 'SELCOLS' :DEGREE = COUNT ;
SQLUPD = 'UPDATE SET' ;
COMMA  = ' ' ;

DO COLUMN_NUMBER = 1 TO DEGREE ;

    EXEC SQL GET DESCRIPTOR 'SELCOLS' VALUE :COLUMN_NUMBER
                                 :COLUMN_NAME = NAME ;
    SQLUPD = SQLUPD || COMMA || COLUMN_NAME || ' = ?' ;
    COMMA = ',' ;

END ;

/* assume an appropriate ALLOCATE :XNAME CURSOR ... has */
/* already been done                                    */

SQLUPD = SQLUPD || ' WHERE CURRENT OF ' || XNAME ;

EXEC SQL PREPARE SQLUPDPREPPED FROM :SQLUPD ;
```

In order to execute the UPDATE, we go through the following steps:

```
EXEC SQL ALLOCATE DESCRIPTOR 'UPD_VALUES' WITH MAX 50 ;
EXEC SQL DESCRIBE INPUT SQLUPDPREPPED
                USING SQL DESCRIPTOR 'UPD_VALUES' ;
```

Suppose that a row has been fetched, displayed, and overtyped by the user on the screen, and suppose that the new column values have been read into an array of small integers called NEW_VALUE. The prepared and described UPDATE statement can now be executed to update the current row, as follows:

```
DO COLUMN_NUMBER = 1 TO DEGREE ;
    COLUMN_VALUE = NEW_VALUE ( COLUMN_NUMBER ) ;
    EXEC SQL SET DESCRIPTOR 'UPD_VALUES' VALUE :COLUMN_NUMBER
                                 DATA = :COLUMN_VALUE ;
END ;

EXEC SQL EXECUTE SQLUPDPREPPED
                USING SQL DESCRIPTOR 'UPD_VALUES' ;
```

How to handle tables whose columns are not all of the same data type is, of course, an added problem, but we have shown how all the information needed by the writer of such a program is available in the SQL descriptor area, and we leave the solution, as they say, as an exercise for the *writer!*

20.6   SESSION DEFAULTS

Consider the case of a generalized "off the shelf" software package that uses dynamic SQL. With such a package, the very same code might be executed by different users, against different databases, on different computer installations, in different organizations, maybe even using different DBMSs.

For such an application, the static SQL rules that determine the default catalog and schema names for the resolution of unqualified table names, domain names, etc., are not at all suitable. Quite apart from anything else, they would require all users always to work with the same defaults! And, of course, analogous remarks apply to the default character set that is used for character string literals and SQL identifiers. Thus, a mechanism is clearly needed to allow programs that use dynamic SQL to specify their defaults at run time. This is the purpose of the operations SET CATALOG, SET SCHEMA, and SET NAMES.*

Each of these operations establishes a default for the current SQL-session. The syntax is:

```
SET { CATALOG | SCHEMA | NAMES } { string | authID-function }
```

Here *string* is a literal, parameter, or host variable, of type character string in each case, and "authID function" is USER, CURRENT_USER, SESSION_USER, or SYSTEM_USER (see Chapter 15). The value specified by *string* is established as the default for the current session for the specified item. *Note:* Each of the three items is set to an implementation-defined "default default" when the SQL-session is initiated, as explained in Chapter 5.

It must be made very clear that the defaults established by these special SET operations apply only to SQL statements that are prepared and/or executed dynamically.† A program that uses a mixture of static and dynamic SQL would have to beware of the possibility that the defaults used for its static statements are not necessarily the same as those used for its dynamic statements.

Note, incidentally, that if a *qualified* schema name is specified as the default in SET SCHEMA, as in the following example—

```
FULL_NAME = CAT_NAME || '.' || SCHEMA_NAME ;
EXEC SQL SET SCHEMA :FULL_NAME ;
```

—then the default catalog name and default schema name for the session are effectively both established, just as if the following statements had both been executed:

```
EXEC SQL SET CATALOG :CAT_NAME ;
EXEC SQL SET SCHEMA  :SCHEMA_NAME ;
```

---

*Obviously SET CATALOG and SET SCHEMA are the operations that specify the default catalog and schema; why the operation that specifies the default character set should be SET *NAMES* is (to this writer, at least) not so obvious.

†And to statements of direct SQL and statements prepared and executed through the Call-Level Interface (see Chapter 23).

21

Information Schemas

21.1 INTRODUCTION

Recall from Chapters 2 and 4 that the SQL-environment includes a set of *catalogs*, each of which includes a set of *schemas*. Each schema in turn has a single *owner*, represented of course by an authID (in general, of course, the same authID can own any number of schemas, in any number of catalogs). The purpose of each schema is to describe a certain collection of base tables, views, etc., that are all owned by the owner of that schema and thus somehow—in some implementation-defined way—constitute some operational unit within the SQL-environment.

Now, the standard does not specify the detailed internal structure and content of schemas in general. However, it does require each catalog to include exactly one particular schema called the *Information Schema* (with unqualified name INFORMATION_SCHEMA), which effectively repeats all of the descriptors contained in all of the other schemas in the catalog in question, but does so in a precisely defined manner.* More specifically, that Information Schema is defined to contain a set of *views* of a hypothetical *Definition Schema*. The SQL-implementation is not required to support the Definition Schema *per se*, but it is required (a) to support *some* kind of Definition Schema, and (b) to support views of that Definition Schema that do look like those Information Schema views.

---

*It also contains descriptors that describe itself; i.e., each Information Schema is *self-describing*.

Note: The standard talks repeatedly in terms of *the* Information Schema. However, such talk is a little misleading, since it obscures the important fact that there is not just one such schema overall, but rather one for each catalog in the environment.

Any given Information Schema is considered to have been created by means of a CREATE SCHEMA operation of the form:

```
CREATE SCHEMA INFORMATION_SCHEMA
          AUTHORIZATION INFORMATION_SCHEMA
```

Despite the AUTHORIZATION clause, such an Information Schema is "globally accessible," at least for retrieval purposes, thanks to a set of implicit GRANTs to PUBLIC (see Section 21.2 below). *Note:* Since the schema name specified in the foregoing CREATE SCHEMA does not include a catalog-name qualifier, a suitable catalog name will be assumed by default, as explained in Chapter 4 (Section 4.2). However, circumstances had better be such as to guarantee that that default is indeed the name of the right catalog!—namely, the catalog that is to contain this particular Information Schema.

Now, given the indisputable facts that (a) existing SQL-implementations most certainly do support something akin to the Definition Schema, but (b) those "Definition Schemas" do vary widely from SQL-implementation to SQL-implementation (even when the SQL-implementations in question come from the same vendor), the idea of requiring only that the SQL-implementation support certain predefined views of its "Definition Schema" clearly makes sense. However, it does also lead immediately to certain anomalies. For example, consider our running example, the suppliers-and-parts database. To define that database, we start with an appropriate CREATE SCHEMA—for example:

```
CREATE SCHEMA S_P_CATALOG . S_P_SCHEMA ...
```

And we go on to create all of the necessary base tables, views, etc., that we want to be described by this particular schema. The descriptors for all of those objects will be included within the schema called S_P_SCHEMA within the catalog called S_P_CATALOG, and those objects will all have fully qualified names of the form

```
S_P_CATALOG . S_P_SCHEMA . xyz
```

(where *xyz* is the object in question).

Note carefully, however, that even though this schema is "our" schema (i.e., "we" created it), *we cannot access it.* For example, to find out what named tables are described by this schema, we *cannot* say (e.g.)

```
SELECT TABLE_NAME
FROM   S_P_CATALOG.S_P_SCHEMA.TABLES
                          -- This is *** ILLEGAL *** !!!
```

(even though such a formulation might seem very natural). Instead, we have to say something like this:

```
SELECT  TABLE_NAME
FROM    S_P_CATALOG.INFORMATION_SCHEMA.TABLES
WHERE   S_P_CATALOG.INFORMATION_SCHEMA.TABLES.TABLE_CATALOG =
        'S_P_CATALOG'
AND     S_P_CATALOG.INFORMATION_SCHEMA.TABLES.TABLE_SCHEMA =
        'S_P_SCHEMA'
```

Note further that a given Information Schema describes only objects that belong to the same catalog as the Information Schema in question, whereas users in general are permitted to access objects belonging to any number of catalogs (provided only that those catalogs all belong to the same "cluster"—see Chapter 4). The standard thus provides no direct means for a given user to see descriptors for all objects that are accessible to that user. More generally, it also does not provide any direct means for some user with higher authorization (e.g., the "database administrator") to see definitions for "all" objects, regardless of the catalog they belong to.

There is another point to be made here also. Most of the Information Schema views are defined in terms of the niladic builtin function CURRENT_USER, which returns the current authID (see Chapter 15). In other words, a given Information Schema effectively describes only those objects that belong to the applicable catalog *and* can be accessed by the current user (loosely speaking). Now, this limitation is probably reasonable, so long as the current authID is the same as the authID of the user that owns the objects in question, which in practice it often will be. Note, however, that the standard thus provides no direct means for a given user *U* to see descriptors for objects that belong to some distinct user *V*, even if *U* has been granted access to those objects by *V*. More generally, it also does not provide any direct means for some user with higher authorization (e.g., the "database administrator") to see definitions for "all" objects, regardless of owner.

21.2   INFORMATION SCHEMA TABLES

In this section, we list all of the named tables (actually views) that are required by the standard to be included in any given Information Schema. For each one, we give a short summary of its content (we leave the details to the official standard document). The SELECT privilege is implicitly granted on each of these views to PUBLIC (with the grant option), but no further privileges are granted—implying, among other things, that the views cannot be the target of an SQL INSERT, UPDATE, or DELETE operation. (Refer to Chapter 15 for an explanation of PUBLIC.)

Note: An Information Schema is expressly permitted to include additional tables, over and above the views required by the standard. Likewise, the views required by the standard are expressly permitted to include additional columns.

For emphasis, we repeat the point that each of the views in a given Information Schema provides information for *one authID* only and *one catalog* only (unless otherwise noted). The authID in question is the authID returned by the niladic builtin function CURRENT_USER. The catalog in question is the catalog in which this particular Information Schema resides.

- INFORMATION_SCHEMA_CATALOG_NAME

    A single-column, single-row table containing the name of the catalog in which this particular Information Schema resides. (Actually this information is repeated in all of the other tables listed below, except for SQL_LANGUAGES, *q.v.*) *Note:* This table, unlike all the other Information Schema tables prescribed by the standard, is a base table, not a view.

- SCHEMATA

    Describes all schemas belonging to this catalog and created by CURRENT_USER.

- DOMAINS

    Describes all domains belonging to this catalog and available to CURRENT_USER or PUBLIC.

- TABLES

    Describes all named tables (base tables and views) belonging to this catalog and accessible to CURRENT_USER or PUBLIC. *Note:* The standard says that TABLES describes only "persistent" tables, but the intent seems to be to describe Type 2 and 3 temporary tables as well. An analogous remark applies to COLUMNS (see below).

- VIEWS

    Describes all views belonging to this catalog and accessible to CURRENT_USER or PUBLIC.

- COLUMNS

    Describes all columns of all named tables belonging to this catalog and accessible to CURRENT_USER or PUBLIC.

- TABLE_PRIVILEGES

    Describes all privileges, on all named tables belonging to this catalog, either granted by CURRENT_USER or granted to CURRENT_USER or PUBLIC.

- COLUMN_PRIVILEGES

    Describes all privileges, on all columns of all named tables belonging to this catalog, either granted by CURRENT_USER or granted to CURRENT_USER or PUBLIC.

- USAGE_PRIVILEGES

Describes all privileges, on all domains, character sets, collations, and translations belonging to this catalog, either granted by CURRENT_USER or granted to CURRENT_USER or PUBLIC.

■ DOMAIN_CONSTRAINTS

Describes all domain constraints belonging to this catalog and created by CURRENT_USER.

Note: There is another slight oddity here, *viz.:* Apparently, user *U* is not allowed to see the constraints that apply to domain *D*, even if *U* is allowed to update—possibly even owns the table containing—some column *C* defined on *D*, unless *U* actually owns *D*. A similar comment applies to TABLE_CONSTRAINTS, REFERENTIAL_CONSTRAINTS, CHECK_ CONSTRAINTS, KEY_COLUMN_USAGE, and ASSERTIONS (see below).

■ TABLE_CONSTRAINTS

Describes all base table constraints belonging to this catalog and created by CURRENT_USER.

■ REFERENTIAL_CONSTRAINTS

Describes all referential constraints belonging to this catalog and created by CURRENT_USER.

■ CHECK_CONSTRAINTS

Describes all check constraints belonging to this catalog and created by CURRENT_USER.

■ KEY_COLUMN_USAGE

Describes all columns participating in candidate keys or foreign keys within base tables belonging to this catalog and created by CURRENT_USER.

■ ASSERTIONS

Describes all general constraints belonging to this catalog and created by CURRENT_USER.

■ CHARACTER_SETS

Describes all character sets belonging to this catalog and available to CURRENT_USER or PUBLIC.

■ COLLATIONS

Describes all collations belonging to this catalog and available to CURRENT_ USER or PUBLIC.

■ TRANSLATIONS

Describes all translations belonging to this catalog and available to CURRENT_ USER or PUBLIC.

- VIEW_TABLE_USAGE

  For all views belonging to this catalog and created by CURRENT_USER, shows which named tables the definitions of those views depend on.

- VIEW_COLUMN_USAGE

  For all views belonging to this catalog and created by CURRENT_USER, shows which columns of which named tables the definitions of those views depend on.

- CONSTRAINT_TABLE_USAGE

  For all constraints belonging to this catalog and created by CURRENT_USER, shows which named tables the definitions of those constraints depend on.

- CONSTRAINT_COLUMN_USAGE

  For all constraints belonging to this catalog and created by CURRENT_ USER, shows which columns of which named tables the definitions of those constraints depend on.

- COLUMN_DOMAIN_USAGE

  For all columns of all named tables belonging to this catalog and accessible to CURRENT_USER or PUBLIC, shows which columns are defined on which domains.

- SQL_LANGUAGES

  Shows which SQL dialects (e.g., SQL/86, SQL/89, SQL/92) the SQL-implementation supports.

  For completeness, we should mention that in addition to the tables (views) just listed, each Information Schema is also considered to contain:

- Certain *domains, viz.* SQL_IDENTIFIER, CHARACTER_DATA, and CARDINAL_NUMBER, consisting of all possible SQL identifiers, all possible SQL_TEXT character strings, and all possible nonnegative integers, respectively.

  Note: More precisely, SQL_IDENTIFIER consists of all possible SQL_TEXT character strings of length not greater than the maximum identifier length; in other words, it includes many character strings that are not legal SQL identifiers. The reason is that (to quote the standard) "there is no way in SQL to specify a domain constraint that would be *true* for any valid SQL identifier and *false* for all other values."

- A general *integrity constraint* called INFORMATION_SCHEMA_CATALOG_ NAME_CARDINALITY, to the effect that the table INFORMATION_ SCHEMA_CATALOG_NAME contains exactly one row.

- The *character set* SQL_TEXT (see Chapter 3), and all other standard- or implementation-defined character sets.*

- All *collations* not explicitly assigned (via an appropriate CREATE statement) to some other schema.

- All *translations* not explicitly assigned (via an appropriate CREATE statement) to some other schema.

- All *form-of-use conversions*.

---

*It is difficult to believe that the standard really intends the character sets *per se* (as opposed to a set of *descriptors* for those character sets) to be components within some Information Schema (especially given the fact that there is a distinct Information Schema in every catalog), but that is what it says.

22

Exception Handling

22.1 STATUS CODES

We remind the reader that (as explained in Chapter 6) after the execution of a given SQL statement, certain *status codes* reflecting the outcome of that execution are returned by means of one or both of the two special parameters (in the module language) or host variables (in embedded SQL) *SQLCODE* and *SQLSTATE*. The SQLCODE value is an integer, the SQLSTATE value is a character string of length 5; the exact data types depend on the applicable host language (at least for embedded SQL)—see the official standard for details. *Note:* As mentioned in Chapter 6, SQLSTATE is preferred over SQLCODE; SQLCODE is now a "deprecated feature," meaning that it is a feature of the standard that is retained only for compatibility with SQL/89 and is likely to be dropped at some time in the future.

To be a little more specific regarding status code values:

- *SQLCODE:* A SQLCODE value of 0 means that the SQL statement completed execution satisfactorily and *either* no errors occurred *or* a warning condition exists; a value of +100 means that no rows were found to satisfy the request; all other values are implementation-defined, except that values representing catastrophic errors must be negative and values representing simple warnings must not. *Note:* As explained in Chapter 6, a *warning* is a noncatastrophic error; for example, a warning is raised on retrieval of a character string value into a target that is too small to hold that string.

■ *SQLSTATE:* SQLSTATE values consist of a two-character *class value* followed by a three-character *subclass value*. Each of the five characters is a digit (0–9) or an upper case letter (A–Z). Class value 00 means that the statement completed execution satisfactorily and no errors occurred (the subclass value will normally be 000 in this case). Class value 01 means that the statement did complete execution satisfactorily but some warning condition exists (e.g., class value 00 with subclass value 003 means that nulls were ignored in the evaluation of an aggregate function reference). Class value 02 means that no data was found (again, the subclass value will normally be 000 in this case). For details of other possible values, see the subsection "SQLSTATE Values" below.

Note: An extensive set of additional status information is also placed in the *diagnostics area* (see Section 22.2).

It follows from the foregoing that, at least in principle, every executable SQL statement (except for GET DIAGNOSTICS, *q.v.*) should be followed by a test of the returned SQLCODE or SQLSTATE value. The WHENEVER statement can be used to simplify this process somewhat in embedded SQL, though not in the module language. Refer to Chapter 6, Section 6.3, for a description of WHENEVER.

Exception vs. Completion Conditions

The standard distinguishes between *exception* and *completion* conditions, as follows:

■ A statement that raises an *exception* condition is defined to have no effect apart from placing the appropriate feedback information into SQLCODE, SQLSTATE, and the diagnostics area. Loosely speaking, therefore, the statement fails—i.e., the requested function is not performed, the database remains unchanged, and no data is returned to the invoking program.

■ A statement that raises a *completion* condition is permitted to have additional effects—e.g., to return data to the invoking program, or to change the state of the database, or to initiate an SQL-transaction, etc. In other words, the statement does complete satisfactorily, but it might nevertheless return a SQLSTATE value other than 00000. *Note:* The standard further divides completion conditions into three categories:

   a. no data (i.e., no rows found; SQLSTATE = 02*xxx*)

   b. warnings (SQLSTATE = 01*xxx*)

   c. successful completion (SQLSTATE = 00*xxx*)

In other words, "exception conditions" in the standard correspond to what are usually called *error* conditions, and "exception conditions" and "completion conditions" taken together correspond (loosely) to what are usually called *exception* conditions! The standard does not seem to have a single term that corresponds to "exceptions" in this broader and more usual sense (the sense, indeed, that is implied by the title of the present chapter).

Note: A single SQL statement execution might give rise to several distinct exceptions simultaneously. In such a situation, the standard requires that the status value returned in SQLCODE and/or SQLSTATE be the most significant, in accordance with the following priority ordering:

1. exceptions causing transaction failure (i.e., rollback)
2. exceptions causing statement failure
3. no data
4. warning
5. successful completion

If a single SQL statement gives rise to two distinct exceptions at the same level simultaneously (and no higher-level exceptions), it is implementation-dependent as to which of the two is reflected in SQLCODE and SQLSTATE (though presumably they must both reflect the same one).

SQLSTATE Values

To repeat, SQLSTATE values consist of a two-character *class* value followed by a three-character *subclass* value. Classes whose values begin with a digit in the range 0–4 or a letter in the range A–H are reserved for conditions explicitly defined in the standard; other classes are reserved for implementation-defined conditions and are called *implementation-defined classes*. Likewise, subclasses whose values begin 0–4 or A–H within classes whose values also begin 0–4 or A–H are reserved for conditions explicitly defined in the standard; other subclasses within such classes, and all subclasses within implementation-defined classes,* are reserved for implementation-defined conditions and are called *implementation-defined subclasses*. *Note:* Implementation-defined classes are reserved for implementation-defined *exceptions* (in the standard's meaning of that term); by contrast, implementation-defined *completions* must be represented by implementation-defined subclass values within one of the class values 00 (successful completion), 01 (warning), or 02 (no data).

---

*Except for subclass value 000, which always means "no subclass." (It is tempting to speculate as to why this case was not represented by *null* instead of 000.)

This is not the place to describe all of the possible SQLSTATE values in detail; we content ourselves here with simply listing the standard *class* values, with their (more or less) self-explanatory generic interpretation in each case. For more information, refer to the official standard.

class value	condition
00	successful completion
01	warning
02	data not found
07	dynamic SQL error
08	connection error
0A	feature not supported
21	cardinality violation
22	data exception
23	constraint violation
24	invalid cursor state
25	invalid transaction state
26	invalid statement name
27	triggered data change violation
28	invalid authID specification
2B	dependent privileges exist
2C	invalid character set name
2D	invalid transaction termination
2E	invalid connection name
33	invalid SQLDA name
34	invalid cursor name
35	invalid condition number
3C	ambiguous cursor name
3D	invalid catalog name
3F	invalid schema name
40	rollback
42	syntax or access error
44	check option violation
HY	Call-Level Interface condition
HZ	Remote Database Access condition

22.2   THE DIAGNOSTICS AREA

Each SQL-agent has an associated diagnostics area, which is used to hold "conditions" (i.e., feedback information relating to the SQL statement most recently executed by that SQL-agent). The area is automatically emptied before each SQL statement starts execution (except for GET DIAGNOSTICS, *q.v.*). The size of the diagnostics area in "conditions"—i.e., its maximum capacity at any time—is established by the SET TRANSACTION statement (see Chapter 5, Section 5.4); for example, the statement

```
SET TRANSACTION DIAGNOSTICS SIZE 5
```

will establish a diagnostics area that is large enough to hold five conditions. The default size is implementation-defined (but must be at least one).

The detailed layout of the diagnostics area is not specified in the standard. Instead, the special statement GET DIAGNOSTICS is provided for the purpose of retrieving information from the diagnostics area in a flexible, disciplined, and pre-cisely defined manner; in other words, SQL diagnostics areas, like SQL descrip-tor areas in dynamic SQL (see Chapter 20), are *encapsulated*.

There are basically two formats of the GET DIAGNOSTICS statement. Format 1 retrieves information relating to the *overall execution* of the immediately preced-ing SQL statement (not counting GET DIAGNOSTICS statements themselves—i.e., a given SQL statement can be followed by any number of GET DIAGNOSTICS statements, each focusing in on one particular aspect of the execution of the original SQL statement). The syntax is:

```
GET DIAGNOSTICS assignment-commalist
```

Each assignment is of the form

```
target = source
```

where "target" is a parameter or host variable, and "source" is one of the following:

```
NUMBER
MORE
COMMAND_FUNCTION
DYNAMIC_FUNCTION
ROW_COUNT
```

NUMBER returns an integer representing the number of conditions raised by the orig-inal SQL statement. MORE returns "Y" or "N"; "Y" means that not all conditions raised were stored in the diagnostics area, "N" means the opposite. COMMAND_ FUNCTION returns a character string identifying the original SQL statement (e.g., "UPDATE WHERE" for a searched UPDATE). DYNAMIC_FUNCTION returns a similar character string identifying the statement executed if the original SQL statement was an EXECUTE or EXECUTE IMMEDIATE. ROW_COUNT returns an integer representing the number of rows directly affected by the original SQL statement (for INSERT, searched UPDATE, and searched DELETE only).

Based on information gleaned from executing one or more Format 1 GET DIAGNOSTICS statements, the user might wish to go on to retrieve more specific information regarding some particular exception(s). This is the purpose of Format 2 of the statement—syntax:

```
GET DIAGNOSTICS EXCEPTION exception assignment-commalist
```

Here "exception" is a literal, parameter, or host variable of type exact numeric with scale zero, whose value, i say, identifies the ith condition in the diagnostics area. Information concerning that ith condition is retrieved in accordance with the specified assignments (see below). *Note:* The first condition ($i = 1$) is required to be the one that corresponds to the values returned in SQLCODE and SQLSTATE; other conditions, if any, appear in an implementation-dependent sequence.

Each assignment is of the form

```
target = source
```

where "target" is a parameter or host variable, and "source" is one of the following:

```
CONDITION_NUMBER
RETURNED_SQLSTATE
CLASS_ORIGIN
SUBCLASS_ORIGIN
SERVER_NAME
CONNECTION_NAME
CONSTRAINT_CATALOG
CONSTRAINT_SCHEMA
CONSTRAINT_NAME
CATALOG_NAME
SCHEMA_NAME
TABLE_NAME
COLUMN_NAME
CURSOR_NAME
MESSAGE_TEXT
MESSAGE_LENGTH
MESSAGE_OCTET_LENGTH
```

Most of these items seem fairly self-explanatory; we elaborate below only on those that seem to require such elaboration.

- RETURNED_SQLSTATE is the SQLSTATE value that would have been returned if this condition had been the only one raised.

- CLASS_ORIGIN is "ISO 9075" (see Appendix G) if the class value of RETURNED_SQLSTATE is one of the SQLSTATE values defined within the standard, and some (different) implementation-defined value otherwise. SUBCLASS_ORIGIN is analogous.

- MESSAGE_TEXT is an implementation-defined character string with length as given by MESSAGE_LENGTH (in characters) and MESSAGE_OCTET_LENGTH (in octets). The intent is, of course, to permit the implementation to provide additional specific information regarding the exception that occurred, perhaps in a form suitable for textual display to an end user.

23

Call-Level Interface

23.1 INTRODUCTION

As explained in Chapter 6, every SQL-implementation is required to support at least one binding style. The subject of this chapter, the *SQL Call-Level Interface* ("SQL/CLI," or just *CLI* for short), is the most recent binding style to be defined.* CLI permits an application written in one of the usual host languages—Ada, C, COBOL, FORTRAN, MUMPS, Pascal, PL/I—to request SQL operations by invoking certain implementation-provided CLI routines. Those routines, which must have been linked to the application in question, will in turn invoke the DBMS by means of dynamic SQL—see Chapter 20—in order to perform the requested SQL operations on the application's behalf. (From the DBMS's point of view, in other words, the CLI routines can be thought of as just another application.)

Advantages of the foregoing scheme include the following:

- It allows applications to be written for which the exact SQL statements to be executed are not known until run time. In other words, it addresses the same general problem as dynamic SQL does; indeed, any application that previously would have used the facilities of dynamic SQL can now use CLI instead. As stated in Chapter 20, however, CLI actually represents a better approach to the

---

*CLI was added to the standard in 1995. It is heavily based on Microsoft Corporation's *Open Database Connectivity* feature (ODBC), and owes much to the work of X/Open and the SQL Access Group (see Chapter 1).

problem than dynamic SQL does (largely because of the advantages identified in the next two paragraphs). For this reason it is probably true to say that dynamic SQL would never have been included in the standard at all if CLI had been defined first.

■   The problem with dynamic SQL is that it is a *source code* standard. Any application using dynamic SQL thus requires the services of some kind of SQL compiler in order to process the operations—PREPARE, EXECUTE, etc.—prescribed by that standard. CLI, by contrast, merely standardizes the details of certain *routine invocations* (i.e., procedure calls, basically); no special compiler services are needed, only the regular services of the standard host language compiler. As a result, applications can be distributed (perhaps by third-party software vendors) in "shrink-wrapped" *object code* form.

■   Furthermore, those applications can be *DBMS-independent*; that is, CLI includes features that permit the creation (again, perhaps by third-party software vendors) of *generic applications* that can be used with several different DBMSs, instead of having to be specific to, or "bound to," some particular DBMS. (In this connection, note the discussion of the CLI routines **GetInfo, GetTypeInfo,** and **GetFunctions** at the end of Section 23.3.)

By way of example, we present a small fragment of C code—accurate, though unrealistically simple—that illustrates the use of CLI. (Since most "real-world" CLI applications are likely to use C as host language, we break with our usual convention in this chapter and use C instead of PL/I as the basis for our examples.) Note that, precisely because it is a standard for invoking routines from a host language, the syntax—though not of course the semantics—of the CLI interface will vary from one host language to another, in general. The variations are not important for the purposes of this book, however.

```
char sqlsource [255] ;

strcpy ( sqlsource, "DELETE FROM SP WHERE SP.QTY < 300" ) ;
rc = SQLExecDirect ( hstmt, (SQLCHAR *)sqlsource, SQL_NTS ) ;
```

Explanation:

1. The name **sqlsource** identifies a C variable in which the application will somehow construct the source form—i.e., character string representation—of some SQL statement (a DELETE statement, in our particular example). *Note:* We follow the CLI specification in using lower case (or mixed upper and lower case) for variable names, routine names, and the like, instead of all upper case as elsewhere in this book. We show such names in **boldface** in the body of the text in order to set them off from surrounding material.

2. The standard C function **strcpy** is invoked to copy the source form of the desired SQL DELETE statement into the C variable **sqlsource**. *Note:* The nor-

mal C convention for referring to functions such as **strcopy** is to show the argument parentheses as well as the function name, thus: **strcopy().** We choose not to follow that convention in this chapter.

3. The C assignment statement then invokes the CLI routine **SQLExecDirect**—the CLI analog of dynamic SQL's EXECUTE IMMEDIATE—to execute the SQL statement contained in **sqlsource,** and assigns the return code resulting from that invocation to the C variable **rc.** (We are not yet in a position to explain the specifics of that CLI routine invocation in any detail, of course, but note that the second argument includes a reference to **sqlsource.**)

As with dynamic SQL, SQL statements to be executed through CLI can include *placeholders* (the official term is *parameters*, or more precisely *dynamic parameters*), represented by question marks ("?"). For example:

```
strcpy ( sqlsource, "DELETE FROM SP WHERE SP.QTY < ?" ) ;
```

The rules regarding the contexts in which such placeholders are legal, etc., are exactly the same as for dynamic SQL (see Chapter 20). Refer to Section 23.7 for a discussion of the means by which arguments can be substituted for such placeholders at run time.

One last preliminary point: In places the specifics of CLI are somewhat tedious, if not downright messy, at the fine detail level (as is only to be expected, given the nature of the task at hand—our remarks are not intended as a criticism). For this reason, we do not aim at quite the same level of completeness in this chapter as we do elsewhere in the book. Rather, our objective is just to give a reasonably comprehensive (and comprehensible) *introduction* to CLI, and thereby to pave the way for a proper and thorough understanding of the CLI specification itself. To this end, every major CLI feature is at least mentioned, and the more important ones are described at some length, with examples and motivating discussion. But we do not hesitate to omit certain less important details, contenting ourselves in such cases with references to the formal specification. We do, however, include both

- a sample "SQLCLI.H" file, and
- a sample CLI application,

(see Sections 23.10 and 23.11, respectively), from which the careful reader might absorb certain details of the CLI interface that are not discussed elsewhere in the chapter.

23.2   WHAT IS THE PROBLEM?

In Chapter 20, Section 20.2, we gave an overview of the general problem that dynamic SQL is intended to address, and much of that overview applies equally well to CLI, *mutatis mutandis*. The reader might therefore care to review that section before continuing with the present chapter. Here we content ourselves with a brief summary of some of the salient points from that overview, plus a few CLI-specific comments.

1. Certain applications of a general-purpose nature need to generate SQL statements at run time; an example might be an interactive database creation utility that allows the end user to enter SQL data definition statements (e.g., CREATE TABLE) from a workstation. This utility cannot be written in static SQL because the SQL statements to be executed are not known until run time. The CLI routine **ExecDirect,** or the two routines **Prepare** and **Execute** taken together, address this problem (see Section 23.5).

    Note: **ExecDirect, Prepare,** and **Execute** here are examples of "generic" CLI routine names. As we will see in Section 23.3, every CLI routine has a two-part name, consisting of a *generic name* (such as **ExecDirect**) and a *prefix* (which is either **SQL** or **SQLR**). It is usual to ignore the prefix in informal contexts.

2. Consider a query utility that allows end users to submit *ad hoc* queries and displays the results of those queries on the screen. In order to display the result of such a query, the utility needs to find out at run time how many columns there are in that result, what the data type of each column is, and much additional information. Like dynamic SQL, CLI provides an elaborate *descriptor* mechanism to address this problem (see Sections 23.6–23.8). *Note:* The descriptors referred to here, like those of dynamic SQL, are nothing to do with the *SQL* descriptors discussed in Chapter 4. Furthermore, of course, we will be using the term "descriptor" throughout this chapter in its CLI sense, not in its SQL sense.

3. That same CLI descriptor mechanism also serves as the means by which arguments corresponding to placeholders are provided at run time (again, see Sections 23.6–23.8).

4. As always in SQL, multi-row retrieval via CLI is done by means of a cursor.* Unusually for SQL, the same is true for *single*-row retrieval under CLI. In neither case, however, does the application have to declare and open a cursor explicitly; instead, a cursor is *implicitly* declared and opened by CLI when the retrieval operation is executed. Rows can then be retrieved via that cursor by means of the CLI routines **Fetch** and **FetchScroll**. They can also be updated or deleted by preparing and executing appropriate positioned UPDATE and DELETE operations. Finally, the cursor can be closed by means of the CLI routine **CloseCursor**. Refer to Section 23.8 for a detailed discussion of these facilities.

---

*Except in direct SQL, of course (though even here there is probably a cursor "under the covers").

5. We remind the reader that in dynamic SQL there are actually two forms of *explicit* "dynamic cursor" declaration—a dynamic version of DECLARE CURSOR *per se* and an operation called ALLOCATE CURSOR (see Chapter 20). As just indicated, CLI does not have, or need, an explicit counterpart to the first of these. In fact, it does not have, or need, an explicit counterpart to the second either (again, see Section 23.8).

6. The special SQL statements used in connection with dynamic SQL to specify the default catalog name, schema name, and character set name for the SQL-session (namely, SET CATALOG, SET SCHEMA, and SET NAMES) are equally applicable to CLI; i.e., it is these *session* defaults that are used in the CLI context, just as it is in the dynamic SQL context.

    Note: Here is as good a place as any to mention that SQL statements prepared and executed via CLI (like "global" prepared statements in dynamic SQL) are considered to belong to the *SQL-session module*, which—as the reader will recall from Chapter 5—is an implementation-defined module that is distinct from all other modules currently existing in the SQL-environment.

We now proceed to examine the features and facilities of CLI in more detail.

23.3 CLI ROUTINES AND PARAMETERS

In this section we discuss a number of important preliminary details relating to CLI routines and parameters.

Functions vs. Procedures

Any given CLI routine can be supported by the implementation either as a function or as a procedure (it is implementation-defined which). Let *CR* be some CLI routine. Then:

- If *CR* is a function, it takes a set of (say) *n* parameters, and of course arguments corresponding to those parameters must be supplied somehow when *CR* is executed. In addition, any given execution of *CR* will return a value of type SMALLINT, representing the *return code* resulting from that execution. The fragment of C code in Section 23.1 shows an example of a routine that is a function. (Return codes are discussed in more detail in Section 23.9.)

- If *CR* is a procedure, an execution of *CR*, by contrast, does not return a value; instead, *CR* now takes an additional—i.e., $(n + 1)$st—parameter called **RetCode,** of type SMALLINT, and $n + 1$ corresponding arguments must now be supplied when *CR* is executed. Any given execution of *CR* will set the **RetCode** argument to the appropriate return code value.

The syntactic difference between a function invocation and a procedure invocation is that the former is just a special case of a scalar expression, while the latter consists of a standalone statement (typically some kind of CALL statement, whence the "Call" in "Call-Level Interface"). For simplicity, we assume throughout the rest of this chapter that CLI routines are functions (where it makes any difference).

Parameter Modes

Each parameter to a CLI routine has a *name*, a *mode*, and a *data type*.

- The *name* depends on the CLI routine under consideration. For example, the parameters to **ExecDirect** are called **StatementHandle** (see Section 23.4 for a discussion of statement—and other—"handles"), **StatementText,** and **TextLength** (also **RetCode,** if the routine is a procedure and not a function). *Note:* Actually there are a few minor discrepancies in the current CLI specification over parameter names (and parameter data types too), but this is not the place to pursue such matters in detail.

- *Data types* are discussed in the next subsection.

- *Modes* are discussed immediately following.

  There are basically two parameter modes, IN and OUT; IN means the parameter represents a *value* the routine will use, OUT means it represents a *variable* the routine will set. (The parameter **RetCode,** if present, will always be an OUT parameter, of course.) Note, incidentally, that functions as well as procedures are permitted to have OUT parameters, which effectively means that invocations of such functions are permitted to have side effects.

  For an *OUT* parameter:

- The value passed on invocation is always a *pointer* to the argument variable *per se*. Depending on the calling conventions of the applicable host language, that value can be specified either by means of a variable of type pointer (in which case the value passed is exactly the value of that pointer variable), or by means of a variable of some other type (in which case the value passed is a reference—i.e., pointer—to that variable).

  For an *IN* parameter:

- If the parameter data type is CHARACTER(n), then the situation is exactly the same* as stated above for OUT parameters (as in the C language, in fact).

- Otherwise, whether the value passed on invocation is a pointer or not depends on whether the CLI routine is a "by reference" routine or a "by value" routine.

---

*Well, not *exactly* the same, because the value corresponding to an IN parameter does not have to be specified by means of a variable *per se* but instead can be specified by means of an arbitrary scalar expression (in general).

"By reference" means the value *is* a pointer (the situation is again as for OUT parameters). "By value" means it is not (the value passed is the actual value specified).

Note: The names of "by reference" routines have the prefix **SQLR,** those of "by value" routines the prefix **SQL.** All host languages are *required* to support "by reference" routines (except for C, where such support is optional). In addition, all host languages are *permitted* to support "by value" routines (except for C, where such support is required, and FORTRAN, where such support is not possible). Either way, it is usual (as already mentioned in Section 23.2) to ignore the prefix in informal contexts and to refer to routines by their generic name alone.

In addition to the two basic modes IN and OUT, there are also three "deferred" variants, namely DEF, DEFIN, and DEFOUT. *Deferred* here essentially means "no dereferencing." In other words, the value passed on invocation is again a pointer, and *the pointer itself* (as opposed to whatever it is that the pointer might be pointing to) is taken to be the actual argument.

■ By way of example, consider the routine **BindCol,** which is used to pass information to the CLI implementation regarding the *target variable* into which some data value is to be retrieved (see Section 23.8). That routine takes a DEFOUT parameter called—somewhat inappropriately!—**TargetValue.** When the routine is invoked, the application passes a value corresponding to this parameter that is a pointer to the desired target variable; and (precisely because the parameter is "deferred") the **BindCol** routine understands that the target variable is indeed the variable pointed to by that pointer, not the variable pointed to by the value in the variable pointed to by that pointer. (It might be worth reading this paragraph twice.)

One final remark regarding the passing of pointer values: Depending on the routine involved, certain of those pointer values might sometimes be specified as zero,* meaning that—for some reason—no corresponding argument is provided at all. (Several examples of such a situation appear at later points in the chapter.) In the case of OUT parameters only, a similar effect can be achieved by specifying a "buffer length" of zero for the argument in question.

Parameter Data Types

The possible CLI parameter data types are INTEGER, SMALLINT, CHARACTER(*n*), and ANY. The table overleaf shows the C types corresponding to each of

---

*A zero pointer value is sometimes called "a null pointer." The term has nothing to do with SQL-style nulls, of course.

these possibilities.* For further information—including, in particular, an explanation of the string length *cn* and the data type mapping rules for other host languages—the reader is referred to the CLI specification.

parameter type	corresponding C type
INTEGER SMALLINT CHARACTER(*n*) ANY	long short char of length *cn* float, double, or any of the above

Note: A character string that is passed as an input value from the application
to a CLI routine can optionally be terminated by the implementation-defined "null
character" (once again, nothing to do with SQL-style nulls) that is used to terminate character strings in C. A character string that is returned as an output value
from a CLI routine to the application either will or will not be "null-terminated,"
depending on whether the "environment NULL TERMINATION attribute" (see
Section 23.4) is set to *true* or *false*. The terminating null character (if present) is
not considered to be part of the string and does not count toward the string length.
(Alternatively, the length of such a string can be specified as –3, a code that is
understood by CLI to mean that the string is null-terminated. The identifier
SQL_NTS—see, e.g., the **ExecDirect** example in Section 23.1—is defined as a
symbolic name for the code value –3.)

Available Routines

For purposes of reference, this subsection lists all available CLI routines in alphabetical order by generic name. Note that the names are usually (though not always!)
fairly self-explanatory. Note too that each routine has an abbreviated name by
which it can be referenced in an implementation that (e.g.) has limitations on the
length of an identifier that would otherwise be exceeded; the abbreviated name
consists of the prefix **SQL** (for a "by value" routine) or **SQR** (for a "by reference"
routine), followed by a two- or three-character abbreviated generic name. The list
below shows each abbreviated generic name alongside the corresponding unab-
breviated one.

---

*Note carefully that this table shows the mappings between C and *CLI* data types, not the mappings
between C and *SQL* data types (the two are not quite the same). The latter mappings are the ones that
would apply if C were used with embedded SQL or the module language as explained in Chapter 6.

AllocConnect	AC	ExecDirect	ED	GetFunctions	GFU
AllocEnv	AE	Execute	EX	GetInfo	GI
AllocHandle	AH	Fetch	FT	GetStmtAttr	GSA
AllocStmt	AS	FetchScroll	FTS	GetTypeInfo	GTI
BindCol	BC	FreeConnect	FC	NumResultCols	NRC
BindParam	BP	FreeEnv	FE	ParamData	PRD
Cancel	CAN	FreeHandle	FH	Prepare	PR
CloseCursor	CC	FreeStmt	FS	PutData	PTD
ColAttribute	CO	GetCursorName	GCN	RowCount	RC
Connect	CON	GetConnectAttr	GCA	SetConnectAttr	SCA
CopyDesc	CD	GetData	GDA	SetCursorName	SCN
DataSources	DS	GetDescField	GDF	SetDescField	SDF
DescribeCol	DC	GetDescRec	GDR	SetDescRec	SDR
Disconnect	DIS	GetDiagField	GXF	SetEnvAttr	SEA
EndTran	ET	GetDiagRec	GXR	SetStmtAttr	SSA
Error	ER	GetEnvAttr	GEA		

Note: The implementation is free to extend this list with its own implementation-defined routines.

We offer a few words of further explanation here regarding three of these routines (since they do not logically belong anywhere else in the chapter), namely **GetInfo, GetTypeInfo,** and **GetFunctions.** Each of these routines is used to obtain certain information regarding the CLI implementation itself. They can thus be used (as mentioned in Section 23.1) in the creation of applications that are *DBMS-independent.* Briefly:

- **GetInfo** provides information such as the name of the supporting DBMS, limits on identifier lengths, limits on statement lengths, limits on table sizes, details of SQL functionality supported, etc., etc.

- **GetTypeInfo** provides information (in the form of an SQL table, in fact) regarding the SQL data types supported, including maximum character string length, radix and maximum and minimum scale for exact numeric types, character set case sensitivity information, etc., etc.

- **GetFunctions** indicates which CLI routines the implementation supports.

23.4   CLI RESOURCES AND RELATED MATTERS

This section describes some further important preliminary concepts, this time having to do with CLI *resources, handles,* and *attributes,* together with certain related matters.

Handles

As explained earlier in this book (principally in Chapters 2 and 5), every SQL application executes in the context of an *SQL-environment.* Within such a context, the application can establish any number of *SQL-connections* (to SQL-servers). And within such a connection, the application can execute any number of *SQL-statements*. Each of these constructs (SQL-environment, SQL-connection, and SQL-statement) requires the CLI implementation to maintain certain control information on the application's behalf (e.g., cursor information, in the case of certain SQL-statements).

The *resources* needed to maintain such control information must be *allocated* by the application before they can be used, and *freed* by the application when they are finished with, using CLI routines provided for the purpose. Allocating such a resource causes CLI to return a *handle* (a value of type INTEGER) that uniquely identifies the resource just allocated. The application must then specify that handle in subsequent CLI routine invocations that make use of the resource.

- For example, suppose the application allocates a resource to manage SQL statements, thereby acquiring a certain "statement handle," *SH* say. Then that handle *SH* must be specified when the application wants to use that resource to execute some SQL statement. (This state of affairs accounts for the **hstmt** argument in the **ExecDirect** example in Section 23.1 and the corresponding **StatementHandle** parameter to **ExecDirect** mentioned in Section 23.3.) *Note:* It is important to understand that a "statement handle" does *not* identify a statement *per se*, it identifies a resource for managing the execution of such a statement. We will return to this point in just a moment.

- As another example, the statement handle specified in a given **Execute** invocation must be the same as the one that was specified in the corresponding **Prepare** invocation (in order to ensure that the **Execute** does in fact execute the statement prepared by that **Prepare**).

To elaborate:

- Almost certainly, the application will have just one *environment* handle, acquired via **AllocEnv** or **AllocHandle** at the start of execution and released via **FreeEnv** or **FreeHandle** at the end of execution. Note that an attempt to release an environment handle will fail if the application still has any unreleased connection handles within that environment (and hence will fail *a fortiori* if it still has any established connections within that environment).

- The application will have one *connection* handle for each connection currently established within the environment,* acquired via **AllocConnect** or **AllocHandle** (each of which requires the application to specify the appropri-

---

*We remind the reader that (as we saw in Chapter 5) an application can have any number of simultaneously established connections (all with different handles, of course, under CLI). Furthermore, the servers involved are not necessarily all distinct—i.e., an application can have two or more simultaneous connections (with different handles once again, under CLI) all involving the same server.

ate environment handle) and released via **FreeConnect** or **FreeHandle.** Note that an attempt to release a connection handle will fail if the corresponding connection still exists (i.e., has not yet been terminated via **Disconnect,** *q.v.*).

Note: An important future objective for CLI (not supported by the current specification) is to allow an application to have *many transactions running simultaneously* (one per established connection), and to be able to commit or roll back those transactions independently of one another. To this end, each individual connection handle has its own distinct set of *descriptor areas* (see Section 23.6) and its own distinct *diagnostics* area (see Section 23.9).*

- Each SQL statement execution requires one *statement* handle, acquired via **AllocStmt** or **AllocHandle** (each of which requires the application to specify the appropriate connection handle) and released via **FreeStmt** or **FreeHandle.** Since the same statement handle can be used repeatedly, however, the application will often have just one such†—though it might have more than one if, e.g., it is supporting the concurrent display of several query results, each in its own window on the screen (implying the existence of several open cursors at the same time).

Note: **AllocStmt** and its **AllocHandle** equivalent also allocate certain *CLI descriptor areas,* each of which also has a unique handle. Contrary to what might have been expected, there is no "AllocDesc" routine for allocating descriptor areas *per se*, but **AllocHandle** can be used to allocate additional descriptor areas without at the same time allocating any further statement resources. Such "additional" descriptor areas are freed by means of **FreeStmt** or its **FreeHandle** equivalent. Refer to Section 23.6 for further discussion.

At this point, the reader might be wondering what the distinction is between the routine **AllocHandle,** on the one hand, and the routines **AllocEnv, AllocConnect,** and **AllocStmt,** on the other. The answer is that **AllocHandle** is a *general* routine and can be used to allocate any type of resource (the required type being specified as an argument when the routine is invoked); the other three routines, by contrast, are specific to the particular type of resource their name suggests. One implication is that **AllocHandle** is *extensible* (meaning that it might be

---

*We should mention another possible future objective (already supported by some commercial products, though not by CLI *per se*)—namely, support for *asynchronous CLI routines,* so that the application might be able to perform several CLI operations concurrently. CLI does include a routine called **Cancel,** one of whose purposes is to cancel a concurrently operating CLI routine; however, the **Cancel** routine constitutes the *only* "asynchronous routine" support explicitly included in CLI at the present time (the specification states that "the method of passing control between concurrently operating programs is implementation-dependent").

†More precisely, we should say that the application will often have one statement handle *per established connection,* since statement handles are "connection-local" (just as connection handles are "environment-local").

extended at some point to deal with additional types of resources), while the other three are not.

Analogous remarks apply to **FreeHandle** *vs.* **FreeEnv, FreeConnect,** and **FreeStmt,** of course.

A note on terminology: The resource allocated by **AllocStmt** is referred to in the CLI specification—very unfortunately, in this writer's opinion—as an *allocated SQL-statement* (and similarly for connections and environments). This terminology is extraordinarily bad, and indeed confusing, since (e.g.) the one thing an "allocated SQL-statement" is quite definitely *not* is an SQL-statement! In this chapter, therefore, we will try to reduce the confusion by using the more neutral terms "E-resource," "C-resource," and "S-resource" (where appropriate) in place of the official terms "allocated environment," "allocated connection," and "allocated statement," respectively.

Resource Attributes

CLI resources (i.e., E-, C-, and S-resources) possess certain *attributes* that can be inspected, and in some cases changed, by the application. The routines for inspecting attributes are **GetEnvAttr, GetConnectAttr,** and **GetStmtAttr;** the routines for changing them are **SetEnvAttr, SetConnectAttr,** and **SetStmtAttr** (of course, the **Env** routines apply to E-resources, the **Connect** routines to C-resources, and the **Stmt** routines to S-resources). Details of most resource attributes are beyond the scope of this chapter; we briefly mention just one of them here, the NULL TERMINATION attribute, which is the sole E-resource attribute currently defined. This attribute is either *true* (meaning output character strings within the environment in question will be null-terminated by the implementation) or *false* (meaning the opposite). It is set to *true* when the E-resource is allocated. It can be inspected at any time by means of **GetEnvAttr** and—so long as there are no currently allocated C-resources in the environment—changed by means of **SetEnvAttr.** Refer to the CLI specification for further discussion.

Connections

Once the application has allocated the C-resource needed to manage a connection, it can go on to *establish* such a connection, using the CLI routine **Connect. Connect** is the CLI analog of SQL's CONNECT operation; it is needed because the latter is not a preparable statement (refer to Chapter 20 if you need to refresh your memory regarding this latter concept). In a like manner, the application can break an established connection by means of the CLI routine **Disconnect** (the CLI analog of SQL's DISCONNECT). Note, however, that there is no direct CLI analog of SQL's SET CONNECTION (which switches from one established connection to another); instead, switching between connections occurs automatically under CLI whenever the application requests an SQL operation on a connection that is currently dormant.

While on the subject of connections, we should mention the CLI routine **DataSources,** which can be used to obtain a list of names of servers (one at a time) to which the application can legally connect. *Note:* The "server names" returned by **DataSources** are the character string values that the application would have to use in the context of an SQL CONNECT operation (or CLI **Connect** routine), as described in Chapter 5.

Transactions

Transaction initiation under CLI is performed in the usual way (i.e., by executing a "transaction-initiating" SQL statement at a time when no transaction is currently in progress—see Chapter 5). Transaction termination under CLI, however, is *not* performed in the usual way (i.e., by executing an SQL COMMIT or ROLLBACK operation); indeed, an attempt to prepare one of those operations via **Prepare,** or execute it via **ExecDirect,** will raise a run-time error. Instead, all transaction terminations under CLI must be performed by means of the CLI routine **EndTran.** This routine takes three parameters:

- **HandleType** (IN SMALLINT): A code that indicates whether the termination applies to just one established connection (2 = connection handle) or to all established connections (1 = environment handle) in the environment
- **Handle** (IN INTEGER): The applicable connection or environment handle
- **CompletionType** (IN SMALLINT): A code that indicates the type of termination (0 = commit, 1 = rollback)

23.5   STATEMENT PREPARATION AND EXECUTION

In this section we discuss the basic **Prepare** and **Execute** routines, which are really the *sine qua non* of CLI. In order to simplify the discussion, we assume that (a) the statement to be prepared and executed does not contain any placeholders, and (b) it is not a retrieval operation. What happens when these restrictions are relaxed is discussed in Sections 23.7 and 23.8, respectively.

The basic purpose of the CLI **Prepare** routine (like that of its dynamic SQL counterpart) is to "prepare" some specified SQL statement for subsequent execution—i.e., to produce a "prepared" (or *object* or *compiled* or *executable* or, very informally, "prepped") form of that SQL statement. **Prepare** takes three parameters:

- **StatementHandle** (IN INTEGER): A statement handle identifying the S-resource under which the preparing is to be done

- **StatementText** (IN CHARACTER(n), where n is the value specified by **TextLength**—see below): The source form of the SQL statement to be prepared
- **TextLength** (IN SMALLINT): The length of the **StatementText** value (possibly specified as –3, meaning the **StatementText** value is null-terminated)

Let the **StatementHandle** and **StatementText** values be *SH* and *ST*, respectively. Then:

- *ST* must be preparable and must not be a COMMIT or ROLLBACK statement. (Also, in accordance with our initial assumptions, it must not be a retrieval operation of any kind, and it must not include any placeholders.)
- *SH* might possibly have any of the following objects currently associated with it: a previously prepared statement; a previously executed statement; a cursor; or a "select source" (see Section 23.8). Any such objects are destroyed. Further, if a cursor is destroyed in this way, then so too are any prepared statements that reference that cursor.
- The prepared version of *ST, PST* say, becomes "the prepared statement associated with *SH*."

Note: It follows from the foregoing discussion that any given statement handle will have at most one prepared statement associated with it at any given time.

We turn now to the CLI **Execute** routine. The basic purpose of **Execute** is (of course) to execute some previously prepared statement. **Execute** takes just one parameter, an IN parameter called **StatementHandle.** Let *SH* be the value of that parameter; *SH* must have a prepared statement, *PST* say, associated with it. *PST* is executed. If that execution is successful, *PST* becomes "the executed statement associated with *SH*" (destroying any previously existing executed statement associated with *SH*). *Note:* A given statement handle will have at most one executed statement associated with it at any given time.

Finally, of course, **ExecDirect** is basically just shorthand for **Prepare** followed by **Execute.** It takes the same parameters as **Prepare.** *Note:* It is worth pointing out explicitly that—owing to the fact that CLI and dynamic SQL have somewhat different mechanisms for dealing with retrieved values and placeholders—**ExecDirect,** unlike its dynamic SQL counterpart, permits the statement that is to be prepared and executed to be a retrieval operation (possibly multi-row) and/or to include placeholders. See Sections 23.7 and 23.8.

23.6   CLI DESCRIPTOR AREAS

The general idea of descriptor areas was explained in Chapter 20 (Section 20.4). Of course, the discussions in that section were specific to dynamic SQL, but the general purpose of the descriptor areas of CLI is very similar to that of "SQL Descriptor Areas" (SQLDAs) in dynamic SQL. To be more specific:

1. CLI *application* descriptor areas contain descriptors for *argument variables* and *target variables* (in particular, they specify the corresponding host data types).

2. CLI *implementation* descriptor areas contain descriptors for *placeholders* and *result columns* (in particular, they specify the corresponding SQL data types).

Note the type conversions between host and SQL data types implied by these descriptors, incidentally (from host argument values to SQL placeholder types and from SQL column values to host target types).

Actually, there are four different kinds of CLI descriptor areas, not two (though all four have the same basic structure, as we will see):

1. *Implementation Parameter Descriptor* areas (IPDs): A given IPD describes a placeholder (recall that CLI uses the term *parameter* to refer to what we call a placeholder).

2. *Application Parameter Descriptor* areas (APDs): A given APD describes the argument that is to be substituted for a given placeholder (CLI unfortunately does not make a clear terminological distinction between "parameters"—i.e., placeholders—and arguments).

3. *Implementation Row Descriptor* areas (IRDs): A given IRD describes the columns of the table that results from a given retrieval operation.

4. *Application Row Descriptor* areas (ARDs): A given ARD describes the target variables into which column values (from rows of the table that results from a given retrieval operation) are to be fetched.

The reader might be forgiven for thinking that the various descriptor area names are not very well chosen. Be that as it may, the general idea is that APDs and ARDs are set by the application and IPDs and IRDs are set by the implementation (though in fact IPDs can also be set by the application; IRDs, however, can indeed be set only by the implementation). The next two sections discuss the setting of descriptor areas in detail.

Suppose, then, that the CLI routine **AllocStmt** is executed to allocate an S-resource and returns a certain handle, *SH* say. As mentioned in Section 23.4, that **AllocStmt** will also "automatically" allocate certain CLI descriptor areas, with additional handles of their own; in fact, it will "automatically" allocate exactly one IPD, one APD, one IRD, and one ARD. Those descriptor areas will become the (initial) current descriptor areas associated with the statement handle *SH*, and their handles will become attributes of the associated S-resource, in the sense of Section 23.4.

Additional APDs or ARDs (but not IPDs or IRDs) can be allocated subsequently, using the CLI routine **AllocHandle,** without having to allocate any corresponding new S-resource.* Such an APD or ARD can then be made "current"

---

*The **AllocHandle** does not even have to specify any existing S-resource. It does, however, have to specify an existing C-resource.

for some existing statement handle by means of the CLI routine **SetStmtAttr** (effectively displacing the previous current descriptor area of the applicable type). In this way, for example, it might be possible to cause different executions of the CLI **Fetch** routine using the same cursor to retrieve data into different target variables. The current descriptor areas for a given statement handle can be determined at any time by means of the CLI routine **GetStmtAttr.**

Note: Such "additional" APDs or ARDs can be freed using the CLI routine **FreeHandle.** Note, however, that freeing any of the initial (automatically allocated) descriptor areas is not allowed. Freeing an "additional" descriptor area that happens to be current for some statement handle causes the applicable initial descriptor area for that handle to become current again.

CLI Descriptor Area Layout

Like their counterparts in dynamic SQL, CLI descriptor areas are *encapsulated* (refer to Chapter 20 for an explanation of this term). Conceptually, however, they can be thought of as being made up of the following fields:

- A COUNT field (SMALLINT), with value N, say (N is greater than or equal to zero and is set to zero when the descriptor area is first allocated)

- An ALLOC_TYPE field (SMALLINT), whose value indicates whether this descriptor area was allocated as part of the process of allocating the corresponding S-resource ("automatic allocation") or was allocated later and independently ("user allocation")

- N individual item descriptor areas, describing N individual placeholders, arguments, columns, or targets (depending on whether the overall descriptor area is an IPD, APD, IRD, or ARD)

  Each item *descriptor area* in turn conceptually consists of a number of named fields, each corresponding to some specific aspect of the item being described. We list below some of the more important of those fields (together with their data type in each case); for a complete list, the reader is referred to the CLI specification. Note that not all fields have meaning in all contexts.

```
NAME                    CHARACTER VARYING (n)
UNNAMED                 SMALLINT
TYPE                    SMALLINT
LENGTH                  INTEGER
PRECISION               SMALLINT
SCALE                   SMALLINT
DATA_POINTER            host variable address (initially 0)
INDICATOR_POINTER       host variable address (initially 0)
```

As the reader will observe, one significant difference between the descriptor areas of dynamic SQL and those of CLI is that the former typically contain *actual data values* (values retrieved from the database, for example), whereas the latter contain *pointers to variables containing* such values.

The CLI routines for retrieving descriptor information are **GetDescField** and **GetDescRec;** the CLI routines for changing it (not allowed in the case of IRDs, which as already mentioned can be set only by the system—actually by **Prepare**) are **SetDescField** and **SetDescRec.** (The term **Rec**—short for *record*—in **GetDescRec** and **SetDescRec** refers to a certain set of fields from within an individual item descriptor area.) In addition, **BindCol** places information into an ARD (see Section 23.8), and **BindParam** places information into an APD and/or an IPD (see Section 23.7).* It is also possible to copy the contents of one descriptor area into another, using the CLI routine **CopyDesc** (but once again the target cannot be an IRD).

23.7 PLACEHOLDERS

We are now in a position to explain how placeholders are dealt with in CLI. Here first is a simple example (repeated from Chapter 20, and therefore expressed in PL/I, not C) involving the use of placeholders in dynamic SQL:

```
SQLSOURCE = 'DELETE FROM SP WHERE SP.QTY > ? AND SP.QTY < ?' ;

EXEC SQL PREPARE SQLPREPPED FROM :SQLSOURCE ;

LOW = 100 ;
HIGH = 300 ;

EXEC SQL EXECUTE SQLPREPPED USING :LOW, :HIGH ;
```

The effect of this example is to delete all shipments with a quantity in the indicated range. Note that:

- The SQL DELETE statement in SQLSOURCE contains two placeholders.
- The prepared version of that statement is assigned to the SQL variable SQLPREPPED.
- The desired argument values corresponding to the two placeholders are assigned to two PL/I variables, LOW and HIGH.
- The EXECUTE statement nominates those two PL/I variables in its USING clause and thereby causes the two argument values to be used in the version of the SQL DELETE statement that is actually executed.

A CLI analog of this example involves the following steps (in outline):

****BindCol** and **BindParam** are both effectively shorthand for a certain sequence of **SetDescField** (or **SetDescRec**) operations.

1. The application builds and prepares the source form of the original SQL statement, with its placeholders.

2. Next, the application uses the CLI routine **BindParam** twice—i.e., once for each placeholder,* or equivalently once for each argument variable—in order to:

   ▪ Place descriptions of the two placeholders into the applicable Implementation Parameter Descriptor (IPD),† and

   ▪ Place descriptions of the variables that will be used to provide corresponding argument values into the applicable Application Parameter Descriptor (APD).

   Note: As noted earlier (in a footnote), the application could alternatively use **SetDescField** and **SetDescRec** instead of **BindParam** to perform this step. These latter routines allow the application to exercise a somewhat finer-grained level of control over the process. **SetDescField,** for example, allows the application to set the descriptor areas on an individual field-by-field basis. (Note that **SetDescField,** like **AllocHandle,** is extensible, while **BindParam,** like **AllocStmt,** is not.)

3. The application assigns the desired argument values to the argument variables now described by the APD.

4. Finally, the application invokes **Execute** on the prepared statement.

We now proceed to discuss this sequence of operations in more detail.

Step 1: The code to prepare the original SQL statement might look like this (omitting declarations and exception handling):

```
strcpy ( sqlsource,
         "DELETE FROM SP WHERE SP.QTY > ? AND SP.QTY < ?" ) ;
rc = SQLPrepare ( hstmt, (SQLCHAR *)sqlsource, SQL_NTS ) ;
```

The prepared version of the statement is now "the prepared statement associated with" the statement handle identified by **hstmt.**

Step 2 (describe the placeholders and argument variables): **BindParam** takes the following parameters:

▪ **StatementHandle** (IN INTEGER): The statement handle with which the prepared statement is associated

▪ **ParameterNumber** (IN SMALLINT): The ordinal position of the placeholder within its containing SQL statement

---

*The term **Param** in the name **BindParam** refers to a placeholder, of course, not to a CLI parameter.

†This portion of the Step 2 task might already have been done "automatically" by **Prepare** in some implementations, in which case there is no need for the application to do it again. See the CLI specification for further details.

- **ValueType** (IN SMALLINT): A code indicating the host language data type of the corresponding argument variable

- **ParameterType** (IN SMALLINT): A code indicating the SQL data type of the placeholder

- **ColumnSize** (IN INTEGER): Placeholder size (e.g., precision, if numeric)

- **DecimalDigits** (IN SMALLINT): Placeholder scale (if numeric)

- **ParameterValue** (DEFIN ANY): Argument variable address

- **StrLen_or_Ind** (DEFIN INTEGER): Associated indicator variable address*

Here then are the necessary **BindParam** invocations for our DELETE example:

```
SQLBindParam ( hstmt,
               1,                       /* first placeholder    */
               SQLSMALLINT,             /* host vble data type */
               SQL_DECIMAL,             /* SQL data type        */
               5,                       /* precision            */
               0,                       /* scale                */
               (SQLPOINTER)low,         /* address of argument */
               0 ) ;                    /* not used here        */

SQLBindParam ( hstmt,
               2,                       /* second placeholder   */
               SQLSMALLINT,             /* host vble data type */
               SQL_DECIMAL,             /* SQL data type        */
               5,                       /* precision            */
               0,                       /* scale                */
               (SQLPOINTER)high,        /* address of argument */
               0 ) ;                    /* not used here        */
```

Let the **StatementHandle** value (i.e., the value of **hstmt**) be *SH*, and let *IPD* and *APD* be the IPD and APD currently associated with *SH*. Then the two invocations of **BindParam** just shown have the effect of placing information into the first two item descriptor areas within each of *IPD* and *APD*. More specifically:

- The first item descriptor area within *IPD* is set to show that the first placeholder in the prepared statement associated with *SH* has SQL data type DECIMAL(5,0);

---

*CLI includes a special feature by which very long character string argument values (sometimes called "character large objects" or CLOBs) can be passed piece by piece instead of all at once. The application signals its intent to use this feature by placing the code value –2 in the indicator variable addressed by **StrLen_or_Ind.** If **Execute** finds this code value at run time, it passes a "data needed" return code back to the application (see Section 23.9). The application can then use the routine **ParamData** to determine which argument has not yet been (completely) supplied, and the routine **PutData** to supply (the next piece of) that argument. This **ParamData/PutData** sequence can be repeated as many times as necessary. The application can also use the routine **Cancel** to terminate execution before the argument has been completely supplied.

Note: It is worth mentioning that the CLI specification refers to arguments supplied in the foregoing manner (using **ParamData** and **PutData**) as "deferred parameter values." This terminology is unnecessarily confusing, however, since the feature under discussion really has nothing to do with the concept of "deferred parameters" as already discussed in Section 23.3.

- The first item descriptor area within *APD* is set to show that the argument corresponding to that first placeholder has C data type **short** ("SQLSMALLINT") and will be found in the C variable **low;**

- The second item descriptor areas within *IPD* and *APD* are set analogously.

Note the implied run-time data type conversions from the C type **short** to the SQL type DECIMAL(5,0).

Step 3: The application assigns values to the argument variables:

```
low = 100 ;
high = 300 ;
```

Step 4: Here at last is the **Execute** invocation:

```
rc = SQLExecute ( hstmt ) ;
```

Execute uses the information placed in *IPD* and *APD* to obtain the necessary argument values and convert them to the appropriate data types before executing the desired SQL statement in its completed form. *Note:* Of course, the application could now assign new values to **low** and **high** and invoke **Execute** again, without having to reinvoke **Prepare** or **BindParam** first.

23.8   RETRIEVAL OPERATIONS

In this section we discuss the special considerations that apply when the SQL statement to be prepared and executed is a data retrieval operation. By way of example, let *SS* be the following SQL SELECT statement:

```
SELECT P.PNO, P.CITY, P.WEIGHT
FROM   P
```

(For simplicity, we deliberately show an example that involves no placeholders.) What is involved in executing this statement via CLI? In outline, the steps the application must go through are as follows.

1. First of all, of course, it must build and prepare the original statement *SS*.

2. Next, it must obtain a description of the result table that will be returned when that prepared statement is executed (for the sake of the example, of course, we assume it does not already have this information, which in general it will not). The CLI routines **NumResultCols, DescribeCol,** and **ColAttribute** are provided for this purpose: **NumResultCols** gives the number of result columns (three in the example), **DescribeCol** gives information about a specific column, and **ColAttribute** gives information about a specific aspect ("attribute") of a specific column. *Note:* The application could alternatively use **GetDescRec** and **GetDescField** instead of **DescribeCol** and **ColAttribute** in performing this step.

3. Next, it must allocate an appropriate set of variables to act as targets into which data can subsquently be retrieved, and then describe those target variables to the system using the CLI routine **BindCol.** This routine places the target variable descriptions in the applicable Application Row Descriptor (ARD). *Note:* The application could alternatively use **SetDescRec** and **SetDescField** instead of **BindCol** in performing this step.

4. Now the prepared form of *SS* can be executed by means of the usual CLI **Execute** routine. A cursor is implicitly declared and opened and positioned before the first result row.

5. The application can now use the CLI routines **Fetch** and (possibly) **FetchScroll** on that cursor to retrieve data from the result table. It can also use prepared forms of the SQL UPDATE and DELETE CURRENT operations to update or delete the current row.

6. Finally, the cursor can be closed via the CLI routine **CloseCursor.**

We now proceed to discuss this sequence of operations in more detail.

Step 1: The code to build and prepare the original SQL retrieval operation might look like this (again omitting declarations and exception handling):

```
strcpy ( sqlsource,
         "SELECT P.PNO, P.CITY, P.WEIGHT FROM P" ) ;
rc = SQLPrepare ( hstmt, (SQLCHAR *)sqlsource, SQL_NTS ) ;
```

Because it is, specifically, a retrieval operation that is being prepared here, **Prepare** will place a description of the columns of the table resulting from that retrieval in the applicable Implementation Row Descriptor (IRD; note that this is fundamentally the *only* way the IRD can be set). The prepared retrieval operation becomes the *select source* associated with the applicable statement handle (even though that retrieval operation is not necessarily an SQL statement *per se*).

Step 2 (obtaining information regarding the result table): **NumResultCols** takes one IN parameter, **StatementHandle,** and one OUT parameter, **ColumnCount.** Hence (e.g.):

```
rc = SQLNumResultCols ( hstmt, &ncols ) ;
```

We omit the details of **ColAttribute** here. **DescribeCol** takes the following parameters, most of which we take to be more or less self-explanatory:

- **StatementHandle** (IN INTEGER)
- **ColumnNumber** (IN SMALLINT)
- **ColumnName** (OUT CHARACTER(n))
- **BufferLength** (IN SMALLINT)
- **NameLength** (OUT SMALLINT)

- **ColumnSize** (OUT INTEGER)
- **DecimalDigits** (OUT SMALLINT)
- **Nullable** (OUT SMALLINT)

Hence (e.g.):

```
for ( i = 0 ; i < ncols ; i++ )
{  rc = SQLDescribeCol ( hstmt, i + 1,
                         colname, sizeof ( colname ),
                         &colnamelen, &coltype,
                         &collen, &scale, &nullable ) ;
   /* code to allocate ith target variable and perform */
   /* BindCol on that target variable goes in here ... */
}
```

Step 3 (describe the target variables): **BindCol** takes the following parameters:

- **StatementHandle** (IN INTEGER): The statement handle with which the prepared statement is associated

- **ColumnNumber** (IN SMALLINT): The ordinal position of the column within its containing table

- **TargetType** (IN SMALLINT): A code indicating the host language data type of the corresponding target variable

- **TargetValue** (DEFOUT ANY): Target variable address

- **BufferLength** (IN INTEGER): Target variable size

- **StrLen_or_Ind** (DEFOUT INTEGER): Associated indicator variable address

Here then are the necessary **BindCol** invocations for the three result columns in the example (we omit the details of allocating the three target variables, since they basically involve only C operations, not CLI routines):

```
SQLBindCol ( hstmt,
             1,                       /* first column        */
             SQLCHAR,                 /* target data type    */
             (SQLPOINTER)&pno,        /* target address      */
             6,                       /* buffer length       */
             0 ) ;                    /* not used here       */

SQLBindCol ( hstmt,
             2,                       /* second column       */
             SQLCHAR,                 /* target data type    */
             (SQLPOINTER)&city,       /* target address      */
             15,                      /* buffer length       */
             0 ) ;                    /* not used here       */

SQLBindCol ( hstmt,
             3,                       /* third column        */
             SQLSMALLINT,             /* target data type    */
             (SQLPOINTER)&weight,     /* target address      */
             2,                       /* buffer length       */
             0 ) ;                    /* not used here       */
```

Let the **StatementHandle** value (i.e., the value of **hstmt**) be *SH*, and let *ARD* be the ARD currently associated with *SH*. Then the three invocations of **BindCol** just shown have the effect of placing information into the first three item descriptor areas within *ARD*. More specifically:

- The first item descriptor area within *ARD* is set to show that the first target for the prepared statement associated with *SH* is the C variable **pno** and has C data type **unsigned char** ("SQLCHAR");

- The second and third item descriptor areas within *ARD* are set analogously.

Step 4: Here now is the **Execute** invocation:

```
rc = SQLExecute ( hstmt ) ;
```

Execute causes a cursor to be declared and opened and associated with *SH;** note that such a cursor is provided even if the retrieval operation is a single-row SELECT. The name of the cursor associated with *SH* can be supplied by the application ahead of time by means of the CLI routine **SetCursorName;** if no such name has been supplied, CLI will invent one anyway. The cursor name for *SH* can be discovered at any time by means of the CLI routine **GetCursorName.** (In a similar manner, the application can use **SetStmtAttr** ahead of time to specify whether the cursor associated with *SH* is a SCROLL cursor—which it must be if **FetchScroll** is to be used—and whether it is INSENSITIVE, and can discover what these specifications are at any time by means of **GetStmtAttr.**)

Step 5: The CLI routines **Fetch** and **FetchScroll** function more or less as expected, and we omit the details here.† As mentioned earlier, the application can also use **Prepare** and **Execute** (or **ExecDirect**) to prepare and execute "preparable forms" of the SQL UPDATE and DELETE CURRENT statements against the current row (refer to Chapter 20 for an explanation of exactly what is meant by the expression "preparable forms of the SQL UPDATE and DELETE CURRENT statements"). Note, however, that preparing and executing those UPDATE and DELETE CURRENT operations must be performed under a statement handle different from that under which the open and fetch operations were performed.

Step 6: The CLI routine **CloseCursor** also functions more or less as expected; again we omit the details here.

---

*In general, of course, **Execute** will also have to go through the process of dealing with placeholders as described in the previous section, but our particular example does not involve any placeholders.

†Another CLI data retrieval routine, **GetData,** can be used to retrieve an individual value from the current row. **GetData** is used for columns for which no target variable has been specified in the ARD (and hence no corresponding value can have been retrieved via **Fetch** or **FetchScroll**). In particular, it can be used to retrieve a long character string value piece by piece instead of all at once. (As mentioned in an earlier footnote, **PutData** can be used somewhat analogously to supply a long character string argument piece by piece.)

23.9   EXCEPTION HANDLING

Return Codes

Executing a CLI routine always raises one or more *conditions* (where by *condition* we mean either a completion condition or an exception condition—refer to Chapter 22 if you need to refresh your memory regarding the meanings of these terms). Those conditions are reflected in the return code passed back from the routine to the application. The following return codes are defined in the CLI specification:

- *Invalid handle* (exception): return code –2
- *Error* (exception): return code –1
- *Data needed* (exception): return code +99*
- *No data found* (completion): return code +100
- *Warning* (completion): return code +1
- *Success* (completion): return code 0

If a single routine execution raises more than one condition, the one appearing first in the foregoing priority sequence is the one reflected in the return code.

In addition to setting the return code, all CLI routines other than **GetDiagField** and **GetDiagRec** (*q.v.*) cause information to be placed in the relevant *diagnostics area* (unless the return code is –2, "invalid handle," in which case no relevant diagnostics area can be identified). See the next subsection.

Diagnostics Areas

Every allocated resource, be it an E-, C-, or S-resource, has an associated (encapsulated) diagnostics area that is used to hold information relating to the most recently executed CLI routine that used that resource. The associated diagnostics area is automatically emptied at the start of execution of every routine that uses the resource in question (except for **Error, GetDiagField,** and **GetDiagRec,** *q.v.*).

Assuming it is populated, a diagnostics area (conceptually) contains certain *header fields* that give general information about the execution of the pertinent CLI routine, together with zero or more *status records* that give further details of that execution. The header fields are as follows:

```
RETURNCODE
NUMBER
MORE
ROW_COUNT
DYNAMIC_FUNCTION
DYNAMIC_FUNCTION_CODE
```

---

*See the footnote in Section 23.7 regarding the piece-by-piece handling of very long string arguments.

And the status record fields are as follows (note the SQLSTATE field specifically):

```
SQLSTATE
NATIVE_CODE
CONDITION_NUMBER
CLASS_ORIGIN
SUBCLASS_ORIGIN
SERVER_NAME
CONNECTION_NAME
CONSTRAINT_CATALOG
CONSTRAINT_SCHEMA
CONSTRAINT_NAME
CATALOG_NAME
SCHEMA_NAME
TABLE_NAME
COLUMN_NAME
CURSOR_NAME
MESSAGE_TEXT
MESSAGE_LENGTH
MESSAGE_OCTET_LENGTH
```

Most of these items seem reasonably self-explanatory (for further discussion, see Chapter 22). They can be retrieved using the CLI routines **GetDiagField** and **GetDiagRec; GetDiagField** retrieves information from an individual field anywhere in the diagnostics area, **GetDiagRec** retrieves information from specified fields within one specified status record in the diagnostics area. In addition, the CLI routine **Error** can be used to retrieve "the next" status record in its entirety (that is, the *i*th execution of **Error** retrieves the *i*th status record, loosely speaking). Mention should also be made of the CLI routine **RowCount,** which can be used to retrieve the ROW_COUNT value specifically (note, however, that ROW_COUNT is meaningful only for INSERT, searched UPDATE, and searched DELETE operations).

23.10   A SAMPLE "SQLCLI.H" FILE

This section shows a typical C header file (**sqlcli.h**). It consists of a lightly edited version of material taken from an "annex" (i.e., appendix) to the CLI specification itself. A genuine header file would have to contain at least all of the information included here (except that the comments can differ, of course).

```
/* C data types */
typedef unsigned char SQLCHAR ;
typedef long          SQLINTEGER ;
typedef short         SQLSMALLINT ;
typedef double        SQLDOUBLE ;
typedef float         SQLREAL ;
typedef void *        SQLPOINTER ;
typedef unsigned char SQLDATE ;
typedef unsigned char SQLTIME ;
typedef unsigned char SQLTIMESTAMP ;
typedef unsigned char SQLDECIMAL ;
typedef unsigned char SQLNUMERIC ;
```

```
/* return code data type */
typedef SQLSMALLINT    SQLRETURN ;

/* handle data types */
typedef SQLINTEGER    SQLHENV ;
typedef SQLINTEGER    SQLHDBC ;
typedef SQLINTEGER    SQLHSTMT ;
typedef SQLINTEGER    SQLHDESC ;

/* special "length or indicator" values */
#define SQL_NULL_DATA          -1
#define SQL_DATA_AT_EXEC       -2

/* return codes */
#define SQL_SUCCESS             0
#define SQL_SUCCESS_WITH_INFO   1
#define SQL_NEED_DATA          99
#define SQL_NO_DATA           100
#define SQL_ERROR              -1
#define SQL_INVALID_HANDLE     -2

/* test for SQL_SUCCESS or SQL_SUCCESS_WITH_INFO */
#define SQL_SUCCEEDED(rc) (((rc)&(-1))==0)

/* null-terminated string codes */
#define SQL_NTS                -3
#define SQL_NTSL               -3L

/* maximum message length */
#define SQL_MAXIMUM_MESSAGE_LENGTH  512

/* maximum identifier length */
#define SQL_MAXIMUM_ID_LENGTH        18

/* datetime lengths; */
/* for time and timestamp, add p+1 if precision p != 0 */
#define SQL_DATE_LENGTH             10
#define SQL_TIME_LENGTH              8
#define SQL_TIMESTAMP_LENGTH        19

/* handle type codes */
#define SQL_HANDLE_ENV    1
#define SQL_HANDLE_DBC    2
#define SQL_HANDLE_STMT   3
#define SQL_HANDLE_DESC   4

/* E-resource attribute */
#define SQL_ATTR_OUTPUT_NTS  10001

/* C-resource attribute */
#define SQL_ATTR_AUTO_IPD    10001

/* S-resource attributes */
#define SQL_ATTR_APP_ROW_DESC        10010
#define SQL_ATTR_APP_PARAM_DESC      10011
#define SQL_ATTR_IMP_ROW_DESC        10012
#define SQL_ATTR_IMP_PARAM_DESC      10013
#define SQL_ATTR_CURSOR_SCROLLABLE    -1
#define SQL_ATTR_CURSOR_SENSITIVITY   -2

/* descriptor area field identifiers */
#define SQL_DESC_COUNT                     1001
#define SQL_DESC_TYPE                      1002
```

```
#define SQL_DESC_LENGTH                          1003
#define SQL_DESC_OCTET_LENGTH_POINTER            1004
#define SQL_DESC_PRECISION                       1005
#define SQL_DESC_SCALE                           1006
#define SQL_DESC_DATETIME_INTERVAL_CODE          1007
#define SQL_DESC_NULLABLE                        1008
#define SQL_DESC_INDICATOR_POINTER               1009
#define SQL_DESC_DATA_POINTER                    1010
#define SQL_DESC_NAME                            1011

#define SQL_DESC_UNNAMED                         1012
#define SQL_DESC_OCTET_LENGTH                    1013
#define SQL_DESC_DATETIME_INTERVAL_PRECISION     1014
#define SQL_DESC_COLLATION_CATALOG               1015
#define SQL_DESC_COLLATION_SCHEMA                1016
#define SQL_DESC_COLLATION_NAME                  1017
#define SQL_DESC_CHARACTER_SET_CATALOG           1018
#define SQL_DESC_CHARACTER_SET_SCHEMA            1019
#define SQL_DESC_CHARACTER_SET_NAME              1020
#define SQL_DESC_PARAMETER_MODE                  1021
#define SQL_DESC_PARAMETER_ORDINAL_POSITION      1022
#define SQL_DESC_PARAMETER_SPECIFIC_CATALOG      1023
#define SQL_DESC_PARAMETER_SPECIFIC_SCHEMA       1024
#define SQL_DESC_PARAMETER_SPECIFIC_NAME         1025
#define SQL_DESC_ALLOC_TYPE                      1099

/* diagnostics area field identifiers */
#define SQL_DIAG_RETURNCODE                         1
#define SQL_DIAG_NUMBER                             2
#define SQL_DIAG_ROW_COUNT                          3
#define SQL_DIAG_SQLSTATE                           4
#define SQL_DIAG_NATIVE                             5
#define SQL_DIAG_MESSAGE_TEXT                       6
#define SQL_DIAG_DYNAMIC_FUNCTION                   7
#define SQL_DIAG_CLASS_ORIGIN                       8
#define SQL_DIAG_SUBCLASS_ORIGIN                    9
#define SQL_DIAG_CONNECTION_NAME                   10
#define SQL_DIAG_SERVER_NAME                       11
#define SQL_DIAG_DYNAMIC_FUNCTION_CODE             12
#define SQL_DIAG_MORE                              13
#define SQL_DIAG_CONDITION_NUMBER                  14
#define SQL_DIAG_CONSTRAINT_CATALOG                15
#define SQL_DIAG_CONSTRAINT_SCHEMA                 16
#define SQL_DIAG_CONSTRAINT_NAME                   17
#define SQL_DIAG_CATALOG_NAME                      18
#define SQL_DIAG_SCHEMA_NAME                       19
#define SQL_DIAG_TABLE_NAME                        20
#define SQL_DIAG_COLUMN_NAME                       21
#define SQL_DIAG_CURSOR_NAME                       22
#define SQL_DIAG_MESSAGE_LENGTH                    23
#define SQL_DIAG_MESSAGE_OCTET_LENGTH              24

/* diagnostics area dynamic function codes */
#define SQL_DIAG_ALTER_DOMAIN                       3
#define SQL_DIAG_ALTER_TABLE                        4
#define SQL_DIAG_CALL                               7
#define SQL_DIAG_CREATE_ASSERTION                   6
#define SQL_DIAG_CREATE_CHARACTER_SET               8
#define SQL_DIAG_CREATE_COLLATION                  10
#define SQL_DIAG_CREATE_DOMAIN                      23
#define SQL_DIAG_CREATE_SCHEMA                      64
#define SQL_DIAG_CREATE_TABLE                       77
#define SQL_DIAG_CREATE_TRANSLATION                79
#define SQL_DIAG_CREATE_VIEW                        84
```

```
#define SQL_DIAG_DELETE_WHERE                         19
#define SQL_DIAG_DROP_ASSERTION                       24
#define SQL_DIAG_DROP_CHARACTER_SET                   25
#define SQL_DIAG_DROP_COLLATION                       25
#define SQL_DIAG_DROP_DOMAIN                          27
#define SQL_DIAG_DROP_SCHEMA                          31
#define SQL_DIAG_DROP_TABLE                           32
#define SQL_DIAG_DROP_TRANSLATION                     33
#define SQL_DIAG_DROP_VIEW                            36
#define SQL_DIAG_DYNAMIC_DELETE_CURSOR                54
#define SQL_DIAG_DYNAMIC_UPDATE_CURSOR                55
#define SQL_DIAG_GRANT                                48
#define SQL_DIAG_INSERT                               50
#define SQL_DIAG_REVOKE                               59
#define SQL_DIAG_SELECT                               41
#define SQL_DIAG_SELECT_CURSOR                        85
#define SQL_DIAG_SET_CATALOG                          66
#define SQL_DIAG_SET_CONSTRAINT                       68
#define SQL_DIAG_SET_NAMES                            72
#define SQL_DIAG_SET_SCHEMA                           74
#define SQL_DIAG_SET_SESSION_AUTHORIZATION            76
#define SQL_DIAG_SET_TIME_ZONE                        71
#define SQL_DIAG_SET_TRANSACTION                      75
#define SQL_DIAG_UNKNOWN_STATEMENT                     0
#define SQL_DIAG_UPDATE_WHERE                         82

/* SQL data type codes */
#define SQL_CHAR            1
#define SQL_NUMERIC         2
#define SQL_DECIMAL         3
#define SQL_INTEGER         4
#define SQL_SMALLINT        5
#define SQL_FLOAT           6
#define SQL_REAL            7
#define SQL_DOUBLE          8
#define SQL_DATETIME        9
#define SQL_INTERVAL       10
#define SQL_VARCHAR        12
#define SQL_BIT            14
#define SQL_BIT_VARYING    15

/* concise codes for datetime and interval types */
#define SQL_TYPE_DATE                                 91
#define SQL_TYPE_TIME                                 92
#define SQL_TYPE_TIME_WITH_TIMEZONE                   93
#define SQL_TYPE_TIMESTAMP                            94
#define SQL_TYPE_TIMESTAMP_WITH_TIMEZONE              95
#define SQL_INTERVAL_DAY                             103
#define SQL_INTERVAL_DAY_TO_HOUR                     108
#define SQL_INTERVAL_DAY_TO_MINUTE                   109
#define SQL_INTERVAL_DAY_TO_SECOND                   110
#define SQL_INTERVAL_HOUR                            104
#define SQL_INTERVAL_HOUR_TO_MINUTE                  111
#define SQL_INTERVAL_HOUR_TO_SECOND                  112
#define SQL_INTERVAL_MINUTE                          105
#define SQL_INTERVAL_MINUTE_TO_SECOND                113
#define SQL_INTERVAL_MONTH                           102
#define SQL_INTERVAL_SECOND                          106
#define SQL_INTERVAL_YEAR                            101
#define SQL_INTERVAL_YEAR_TO_MONTH                   107

/* GetTypeInfo request for all data types */
#define SQL_ALL_TYPES       0
```

```
/* BindCol/BindParam default conversion code */
#define SQL_DEFAULT        99

/* GetData code indicating that APD specifies data type */
#define SQL_ARD_TYPE      -99

/* datetime type subcodes */
#define SQL_CODE_DATE              1
#define SQL_CODE_TIME              2
#define SQL_CODE_TIMESTAMP         3
#define SQL_CODE_TIME_ZONE         4
#define SQL_CODE_TIMESTAMP_ZONE    5

/* interval qualifier codes */
#define SQL_DAY                    3
#define SQL_DAY_TO_HOUR            8
#define SQL_DAY_TO_MINUTE          9
#define SQL_DAY_TO_SECOND         10
#define SQL_HOUR                   4
#define SQL_HOUR_TO_MINUTE        11
#define SQL_HOUR_TO_SECOND        12
#define SQL_MINUTE                 5
#define SQL_MINUTE_TO_SECOND      13
#define SQL_MONTH                  2
#define SQL_SECOND                 6
#define SQL_YEAR                   1
#define SQL_YEAR_TO_MONTH          7

/* option codes */
#define SQL_FALSE                  0
#define SQL_TRUE                   1
#define SQL_NONSCROLLABLE          0
#define SQL_SCROLLABLE             1

/* parameter modes */
#define SQL_PARAM_MODE_IN          1
#define SQL_PARAM_MODE_OUT         4
#define SQL_MODE_INOUT             2
#define SQL_PARAM_MODE_NONE        0

/* NULLABLE codes */
#define SQL_NO_NULLS               0
#define SQL_NULLABLE               1

/* values returned by GetTypeInfo for SEARCHABLE column */
#define SQL_PRED_NONE              0
#define SQL_PRED_CHAR              1
#define SQL_PRED_BASIC             2

/* values of UNNAMED field in descriptor area */
#define SQL_NAMED                  0
#define SQL_UNNAMED                1

/* values of ALLOC_TYPE field in descriptor area */
#define SQL_DESC_ALLOC_AUTO        1
#define SQL_DESC_ALLOC_USER        2

/* EndTran codes */
#define SQL_COMMIT                 0
#define SQL_ROLLBACK               1

/* FreeStmt options */
#define SQL_CLOSE                  0
```

```
#define SQL_DROP                      1
#define SQL_UNBIND                    2
#define SQL_RESET_PARAMS              3

/* "null" handles returned if AllocHandle fails */
#define SQL_NULL_HENV                 0
#define SQL_NULL_HDBC                 0
#define SQL_NULL_HSTMT                0
#define SQL_NULL_HDESC                0

/* GetFunctions codes to identify CLI routines */
#define SQL_API_SQLALLOCCONNECT       1
#define SQL_API_SQLALLOCENV           2
#define SQL_API_SQLALLOCHANDLE     1001
#define SQL_API_SQLALLOCSTMT          3
#define SQL_API_SQLBINDCOL            4
#define SQL_API_SQLBINDPARAM       1002
#define SQL_API_SQLCANCEL             5
#define SQL_API_SQLCLOSECURSOR     1003
#define SQL_API_SQLCOLATTRIBUTE       6
#define SQL_API_SQLCONNECT            7
#define SQL_API_SQLCOPYDESC        1004
#define SQL_API_SQLDATASOURCES       57
#define SQL_API_SQLDESCRIBECOL        8
#define SQL_API_SQLDISCONNECT         9
#define SQL_API_SQLENDTRAN         1005
#define SQL_API_SQLERROR             10
#define SQL_API_SQLEXECDIRECT        11
#define SQL_API_SQLEXECUTE           12
#define SQL_API_SQLFETCH             13
#define SQL_API_SQLFETCHSCROLL     1021
#define SQL_API_SQLFREECONNECT       14
#define SQL_API_SQLFREEENV           15
#define SQL_API_SQLFREEHANDLE      1006
#define SQL_API_SQLFREESTMT          16
#define SQL_API_SQLGETCONNECTATTR  1007
#define SQL_API_SQLGETCURSORNAME     17
#define SQL_API_SQLGETDATA           43
#define SQL_API_SQLGETDESCFIELD    1008
#define SQL_API_SQLGETDESCREC      1009
#define SQL_API_SQLGETDIAGFIELD    1010
#define SQL_API_SQLGETDIAGREC      1011
#define SQL_API_SQLGETENVATTR      1012
#define SQL_API_SQLGETFUNCTIONS      44
#define SQL_API_SQLGETINFO           45
#define SQL_API_SQLGETSTMTATTR     1014
#define SQL_API_SQLGETTYPEINFO       47
#define SQL_API_SQLNUMRESULTCOLS     18
#define SQL_API_SQLPARAMDATA         48
#define SQL_API_SQLPREPARE           19
#define SQL_API_SQLPUTDATA           49
#define SQL_API_SQLROWCOUNT          20
#define SQL_API_SQLSETCONNECTATTR  1016
#define SQL_API_SQLSETCURSORNAME     21
#define SQL_API_SQLSETDESCFIELD    1017
#define SQL_API_SQLSETDESCREC      1018
#define SQL_API_SQLSETENVATTR      1019
#define SQL_API_SQLSETSTMTATTR     1020

/* info requested by GetInfo */
#define SQL_MAXIMUM_DRIVER_CONNECTIONS        0
#define SQL_MAXIMUM_CONCURRENT_ACTIVITIES     1
#define SQL_DATA_SOURCE_NAME                  2
```

```
#define SQL_FETCH_DIRECTION                      8
#define SQL_SERVER_NAME                          13
#define SQL_DBMS_NAME                            17
#define SQL_DBMS_VERSION                         18
#define SQL_CURSOR_COMMIT_BEHAVIOR               23
#define SQL_DATA_SOURCE_READ_ONLY                25
#define SQL_DEFAULT_TRANSACTION_ISOLATION        26
#define SQL_IDENTIFIER_CASE                      28
#define SQL_MAXIMUM_COLUMN_NAME_LENGTH           30
#define SQL_MAXIMUM_CURSOR_NAME_LENGTH           31
#define SQL_MAXIMUM_SCHEMA_NAME_LENGTH           32
#define SQL_MAXIMUM_CATALOG_NAME_LENGTH          34
#define SQL_MAXIMUM_TABLE_NAME_LENGTH            35
#define SQL_SCROLL_CONCURRENCY                   43
#define SQL_TRANSACTION_CAPABLE                  46
#define SQL_USER_NAME                            47
#define SQL_TRANSACTION_ISOLATION_OPTION         72
#define SQL_INTEGRITY                            73
#define SQL_GETDATA_EXTENSIONS                   81
#define SQL_NULL_COLLATION                       85
#define SQL_ALTER_TABLE                          86
#define SQL_ORDER_BY_COLUMNS_IN_SELECT           90
#define SQL_SPECIAL_CHARACTERS                   94
#define SQL_MAXIMUM_COLUMNS_IN_GROUP_BY          97
#define SQL_MAXIMUM_COLUMNS_IN_ORDER_BY          99
#define SQL_MAXIMUM_COLUMNS_IN_SELECT            100
#define SQL_MAXIMUM_COLUMNS_IN_TABLE             101
#define SQL_MAXIMUM_STATEMENT_LENGTH             105
#define SQL_MAXIMUM_TABLES_IN_SELECT             106
#define SQL_MAXIMUM_USER_NAME_LENGTH             107
#define SQL_OUTER_JOIN_CAPABILITIES              115

#define SQL_CURSOR_SENSITIVITY                   10001
#define SQL_DESCRIBE_PARAMETER                   10002
#define SQL_CATALOG_NAME                         10003
#define SQL_COLLATING_SEQUENCE                   10004
#define SQL_MAXIMUM_IDENTIFIER_LENGTH            10005

/* S-resource attribute values for cursor sensitivity */
#define SQL_UNSPECIFIED                 0x00000000L
#define SQL_INSENSITIVE                 0x00000001L

/* "null handle" used when allocating E-resource */
#define SQL_NULL_HANDLE                          0L

/* SQL_ALTER_TABLE bitmasks */
#define SQL_AT_ADD_COLUMN               0x00000001L
#define SQL_AT_DROP_COLUMN              0x00000002L
#define SQL_AT_ALTER_COLUMN             0x00000004L
#define SQL_AT_ADD_CONSTRAINT           0x00000008L
#define SQL_AT_DROP_CONSTRAINT          0x00000010L

/* SQL_CURSOR_COMMIT_BEHAVIOR values */
#define SQL_CB_DELETE                            0
#define SQL_CB_CLOSE                             1
#define SQL_CB_PRESERVE                          2

/* SQL_FETCH_DIRECTION bitmasks */
#define SQL_FD_FETCH_NEXT               0x00000001L
#define SQL_FD_FETCH_FIRST              0x00000002L
#define SQL_FD_FETCH_LAST               0x00000004L
#define SQL_FD_FETCH_PRIOR              0x00000008L
#define SQL_FD_FETCH_ABSOLUTE           0x00000010L
#define SQL_FD_FETCH_RELATIVE           0x00000020L
```

```
/* SQL_GETDATA_EXTENSIONS bitmasks */
#define SQL_GD_ANY_COLUMN                    0x00000001L
#define SQL_FD_ANY_ORDER                     0x00000002L

/* SQL_IDENTIFIER_CASE values */
#define SQL_IC_UPPER                                    1
#define SQL_IC_LOWER                                    2
#define SQL_IC_SENSITIVE                                3
#define SQL_IC_MIXED                                    4

/* SQL_NULL_COLLATION values */
#define SQL_NC_HIGH                                     1
#define SQL_NC_LOW                                      2

/* SQL_OUTER_JOIN_CAPABILITIES bitmasks */
#define SQL_OUTER_JOIN_LEFT                  0x00000001L
#define SQL_OUTER_JOIN_RIGHT                 0x00000002L
#define SQL_OUTER_JOIN_FULL                 0x00000004L
#define SQL_OUTER_JOIN_NESTED               0x00000008L
#define SQL_OUTER_JOIN_NOT_ORDERED          0x00000010L
#define SQL_OUTER_JOIN_INNER                0x00000020L
#define SQL_OUTER_JOIN_ALL_COMPARISON_OPS   0x00000040L

/* SQL_SCROLL_CONCURRENCY bitmasks */
#define SQL_SCCO_READ_ONLY                  0x00000001L
#define SQL_SCCO_LOCK                       0x00000002L
#define SQL_SCCO_OPT_ROWVER                 0x00000004L
#define SQL_SCCO_OPT_VALUES                 0x00000008L

/* SQL_TRANSACTION_CAPABLE values */
#define SQL_TC_NONE                                     0
#define SQL_TC_DML                                      1
#define SQL_TC_ALL                                      2
#define SQL_TC_DDL_COMMIT                               3
#define SQL_TC_DDL_IGNORE                               4

/* SQL_TRANSACTION_ISOLATION bitmasks */
#define SQL_TRANSACTION_READ_UNCOMMITTED    0x00000001L
#define SQL_TRANSACTION_READ_COMMITTED      0x00000002L
#define SQL_TRANSACTION_REPEATABLE_READ     0x00000004L
#define SQL_TRANSACTION_SERIALIZABLE        0x00000008L

/* CLI function signatures */

SQLRETURN  SQLAllocConnect
        ( SQLHENV       EnvironmentHandle,
          SQLHDBC       *ConnectionHandle ) ;

SQLRETURN  SQLAllocEnv
        ( SQLHENV       *EnvironmentHandle ) ;

SQLRETURN  SQLAllocHandle
        ( SQLSMALLINT   HandleType,
          SQLINTEGER    InputHandle,
          SQLINTEGER    *OutputHandle ) ;

SQLRETURN  SQLAllocStmt
        ( SQLHDBC       ConnectionHandle,
          SQLSTMT       *StatementHandle ) ;

SQLRETURN  SQLBindCol
        ( SQLHSTMT      StatementHandle,
          SQLSMALLINT   ColumnNumber,
```

```
              SQLSMALLINT  BufferType,
              SQLPOINTER   Data,
              SQLINTEGER   BufferLength,
              SQLINTEGER   *StrLen_or_Ind ) ;

SQLRETURN  SQLBindParam
           ( SQLHSTMT      StatementHandle,
             SQLSMALLINT  ParamNumber,
             SQLSMALLINT  ValueType,
             SQLSMALLINT  ParameterType,
             SQLINTEGER   ColumnSize,
             SQLSMALLINT  DecimalDigits,
             SQLPOINTER   ParameterValue,
             SQLINTEGER   *StrLen_or_Ind ) ;

SQLRETURN  SQLCancel
           ( SQLHSTMT      StatementHandle ) ;

SQLRETURN  SQLCloseCursor
           ( SQLHSTMT      StatementHandle ) ;

SQLRETURN  SQLColAttribute
           ( SQLHSTMT      StatementHandle,
             SQLSMALLINT  ColumnNumber,
             SQLSMALLINT  FieldIdentifier,
             SQLCHAR      *CharacterAttribute,
             SQLINTEGER   BufferLength,
             SQLINTEGER   *StringLength,
             SQLINTEGER   *NumericAttribute ) ;

SQLRETURN  SQLConnect
           ( SQLHDBC       ConnectionHandle,
             SQLCHAR      *ServerName,
             SQLSMALLINT  NameLength1,
             SQLCHAR      *UserName,
             SQLSMALLINT  NameLength2,
             SQLCHAR      *Authentication,
             SQLSMALLINT  NameLength3 ) ;

SQLRETURN  SQLCopyDesc
           ( SQLHDESC      SourceDescHandle,
             SQLHDESC      TargetDescHandle ) ;

SQLRETURN  SQLDataSources
           ( SQLHENV       EnvironmentHandle,
             SQLSMALLINT  Direction,
             SQLCHAR      *ServerName,
             SQLSMALLINT  BufferLength1,
             SQLSMALLINT  *NameLength1,
             SQLCHAR      *Description,
             SQLSMALLINT  BufferLength2,
             SQLSMALLINT  *NameLength2 ) ;


SQLRETURN  SQLDescribeCol
           ( SQLHSTMT      StatementHandle,
             SQLSMALLINT  ColumnNumber,
             SQLCHAR      *ColumnName,
             SQLSMALLINT  BufferLength,
             SQLSMALLINT  *NameLength,
             SQLSMALLINT  *DataType,
             SQLINTEGER   *ColumnSize,
             SQLSMALLINT  *DecimalDigits,
```

```
                    SQLSMALLINT *Nullable ) ;

SQLRETURN   SQLDisconnect
          ( SQLHDBC        ConnectionHandle ) ;

SQLRETURN   SQLEndTran
          ( SQLSMALLINT  HandleType,
            SQLINTEGER   Handle,
            SQLSMALLINT  CompletionType ) ;

SQLRETURN   SQLError
          ( SQLHENV      EnvironmentHandle,
            SQLHDBC      ConnectionHandle,
            SQLSTMT      StatementHandle,
            SQLCHAR      *Sqlstate,
            SQLINTEGER   *NativeError,
            SQLCHAR      *MessageText,
            SQLINTEGER   BufferLength,
            SQLINTEGER   *TextLength ) ;

SQLRETURN   SQLExecDirect
          ( SQLHSTMT     StatementHandle,
            SQLCHAR      *StatementText,
            SQLSMALLINT  TextLength ) ;

SQLRETURN   SQLExecute
          ( SQLHSTMT     StatementHandle ) ;

SQLRETURN   SQLFetch
          ( SQLHSTMT     StatementHandle ) ;

SQLRETURN   SQLFetchScroll
          ( SQLHSTMT     StatementHandle,
            SQLSMALLINT  FetchOrientation,
            SQLINTEGER   FetchOffset ) ;

SQLRETURN   SQLFreeConnect
          ( SQLHDBC      ConnectionHandle ) ;

SQLRETURN   SQLFreeEnv
          ( SQLHENV      EnvironmentHandle ) ;

SQLRETURN   SQLFreeHandle
          ( SQLSMALLINT  HandleType,
            SQLINTEGER   Handle ) ;

SQLRETURN   SQLFreeStmt
          ( SQLHSTMT     StatementHandle,
            SQLINTEGER   Option ) ;

SQLRETURN   SQLGetConnectAttr
          ( SQLHDBC      ConnectionHandle,
            SQLINTEGER   Attribute,
            SQLPOINTER   Value,
            SQLINTEGER   BufferLength,
            SQLINTEGER   *StringLength ) ;

SQLRETURN   SQLGetCursorName
          ( SQLHSTMT     StatementHandle,
            SQLCHAR      *CursorName,
            SQLSMALLINT  BufferLength,
            SQLSMALLINT  *NameLength ) ;
```

```
SQLRETURN   SQLGetData
        ( SQLHSTMT       StatementHandle,
          SQLSMALLINT    ColumnNumber,
          SQLSMALLINT    TargetType,
          SQLPOINTER     TargetValue,
          SQLINTEGER     BufferLength,
          SQLINTEGER     *StrLen_or_Ind ) ;

SQLRETURN   SQLGetDescField
        ( SQLHDESC       DescriptorHandle,
          SQLSMALLINT    RecordNumber,
          SQLSMALLINT    FieldIdentifier,
          SQLPOINTER     Value,
          SQLINTEGER     BufferLength,
          SQLINTEGER     *StringLength ) ;

SQLRETURN   SQLGetDescRec
        ( SQLHDESC       DescriptorHandle,
          SQLSMALLINT    RecordNumber,
          SQLCHAR        *Name,
          SQLSMALLINT    BufferLength,
          SQLSMALLINT    *NameLength,
          SQLSMALLINT    *Type,
          SQLSMALLINT    *SubType,
          SQLINTEGER     *Length,
          SQLSMALLINT    *Precision,
          SQLSMALLINT    *Scale,
          SQLSMALLINT    *Nullable ) ;

SQLRETURN   SQLGetDiagField
        ( SQLSMALLINT    HandleType,
          SQLINTEGER     Handle,
          SQLSMALLINT    RecordNumber,
          SQLSMALLINT    DiagIdentifier,
          SQLPOINTER     DiagInfo,
          SQLSMALLINT    BufferLength,
          SQLSMALLINT    *StringLength ) ;

SQLRETURN   SQLGetDiagRec
        ( SQLSMALLINT    HandleType,
          SQLINTEGER     Handle,
          SQLSMALLINT    RecordNumber,
          SQLCHAR        *Sqlstate,
          SQLINTEGER     *NativeError,
          SQLCHAR        *MessageText,
          SQLSMALLINT    BufferLength,
          SQLSMALLINT    *TextLength ) ;

SQLRETURN   SQLGetEnvAttr
        ( SQLHENV        EnvironmentHandle,
          SQLINTEGER     Attribute,
          SQLPOINTER     Value,
          SQLINTEGER     BufferLength,
          SQLINTEGER     *StringLength ) ;

SQLRETURN   SQLGetFunctions
        ( SQLHDBC        ConnectionHandle,
          SQLSMALLINT    FunctionId,
          SQLSMALLINT    *Supported ) ;

SQLRETURN   SQLGetInfo
        ( SQLHDBC        ConnectionHandle,
```

```
                    SQLSMALLINT   InfoType,
                    SQLPOINTER    InfoValue,
                    SQLINTEGER    BufferLength,
                    SQLINTEGER    *StringLength ) ;

SQLRETURN   SQLGetStmtAttr
          ( SQLHSTMT      StatementHandle,
            SQLINTEGER    Attribute,
            SQLPOINTER    Value,
            SQLINTEGER    BufferLength,
            SQLINTEGER    *StringLength ) ;

SQLRETURN   SQLGetTypeInfo
          ( SQLHSTMT      StatementHandle,
            SQLSMALLINT   DataType ) ;

SQLRETURN   SQLNumResultCols
          ( SQLHSTMT      StatementHandle,
            SQLSMALLINT   *ColumnCount ) ;

SQLRETURN   SQLParamData
          ( SQLHSTMT      StatementHandle,
            SQLPOINTER    *Value ) ;

SQLRETURN   SQLPrepare
          ( SQLHSTMT      StatementHandle,
            SQLCHAR       *StatementText,
            SQLSMALLINT   TextLength ) ;

SQLRETURN   SQLPutData
          ( SQLHSTMT      StatementHandle,
            SQLPOINTER    Data,
            SQLINTEGER    StrLen_or_Ind ) ;

SQLRETURN   SQLRowCount
          ( SQLHSTMT      StatementHandle,
            SQLINTEGER    *RowCount ) ;

SQLRETURN   SQLSetConnectAttr
          ( SQLHDBC       ConnectionHandle,
            SQLINTEGER    Attribute,
            SQLPOINTER    Value,
            SQLINTEGER    StringLength ) ;

SQLRETURN   SQLSetCursorName
          ( SQLHSTMT      StatementHandle,
            SQLCHAR       *CursorName,
            SQLSMALLINT   NameLength ) ;

SQLRETURN   SQLSetDescField
          ( SQLHDESC      DescriptorHandle,
            SQLSMALLINT   RecordNumber,
            SQLSMALLINT   FieldIdentifier,
            SQLPOINTER    Value,
            SQLINTEGER    BufferLength ) ;

SQLRETURN   SQLSetDescRec
          ( SQLHDESC      DescriptorHandle,
            SQLSMALLINT   RecordNumber,
            SQLSMALLINT   Type,
            SQLSMALLINT   SubType,
            SQLINTEGER    Length,
            SQLSMALLINT   Precision,
```

```
            SQLSMALLINT  Scale,
            SQLPOINTER   Data,
            SQLINTEGER   *StringLength,
            SQLSMALLINT  *Indicator ) ;

SQLRETURN   SQLSetEnvAttr
          ( SQLHENV      EnvironmentHandle,
            SQLINTEGER   Attribute,
            SQLPOINTER   Value,
            SQLINTEGER   StringLength ) ;

SQLRETURN   SQLSetStmtAttr
          ( SQLHSTMT     StatementHandle,
            SQLINTEGER   Attribute,
            SQLPOINTER   Value,
            SQLINTEGER   StringLength ) ;
```

23.11 A SAMPLE CLI APPLICATION

This section shows a sample CLI application. Like the previous section, it consists of a lightly edited version of material taken from an annex to the CLI specification itself. The application uses CLI to create a base table, insert a single row into that table, and then retrieve it. *Note:* The application is not meant to be particularly realistic; rather, it has deliberately been written to illustrate several distinct aspects of CLI (including some not discussed in any detail in earlier parts of the chapter). Note too that much of the error checking that would be needed in practice has been omitted.

```
#include <stddef.h>
#include <string.h>
#include <sqlcli.h>

#define namelen 50

int print_err ( SQLSMALLINT handletype, SQLINTEGER handle ) ;

int example ( SQLCHAR *server,
              SQLCHAR *uid,
              SQLCHAR *authen )
{
SQLHENV     henv ;
SQLHDBC     hdbc ;
SQLHDESC    hdesc0 ;
SQLHDESC    hdesc1 ;
SQLHDESC    hdesc2 ;
SQLHSTMT    hstmt ;
SQLINTEGER  id ;
SQLSMALLINT idind ;
SQLCHAR     name [namelen+1] ;
SQLINTEGER  namelen ;
SQLSMALLINT nameind ;
```

```
SQLCHAR      sqlsource0 [255] ;
SQLCHAR      sqlsource1 [255] ;
SQLCHAR      sqlsource2 [255] ;

SQLAllocEnv ( &henv ) ;
SQLAllocConnect ( henv, &hdbc ) ;

/* establish connection */
if ( SQLConnect
     ( hdbc, server, SQL_NTS, uid, SQL_NTS, authen, SQL_NTS )
                                        != SQL_SUCCESS )
   return ( print_err ( SQL_HANDLE_DBC, hdbc ) ) ;

SQLAllocStmt ( hdbc, &hstmt ) ;

/* what follows is a CLI analog of :          */
/* EXEC SQL CREATE TABLE NAMEID               */
/*               ( ID     INTEGER,            */
/*                 NAME   CHARACTER VARYING (50), */
/*                 PRIMARY KEY ( ID ) ) ;     */
{
   SQLCHAR sqlsource0[] =
          "CREATE TABLE NAMEID "
             "( ID     INTEGER, "
               "NAME   CHARACTER VARYING (50), "
               "PRIMARY KEY ( ID ) )" ;
   if ( SQLExecDirect ( hstmt, sqlsource0, SQL_NTS )
                                        != SQL_SUCCESS )
      return ( print_err ( SQL_HANDLE_STMT, hstmt ) ) ;
}

/* commit the CREATE TABLE */
SQLEndTran ( SQL_HANDLE_ENV, henv, SQL_COMMIT ) ;

/* now insert a data row */
{
   SQLCHAR sqlsource1[] =
      "INSERT INTO NAMEID ( ID, NAME ) VALUES ( ?, ? )" ;
   if ( SQLPrepare ( hstmt, sqlsource1, SQL_NTS )
                                        != SQL_SUCCESS )
      return ( print_err ( SQL_HANDLE_STMT, hstmt ) ) ;

   /* get handle of automatically allocated APD */
   SQLGetStmtAttr ( hstmt, SQL_ATTR_APP_PARAM_DESC,
                    &hdesc1, 0L, (SQLINTEGER *)NULL ) ;
   /* place argument variable descriptions into APD */
   SQLSetDescRec ( hdesc1, 1, SQL_INTEGER, 0, 0L, 0, 0,
                   (SQLPOINTER)&id, (SQLINTEGER *)NULL,
                                   (SQLSMALLINT *)NULL ) ;
   SQLSetDescRec ( hdesc1, 2, SQL_CHAR, 0, namelen, 0, 0,
                   (SQLPOINTER)name, (SQLINTEGER *)NULL,
                                   (SQLSMALLINT *)NULL ) ;

   /* get handle of automatically allocated IPD */
   SQLGetStmtAttr ( hstmt, SQL_ATTR_IMP_PARAM_DESC,
                    &hdesc2, 0L, (SQLINTEGER *)NULL ) ;
   /* place placeholder descriptions into IPD */
   SQLSetDescRec ( hdesc2, 1, SQL_INTEGER, 0, 0L, 0, 0,
                   (SQLPOINTER)NULL, (SQLINTEGER *)NULL,
                                   (SQLSMALLINT *)NULL ) ;
   SQLSetDescRec ( hdesc1, 2, SQL_VARCHAR, 0, namelen, 0, 0,
                   (SQLPOINTER)NULL, (SQLINTEGER *)NULL,
                                   (SQLSMALLINT *)NULL ) ;
```

```
    /* assign values to arguments */
    id = 410118 ; /* say */
    (void) strcopy ((char *)name, "Dolores") ; /* say */

    /* execute the INSERT */
    if ( SQLExecute ( hstmt ) != SQL_SUCCESS )
       return ( print_err ( SQL_HANDLE_STMT, hstmt ) ) ;
}

/* commit the INSERT */
SQLEndTran ( SQL_HANDLE_ENV, henv, SQL_COMMIT ) ;

/* get ready to retrieve the row */
{
    SQLCHAR sqlsource2[] =
          "SELECT ID, NAME FROM NAMEID" ;
    if ( SQLExecDirect ( hstmt, sqlsource2, SQL_NTS )
                                        != SQL_SUCCESS )
       return ( print_err ( SQL_HANDLE_STMT, hstmt ) ) ;
}

/* allocate an ARD */
SQLAllocHandle ( SQL_HANDLE_DESC, hdbc, &hdesc0 ) ;
/* place target variable descriptions into ARD */
SQLSetDescRec ( hdesc0, 1, SQL_INTEGER, 0, 0L, 0, 0,
               (SQLPOINTER)&id, (SQLINTEGER *)NULL,
                             (SQLSMALLINT *)&idind ) ;
SQLSetDescRec ( hdesc0, 2, SQL_CHAR, 0, namelen, 0, 0,
               (SQLPOINTER)&name, (SQLINTEGER *)&namelen,
                             (SQLSMALLINT *)&nameind ) ;

/* associate descriptor with statement handle */
SQLSetStmtAttr ( hstmt, SQL_ATTR_APP_ROW_DESC, &hdesc0, 0 ) ;

/* fetch the row */
SQLFetch ( hstmt ) ;

/* code to display the row might go in here */

SQLCloseCursor ( hstmt ) ;

/* commit the transaction */
SQLEndTran ( SQL_HANDLE_ENV, henv, SQL_COMMIT ) ;

SQLFreeHandle ( SQL_HANDLE_STMT, hstmt ) ;

SQLFreeHandle ( SQL_HANDLE_DESC, hdesc0 ) ;
SQLFreeHandle ( SQL_HANDLE_DESC, hdesc1 ) ;
SQLFreeHandle ( SQL_HANDLE_DESC, hdesc2 ) ;

SQLDisconnect ( hdbc ) ;

SQLFreeHandle ( SQL_HANDLE_DBC, hdbc ) ;

SQLFreeHandle ( SQL_HANDLE_ENV, henv ) ;

return ( 0 ) ;
}
```

Appendixes

The appendixes that follow cover a somewhat mixed bag of topics. Appendix A presents an SQL BNF grammar. Appendix B discusses the question of compliance with the standard. Appendix C discusses ways in which SQL/92 differs from the previous version of the standard (SQL/89). Appendix D is the list, promised in the preface to this book, of issues that do not seem to be satisfactorily defined or described in the standard at the present time. Appendix E discusses the planned *Persistent Stored Modules* feature (PSM) in some depth. Appendix F presents an overview of the proposed extensions to the standard known informally as "SQL3," including in particular a brief look at the extensions for incorporating certain object-oriented features into SQL. Finally, Appendix G provides a list of references and suggestions for further reading.

An SQL Grammar

A.1 INTRODUCTION

Any formal language definition, standard or otherwise, necessarily involves at least two parts, a syntactic part and a semantic part—where, loosely, *syntax* is how you say it and *semantics* is what it means. In the SQL standard (and in this book), the syntactic part of the language is defined by means of a BNF grammar, together with certain additional "syntax rules" expressed in English prose; the semantic part is defined purely by a set of "general rules" expressed (again) in English prose.* We remark in passing that other, more formal, definitional techniques do exist; however, such matters are beyond the scope of this book.

A language is thus certainly not just syntax. Nevertheless, it is always convenient to have a summary of the syntax of a language—i.e., a complete BNF grammar—for purposes of reference. Despite this fact, the official standard document does not include any such summary. We therefore present one (or at least an approximation to one) in this appendix.

The grammar that follows deliberately does not try to use the same terminology as the official standard, for reasons explained in Chapter 3, Section 3.6; in fact, it does not always use the same terminology as the body of the book, because of

---

*Actually, the distinction between syntax rules and general rules is not nearly as clearcut in the standard as this simple characterization would suggest.

certain terminological conflicts that would arise if it did. It does use the "list" and "commalist" constructs (again, see Chapter 3, Section 3.6, for details). It also uses a few simplifying abbreviations, as follows:

```
exp    for    expression
cond   for    condition, conditional
ref    for    reference
def    for    definition
```

The following are all defined to be *identifiers* in this grammar:

```
catalog
column
cursor
host-variable (except that a colon prefix is required)
module
parameter (except that a colon prefix is required)
prepped-statement-container
procedure
range-variable
user
```

The following are terminal categories (i.e., are undefined) with respect to this grammar:

```
data-type
identifier
integer
literal
scalar-function-ref
```

(though it is perhaps worth mentioning explicitly that "scalar function ref" is intended to include both CASE and CAST expressions, and that "identifier" is intended—sometimes!—to include an associated null indicator). We present the grammar top-down, more or less.

Note: In the interests of clarity and brevity, our grammar is indeed (as suggested above) only an approximation to a true grammar for the SQL language. It differs from a fully accurate SQL grammar in at least the following three respects.

1. First, it does not attempt to reflect all of the syntactic limitations of SQL but is instead quite permissive, in the sense that it allows the generation of many constructs that are not legal in genuine SQL. For example, it permits the argument to an aggregate function such as AVG to be specified as a reference to another such function, which SQL does not in fact allow.

2. It also does not bother to show all possible syntactic permutations in cases where such permutations do not affect the meaning. For example, the ON DELETE and ON UPDATE specifications in a foreign key definition can actually appear in either order, but our grammar does not show as much.

3. Finally, it simply omits some of the more esoteric features of the language. For example, a grouping column (in a GROUP BY clause) can optionally have an

associated COLLATE clause if and only if that grouping column is of type character string, but our grammar does not show this possibility.

Our reason for making all of these simplifications is that SQL is a highly context-sensitive language, and attempts to reflect context sensitivity in BNF tend to lead to a rather unwieldy set of production rules.

Despite all of the foregoing inaccuracies, we still believe that a syntax summary such as the one that follows is a useful thing to have, but the reader is cautioned against taking it as gospel. Where there is a discrepancy between this appendix and the body of the book, the body of the book must be regarded as taking precedence.

A.2   SESSIONS, CONNECTIONS, AND TRANSACTIONS

```
connect
    ::=    CONNECT TO { DEFAULT
                  | lit-param-or-var [ AS lit-param-or-var ]
                                     [ USER lit-param-or-var ] }

set-connection
    ::=    SET CONNECTION { DEFAULT | lit-param-or-var }

disconnect
    ::=    DISCONNECT { DEFAULT | CURRENT | ALL
                               | lit-param-or-var }

set-catalog
    ::=    SET CATALOG { lit-param-or-var | authID-function-ref }

set-schema
    ::=    SET SCHEMA { lit-param-or-var | authID-function-ref }

set-names
    ::=    SET NAMES { lit-param-or-var | authID-function-ref }

set-authorization
    ::=    SET SESSION AUTHORIZATION
                  { lit-param-or-var | authID-function-ref }

set-time-zone
    ::=    SET TIME ZONE { interval-exp | LOCAL }

commit
    ::=    COMMIT [ WORK ]

rollback
    ::=    ROLLBACK [ WORK ]

set-transaction
    ::=    SET TRANSACTION option-commalist

option
    ::=    DIAGNOSTICS SIZE integer
         | { READ ONLY | READ WRITE }
         | ISOLATION LEVEL { READ UNCOMMITTED
                             READ COMMITTED
                             REPEATABLE READ
                             SERIALIZABLE }
```

A.3   DATA DEFINITION

```
schema-def
   ::=   CREATE SCHEMA [ schema ] [ AUTHORIZATION user ]
              [ DEFAULT CHARACTER SET character-set ]
              [ schema-element-list ]

schema-element
   ::=   domain-def
       | base-table-def
       | view-def
       | authorization-def
       | general-constraint-def
       | character-set-def
       | collation-def
       | translation-def

domain-def
   ::=   CREATE DOMAIN domain [ AS ] data-type
              [ default-def ]
              [ domain-constraint-def ]

default-def
   ::=   DEFAULT { literal | niladic-function-ref | NULL }

base-table-def
   ::=   CREATE [ { GLOBAL | LOCAL } TEMPORARY ] TABLE
                  base-table
              ( base-table-element-commalist )
              [ ON COMMIT { DELETE | PRESERVE } ROWS ]

base-table-element
   ::=   column-def | base-table-constraint-def

column-def
   ::=   column { data-type | domain }
              [ default-def ]
              [ column-constraint-def-list ]

view-def
   ::=   CREATE VIEW view [ ( column-commalist ) ]
              AS table-exp
                  [ WITH [ CASCADED | LOCAL ] CHECK OPTION ]

authorization-def
   ::=   GRANT { privilege-commalist | ALL PRIVILEGES }
                  ON accessible-object TO grantee-commalist
                              [ WITH GRANT OPTION ]

general-constraint-def
   ::=   CREATE ASSERTION constraint CHECK ( cond-exp )
                                      [ deferrability ]

deferrability
   ::=   INITIALLY { DEFERRED | IMMEDIATE }
                          [ NOT ] DEFERRABLE

privilege
   ::=   SELECT
       | INSERT [ ( column-commalist ) ]
       | UPDATE [ ( column-commalist ) ]
       | DELETE
       | REFERENCES [ ( column-commalist ) ]
       | USAGE
```

```
accessible-object
    ::=    DOMAIN domain
         | [ TABLE ] table
         | CHARACTER SET character-set
         | COLLATION collation
         | TRANSLATION translation

grantee
    ::=    user | PUBLIC

character-set-def
    ::=    CREATE CHARACTER SET character-set [ AS ]
               GET character-set
         [ COLLATE collation
         | COLLATION FROM collation-source ]

collation-source
    ::=    EXTERNAL ( 'collation' )
         | collation
         | DESC ( collation )
         | DEFAULT
         | TRANSLATION translation [ THEN COLLATION collation ]

collation-def
    ::=    CREATE COLLATION collation
               FOR   character-set
               FROM collation-source

translation-def
    ::=    CREATE TRANSLATION translation
               FOR   character-set
               TO    character-set
               FROM translation-source

translation-source
    ::=    EXTERNAL ( 'translation' )
         | IDENTITY
         | translation

domain-alteration
    ::=    ALTER DOMAIN domain domain-alteration-action

domain-alteration-action
    ::=    domain-default-alteration-action
         | domain-constraint-alteration-action

domain-default-alteration-action
    ::=    SET default-def
         | DROP DEFAULT

domain-constraint-alteration-action
    ::=    ADD domain-constraint-def
         | DROP CONSTRAINT constraint

base-table-alteration
    ::=    ALTER TABLE base-table base-table-alteration-action

base-table-alteration-action
    ::=    column-alteration-action
         | base-table-constraint-alteration-action

column-alteration-action
    ::=    ADD [ COLUMN ] column-def
         | ALTER [ COLUMN ] column
               { SET default-def | DROP DEFAULT }
         | DROP [ COLUMN ] column { RESTRICT | CASCADE }
```

```
base-table-constraint-alteration-action
   ::=    ADD base-table-constraint-def
        | DROP CONSTRAINT constraint { RESTRICT | CASCADE }

schema-drop
   ::=    DROP SCHEMA schema { RESTRICT | CASCADE }

domain-drop
   ::=    DROP DOMAIN domain { RESTRICT | CASCADE }

base-table-drop
   ::=    DROP TABLE base-table { RESTRICT | CASCADE }

view-drop
   ::=    DROP VIEW view { RESTRICT | CASCADE }

authorization-drop
   ::=    REVOKE [ GRANT OPTION FOR ] privilege-commalist
                  ON accessible-object FROM grantee-commalist
                                       { RESTRICT | CASCADE }

general-constraint-drop
   ::=    DROP ASSERTION constraint

character-set-drop
   ::=    DROP CHARACTER SET character-set

collation-drop
   ::=    DROP COLLATION collation

translation-drop
   ::=    DROP TRANSLATION translation
```

A.4   MODULES

```
module-def
   ::=    MODULE [ module ] [ NAMES ARE character-set ]
          LANGUAGE { ADA | C | COBOL | FORTRAN
                                    | MUMPS | PASCAL | PLI }
        [ SCHEMA schema ] [ AUTHORIZATION user ]
        [ temporary-table-def-list ]
          module-element-list

temporary-table-def
   ::=    DECLARE LOCAL TEMPORARY TABLE MODULE . base-table
              ( base-table-element-commalist )
              [ ON COMMIT { PRESERVE | DELETE } ROWS ]

module-element
   ::=    cursor-def
        | dynamic-cursor-def
        | procedure-def

procedure-def
   ::=    PROCEDURE procedure
        { parameter-def-list | ( parameter-def-commalist ) } ;
          SQL-statement ;
```

Note: "SQL-statement" is defined in Chapter 6, Section 6.2.

```
parameter-def
   ::=    parameter data-type
      |   SQLCODE
      |   SQLSTATE
```

A.5   DATA MANIPULATION

```
single-row-select
   ::=    SELECT [ ALL | DISTINCT ] select-item-commalist
          INTO   target-commalist
          FROM   table-ref-commalist
      [ WHERE   cond-exp ]
      [ GROUP   BY column-ref-commalist ]
      [ HAVING cond-exp ]

insert
   ::=    INSERT INTO table
          { [ ( column-commalist ) ] table-exp
                              | DEFAULT VALUES }

searched-update
   ::=    UPDATE table
          SET    update-assignment-commalist
      [ WHERE   cond-exp ]

update-assignment
   ::=    column = { scalar-exp | DEFAULT | NULL }

searched-delete
   ::=    DELETE
          FROM    table
      [ WHERE   cond-exp ]

cursor-def
   ::=    DECLARE cursor [ INSENSITIVE ] [ SCROLL ] CURSOR FOR
                    table-exp
                 [ ORDER BY order-item-commalist ]
      [ FOR { READ ONLY | UPDATE [ OF column-commalist ] } ]
```

Note: The construct "table-exp [ORDER BY order-item-commalist]" can also be used in direct SQL as a multi-row retrieval statement.

```
order-item
   ::=    { column | integer } [ ASC | DESC ]

open
   ::=    OPEN cursor

fetch
   ::=    FETCH [ [ row-selector ] FROM ] cursor
                              INTO target-commalist

row-selector
   ::=    NEXT | PRIOR | FIRST | LAST
                 | ABSOLUTE number | RELATIVE number

positioned-update
   ::=    UPDATE table
          SET    update-assignment-commalist
          WHERE   CURRENT OF cursor
```

```
positioned-delete
   ::=    DELETE
          FROM    table
          WHERE   CURRENT OF cursor

close
   ::=    CLOSE cursor
```

A.6   TABLE EXPRESSIONS

```
table-exp
   ::=    join-table-exp | nonjoin-table-exp

join-table-exp
   ::=    table-ref CROSS JOIN table-ref
        | table-ref [ NATURAL ] [ join-type ] JOIN table-ref
                  [ ON cond-exp | USING ( column-commalist ) ]
        | ( join-table-exp )

table-ref
   ::=    join-table-exp
        | table [ [ AS ] range-variable
                       [ ( column-commalist ) ] ]
        | ( table-exp ) [ AS ] range-variable
                            [ ( column-commalist ) ]

join-type
   ::=    INNER
        | LEFT [ OUTER ]
        | RIGHT [ OUTER ]
        | FULL [ OUTER ]
        | UNION

nonjoin-table-exp
   ::=    nonjoin-table-term
        | table-exp { UNION | EXCEPT } [ ALL ]
                  [ CORRESPONDING [ BY ( column-commalist ) ] ]
                         table-term

nonjoin-table-term
   ::=    nonjoin-table-primary
        | table-term INTERSECT [ ALL ]
                  [ CORRESPONDING [ BY ( column-commalist ) ] ]
                         table-primary

table-term
   ::=    join-table-exp
        | nonjoin-table-term

table-primary
   ::=    join-table-exp
        | nonjoin-table-primary

nonjoin-table-primary
   ::=    ( nonjoin-table-exp )
        | select-exp
        | TABLE table
        | table-constructor

table-constructor
   ::=    VALUES row-constructor-commalist
```

```
row-constructor
    ::=    scalar-exp
        |  ( scalar-exp-commalist )
        |  ( table-exp )
```

Note: The parenthesized table expression here is actually a row subquery.

```
select-exp
    ::=    SELECT [ ALL | DISTINCT ] select-item-commalist
               FROM table-ref-commalist
                 [ WHERE cond-exp ]
                   [ GROUP BY column-ref-commalist ]
                     [ HAVING cond-exp ]
```

```
select-item
    ::=    scalar-exp [ [ AS ] column ]
        |  [ range-variable . ] *
```

A.7   CONDITIONAL EXPRESSIONS

```
cond-exp
    ::=    cond-term
        |  cond-exp OR cond-term
```

```
cond-term
    ::=    cond-factor
        |  cond-term AND cond-factor
```

```
cond-factor
    ::=    [ NOT ] cond-test
```

```
cond-test
    ::=    cond-primary
             [ IS [ NOT ] { TRUE | FALSE | UNKNOWN } ]
```

```
cond-primary
    ::=    simple-cond | ( cond-exp )
```

```
simple-cond
    ::=    comparison-cond
        |  between-cond
        |  like-cond
        |  in-cond
        |  match-cond
        |  all-or-any-cond
        |  exists-cond
        |  unique-cond
        |  overlaps-cond
        |  test-for-null
```

```
comparison-cond
    ::=    row-constructor comparison-operator row-constructor
```

```
comparison-operator
    ::=    = | < | <= | > | >= | <>
```

```
between-cond
    ::=    row-constructor [ NOT ] BETWEEN row-constructor
                                     AND row-constructor
```

```
like-cond
   ::=   character-string-exp
         [ NOT ] LIKE character-string-exp
               [ ESCAPE character-string-exp ]

in-cond
   ::=   row-constructor [ NOT ] IN ( table-exp )
       | scalar-exp [ NOT ] IN ( scalar-exp-commalist )

match-cond
   ::=   row-constructor MATCH [ UNIQUE ]
                         [ PARTIAL | FULL ] ( table-exp )

all-or-any-cond
   ::=   row-constructor
             comparison-operator { ALL | ANY | SOME }
                                       ( table-exp )

exists-cond
   ::=   EXISTS ( table-exp )

unique-cond
   ::=   UNIQUE ( table-exp )

overlaps-cond
   ::=   ( scalar-exp, scalar-exp )
                    OVERLAPS ( scalar-exp, scalar-exp )

test-for-null
   ::=   row-constructor IS [ NOT ] NULL
```

A.8   CONSTRAINTS

```
domain-constraint-def
   ::=   [ CONSTRAINT constraint ] CHECK ( cond-exp )
                                       [ deferrability ]

base-table-constraint-def
   ::=   [ CONSTRAINT constraint ]
         candidate-key-def [ deferrability ]
       | [ CONSTRAINT constraint ]
         foreign-key-def [ deferrability ]
       | [ CONSTRAINT constraint ]
         check-constraint-def [ deferrability ]

candidate-key-def
   ::=   { PRIMARY KEY | UNIQUE } ( column-commalist )

foreign-key-def
   ::=   FOREIGN KEY ( column-commalist ) references-def

references-def
   ::=   REFERENCES base-table [ ( column-commalist ) ]
             [ MATCH { FULL | PARTIAL } ]
             [ ON DELETE referential-action ]
             [ ON UPDATE referential-action ]

referential-action
   ::=   NO ACTION | CASCADE | SET DEFAULT | SET NULL
```

```
check-constraint-def
   ::=   CHECK ( cond-exp )

column-constraint-def
   ::=   [ CONSTRAINT constraint ]
           NOT NULL [ deferrability ]
       | [ CONSTRAINT constraint ]
           { PRIMARY KEY | UNIQUE } [ deferrability ]
       | [ CONSTRAINT constraint ]
           references-def [ deferrability ]
       | [ CONSTRAINT constraint ]
           CHECK ( cond-exp ) [ deferrability ]

set-constraints
   ::=   SET CONSTRAINTS { constraint-commalist | ALL }
                                  { DEFERRED | IMMEDIATE }
```

A.9   DYNAMIC SQL

```
execute-immediate
   ::=   EXECUTE IMMEDIATE param-or-var

prepare
   ::=   PREPARE prepared FROM param-or-var

prepared
   ::=   prepped-statement-container | param-or-var

deallocate-prepare
   ::=   DEALLOCATE PREPARE prepared

execute
   ::=   EXECUTE prepared [ INTO places ] [ USING arguments ]

places
   ::=   target-commalist | SQL DESCRIPTOR descriptor

arguments
   ::=   target-commalist | SQL DESCRIPTOR descriptor

descriptor
   ::=   lit-param-or-var

allocate-descriptor
   ::=   ALLOCATE DESCRIPTOR descriptor
                  [ WITH MAX lit-param-or-var ]

deallocate-descriptor
   ::=   DEALLOCATE DESCRIPTOR descriptor

describe-input
   ::=   DESCRIBE INPUT prepared
                  USING SQL DESCRIPTOR descriptor

describe-output
   ::=   DESCRIBE [ OUTPUT ] prepared
                  USING SQL DESCRIPTOR descriptor

get-descriptor-1
   ::=   GET DESCRIPTOR descriptor target = COUNT
```

```
get-descriptor-2
  ::=    GET DESCRIPTOR descriptor
             VALUE number get-assignment-commalist

get-assignment
  ::=    target = item-descriptor-component
```

Note: "Item-descriptor-component" is explained in Chapter 20, Section 20.4.

```
set-descriptor-1
  ::=    SET DESCRIPTOR descriptor COUNT = lit-param-or-var

set-descriptor-2
  ::=    SET DESCRIPTOR descriptor
             VALUE number set-assignment-commalist

set-assignment
  ::=    item-descriptor-component = lit-param-or-var
```

Note: "Item-descriptor-component" is explained in Chapter 20, Section 20.4.

```
dynamic-cursor-def
  ::=    DECLARE cursor [ INSENSITIVE ] [ SCROLL ] CURSOR
         FOR prepared

allocate-cursor
  ::=    ALLOCATE param-or-var [ INSENSITIVE ] [ SCROLL ]
                  CURSOR FOR prepared

dynamic-open
  ::=    OPEN dynamic-cursor [ USING arguments ]

dynamic-cursor
  ::=    cursor | param-or-var

dynamic-close
  ::=    CLOSE dynamic-cursor

dynamic-fetch
  ::=    FETCH [ [ row-selector ] FROM ] dynamic-cursor
                INTO places

dynamic-positioned-delete
  ::=    DELETE [ FROM table ]
         WHERE CURRENT OF dynamic-cursor

dynamic-positioned-update
  ::=    UPDATE [ table ] SET update-assignment-commalist
         WHERE CURRENT OF dynamic-cursor
```

A.10 SCALAR EXPRESSIONS

```
scalar-exp
  ::=    numeric-exp
       | character-string-exp
       | bit-string-exp
       | datetime-exp
       | interval-exp
```

```
numeric-exp
   ::=    numeric-term
      |  numeric-exp { + | - } numeric-term

numeric-term
   ::=    numeric-factor
      |  numeric-term { * | / } numeric-factor

numeric-factor
   ::=    [ + | - ] numeric-primary

numeric-primary
   ::=    column-ref
      |  lit-param-or-var
      |  scalar-function-ref
      |  aggregate-function-ref
      |  ( table-exp )
      |  ( numeric-exp )
```

Note: The parenthesized table expression here (also that under "character string primary," "bit string primary," "datetime primary," and "interval primary," *q.v.*) is actually a scalar subquery.

```
aggregate-function-ref
   ::=    COUNT(*)
      |  { AVG | MAX | MIN | SUM | COUNT }
            ( [ ALL | DISTINCT ] scalar-exp )

character-string-exp
   ::=    character-string-concatenation
      |  character-string-primary

character-string-concatenation
   ::=    character-string-exp || character-string-primary
```

Note: The symbol "‖" here represents the concatenation operator—it should not be confused with the vertical bar "|" that is used to separate alternatives in the grammar.

```
character-string-primary
   ::=    column-ref
      |  lit-param-or-var
      |  authID-function-ref
      |  scalar-function-ref
      |  aggregate-function-ref
      |  ( table-exp )
      |  ( character-string-exp )

bit-string-exp
   ::=    bit-string-concatenation
      |  bit-string-primary

bit-string-concatenation
   ::=    bit-string-exp || bit-string-primary
```

Note: The symbol "‖" here represents the concatenation operator—it should not be confused with the vertical bar "|" that is used to separate alternatives in the ·
grammar.

```
bit-string-primary
    ::=    column-ref
         | lit-param-or-var
         | scalar-function-ref
         | aggregate-function-ref
         | ( table-exp )
         | ( bit-string-exp )

datetime-exp
    ::=    datetime-term
         | interval-exp + datetime-term
         | datetime-exp { + | - } interval-term

datetime-term
    ::=    datetime-primary
                [ AT { LOCAL | TIME ZONE interval-primary } ]

datetime-primary
    ::=    column-ref
         | lit-param-or-var
         | datetime-function-ref
         | scalar-function-ref
         | aggregate-function-ref
         | ( table-exp )
         | ( datetime-exp )

interval-exp
    ::=    interval-term
         | interval-exp { + | - } interval-term
         | ( datetime exp - datetime-term ) start [ TO end ]
```

Note: The values "start" and "end" here are datetime fields. See Chapter 17.

```
interval-term
    ::=    interval-factor
         | interval-term { * | / } numeric-factor
         | numeric-term * interval-factor

interval-factor
    ::=    [ + | - ] interval-primary [ start [ TO end ] ]
```

Note: The values "start" and "end" here are datetime fields, and appear only in the context of certain dynamically prepared SQL Statements. See Chapters 17, 20, and 23.

```
interval-primary
    ::=    column-ref
         | lit-param-or-var
         | scalar-function-ref
         | aggregate-function-ref
         | ( table-exp )
         | ( interval-exp )
```

A.11 GET DIAGNOSTICS

```
get-diagnostics-1
    ::=    GET DIAGNOSTICS diagnostics-1-assignment-commalist
```

Note: "Diagnostics-1-assignment" is explained in Chapter 22, Section 22.2.

```
get-diagnostics-2
   ::=    GET DIAGNOSTICS EXCEPTION number
                       diagnostics-2-assignment-commalist
```

Note: "Diagnostics-2-assignment" is explained in Chapter 22, Section 22.2.

A.12   MISCELLANEOUS

```
schema
   ::=    [ catalog . ] identifier

domain
   ::=    [ schema . ] identifier

table
   ::=    base-table | view

base-table
   ::=    [ schema . ] identifier

view
   ::=    [ schema . ] identifier

constraint
   ::=    [ schema . ] identifier

character-set
   ::=    [ schema . ] identifier

collation
   ::=    [ schema . ] identifier

translation
   ::=    [ schema . ] identifier

conversion
   ::=    [ schema . ] identifier

column-ref
   ::=    [ column-qualifier . ] column

column-qualifier
   ::=    table | range-variable

param-or-var
   ::=    parameter [ [ INDICATOR ] parameter ]
       | host-variable [ [ INDICATOR ] host-variable ]

lit-param-or-var
   ::=    literal | param-or-var

target
   ::=    param-or-var

number
   ::=    lit-param-or-var
```

```
niladic-function-ref
   ::=   authID-function-ref
       | datetime-function-ref

authID-function-ref
   ::=   USER
       | CURRENT_USER
       | SESSION_USER
       | SYSTEM_USER

datetime-function-ref
   ::=   CURRENT_DATE
       | CURRENT_TIME [ ( integer ) ]
       | CURRENT_TIMESTAMP [ ( integer ) ]
```

Language Levels
and Conformance

B.1 INTRODUCTION

The official SQL standard document defines three language *levels*: Full SQL, Intermediate SQL, and Entry SQL. The general idea is that *Full* SQL is the entire standard, *Intermediate* SQL is a proper subset of Full SQL, and *Entry* SQL is a proper subset of Intermediate SQL. The intent is to permit implementations to be staged, so that over time the level of support can progress from Entry to Intermediate to Full SQL (see below). Section B.2 summarizes the major features of Full SQL that are omitted from Intermediate SQL, and Section B.3 summarizes the major features of Intermediate SQL that are additionally omitted from Entry SQL.

The SQL language defined by the standard is said to be *conforming SQL language*. An implementation is said to be a *conforming SQL implementation* if it processes conforming SQL language according to the specifications of the standard. Thus, a conforming SQL implementation must support conforming SQL language to at least Entry level. Such an implementation must also support at least one *binding style* (module, embedded SQL, CLI, or direct), and, except in the case of direct SQL, at least one of the official host languages (Ada, C, COBOL, FORTRAN, MUMPS, Pascal, or PL/I). Furthermore, such an implementation must also provide documented definitions for all features of conforming SQL language that are stated by the standard to be implementation-defined.

Note, however, that a conforming implementation is explicitly permitted:

- To provide support for additional facilities or options not specified at the level of the standard to which conformance is claimed;

- To provide options to process conforming SQL language in a nonconforming manner; and

- To provide options to process nonconforming SQL language.

On the other hand, an implementation that claims conformance to the standard at any level, except possibly Entry level, is also required to provide an *SQL Flagger* option to flag items that do not conform to the specified level. See Section B.4.

Then again, many aspects of the standard are explicitly stated to be "implementation-dependent" (that is, undefined); in fact, certain aspects seem—presumably unintentionally—to be *im*plicitly undefined also (see Appendix D). Even if two implementations can both legitimately claim to be conforming, therefore, there can be no guarantee of application portability between the two.

Note that the standard specifically does not define the method by which an application program containing embedded SQL statements is compiled or otherwise processed. To quote: "Although the processing of [such a program] is defined in terms of derivation of a program compliant with [some] programming language standard and a module [in the module language], implementations of SQL are not constrained to follow that method [of processing such a program], provided [that defined effect] is achieved."

B.2   INTERMEDIATE SQL

In this section we list some of the major differences between Full SQL and Intermediate SQL. Please note that we are *not* aiming at completeness in what follows; the intent is merely to give the reader a general idea of how Full SQL and Intermediate SQL differ. For the specifics, the reader is referred to the standard document *per se*.

First, here is a list of Full SQL constructs that are omitted entirely from Intermediate SQL:

- Identifiers in which the final character is an underscore.
- Hexadecimal literals.
- Explicit catalog names.
- SET CATALOG, SET SCHEMA, SET NAMES.
- CONNECT, SET CONNECTION, DISCONNECT.

- Bit strings.
- Translations, conversions, and (explicit) collations.
- Explicit precision specification for TIMEs and TIMESTAMPs.
- POSITION, UPPER, LOWER.
- CROSS JOIN, UNION JOIN.
- IS [NOT] TRUE, IS [NOT] FALSE, IS [NOT] UNKNOWN.
- MATCH conditions and MATCH in foreign key definitions.
- General constraints (CREATE and DROP ASSERTION).
- Domain or base table constraints that involve a subquery.
- ON UPDATE in foreign key definitions.
- SET CONSTRAINTS.
- Temporary tables.
- Column-specific INSERT privileges.
- LOCAL or CASCADED in check options (though CASCADED must be supported implicitly).
- ALTER DOMAIN.
- INSENSITIVE cursors.
- Table expressions of the form "TABLE table."
- Dynamic SQL descriptor area names specified by means of a parameter or host variable.
- User-generated statement and cursor names.
- DEALLOCATE PREPARE, DESCRIBE INPUT, and (in EXECUTE) INTO "places."

And here is a list of additional restrictions:

- A table reference cannot be a table subquery (i.e., a table expression in parentheses).
- The operator DISTINCT is permitted within a table expression at most once at each level of nesting.
- A row constructor must include exactly one component, *except* in the special case in which the row constructor is a component within a table constructor (in which case it must be the *only* such component) *and* that table constructor is being used to define the source for an INSERT operation.
- The list of comparands on the right hand side of an IN condition must not include any scalar expression more complex than a literal, a column reference, or a reference to a niladic builtin function.

- If the argument expression in an aggregate function reference specifies DISTINCT, then the argument to that DISTINCT must be specified as a simple column reference.

- The REFERENCES privilege is not required for columns referenced in an integrity constraint. *Note:* This is actually the *opposite* of a restriction. It implies that Intermediate SQL is not quite a "proper subset" of Full SQL after all.

- If a cursor definition includes FOR UPDATE, neither SCROLL nor ORDER BY can be specified.

- An INSERT, searched UPDATE, or searched DELETE statement cannot include a WHERE clause that references the table that is the target of that INSERT, UPDATE, or DELETE statement.

B.3   ENTRY SQL

In this section we list some of the additional features of Full SQL that are omitted from Entry SQL, over and above those already omitted from Intermediate SQL. Please note once again, however, that we are *not* aiming at completeness here; the intent again is just to give the general idea.

- Identifiers of more than 18 characters.

- Lower case letters in identifiers.

- SET SESSION AUTHORIZATION.

- Varying length character strings.

- Character string literals that span several lines.

- Implementation-defined character sets, including national character sets.

- Datetimes and intervals.

- Domains.

- Explicit constraint names.

- CURRENT_USER, SESSION_USER, and SYSTEM_USER (USER is supported, however).

- CHARACTER_LENGTH, OCTET_LENGTH.

- SUBSTRING, TRIM.

- Concatenation.

- CASE and CAST.

- DEFAULT in INSERT and UPDATE.

- JOIN.

- EXCEPT and INTERSECT.

- UNION CORRESPONDING.
- The key word AS preceding a range variable in the FROM clause.
- The parenthesized column-commalist following a range variable in the FROM clause.
- Select-items of the form "R.*".
- UNIQUE conditions.
- DROP SCHEMA.
- ALTER and DROP TABLE.
- ON DELETE in foreign key definitions.
- DROP VIEW.
- REVOKE.
- SET TRANSACTION.
- Dynamic SQL.
- SCROLL cursors.
- FOR UPDATE on a cursor definition.
- Conversion between exact and approximate numeric on assignment.
- Information Schemas.
- GET DIAGNOSTICS.
- Host language MUMPS.

And here is a list of additional restrictions:

- A cursor or view whose definition involves a subquery is not SQL-updatable.
- A view definition cannot include UNION. (By contrast, a cursor definition apparently can.)
- A subquery cannot include UNION.
- The argument expression in a COUNT reference must specify DISTINCT.
- If the FROM clause in a select-expression references a view whose definition involves a GROUP BY or HAVING clause, then:
  a. That FROM clause must not mention any other tables.
  b. That select-expression cannot include a WHERE, GROUP BY, or HAVING clause.
  c. The SELECT clause in that select-expression must not include any aggregate function references.
- A single-row SELECT statement cannot include a GROUP BY or HAVING clause and cannot reference a view whose definition involves a GROUP BY or HAVING clause.

- If either comparand of a comparison condition is a select-expression in parentheses, that select-expression must not contain a GROUP BY or HAVING clause and must not reference a view whose definition contains a GROUP BY or HAVING clause.

- For UNION, the data types of corresponding columns must be *exactly* the same (and NOT NULL must apply to both or to neither). Note that this rule implies that, e.g., data types CHAR(3) and CHAR(4) are not compatible for the purposes of UNION in Entry SQL.

- In a LIKE condition, the first operand must be a column reference and "pattern" and "escape" must each be a literal, parameter, or host variable.

- In a test for null, the operand must be a column reference.

- CREATE SCHEMA must include an AUTHORIZATION clause and must not include a schema name.

- A module definition must include an AUTHORIZATION clause and must not include a SCHEMA clause.

- Every column mentioned in a candidate key definition must be explicitly defined to be NOT NULL.

- The key word TABLE must not appear in GRANT.

- COMMIT and ROLLBACK must include the noiseword WORK.

For a brief note on what is left in Entry SQL after all of the foregoing omissions, see Appendix C, Section C.2, subsection "A Note on Entry SQL."

B.4   SQL FLAGGER

As mentioned in Section B.1, an implementation that claims conformance to the standard at any level, except possibly Entry level, is required to provide an *SQL Flagger*. The purpose of the Flagger is to flag any implementation-specific SQL constructs—i.e., SQL constructs that are recognized and supported by the implementation but do not conform to the level of the standard to which conformance is claimed. The intent is to identify SQL features that might produce different results in different environments—i.e., features that might require attention if applications or SQL requests are moved from one environment to another. Such considerations might be relevant, for example, if an application is developed on a workstation for execution on a mainframe.

An implementation that claims *Full SQL* conformance must provide an SQL Flagger that supports the following options:

- *Entry SQL flagging* (i.e., an option to flag SQL constructs that do not conform to Entry SQL);

- *Intermediate SQL flagging* (i.e., an option to flag SQL constructs that do not conform to Intermediate SQL);

- *Full SQL flagging* (i.e., an option to flag SQL constructs that do not conform to Full SQL).

It must also support both "syntax only" and "catalog lookup" checking options. "Syntax only" checking means that the implementation is required only to perform those checks that are possible without access to the Definition Schema (see Chapter 21). "Catalog lookup" checking means that the implementation is additionally required to perform those checks (except privilege checks) that are possible if the Definition Schema is available. *Note:* In both cases, the intent is that the checking be "static" (i.e., "compilation time") checking only; there is no requirement for the Flagger to check for deviations that cannot be determined until execution time.

An implementation that claims *Intermediate SQL* conformance must provide an SQL Flagger that supports Entry SQL and Intermediate SQL flagging, and must support at least "syntax only" checking.

An implementation that claims *Entry SQL* conformance can optionally provide an SQL Flagger that supports at least "syntax only" Entry SQL flagging.

SQL/92 vs. SQL/89

C.1 INTRODUCTION

For the benefit of readers who might be familiar with the previous version of the standard, *viz.* "SQL/89," we present in this appendix a brief summary of the major differences between that version and the current standard, *viz.* "SQL/92." Section C.2 lists the major extensions—i.e., features of SQL/92 that had no counterpart in SQL/89. Section C.3 describes all known incompatibilities between the two versions (ignoring previously known incompatibilities between Level 1 and Level 2 of SQL/89). Finally, Section C.4 gives a list of "deprecated features" (officially so designated) of SQL/92.

C.2 EXTENSIONS

In this section we summarize the major new features introduced in SQL/92.

- Everything to do with the Call-Level Interface.
- Everything to do with embedded SQL. *Note:* Embedded SQL was the subject of a separate ANSI standard, "Database Language Embedded SQL," but was never part of SQL/89 *per se*, nor was it an ISO standard. Furthermore, that separate ANSI standard did not include MUMPS support, and SQL/89 did not include Ada or C support either.

- Everything to do with catalogs, and almost everything to do with schemas. SQL/89 did have a statement called CREATE SCHEMA—but no DROP SCHEMA!—and all CREATE TABLEs, CREATE VIEWs, and GRANTs had to be specified as "schema elements" within such a CREATE SCHEMA statement (i.e., there was no concept of executing such statements independently, as there is in SQL/92). However, the schema concept *per se* was essentially undefined. Note too that CREATE TABLE, CREATE VIEW, and GRANT were the *only* data definition operations in SQL/89; DROP TABLE, ALTER TABLE, etc., did not exist.

- The ability to include all kinds of SQL statements within a module. As already mentioned, CREATE TABLE, CREATE VIEW, and GRANT had to be executed as components of a CREATE SCHEMA operation in SQL/89; in fact, CREATE SCHEMA, CREATE TABLE, CREATE VIEW, and GRANT together constituted a separate "schema language" that was quite distinct from the "module language." That undesirable and unnecessary distinction between schema language and module language has been (almost) eliminated in SQL/92.

- The ability to include all kinds of SQL operations—in particular, the ability to mix data definition and data manipulation operations—in a single transaction. Because of the separation between schema and module languages mentioned in the previous paragraph, SQL/89 did not have this capability.

- Everything to do with SQL-connections and SQL-sessions.

- The SET TRANSACTION statement, including in particular the ability to specify an isolation level (SQL/89 supported SERIALIZABLE only, and that only implicitly).

- Everything to do with domains, including CREATE, ALTER, and DROP DOMAIN.

- ALTER and DROP TABLE.

- Everything to do with temporary tables.

- CASCADED and LOCAL variants of the check option on CREATE VIEW.

- DROP VIEW.

- Almost everything to do with integrity constraints, except for candidate key and foreign key definitions and one simple form of base table check constraint. SQL/89 did have candidate keys and foreign keys, and it did have single-row check constraints (i.e., constraints that could be tested for a given row by examining just that row in isolation). However, it did not have general (multi-row) constraints, it did not have FULL *vs.* PARTIAL matching on foreign keys, it did not have any explicit referential actions, and it did not have any deferred checking (DEFERRABLE, INITIALLY DEFERRED, SET CONSTRAINTS, etc.).

- REVOKE.

- Varying length character strings.

- Bit strings, both fixed and varying length.

- Everything to do with dates and times.

- Almost everything to do with character sets, collations, translations, and conversions (including national character set support and character sets for identifiers). SQL/89 did support a fixed-length character string data type, together with an associated set of assignment and comparison rules and operators, but that was about all; in particular, the character set and collating sequence were essentially implementation-defined.

- All scalar operators and functions (except "+", "−", "*", "/", and USER), including in particular the CASE operator, and CAST for controlling data type conversions.

- Greatly improved orthogonality in scalar expressions, including in particular the ability to use scalar values from the database as operands within such an expression. (See the subsection "A Note on Orthogonality" at the end of this section for a brief explanation of the concept of orthogonality.)

- The FOR UPDATE, SCROLL, and INSENSITIVE specifications on DECLARE CURSOR.

- Greatly improved orthogonality in table expressions, including (a) the ability to introduce result column names and table names, (b) a set of column name inheritance rules for derived tables, and (c) the ability to nest table expressions.

- Explicit support for INTERSECT, EXCEPT, and JOIN (including natural join and outer join).

- Row constructors, including in particular the ability to use such constructors in conditional expressions.

- New MATCH and UNIQUE conditions.

- New IS [NOT] TRUE, IS [NOT] FALSE, and IS [NOT] UNKNOWN conditions.

- Everything to do with dynamic SQL.

- Information Schemas.

- SQLSTATE and everything to do with the diagnostics area.

- A more comprehensive treatment of direct SQL (though many of the specifics are still implementation-defined).

A Note on Entry SQL

It is worth pointing out that most of the foregoing list of extensions do *not* apply to Entry SQL (see Appendix B). Basically, the only functionality that Entry SQL provides over SQL/89 is the following:

- Support for Ada and C.
- The parenthesized commalist form of specification for parameters to a procedure.
- SQLSTATE.
- The AS clause on a select-item.
- Delimited identifiers.

A Note on Orthogonality

Orthogonality means *independence*. A language is orthogonal if independent concepts are kept independent and not mixed together in confusing ways. An example of *lack* of orthogonality in SQL/89 was provided by the rule that a scalar value in an INSERT statement had to be represented by a simple variable or literal, not by an arbitrary scalar expression (this restriction is eliminated in SQL/92). Orthogonality is desirable because the less orthogonal a language is, the more complicated it is and—paradoxically but simultaneously—the less powerful it is. "Orthogonal design maximizes expressive power while avoiding deleterious superfluities" (from A. van Wijngaarden *et al.*, eds., *Revised Report on the Algorithmic Language Algol 68,* Springer-Verlag, 1976).

C.3   INCOMPATIBILITIES

The SQL/92 document includes an "annex" (i.e., appendix) identifying a number of incompatibilities between SQL/92 and SQL/89. We list those incompatibilities below. *Note:* It is not always clear exactly what it is that constitutes an incompatibility; in some respects the concept is rather elusive. For example, consider the specification PRIMARY KEY, which implies NOT NULL in SQL/92 but not in SQL/89. There is clearly an incompatibility here of a kind. However, SQL/89 had an additional rule to the effect that every column mentioned in a PRIMARY KEY specification must be *explicitly defined* to be NOT NULL; hence a program that did not produce an error in this area in SQL/89 will also not produce an error in this area in SQL/92, and so the incompatibility is presumably unimportant. On the other hand, of course, a program that was deliberately intended to produce some specific error in SQL/89 might fail to do so in SQL/92.

Here anyway are the incompatibilities identified in the SQL/92 specification:

■ First, SQL/92 has well over 100 additional reserved words. For specifics, the reader is referred to the standard document.

■ In SQL/89, the implied module for embedded SQL had an implementation-defined authID; in SQL/92, it has no authID at all.

■ Parameter names did not have a colon prefix in SQL/89. Such a prefix is required in SQL/92.

■ SQL/89 allowed two distinct candidate key definitions for the same base table to specify the same set of columns. SQL/92 does not.

■ In SQL/89, the only legal SQLCODE values were 0, +100, and implementation-defined negative integers (these latter indicating a catastrophic error). SQL/92 additionally permits implementation-defined positive integers (to indicate warning conditions).

■ SQL/89 did not preclude the possibility of defining a view recursively, i.e., in terms of itself. SQL/92 does preclude such a possibility.

■ The semantics of WITH CHECK OPTION were ambiguous in SQL/89 but have been clarified in SQL/92. (At least, this is what the SQL/92 document claims. It would be more accurate to say that the check option was not inheritable in SQL/89 but is so in SQL/92—i.e., if view *V2* is defined on top of view *V1*, where *V2* and *V1* are both SQL-updatable and *V1* has the check option, then updates on *V2* are ALWAYS checked against the view-defining condition for *V1* in SQL/92 but were not necessarily so in SQL/89. In other words, this change is truly an incompatibility, not just a "clarification." See the discussion of LOCAL and CASCADED in Chapter 13.)

■ Let cursor *C* be declared without an ORDER BY clause, and let cursor *C* be opened several times within the same SQL-transaction. In SQL/89, the rows accessed by cursor *C* had to be returned in the same order on each opening. In SQL/92, the order is implementation-dependent on each opening, and thus can differ from one opening to the next.

    Note: A similar remark presumably applies if ORDER BY *is* specified but does not define a total ordering for the rows (see Chapter 10), but the SQL/92 standard does not explicitly say as much.

■ In SQL/89, if a cursor is on or before some row and that row is deleted, the cursor is positioned before the next row or (if there is no next row) after the last row. In SQL/92, this cursor state change is defined only if the DELETE is done via the cursor in question; otherwise the effect on the cursor is implementation-dependent. See Appendix D for further discussion of this question.

■ In SQL/89, integrity constraints were permitted to include references to the niladic builtin function USER. In SQL/92 they are not.

- In SQL/89, the SELECT privilege was required only for tables accessed via FETCH or single-row SELECT statements. In SQL/92, it is additionally required for tables mentioned in certain table expressions, conditional expressions, and scalar expressions.

- Finally, the SQL/92 document identifies one additional known incompatibility, which (as with a couple of other aspects of the standard—see, e.g., the explanation of CREATE TEMPORARY TABLE in Chapter 18) we cannot do better than describe in a slight paraphrase of the standard's own words:*

  "[SQL/89] did not preclude the possibility of using outer references in <set function specification>s in <subquery>s contained in the <search condition> of a <having clause>, but did not define the semantics of such a construction. [SQL/92] adds a Syntax Rule in [the definition of] <set function specification> and a Syntax Rule in [the definition of] <where clause> to preclude that possibility."

  Note: The term "<set function specification>" corresponds to what we have been calling an aggregate function reference in this book.

  The Syntax Rules referred to are as follows. First, in the definition of <set function specification> we find the following:

  "If the [argument expression] contains a <column reference> that is an outer reference, then that outer reference shall be the only <column reference> contained in the [argument expression] ... [and] ... the <set function specification> shall be contained in either:

  "(a) a <select list>, or

  "(b) a <subquery> of a <having clause>, in which case the scope of the explicit or implicit <qualifier> of the <column reference> shall be a <table reference> that is directly contained in the [select-expression] that directly contains the <having clause>."

  And in the definition of <where clause> we find:

  "If a [scalar-expression] directly contained in the <search condition> is a <set function specification>, then the <where clause> shall be contained in a <having clause> or <select list> and the <column reference> in the <set function specification> shall be an outer reference ... No <column reference> contained in a <subquery> in the <search condition> that references a column of *T* shall be specified in a <set function specification>." (*T* here refers to the table that results from evaluation of the FROM clause immediately preceding the WHERE clause in question.)

  Note: The term "<select list>" corresponds to what we have been calling a select-item-commalist in this book.

---

*Though we did make an attempt at a better description in Chapter 7, Section 7.5. See paragraph number 8 following the definition of the syntax of "aggregate function reference" in that section.

The foregoing is intended to be an exhaustive list; to quote the SQL/92 document, "unless specified in this Annex, features and capabilities of [SQL/92] are compatible with [those of SQL/89]." However, there seem to be a few additional areas where SQL/92 and SQL/89 are in some disagreement:

- As mentioned in Section C.2, SQL/89 consisted of two distinct languages, a module language and a schema language (more precisely, a schema *definition* language). CREATE TABLE, CREATE VIEW, and GRANT statements could appear only as elements within a CREATE SCHEMA statement, and that statement in turn was a schema definition language statement; thus, CREATE SCHEMA (and hence CREATE TABLE, CREATE VIEW, and GRANT, *a fortiori*) could *not* appear within a module. In what seems to be an attempt to remain compatible with this rather curious state of affairs, SQL/92 does refer repeatedly to the idea that a CREATE SCHEMA statement might be "standalone," i.e., not included within a module; however, there does not seem to be any way that such a possibility can occur (as explained in Chapter 6, there is *always* a module, at least implicitly).

- In SQL/89, the REFERENCES privilege was required only for candidate keys that were referenced by some foreign key. In SQL/92, it is required for every column that is mentioned in some integrity constraint.

- SQL/89 permitted qualified column names in the ORDER BY clause. SQL/92 does not. *Note:* This change is perhaps better regarded as a correction rather than an incompatibility. Qualified column names in ORDER BY were a mistake in SQL/89, since the scope of the relevant range variable did not include (or, at least, should not have included) the ORDER BY clause.

- In SQL/92 USER returns the current authID, not a schema or module authID. In SQL/89 it returned the module authID.
  Note: This is certainly a definitional change, but perhaps it should not be regarded as an incompatibility *per se* (i.e., it should not cause an SQL/89 program to fail under SQL/92, thanks to SQL/92's system of defaults).

- In SQL/89, the high-level qualifier for (e.g.) base table names was an authID. In SQL/92 it is a schema name, which in turn includes a possibly implicit catalog name as another (next higher level) qualifier.
  Note: Like the previous point, this is certainly a definitional change, but perhaps it should not be regarded as an incompatibility *per se*.

C.4   DEPRECATED FEATURES

The SQL/92 document also includes an annex identifying "deprecated features"— i.e., features that are retained in SQL/92 only for compatibility with SQL/89 and are likely to be dropped in some future version of the standard. We list those features below.

- SQLCODE (SQLSTATE is preferred). Consequently, a COBOL integer variable defined as USAGE IS COMPUTATIONAL is also deprecated, since this USAGE is supported only for SQLCODE.

- Unsigned integers as order-items within an ORDER BY clause (the use of column names, perhaps introduced via an AS clause on the relevant select-items, is preferred).

- Unparenthesized lists of parameter definitions in procedures (parenthesized commalists are preferred).

Some Outstanding Issues

If you're not confused by all this,
it just proves you're not thinking clearly (anon).

D.1   INTRODUCTION

As mentioned in the preface to this book, there are many aspects of the standard that seem to be inadequately defined, or even incorrectly defined, at this time. Despite the fact that it has been formally ratified, therefore, it is likely that a number of formal follow-up documents will be needed to clarify and elaborate on various specific aspects of the standard over the next few years. In this appendix, therefore, we identify and comment on a variety of features that seemed to the present authors, during the writing of this book, to be insufficiently or incorrectly specified—in other words, features that constitute outstanding or unresolved issues. It is our hope that such a list of issues will serve two broad purposes:

- For *implementers*, it should serve to pinpoint aspects of the standard that (at the very least) deserve further study, and perhaps omission from a first product release in some cases.

- For *users*, it should serve as a checklist of features that should be used with some circumspection, or perhaps even avoided for the time being.

Note: Since the previous edition of this book, two follow-up documents, *SQL Technical Corrigendum 1* and *SQL Technical Corrigendum 2*, have in fact appeared (see Appendix G). A few words regarding those two documents are appropriate here.

- The original SQL/92 specification consisted of some 624 pages (16 introductory pages, 28 pages of index, and 580 pages in the body of the document *per se*). The corrigenda affect very nearly every third page of that original!—actually 190 pages out of the 580 in the body. And some of the changes are quite extensive. The definition of REVOKE, for example, originally involved 18 syntax rules and nine general rules. Six of those 18 syntax rules have now been revised, and eight new ones have been added; in addition, four of those nine general rules have now been revised, and one new one has been added.

- The corrigenda themselves have clear errors in them (albeit minor ones, for the most part). For example, Information Schema tables are referred to fairly consistently without underscores in their names (e.g., DOMAIN CONSTRAINTS instead of DOMAIN_CONSTRAINTS).

- They often give the rationale for a revision as "editorial" or "clarification" when "correction" would be more honest. For example, one "editorial" change replaces the expression $L/(B + 1)$ by the expression $(L/B) + 1$. Indeed, they sometimes radically change the semantics of some construct; for instance, the definition—the *semantic* definition, that is—of the check option for SQL-updatable views is now quite different from that originally given in the SQL/92 standard *per se*.

- Most important of all, they fail to correct most of the problems identified in this appendix in the previous edition of this book. Thus, most of the issues identified in that previous edition remain unresolved at the time of writing.*

A couple of further preliminary remarks:

1. In the interests of brevity, we concentrate on issues over which there might genuinely be some confusion, ignoring items that are wrong only in some trivially obvious way. For example, the standard states that "[A scalar] value is primitive in that it has no logical subdivision within this [standard]." Now, this statement is clearly incorrect in the case of datetime and interval values, and arguably in the case of other scalar values also, such as strings; however, the error is not very significant, and is thus scarcely worth discussing further. The standard contains literally dozens of such "trivially" incorrect statements, and there is just no point in trying to deal with them all here.

---

*In this connection, it is worth mentioning that *SQL Technical Corrigendum 3* is currently in production. This document—which is already bigger than the entire first version of the standard!—is likely to be published sometime around the middle of 1997.

2. Since it looks as if the standard is necessarily going to be the subject of a continual revision and clarification process for some time to come, it is possible that some of the remarks in this appendix might no longer be valid by the time this book appears in print, or by the time it reaches the reader's hands. Also, of course, it is possible that we might have misconstrued the standard in the first place and that some of our remarks might therefore be incorrect. If so, we apologize.

Hugh Darwen adds a personal statement: In endorsing this list of criticisms, which I have carefully reviewed, I find myself in a rather strange and possibly embarrassing position, for I have been, since 1988, an active and contributing member of the ISO committee responsible for the SQL standard. Personally, I lay most of the blame for the following problems (if problems they be) firmly on SQL itself. If the world needs a better database standard, it should prepare itself to move to a better database *language*.

D.2   THE ISSUES

In this section we present the list of issues, in a sequence that approximates the sequence in which the relevant topics were first discussed in the body of the text (although the assignment of issues to categories is sometimes a little arbitrary). Some of the points, and some of the commentary thereon, are essentially just a repetition of material from the main part of the book; other items are new.

Basic Terminology

■   In Chapter 1 we introduced the important terms "implementation-defined" and "implementation-dependent." Here are the standard's definitions of these terms:

a. *Implementation-defined:* Possibly differing between SQL-implementations, but specified . . . for each particular SQL-implementation.

b. *Implementation-dependent:* Possibly differing between SQL-implementations, but not specified by this International Standard and not required to be specified . . . for any particular SQL-implementation.

The trouble with these definitions is that they effectively confuse the notions of an *implementation* as such and an implementation *instance* (or DBMS and DBMS instance, to make matters more concrete). For example, the maximum length of a character string and the default SQL-server are both stated by the standard to be implementation-defined. However, the former will surely be the same for all instances of a given implementation, while the latter will vary from one instance of a given implementation to another. National character sets and default time zones are other important examples of "implementation-defined" constructs that will clearly vary from instance to instance, in general.

Basic Language Elements

- According to the standard, "&" (ampersand) is an SQL special character, while "[" and "]" (left and right bracket) are SQL embedded language characters. This slight discrepancy is a trifle mysterious, given that the only use within SQL* for all three characters is in embedded SQL programs (ampersand in MUMPS, and left and right bracket in Pascal and C).

- The rule by which it is determined within the standard that one key word is reserved while another is not is unclear.

- We pointed out in Chapter 19, Section 19.8, that, although the standard does avoid the possible need for an infinite *sequence* of identifier "introducers" (i.e., character set name prefixes such as _FRANCAIS), it does not avoid the possible need for an infinite *nest* of them.

Catalogs and Schemas

- We stated in Chapter 3 that catalog names are supposed to be unique within the environment. Actually the standard says only that catalog names must be unique within their containing *cluster*. On the other hand, catalog names have no high-level "cluster name" qualifier, and in any case clusters have no names!—or, at best, have names that are implementation-defined. It looks very much as if the cluster notion was grafted on to the standard at a late stage in its development and was never properly integrated with other features. Indeed, it is really not clear why the concept is present at all; there is just one reference to it in the body of the standard, in the form of a sentence stating that "an instance of a Definition Schema describes an instance of a cluster of catalogs" (a sentence that manages to include two further undefined notions, "Definition Schema instance" and "cluster instance"!).

- As mentioned in Appendix C and elsewhere, the standard refers repeatedly to the idea that a CREATE SCHEMA statement might be "standalone," i.e., not included within a module, yet there does not seem to be any way that such a possibility can occur (there is *always* supposed to be a module, at least implicitly).

- As explained in Chapter 4, the elements within a single CREATE SCHEMA operation must somehow be thought of as all being executed simultaneously.

---

*The ampersand is also used in arguments to CLI calls, but CLI calls are not part of the SQL language *per se.*

In particular, therefore, it must be possible for (e.g.) two CREATE TABLE operations within a single CREATE SCHEMA operation each to include a foreign key definition that references the other. The full implications of such circular references and such simultaneity of execution are not clear.

■ A specific instance of the foregoing arises in connection with CREATE CHARACTER SET and CREATE COLLATION (see Chapter 19). Consider the following:

```
CREATE CHARACTER SET CHARSET1 AS
       GET ...
       COLLATE COLL1

CREATE COLLATION COLL1
       FOR CHARSET1
       FROM ...
```

Since every character set has one default collation and every collation has one associated character set, some circularity of reference is unavoidable. Thus, it appears that the two CREATEs above cannot possibly be executed independently but *must* be included within a CREATE SCHEMA operation (in fact, within the *same* CREATE SCHEMA operation).

Connections, Sessions, and Transactions

■ There seems to be a considerable amount of confusion over the "SQL-environment" and "SQL-implementation" concepts. First, an SQL-environment is defined to consist of an SQL-implementation (and the indefinite article *an* here strongly suggests the interpretation *exactly one*), together with certain catalogs, modules, data, and authIDs. An SQL-implementation, in turn, is defined to be a database management system (DBMS) that conforms to the standard.* So far, therefore, we would seem to be justified in thinking of the SQL-environment concept as essentially just an abstraction of the notion of an operational DBMS instance at a single computer site.

Following on from the foregoing, it would seem reasonable to regard a system that supports some form of multi-site or distributed processing as one that involves several SQL-environments, and hence several SQL-implementations, that are somehow capable of communication with one another.

However, the standard goes on to say: "As perceived by an SQL-agent, an SQL-implementation consists of one or more SQL-servers and one SQL-client through which SQL-connections can be made to the SQL-servers." So if the SQL-client and SQL-servers are at different sites, then the SQL-implementation spans all of those sites, and so therefore does the SQL-environment. Yet each of those SQL-servers surely corresponds to what

---

*This definition appeared in the original SQL/92 standard but was deleted by Technical Corrigendum 1 on the grounds that it was "unnecessary" (?).

is usually thought of as a single DBMS (i.e., single DBMS *instance*). So now it looks as if a single SQL-environment, and a single SQL-implementation, can include any number of DBMS instances and can span any number of sites.

Note that the distinction between these two interpretations (one site *vs.* many per environment and implementation) is certainly significant, given that catalog names, authIDs, and module names are all required to be "unique within the SQL-environment." This requirement might be quite difficult to satisfy if the "many sites per environment" interpretation is indeed the correct one.

Of course, it is easy to speculate as to the source of the foregoing confusion. It seems to this writer extremely likely that the historical development of the concepts went somewhat as follows:

a. Originally the "environment" idea was indeed supposed to be an abstraction of a single-site system.

b. However, somebody pointed out that, increasingly, real systems were beginning to support various kinds of distributed processing (especially client/server processing).

c. The environment notion was therefore extended to include the client and server concepts; i.e., "environment" was redefined to include a *client*, together with one or more servers that were at least conceptually distinct from the client and from one another.

d. In order to support this change, the definition of the CONNECT operation was revised to say that a connection was established to a *server*, instead of to an *environment*. (An analogous revision was made to SET CONNECTION also.) *Note:* These particular revisions certainly did occur, as the historical record shows.

e. At the time of the foregoing revisions, the point was overlooked that (as stated above) authIDs, catalog names, and module names were defined to be unique within the *environment*, not (e.g.) within the *server*.

■ *(This point follows on from the previous one:)* If a single SQL-implementation can truly span many servers, the possibility arises that those servers might come from different implementers (i.e., different DBMS vendors). If such is the case, the concepts "implementation-dependent" and (more importantly) "implementation-defined" become very suspect indeed.

■ The session context information does not include any identification of the relevant cluster, though logically it should (because, to quote the standard, "exactly one cluster is associated with [each] SQL-session"). Perhaps this fact can be seen as further evidence that the cluster concept should not have been part of the standard in the first place.

■ The session context information includes the "current" authID but not the "session" authID. Surely it should include both.

- As explained in Chapter 5, a single SQL-transaction is optionally allowed to span several SQL-servers, and hence to span multiple *sessions* also (so the relationship between transactions and sessions is many-to-many, in general). This state of affairs does not fit well with the usual intuitive interpretation of the terms "transaction" and "session," according to which a given transaction would execute entirely within a single session (but could establish any number of *connections* to servers). But the standard states quite explicitly that "an SQL-session is associated with an SQL-connection" and that "an SQL-session involves an SQL-agent, an SQL-client, and an SQL-server." In other words, *one* session has *one* corresponding connection, not many.

- Indeed, there is a one-to-one lockstep relationship between sessions and connections: One session has one corresponding connection, one connection has one corresponding session. This fact strongly suggests that one of the two concepts could be deleted without significant loss.

- The optional support for multi-server transactions really does seem to have been added at a late stage in the development of the standard. Whether or not such was the case, it is certain that some implications of that support were not fully thought through. For example, COMMIT and ROLLBACK should probably make all active SQL-connections inactive, but the standard does not say as much. As another example, the constraint modes *immediate* and *deferred* are defined with respect to a given transaction, but they ought to be defined with respect to *a given session within* a given transaction. Likewise, the initial mode of a given constraint is defined to be the mode that applies at the start of every transaction, but it ought to be the mode that applies at the start of *every session within* every transaction. *Note:* The SET CONSTRAINTS statement, by contrast, is correctly defined in the standard to be "session-local" rather than "transaction-wide".*

- The standard provides a variety of "SET" statements—SET CONNECTION, SET CATALOG, SET SCHEMA, SET SESSION AUTHORIZATION, SET TIME ZONE, and SET NAMES—each of which can be regarded as assigning a value to one or more hidden "system variables" (e.g., a system variable containing the name of the default catalog for the SQL-session, in the case of SET CATALOG). With one exception, however, the standard does not provide any way of discovering the current value of any of those system variables (the exception is SESSION AUTHORIZATION, whose value is returned by the niladic builtin function SESSION_USER). Note in particular that there is no CURRENT_TIMEZONE function (such a function might have been

---

*Precisely because of this fact, we pointed out in the previous edition of this book that COMMIT should cause an implicit SET CONSTRAINTS ALL IMMEDIATE *for every active session,* not just for the current session as the standard stated at that time. This problem was corrected by Technical Corrigendum 1.

expected, given that the standard does provide CURRENT_DATE, CURRENT_TIME, and CURRENT_TIMESTAMP functions). *Note:* The value of the "current time zone" system variable can be *referenced*, however, via the AT LOCAL option in a datetime expression. Likewise, the "current connection" system variable can be referenced via the CURRENT option on DISCONNECT.

- SET TRANSACTION is defined to be "transaction wide," yet the values established by that statement (isolation level, diagnostics area size, and READ ONLY *vs.* READ WRITE) are defined to be part of the *session* context information—suggesting that (e.g.) a multi-session transaction might have different isolation levels in different sessions (and hence at different servers).

- The standard fails to prohibit *dirty write* (defined as the possibility that two transactions *T1* and *T2* might both perform an update on the same row before either transaction terminates).

- The standard tends to suggest, but never quite states explicitly, that isolation level READ UNCOMMITTED guarantees that no concurrent transaction will be permitted to UPDATE or DELETE a row to which the READ UNCOMMITTED transaction has addressability (i.e., a row the READ UNCOMMITTED transaction has a cursor positioned on). To put it another way, it is not clear exactly what READ UNCOMMITTED does guarantee.

- The specification READ ONLY on SET TRANSACTION prohibits updates to tables (other than temporary tables). The standard does not say whether it prohibits "SQL schema statements," which imply updates to *schemas* (and catalogs)—to Information Schemas in particular, which are explicitly defined to consist of tables (actually views).

- The standard ought probably to say (but does not) that if a transaction is initiated for which no corresponding SET TRANSACTION has been performed, the effect is as if such a SET TRANSACTION *had* been performed with all options set to their default value.

- The standard never seems to state explicitly that changes made by a given SQL-transaction *T1* do not become visible to any distinct transaction (other than a READ UNCOMMITTED transaction) *T2* until and unless transaction *T1* terminates successfully (i.e., "with commit").

Binding Styles

- The standard contradicts itself on the question of whether or not DECLARE CURSOR and DECLARE TEMPORARY TABLE are SQL data statements.

- We stated in the body of the text that there is always a module, at least conceptually, but the standard does not seem to say as much explicitly in the case of direct SQL. Presumably the module *ought* to be the "SQL-session module" in this case, but, to repeat, the standard does not say (it does say that the current authID for direct SQL is the session authID, however).

- Let *p* be a parameter, other than SQLCODE or SQLSTATE, to procedure *P*. Then according to the standard:

    a. The presence within *P* of a statement that assigns a value to *p* means that *p* is an *output parameter*;

    b. The presence within *P* of an expression that includes a reference to the value of *p* means that *p* is an *input parameter*;

    c. The presence of both means that *p* is both an input parameter and an output parameter; and

    d. The presence of neither means that *p* is neither an input parameter nor an output parameter.

    The standard thus defines the strange concept of a parameter that is neither input nor output. The point of such a concept is unclear to this writer (certainly the standard makes no use of it or further reference to it).

Scalar Objects, Operators, and Expressions

- The standard states that "a numeric data type descriptor contains ... the name of the specific numeric data type (NUMERIC, DECIMAL, INTEGER, SMALLINT, FLOAT, REAL, or DOUBLE PRECISION)"—implying among other things that it is not quite accurate to say that REAL and DOUBLE PRECISION are just shorthands for FLOAT with a specific precision. The full implications of this point are unclear.

- The rules given in Chapter 7 regarding bit string assignment were really no more than an educated guess on the part of the writers. This is what the standard has to say on the subject: "Assignment of a bit string to a bit string variable is performed from the most significant bit to the least significant bit in the source string to the most significant bit in the target string, one bit at a time."

Domains and Base Tables

- The reader is cautioned that the behavior of the different varieties of DROP is very inconsistent. In particular, DROP SCHEMA, DROP DOMAIN, DROP TABLE, DROP CHARACTER SET, DROP COLLATION, and DROP TRANSLATION all behave differently with respect to their CASCADE effects (or lack of same). Refer to the body of the book for the specifics.

Noncursor Operations

- It is not clear why a single-row SELECT statement *is* in fact basically a select-expression and not a general table expression—i.e., is not allowed to involve any JOIN, UNION, INTERSECT, or EXCEPT operators (at the outermost level). The rule is particularly strange, given that "SELECT ... FROM *T*," where *T* in turn is an arbitrarily complex table expression (possibly involving JOIN, etc.) enclosed in parentheses, *is* a legal single-row SELECT, at least syntactically.

Cursor Operations

- The standard requires the *n* in "ABSOLUTE *n*" or "RELATIVE *n*" (within a FETCH statement) to be a literal, parameter, or host variable, not a general numeric expression. It is not clear why this should be so.

- The standard says that UPDATE CURRENT cannot be used on column *C* if column *C* was mentioned in the ORDER BY clause for the relevant cursor. Why is there not a syntax rule for DECLARE CURSOR that says that no column mentioned in the ORDER BY clause can be explicitly mentioned in the FOR UPDATE clause? And why is not FOR UPDATE without a column-commalist defined to be shorthand for a FOR UPDATE clause with a column-commalist that specifies all and only those columns not mentioned in the ORDER BY clause?

- It is not clear why the SCROLL option is provided. For suppose cursors *A* and *B* have identical definitions, except that *A* has the SCROLL option and *B* does not. Then *A* provides all of the functionality of *B* and more besides. So what is the point of *not* specifying SCROLL?

  Note: Some possible answers—none of them very good!—to the question of why SCROLL is supported are as follows:

  a. It provides a differentiation between Intermediate SQL and Entry SQL (SCROLL is included in Intermediate SQL but not Entry SQL).

  b. It helps in performance (if SCROLL is *not* stated for a given cursor, the implementation knows that certain operations will never be requested against that cursor, and hence might be able to avoid certain overheads in operations involving that cursor).

  c. It provides compatibility with SQL/89, which did not include the SCROLL option—but this objective could be met by making SCROLL the default (at the same time dropping the rule that SCROLL implies FOR READ ONLY in the absence of an explicit FOR UPDATE specification).

- Consider the following example, which is based (as usual) on the suppliers-and-parts database.

```
DECLARE X CURSOR
   FOR SELECT SP.SNO, SP.QTY
       FROM   SP
```

Note that (a) "cursor X is updatable"; (b) the table that is accessible via cursor X permits duplicate rows; (c) the underlying table (table SP) does *not* permit duplicate rows. Now suppose that a positioned UPDATE or DELETE operation is executed on cursor X (UPDATE or DELETE ... WHERE CURRENT OF X). Then there is no way, in general, to say precisely which row of table SP is being updated or deleted by that operation.

■   The standard states that if a cursor C is on some row and that row is deleted via a DELETE ... WHERE CURRENT OF C, then cursor C is positioned before the next row or (if there is no next row) after the last row. But as we pointed out in Chapter 10:

a. Updates via some distinct cursor, also updates that do not use a cursor at all, have similar potential for changing cursor state and positioning in a "side effect" kind of way.

b. However, all the standard has to say on this possibility is that if the row that is the target of some UPDATE or DELETE ... WHERE CURRENT OF C has been subjected to such a side effect,* then a warning is raised, but the UPDATE or DELETE ... WHERE CURRENT completes execution in the usual way.

c. Further, the standard is not explicit regarding exactly which updates can have such a side effect.

Here for purposes of reference are some examples of updates that might have such a side effect. We assume that cursor C is currently associated with a certain ordered collection of rows, and further that the ordering of that collection is defined by values of a certain column K. Then:

a. If C is "before $R1$" (so C has just been used to delete some old row R) and a new row R is inserted with a value of K such that R logically belongs between $R1$ and $R1$'s predecessor (if any), what happens to C?

b. Does it make any difference if the new row R logically precedes or logically follows the old row R that C was positioned on before that old row R was deleted?

c. Does it make any difference if the new row R is not the result of an INSERT but the result of an UPDATE?

d. If C is positioned on row R and the value of column K in that row R is updated (not via cursor C), what happens to C?

e. If C is "before $R1$" and row $R1$ is deleted (not via cursor C), what happens to C?

---

*Presumably while cursor C was positioned on it, though the standard does not actually say as much.

f. If *C* is "before *R1*" and the value of column *K* in row *R1* is updated (not
    via cursor *C*), what happens to *C*?

The foregoing list is not guaranteed to be exhaustive.

Table Expressions

■   We pointed out several times in Chapter 11 that SQL has a syntax rule to the
    effect that a table reference (within a FROM clause or a join expression) that
    is specified as a table expression in parentheses *must* have an associated AS
    clause that explicitly introduces a range variable, even though that range vari-
    able is often never referenced. What is the point of this rule?

■   Part of the standard's explanation of the FROM clause reads as follows: "The
    extended Cartesian product, *CP*, is the multiset of all rows *R* such that *R* is the
    concatenation of a row from each of the identified tables . . . ." Note carefully,
    therefore, that *CP* is not well-defined!—despite the fact that the standard goes
    on to say that "The cardinality of *CP* is the product of the cardinalities of the
    identified tables." Consider the tables T1 and T2 shown below:

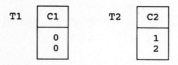

Either of the following fits the above definition for "the" extended Cartesian
product *CP* of T1 and T2 (i.e., either one could be "the" multiset referred to):

C1	C2		CP2	C1	C2
0	1			0	1
0	1			0	2
0	2			0	2
0	2			0	2

Note, moreover, that the only way to resolve the ambiguity is by effectively
defining a mapping from each of the (multiset) argument tables to a proper set,
and likewise defining a mapping of the (multiset) result table—i.e., the desired
extended Cartesian product—to a proper set. In other words, this whole area
serves to emphasize the point once again that one of the most fundamental
concepts in the entire SQL language (namely, the concept that tables should
permit duplicate rows) is *fundamentally flawed*—and cannot be repaired without, in effect, dispensing with the concept altogether.

■   (This item is an illustration of the point mentioned briefly in a footnote in
    Chapter 11, Section 11.6, subsection "The HAVING Clause.") Let MT be an
    empty table (i.e., a table with no rows), and consider the following query:

```
SELECT COUNT(*) AS X
FROM    MT
HAVING 0 = 0
```

The logically correct result is a table of one column and no rows. However, SQL gives a table of one column and *one row*, containing the value zero. To elaborate: The presence of a HAVING clause in the absence of a GROUP BY clause effectively implies "GROUP BY no columns." "GROUP BY no columns," in turn, should logically produce a grouped table containing exactly one group if its operand (i.e., the result of evaluating the relevant FROM and WHERE clauses) contains any rows at all, but a grouped table containing *no groups at all* if that operand contains no rows at all. In the example, therefore, there are logically no groups to which the HAVING can be applied, and hence there should be no rows in the overall result (because "SELECTing" from a grouped table always produces as many rows in the output as there are groups in the input).

- It is still the case in SQL/92 (as it was in SQL/89, though it was never clear why) that in a SELECT clause of the form "SELECT *" (where the "*" is unqualified), the commalist of items following the key word "SELECT" must consist of just that "*" and nothing else. Why? *Note:* Not only does this rule seem to have no good justification, it is actively annoying. For example, it means that the following perfectly reasonable and useful query is *** *ILLEGAL* ***:

```
SELECT *, QTY/10 AS TENTH        -- This is *** ILLEGAL *** !!!
FROM    S, SP
WHERE   S.SNO = SP.SNO
```

And so is this one:

```
SELECT *, QTY/10 AS TENTH        -- This is *** ILLEGAL *** !!!
FROM    SP
```

By contrast, the following is legal:

```
SELECT SP.*, QTY/10 AS TENTH
FROM    SP
```

- The standard gives rules defining the data type of each column of the result of evaluating a given table expression, but those rules overlook the fact that such a column might correspond to the NULL or DEFAULT specification in an expression of the form

```
VALUES ( ..., NULL, ... )
```

or

```
VALUES ( ..., DEFAULT, ... )
```

What are the result column data types in these cases? *Note:* This is not a burning issue, since DEFAULT and NULL can be specified only in the context of an INSERT operation, implying that, no matter what the result column data type is, it will be converted to that of the corresponding column of the INSERT target anyway.

■   In Chapter 19, we gave the standard's rules for deciding whether a given table expression is indeterminate (the standard term is "possibly nondeterministic"). For reference, we repeat those rules here. A given table expression, *T* say, is considered to be *indeterminate* ("possibly nondeterministic") if and only if any of the following is true:

a.   *T* is a union (without ALL), intersection, or difference, and the operand tables include a column of type character string.

b.   *T* is a select-expression, the commalist of select-items in that select-expression includes a select-item (*C* say) of type character string, and:

   ▪   The commalist of select-items is preceded by the key word DISTINCT, *or*

   ▪   *C* involves a MAX or MIN reference, or

   ▪   *T* directly includes a GROUP BY clause and *C* is one of the grouping columns.

c.   *T* is a select-expression that directly includes a HAVING clause and the conditional expression in that HAVING clause includes *either* a reference to a grouping column of type character string *or* a MAX or MIN reference in which the argument is of type character string.

However, these rules seem to be neither accurate nor complete. For example:

a.   A union *with* ALL is surely still indeterminate if one of its operands is a "possibly nondeterministic" select-expression.

b.   An explicit NATURAL JOIN or JOIN USING has exactly the same potential for indeterminacy as (e.g.) an intersection.

c.   A difference with ALL cannot possibly be indeterminate if its first operand is not.

Furthermore, the rules are certainly stronger than they need to be in some cases; for example, suppose NO PAD applies, and the collation in effect is one in which there are no characters that are "equal but distinguishable."

Views

■   As we explained in Chapter 13, if all views have a check option, then all updates will be handled correctly, and it makes no difference whether those check options are specified as LOCAL or CASCADED or any mixture. But if any view is permitted to have no check option at all, then (in general) certain updates will be treated incorrectly; further, more updates will be treated incorrectly if some views have only a LOCAL check option instead of a CASCADED one (again in general). The following questions arise:

a. Why are views without a check option supported at all? *Note:* The (bad!) answer here is probably "backward compatibility with SQL/89."

b. Why is the LOCAL check option supported? *Note:* The answer here cannot be "backward compatibility," because such an option was not supported in SQL/89.

- The SQL rules for view updatability would apparently say that the following view STC is SQL-updatable:

```
CREATE VIEW STC AS
      SELECT STATUS, CITY
      FROM   S
```

If column S.SNO has no default, however, an INSERT into this view will necessarily fail. Why is it necessary to wait until run time to discover this fact? Or *is* it necessary?

Integrity

- The following is an excerpt from the standard:

"Let *D1* be some domain. *D1* is *in usage by* a domain constraint *DC* if and only if the <search condition> of *DC* generally contains the <domain name> either of *D1* or of some domain *D2* such that *D1* is in usage by some domain constraint of *D2*. No domain shall be in usage by any of its own constraints."

The broad intent of this rule seems to be to prohibit some kind of circularity of reference among domains (and we stated as much in Chapter 13). It is not clear that the rule actually achieves this objective, however. The phrase *generally contains* is a technical term, defined in the standard as follows: A given syntax element *A generally contains* another syntax element *B* if *A* contains a view name *V* and *B* is, or is generally contained in, the defining expression for *V*. Thus, "general containment" has to do with views, not domains, and its relevance to the problem at hand is unclear.

So consider the following definitions (which certainly do involve circular references between domains D1 and D2). Are they legal? If so, what do they mean? If not, where does the standard prohibit them?

```
CREATE DOMAIN D1 ... CHECK ( VALUE IN ( SELECT C1 FROM T1 ) )

CREATE TABLE T1 ( C1 D2 )

CREATE DOMAIN D2 ... CHECK ( VALUE IN ( SELECT C2 FROM T2 ) )

CREATE TABLE T2 ( C2 D1 )
```

- There are various subtle differences between stating a constraint "in line" in (e.g.) a base table definition and stating that very same constraint "out of line" in CREATE ASSERTION. For example, an attempt to drop column *C* (specifying RESTRICT) will succeed if

  a. *C* is referenced in exactly one integrity constraint, and

  b. That integrity constraint is specified as part of the CREATE TABLE for the base table that contains *C*, and

  c. That integrity constraint does not reference any other columns, and yet

  d. Will fail if that very same integrity constraint is specified via CREATE ASSERTION instead.

  The full extent of such differences is unclear, and so are the full implications.

- The standard says that conditional expressions within domain and base table constraints are not allowed to contain any aggregate function references except inside subqueries. It does *not* say that the same restriction applies to general constraints. Are we to infer that it does not? If so, why not?

  In any case, it is hard to imagine what a constraint that involved an aggregate function reference *not* inside a subquery would look like.

- It is strange that a column check constraint can reference only the column in whose definition the constraint appears, whereas a domain constraint is allowed almost unrestricted access to any part of the database. Certainly there are those (the present writer included) who would argue that it should be the other way around.

  Note: This difference between the two kinds of constraints explains the remark we made in Chapter 14 to the effect that it is not possible, in general, to derive a column check constraint from a domain constraint by simply replacing each occurrence of VALUE by the relevant column name.

- When dropping a base table constraint via ALTER TABLE, the user is required to specify a RESTRICT *vs.* CASCADE option. But RESTRICT and CASCADE are both meaningless for base table constraints other than candidate key definitions. Why is such a specification required when it is meaningless?

- The standard requires each column of a given foreign key to have the same data type as the corresponding column of the corresponding candidate key (the standard explicitly says the *same* data type, not just *compatible* types). The question is, what does it mean for two data types to be "the same"? At one point the standard says that there are exactly six types, *viz.* character strings, national strings, bit strings, numbers, datetimes, and intervals—implying that, e.g., all numbers are of the same type.* At another point it talks about ". . . the specific numeric data type (NUMERIC, DECIMAL, INTEGER, SMALLINT,

---

*It is relevant to point out that dates and times, though both subsumed under "datetimes," are clearly *not* of the same type, since neither can be converted to the other.

FLOAT, REAL, or DOUBLE PRECISION)"—implying among other things that numbers are not all of the same type. Perhaps all exact numeric types are "the same type," and likewise for all approximate numeric types, but exact numeric and approximate numeric are different types? What *is* the true state of affairs?

It is also not clear whether, e.g., CHAR(3) and CHAR(4) are different types, or whether CHAR(3) and CHAR(3) VARYING are.

■ It is strange that integrity constraints can refer to views but not be stated as part of a view definition (contrast the situation with respect to base tables). For example, the following is legal—

```
CREATE VIEW GOODSUPPS
    AS SELECT SNO, STATUS, CITY
       FROM   S
       WHERE  STATUS > 15

CREATE ASSERTION GOODSUPPS_CK
       CHECK ( UNIQUE ( SELECT SNO FROM GOODSUPPS ) )
```

—whereas the following is not:

```
CREATE VIEW GOODSUPPS
    AS SELECT SNO, STATUS, CITY
       FROM   S
       WHERE  STATUS > 15
    UNIQUE ( SNO )                 -- This is *** ILLEGAL !!! ***
```

Security

■ The standard states that the mapping of authIDs to operating system users is implementation-dependent. Should not that be implementation-*defined*?

■ The standard says that if a module has a module authID (specified via the AUTHORIZATION clause on the module definition), then that authID is used as the current authID "for the execution of all <procedure>s in the <module>." However, it also says that if a schema has a schema authID (specified via the AUTHORIZATION clause on CREATE SCHEMA), then that authID is used as the current authID "for the creation of the schema" (presumably including CREATE TABLE operations, GRANT operations, etc., that are specified as schema elements within the CREATE SCHEMA). So what happens if the (sole) statement within a procedure is a CREATE SCHEMA statement?

■ The standard's definition of the GRANT and REVOKE statements is very complicated and appears to suffer from numerous problems. However, those problems are so complex, and so much interwoven with one another, that they do not admit of succinct description here. Careful reading of the relevant sections of the standard is recommended.*

---

*It is relevant to mention that these statements were the subject of extensive revisions in the technical corrigenda.

- The standard's discussion of security makes use of a concept called "applicable privileges." Here is the text from the standard that introduces this term:

  "The phrase *applicable privileges* refers to the privileges defined by the privilege descriptors that define privileges granted to the current <authorization identifier>.

  "The set of applicable privileges for the current <authorization identifier> consists of the privileges defined by the privilege descriptors associated with that <authorization identifier> and the privileges defined by the privilege descriptors associated with PUBLIC."

  Questions and comments:

  a. Note first that we have two consecutive paragraphs giving two (slightly) conflicting definitions of the same thing.

  b. Second, the phrase "privileges defined by the privilege descriptors that define privileges" could surely be abbreviated to just "privileges" without significant loss.

  c. Third, what does "associated with" mean here?

  d. Finally, why is the term "authorization identifier" repeatedly enclosed in angle brackets?

Missing Information and Nulls

In principle, the number of anomalies that can arise in connection with SQL-style nulls is quite literally infinite. Readers will probably be familiar with many such anomalies, however. In what follows, therefore, we merely present a few nulls-related peculiarities—in particular, peculiarities introduced with SQL/92—that might perhaps be less familiar than most.

- The BETWEEN condition "*x* BETWEEN +1 AND –1" ought always to evaluate to *false**—yet, if *x* happens to be null, it evaluates not to *false* but to *unknown*.

  The reason we mention this particular anomaly is that the standard goes out of its way to avoid certain similar anomalies in connection with OVERLAPS, and OVERLAPS is analogous to BETWEEN in some respects (though more complex). For example, an OVERLAPS condition of the form

```
( TIME '08:00:00', TIME '09:00:00' )
  OVERLAPS
( TIME '08:30:00',         NULL      )
```

---

*Note that BETWEEN is asymmetric; thus, e.g., the expressions "*x* BETWEEN +1 AND –1" and "*x* BETWEEN –1 AND +1" are not equivalent (another trap for the unwary!).

(not intended to be valid SQL syntax) is defined to evaluate to *true*, not *unknown*. (This is one reason why the definition of OVERLAPS is so complex. See the subsection "Dates and Times" later in this appendix.)

- There is definitely an inconsistency of approach here. If the foregoing treatment of OVERLAPS is regarded as reasonable, then surely the (much simpler) expression *A* LIKE '%' should by analogy be defined to return *true* for any *A*, even if *A* is null. And *A – A* should return zero even if *A* is null. And *A = A* should return *true* even if *A* is null. And *A* / 0 should be a "zero divide" error even if *A* is null. And so on.

- If column *C* is defined to be of data type CHAR(5), say, then the expression CHAR_LENGTH(*C*) should surely always return 5, even if *C* happens to be null. And then, if *C1* and *C2* are both of data type character string, and if CHAR_LENGTH(*C1*) <> CHAR_LENGTH(*C2*), and if NO PAD applies, then "*A = B*" should always return *false*, and "*A <> B*" should always return *true*, even if *A* or *B* is null. And so on.

Dates and Times

- There seems to be some fundamental confusion in the standard over the intended interpretations of the data types DATE, TIME, and TIMESTAMP. One possible interpretation—one that seems highly reasonable to this writer— is to regard dates and timestamps as conceptually similar, but times as very different. After all, a date might well be thought of as a timestamp with precision only down to the nearest day (whereas a timestamp has precision down to the second or even fractions thereof); both represent absolute positions on the timeline. Times, by contrast, are relative; they do *not* represent absolute positions on the timeline ("7:00 AM" in London is not the same point in time as "7:00 AM" in San Francisco; further, "7:00 AM on Monday" is not the same point in time as "7:00 AM on Tuesday").

  The standard seems partly to agree with the foregoing interpretation and partly not. For example, conversions (CASTs) are defined between dates and timestamps and not between dates and times; yet conversions are defined between times and timestamps. Also, times and timestamps have a time zone component, while dates do not (we will return to this particular point in a moment).

- The YEAR component in a date or timestamp must be in the range 0001 to 9999. Why? In other words, why does the standard outlaw (a) all BC dates*

---

*One consequence of this particular omission is that SQL is unable to represent the presumptive date of birth of the historical figure on which its own calendar is based!—generally accepted to have been sometime around the year 4 BC.

and (b) AD dates greater than or equal to 10,000 AD? The point is particularly puzzling, given that intervals are not analogously constrained. *Note:* Indeed, it is rather surprising to find such a mistake being made at a time when there is universal concern over the imminent "millenium problem" (i.e., the problem of incorrect date wrapover from 1999 to 2000 AD).

- We stated in Chapter 17 that datetime field values are decimal integers (except possibly for SECOND values, which optionally include a fractional part). Actually, the standard says only that they are *integers* (except, again, for SECOND values), not that they must be decimal. Further, EXTRACT is defined to return exact numeric values, not necessarily decimal values. However, the various precision specifications—e.g., the precision for the "start" component of an interval—are specifically defined to give the relevant precision as a number of *decimal* digits.

- We also stated in Chapter 17 that to convert a given local time value to UTC, it is necessary to subtract the appropriate time zone displacement value from that local time value; that is,

```
UTC time  =  local time - time zone displacement
```

The standard contradicts itself on this issue, however, stating at some points that the arithmetic should go the other way; that is,

```
UTC time  =  local time + time zone displacement
```

So which is it?

- Following on from the previous point: The standard makes use of the term "normalized to UTC," but does not seem to define that term anywhere. Of course, it is possible to guess at the meaning ("converted to UTC if necessary"?). But it is also possible to guess wrong.

- The standard does not adequately define the data type of the result of an arbitrary datetime expression. Specifically, it fails to consider the effect of explicit WITH TIME ZONE declarations. For example, let column C of base table T be declared to be of type TIME WITH TIME ZONE, and let i be an interval. What exactly is the data type of the result of the expression $T.C - i$?

- In the real world, time zones are relevant to dates as well as times and timestamps (for example, the date might simultaneously be January 1st in Helsinki and December 31st—of the prior year!—in San Francisco). Yet:

  a. The standard explicitly states that "[values of] datetime data types that contain time fields (TIME and TIMESTAMP) are maintained in ... UTC," with the clear implication that *date* values are not so maintained (i.e., not "normalized to UTC"?).

  b. Also, the standard does not provide a WITH TIME ZONE option on a DATE data type definition.

   c. Nor does it allow a time zone component within a DATE literal.

   d. Nor does it permit AT LOCAL or AT TIME ZONE to be specified in a datetime expression if that expression represents a date instead of a time or timestamp. In other words, it does not provide for dates to be converted to some particular time zone when they are referenced, unlike times and timestamps.

The only possible mention of the point (that time zones might be relevant to dates too) in the standard occurs when it says that "when a datetime is specified . . . it has an implied or explicit time zone specifier associated with it"—a date, of course, being a special case of a datetime. (Incidentally, the term "time zone specifier" refers to a LOCAL *vs.* TIME ZONE specification, which does not seem to make much sense in this context.)

- Let column *C* be of type TIME WITH TIME ZONE. Then just what it is that constitutes a value in such a column is not clear from the standard—sometimes it is considered to be the combination of the time value and the associated time zone displacement value, sometimes it is just the time value *per se*.

- The standard is also ambivalent over the question of whether or not TIMEZONE_HOUR and TIMEZONE_MINUTE are considered to be datetime fields. For instance, the definition of EXTRACT calls them "time zone fields" and clearly distinguishes between them and datetime fields. On the other hand, the table in the standard that explains what datetime fields are does include TIMEZONE_HOUR and TIMEZONE_MINUTE. The point is significant, because the standard states (among other things) that "[values] of type datetime are mutually comparable only if they have the same <datetime field>s." So is it legal to compare (e.g.) a TIME value and a TIME WITH TIME ZONE value?

- The standard says that *every* time value and timestamp value always has a certain time zone displacement value associated with it, even values in TIME or TIMESTAMP columns to which WITH TIME ZONE does not apply: "[values of] datetime data types that contain time fields (TIME and TIMESTAMP) are maintained in [UTC] . . . *with an explicit or implied time zone part* [emphasis added] ... A TIME or TIMESTAMP that does not specify WITH TIME ZONE has an implicit time zone equal to the local time zone for the SQL-session." And elsewhere it says: "If WITH TIME ZONE is not specified, then the time zone displacement of the datetime data type is effectively the current default time zone displacement of the SQL-session."

Questions and comments:

   a. Let *t* be a value in a TIME column to which WITH TIME ZONE does not apply, and let *tz* be the (implied) time zone displacement value associated with *t*. What exactly *is* the value *tz*?—i.e., what does *current* mean in the phrase "effectively the current default time zone displacement of the

SQL-session"? If it means "at the time the value is entered into the database," then different values in the same column can have different implied *tz* values.

b. Yet there does not seem to be any place to *hold* those different *tz* values, because *t* does not include any TIMEZONE_HOUR and TIMEZONE_MINUTE components.* So does *current* perhaps mean "at the time the column is defined"? If it does, all values in the column will at least have the same time zone displacement value, and that value could plausibly be held in the appropriate schema along with the relevant column descriptor.

c. Regardless of which of the foregoing interpretations of *current* is correct, the standard states that an attempt to EXTRACT the TIMEZONE_HOUR or TIMEZONE_MINUTE component of a value such as the value *t* referred to above is an error. So apparently *t* has no time zone displacement value associated with it after all? What then does it mean to say that *t* has an "implied time zone part"?

   Note: Actually, the standard seems to contradict itself on this point; it states elsewhere that EXTRACT is used to extract the *implicit or explicit* time zone (emphasis added) "associated with" a given datetime value. By the way, what exactly does "associated with" mean here?

d. In any case, it could be argued that the question of whether or not *t* has an associated *tz* value is largely irrelevant. Assume for the sake of discussion that it does have such an associated value. Then that associated value will (necessarily) either be or not be the same as if WITH TIME ZONE applied. It surely cannot be the same, for then there would be no point in ever specifying WITH TIME ZONE. Therefore it must be different. But then it serves no useful purpose!—since it will always effectively be overridden when the value *t* is referenced (as we saw in Chapter 17, the UTC value is always converted to a local time when it is referenced, using either the *session* time zone or a time zone explicitly specified by the user, not the value *tz*).

■ A datetime term representing a time or a timestamp can include an AT LOCAL or AT TIME ZONE qualifier. If it does not, then:

a. AT LOCAL is assumed if the datetime term is of data type TIME or TIMESTAMP *without* the WITH TIME ZONE option.

b. But the standard does not say what happens if the datetime term is of data type TIME or TIMESTAMP *with* the WITH TIME ZONE option.

---

*The standard defines values of type TIME to be eight "positions" long and values of type TIME WITH TIME ZONE to be 14 "positions" long (ignoring fractional SECOND values in both cases). (*Note:* The length in positions of a datetime value is defined to be "the number of characters from the character set SQL_TEXT that it would take to represent [that] value.") Clearly it is the TIMEZONE_HOUR and TIMEZONE_MINUTE components that account for the difference. See also the discussion of EXTRACT in paragraph c.

- We remark on an ugly asymmetry in the definition of OVERLAPS. Let the two time periods be *Left* and *Right*, with start points *Ls* and *Rs* and end points *Le* and *Re*, respectively. Then a symmetric definition would say that the OVERLAPS condition is equivalent to

```
Re > Ls AND Rs < Le
```

The standard, however, says it is equivalent to

```
( Ls > Rs AND ( Ls < Re OR Le < Re ) ) OR
( Rs > Ls AND ( Rs < Le OR Re < Le ) ) OR
( Ls = Rs AND Le IS NOT NULL AND Re IS NOT NULL )
```

One implication is that if *Right* is a time period of zero length that happens to coincide with either *Le* or *Ls*, the symmetric definition yields *false* (no overlap); the standard's definition yields *false* (no overlap) if *Right* coincides with the end point of *Left*, but *true* (overlap) if it coincides with the start point.

Temporary Tables

- Why must a GRANT against a "created" temporary table specify ALL PRIVILEGES?

- Temporary tables can have associated base table constraints but cannot be referenced in "general" constraints (specified via CREATE ASSERTION). This is a rather strange restriction, given that any base table constraint can in principle be rewritten as a general constraint and *vice versa*. It is true that "temporary" base table constraints are not allowed to reference permanent base tables (whether this rule is reasonable is another matter); however, a precisely analogous rule could be specified for general constraints, if desired.

- We remind the reader that CREATE TABLE does *not* create a table at all, if the table in question is TEMPORARY; it "primes the pump" for the actual creation, which is done at some later (and conceptually quite distinct) time. See Chapter 18 for further discussion.

Character Data

- The standard states that a character string value, *B* say, can be assigned to a character string target (e.g., a character string variable), *A* say, "if and only if [*A* and *B* have] the same [character] repertoire." Should not "character repertoire" here be "character *set*" (as stated in Chapter 19)? For otherwise there is an implication that if *A* and *B* have different forms-of-use, the assignment will cause an implicit form-of-use conversion to be performed, which is a little hard to believe (especially since the system might not even have knowledge of how to perform such a conversion).

- To follow on from the previous point: Actually, it is not even clear what the phrase "the same character set" means. Are character sets *C1* and *C2* "the same" if they have the same character repertoire and the same form-of-use, but different names? Are they "the same" if they have repertoires *R1* and *R2* respectively, but *R1* and *R2* each involve exactly the same collection of characters? Etc.

- Another related point: The standard states (indirectly) that if two character strings are concatenated, they must be drawn from the same character repertoire. Surely (again) it should be "from the same character *set*"?—for otherwise, what form-of-use applies to the result?

- And another: The standard says that two character strings can be compared if and only if they are "mutually assignable" and can be coerced to have the same collation. But if they can be coerced to have the same collation, they must have the same *character set* (not just the same character repertoire), because every collation has just one associated character set. And if they have the same character set, they are certainly "mutually assignable." So it is redundant, and arguably much too weak, to say that they must be "mutually assignable."

- For CONVERT, the two character repertoires are required to be identical. Is this ever the case? Note in particular that it is not the case for EBCDIC and ASCII (despite the fact that converting from EBCDIC to ASCII or *vice versa* is the very example quoted in the standard itself).

- Why is CONVERT provided anyway? Its functionality appears to be totally subsumed by that of TRANSLATE (i.e., there does not seem to be anything that can be done with CONVERT that cannot equally well be done with TRANSLATE).

- The default collation for a given character set is specified either by the COLLATE option or by the COLLATION FROM option in the CREATE CHARACTER SET statement. It is not clear why two distinct options (COLLATE and COLLATION FROM) are provided. Perhaps the intent was that the COLLATE option *must* specify a user-defined collation (i.e., a collation explicitly created via CREATE COLLATION), and the COLLATION FROM clause *must* specify one defined "externally" (i.e., a collation defined outside the framework of SQL *per se*). Indeed, having two distinct options would seem to make sense only if the possible COLLATE specifications and the possible COLLATION FROM specifications formed two disjoint sets. Yet such does not seem to be the case.

- A parameter definition, a host variable definition, and the target data type specification in a CAST expression can all include the specification "CHARACTER SET character-set"; if that specification is omitted, an implementation-defined character set is assumed by default. It would be more consistent, and more user-friendly, to assume the default character set for the module instead (or possibly the default character set for the schema, in the case of CAST, if the CAST expression appears within a CREATE SCHEMA statement).

- In its explanation of DROP TRANSLATION, the standard says that (a) the translation to be dropped must not be referenced by any collation, and then goes on to say that (b) any collation that references that translation is implicitly dropped.

Dynamic SQL

- We mentioned the point in Chapter 3 that the LOCAL *vs.* GLOBAL key words (on, for example, the "prepped statement name container" in PREPARE, second format) are not well chosen.* LOCAL means the scope is the module and GLOBAL means it is the session. But sessions and modules do not have a global-to-local kind of relationship: One session can involve many modules and one module can involve many sessions. (We note too that LOCAL refers to the *session*, not the module, in the context of date and time support.)

- In Chapter 20, we stated that a preparable statement cannot include any parameters or host variables. This statement is surely correct; however, the only hint of a suggestion of a mention of the matter in the standard is in the definition of two constructs called "<value specification>" and "<target specification>," where we find the following (part of a syntax rule):

    "Each <parameter name> shall be contained in a <module>. Each <embedded variable name> shall be contained in an <embedded SQL statement>."

    If these two sentences are indeed intended to imply that parameters and host variables cannot appear in preparable statements, then there must surely be a clearer way of stating this important fact. Furthermore, it would surely have been better to state that fact as part of the definition of the construct called "<preparable statement>."

- We also stated in Chapter 20 that the character set for a character string placeholder (denoted by a question mark) in dynamic SQL was the default character set for the SQL-session. Actually the standard does not seem to address this question at all.

- Following on from the previous point: Why cannot a character string placeholder have an "introducer" to override the default character set, whatever that might be?

Information Schemas

- The standard provides no direct means for a given user *U* to see descriptors for all objects accessible to that user *U*. More generally, it does not provide any

---

*An analogous remark applies to the use of the same key words in the context of temporary table definitions (see Chapter 18).

direct means for some user with higher authorization to see definitions for "all" objects, regardless of the catalog they belong to.

- The standard provides no direct means for a given user U to see descriptors for objects that belong to some distinct user V, nor more generally for some user with higher authorization to see definitions of "all" objects, regardless of owner.

- (A particular, and peculiar, illustration of the previous point:) Let user V be the owner of a base table B, and suppose V has created an integrity constraint C on B. Suppose also that V has granted UPDATE on B to some other user U. Then U is constrained by C, and yet U is not allowed to see the definition of C.

- Despite the name, Definition Schemas are not true SQL-schemas and are not contained in catalogs (in fact a given Definition Schema spans many catalogs, in general). It is still the case, however, that no SQL-schema can have an unqualified name of DEFINITION_SCHEMA.

Exception Handling

- Why is there no SQLWARNING option on WHENEVER? Could this be just an oversight?

- There is exactly one diagnostics area per SQL-agent, yet its size varies from SQL-transaction to SQL-transaction; why?

- In fact, we have already mentioned the fact that diagnostics area size is part of the *SQL-session* context information, suggesting that the size might vary *from session to session* within one transaction. (On the other hand, Technical Corrigendum 2 explicitly states that operations that can affect several SQL-servers—e.g., COMMIT, DISCONNECT ALL—can lead to several sets of "conditions" within the [sole] diagnostics area.)

Language Levels and Conformance

- *(This point was first noted by Ed Dee:)* In Entry SQL, the USER function returns a character string whose associated character set is implementation-defined. In Intermediate and Full SQL, it returns a character string whose associated character set is SQL_TEXT.*

---

*Technical Corrigendum 1 does not fix this problem, but simply notes that it *is* a problem! To quote: "In an environment where the SQL-implementation conforms to Entry SQL, conforming SQL language that contains [a USER reference] will become nonconforming in an environment where the SQL-implementation conforms to Intermediate SQL or Full SQL, unless the character repertoire of the implementation-defined character set in that environment is identical to the character repertoire of SQL_TEXT."

APPENDIX E

Persistent Stored Modules

E.1 INTRODUCTION

A well known shortcoming of the SQL/92 standard as originally defined was that it did not include any support for *user-defined functions and procedures.* Commercial SQL products, by contrast, have been offering such a capability for years (usually in the form of "stored procedures" or something of that nature). There are two broad reasons for providing such a capability: improved *functionality* and improved *performance.*

1. *Improved functionality:* Every SQL product does provide a set of builtin operators and functions—the standard itself prescribes support for "+", "*", SUBSTRING, TRIM, and many others (see Chapter 7), and some products have gone considerably beyond the standard in this regard. But there will always be applications that require facilities over and above those provided by the builtin set, no matter how comprehensive that set might be. There is thus a clear need for a feature that would permit suitably skilled users to add their own extensions to the builtin set—in other words, a feature that would allow users to define their own functions and procedures. In particular, a third-party vendor could use such a feature to build and market special-purpose function packages: sophisticated string-handling functions, perhaps, for analysis of text, or esoteric mathematical functions for scientific purposes.

2. *Improved performance:* Recall from Chapter 6 that SQL statements are always contained within some module, at least conceptually. Now, all of the modules

discussed in the body of the book were *client* modules, so called (informally) because they can be thought of (again informally) as being stored at the applicable SQL-client site. In order to execute an SQL statement contained within such a module, however, it is clear that communication will be needed with the relevant SQL-server site; and such communication can represent significant overhead, particularly if the client and server sites are some distance apart. Also, the decision as to whether to execute a given SQL statement often depends on the current state of the database, and this fact can lead to further overhead, because data will have to be transferred from the server to the client in order for the decision in question to be made.

The obvious solution to these overhead problems is to allow SQL statements—or, rather, functions or procedures containing such statements—to be kept in *server* modules (i.e., modules that are stored at the server site instead of the client site), and then to let those functions and procedures be invoked from the client site.* Thus, the feature already identified as desirable under 1. above for functionality reasons (*viz.,* the ability for users to define their own functions and procedures) becomes desirable for performance reasons too, if those functions and procedures can be stored at a remote site.

Incidentally, such a feature might offer another, subsidiary benefit as well: Storing a module once at a server site, instead of once at each of several client sites, could help to guarantee that those client sites all use the same version of the module in question, without the need for carefully coordinated distribution of copies of that module.

Now, current commercial "stored procedure" support typically includes the following:

1. The ability to create user-defined *functions* and to invoke such functions from within scalar expressions—e.g., in SELECT clauses and WHERE clauses in queries and constraints;

2. The ability to create user-defined *procedures* and to invoke such procedures by means of a new SQL statement (typically CALL);

3. The provision of a proprietary *programming language* for defining such functions and procedures.

We elaborate on this last point briefly. There are several reasons to prefer a special-purpose language over traditional languages such as PL/I for the purpose at hand:†

---

*More precisely, they will be *SQL-invoked* (see Section E.2)—i.e., invoked from *within the client module* at the client site.

†One reviewer (Nelson Mattos) pointed out that there are advantages to using a traditional language, too. They include (a) the ability to use the very same code both within an application program and as a stored procedure; (b) the ability to use functions from existing function libraries (e.g., a FORTRAN scientific library) as stored procedures; (c) the ability to execute user-defined functions on the client as well as on the server.

- Awkward conflicts between host and SQL data types can be avoided. *Note:* Such conflicts constitute one aspect of what is sometimes called the *impedance mismatch* problem.

- Conditional expressions in flow control statements (e.g., IF–THEN–ELSE) can reference database data directly; so too can scalar expressions in assignment statements and elsewhere. As another example, it might be possible to write a loop that iterates directly over the rows of a table.

- The DBMS can more readily assess the resources required to execute code written in a special-purpose language. In particular, the optimizer can more readily assess the impact of invoking a given function—e.g., within a query— because the code that implements that function will already have been analyzed by the DBMS's own compiler. (Indeed, it might be possible to "merge" the function and the query, thereby allowing the two to be optimized together as a unit.)

The subject of this appendix, the SQL *Persistent Stored Modules* feature ("SQL/PSM" or just *PSM* for short), represents the approach to such matters proposed for the SQL standard. The structure of the appendix is as follows. Following this introductory section, Section E.2 provides a fairly extensive overview of the PSM feature; in particular, it describe the PSM *routine* concept (PSM "routines" subsume both functions and procedures). Section E.3 explains the relationship between the new routine construct on the one hand and the existing module and schema constructs on the other. Sections E.4 and E.5 then examine the complicated issues of *type precedence* and *subject routine determination.* Section E.6 describes the new general-purpose programming language statements (IF–THEN–ELSE, etc.) introduced into SQL by PSM. Section E.7 is devoted to a consideration of PSM exception handling. Section E.8 discusses the special considerations that apply to PSM routines that are coded in some "external" language (i.e., a language other than SQL). Finally, Section E.9 deals with a number of miscellaneous matters (new key words, new Information Schema tables, etc.).

A note on terminology: For convenience and brevity, we use the term "PSM" throughout this appendix as shorthand for both the PSM feature *per se* and the current PSM draft specification. We feel bound to say, however, that "PSM"—standing as it does for "Persistent Stored Modules"—is a most inapt choice for the feature in question:*

- Regarding "persistent": In fact, of course, *all* modules "persist" (in the sense that they outlive individual program executions), in general, regardless of whether they are PSM modules specifically or the modules of the module language already discussed in Chapter 6.

---

*Some might feel our criticisms here to be mere nitpicking. But it is surely undeniable that bad terminology makes a topic unnecessarily hard to teach, learn, understand, and remember.

- Regarding "stored": The question of "storing" modules, though unquestionably important from a practical point of view, is—quite rightly—not addressed at all in the PSM specification. In particular, the specification has nothing to say on the question of whether modules are "stored at the server." It is true that PSM modules are, by definition, "server modules," but all this terminology means is that the modules in question belong to some schema. (Of course, it would make little sense in practice for PSM modules—or "schema objects" in general, come to that—*not* to be stored at the server, but where objects happen to be stored is properly an implementation matter, not a concern of the SQL standard.)

- Regarding "modules": Not all PSM routines belong to modules (though they do all persist and in practice will presumably be stored at the server site).

- Finally, the name makes no mention at all of the most important *logical* aspect of the PSM feature!—namely, the ability to create user-defined functions (and procedures).

Further support for our suggestion that the name "PSM" does not adequately convey the scope of the PSM feature is provided by the fact that the current draft currently contains nineteen chapters (the official term is "clauses"), of which exactly one is called "Persistent Stored Modules."

CAVEAT: It was originally hoped that PSM would be ratified as an official standard by late 1996. However, it now seems possible that this goal will not be met, owing to the large number of technical issues that still remain unresolved. Nevertheless, we felt it was worth discussing PSM in some detail in this book, on the grounds that (a) *some* version of PSM will eventually become a standard, and (b) that version will probably not differ all that much at the overall design level from the version currently "defined" in the draft PSM document. But the reader is warned that changes at the detail level are a virtual certainty.

E.2   OVERVIEW

As already mentioned, PSM uses the term *routine* to cover both functions and procedures. The reader is surely familiar with these two concepts, but we begin by reviewing them briefly:

- A *function* is a routine whose invocation returns a value (and might have side effects, though such side effects are usually deprecated). A function invocation is a special case of a scalar expression; such invocations are represented syntactically by means of prefix operators (consider, e.g., the builtin functions SUBSTRING, TRIM, etc.). They can appear wherever a scalar literal of the appropriate data type can appear, generally speaking (though as with scalar expressions in general—see Chapter 7—there are, regrettably, certain exceptions to this general rule).

- A *procedure* is a routine whose invocation does not return a value (and so *must* have side effects—typically including updates to the database—if it is to achieve any useful purpose). Since it returns no value, a procedure invocation is *not* a scalar expression; instead, procedures are invoked by means of an explicit CALL statement.

In other respects, PSM functions and procedures are very similar:

- The same *programming languages*—including, primarily, SQL itself, with its new "control statements" (see Section E.6) and other extensions—are available for their definition.

- In both cases, that definition includes the definition of *parameters*, and corresponding invocations involve the provision of *arguments* in one-to-one correspondence with those parameters.

- They are subject to the same *packaging* methods (see Section E.2).

- They are subject to the same *authorization* mechanism.

- They both have *names*. In fact, several distinct routines can have the same name; the *subject routine determination* rules that determine which of possibly many routines with the same name is actually to be executed for a given invocation are the same—more or less—for both functions and procedures (see Section E.5).*

We now proceed to examine these points in more depth. We begin with an introductory example.

A Function Example

Example 1: The following PSM statement defines a function called FIRST_WORD, which extracts the first word from a given block of text. (More precisely, an invocation of FIRST_WORD takes as its argument a character string consisting of a sequence of words separated by spaces, and returns a copy of the first word in that sequence, defined as the character string up to but excluding the first space in that sequence.)

```
FUNCTION
   FIRST_WORD ( :X CHAR VARYING (1000) )
   RETURNS CHAR VARYING (40)
   RETURN
      TRIM
      ( SUBSTRING
        ( ( :X || ' ' )
          FROM 1
          FOR POSITION ( ' ' IN ( :X || ' ' ) ) ) )
```

---

*It is worth mentioning that the proposed SQL3 support for *objects* (see Appendix F) uses PSM as the basis for defining what the object community calls *methods* for operating on those objects, and the subject routine determination rules have been defined with this fact in mind.

Example 1 illustrates just those syntax elements that are minimally required to define a PSM routine:

- The key word FUNCTION indicates the *routine type* of the routine being defined (the alternative is PROCEDURE).

- FIRST_WORD is the *routine name*. More precisely, it is the name by which the routine will be invoked. As we will see in Section E.3, routines generally have two names, a "generic" or *invocation* name (not official terminology) and a possibly implicit "specific" name; specific names are required to be unique, but invocation names need not be. (In other words, invocation names can be *overloaded.* See Section E.4.) In the example, FIRST_WORD is the invocation name, and no explicit specific name is shown.

- The name is immediately followed by a parenthesized commalist of *parameter definitions.* In the example, there is just one parameter, called :X—note the customary colon prefix*—of data type CHAR VARYING (40) (an *SQL* data type, please note, exactly as it would be in the module language of Chapter 6).

  Note: Since parameter data types are, specifically, SQL data types, it follows that PSM does not support the extremely useful feature, found in some languages, that permits a parameter type to be specified as, e.g., CHAR(*)—meaning a generic CHAR string of arbitrary length, where the actual length is taken from that of the corresponding argument at run time. Such a feature would allow (e.g.) a version of FIRST_WORD to be defined that would work on CHAR strings of any length, not just ones of maximum length 1000. Note that the *builtin* functions, by contrast, are "generic" in this sense (in general).

- Since the routine type is FUNCTION, not PROCEDURE, the parameter definition list is followed by a RETURNS clause, indicating that the data type of the result of invoking the routine is CHAR VARYING (40)—also an SQL data type, since the routine will be invoked from within SQL expressions. (The invoking SQL expression might be contained within either a client module or another PSM routine.)

  Note: Since the result type is, specifically, an SQL data type, it follows that PSM does not permit a user-defined function to return *true* or *false* (since there is no SQL "truth values" data type), and hence that, e.g., WHERE clauses of the form WHERE CONDX(...), where CONDX is a user-defined function, are also not supported.†

- The remainder of the definition consists of the routine *body,* i.e., the code—actually a single SQL statement (RETURN in the example)—that specifies

---

*Actually there is some debate over whether such a prefix should be required, but at the time of writing the PSM draft says it is.

†An SQL "truth values" data type is proposed for SQL3 (see Appendix F).

what the routine is to do when it is invoked. *Note:* RETURN applies only to functions, not to procedures.

Here is an example of an SQL expression that includes an invocation of FIRST_WORD:

```
SELECT LINENO, TEXT_LINE
FROM    TEXT_LINES
WHERE   FIRST_WORD ( TEXT_LINE ) = 'Dolores'
```

A number of further points arise in connection with Example 1:

1. Note first that—in this particular example—the expression in the RETURN statement is a legal SQL/92 expression; that is, it uses only operators already available in SQL/92 without PSM.

2. Any language that supports functions (or procedures) clearly needs a set of rules to define the process of matching arguments and parameters, and PSM is no exception. In particular, rules are needed to specify the legal data types for the argument that corresponds to a parameter of a given data type. In the case of PSM, for example, is it legal to invoke FIRST_WORD with an argument of type CHAR VARYING(500)? What about CHAR VARYING(1500)? What about a character string of fixed length, not varying length? These issues are addressed in Sections E.4 and E.5.

3. It is at first a little surprising to learn that (as suggested in the introduction to this section) routine names—or, rather, routine *invocation* names, as we call them in this appendix—are not required to be unique within any particular scope. In the example, therefore, a second routine with invocation name FIRST_WORD could also be defined (perhaps within the same PSM module), provided only that:

   ▪ *Either* it did not also have just one parameter;

   ▪ *Or,* if it did, the data type of that parameter was not CHAR VARYING (1000).

   Further, it is not necessary for every routine with invocation name FIRST_WORD to specify the data type of its result as CHAR VARYING (40). It is not even necessary for every such routine to be a function. In other words, routines are identified not by their invocation name alone, but rather by their *signature*, defined as the combination of invocation name, routine type, and parameter definitions.* Refer to Section E.5 for further discussion.

4. Note that all routine parameters and results are scalars, not, e.g., arrays or rows or tables. In particular, therefore, PSM does not currently support user-defined *aggregate* functions.

---

*We note that the term *signature* is defined but nowhere used in the current PSM draft. The concept is probably included in anticipation of future support for supertypes and subtypes (see Appendix F).

5. The definition of a niladic routine—i.e., one involving no parameters—must include a "parenthesized parameter definition commalist" that consists of a pair of parentheses enclosing nothing. *Note:* Invocation of such a routine will also involve a pair of parentheses enclosing nothing, of course. We remark that, by contrast, invocations of niladic *builtin* functions consist of the function name alone (no arguments and no parentheses).

Routine Classification

Routines in general can be classified into four broad categories, according to (a) the language in which they are written and (b) the language from which they are invoked, as the following table indicates:

	written in SQL	written in nonSQL	
invoked from SQL	Case 1	Case 2	PSM routines
invoked from nonSQL	Case 3	Case 4	nonPSM routines

As the table suggests, only Case 1 or Case 2 routines ("SQL-invoked routines") are truly part of PSM as such; for completeness, however, we briefly examine all four cases below.

■ *Case 1:* Written in and invoked from SQL

A routine that is written in SQL is said to be an *SQL routine;* the body of such a routine consists of a single SQL statement, possibly compound (where the name "SQL" refers to SQL/92 augmented by the facilities of PSM—see Section E.6). A routine that is meant to be invoked from SQL is said to be an *SQL-invoked routine.* Routine FIRST_WORD in Example 1 is an SQL routine and an SQL-invoked routine. *Note:* Compound SQL statements are illustrated in Example 2 in the next subsection below.

■ *Case 2:* Written in some other language, invoked from SQL

PSM allows SQL-invoked routines to be written in some language other than SQL (e.g., PL/I). Such a routine is said to be an *external routine* ("nonSQL routine" might have been a better term). The PSM routine definition for such a routine contains, not the code that actually implements that routine, but rather an EXTERNAL clause that (among other things) tells the system where that code can be found. Note that external routines are likely to suffer from the problems of impedance mismatch (etc.) mentioned briefly in Section E.1.

■ *Case 3:* Written in SQL, invoked from some other language

SQL routines can also be invoked from some language other than SQL (e.g., PL/I). Such a routine is said to be an *externally invoked routine* ("nonSQL-invoked routine" might have been a better term). Note, therefore, that the procedures of the module language described in Chapter 6 are precisely—by definition—externally invoked SQL routines (although those procedures can now make use of the new SQL statements introduced by PSM); in fact, the procedures of the module language are the *only* externally invoked SQL routines.* Note carefully, therefore, that such routines are not considered to be PSM routines as such.

- *Case 4:* Written in and invoked from some other language

  The concept of a routine that is both external (i.e., not written in SQL) and externally invoked (i.e., not invoked from SQL) also exists, at least notionally. However, no syntax is provided for defining such a thing. None is needed, of course, because the concept can refer only to routines defined and implemented in a nonSQL environment, invoked by programs also defined and implemented in a nonSQL environment. *Note:* It might possibly be argued that the routines of CLI (see Chapter 23) fall into this category.

From the foregoing overview, it should be clear that Case 1 is the most important so far as this appendix is concerned, and so we focus our attention on that case. From this point forward, therefore, we will simply assume (where it makes any difference) that all routines are Case 1 routines, barring explicit statements to the contrary. We will say a little more regarding Case 2 in Section E.8. As for the other two cases, Case 3 is adequately covered by Chapter 6, and there is nothing more to say regarding Case 4.

We close this subsection by returning to Example 1 to make a few additional points. As explained above, FIRST_WORD is an SQL routine and an SQL-invoked routine. The fact that it is an SQL routine can be stated explicitly by means of the specification LANGUAGE SQL, as here:

```
FUNCTION
    FIRST_WORD ( :X CHAR VARYING (1000) )
    RETURNS CHAR VARYING (40)
    LANGUAGE SQL
    RETURN etc.
```

LANGUAGE SQL is implied if no LANGUAGE specification is stated explicitly (unless the routine definition appears within a module definition—see the subsection "Routine Packaging" later in this section—in which case the routine effectively inherits the LANGUAGE specification of the containing module).

Some Procedure Examples

Example 2: Thus far, we have described some general aspects of routines with reference to an example that is a function. That example necessarily shows syntax that

---

*It follows that (by contrast) *functions* are always SQL-invoked, and hence always PSM routines specifically.

is special to functions and omits syntax that is special to procedures. We turn now
to the procedure case. Here is an example of a procedure definition:

```
PROCEDURE
    TRANSFER  ( :FROM    CHAR(7),
                :TO      CHAR(7),
                :AMOUNT DECIMAL(7,2) )

    BEGIN

        UPDATE ACCOUNTS
        SET    BALANCE = BALANCE - :AMOUNT
        WHERE  ACCOUNT_ID = :FROM ;

        UPDATE ACCOUNTS
        SET    BALANCE = BALANCE + :AMOUNT
        WHERE  ACCOUNT_ID = :TO ;

    END
```

Example 2 shows a more or less self-explanatory procedure called TRANSFER.
Points to note:

1. Because TRANSFER is a procedure, there is no RETURNS clause and no
   RETURN statement in the procedure body (in fact, the body of a procedure
   is not allowed to contain such a statement).

2. If the body of a PSM routine (function or procedure) is written in SQL, that
   body—just like that of a procedure as described in Chapter 6—is required to
   consist of a single SQL statement. However, that statement is allowed to be
   compound (as it is in the example, in fact); i.e., it can consist of a sequence of
   SQL statements, each followed by a semicolon,* the whole sequence being
   bracketed by the key words BEGIN and END. Compound statements are discussed in detail in Section E.6.

3. The parameters :FROM, :TO, and :AMOUNT are all *input parameters;* that
   is, they all represent values—i.e., *arguments*—that will be provided as input
   to the procedure when it is invoked. Here is an example of such an invocation
   (part of an application program using embedded SQL):

```
EXEC SQL CALL TRANSFER ( 'A123456', 'B987654', 99.95 ) ;
```

   In this invocation, the necessary input values are provided by the three arguments A123456 (the FROM account number), B987654 (the TO account
   number), and 99.95 (the AMOUNT value).

Example 3: In fact, PSM supports *output* parameters also. Suppose TRANSFER
is required not only to effect the desired transfer of funds but also to place the

---

*We remark that the syntax of PSM makes heavy but rather unsystematic (and certainly very confus-
ing) use of semicolons, as will be seen.

resulting balances into certain host variables. Then the definition of TRANSFER might look like this:

```
PROCEDURE
    TRANSFER ( IN   :FROM         CHAR(7),
               IN   :TO           CHAR(7),
               IN   :AMOUNT       DECIMAL(7,2),
               OUT  :FROM_BALANCE DECIMAL(9,2),
               OUT  :TO_BALANCE   DECIMAL(9,2) )

    BEGIN

        UPDATE ACCOUNTS
        SET    BALANCE = BALANCE - :AMOUNT
        WHERE  ACCOUNT_ID = :FROM ;

        UPDATE ACCOUNTS
        SET    BALANCE = BALANCE + :AMOUNT
        WHERE  ACCOUNT_ID = :TO ;

        SELECT F.BALANCE, T.BALANCE
        INTO   :FROM_BALANCE, :TO_BALANCE
        FROM   ACCOUNTS F, ACCOUNTS T
        WHERE  F.ACCOUNT_ID = :FROM
        AND    T.ACCOUNT_ID = :TO ;

    END
```

Example 3 has the same input parameters as Example 2, but this time we have explicitly defined them to be input parameters by including the key word IN in their definitions. By contrast, we have explicitly defined FROM_BALANCE and TO_BALANCE to be output parameters, by including the key word OUT in their definitions. It is also possible to specify a parameter that is both input and output, using the key word INOUT. IN is the default if nothing is specified. *Note:* These *parameter modes* can be specified only for procedures; for functions, all parameters are IN parameters by definition, and explicit specification of a parameter mode is not allowed. Note too that (a) assignment to an IN parameter is not allowed, and (b) reference to the value of an OUT parameter is not allowed.

Arguments corresponding to input parameters can be specified as arbitrary scalar expressions; arguments corresponding to output parameters, by contrast, must be specified as simple host variables.* An invocation of (the revised version of) procedure TRANSFER might thus look like this:

```
EXEC SQL CALL TRANSFER
            ( 'A123456', 'B987654', 99.95, :X, :Y ) ;
```

The effect of this invocation will be to perform the desired transfer of funds and to set host variables X and Y to contain the resulting FROM account balance and TO account balance, respectively.

---

*Or SQL variables—see Section E.6—or (if the invocation is from within another routine, possibly from within a client module) parameters.

We have now shown two examples of the use of the new SQL CALL statement to invoke a procedure. Note that even if the program containing those invocations is written in some host language such as Pascal or PL/I, the invoked procedure is still an SQL-invoked routine, because the CALL statement that performs the actual invocation is an SQL statement, not a Pascal or PL/I statement. Note further that, precisely because they are SQL-invoked, such procedures do not need—and in fact are not permitted to have—an SQLCODE or SQLSTATE parameter; instead, the invoking routine can and should use GET DIAGNOSTICS statements, augmented by the exception-handling features described in Section E.7, to determine the success or otherwise of the procedure invocation. *Note:* The question of *functions* having an SQLCODE or SQLSTATE parameter does not arise (why not?).

Routine Packaging

Every PSM routine belongs either to a schema or to a module that in turn belongs to a schema.* *Note:* The reason for providing two alternative packaging methods, and the rationale by which a choice is made between the two in any given situation, are both extremely unclear to this writer. What is more, the fact that there *are* two alternative is the source of much complexity, as will be seen.

We discuss modules first (the *M* in "PSM" does stand for *modules,* after all). The module concept is not new, of course, but PSM modules—"server modules"—do differ somewhat from the "client" modules of the existing module language as discussed in Chapter 6. To be more specific:

1. Every PSM module (the official term is *SQL-server module*) has an associated *search path,*† specifying which schemas, in which order, are to be searched to find the specific routine that is to be executed as the result of some routine invocation from within the module (unless the routine invocation in question specifies a qualified invocation name, in which case no such search is needed). See Section E.5.

2. PSM modules can contain functions as well as (or instead of) procedures. Furthermore, those functions and procedures can include external routines as well as SQL routines (i.e., one PSM module can contain a mixture of both).

3. PSM modules ("server modules") belong to schemas and hence are presumably stored at the server site. They are created and destroyed by means of new

---

*There is a conceptual difference between the concepts "belonging to a module" and "belonging to a schema," as follows. Modules can be perceived as *actually containing* the corresponding objects. Schemas, by contrast, contain only *descriptors* of the corresponding objects. Whether this distinction is important in the present context is unclear.

†The same is true of client modules also under PSM.

CREATE and DROP MODULE statements. *Note:* As stated in Section E.1, PSM never explicitly says that client modules are stored at the client site and server modules at the server site; in particular, there is no prohibition against storing a "client" module at the server site. Note too that (as already mentioned) it is also possible for a routine to belong to a schema instead of to a module. Such routines are *not* referred to as "server routines" (instead they are called "schema routines"), but they do enjoy a kind of "server" status—they can be created and destroyed by new CREATE and DROP statements, and presumably they can also be stored at the server site.

4. Like all schema elements, server modules (and schema routines) have names that consist of an identifier preceded by a qualifier that is the name of the relevant schema (separated from the identifier by a period).

Example 4: We illustrate the packaging of routines into a PSM ("server") module. Module STRING_FUNCS is intended to consist of a package of commonly desired (but not so commonly provided!) functions on character strings. We show three such functions below: REVERSE, which returns the reverse of its argument (e.g., "SQL" yields "LQS"); FIRST_WORD, which returns the first word of its argument; and LAST_WORD, which returns the last word of its argument. We do not show the containing schema for the module, though such a schema must of course exist.

```
CREATE MODULE STRING_FUNCS
   LANGUAGE SQL

DECLARE FUNCTION
   REVERSE ( :X CHAR VARYING (1000) )
   RETURNS CHAR VARYING (1000)
   RETURN
   CASE CHAR_LENGTH ( :X )
      WHEN 0 THEN :X
      WHEN 1 THEN :X
      ELSE SUBSTRING ( :X FROM CHAR_LENGTH ( :X ) ) ||
              REVERSE ( SUBSTRING ( :X FROM 1 FOR
                                    CHAR_LENGTH ( :X ) - 1 ) )
   END ;

DECLARE FUNCTION
   FIRST_WORD ( :X CHAR VARYING (1000) )
   RETURNS CHAR VARYING (40)
   RETURN TRIM
       ( SUBSTRING
         ( ( :X || ' ' )
           FROM 1
           FOR POSITION ( ' ' IN ( :X || ' ' ) ) ) ) ;

DECLARE FUNCTION
   LAST_WORD ( :X CHAR VARYING (1000) )
   RETURNS CHAR VARYING (40)
   RETURN REVERSE ( FIRST_WORD ( REVERSE ( :X ) ) ) ;

END MODULE
```

Points to note:

1. Unlike client module definitions, server module definitions must begin with CREATE MODULE (instead of just MODULE) and end with END MODULE.

2. Every routine definition in the example begins with DECLARE FUNCTION, instead of (as in Example 1) just FUNCTION alone. DECLARE is an optional noiseword, permitted if and only if the routine definition appears within a module definition.

3. Every routine body terminates in a semicolon. Such semicolons are required if and only if the routine definition appears within a module definition.

4. The specification LANGUAGE SQL appears at the level of the overall module, implying that every routine defined therein is an SQL routine unless it explicitly specifies otherwise.

5. We point out that the function REVERSE is recursive. PSM does not explicitly state that recursive routines are allowed, but nor does it prohibit them.*

6. The line WHEN 1 THEN :X could be omitted from the body of REVERSE without changing the semantics of the function. We include it merely for performance reasons.

Example 5: Packaging routines into a PSM module as illustrated in Example 4 might be best suited to third-party organizations that wish to sell "shrink-wrapped" software to SQL database users. Database administrators, providing customized routines for use at their own installations, might possibly prefer such routines to belong to schemas (perhaps to modules "within" such schemas) instead. PSM has some extensions to the CREATE SCHEMA statement for this purpose. For example:

```
CREATE SCHEMA ACCT_PROCS

CREATE PROCEDURE
   TRANSFER ( :FROM    CHAR(7),
              :TO      CHAR(7),
              :AMOUNT DECIMAL(7,2) )

   BEGIN

      UPDATE ACCOUNTS
      SET    BALANCE = BALANCE - :AMOUNT
      WHERE  ACCOUNT_ID = :FROM ;

      UPDATE ACCOUNTS
      SET    BALANCE = BALANCE + :AMOUNT
      WHERE  ACCOUNT_ID = :TO ;

   END
```

---

*As this book was going to press, we discovered that PSM does *implicitly* include a prohibition against recursion (an unfortunate prohibition, in our opinion), because "subject routine determination"—see Section E.5—is performed at routine creation time. REVERSE is thus not a legal PSM function.

```
CREATE PROCEDURE
    ADJUST ( :TO       CHAR(7),
             :AMOUNT DECIMAL(7,2) )

    BEGIN

        UPDATE ACCOUNTS
        SET    BALANCE = BALANCE + :AMOUNT
        WHERE  ACCOUNT_ID = :TO ;

        INSERT
        INTO   ADJUSTMENTS ( ACCOUNT_ID, AMOUNT, ADJUST_TIME )
        VALUES ( :TO, :AMOUNT, CURRENT_TIMESTAMP ) ;

    END
```

Points to note:

1. The routine definitions begin with CREATE instead of DECLARE. In fact, routine definitions that appear directly within a schema instead of within a module definition *must* begin with the key word CREATE. Such routines (only) can be dropped by means of an explicit DROP statement.

2. LANGUAGE specifications can appear at the routine level (though the example does not show any). Such a specification is not permitted at the schema level.

E.3   ROUTINES, MODULES, AND SCHEMAS

In this section, we describe the syntax and semantics of (the relevant aspects of) routine, module, and schema creation and destruction in detail, without however unnecessarily repeating material already covered in the previous section. We also briefly discuss a few related matters.

Routine Definition

```
routine-definition
    ::=    [ CREATE | DECLARE ] { PROCEDURE | FUNCTION }
           routine ( [ parameter-definition-commalist ] )
           [ RETURNS data-type ]
           [ LANGUAGE language ]
           [ SPECIFIC routine ]
           SQL-statement

parameter-definition
    ::=    [ IN | OUT | INOUT ] parameter data-type
```

Points to note:

1. The key word CREATE is required if the routine definition is immediately contained within a schema. The key word DECLARE is permitted (though not

required) if the routine definition is immediately contained within a module definition.

2. The syntax element *routine* appearing after the PROCEDURE or FUNCTION key word is the name by which the routine in question will be invoked (referred to as the *invocation name* in this appendix). In order to support what is commonly called "overloading" (see Sections E.4 and E.5), distinct routines are allowed to have the same invocation name. However, every routine is required to have a unique *specific* name, defined by means of the SPECIFIC clause, that is unique with respect to all such names within the schema that directly or indirectly contains the definition of the routine in question.* (If the SPECIFIC clause is omitted, an implementation-defined default—presumably derived from the invocation name in some straightforward way—is provided.) As already explained, routine invocation is performed in terms of the (not necessarily distinct) invocation name; the specific name, by contrast, is used in operations that are intended to drop the routine or grant or revoke authorization on it.

3. Let routine *R* have invocation name *I*. Then:

   - If *R* belongs to schema *S*, then the name *I* can be qualified by the schema name *S* in the usual way. For example, if *R* happened to be a procedure, then CALL *S.I* (...) would be a legal procedure invocation.

   - If *R* additionally belongs to module *M*, then the name *I* can instead be qualified by the key word MODULE (*cf.* "Type 1 temporary tables" in Chapter 18). Thus, if (again) *R* happened to be a procedure, then CALL MODULE.*I* (...) would be a legal procedure invocation—though only from within module *M*.

4. As already explained in Section E.2, the *data type* specifications within parameter definitions and the RETURNS clause must be SQL data types (or domains), not host language data types.

5. For an explanation of the LANGUAGE specification, see Sections E.2 and E.8.

6. The routine body consists of a single SQL statement, and can be any of the following:

   - An SQL data manipulation statement
   - An SQL session statement
   - An SQL diagnostics statement

---

*If the specific name is qualified by a schema name, then that schema name must identify the schema that would have been assumed by default anyway, *viz.* the schema being created (if the routine definition is contained within a CREATE SCHEMA) or the schema associated with the module (if the routine definition is contained within a CREATE MODULE). See Chapters 4 and 6.

- An SQL dynamic statement
- An SQL control statement

Most of these categories were explained in the body of the book (principally in Chapter 6). Note, however, that the *SQL session statements* now include SET PATH (see Section E.9), and the *SQL diagnostics statements* now include SIGNAL and RESIGNAL (see Section E.7). The *SQL control statements*—CALL, RETURN, assignment (SET), CASE, IF, LOOP, LEAVE, WHILE, REPEAT, FOR, and compound statements—are explained in Section E.6.

Server Module Definition

```
server-module-definition
   ::=    CREATE MODULE [ module ]
        [ NAMES ARE character-set ]
          LANGUAGE language
        [ SCHEMA schema ] [ AUTHORIZATION user ]
        [ PATH schema-commalist ]
        [ temporary-table-definition-list ]
          module-element-list
          END MODULE
```

The SQL/92 syntax for *client* module definition was given in Chapter 6. Server modules extend that syntax somewhat, as follows:

1. The CREATE and END MODULE key words must be specified.

2. The LANGUAGE specification indicates the language in which routines in this module are written (*not* the language from which they are invoked, as it does for a client module). As previously mentioned, this specification can be overridden at the individual routine level.

3. The optional clause PATH *schema-commalist* specifies the module *default search order* or "search path"—that is, which schemas, in which order, are to be searched to find the specific routine that is to be executed as the result of some routine invocation from within the module (unless the routine invocation in question specifies a qualified invocation name, in which case no such search is needed). All schemas in the path must belong to the catalog that contains the schema associated with the module in question (see Chapter 6 for an explanation of what it means for a schema to be "associated with" a module). If no default path is specified explicitly, an implementation-defined path is assumed by default; that default path must include the schema associated with the module in question. See Section E.5 for further discussion.

4. The legal "module elements" are as follows:

- cursor definitions
- dynamic cursor definitions
- routine definitions

Cursor definitions, dynamic or otherwise, were discussed earlier in this book, in Chapters 20 and 10, respectively; routine definitions were discussed in the previous subsection. Note that routine definitions immediately contained within a module definition must have a semicolon terminator.

Schema Definition

```
schema-definition
    ::=   CREATE SCHEMA [ schema ] [ AUTHORIZATION user ]
                [ DEFAULT CHARACTER SET character-set ]
                [ PATH schema-commalist ]
                [ schema-element-list ]
```

The SQL/92 syntax for schema definition was given in Chapter 4. PSM extends that syntax somewhat, as follows:

1. The optional clause PATH *schema-commalist* specifies the schema *default search order* or "search path"—that is, which schemas, in which order, are to be searched to find the specific routine that is to be executed as the result of some routine invocation from within some routine, possibly within some module, defined within this CREATE SCHEMA (unless the routine invocation in question specifies a qualified invocation name, in which case no such search is needed). All schemas in the path must belong to the same catalog as the schema being defined. If no default path is specified explicitly, an implementation-defined path is assumed by default; that default path must include the schema being defined. See Section E.5 for further discussion.

2. The schema elements can now include one or more module definitions, each of which *must* include the CREATE and END MODULE key words. Those modules are server modules, by definition.

3. The schema elements can now include one or more routine definitions, each of which *must* begin with the key word CREATE.

Routine and Module Destruction

Modules and routines can be destroyed by means of appropriate DROP statements—syntax:

```
DROP MODULE module { RESTRICT | CASCADE }

DROP [ SPECIFIC ] { ROUTINE | FUNCTION | PROCEDURE } routine
                                    { RESTRICT | CASCADE }
```

Destroying a module automatically destroys all routines belonging to that module, of course; likewise, destroying a schema automatically destroys all modules and routines belonging to that schema. In the case of "DROP ... routine," *routine* must be a specific name if SPECIFIC is specified, an invocation name otherwise (further, that invocation name can be followed, if necessary, by a parenthesized commalist of parameter data type specifications—not shown in the syntax above—in order to pin down the corresponding specific name precisely).

Note: As usual, if RESTRICT is specified, the DROP will succeed only if it has no side effects (loosely speaking). If CASCADE is specified, on the other hand, the DROP will always succeed, even if there exists some invocation somewhere of the now dropped routine or of a routine within the now dropped module. What happens if any such invocations exist is the following:

- An invocation that is part of the DEFAULT clause of a domain or column definition causes an implicit ALTER DOMAIN ... DROP DEFAULT for that domain or an implicit ALTER TABLE ... ALTER COLUMN ... DROP DEFAULT for that column.

- An invocation that is part of the body of some routine causes an implicit DROP SPECIFIC ROUTINE ... CASCADE for that routine!—an action that appears so drastic that (as with DROP SCHEMA in the body of the book) we respectfully suggest that CASCADE be reserved for very special occasions indeed.

The EXECUTE Privilege

Very loosely speaking, EXECUTE is the privilege that is required on a given routine in order to be allowed to invoke that routine (see below for further discussion). More precisely, the EXECUTE privilege applies to:

- Routines within schemas;
- Routines within server modules (in this case, however, the privilege is granted or revoked at the level of the overall module, not that of the individual routine).

No other privileges are defined for routines and modules, nor does EXECUTE apply to anything other than routines and modules.

The syntax for granting the EXECUTE privilege is:

```
GRANT EXECUTE ON object TO users [ WITH GRANT OPTION ]
```

Here "object" is either an expression of the form "MODULE module" or an expression of the form

```
[ SPECIFIC ] { ROUTINE | FUNCTION | PROCEDURE } routine
```

(possibly followed by a parenthesized commalist of parameter data type specifications, as for DROP). And here is the corresponding REVOKE syntax:

```
REVOKE [ GRANT OPTION FOR ] EXECUTE ON object FROM users
                          { RESTRICT | CASCADE }
```

Note: Destroying a module or routine automatically causes all EXECUTE privileges on that module or routine to be revoked, of course.

Let us examine the EXECUTE privilege a little more closely. The fact is, the semantics of EXECUTE are subtly and importantly different from those of other privileges. It might be expected that the possession or otherwise of the EXECUTE privilege on routine *R* would determine whether or not an invocation of *R* is permitted (*R* here being an invocation name). However, matters are not quite so straightforward. Suppose for definiteness that routine *R* belongs to some schema *S*. Then schema *S* might contain several distinct routines, with (say) specific names *R1, R2,* and so on, all having the same invocation name *R*. So long as the user holds the EXECUTE privilege on *at least one* of *R1, R2,* etc., an invocation of *R* by that user is permissible.

This discussion brings us to the delicate topic of *subject routine determination*—i.e., the process of determining which specific routine is to be executed in response to a given routine invocation. Section E.5 addresses that topic in detail. First, however, it is necessary to say something (in Section E.4) regarding the related topic of *type precedence*. But it is only fair to say that sections E.4 and E.5 are both fairly detailed and complex; the reader might prefer to skip them on a first reading, going straight on to the simpler Section E.6, "SQL Control Statements."

E.4   TYPE PRECEDENCE

The *type precedence* concept has to do with the issue, already mentioned briefly in Section E.2, of *matching arguments and parameters.* More specifically, it has to do with questions such as the following: If function FIRST_WORD is defined with a parameter of type CHAR VARYING, can it be invoked with an argument of type CHAR—i.e., a fixed length string instead of a varying one? (The answer to this particular question, by the way, is *yes.*)

We being with the notion of a *type precedence list,* which is basically just an ordered list of data types. The first type in such a list is said (prosaically enough) to *precede* the second, and the second the third, and so on, with the exception that consecutive elements are permitted to be *equal in precedence.* Let *A, B, C* be types in the same precedence list. Then, if *A* precedes *B* and *B* precedes or is equal in precedence to *C*, then *A* precedes *C*; similarly, if *A* is equal in precedence to *B* and *B* precedes *C*, then again *A* precedes *C*.

Type precedence lists are based on defined complete orderings for the data types of various "generic" data types—numeric, character string, and so on. The type precedence list for some specific type *T* is exactly the type precedence list for the generic type to which *T* belongs, minus the types that precede *T* in that generic list. Every specific type is thus the first or equal first element of exactly one type precedence list, so we can, and do, speak unambiguously of *the* type precedence list for any given type.

The primary purpose of defining type precedence lists is to allow developers of user-defined routines some of the same freedoms that implementers of SQL builtin functions already enjoy. Recall, for example, that SQL builtin numeric operators such as "+" and "−" apply to all numeric data types; e.g., the expression $X + Y$ is equally permissible when the data types of X and Y are INTEGER and when they are REAL (or, indeed, when X is INTEGER and Y is REAL). In the same way, we might specify the single parameter to the user-defined function ABS ("absolute value") to be of type REAL and yet expect invocations such as ABS(I) to work as expected, and not be syntax errors, even when the data type of I is INTEGER. And indeed so we can, because the type precedence list for type INTEGER includes type REAL (see below). In other words, argument A can be thought of as "matching" parameter P if the type precedence list for the actual type of A includes the declared type of P.*

Note: Let us stay with the ABS example a moment longer. Suppose the definition of ABS is such that its single parameter and its result are both of type REAL. Then an invocation such as ABS(I), where I is of type INTEGER, will indeed be legal, thanks to the type precedence rules; however, the result will be of type REAL, not INTEGER. If we want ABS(I) to return an *integer,* we will have to *overload* the function—i.e., we will have to define two distinct routines with the same invocation name (ABS), one with parameter and result types both REAL and the other with them both INTEGER.

We now explain the various generic type precedence lists in detail. The only case that is less than straightforward is that of the generic type "numeric"; we therefore dispose of the other cases first.

- *Character strings:* The ordering is

  ```
  1. CHARACTER
  2. CHARACTER VARYING
  ```

- *Bit strings:* The ordering is

  ```
  1. BIT
  2. BIT VARYING
  ```

- *Datetimes and intervals:* The type precedence list for any given datetime or interval type is a singleton list containing just the datetime or interval type in question (though whether, e.g., TIME and TIME WITH TIME ZONE are considered to be two types or one is currently unclear).

- *Numbers:* In principle, the numeric types are ordered as follows:

---

*We assume here that P is an input parameter. If instead it is an output parameter, the types of A and P are required to be "the same" (though we note that the concept of two types being "the same" is itself somewhat problematic—see Appendix D).

```
1. SMALLINT
2. INTEGER
3. NUMERIC
4. DECIMAL
5. REAL
6. FLOAT
7. DOUBLE PRECISION
```

For historical reasons, however, PSM permits this ordering to vary somewhat from implementation to implementation. To be more specific, the following deviations are permitted (except that if the implementation-defined precision or maximum precision of type *T1* is less than that of type *T2*, then *T1* is required to precede *T2* in the ordering).

- SMALLINT and INTEGER can be equal in precedence.
- INTEGER and DECIMAL can be equal in precedence.
- DECIMAL can precede INTEGER (and possibly SMALLINT too).
- NUMERIC can precede INTEGER (and possibly SMALLINT).
- NUMERIC and DECIMAL can be equal in precedence.
- NUMERIC can precede DECIMAL.
- FLOAT and REAL can be equal in precedence.
- FLOAT can precede REAL.
- FLOAT and DOUBLE PRECISION can be equal in precedence.
- FLOAT can precede REAL.
- FLOAT and DOUBLE PRECISION can be equal in precedence.
- DOUBLE PRECISION can precede FLOAT.

Note: When a given routine is actually invoked, argument values are assigned to input parameters in accordance with the rules for update assignments (see Chapter 7). And when it completes execution, output parameters are assigned to argument variables in accordance with the rules for retrieval assignments (again, see Chapter 7).

We now move on to examine the process of "subject routine determination," and in particular to explain the role played by the notion of type precedence in that process.

E.5   SUBJECT ROUTINE DETERMINATION

The material of this section, perhaps more than other aspects of PSM, is almost certain to change before PSM does eventually become a standard. But the basic idea is quite simple, and can easily be explained by means of an example. Suppose there are two routines with the same invocation name (*R*, say). Suppose further that both routines have two parameters, of types INTEGER and REAL in the first case and REAL and INTEGER in the second case. Suppose finally that the user attempts a routine invocation of the form $R(A1,A2)$, where $A1$ and $A2$ are both of type DEC-IMAL. Which of the two routines is invoked? How does the system decide? This is the problem of *subject routine determination.*

Consider, then, the general invocation

```
routine ( argument-commalist )
```

(of course, this invocation will appear within a CALL statement if "routine" is in fact a procedure). Suppose some user attempts such an invocation, *RI* say. Note that the invocation name in *RI*, *R* say, might be qualified. Now, there can be any number of routines with invocation name *R*. Let *S1* be the set of all such routines. Then PSM specifies a sequence of rules for eliminating routines from *S1* until at most one—the *subject routine*—remains (it is an error if the rules do not yield exactly one subject routine). The rules (slightly simplified) are as follows.*

1. Eliminate all functions (if *RI* is the operand of a CALL statement) or procedures (otherwise) with invocation name *R* from *S1,* yielding the set *S2.*

2. Eliminate all routines from *S2* for which the user in question does not have the EXECUTE privilege, yielding the set *S3.*

3. Eliminate all routines from *S3* whose parameter data types do not match the corresponding argument data types, yielding the set *S4. Note:* "Match" here does not necessarily mean that the parameter and argument types have to be identical. In fact, for output parameters they do have to be identical; for input parameters, however, the parameter type need only be a member of the argument's type precedence list (see Section E.4). For character strings, the parameter and argument character sets must be the same.

4. If the invocation name *R* is unqualified, then (a) if *RI* appears in a module *M* and *M* contains at least one of the routines in *S4,* eliminate routines that do not belong to *M* from *S4*, yielding the set *S5*; (b) if *RI* appears in a module *M* but *M* contains none of the routines in *S4,* eliminate routines that do not belong to some schema in the search path of *M* from *S4,* yielding the set *S5.*

5. Let the *i*th argument of *RI* be of type *Ti* ($i = 1, 2, ..., n$). For each pair of routines, *RA* and *RB* say, in *S5*, where the type of the *i*th parameter of *RA* precedes that of the *i*th parameter of *RB* in the type precedence list of *Ti*, eliminate *RB* from *S5*. Let *S6* be the set resulting from all such eliminations.

   Note, incidentally, that this rule gives priority to parameters according to their left-to-right ordering. Consider the invocation R(X,Y), where the data

---

*There is a move afoot at the time of writing to limit PSM's support for overloaded routines to functions only. If this change occurs, the rules will require some further (minor) simplification.

types of X and Y are DECIMAL and SMALLINT, respectively. Then the definition R (... FLOAT, ... DOUBLE PRECISION) will be chosen over the definition R (... DOUBLE PRECISION, ... SMALLINT) because the latter will be eliminated when the first argument to the invocation is considered, even though it has an exact match for the second argument while the first definition has the poorest possible match.

6. Set *S6* will contain either just one routine or no routines at all. If it contains just one, that one is the subject routine. If it contains none at all, an error is raised.

E.6   SQL CONTROL STATEMENTS

The term *SQL control statements* refers to the new procedural programming statements introduced into SQL by PSM*—*viz.,* the CALL, RETURN, SET, CASE, IF, LOOP, LEAVE, WHILE, REPEAT, FOR, and compound statements. Since those statements make use of the normal imperative style, with familiar key words and semantics, we take the liberty of just presenting the syntax, for the most part, making only such brief additional commentary as seems warranted.

Note: It is worth pointing out explicitly that, since they are part of the SQL language, all of the SQL control statements—along with the associated exception-handling constructs defined in Section E.7 and the ability to define SQL variables (see later in this section)—can be used in a host program with embedded SQL or in a client module. It is worth pointing out also that the facilities introduced by PSM have the effect of converting the SQL "data sublanguage" into a computationally complete, general-purpose programming language; in principle, therefore, entire applications can now be coded in SQL.

CALL

```
CALL routine-invocation
```

The specified routine must be a procedure, not a function. The effects of the CALL are, precisely, the "side effects" of the procedure invocation. Such side effects can include updates to the database, assignments to SQL variables (see the subsection "SQL Variables" at the end of this section), and assignments to output parameters (or rather, more accurately, assignments to the arguments corresponding to such parameters).

RETURN

```
RETURN scalar-expression
```

---

*It has nothing to do with the term "data control" as used in the body of this book!—in Part IV in particular.

RETURN is permitted only within the body of a function. Its effect is to establish the result to be returned to the invoking routine and to pass control back to that routine. The key word NULL can appear in place of the scalar expression, with the obvious interpretation.

Assignment (SET)

```
SET target = scalar-expression
```

The target can be an output parameter or an SQL or host variable. The key word NULL can appear in place of the scalar expression, with the obvious interpretation.

CASE

There are two formats of the CASE statement. The more general is

```
CASE
    when-clause-list
  [ ELSE nested-SQL-statement-list ]
END CASE
```

where a "when clause" takes the form

```
WHEN conditional-expression THEN nested-SQL-statement-list
```

and a "nested SQL statement" is an SQL statement followed by a semicolon (see below). The WHEN clauses are processed in sequence as written. As soon as one is found for which the conditional expression evaluates to *true,* the evaluation process stops, and control is passed to the corresponding list of SQL statements. (As always, *true* here means what it says—i.e., not *false* and not *unknown*.) If none of the conditional expressions evaluates to *true*, then:

- If an ELSE clause is specified, control is passed to the corresponding list of SQL statements;
- Otherwise, the statement is in error.

The second CASE statement format effectively serves as shorthand for a special case of the first. The syntax is

```
CASE scalar-expression-1
    type-2-when-clause-list
  [ ELSE nested-SQL-statement-list ]
END CASE
```

where a "type 2 when clause" takes the form

```
WHEN scalar-expression-2 THEN nested-SQL-statement-list
```

This CASE format is defined to be equivalent to a CASE statement of the first format in which each WHEN clause includes a conditional expression of the form "scalar-expression-1 = scalar-expression-2."

As for the construct "nested SQL statement list": In fact, that construct appears as part of the syntax of several of the SQL control statements, not just the CASE statement *per se*. The intent in all cases is simply that if control is passed to that list of statements, then those statements are to be executed in sequence as written.* (Actually it is not clear why the construct exists at all, given that under PSM a single SQL statement can be a compound statement anyway. E.g., it is not clear why the WHEN clause of the CASE statement is not defined just to be of the form "WHEN conditional-expression THEN SQL-statement.")

Observe, incidentally, that CASE *statements* terminate in END CASE, while CASE *operations* (see Chapter 7) terminate in just plain END.

IF

```
IF conditional-expression
   THEN nested-SQL-statement-list
      [ elseif-clause-list ]
   [ ELSE nested-SQL-statement-list ]
END IF
```

The PSM IF statement is basically the familiar IF–THEN–ELSE construct found in many other programming languages, except that it can include a list of "elseif clauses" of the form

```
ELSEIF conditional-expression
   THEN nested-SQL-statement-list
```

Here ELSEIF is short for ELSE IF, with an implied END IF appearing (logically) immediately before the explicit one. Thus, for example, the statement

```
IF c1 THEN s11
      ELSEIF c2 THEN s12
                  ELSE s13
   END IF
```

is equivalent to the statement

```
IF c1 THEN s11
      ELSE IF c2 THEN s12
                  ELSE s13
            END IF
   END IF
```

---

*We remind the reader that (as explained in Chapter 17), within any given SQL statement execution, all references to the builtin functions CURRENT_DATE, CURRENT_TIME, and CURRENT_TIMESTAMP are effectively evaluated simultaneously (i.e., they are all based on a single reading of the local clock). This rule clearly requires certain revisions, given the possibility that a single SQL statement can now include many other SQL statements nested inside itself (and so on, recursively). The details of those revisions are beyond the scope of this appendix, however.

Likewise, the statement

```
IF c1 THEN s11
      ELSEIF c2 THEN s12
                    ELSEIF c3 THEN s13
                              ELSE s14
      END IF
```

is equivalent to the statement

```
IF c1 THEN s11
      ELSE IF c2 THEN s12
                    ELSE IF c3 THEN s13
                                 ELSE s14
                          END IF
               END IF
      END IF
```

(and so on). The reader might observe that these two examples are also equivalent to the statements

```
CASE
    WHEN c1 THEN s11
    WHEN c2 THEN s12
    ELSE         s13
END CASE
```

and

```
CASE
    WHEN c1 THEN s11
    WHEN c2 THEN s12
    WHEN c3 THEN s13
    ELSE         s14
END CASE
```

(respectively) and thus, like the present writer, question the justification for including ELSEIF in the language at all.

LOOP

```
[ beginning-label : ] LOOP
                     nested-SQL-statement-list
              END LOOP [ ending-label ]
```

We defer discussion of the beginning and ending labels for a moment. The "nested SQL statement list" is executed repeatedly *ad infinitum*. It might thus appear that a LOOP statement is a guaranteed recipe for an infinite loop; however, a device is available to permit exit from the loop, in the form of the LEAVE statement. Consider the following example.

Example 6: In the code fragment that follows, loop L1 will be executed just as many times as there are characters in the character string X (assumed to be a parameter). Note the use of an SQL variable, L (see later in this section).

```
DECLARE LOCAL TEMPORARY TABLE TTT
      ( III INTEGER, CCC CHAR(1),
        PRIMARY KEY ( III ) ) ;

BEGIN
    DECLARE L INTEGER ;
    SET L = 1 ;
L1: LOOP
        IF L > CHAR_LENGTH ( :X )
        THEN LEAVE L1 ;
        ELSE INSERT
             INTO   TTT ( III, CCC )
             VALUES ( L, SUBSTRING ( :X FROM L FOR 1 ) ) ;
             SET L = L + 1 ;
        END IF ;
    END LOOP L1 ;
END
```

Incidentally, the current PSM draft allows DECLARE LOCAL TEMPORARY TABLE statements to appear within a module but not within a compound statement, and hence not within a routine. Analogous remarks apply to DECLARE CURSOR also. However, this state of affairs is probably just an oversight and might well change before PSM becomes a standard.

As for the question of *beginning* and *ending labels:* Such labels are identifiers in the usual sense. Note, however, that not all SQL statements can be labeled; in fact, the only ones that can be are *compound* statements and the various *looping* statements (WHILE, REPEAT, FOR, and LOOP itself). The foregoing example illustrates perhaps the major reason for giving a statement a "beginning label": That label can then be used in a LEAVE statement within the body of the statement—which, to repeat, must be a loop or compound statement—to cause control to pass out of the statement identified by that label.

Statements with a beginning label can also have an ending label, but if they do, then that ending label must be identical to the corresponding beginning label (the intent seems to be a matter of documentation merely).

LEAVE

```
LEAVE label
```

The specified label must be the beginning label of some SQL statement (a looping or compound statement) that contains the LEAVE statement. Execution of the statement identified by the label is terminated. Note that if statement *L1* contains statement *L2* (at any level of nesting), statement *L2* can contain the statement LEAVE *L1*.

WHILE

```
[ beginning-label : ] WHILE conditional-expression DO
                          nested-SQL-statement-list
                      END WHILE [ ending-label ]
```

The WHILE statement

```
W: WHILE c DO
       sl
    END WHILE W
```

is defined to be equivalent to the LOOP statement

```
W: LOOP
       IF c
          THEN sl
          ELSE LEAVE W ;
       END IF ;
    END LOOP W
```

(we assume here that some arbitrary statement label *W* is supplied by the implementation if no such label is stated explicitly).

REPEAT

```
[ beginning-label : ] REPEAT
                         nested-SQL-statement-list
                      UNTIL conditional-expression
                      END REPEAT [ ending-label ]
```

The REPEAT statement

```
R: REPEAT
       sl
    UNTIL c
    END REPEAT R
```

is defined to be equivalent to the LOOP statement

```
R: LOOP
       sl
       IF c
          THEN LEAVE R ;
       END IF ;
    END LOOP R
```

(we assume here that some arbitrary statement label *R* is supplied by the implementation if no such label is stated explicitly).

FOR

```
[ beginning-label : ] FOR variable AS
                         [ cursor [ INSENSITIVE ] CURSOR FOR ]
                         cursor-specification
                         DO nested-SQL-statement-list
                      END FOR [ ending-label ]
```

CAVEAT: There are clear problems with the FOR statement at the time of writing; it might even be deleted entirely by the time PSM becomes a standard. We therefore do not attempt a very thorough explanation of it here. But the basic idea is simply that the "nested SQL statement list" is to be executed once for each row in the result of evaluating the cursor specification. For each column in that result, an SQL variable is implicitly defined with the same name and data type as that column; the ith iteration of the loop starts with an implicit FETCH that assigns values from the ith row to those variables.

Example 7: The following example is an inverse of Example 6, reconstructing the character string that Example 6 dissects.

```
BEGIN
    SET :X = '' ;
    FOR F1 AS SELECT TTT.III, TTT.CCC
              FROM    TTT
              ORDER   BY III
          DO
              SET :X = :X || CCC ;
    END FOR ;
END
```

Note the use of variable CCC, whose existence and data type are implied by the existence and data type of column CCC within the result of evaluating the select-expression referencing temporary table TTT (see Example 6). Note too that the (required) "for loop variable"—F1 in the example—is never referenced!

Compound Statements

```
[ beginning-label : ] BEGIN
    [ [ NOT ] ATOMIC ]
    [ SQL-variable-definition-list ]
    [ condition-definition-list ]
    [ handler-definition-list ]
    [ nested-SQL-statement-list ]
                        END [ ending-label ]
```

SQL variable definitions are discussed at the end of the present section; condition and handler definitions are discussed in Section E.7. *Note:* Despite the syntax as shown above, PSM allows SQL variable and condition definitions to be arbitrarily interspersed.

Compound statements serve several more or less unrelated purposes:

- A sequence of one or more SQL statements can be given semicolon terminators and then bracketed by BEGIN and END (those BEGIN and END brackets *not* having semicolon terminators, observe) and thereby treated as a unit. That unit can optionally be executed within an "atomic execution context." (The meaning of this latter term might perhaps be guessed but is not defined in the current PSM draft. Whatever it means, the intent seems to be that ATOMIC specifies such a context and NOT ATOMIC does not; NOT ATOMIC is the default.)

■ A compound statement can include definitions of various "local" items—SQL variables, conditions, and handlers—whose scope is just the compound statement in question, overriding definitions of items that have the same name* and would otherwise be inherited from some "outer" or encompassing compound statement.

■ As we have already seen, a compound statement can have a statement label. We have already illustrated the use of such labels in connection with the LEAVE statement. Such labels can also be used as high-level qualifiers on references to local variables; however, we find such a usage rather unorthodox, to say the least, and choose not to discuss it any further here.

SQL Variables

An SQL variable definition takes the following form:

```
DECLARE SQL-variable-commalist
        { data-type | domain } [ DEFAULT default ] ;
```

As the syntax suggests, any number of SQL variables† can be defined within a single DECLARE, all of them having exactly the same data type and the same initial value (specified by "default," which can be any legal SQL/92 default, or an invocation of a user-defined function, or an invocation of the new niladic builtin function CURRENT_PATH discussed in Section E.9; the "default default" is—surprise!—null). Note that an SQL domain can be used to specify the data type; alas, such a specification means nothing more than that the data type is that on which the domain is defined—any domain constraints on that domain are ignored, as is also (curiously enough) the DEFAULT specification, if any, for that domain.

E.7   EXCEPTION HANDLING

Note: As in the body of the book (Chapter 22 in particular), we use the term "exception" in the present section to refer to both what SQL/92 calls exceptions (which are really *errors*) and also what it calls *completions*.

---

*Or items that handle a condition with the same name, in the case of handlers—handlers (very unfortunately, in this writer's opinion) having no names of their own.

†Note that, unlike the "SQL variables" discussed in Chapter 20 in connection with dynamic SQL, the SQL variables of PSM must be explicitly declared. Note too that (like parameters, and for the same reason) such variables probably ought to require a colon prefix; however, the current PSM draft says they do not.

PSM routines—more precisely, compound statements within PSM routines—can make their own arrangements for handling exceptions that might arise during execution of the compound statement in question. The relevant PSM facilities are as follows:

- The DECLARE CONDITION statement, which is used to define condition names;*

- The DECLARE HANDLER statement, which is used to define exception handlers for specified conditions;

- The SIGNAL statement, which is used to force the raising of a specified condition;

- The RESIGNAL statement, which (like SIGNAL) is used to force the raising of a condition, but only from within an exception handler execution. *Note:* Other, more detailed, differences between SIGNAL and RESIGNAL are explained later.

We examine these ideas in some depth in the subsections that follow. First, however, we remark that since an individual PSM statement can invoke another PSM routine, and that routine can in turn invoke other, lower-level routines (and so on), the SQL/92 concept of "one diagnostics area per SQL-agent" is a rather crude approach to dealing with feedback information. It might have been better to replace that concept by some kind of *stack* of diagnostics areas; invoking a routine would then add a new entry to the stack, which would later be deleted when that invocation completes.† However, such does not appear to be the mechanism proposed for PSM.

Condition Definition

```
DECLARE condition CONDITION [ FOR string ] ;
```

The purpose of the DECLARE CONDITION statement is simply to introduce a *name* ("condition") that can be used in subsequent DECLARE HANDLER, SIGNAL, and RESIGNAL statements. The DECLARE CONDITION must physically precede any DECLARE HANDLER that refers to the condition name in question. If the FOR option is specified, the condition name stands for the particular condition identified by the specified SQLSTATE value; "string" must be a character string literal representing one of the standard SQLSTATE values (not

---

*The term "condition" here has nothing to do with the conditional expressions discussed in Chapter 12. Rather, it simply means an *exception*.

†Analogous remarks apply to various aspects of the SQL-session context information, such as the current time zone (see Chapter 5).

00000). If the FOR option is omitted, the condition name stands merely for some condition whose meaning is, presumably, understood by the user but not by SQL *per se*. Here are examples of both cases (note the semicolons!):

```
DECLARE ZERODIVIDE CONDITION FOR '22012' ;

DECLARE ORDER_LIMIT_EXCEEDED CONDITION ;
```

The scope of a condition name is the compound statement in which it is declared, excluding any inner compound statements in which another DECLARE CONDITION appears specifying the same condition name. No two condition names in the same scope can refer to the same SQLSTATE value.

Handler Definition

```
DECLARE [ CONTINUE | EXIT | UNDO ] HANDLER
     FOR exception-commalist
         action ;
```

Again note the semicolon. Observe too that (as previously noted) handlers have no name. The "action" is a single SQL statement (exactly as in a routine body); that statement is to be executed if any of the specified "exceptions" occur.* Legal "exceptions" are as follows:

```
SQLEXCEPTION
SQLWARNING
NOT FOUND
SQLSTATE [ VALUE ] string-commalist
condition
```

SQLEXCEPTION corresponds to SQLSTATE values with a class value other than 00, 01, or 02; SQLWARNING corresponds to SQLSTATE values with class value 01; NOT FOUND corresponds to SQLSTATE values with class value 02.† VALUE is just a noiseword. "String" and "condition" are as for DECLARE CONDITION.

Let *H* be a handler defined within compound statement *S1* (we pretend for the sake of the discussion that handlers do in fact have names after all, so that expressions like "let *H* be a handler" can make some sense). Then *H* effectively defines one or more *condition:action* pairs with scope *S1* (excluding any inner compound

---

*It might help to point out that the "action" will almost certainly consist of a compound statement, the component statements of which will include (a) one or more GET DIAGNOSTICS statements, and perhaps (b) one or more RESIGNAL statements to invoke other actions if other errors occur during execution of the particular action under consideration.

†We remark in passing that the WHENEVER statement of embedded SQL supports SQLERROR and NOT FOUND, whereas DECLARE HANDLER supports SQLEXCEPTION, SQLWARNING, and NOT FOUND. SQLERROR and SQLEXCEPTION seem to mean the same thing. There is no WHENEVER analog of SQLWARNING.

statement *S2* in which another handler is defined for the same condition). What this means is that if *H* defines the condition:action pair *C:A1* (say) and condition *C* arises while that pair is "in scope," then action *A1* will be executed. But if *S1* contains a compound statement *A2* in which another DECLARE HANDLER specifies some new action *A2* for condition *C*, then the pair *C:A2* replaces *C:A1* within *S2*. No condition can be paired with more than one action in the same scope.

The optional "handler type" (CONTINUE or EXIT or UNDO) specifies what the system is to do before and after execution of the specified action (*A*, say):

- *CONTINUE:* No action before *A*. On successful completion of *A*, pass control to the statement immediately following the one that raised the condition that caused *A* to be invoked.

- *EXIT:* No action before *A*. On successful completion of *A*, pass control to the end of the compound statement that most immediately contains the statement that caused *A* to be invoked.

- *UNDO:* Before executing *A*, undo all changes made to SQL-data and SQL-schemas during the execution of the compound statement that most immediately contains the statement that caused *A* to be invoked. On successful completion of *A*, pass control to the end of that compound statement.

Let *s* be the SQLSTATE value produced by execution of *A*. If that execution was in fact successful (*s* = 00*xxx*), then the condition that caused *A* to be invoked is deemed to have been successfully handled. Otherwise, the system forces an implicit RESIGNAL; that RESIGNAL has no explicit operand (see the next subsection below for the significance of this remark), but is implicitly for that SQLSTATE value *s*. (Note that "SIGNAL *s*" would *not* work well here, because it would delete existing feedback information in the diagnostics area, as explained in the next subsection.)

SIGNAL and RESIGNAL

Both these statements force an exception to be raised. The syntax is:

```
SIGNAL { condition | string }
RESIGNAL [ condition | string ]
```

where, once again, "condition" and "string" are as for DECLARE CONDITION. Examples:

```
SIGNAL ORDER_LIMIT_EXCEEDED
RESIGNAL ZERODIVIDE
RESIGNAL
```

The important differences between SIGNAL and RESIGNAL are as follows:

- SIGNAL is always valid. RESIGNAL is valid only during execution of the "action" portion of some handler definition.

- SIGNAL sets the diagnostics area to contain just one entry, corresponding to the "condition" or "string" specified as the (required) SIGNAL operand; any previous entries are discarded.* RESIGNAL retains existing entries; if and only if "condition" or "string" is specified, it pushes those existing entries down and adds a new one (corresponding to that RESIGNAL operand) as entry number 1.

- If "condition" is specified, SIGNAL and RESIGNAL both set the CONDITION_IDENTIFIER value (introduced with PSM) for entry number 1 in the diagnostics area to indicate the specified condition. If "string" is specified (or if "condition" is specified and that condition stands for an SQLSTATE value), SIGNAL and RESIGNAL both set the RETURNED_SQLSTATE value for entry number 1 accordingly.

After the diagnostics area has been set as necessary, SIGNAL and RESIGNAL both cause the applicable handler action (if any) to be invoked. If no such action has been defined, the statement—SIGNAL itself, in the case of SIGNAL, or the statement that caused the handler action containing the RESIGNAL to be invoked, in the case of RESIGNAL—terminates with an "unhandled condition" exception.

E.8   EXTERNAL ROUTINES

In this section we take care of some unfinished business: namely, the specifics of *external* or "Case 2" routines (i.e., routines that are SQL-invoked but not written in SQL). The body of the PSM definition of such a routine consists not of an SQL statement, as that of a "Case 1" (or "Case 3") routine does, but rather of an EXTERNAL clause. And an EXTERNAL clause in turn consists primarily of a reference to a piece of code written in one of the standard host programming languages and stored somewhere else in the system. Here is an example.

Example 8: Suppose the code for function FIRST_WORD is written in PL/I and the executable version of that code is to be found in an operating system file called FIRST_WORD.EXE. Then the PSM definition of that function might look like this:

```
FUNCTION
    FIRST_WORD ( CHAR VARYING (1000) )
    RETURNS CHAR VARYING (40)
    LANGUAGE PLI
    EXTERNAL NAME FIRST_WORD.EXE
```

---

*Diagnostics area entries are called "conditions" in SQL/92!—see Chapter 22.

Points to note:

1. The parameter is unnamed. Parameters of external routines can be named but do not have to be; any such names would have no operational significance anyway but would serve as documentation merely (see the discussion of PARAMETER STYLE in the subsection "The EXTERNAL Clause" below).

2. The parameter data type is still an SQL data type, since the function will be invoked from SQL; however, the PL/I code that implements that function will expect a PL/I data type, of course. Refer to Chapter 6 for a discussion of the correspondences between SQL data types and those of "external" languages such as PL/I.

3. If and only if the routine is a procedure rather than a function, then explicit parameter modes—IN, OUT, or INOUT—should normally be specified (though IN will be assumed for any parameter for which no mode is stated explicitly).

4. As always (in PSM), the LANGUAGE specification indicates the language in which the routine is written—"PLI" in the example.

5. The EXTERNAL clause specifies that the executable version of function FIRST_WORD is to be found in the indicated operating system file. *Note:* PSM does not specify any syntax rules for the character string that follows the key word NAME. Our suggestion, FIRST_WORD.EXE, is not guaranteed to be appropriate. If the NAME clause is omitted, a string identical to the unqual-ified routine invocation name is assumed (it would be just FIRST_WORD in the example).

The EXTERNAL Clause

Here then is the full syntax for the EXTERNAL clause:

```
EXTERNAL [ NAME string ]
         LANGUAGE language
         [ PARAMETER STYLE { GENERAL | SQL } ]
         [ [ NOT ] DETERMINISTIC ]
         [ { READS | MODIFIES } SQL DATA ]
```

PARAMETER STYLE: The PARAMETER STYLE specification—SQL or GENERAL—concerns the protocol for passing information between invoking routines (necessarily SQL routines) and the external routine, catering for nulls and a few implicit extra parameters that are general to all external routines. Let the term "effective parameter definition commalist" ("effective commalist" for short) refer to the parameter definition commalist as understood by the code of the external routine. The structure of that effective commalist depends on (a) whether

GENERAL or SQL is specified for PARAMETER STYLE, and (b) whether the routine is a function or a procedure (a function requires an additional output parameter to deal with the returned value).

- If GENERAL is specified, the effective commalist is the same as the one explicitly stated. The disadvantage (or advantage, depending on one's point of view) of this case is that an exception will be raised on invocation if any argument is null.

- If SQL (the default) is specified, the effective commalist is defined as follows:

  a. The first n parameters are the n explicitly defined ones.

  b. If and only if the routine is a function, the next parameter is an output parameter corresponding to the result to be returned.

  c. The next n parameters ($n + 1$ if the routine is a function) are "null indicator" parameters (see Chapter 16), in 1:1 correspondence with the first n (or $n + 1$) "regular" parameters. The precise data type of such indicator parameters is implementation-defined but must be exact numeric with scale zero. The parameter mode for each such indicator parameter is the same as that of its corresponding regular parameter.

  d. The next parameter is both an input parameter and an output parameter; it is used to pass the "exception data item" (a term not further defined in PSM). Its data type must be some character type with length 5 and character set SQL_TEXT.

  e. The next parameter is an input parameter; it is used to pass the invocation name of the external routine to be invoked. Its data type must be some character type with implementation-defined length and character set SQL_TEXT.

  f. The next parameter is an input parameter; it is used to pass the specific name of the external routine to be invoked. Its data type must be some character type with implementation-defined length and character set SQL_TEXT.

  g. The final parameter is both an input parameter and an output parameter; it is used to pass the "message text data item" (another term not further defined in PSM). Its data type must be some character type with implementation-defined length and character set SQL_TEXT.

DETERMINISTIC: We pointed out in Section E.2 that external routines are likely to suffer from certain problems, especially since the SQL-implementation does not "see" the external code. For this reason, commercial products often provide extra syntax whereby the routine definer can inform the system of certain important properties the routine might possess. PSM provides one such piece of additional syntax, the DETERMINISTIC *vs.* NOT DETERMINISTIC option. DETERMINISTIC (the default) means the routine is guaranteed always to produce the same effects when invoked with the same arguments; NOT DETERMINISTIC means the opposite. For example:

```
FUNCTION
    FIRST_WORD ( CHAR VARYING (1000) )
    RETURNS CHAR VARYING (40)
    LANGUAGE PLI
    EXTERNAL NAME FIRST_WORD.EXE
            DETERMINISTIC
```

If DETERMINISTIC is specified when NOT DETERMINISTIC should have been, PSM merely observes, sagely, that "results are implementation-dependent." *Note:* At the time of writing, the DETERMINISTIC *vs.* NOT DETERMINISTIC option does not apply to SQL routines (though this situation might well change before PSM is finalized); instead, the implementation is expected to be able to work out for itself whether or not such a routine suffers from being "not deterministic" (or "indeterminate," a term the present writer would prefer—see Chapter 19).

READS or MODIFIES SQL DATA: A routine that intends to (read and) update SQL data must specify MODIFIES SQL DATA. A routine that intends to read but not update SQL data must specify READS SQL DATA. A routine that does not specify either READS or MODIFIES will not be allowed to access SQL data at all. *Note:* It is likely that such specifications will also be required of SQL routines in the final version of PSM.

The CAST FROM Clause

In the case of an external function, the RETURNS clause has an optional extension, the CAST FROM option, thus:

```
RETURNS data-type [ CAST FROM data-type ]
```

As indicated, CAST FROM applies only if the external routine is a function. Because it is a function, it returns a value; because it is external, that returned value might be of some SQL data type that is not directly available in the language in which the function is coded. Suppose, for example, that the result type is DATE and the external language is PL/I. Then the PL/I code might return its computed date in some character representation, in which case RETURNS DATE CAST FROM CHAR VARYING (30) might be an appropriate specification for the RETURNS clause.

E.9 MISCELLANEOUS TOPICS

In this final section we take care of a few miscellaneous PSM-related matters.

Key Words

PSM adds the following new key words:

ATOMIC	INOUT	RETURNS
CALL	LEAVE	ROUTINE
CONDITION	LOOP	SIGNAL
CURRENT_PATH	MODIFIES	SPECIFIC
DETERMINISTIC	OUT	SQLEXCEPTION
DO	PARAMETER	SQLWARNING
ELSEIF	PATH	STYLE
EXIT	READS	UNDO
FUNCTION	REDO	UNTIL
GENERAL	REPEAT	WHILE
HANDLER	RESIGNAL	
IF	RETURN	

Of these, all except ATOMIC, GENERAL, and STYLE are reserved words. We remark that the key word REDO is not used anywhere (it is probably a hangover from an earlier version of PSM in which DECLARE HANDLER supported an additional handler type).

Identifiers and Names

PSM introduces various new kinds of names—routine names, condition names, SQL variable names, and statement labels, all of which in their unqualified form are just identifiers (in the usual sense of that term). However, the rules regarding name qualification and scope of uniqueness are unfortunately not clear at this time. The general intent seems to be to support some kind of block-structured scoping, but the current PSM draft does not appear to spell out the rules in detail anywhere. In at least one respect, moreover—*viz.,* the use of statement labels as qualifiers on names of variables—it seems to have adopted a technique that is a trifle unconventional, to say the least.

Statement Categories

The statements introduced by PSM are categorized as follows. First, an entirely new category, the *SQL control statements,* is introduced, consisting of the following:

```
CALL, RETURN
IF, CASE
LOOP, WHILE, REPEAT, FOR, LEAVE
assignment (SET)
compound statement
```

The following are additional *SQL schema statements:*

```
CREATE MODULE, DROP MODULE
[ CREATE | DECLARE ] routine, DROP routine
```

The following is an additional *SQL session statement:*

```
SET PATH
```

The following are additional *SQL diagnostics statements:*

```
SIGNAL, RESIGNAL
```

PSM does not say whether or not any of the SQL control statements are preparable; the other new statements presumably are so, except for SIGNAL and RESIGNAL (SQL/92 says that SQL diagnostics statements are not preparable). As for the question as to which statements are transaction-initiating, the current PSM draft has only this to say:

> "The <return statement> is an additional transaction-initiating SQL-statement. If an <SQL control statement> causes the evaluation of a <subquery> and there is no current SQL-transaction, then an SQL-transaction is initiated before evaluation of the <subquery>."

We leave these—in our opinion, somewhat astounding—remarks as a topic for the reader to meditate on.

Dynamic SQL

For a note on the question as to which of the new PSM statements are preparable, see the previous subsection. Apart from this question, PSM adds just a little to the topic of dynamic SQL, having to do with *search paths* (see Section E.5) and *SQL descriptor areas* (see Chapter 20, Section 20.4). We discuss the first of these matters only, since the second does not currently seem to be very sensibly defined.

When an SQL statement *S* is the object of a PREPARE or EXECUTE IMMEDIATE statement, the search path for any routine invocation in *S* is the "default path" (part of the context information associated with the current SQL-session). The default path is set to an implementation-defined "default default" when the SQL-session is initiated, but can subsequently be changed by means of a SET PATH statement:

```
SET PATH string
```

String here is (typically) a literal, parameter, or SQL or host variable,* of type character string, whose value is a commalist of schema names. All identified schemas must be part of the default catalog for the current SQL-session.

---

*It can also be CURRENT_PATH, one of the niladic "user" builtin functions (CURRENT_USER, etc.), or a PSM routine invocation.

A new niladic builtin function, CURRENT_PATH, returns the current default path as a character string representing a commalist of schema names.

Information Schema Tables

The following additional Information Schema tables (actually views) are defined:

- MODULES

  Describes all modules belonging to schemas in this catalog and accessible to CURRENT_USER or PUBLIC.

- ROUTINES

  Describes all routines belonging to schemas in this catalog (or within modules belonging to schemas in this catalog) and accessible to CURRENT_USER or PUBLIC.

- PARAMETERS

  Describes all parameters for all routines listed in ROUTINES.

SQLSTATE Class Values

The following additions are made to the table of SQLSTATE class values given in Chapter 22:

class value	condition
0E	invalid schema name commmalist exception
20	case not found for CASE statement
2F	SQL routine exception
2G	routine invocation exception
38	external routine exception
39	external routine invocation exception
45	unhandled user-defined exception

Conformance

Conformance to PSM includes conformance to at least the Entry level of SQL/92 as described in Appendix B, together with full support for SQL routines and at least one of the specified languages for writing external routines.

An Overview of SQL3

F.1 INTRODUCTION

The previous edition of this book was written in 1992. In that edition, we explained how the content of *SQL2,* as SQL/92 was then known, was "frozen" in 1989, and how various items previously under consideration for SQL2 were thereby deferred to something called *SQL3.* At the time of writing, there is still something called SQL3, but there is also something called *SQL4* . . . What is more, the current version of SQL3 differs significantly from that of 1992, while the current version of SQL4 is in some respects very similar to the SQL3 of 1992! In this appendix, we present a broad overview of the current (1996) version of SQL3 (we choose to ignore SQL4, for the most part).

Note: SQL3 by definition includes the whole of SQL/92 as a proper subset. In this appendix, however, we follow the conventional path of taking the name "SQL3" to refer primarily to those features that are *not* already part of SQL/92.

SQL3 is still no more than a draft. It will be several years before it is published. It is less mature than the 1989 draft of SQL2 in that, among other things, the scope and functional content have not yet been "frozen" (quite). That observation alone tends to suggest a publication date of about 1999. Moreover, consideration of certain other factors might give grounds to be still more pessimistic:

- The current draft (encompassing both SQL3 and SQL4) is over 1500 pages long, while SQL/92 was "only" about one third that size. There is thus considerably more work to be done to finalize SQL3 than was done to finalize SQL2 between 1989 and 1992.

■   Some of the material was already drafted in 1989, but did not appear in SQL/92 because it was difficult to specify and needed more work than the committees thought there was time for. Thus, there is not only considerably more work to be done, but much of it is proving to be significantly more difficult than the SQL/92 work did.

■   Many of the national body committees have fewer people engaged in this work than they did in 1989–92 (a good thing, some might say, but the fact is that after a certain point—when the arguments are over and all that remains to be done is to clean up the text—"many hands make light work" becomes a more applicable proverb than "too many cooks spoil the broth").

Note: The previous edition included the following caveat, which must still stand:

In presenting a brief summary of the salient new features of [SQL3], we do not risk any predictions about the relative probabilities of appearance of this or that feature in any future version of the standard.

The current "salient new features" can be categorized as follows.

1. Data definition and manipulation
    ■   New builtin data types
    ■   User-defined data types
    ■   Subtables and supertables
    ■   CREATE TABLE LIKE
    ■   Temporary views
    ■   SENSITIVE cursors
    ■   WITH HOLD cursors
2. Functions and operators
    ■   Recursive table expressions
    ■   New quantifiers
    ■   SIMILAR condition
    ■   DISTINCT condition
    ■   Cross tabulation
3. Integrity
    ■   Referential action RESTRICT
    ■   Triggered actions

4. Security
   - User-defined roles
   - Column-specific SELECT privileges
5. Transactions
   - Transaction savepoints

F.2   DATA DEFINITION AND MANIPULATION

New Builtin Data Types

There are three new builtin scalar data types, BOOLEAN, BLOB ("binary large object"), and CLOB ("character large object"); there are also several *type constructors* for specifying "period" and "structured" types.* We consider BOOLEAN first. With the advent—at long last, many will say—of this type, truth-valued, logical, or conditional expressions (see Chapter 12) will finally be generating values of a type that is known to the SQL language. Thus, parameters, SQL variables (see Appendix E), and columns in base tables can all be defined to be of this type, and columns in derived tables (i.e., final or intermediate results) can get their values from arbitrary truth-valued expressions.

A word of warning is appropriate here, however. Although (as explained in Chapter 16) SQL is largely based on three-valued logic, BOOLEAN comprises only two values, *true* and *false;* the third truth value, *unknown,* is represented (quite incorrectly!) by NULL. To understand the seriousness of this flaw, the reader might care to meditate on the analogy of a numeric type that used null instead of zero to represent zero. *Note:* Further discussion of the difference between *unknown* and NULL can be found in the paper "NOT Is Not "Not"! (Notes on Three-Valued Logic and Related Matters)," in C. J. Date, *Relational Database Writings 1985–1989* (Addison-Wesley, 1990).

Next, the "large object" types BLOB and CLOB represent variable-length binary (BLOB) or character (CLOB) strings that might be very lengthy indeed. They come with operators, involving a "locator" mechanism, for handling such strings a manageable portion at a time. The reader will probably be aware that many products already provide such facilities. *Note:* Binary strings are a new SQL concept; they should not be confused with bit strings. A binary string is a sequence not of bits, but of *octets* (i.e., bytes, loosely speaking).

The type constructor PERIOD is defined in a comparatively recent addition to the SQL3 draft called *SQL/Temporal* (see Appendix G). In principle, given any

---

*The term *interval* would have been more apt than *period* but had already been used, in a different sense, in SQL/92 (see Chapter 17).

totally ordered "element type" T (e.g., type INTEGER), the type PERIOD(T) could usefully be defined; a PERIOD(T) value would represent an "anchored interval" made up of values of type T. For example, the interval 19 through 33 would be a value in the type PERIOD(INTEGER). Currently, however, the "element type" T is constrained to be some DATE, TIME, or TIMESTAMP type.

There are three collection type constructors, *viz.* SET, MULTISET, and LIST; the "element type" in each case can be any known type. For example, LIST(CHAR VARYING(20)) is a type whose values are *lists,* and the elements in those lists are varying length character strings of maximum length 20 characters. Similarly, the values of SET types are *sets,* and the values of MULTISET types are *bags* ("multisets"). Nested structures such as SET(LIST(INTEGER)) are permitted.

Tuple types can also be constructed, though for obvious reasons SQL uses the key word ROW instead of TUPLE. The ROW constructor takes a list of element types, each paired with what SQL calls a *field name* (rather than attribute name or column name, these terms being used elsewhere in the language already).

Note: The reader might be wondering at this point whether there is any connection between (e.g.) the type

```
MULTISET ( ROW ( EMPNO CHAR(5), SALARY DECIMAL(6,2) ) )
```

and the table defined by

```
CREATE TABLE EMP ( EMPNO CHAR(5), SALARY DECIMAL(6,2) )
```

Indeed there is; in fact, the type constructor TABLE is defined to be shorthand for MULTISET(ROW(...)). *Note:* The rather more respectable SET(ROW(...)) is currently left out in the cold, a state of affairs the standardizers hope to remedy in the fullness of time.

We close this subsection with a brief mention of a recent proposal to introduce the concept of *named* row types. The intent behind that proposal is to try a fresh approach to the provision of "object support" in SQL (see the next subsection below). For example, we might define a named row type EMP_TYPE as follows:

```
EMP_TYPE ( EMPNO CHAR(5), SALARY DECIMAL(6,2) )
```

Then we could define a base table as follows:

```
CREATE TABLE EMP OF EMP_TYPE ...
```

Other components of this approach include reference (REF) types, system-generated primary key values,* and explicit operators for referencing and dereferencing.

---

*We support the idea of system-generated primary key values but feel bound to point out that they are (or should be) orthogonal to the question of object support. By contrast, we emphatically do *not* support the idea of named row types, even though they too really have (or should have) nothing to do with object support as such.

While it is possible that this approach might eventually become an important part of SQL3, at the time of writing it raises too many unanswered questions; we therefore choose not to discuss it any further here.

User-Defined Data Types

In the counterpart to this subsection in the previous edition of this book, we said: "It would be more fashionable to have the word *object* somewhere in the heading of this subsection, but the extent to which SQL3 will actually embrace the object paradigm is still a subject of hot debate." Four years on, this sentence still applies! However, the text that previously followed that sentence now hardly applies at all. The current state of affairs is described below.

First of all, SQL3 introduces two statements, CREATE TYPE and CREATE DISTINCT TYPE, for adding arbitrary type definitions to those that can be specified using the builtin types and type constructors. We discuss CREATE TYPE first (though we remark in passing that CREATE DISTINCT TYPE really is a different operation altogether, not just a qualified form of CREATE TYPE). CREATE TYPE includes facilities for specifying all of the following:

- The (encapsulated) representation of values of the new type;
- Optionally, one or more supertypes for the new type;
- Optionally, the definition of an "=" operator for values of the new type (if no such definition is provided, a standard default definition is assumed, since every data type *must* support an "=" operator);
- Optionally, the definition of a "<" operator for values of the new type (if no such definition is provided, the type is unordered, meaning that "<", and therefore ORDER BY, are undefined);

and several other less important features that might or might not survive.

Types defined via CREATE TYPE are called *abstract* data types or *ADTs*. Points to note:

- All values of a given ADT have the same representation. The representation is specified as a list of *attributes,* each defined as a name:type pair. An attribute can be of any known type (possibly an ADT).
- The representation for an ADT that is a subtype of one or more other ADTs is the union of the representations for the supertypes and any additional attributes specified for the subtype.
- The functions and/or procedures available in connection with an ADT are precisely those PSM functions and/or procedures that are defined to have at least one parameter of that type (or any supertype thereof) or to return a result of that type (or any subtype thereof). See Appendix E for a detailed discussion of PSM functions and procedures.

- SQL3 embraces the principle of *substitutability,* whereby, if type *B* is a subtype of type *A*, then a value of type *B* is permitted in all contexts in which a value of type *A* is permitted. In particular, a value of type *B* can appear:

  a. In a table, in a column defined to be of type *A*;

  b. As a value of an SQL variable (see Appendix E) of declared type *A*;

  c. As an argument to a routine invocation (again, see Appendix E) if the declared type of the corresponding parameter is *A*.

Note: Alas, the foregoing ideas apply only in connection with abstract types, not builtin types. What this writer has referred to elsewhere as the *Shackle of Compatibility* has meant that subtyping and substitutability could not be retrofitted to the builtin types and constructors.

While on the question of object support, we should say a word regarding *object identifiers*. It is now recognized that this concept is orthogonal to that of types. Various proposals involving the concept have been made over the years and embraced in text that has come and gone in the draft. The one that is most likely to see the light of day involves explicit referencing and dereferencing. It is not surprising to this writer that the favored (by some) but, we think, unsound implicit referencing and dereferencing found in some object-oriented database systems proved too problematical for SQL. (We should add too that, despite the agreement over orthogonality, it is likely that object identifiers will be restricted to certain special types in SQL3. Because of such difficulties, object support is currently described in a separate document and might possibly be published later than other portions of SQL3. It is in this separate document that the specifications for named row types, reference types, system-generated keys, and the associated operators reside.)

We turn now to CREATE DISTINCT TYPE. The syntax is:

```
CREATE DISTINCT TYPE distinct-type AS underlying-type
```

Note that the "underlying" type must not be another "distinct" type.

The current SQL3 distinct type specifications are somewhat incomplete, but the following aspects, at least, *are* specified:

- A distinct type can be used as the basis for a column definition.

- The (encapsulated) representation of values of a given distinct type is the same as that of values of the underlying type.

- Values of a given distinct type are comparable with each other *and nothing else* (note in particular that they are not comparable with values of the underlying type). The applicable comparison operators are inherited from the underlying type.

- Values of a given distinct type can be assigned only to targets of that same type.

- If the underlying type is an ADT, the descriptor for the distinct type includes everything that is included in the descriptor of that ADT. This fact suggests that the distinct type is meant to inherit all of the operators (not just the comparison operators) that apply to the ADT, but the specifications are unclear on this point.

- Aggregate functions such as SUM are explicitly defined not to apply to distinct types. It is clear, then, that a distinct type does not inherit the builtin aggregate functions, even when those functions do apply to the underlying type. The specifications have nothing to say on the question of whether a distinct type can inherit any of the builtin *scalar* functions, such as TRIM.

- A distinct type cannot have any subtypes or supertypes, though the underlying type is not prohibited from having supertypes.

- If the source value in a CAST operation is of some distinct type, then the target type *must* be the corresponding underlying type. Likewise, if the target type in a CAST operation is some distinct type, then the source value *must* be of the corresponding underlying type.

Subtables and Supertables

Given a base table called SUPER (say), it is possible to create another base table, called SUB perhaps, that is defined to be a "subtable" of SUPER (and, yes, SUPER is said to be a "supertable" of SUB). SUB inherits all the columns of SUPER, plus its primary key (SUPER must *have* a primary key); however, the inherited columns can be renamed in SUB, and any number of additional columns and constraints can be defined for SUB. Every row in SUB has exactly one corresponding row in SUPER (identified by the inherited primary key value), from which it inherits values for all its inherited columns.

A supertable can have any number of subtables. In addition, of course, a subtable can be another subtable's supertable, and so on, to any depth.

The full implications of the foregoing ideas are extremely unclear at this time. We therefore choose not to go into any further details here.

CREATE TABLE LIKE

In common with some current SQL implementations, SQL3 supports a LIKE operator on CREATE TABLE, permitting some or all of the column definitions of a new base table to be inherited from some existing named table (note the word "named" here—it is not possible to specify an arbitrary table expression).

Temporary Views

The basic idea of temporary tables—i.e., the ability to create a new base table that will be implicitly destroyed at the end of the SQL-session, as described in Chapter 18—is extended to views.

SENSITIVE Cursors

In SQL/92 a cursor can be declared to be INSENSITIVE, in which case (as explained in Chapter 10) OPEN effectively causes the cursor to access a private copy of the data, implying that updates made through other cursors, or made without cursors at all, will not be visible through this opening of this cursor. In SQL3 a cursor can alternatively be declared to be SENSITIVE, in which case the user is asking that the cursor access "the real data," and hence that updates made through other cursors, or made without cursors at all, should be visible (if appropriate) through the cursor. *Note:* The default is neither SENSITIVE nor INSENSITIVE but "don't care."

Implementations are not required to support the semantics of SENSITIVE, but they are required at least to permit SENSITIVE as an option on a cursor declaration, and to generate a special exception on OPEN if the declared sensitivity cannot be provided.

WITH HOLD Cursors

A cursor can be defined to be WITH HOLD, in which case COMMIT does not close the cursor; instead, it leaves it open, positioned such that the next FETCH will move it to the next row in sequence. The possibly complex repositioning code that might otherwise be needed on the next OPEN is thus no longer required.

F.3   FUNCTIONS AND OPERATORS

Recursive Table Expressions

The previous edition of this book mentioned an operator called RECURSIVE UNION. That operator has now been dropped and a radically different approach to recursion adopted in its place. The new approach exploits another recent SQL3 extension, namely the ability to define, within a given table expression *TE1*, a name for some other table expression *TE2*. Let *TEN* be such a name. Then *TEN* can be used subsequently within *TE1* wherever *TE2* is required. Thus, *TEN* is very much like a view name, except that its scope is confined to the table expression in which it is defined.

Here is a simple example, showing the definition and use of a "query name" (as SQL3 calls it) in a table expression that returns, for each employee *e* who has been with the company for a certain minimum length of time, *e*'s employee number and a count of other similar employees in the same department as *e*:

```
WITH LONG_TERM_EMPS AS
   ( SELECT *
     FROM    EMP
     WHERE   DATE_HIRED < DATE '1980-01-01' )
```

```
SELECT EMPNO, LONG_TERM_CT - 1 AS NO_OF_FELLOW_LONG_TERM_EMPS
FROM   LONG_TERM_EMPS AS L1,
     ( SELECT DEPTNO, COUNT(*) AS LONG_TERM_CT
       FROM   LONG_TERM_EMPS
       GROUP  BY DEPTNO ) AS L2
WHERE  L1.DEPTNO = L2.DEPTNO
```

The effect of the WITH clause is similar to that of a CREATE VIEW statement specifying the same name and table expression, but localized to the containing table expression. *Note:* Since it is part of the syntax of table expressions and table expressions can be nested, a WITH clause can appear at any level of nesting (the level in question determining the scope of the defined name).

Even without recursion, this new feature appears to be very useful, satisfying a requirement that has been strongly expressed elsewhere by the present writer; see, for example, Chapter 20, "Chivalry," by Hugh Darwen (writing as Andrew Warden), in C. J. Date, *Relational Database Writings 1985–1989,* Addison-Wesley (1990). Furthermore, of course, it can also be used to formulate *recursive* queries (and to do so, moreover, in a manner more familiar and intuitive than that of RECURSIVE UNION). *Note:* Such recursive query formulations are unfortunately subject to certain restrictions. The precise statement of those restrictions is somewhat complicated, but in fact the restrictions themselves are fairly intuitive and reasonable.

Here is an example. We are given the table PARENT_OF (PARENT, CHILD). The requirement is to find all pairs of people (*a,b*) such that *a* is an ancestor of *b*:

```
WITH RECURSIVE ANCESTOR_OF ( ANCESTOR, DESCENDANT )
AS ( SELECT PARENT, CHILD
     FROM   PARENT_OF
     UNION
     SELECT A.PARENT, P.CHILD
     FROM   ANCESTOR_OF AS A, PARENT_OF AS P
     WHERE  A.CHILD = P.PARENT )

SELECT *
FROM   ANCESTOR_OF
```

Note: The "justification" for the (required) key word RECURSIVE is that it serves to protect against any accidental recursion that might otherwise arise through typographical errors. Also, support is provided for detecting cycles in the data and for specifying the order, depth first or breadth first, in which the "search" (as SQL3 calls it) is to be conducted. Such aspects are beyond both the scope of this appendix and the taste of the present writer.

It is worth pointing out that this approach to recursive queries also permits *mutual* recursion, as in the case where the table expression of query name *Q1* references query name *Q2* and *vice versa.* Suppose, for example, that we are given the tables WORKS_IN (EMPNO, DEPTNO) and MANAGES (DEPTNO, MGRNO). Consider the following recursive expression:

```
WITH RECURSIVE

REPORTS_TO ( EMPNO, MGRNO )
AS ( SELECT EMPNO, MGRNO
     FROM    MANAGES AS M, WORKS_IN AS W
     WHERE   M.DEPTNO = W.DEPTNO
     UNION
     SELECT W.EMPNO, B.MGRNO
     FROM    WORKS_IN AS W, BELONGS_TO AS B
     WHERE   W.DEPTNO = B.DEPTNO ) ,
  BELONGS_TO ( DEPTNO, MGRNO )
  AS ( SELECT M.DEPTNO, R.MGRNO
       FROM    MANAGES AS M, REPORTS_TO AS R
       WHERE   M.MGRNO = R.EMPNO )

SELECT ...
```

REPORTS_TO pairs every EMPNO with the MGRNO of every manager that employee EMPNO reports to, directly or indirectly. BELONGS_TO pairs every MGRNO with the DEPTNO of every department that manager MGRNO is responsible for, again either directly or indirectly. Both names, REPORTS_TO and BELONGS_TO, can be referenced within the omitted portion of the overall table expression.

New Quantifiers

The new quantifiers FOR SOME and FOR ALL are supported, with syntax as follows:

```
FOR { SOME | ALL } table-expression-commalist
                       ( conditional-expression )
```

They are both three-valued, unlike the EXISTS of existing SQL.* The commalist of table expressions defines the same table as it would if it were specified in a FROM clause, *viz.* the Cartesian product of the tables that result from evaluating the individual table expressions. Let that table be *T*, and let the specified conditional expression be *C*. Then:

- FOR SOME returns *true* if *C* evaluates to *true* for at least one row of *T*, *false* if *C* evaluates to *false* for every row of *T*, and *unknown* otherwise.

- FOR ALL returns *true* if *C* evaluates to *true* for every row of *T*, *false* if *C* evaluates to *false* for at least one row of *T*, and *unknown* otherwise.

For example, the expression

```
FOR SOME ( SELECT * FROM S SX ) ( SX.CITY = 'London' )
```

returns *true* if at least one supplier is located in London. And the expression

---

*Indeed, FOR SOME was probably introduced precisely because EXISTS "does not work right" (as explained in Chapter 16). FOR ALL is useful, representing as it does direct support for the *universal* quantifier of (three-valued) logic.

```
    FOR ALL ( SELECT * FROM S SX ) ( SX.CITY = 'London' )
```

returns *true* if every supplier is located in London (note in particular that "every supplier is located in London" is considered to be *true* if there are no suppliers at all).

SIMILAR Condition

SIMILAR, like LIKE, is intended for character string pattern matching—i.e., for testing a given character string to see whether it conforms to some prescribed pattern. The difference is that SIMILAR supports a much more extensive range of possibilities ("wild cards," etc.) than LIKE does. The syntax is:

```
    character-string-expression [ NOT ] SIMILAR TO pattern
                                       [ ESCAPE escape ]
```

The "pattern" and "escape" specifications are essentially as for LIKE, except that "pattern" can involve additional special characters—not just "%" (percent) and "_" (underscore) as in LIKE, but also "*" (asterisk), "+" (plus), "–" (minus), and many others. The general intent seems to be to support the parsing of syntax strings in some formal language. *Note:* It is worth mentioning that the rules for SIMILAR were copied from the similar function in POSIX.

DISTINCT Condition

SQL3 also provides a new DISTINCT condition (not to be confused with the existing UNIQUE condition) for testing whether two rows are "distinct." Let the two rows in question be *Left* and *Right; Left* and *Right* must contain the same number, n say, of scalar components each. Let i range from 1 to n, and let the ith components of *Left* and *Right* be Li and Ri, respectively. The type of Li must be compatible with the type of Ri. Then the expression

```
    Left IS DISTINCT FROM Right
```

returns *false* if and only if, for all i, either (a) "$Li = Ri$" is *true*, or (b) Li and Ri are both null; otherwise it returns *true*. (In other words, *Left* and *Right* are "distinct" if and only if they are not "duplicates" of one another. See Chapter 16.) Note that a DISTINCT condition never evaluates to *unknown*.

Cross Tabulation

A move is under way at the time of writing to extend GROUP BY with syntax involving new key words (such as CUBE and ROLLUP) in support of *cross tabulation,* a function formerly found in report writers rather than in purportedly relational languages. These proposals will probably be accepted for SQL3, thanks to the high degree of attention focused on such functions in the currently fashionable arena(s) known variously as "data warehousing," "data mining," "online analytical processing" (OLAP), "multidimensional data analysis," and "the hypercube." By way of example, consider a table expression that calculates sales statistics by product, area, and week number. Report writers have typically allowed the report to include "rolled up" statistics for product and area, product and week number, area and week number, product alone, area alone, week number alone, and possibly "grand totals" too. To combine all such information into a single SQL table requires a series of outer joins (or contrived unions, if outer join is not directly supported). Such a table involves an unprecedented number of nulls, where the report writers merely produced innocent white space. The present writer seriously questions the wisdom of treating such an object as a table, but no doubt the proposed shorthands will be extremely popular, not only with people who use them cautiously but also with others.

F.4   INTEGRITY

Referential Action RESTRICT

In addition to the referential actions specified for SQL/92 (CASCADE, SET NULL, SET DEFAULT, and NO ACTION), SQL3 supports a new one, RESTRICT. RESTRICT is very similar—but not quite identical—to NO ACTION. The subtle difference between them is as follows. *Note:* To fix our ideas, we concentrate here on the delete rule; the implications for the update rule are essentially similar, *mutatis mutandis.*

- Let *T1* and *T2* be the referenced table and the referencing table, respectively; let *R1* be a row of *T1*, and let *R2* be a row of *T2* that corresponds to row *R1* under the referential constraint in question. What happens if an attempt is made to delete row *R1*?

- Under NO ACTION, as explained in Chapter 14, the system—conceptually, at least—actually performs the requested DELETE, then discovers that row *R2* now violates the constraint, and so undoes the DELETE (thereby reinstating the deleted row *R1*).

- Under RESTRICT, by contrast, the system realizes "ahead of time" that row *R2* exists and will violate the constraint if *R1* is deleted, and so rejects the DELETE out of hand.

Triggered Actions

Cascaded deletes and updates are examples of integrity features in SQL/92 where actions can be specified to be executed when "triggered" by specified events. SQL3 provides several new features having to do with "triggered actions," including in particular a CREATE TRIGGER statement, which defines a *trigger*—i.e., a combination of an *event* specification and an *action* specification, where:

- An "event" is an INSERT, UPDATE (optionally of specified columns), or DELETE against a specified named table.

- The "action" is an action (in effect, a procedure) to be performed AFTER or BEFORE the specified event occurs.

More precisely, the "action" consists of an optional conditional expression (defaulting to *true*), and a list of SQL statements that will be executed if and only if the condition is *true* when the event occurs. The user can specify whether the action is to take place just once per occurrence of the event, or once FOR EACH ROW of the table with which the event is associated. Furthermore, the action specification can refer to "before" and "after" values in the table associated with the specified event, thus providing a kind of support for *transition constraints*.

F.5   SECURITY

User-Defined Roles

The new CREATE ROLE statement supports the creation of named *roles*. An example might be "DBADM" ("database administration"). Role names must be unique, not only with respect to the set of role names, but also with respect to the set of authorization identifiers in the environment. Once created, a role can be granted privileges, just as if it were an authID. Furthermore, roles can be granted, like privileges, and, like all privileges, they can be granted either to an authID or to another role.

Column-Specific SELECT Privileges

The new "SELECT(x)" privilege allows the holder to reference a specific column x of a specific named table within a table expression (e.g., within a select-item in a SELECT clause).

F.6   TRANSACTIONS

Transaction Savepoints

The SQL3 savepoint mechanism allows transactions to be *partially* rolled back (on user request). The SAVEPOINT statement allows the user to establish a named "savepoint" within a transaction. Subsequently, a special form of the ROLLBACK statement—"ROLLBACK TO *savepoint*"—allows the user to undo all updates performed since the specified savepoint, while at the same time preserving updates performed prior to that point. Note that "ROLLBACK TO *savepoint*" (unlike the ordinary ROLLBACK statement) does not terminate the transaction.

The foregoing facility might be useful in certain kinds of "what if" processing.

References
and Bibliography

1. International Organization for Standardization (ISO): *Database Language SQL*. Document ISO/IEC 9075:1992. Also available as American National Standards Institute (ANSI) Document ANSI X3.135-1992.

The original ISO/ANSI "SQL/92" standard definition (known to the cognoscenti as *ISO/IEC 9075*, or sometimes just *ISO 9075*). The original single-part document has since been expanded into an open-ended series of separate parts, under the general title *Information Technology—Database Languages—SQL*. At the time of writing, the following parts have been defined (though certainly not all completed):

Part 1: Framework (SQL/Framework)
Part 2: Foundation (SQL/Foundation)
Part 3: Call-Level Interface (SQL/CLI)
Part 4: Persistent Stored Modules (SQL/PSM)
Part 5: Host Language Bindings (SQL/Bindings)
Part 6: XA Specialization (SQL/Transaction)
Part 7: Temporal (SQL/Temporal)

Most of the present book is based on material that will eventually form Parts 1–3 and 5 of this restructured version of the standard. The text of Appendix E is based on the most recent draft of Part 4 (June 1996, not yet generally available). The "global transaction" concept, mentioned briefly in Chapter 5, is taken from Part 6. The discussion of the "period" type constructor in Appendix F is taken from Part 7. Certain other planned features (e.g., the proposed SQL3 "object support") have yet to be officially pinned down as a formal part of the series.

2. International Organization for Standardization (ISO): *Information Technology— Database Languages—SQL—Technical Corrigendum 1.* Document ISO/IEC 9075:1992/Cor.1:1994(E).

   Contains a large number of revisions and corrections to reference [1]. *Note:* This document is subsumed by reference [3].

3. International Organization for Standardization (ISO): *Information Technology— Database Languages—SQL—Technical Corrigendum 2.* Document ISO/IEC 9075:1992/Cor.2:1996(E).

   An expanded version of reference [2].

4. International Organization for Standardization: *Database Language SQL.* Document ISO/IEC 9075:1987. Also available as American National Standards Institute (ANSI) Document ANSI X3.135-1986.

   The ISO/ANSI "SQL/86" definition.

5. International Organization for Standardization: *Database Language SQL.* Document ISO/IEC 9075:1989. Also available as American National Standards Institute (ANSI) Document ANSI X3.135-1989.

   The ISO/ANSI "SQL/89" definition. Note: SQL/89 = SQL/86 plus the optional *Integrity Enhancement Feature* (IEF).

6. American National Standards Institute: *Database Language Embedded SQL.* Document ANSI X3.168-1989.

   The ANSI embedded SQL standard definition.

7. X/Open: *Structured Query Language (SQL): CAE Specification C201* (September 1992).

   The X/Open SQL standard definition. It corresponds more or less to the Entry level of SQL/92 but includes a number of extensions (e.g., CREATE and DROP INDEX) and certain Intermediate SQL features (e.g., GET DIAGNOSTICS).

8. US Department of Commerce, National Institute of Standards and Technology: *Database Language SQL.* FIPS PUB 127-2 (1992).

   The Federal Information Processing SQL standard definition. Like the X/Open standard, it corresponds to the Entry level of SQL/92 but includes a few additional specifications, such as prescribed lower limits on certain implementation-defined values.

9. IBM Corp.: *Systems Application Architecture Common Programming Interface: Database Reference.* IBM Document No. SC26-4348.

   The IBM SAA SQL standard definition.

10. E. F. Codd: "A Relational Model of Data for Large Shared Data Banks." *Communications of the ACM 13,* No. 6 (June 1970); republished in *Communications of the ACM 26,* No. 1 (January 1983).

    The paper that (apart from some early internal IBM papers, also by Codd) first proposed the ideas of the relational model.

11. C. J. Date: *An Introduction to Database Systems,* 6th edition (Addison-Wesley, 1995).

    This book provides a basis for a comprehensive education in the foundations of database technology. In particular, it includes a very detailed treatment of the relational approach.

12. D. D. Chamberlin and R. F. Boyce: "SEQUEL: A Structured English Query Language." Proc. ACM SIGMOD Workshop on Data Description, Access, and Control, Ann Arbor, Mich. (May 1974).

    The paper that first introduced the SQL language (or SEQUEL, as it was originally called).

13. M. M. Astrahan and R. A. Lorie: "SEQUEL-XRM: A Relational System." Proc. ACM Pacific Regional Conference, San Francisco, Calif. (April 1975).

    Describes the first prototype implementation of SEQUEL.

14. D. D. Chamberlin *et al.*: "SEQUEL/2: A Unified Approach to Data Definition, Manipulation, and Control." *IBM J.R&D 20,* No. 6 (November 1976). See also errata in January 1977 issue.

    Describes the revised version of SEQUEL called SEQUEL/2.

15. M. M. Astrahan *et al.*: "System R: Relational Approach to Database Management." *ACM Transactions on Database Systems 1,* No. 2 (June 1976).

    System R was a major prototype implementation of the SEQUEL/2 (later SQL) language. This paper describes the architecture of System R as originally planned.

16. D. D. Chamberlin: "A Summary of User Experience with the SQL Data Sublanguage." Proc. International Conference on Databases, Aberdeen, Scotland (July 1980).

    Includes details of several enhancements and revisions to SQL (previously SEQUEL/2) that were made during the lifetime of the System R project.

17. D. D. Chamberlin *et al.*: "A History and Evaluation of System R." *Communications of the ACM 24,* No. 10 (October 1981).

    Describes the pioneering work on relational implementation technology (in particular, optimization technology) done as part of the System R project.

18. C. J. Date: *Relational Database: Selected Writings* (Addison-Wesley, 1986); *Relational Database Writings 1985–1989* (Addison-Wesley, 1990); (with Hugh Darwen) *Relational Database Writings 1989–1991* (Addison-Wesley, 1992); *Relational Database Writings 1991–1994* (Addison-Wesley, 1995).

    These four books contain a collection of papers on various aspects of relational database management, including several (mostly somewhat critical) that discuss the SQL language. See in particular the papers "A Critique of the SQL Database Language" in the first volume, "What's Wrong with SQL?" and "EXISTS Is Not Exists!" in the second, "Oh No Not Nulls Again" and "Without Check Option" in the third, and "How We Missed the Relational Boat" in the fourth.

19. C. J. Date: *A Guide to INGRES* (Addison-Wesley, 1987); (with Colin J. White) *A Guide to SQL/DS* (Addison-Wesley, 1988); (with Colin J. White) *A Guide to DB2* (4th

edition, Addison-Wesley, 1992). David McGoveran (with C. J. Date): *A Guide to SYBASE and SQL Server* (Addison-Wesley, 1992).

Detailed descriptions of some commercially significant SQL implementations.

20. David Rozenshtein, Anatoly Abramovich, and Eugene Birger: *Optimizing Transact-SQL: Advanced Programming Techniques* (SQL Forum Press, 1995).

Transact-SQL is the dialect of SQL supported by the SYBASE and SQL Server products. This book presents a series of programming techniques for Transact-SQL based on the use of *characteristic functions* (defined by the authors as "devices that allow programmers to encode conditional logic as scalar expressions within SELECT, WHERE, GROUP BY, and SET clauses"). Although aimed at Transact-SQL specifically, the ideas are actually of wider applicability.

21. Raymond A. Lorie and Jean-Jacques Daudenarde: *SQL and Its Applications* (Prentice-Hall, 1991).

Another SQL "how to" book. Almost half of the book consists of a detailed series of case studies involving realistic applications.

22. Joe Celko: *SQL for Smarties: Advanced SQL Programming* (Morgan Kaufmann, 1995).

"This is the first advanced SQL book available that provides a comprehensive presentation of the techniques necessary to support your progress from casual user of SQL to expert programmer" (from the book's own cover).

23. Jim Melton and Alan R. Simon: *Understanding the New SQL: A Complete Guide* (Morgan Kaufmann, 1993).

A tutorial on SQL/92 (original version). Jim Melton was the editor of the original SQL/92 specification [1]. This book and the next [24] are thus competitors to the present book.

24. Stephen Cannan and Gerard Otten: *SQL—The Standard Handbook* (McGraw-Hill, 1993).

"[Our] objective . . . is to provide a reference work explaining and describing [the original version of SQL/92] in a much less formal and very much more readable way than the standard itself" (from the book's introduction).

Index